"WHIP THE REBELLION"

* * * * * * * * * * * * * *

BOOKS BY GEORGE WALSH

*"Whip the Rebellion":
Ulysses S. Grant's Rise to Command

*"Damage Them All You Can":
Robert E. Lee's Army of Northern Virginia

Public Enemies:
The Mayor, the Mob, and the Crime That Was

Gentleman Jimmy Walker:
Mayor of the Jazz Age

*denotes a Forge Book

"WHIP THE REBELLION"

* * * * * * * * * * * * * * * * *

ULYSSES S. GRANT'S RISE TO COMMAND

GEORGE WALSH

A TOM DOHERTY ASSOCIATES BOOK

NEW YORK

"WHIP THE REBELLION": ULYSSES S. GRANT'S RISE TO COMMAND

Copyright © 2005 by George Walsh

This book is printed on acid-free paper.

A Forge Book
Published by Tom Doherty Associates, LLC
175 Fifth Avenue
New York, NY 10010

www.tor.com

Forge® is a registered trademark of Tom Doherty Associates, LLC.

Library of Congress Cataloging-in-Publication Data

Walsh, George, 1931–
    Whip the rebellion : George Walsh.—1st. ed.
        p. cm.
    "A Tom Doherty Associates book."
    ISBN 0-765-30526-7 (alk. paper)
    EAN 978-0765-30526-8
    1. Grant, Ulysses S. (Ulysses Simpson), 1822–1885—Military leadership.
    2. Grant, Ulysses S. (Ulysses Simpson), 1822–1885—Friends and associates.
    3. United States—History—Civil War, 1861–1865—Campaigns. 4. Command
    of troops—Case studies. 5. Generals—United States—Biography. 6. United
    States. Army—Biography. I. Title.

    E672.W35   2005
    973.7'3'092—dc22
    [B]   2004056300

First Edition: February 2005

Printed in the United States of America

0 9 8 7 6 5 4 3 2 1

For Grail and Chris, Simon and Jane

CONTENTS

PREFACE

Before I began researching Ulysses S. Grant's surprising rise to command during the Civil War, I thought of him as a diligent but somewhat plodding man whose greatest strength was the Union's superiority in manpower and matériel—someone, in effect, who had greatness thrust upon him. I could not have been more wrong. With the outbreak of hostilities this former West Pointer, who had been forced to resign from the peacetime army for drinking and thereafter failed in one civilian pursuit after the other, came to the forefront through his own unique abilities. What he knew best, it turned out, was how to wage war—relentlessly and with irresistible force.

From the time his Galena, Illinois, congressman insisted that the unprepossessing Grant be named a colonel of volunteers, and then a brigadier, he made the most of his chances. In 1862, with the war a year old and both sides in Tennessee reluctant to fight, he took the initiative and captured Fort Donelson, gaining national attention.

Subsequently he survived and repulsed the Rebel attack at the desperate Battle of Shiloh, and the newspaper calumnies that followed. The next year, in Mississippi, he conducted the arduous, brilliant campaign against Vicksburg, cutting the Confederacy in half. During this period he simultaneously coped with jealous rivals, Washington politics, and resentful subordinates.

For his victories, Grant late in 1863 was named commander in the West and sent to relieve the siege at Chattanooga. This he did, putting the Rebels to rout and setting the stage the next year for his first meeting with President Abraham Lincoln and his promotion to general-in-chief. "The particulars of your plans I neither know nor seek to know," Lincoln told him. "You are vigilant and self-reliant; and, pleased with this, I wish not to obtrude any constraints or restraints upon you. . . ."

Grant then moved to the East and joined the Army of the Potomac, pushing the climactic campaign against Robert E. Lee and the Army of Northern Virginia, accepting massive casualties but bringing Lee to bay. Meanwhile with his trusted lieutenant William Sherman, whom he left in command in the West, he devised the strategy for the Atlanta Campaign and the March to the Sea, devastating the South's interior and revealing its helplessness.

No one summed up Grant better than Bruce Catton, his preeminent military biographer, writing some forty-five years ago: "There was nothing about Ulysses S. Grant that struck the eye; and this puzzled people, after it was all over, because it seemed reasonable that greatness, somewhere along the line, should look like greatness. Grant could never look like anything, and he never could make the things that he did look very special; and afterward men could remember nothing more than the fact that when he came around things seemed to happen. . . ."

Those events "that seemed to happen" I hope will be made more meaningful in this narrative, enhanced by the words of the participants and the insights of modern scholarship. "Whip the Rebellion" was Grant's creed during every day of the Civil War, and he embraced it with his usual resolve. In so doing, he preserved the Republic.

My sources in writing this book included the indispensable *War of the Rebellion, A Compilation of the Official Records of the Union and Confederate Armies* (128 volumes); *Battle and Leaders of the Civil War* (4 volumes); and innumerable firsthand accounts and manuscripts. Included in the last category are Grant's and Sherman's *Memoirs,* both of which should be required reading for every student of American history (and every citizen as well). My special thanks to the late Bruce Catton, whose evocative books, *Grant Goes South* and *Grant Takes Command,* are landmark works in the field. To all fellow Civil War historians I acknowledge my debt, and I cite their contributions when appropriate in the Notes.

Let me acknowledge my special appreciation to the late Staige Blackford. Staige was a longtime friend, a southern liberal, and his comments contributed significantly to this northern conservative's understanding of the conflict. Finally, I wish to thank the agent Ted Chichak for his untiring efforts in guiding to publication both *"Whip the Rebellion"* and its companion volume, *"Damage Them All You Can": Robert E. Lee's Army of Northern Virginia.*

—New York, July 22, 2004

1862

ONE

* * * *

GRANT, SHERMAN, AND HALLECK

With the Civil War entering its second year, the Federal military situation in the West—that vast, sprawling expanse from the Appalachian Mountains to the Mississippi River and beyond—remained a puzzlement. The border states of Missouri and Kentucky had been held in the Union, but immediately south of them lay rebellious Tennessee, blocking any advance into the Confederacy. Compounding the problem was the command situation in the area. Henry Wager Halleck, positioned to direct Federal operations in Missouri and west Tennessee from his base in St. Louis, and Don Carlos Buell, poised opposite east Tennessee with his headquarters in Louisville, Kentucky, were all but autonomous and loath to act in concert. Ruefully remarked President Abraham Lincoln of this and other such rivalries: "It has been said that one bad general is better than two good ones; and the saying is true . . . an army is better directed by a single mind, though inferior, than by two superior ones, at variance and cross-purposes with each other."

But this early part of our story deals only incidentally with the competition between Halleck and Carlos Buell. Rather it focuses on Halleck and his then subordinates Ulysses S. Grant and William Tecumseh Sherman—West Pointers but disparate personalities all—and how their abilities and ambitions complemented and clashed with results that no one could have foretold.

Halleck, forty-seven years old in 1862, was the oldest of the three. Intellectual, analytic, dispassionate—these were the qualities that admirers saw in him. "General Halleck was a man of great capacity, of large acquirements," said Sherman, who knew him well, "and at the time possessed the confidence of the country, and of most of the army. I held him in high estimation." Others felt differently. They viewed Halleck as cold and calculating, called him Old Brains and complained that he "takes no responsibility, plans nothing, suggests nothing, is good for nothing." The forty-two-year-old, mercurial Sherman, of course, had reason to be grateful to Halleck. The year before, while commanding in Kentucky before being relieved by Buell, he had suffered what amounted to a nervous breakdown. Halleck had rescued his career, granting him leave and then assigning him to training-camp duty in Missouri. Old Brains even made light of the occurrence, telling Sherman's wife that he would "take all that is said against [Sherman] if he will take all that is said against me. I am certain to make 50 percent profit by the exchange."[1]

Halleck's ranking field general in the area was the quiet, rumpled, forty-year-old Grant, who was stationed in Cairo, Illinois, just north of the Missouri-Kentucky line at the junction of the Ohio and Mississippi Rivers. The two men had an uneasy relationship. Halleck appreciated Grant's talent for organization and insistence on discipline, but thought him overly willing to risk men in battle. He also worried about his supposed binges. Years before, Grant had been forced to resign from the army because of excessive drinking—or so the rumors had it—and he and his family had been living what amounted to a hand-to-mouth existence ever since. Perhaps these factors accounted for Halleck's curt attitude when Grant first outlined his strategy for going on the offensive in Tennessee. "I had known General Halleck very slightly in the old army, not having met him either at West Point or during the Mexican War," Grant remembered. "I was received by him with so little cordiality that I perhaps stated the object of my visit with less clearness than I might have done, and I had not uttered many sentences before I was cut short as if my plan was preposterous."

Grant had not yet commanded Sherman in combat, nor developed the close rapport with him that resulted in Sherman becoming his chief lieutenant. But that soon would come. Commenting on the Battle of Shiloh, Grant would remark, "During the whole of Sunday I was continuously engaged in passing from one part of the field to another, giving directions to division commanders. In thus moving along the line, however, I never deemed it important to stay long with Sherman. Although his troops were then under fire for the first time, their commander, by his constant presence with them, inspired a confidence in officers and men that enabled them to render services on that bloody battlefield worthy of the best of veterans." Sherman, writing to his wife, would return the tribute. "[Grant] is as brave as any man should be, he has won several victories such as [Fort] Donelson which ought to entitle him to universal praise," he would say, "but his rivals have almost succeeded through the instrumentality of the press in pulling him down." Sherman, who despised reporters, continued: "[Grant] is not a brilliant man and has himself thoughtlessly used the press to give him eclat in Illinois, but he is a good & brave soldier . . . is sober, very industrious, and as kind as a child. Yet he has been held up as careless, criminal, a drunkard, tyrant and everything horrible."[2]

These then were the Federal generals fronting west Tennessee whose relationships with one another will directly shape our story in 1862. Before we take up their campaigns, however, let us look at their backgrounds and personalities, and how they came to their commands.

Hiram Ulysses Grant—that was how he was christened—was born in Point Pleasant, Ohio, on April 27, 1822, the first of six children of Jesse and Hannah Simpson Grant. He was an eighth-generation American of English descent whose great-grandfather had died and grandfather had fought, respectively, in the French and Indian and Revolutionary Wars, and whose antecedents had steadily moved west. His father, a farmer and tradesman, was gregarious and shrewd, his mother silent and reserved. He was named in part for the Greek hero, and from his earliest days called Ulysses.

Jesse Grant soon after his son's birth started up a successful tannery in Georgetown, Ohio, and there the youngster grew up. His early education was typical of the time. "There were no free schools," Grant would say, "and none in which the scholars were classified. They were all supported by subscription, and a single teacher—who was often a man or woman incapable of teaching much, even if they imparted all they knew—would have thirty or forty scholars, male and female, from the infant learning the ABC's up to the young lady of eighteen and the boy of twenty, studying the highest branches taught—the three R's, 'Reading, 'Riting, 'Rithmetic." His childhood was a happy one, and he had "no recollection of ever having been punished at home, either by scolding or the rod." School was a different matter. "The rod was freely used there, and I was not exempt from its influence. . . . Switches were brought in bundles. . . . Often a whole bundle would be used up in a single day."

Ulysses disliked the tedium of the tannery, but "was fond of agriculture, and of all employment in which horses were used. . . . When I was seven or eight years of age, I began hauling all the wood used in the house and shops." By the time he was eleven, "I was strong enough to hold a plow." Thereafter he "did all the work done with horses, such as breaking up the land, furrowing, ploughing corn and potatoes, bringing in the crops." So adept did he become in handling horses that farmers from miles around Georgetown asked him to break in their colts and fillies. Explained one biographer: "He could train a horse to trot, rack, or pace, apparently at will."[3]

Once, on a visit to Flat Rock, Kentucky, Ulysses found those skills severely tested. He had gone there with a neighbor, driving a two-horse carriage, and had swapped one of the two for a saddle horse that caught his eye, thinking he would hitch him up for the return trip. This he did, even though the new horse had not worn harness before. The journey started out badly for Ulysses and his companion and only got worse. "We encountered a ferocious dog that frightened the horses and made them run. The new animal kicked at every jump [the dog] made." He reined in the team, settled them down, and started anew. "That instant the new horse kicked, and started to run once more. The road we were on struck the turnpike within half a mile . . . [where] there was an embankment twenty or more feet deep. . . . I got the horses stopped on the very brink of the precipice." His untrained horse "was trembling like an aspen," and so was his companion, who left him for a seat on a freight wagon. Subsequently, every time the youngster tried to resume the trip, the animal would rear and kick. But he persevered—as he would through his life. "I was in quite a dilemma for a time. . . . Finally I took out my bandana—the style of handkerchief in use then—and with this blindfolded my horse." In this manner he made his way home.

One more incident from Grant's youth merits retelling. He desperately wanted to buy a colt, but his father thought the animal worth no more than twenty dollars and the owner wanted twenty-five dollars. After much cajoling Jesse Grant agreed his son could offer the higher sum, but only after starting at twenty dollars. If it was rejected he was authorized "to offer twenty-two and a half, and if that would not get him, to give the twenty-five." The boy wasted no time with lengthy negotiations. "Papa says I may offer you twenty dollars for the colt," he told the owner, "but if you won't take that, I am to offer twenty-two and a half, and if you won't take that, to give you twenty-five." For Jesse the occasion indicated that his son had no head for business—as later events would prove. "The story got out among the boys of the village," Grant would admit, "and it was a long time before I heard the last of it." But the tale was added evidence of his tenacity. "I certainly showed very plainly," he would say, "that I had come for the colt and I meant to have him."[4]

His appointment to West Point, which he entered in 1839, came as a complete surprise to him. His father had arranged it, and made it plain the lad had no choice in the matter. "A military career had no charms for me," Grant admitted, "and I had not the faintest idea of staying in the army even if I should be graduated, which I did not expect." Early on at the academy, because of a clerical mix-up, Hiram Ulysses Grant was enrolled as "Ulysses S. Grant." In short order, the other cadets were calling him "United States" and "Uncle Sam" and, finally, just "Sam." Cadet life was, as Grant expected, both rigorous and, for him, unrewarding. "My pants sit as tight to my skin as bark to a tree," he wrote a cousin. "And if I do not walk *military*, that is if I bend over quickly or run, they are very apt to crack with a report as loud as a pistol."

During Grant's plebe year at the academy, Sherman was a first classman, and the two saw little of each other. His closest friend at West Point turned out to be James Longstreet of Georgia, who was one year ahead of him and who next to Stonewall Jackson would be Robert E. Lee's most notable commander. They made a striking contrast. Grant stood no more than five feet one inch—although he would grow six inches over the next four years—was well but slightly built and modest in manner. Longstreet was six feet two, muscular and athletic, and boisterous as well. "We became fast friends at our first meeting," Longstreet would say. "[He possessed] a noble, generous heart, a loveable character and a sense of honor so perfect . . . that in the numerous cabals which were often formed his name was never mentioned." Reminisced another classmate: "[Grant's] hair was reddish-brown and his eyes gray-blue. We all liked him. He had no bad habits . . . [but] he had no facility in conversation with the ladies, a total absence of elegance, and naturally showed off badly with the young Southern men, who prided themselves in being finished in the ways of the world."

Sam Grant's academy years were undistinguished. He piled up demerits for various infractions of the rules, graduated twenty-first in a class of thirty-nine and, intriguingly, spent as much time reading novels (Bulwer-Lytton, Fenimore Cooper, Washington Irving) and taking drawing courses as he did studying artillery and engineering. Much to the chagrin of his hard-riding Southern colleagues, however, he was the best horseman in the class. This was obvious on graduation day when, following the usual mounted exercises, Grant was called on to deliver the pièce de résistance—taking the high jump on York, a massive beast only he could control. "A clean-faced, slender young fellow," said one cadet who was there, "weighing about one hundred and twenty pounds, dashed from the ranks on a powerfully built chestnut-sorrel horse." From the far end of the riding hall, while the spectators leaned forward in their seats, Grant and York came galloping down the approach. Continued the cadet: "The horse increased his pace . . . bounded into the air, and cleared the bar, carrying his rider as if man and beast were welded together. The spectators were breathless." Grant's jump would remain an academy record for the next quarter century but, characteristically, he gave the credit to his mount. "York was a wonderful horse," he would recall. "I could *feel* him gathering under me as he approached the bar."[5]

Returning to Ohio on leave, Grant, elated to be wearing his brand-new dress blues, suffered two indignities. The first came when he passed through Cincinnati and rode by a jeering street urchin, "bareheaded, barefooted, with dirty and ragged pants held up by a single gallows—that's what suspenders were called then—and a shirt that had not seen a washtub for weeks."

"Soldier! Will you work?" the boy cried out, much to the self-conscious new officer's discomfort. "No, sir-ee; I'll sell my shirt first." The few observers laughed heartily, adding to Grant's unease.

The second slight came when he reached home. There a shabby stableman, "rather dissipated but possessed of some humor," had prepared a less than kindly welcome. "I found him parading the streets, and attending in the stable, barefooted, but in a pair of sky-blue nankeen pantaloons—just the color of my uniform trousers—with a strip of white cotton sheeting sewed down the outside seams in imitation of mine." For many of the townspeople, Grant concluded, "the joke was a huge one . . . but I did not appreciate it so highly." For the rest of his military career, he shunned dress uniforms.[6]

Though Lieutenant Grant thirsted for cavalry duty, his class standing doomed him to the infantry. In the fall of 1843 he reported to Jefferson Barracks near St. Louis, where the next year he began courting Julia Dent, the seventeen-year-old daughter of a well-off—and slaveholding—planter and merchant, and the sister of Frederick Dent, a West Point roommate. (She was also a cousin of Longstreet's, who was likewise stationed at Jefferson Barracks.) Julia was not beautiful—one historian ungallantly remarked that "she had more neck than chin"—but to Grant she was sprightly, cheerful, and altogether captivating. He was smitten. By mid-1844 the couple was informally engaged, but they would not marry for four more years. "When he spoke of marriage," said Julia, "I simply told him I thought it would be charming to be engaged, but to be married—no! I would rather be engaged. I do not think he liked this arrangement."

For Grant this interval, during which he and Julia kept up "a constant correspondence," was spent on duty in Louisiana and Texas, and then fighting with the 4th Infantry Regiment in the Mexican War. In that conflict he first served in 1846 under General Zachary Taylor, who was pursuing the dubious strategy of advancing on Mexico City, some 800 rugged, sun-baked miles away, from Texas and the Rio Grande. His initial battle, at Palo Alto, could have been his last. "One cannon ball passed through our ranks, not far from me," he said. "It took off the head of an enlisted man, and the under jaw of Captain Page of my regiment, while the splinters from the musket of the killed soldier, and his brains and bones, knocked down two or three others." Later, at Monterey, when his regiment was low on ammunition, Grant rode through a gamut of Mexican marksmen to get more. "I adjusted myself on the side of my horse furthest from the enemy, and with only one foot holding to the cantel of my saddle, and an arm over the neck of the horse exposed, I started at full run." Most of the danger came at street corners, "but these I crossed at such a flying rate that generally I was past and under cover of the next block of houses before the enemy fired."[7]

In the battle's aftermath, responding to a letter he had received from Julia, Grant emphasized how much he continued to yearn for their marriage. "What made you ask the question Dearest Julia 'if I thought absence could conquer love?'" he wrote. "You ought to be just as good a judge as me! I can only answer for myself alone, that Julia is as *dear* to me today as she was the day we visited St. Louis together, more than two years ago, when I first told her of my love. From that day to this I have loved you constantly and the same, and with the hope too that long before this time I would have been able to call you *Wife*."

Within months General Winfield Scott took overall charge of U.S. forces and Grant's regiment was transferred to his command. Scott's strategy, far sounder than Taylor's, called for landing at Vera Cruz on the Gulf of Mexico, and driving inland less than 200 miles to the capital. Grant fought in several battles en route, and then, in September of 1847, took part in the successful assault on Mexico City. There near the San Cosme road, helped by a dozen volunteers, he managed to get a howitzer up a church belfry overlooking the foe. "We were not more than two or three hundred yards from San Cosme," he said. "The shots from our little gun dropped in upon

the enemy and created great confusion. Why they did not send out a small
party and capture us, I do not know. We had no infantry or other defenses." General William Worth, Grant's division head, was so impressed
with his initiative that he personally congratulated him and sent him a second howitzer. "I could not tell the General that there was not room enough
in the steeple for a second gun," said Grant, already wise in the ways of
command, "because he probably would have looked upon such a statement as a contradiction from a second lieutenant."[8]

On the whole, however, the self-effacing Grant—though promoted to
first lieutenant and then to the brevet, or temporary, rank of captain—
attracted no more attention in Mexico than he had at West Point. That did
not keep him from making some observations about his superiors. General
Worth he found wanting. He "was nervous, impatient and restless on the
march, or when important and responsible duty confronted him." Zachary
Taylor "never wore uniform, but dressed himself entirely for comfort. . . .
Often he would be without staff officers. . . . Taylor was not a conversa-
tionalist, but on paper he could put his meaning so plainly that there could
be no mistaking it." Winfield Scott "was the reverse in all these particulars. He always wore all the uniform prescribed or allowed by law when
he inspected his lines. . . . On these occasions he wore his dress uniform,
cocked hat, aiguillettes, sabre and spurs. . . . General Scott was precise in
language . . . was proud of his rhetoric." Obviously Grant, though he
liked both Scott and Taylor, saw himself in the mold of the latter. "Both
were pleasant to serve under—Taylor was pleasant to serve with," he
summed up. "Scott saw more through the eyes of staff officers . . . Taylor
saw for himself."[9]

For West Pointers, almost 300 of whom died in the conflict, the Mexican War provided critical preparation for the Civil War to come. "Besides
the many practical lessons it taught," said Grant, "the war brought nearly
all the officers of the regular army together so as to make them personally
acquainted." Former comrades learned the strengths and weaknesses of
those they would soon call enemies. "The natural disposition of most people is to clothe a commander of a large army whom they do not know,
with almost superhuman abilities. A large part of the [Federal] army, for
instance, and most of the press of the country, clothed General Lee with
just such qualities, but I had known him personally, and knew that he was
mortal." Moreover, for those officers who had the good sense to learn, the
Mexican War highlighted the divide between classroom tactics and battlefield truths. Grant would perceive and accept these lessons; theorists like
Henry Halleck would not.

In August of 1848, following his return to the U.S., Grant and Julia were wed at the Dent home in St. Louis, with James Longstreet as best man. Garrison duty in Upstate New York and Detroit came next, and a first child (Fred) was born. Then in late 1852, posted to the Pacific Northwest, Grant made the fateful decision to leave behind his wife, pregnant with their second child. "I was indignant at this and said I would go, I would; for him to hush. . . . And, of course, I shed tears," said Julia. "He said: 'You know how loath I am to leave you, but crossing Panama is an undertaking for one in robust health; and then my salary is so small, how could you and my little boy have even the common necessities of life out there?' "[10]

Grant's two years without his family at Fort Vancouver in Oregon, and then at Fort Humboldt in northern California, touched off a downslide in his life. Everything seemed to go wrong. First he financed a casual acquaintance named Elijah Camp with his accumulated back pay, some $1,500, to start up a general store in San Francisco. Soon the man, claiming he could not sleep at night for fear Grant would come to him for the money, talked him into tearing up the promissory note. Later Camp skipped town and went back to New York. "I chided Ulys when he told me this," Julia said long afterward, "telling him that the Vicar of Wakefield's Moses [Moses Primrose, the naive vicar's son in the Oliver Goldsmith novel] was a financier beside him. Ulys should have given him something to *make* him sleep: the poker."

Next Grant and two fellow officers invested in seed potatoes and other vegetables, hoping to make money farming. He also invested in timber. But the Columbia River flooded, destroying the crops and rotting the wood. Still a third quixotic enterprise followed. Grant and another friend, noting the single men flocking to California in the aftermath of the Gold Rush, decided to open a social club in San Francisco. The fellow they hired to run the operation took their lease money and then disappeared. "Neither Grant nor myself," admitted the friend, "had the slightest suggestion of business talent. He was the perfect soul of honor and truth, and believed everyone as artless as himself."[11]

Grant's letters to Julia in 1854 indicated his growing despondency. "Imagine a place," he wrote her in January of desolate Fort Humboldt, located on the cliffs high above the Pacific, "closed in by a bay that can be entered only with certain winds." His second son, Ulysses Jr. (called Buck), had been born, and he had yet to see the child. "You do not know how forsaken I feel here!" he said the next month. ". . . I feel again as if I have been separated from you and Fred long enough, and as to Ulys I have never seen him. . . . I do nothing but [sit] in my room and read and occasionally take a short ride." In March, he first raised the possibility of leaving the army. "I sometimes get so anxious to see you, and our little boys, that I am almost tempted to resign and trust to Providence, and my own exertions, for a living where I can have you and them with me." Then on April 11, the same day his rank of captain became official, Grant abruptly submitted his resignation.

His decision, however, was not entirely voluntary. Explained Lieutenant Henry Hodges, who was serving with him at the time: "One day when his company was being paid off, Captain Grant was at the pay table, slightly under the influence of liquor. This came to the knowledge of Colonel Buchanan; he gave Grant the option of resigning or having charges preferred against him." Drinking was the rule rather than the exception on the frontier but Colonel Robert Buchanan, Grant's commanding officer, was something of a martinet. Rufus Ingalls of Maine, a classmate of Grant's at West Point and a lifetime intimate, backed up this account. "Grant, finding himself in dreary surroundings, without his family, and with but little to occupy his attention, fell into dissipated habits. . . . [His] friends at the time urged him to stand trial, and were confident of his acquittal; but, actuated by a noble spirit, he said he would not for all the world have his wife know that he had been tried on such a charge."[12]

Grant arrived back in New York in June but, perhaps unsure of his welcome, did not immediately rejoin Julia in St. Louis. Badly needing funds, he obtained a loan from still another classmate, Captain Simon Bolivar Buckner of Kentucky, then journeyed upstate in a vain effort to get his money back from Elijah Camp. "The fear of poverty was still stronger than his need to admit to it and return home," said a biographer. "The slips of paper that pathetically marked inept California speculations still stuck to his fingers." But a loving letter from Julia soon allayed Grant's misgivings, and by late summer of 1854 he was with his family in Missouri. There for the next few years he eked out a living by clearing sixty acres of land given his wife by her father (he became a familiar figure selling firewood on the streets of St. Louis), and by farming. He and Julia had their third child, called Nellie, and he built with his own hands a rough, two-story house he named, with biting humor, Hardscrabble. West Pointers who met him during this period found him abstemious to a fault. "He will go into the bar with you," complained one such officer, "but he will not touch anything."

The financial Panic of 1857, which roiled the economy and caused commodity prices to plummet, brought disaster to Grant's already-dim farming prospects. In December he was forced to pawn his gold watch, for twenty-two dollars, so his family could have some semblance of a Christmas celebration. The following year Julia gave birth to their fourth and last child, Jesse, and Grant, after being wracked for months "by fever and ague," found he had little choice but to sell "stock, crops and farming utensils at auction, and [give] up farming." That summer he encountered then Major Longstreet, who was passing through St. Louis. One of the officers in the latter's party, finding they needed a fourth for cards, went out to find a recruit. "In a few minutes," Longstreet remembered, "he came back with a man poorly dressed in citizen's clothes and in whom we recognized our old friend." The reunion was a convivial one, but he could not help noting that Grant "had been unfortunate," and "was really in needy circumstances."

When Longstreet left his hotel the next morning, he came "face to face again with Grant who, placing in the palm of my hand a five dollar gold piece, insisted that I should take it in payment of a debt of honor fifteen years old. I peremptorily declined . . . alleging that he was out of the service and more in need of it than I."

"You must take it," Grant replied. "I cannot live with anything in my possession which is not mine."

"Seeing the determination in [his] face," said Longstreet, "and in order to save him mortification, I took the money, and shaking hands we parted."[13]

Late in 1858 Grant tried his hand at real estate, forming a partnership with Harry Boggs, a cousin of Julia's. It was an unwise decision, for he was "too tenderhearted to be a rent collector and too candid to sell real estate," and he and the blustery Boggs were like oil and water. In 1860, when the business failed, Grant reluctantly petitioned his father for help. Despite his misgivings about his son's business sense, Jesse responded quickly and positively, offering him a $600-a-year clerkship in the family's thriving tannery and leather-goods operation, which now had its headquarters in Galena, Illinois. Though he had avoided the tannery since childhood, and would work under his two younger brothers, Grant was grateful for the job. "While living in Galena, I was nominally only a clerk," he said, putting the best possible face on the matter, "supporting myself and family on a stipulated salary. In reality the position was different. . . . When I went there it was my father's intention to give up all connection with the business himself, and to establish his three sons in it."

Grant then had no way of knowing, of course, but the move to Galena

would be his salvation. There, on the eve of the Civil War, his military career would begin to come into its own. "During the eleven months that I
lived in Galena prior to the first call for volunteers, I had been strictly at-
tentive to my business," he said, "and had made but few acquaintances."
When the presidential election took place in November 1860, Grant could
not even vote; he had not been a resident of Illinois long enough. "The
contest was really between Mr. [John] Breckinridge and Mr. Lincoln; between minority rule and rule by the majority. I wanted . . . to see Mr. Lincoln elected."[14]

Even before Lincoln's inauguration in March of 1861, however, all the
states of the Deep South—South Carolina, Mississippi, Florida, Alabama,
Georgia, Louisiana, and Texas—had voted to secede. Virginia, Arkansas,
North Carolina, and Tennessee soon would follow. "Emancipation had
become a creed," one historian commented, "states' rights a dogma." The
shelling and surrender in April of Fort Sumter in Charleston, South Carolina, one of the few Federal outposts not yet in Rebel hands, made the
conflict inevitable. Lincoln promptly called for 75,000 volunteers, then
asked for 300,000 more. "Galena was throbbing with patriotism," Julia
said. "The men were holding meetings and asking for volunteers. The
boys were playing at war, wearing military caps, beating small drums. . . ."
Grant was active in recruiting and training in Galena, and thereby attracted the attention of Elihu B. Washburne, the area's influential U.S.
congressman and a longtime friend of Lincoln's. This was fortunate, because Grant's own efforts to secure a commission in the regular army during this period were ignored. But Washburne saw something in him, and
backed him for command. In June, the shaggy-bearded, steady-eyed Grant
was named colonel of the 21st Illionis Volunteers, a regiment of rugged,
rowdy farmboys. He began drilling them immediately, wearing an old
blue coat and slouch hat but no sign of rank. "I found it very hard work
for a few days to bring all the men into anything like subordination," he
said, "but the great majority favored discipline, and by the application of
a little regular army punishment, all were reduced to as good discipline as
one could ask."

Grant was being modest. In all the volunteer regiments and brigades,
both North and South, discipline could be instilled and maintained only if
the colonels and brigadiers in command earned the men's respect. When a
particularly truculent soldier turned out for duty one morning "drunk and
disorderly," Grant brooked no nonsense, ordering him to the guardhouse.

"For every minute I stand here I'll have an ounce of your blood," the soldier snarled.

Grant's unruffled response was to tell the guards to bind and gag the man, and then to spend most of the day on other concerns. When he returned to the guardhouse, he unbound the prisoner himself, and the soldier, who had slept off his rage and doubtless regretted his outburst, tamely went back on duty. From that moment on, "all question of Grant's power to command both himself and his men" ceased, and everyone in the 21st Illinois—officer and enlisted man—knew who was in charge.[15]

In early summer he and his regiment crossed into slaveholding Missouri, reinforcing the Federal troops who controlled that state and its divided populace. There Grant, given added responsibilities, kept a tight rein on other units as well. "My arrival . . . had been preceded by two or three regiments in which proper discipline had not been maintained," he said, "and the men had been in the habit of visiting houses without invitation and helping themselves to food and drink. . . . They carried their muskets while out of camp and made every man they found take the oath of allegiance to the government." He at once ordered these practices stopped. "The people were no longer molested or made afraid. I received the most marked courtesy from the citizens . . . as long as I remained there."

Meanwhile he stepped up the drilling of the 21st Illinois, proceeding from company formations to complicated battalion movements. Unfortunately, he had given these subjects little attention at West Point. To remedy this deficiency, he opened the standard text of the time—*Hardee's Tactics*—and read the first lesson, intending to stay one chapter ahead of his men. "We were encamped just outside of town on the common," he wrote of this stopover in Mexico, Missouri, "among scattering suburban houses with enclosed gardens . . . and I soon saw that if I [followed] the lesson . . . I would have to clear away some of the houses and garden fences to make room." Ever the pragmatist, Grant tossed aside the textbook and adapted the drill to close quarters. "I found no trouble in giving commands that would take my regiment where I wanted it to go and carry it around all obstacles," he remarked. "I do not believe that the officers of the regiment ever discovered that I had never studied the tactics that I used."

In early August James Crane, chaplain of the 21st, picked up a copy of the *Daily Missouri Democrat* and read some unexpected news. Grant had been named a brigadier general. Crane lost no time informing his commander, who seemed more bemused than elated by the promotion. "Well, sir, I had no suspicion of it," he said. "It never came from any request of mine. That's some of Washburne's work. . . . [He] had something to do with having me commissioned colonel . . . and I suppose this is more of his work." Elihu Washburne had indeed been busy. Illinois was entitled to four brigadiers in the expanding Union forces, and the Galena congressman had made sure that Grant—the Galena resident—was one of them. The other newly minted generals were Stephen Hurlbut, Benjamin Prentiss, and John McClernand, all prominent politicians. Grant was the sole West Pointer. All three men would serve under him and one, McClernand, would despite his courage become a constant irritant.[16]

Some days later Grant, now comfortable in his new rank, made a call on Harry Boggs in St. Louis. His former real estate partner, a Southern sympathizer, was accustomed to seeing Grant in straitened circumstances. The fact that he was a general, and a *Yankee* general at that, sent Boggs into a rage. "He cursed and went on like a Madman," Grant contentedly wrote his wife. "Told me I never would be welcome in his house; that the people of Illinois were a poor miserable set of Black Republicans, abolition paupers that had to invade [Missouri] to get something to eat. . . . Harry is such a pitiful insignificant fellow that I could not get mad at him and told him so. . . ."

Grant was no fire-breathing abolitionist, however, nor would he become one. Instead his views were much like Lincoln's: keeping the Union together was the paramount goal, eliminating slavery was secondary. "My inclination is to whip the rebellion into submission," he would tell his father, "preserving all constitutional rights. If it cannot be whipped in any other way than through a war against slavery let it come to that legitimately. If it is necessary that slavery should fall that the Republic may continue its existence, let slavery go. . . ."[17]

Grant's rise in the military pecking order continued apace. On September 1, 1861, he was named commander of the District of Southeast Missouri—despite lingering reservations about his drinking habits—serving under the ineffectual Major General John C. Fremont, then head of the Department of the West. He forthwith made his headquarters in strategically important Cairo, Illinois, located on the Mississippi just north of the Missouri-Kentucky line. There he would be joined by his new chief of staff, a Galena lawyer named John A. Rawlins, whose father had died an alcoholic and who, understandably, was a passionate teetotaler. "Rawlins had no lighter side," wrote a historian, "he was the sworn enemy of all who brought liquor to headquarters, and in his stern dedication to Grant he took on the responsibility of making certain that there would not be any basis for a revival of the old rumors about [him]. He was a confidante of Congressman Washburne, and kept him posted on this matter, and on others." We will subsequently hear more of Rawlins.

Learning that Confederate troops under Leonidas Polk—an Episcopal bishop turned general—had moved into Columbus, Kentucky, just eighteen miles below Cairo, Grant within days moved to checkmate the advance. Without waiting for orders he sent troops east into Paducah, at the mouth of the Tennessee River, occupying the town and blocking further incursions. "I have come among you, not as an enemy, but as your friend and fellow-citizen," he told the townspeople, most of whom were Southern loyalists. Then he prepared his command for war. "By the first of November," he said, "I had not fewer than 20,000 men, most of them under good drill and ready to meet any equal body of men who, like themselves, had not yet been in an engagement."[18]

That first encounter occurred on November 7. Grant, who had received orders from Fremont merely to demonstrate against the Rebels at Columbus, instead took it upon himself to attack. He steamed down the Mississippi with some 3,000 men aboard transports, convoyed by two gunboats, and debarked the troops across the river from Columbus at Belmont, Missouri, where the Confederates had an outpost. His intent was to destroy the camp and then withdraw, in good order, before reinforcements could cross the river. The fighting began about 10:00 A.M. when the Rebels, who were in greater strength than Grant anticipated, rushed forward to repel the assault. It continued, he stated, "growing fiercer and fiercer, for about four hours, the enemy being forced back gradually until he was driven into his camp." When one horse was shot from under him, Grant commandeered another. The turning point came when he massed his artillery on the exposed Confederate center, bringing on a rout. "Veterans could not have behaved better than they did," he said of his command, "up to the moment of reaching the enemy camp. . . . [Then] they became demoralized from their victory and failed to reap its full reward. The enemy had been followed so closely that when he reached the clear ground on which his camp was pitched he beat a hasty retreat over the river bank, which protected him from our shots and from view."

Thinking the fighting over, the Federals began to celebrate, pillaging and looting the Rebel tents. "All this time," said Grant, "the troops we had been engaged with . . . lay crouched under the cover of the river bank, ready to come up and surrender if summoned to do so; but finding they were not pursued, they worked their way up the river and came up on the bank between us and our transports." Then he saw two ships loaded with fresh troops steaming out from the Columbus side of the river. "Some of my men were engaged in firing from captured guns at empty steamers down the river, out of range, cheering at every shot. I tried to get them to turn their guns upon the loaded steamers. . . . My efforts were in vain."[19]

Grant forthwith ordered his staff officers to torch the camp. "This drew the fire of the enemy's guns located on the heights of Columbus. They had abstained from firing before, probably because they were afraid of hitting their own men." By now the Federals were in danger of being surrounded, with Rebels between them and their transports and reinforcements about to land behind them. "The alarm 'surrounded' was given," Grant said. "The guns of the enemy, and the report of being surrounded, brought officers and men completely under control. At first some of the officers seemed to think that [they were] in a hopeless position. . . . But when I announced that we had cut our way in and could cut our way out just as well, it seemed a . . . revelation." His troops rapidly formed up and, led by the exhortations of Colonel John "Black Jack" Logan of the 31st Illinois—"Follow the flag and myself!"—fought their way to the transports. "The enemy was soon encountered," said Grant, "but his resistance this time was feeble. I now set the troops to bringing their wounded to the boats."

The pursuing Confederates, understandably, contradicted this matter-of-fact account of the withdrawal. "The route over which we passed," said Polk of his adversaries, "was strewn with the dead and wounded. . . . On arriving where [Grant's] transports lay, I ordered the column . . . to be deployed within easy range of the boats. . . . Under this galling fire he cut his lines and retreated from the shore, many of his soldiers driven overboard by the rush of those behind them."

While this bloodshed was going on, Grant had retraced his column's escape route, entirely alone, to reconnoiter and inspect his rear guard, "knowing the enemy had crossed over from Columbus in considerable numbers and might be expected to attack us as we were embarking." To his chagrin, he found that his guard had already moved out. Narrowly escaping capture by taking refuge in a field of towering cornstalks, he did not make it back to the embarkation point until sunset, as the last of the boats was leaving. "I was the only man of the National army between the Rebels and our transports. The captain of a boat that had just pushed off but had not started . . . had a plank run out for me. My horse seemed to take in the situation. There was no path down the bank and everyone acquainted with the Mississippi knows that its banks . . . do not vary at any great angle from the perpendicular." Grant and his mount never hesitated. "My horse," he said proudly, "put his fore feet over the bank . . . and with his hind feet well under him, slid down the bank and trotted aboard the boat, twelve or fifteen feet away, over a single gang plank."[20]

From his vantage point overlooking the transports, Leonidas Polk had noted Grant's impromptu escape and, though he had no idea who the horseman was, had remarked to some aides: "There is a Yankee; you may try your marksmanship on him if you wish." No one did, and he embarked without a scratch.

The Battle of Belmont was costly, particularly for a supposed demonstration; each side suffered some 600 casualties—dead, wounded, and missing—out of the 4,000 Confederates and 3,000 Federals involved. Overall the affair burnished Grant's reputation as a forceful leader, albeit one perhaps too willing to accept losses. The *Chicago Tribune* initially was critical, printing the casualty lists and editorializing, "It may be said of these victims, 'They have fallen, but to what end?' " But *The New York Times* trumpeted that the battle "is considered in high degree creditable . . . and the success of the brilliant movement is due to Gen. Grant." The *St. Louis Republican* and the *New York Herald* echoed the praise, the former saying the commander was "present where the balls fell thickest, directing every movement as if on parade," and the latter insisting that Belmont was a victory "as clear as ever warriors gained."

Grant soon learned that he would have a new commander: Henry Halleck had superceded John Fremont. He gave the report scant attention. Calmly and purposefully, the onetime seller of firewood on the streets of St. Louis continued to get ready for war. "From the battle of Belmont until early in February 1862," he wrote, "the troops under my command did little except prepare for the long struggle which proved to be before them."[21]

Tecumseh Sherman, whose English forbears had arrived in Massachusetts and Connecticut in the 1600s—and one of whom had signed the Declaration of Independence—was born on February 8, 1820, in Lancaster, Ohio, the sixth child (there ultimately would be eleven) of Charles and Mary Hoyt Sherman. Idiosyncratically named for the great Shawnee chieftain and warrior, he was simply called Cump. His father, a respected circuit court judge, had long been debt ridden, and his sudden death of typhoid fever in 1829 forced Mary Sherman to parcel out her brood to family and friends. Though he would continue to see his mother through the years, nine-year-old Cump was sent the road to the home of Thomas Ewing, a wealthy lawyer who would soon serve as a U.S. senator and, later, a cabinet officer in two administrations. The Ewings had four children of their own (and would have two more), so he did not lack for youthful companionship. Remembered one of the Ewing offspring, five-year-old Ellen, "I peeped at him with great interest." She subsequently would become his wife.

Tom Ewing's wife Maria, a devout Catholic, insisted that Cump be baptized as one—even though he came from a Protestant household. The impasse, of course, was that the name Tecumseh was nowhere to be found in the lexicon of Catholic saints. Noting it was St. William's Day, the Dominican performing the rite forthwith named the boy William Tecumseh. Perhaps because the baptism was coerced, it did not take root, and Cump never did become a practicing Catholic. Maria Ewing was more successful in furthering the boy's education. She saw to it he studied Latin and Greek, read Shakespeare and Sir Walter Scott, and delved into mathematics and science. Though the Ewings treated him the way they did all their children, with love and affection, his feelings for them—and particularly Mr. Ewing—were ambivalent. "Cump wanted to stand on his own and be free of his foster father's support," wrote a biographer. "He appreciated Ewing's help but disliked having to receive it, perhaps unconsciously feeling it was not his birthright."[22]

In 1836, through Thomas Ewing's contacts, a curious Sherman received an appointment to West Point, of which he knew very little, "except that it was very strict, and that the army was its natural consequence." But off he went, taking the stagecoach from Lancaster to the East, "a tall, slim, loose-jointed lad, with red hair, fair, burned skin, and piercing black eyes." His academy years, like Grant's, would be notable mostly for the demerits both men amassed—in part because of their independent natures. "I was not considered a good soldier," he said, "for at no time was I selected for any office, but remained a private through the whole four years. Then, as now, neatness in dress and form, with a strict conformity to the rules, were the qualifications . . . and I suppose I was found not to excel in any of these." His strongest challenge to authority occurred one New Year's Eve, when he and some other cadets hauled up a cannon to the top floor of a barracks and, for good measure, raised some fifes and drums to the top of a flagpole. "There was no reveille *that* morning," he exulted.

Unlike Grant, a man of few words, Sherman was a rapid-fire talker, given to expressing his opinions in short but frequent bursts. He was a superior student as well, who on graduation in 1840 ranked sixth in a class of forty-three and, but for the demerits, would have been even higher. "In studies I always held a respectable reputation with the professors, and ranked among the best, especially in drawing, chemistry, mathematics, and natural philosophy."[23]

Commissioned in the artillery, Sherman first served in Florida during the continuing war against the Seminoles, and then during 1842 to 1843 was stationed in Alabama and South Carolina, giving him the opportunity to travel through Louisiana, Georgia, and North Carolina. He made many Southern friends, and came to understand their beliefs. Nonetheless, he felt secession could not be tolerated. "Charleston was then a proud, aristocratic city," he would write of his posting in South Carolina. "On more than one occasion previously, the inhabitants had almost inaugurated Civil War, by their assertion and professed belief that each state had . . . reserved to itself the right to withdraw from the Union at its own option. . . . We used to discuss these things at our own mess-tables, vehemently and sometimes quite angrily. . . ." Meanwhile, as he had throughout his years at West Point, he corresponded with his foster sister Ellen—a sweet-faced, serene young woman—and continued to see her in Lancaster while on furlough. Now they began to discuss marriage.

In 1844 Ellen committed herself, and Tom Ewing gave his consent. Both she and her father, however, urged him to resign from the army and turn to civilian pursuits, where he would earn more money. This was a continual strain on the relationship.

Complicating the situation was Ellen's devotion to religion and her dependence on her parents. Not only was she as dutiful a Catholic as her mother, and hoped that Sherman would share her beliefs, but she dreaded leaving Lancaster, the family home, for the distant postings the army demanded. Sherman must have felt that marriage and children would overcome the latter difficulty, but he offered Ellen scant hope that he would accept her faith. Since leaving the Ewing household, he told her, "I have practiced or professed no particular creed, believing firmly in the main doctrines of the Christian religion, the purity of its morals, the almost absolute necessity for its existence and practice. . . . Yet I cannot, with due reflection, attribute to minor points of doctrine the importance usually attached to them. I believe in good works rather than faith, and I believe them to constitute the basis of true religion."[24]

Primarily for these reasons, the couple put off their marriage for six years. In the interim, Lieutenant Sherman despite strenuous efforts failed to see action in the Mexican War. Instead in 1846 he found himself ordered to California, making a seven-month-long, arduous trip around Cape Horn in the company of Lieutenant Henry Halleck and other officers. "When others were struggling to kill time," he would say admiringly of Halleck, who already was the author of the well-received *Elements of Military Art and Science,* "he was using it in hard study. . . . He stood on a stool, his book and candle on the upper berth and a bed strap round his middle secured to the frame, to support him in the wild tossing of the ship."

Once in California, Sherman served as an aide to Colonel Richard B. Mason, the military governor during the tumultuous Gold Rush era. "As the spring and summer of 1848 advanced," he said, "the reports came faster and faster from the gold-mines at Sutter's saw-mill. Stories reached us of fabulous discoveries, and spread throughout the land. Everyone was talking of 'Gold! Gold!' until it assumed the character of a fever." He personally visited the mines, then drafted the report to the War Department detailing the tidings. Later he served under Mason's successor, helping him cope with the problems that the Gold Rush engendered. On one occasion, when twenty-eight men in the 2nd Infantry deserted to try their luck in the mines, Sherman led the pursuit, capturing six of them within hours and the rest the next morning. "I doubt not this prevented the desertion of the bulk of the 2nd Infantry that spring," he said, "for at that time so demoralizing was the effect of the gold mines that everybody not in the military justified desertion, because a soldier, if free, could earn more money in a day than he received per month."

By 1850 Sherman was back in Washington, doubtless through the influence of now Secretary of the Interior Tom Ewing, combining both military and marital affairs. He bore with him dispatches for General-in-Chief Winfield Scott and President Zachary Taylor, both of whom he briefed on developments in California. His long-postponed marriage to Ellen took place on May 1 at Blair House, and it was one of the capital's premier social events. The president of Georgetown University, a Jesuit, officiated, and the guests included President Taylor, various cabinet members, and such senators as Henry Clay, Daniel Webster, and Stephen Douglas. Promoted to captain, Sherman served the next two years in St. Louis and New Orleans. Two children were born, Maria (called Minnie) and Elizabeth (called Lizzie), with Ellen in various stages of pregnancy shuttling back and forth to Lancaster.

Finally in 1853 Sherman acceded to his wife's pleas, resigning from the army and taking a position as a bank manager in then booming San Francisco. Ellen and Lizzie soon joined him, although Minnie stayed with the Ewings in Ohio, enlarging the list of family separations. During 1854–1856 a third child, William (Willie) was born, Ellen returned to Lancaster for a six-month visit—leaving Lizzie and Willie with their father—and a beleaguered Sherman, with San Francisco's economy now in the doldrums, barely survived a run on the banks. "This run" he dryly wrote, "presented all the features, serious and comical, usual to such occasions." One of his depositors, a Frenchman, "was nearly squeezed to death in getting to the counter and, when he received his money, did not know what to do with it."

"If you got the money I no want him," the man yelled in his best English, "but if you no got him, I want it like the devil!"[25]

Sherman's bank emerged from the run intact, but he was becoming disillusioned with San Francisco. "Politics had become a regular and profitable business," he lamented, "and politicians were more than suspected of being corrupt. . . . All sorts of dishonesty were charged and believed, especially of 'ballot-box stuffing,' and too generally the better classes avoided the elections . . . so that the affairs of the city government necessarily passed into the hands of a low set of professional politicians." One such hack was James Casey, who also edited a newspaper on the third floor of the building where Sherman had his bank offices—a fact that perhaps fostered the latter's contempt for the press. Soon after reading an article in Casey's paper "so full of falsehood and malice, that we construed it as an effort to black-mail the banks generally," Sherman took direct action. "I went upstairs, found Casey . . . told him plainly I would not tolerate his attempt to print and circulate slanders . . . and, if he repeated it, I would cause him and his press to be thrown out of the windows. He took the hint. . . ."

With business conditions continuing to deteriorate, Sherman during the Panic of 1857 closed the bank and left with his family (including a fourth child—Thomas Ewing Sherman) for New York, whereupon Ellen decamped for Lancaster.

Financial turmoil now was nationwide, and Sherman was growing increasingly concerned about his civilian career. For the next few years, despite his connections, he flailed about. He mulled over the standing offer of his father-in-law to run the family's salt works in Ohio, became a member of the Kansas bar and moved with Ellen to Leavenworth to practice law with two of his brothers-in-law, and even wrote the War Department for reinstatement. His fifth child, Ellie, was born, adding to his obligations. In effect he began to despair of supporting Ellen in Tom Ewing's style and, just as importantly, of escaping his father-in-law's paternalism.

"I am doomed to be a vagabond," he said. "I look upon myself as a dead cock in the pit, not worthy of further notice."[26]

In 1860 Sherman found what he thought the ideal fit for his talents. Supported by such West Point friends and native Louisianans—and future adversaries—as Braxton Bragg and Pierre Beauregard, he was named superintendent of the newly established Louisiana State Seminary and Military Academy (later Louisiana State University), turning down a better offer—arranged through Ewing—to manage an American bank in London. "If you hear I have concluded to stay here," he told his wife, who was again in Lancaster, "just make up your mind to live and die here, because I am going to take the bit in my mouth, and resume my military character, and control my own affairs. . . . Therefore, if Louisiana will endow this college properly, and . . . give me $5,000 a year, we will drive our tent pins and pick out a magnolia under which to sleep."

Sherman poured his energies into the academy's operations, instructing the fifty-six privileged cadets in West Point curriculum and drill. They were "the sons of wealthy planters from the rivers, and aristocratic Creoles from the south, the nimble pony-riding Cajeans from the prairies, and the diligent, quiet fellows from the pine woods." In short order he had them responding to, even enjoying, the regimen. Malcontents he culled out. "We have just passed through a critical week," he wrote Ellen, "the struggle for mastery resulting in five [cadets] being gone. . . . I am now rid of five noisy, insubordinate boys. . . . I must rest satisfied with the title of the 'Old Man.' "

The Louisiana elite was suitably impressed, and Sherman became a frequent guest at its dinner parties. There he made it clear that, while he was opposed to secession, he had few objections to slavery. During one such event, at the home of Governor Thomas Moore, his host referred to Sherman's brother, John, a member of the U.S. House of Representatives who, backed by the abolitionists, was running for Speaker, and inquired whether Sherman shared his views.

"Now you are at my table. . . ." said Moore. "Won't you speak your mind freely on this question of slavery?"

"Governor Moore," demurred Sherman, "you mistake in calling my brother, John Sherman, an abolitionist. . . . It is possible [he and I] may differ in general sentiment, but I deny that he is considered at home an abolitionist; and, although he prefers the free institutions under which he lives to those of slavery which prevail here, he would not of himself take from you by law or force any property whatever, even slaves."

"Give us your own views of slavery as you see it here," said Moore, while the guests listened intently.

"The people of Louisiana were hardly responsible for slavery, as they had inherited it," Sherman responded. "[But] were I a citizen of Louisiana, and a member of the legislature, I would deem it wise to bring the legal condition of the slaves more near the status of human beings under all Christian and civilized governments. . . . I would forbid the separation of families. . . . I would advise the repeal of the statute which enacted a severe penalty for even the owner to teach his slave to read or write. . . ."

"By God, he is right!" said one guest, striking his fist on the table, and with that the discussion went on the rest of the evening.

In point of fact, Sherman's views on slavery were much like those of his fellow dinner guests. Slaves in the South were not people, they were property. They should be well treated, of course, because that only enhanced their value. Morality had no place in the debate. "I don't know that I would materially change the actual relation of master and slave," Sherman would write. "Negroes in the great numbers that exist [in the South] must of necessity be slaves."[27]

When Louisiana seceded in January of 1861, Sherman as a loyal Unionist had no recourse but to resign, and he returned north, once again looking for employment. "It may be that Louisiana's honor compelled her to this course," he wrote one of the trustees on the eve of his departure, "but I see it not, and must think it is the rash result of excited men. . . . War seems to be courted by those who understand not its cost. . . ." It was in this depressed frame of mind during a stopover in Washington that he was introduced, through his brother John—now an U.S. senator from Ohio—to the newly inaugurated Lincoln.

"Mr. President, this is my brother, who is just up from Louisiana, he may give you some information you want," said John Sherman, alluding to the secession crisis.

"Ah!" said Lincoln, "how are they getting along down there?"

"They think they are getting along swimmingly—they are preparing for war," replied the outspoken Sherman.

"Oh well," allowed Lincoln in his affable politician's way, "I guess we'll manage to keep house."

The president's comment infuriated Sherman, who considered it flippant. Once the meeting was over, "I broke out on John, damming politicians generally, saying, 'You have got things in a hell of a fix, and you may get them out as you best can,' adding that the country was sleeping on a volcano that might burst forth at any minute."

In the days that followed, Sherman's dark mood persisted. Unconvinced that the country's leadership would deal forcefully with secession, he rejected the chief clerkship of the War Department, a post that would have led to his being named assistant Secretary of War. On April 14, however, the bombardment of Fort Sumter clarified the issues. His brother and the Ewing family saw to it that Sherman was named colonel of the 13th Regular Infantry—a unit, unfortunately, that did not exist. Soon he was put in charge of a brigade of volunteers. To his men, he was an odd-looking figure. Tall and gaunt, he affected a broad-brimmed straw hat and an ill-fitting, nondescript blue coat. His eyes were sharp and piercing, his forehead bulging and his cheeks hollow, his reddish-brown hair and beard uncombed and untrimmed. But his emphasis on drill and discipline, together with his unpretentious manner, quickly won them over. Within weeks he would be commanding them in the first major engagement of the war.[28]

The battle of First Bull Run—called First Manassas by the South—took place on July 21, 1861. There some 37,000 Federals led by General Irvin McDowell pushed down the Warrenton Turnpike from Washington through Centreville in stifling heat to cross over Bull Run Creek and assail almost as many Confederates, led by Joseph Johnston and Pierre Beauregard, at the Manassas rail junction. The Union plan called for two divisions to surprise and flank the Rebel left at Sudley Ford, while a smaller force, including Sherman's unit, feinted against the center at the Stone Bridge. All morning the battle raged back and forth on the enemy left, until about 1:00 P.M. it converged on Henry Hill, where Confederate general Thomas Jackson, "standing like a stone wall," first earned his sobriquet. Finally ordered into action Sherman rushed his men across Bull Run and toward the hill, whereupon the Rebels, hidden in some nearby woods, stopped them cold with a withering hail of musketry. "Here my regiments came into action well, but successively, and were driven back, each in its turn," he said. "For two hours we continued to dash at the woods . . . which were full of Rebels; but I was convinced their organization was broken, and that they had simply halted there and taken advantage of the woods as a cover."

Sherman was far too optimistic, for the Confederates had held their lines on Henry Hill and the Federals had lost heart. "I had no idea that we were beaten, but reformed the regiments in line in their proper order, and only wanted a little rest, when I found that my brigade was almost alone. . . . I then realized that the whole army was 'in retreat,' and that my own men were individually making back for the Stone Bridge." He rallied what was left of his command, then realized the situation was hopeless. "[We] formed the brigade into an irregular square, but it fell to pieces; and along with a crowd, disorganized but not much scared, the brigade got back to Centreville to our former camps." Stated one historian: "The wonder was not that the Union troops were repulsed, but that they had kept up their spasmodic efforts for so long. There was certainly no irresistible charge sweeping [the Federals] off the hill. . . . If the defeated gradually became . . . a confused mob of stragglers, it was not under shock pressure but under the influence of mass suggestion." The Federals incurred some 2,900 casualties, of whom 600 were in Sherman's command; the Confederates, 2,000.

Taking the defeat as a personal failure, Sherman wrote to Ellen: "Well, as I am sufficiently disgraced now, I suppose I can sneak into some quiet corner. I was under heavy fire for hours—brushed on the knee & shoulder— my horse shot through the leg, and was every way exposed and cannot imagine how I escaped, except to experience the mortification of a retreat route. . . ."[29]

Within days, however, he had recovered his composure, stating that his brigade was "about as well governed as any in the army," but admitting "most of the ninety-day men . . . had become extremely tired of the war, and wanted to go home." Following roll call one morning he fell in step with an officer who told him: "Colonel, I am going to New York today. What can I do for you?"

"How can you go to New York?" Sherman replied. "I do not remember to have signed a leave for you. [The officer] said, 'No, he did not want a leave. He had engaged to serve three months . . . he was a lawyer, and had neglected his business long enough, and was going home.' "

Sherman noticed that the troops had gathered around and were listening, and he knew that if he allowed this officer to defect, they would too.

"Captain . . ." he said sharply, "You are a soldier and must submit to orders till you are properly discharged. If you attempt to leave without orders it will be mutiny, and I will shoot you like a dog!"

The officer looked at him, paused a moment, and then turned back to his quarters.

That same day President Lincoln visited Sherman's camp. "Mr. Lincoln was full of feeling," said Sherman, who was invited to ride in his carriage, "and wanted to encourage our men. I asked if he intended to speak to them, and he said he would like to. I asked him then to discourage all cheering . . . that we had had enough of it before Bull Run to ruin any set of men, and that what we needed were cool, thoughtful, hard-fighting soldiers—no more hurrahing, no more humbug. He took my remarks in the most perfect good humor."

Standing up in the carriage, Lincoln then made what Sherman called "one of the neatest, best . . . addresses I ever listened to, referring to our late disaster at Bull Run . . . and the brighter days yet to come."

When the inevitable cheers began to be heard, Lincoln checked them: "Don't cheer, boys. I confess I rather like it myself, but Colonel Sherman here says it's not military, and I guess we had better defer to his opinion."

With that the president rode to each of Sherman's regiments in turn, echoing the same sentiments. When he finished the last of his talks, the officer Sherman earlier had confronted approached Lincoln's carriage.

"Mr. President," he said, "I have a cause of grievance. This morning I went to speak with Colonel Sherman, and he threatened to shoot me."

Lincoln, still standing in the carriage, said, "Threatened to shoot you?"

"Yes, sir, he threatened to shoot me."

Lincoln looked at the officer, then at Sherman, then leaned toward the complainant and said, in a loud voice all the troops could hear, "Well, if I were you, and he threatened to shoot [me], I would not trust him, for I believe he would do it." The officer departed amid hoots of laughter.

When the carriage drove on, Sherman explained to the president the circumstances behind his warning. "Of course I didn't know anything about it," Lincoln responded, "but I thought you knew your own business best." The next month Sherman was promoted to brigadier general.[30]

Cump soon would be ordered to the West. By September 1861 he was second in command to General Robert Anderson in slaveholding Kentucky, which like Missouri was mostly under Federal control, but where Rebel sentiment ran perhaps three to one in favor of secession. One month later, when Anderson—who had led the garrison at Fort Sumter—resigned because of failing health, Sherman was named to replace him.

Grant's occupation of Paducah had blocked Confederate incursions into western Kentucky, but the situation below Louisville, where Sherman had his headquarters, was more precarious—or so he thought. There, in the central part of the state, he fretted that he would be attacked at any moment by vastly superior numbers. In truth, however, Albert Sidney Johnston—his Confederate adversary—had similar concerns; each man was overestimating the other's strength. Sherman tried to bury his worries in round-the-clock activity, all but forgetting to eat, sleep, or change his clothes in the midst of making plans and bolstering fortifications. But his anxiety only increased. "I am afraid you are too late to save Kentucky," he told his senator brother. "The young active element is all secession. The older stay-at-homes are for Union & Peace [but] they will not take part. In the meantime the [South] . . . has armed, organized, equipped & have the railroads so disposed that by concentration they can overwhelm any part."

So frequent and strident were his warnings that, on October 17, Secretary of War Simon Cameron and Adjutant General Lorenzo Thomas journeyed to Louisville to confer with him.

"Now, General Sherman, tell us of your troubles," Cameron said, while his entourage, who included some newspapermen, settled into their seats. Cump objected, saying he preferred not to discuss business with so many strangers present.

"They are friends, all members of my family, and you may speak your mind freely and without restraint," Cameron assured him.

"I complained," said Sherman "that the new levies of Ohio and Indiana were diverted East and West, and we got scarcely anything . . . that, if Johnston chose, he could march to Louisville any day."

"You astonish me!" Cameron said. "Our informants, the Kentucky Senators and members of Congress, claim they have in Kentucky plenty of men, and all they want are arms and money."

"I then said it was not true," Sherman replied, "for the young men were arming and going out in broad daylight to the Rebel camps, provided with good horses and guns by their fathers." He took out a large map to illustrate the situation. "[I] showed that [George] McClellan was on the left [in Virginia], having a frontage of less than a hundred miles, and Fremont the right [in Missouri], about the same; whereas I, the centre, had from the Big Sandy to Paducah, over three hundred miles of frontier; that McClellan had 100,000 men, Fremont 60,000, whereas to me had been allotted about 18,000." Just to defend his lines, he maintained, he needed 60,000 men; to go on the offense and push deep into the South, he required 200,000.

"Great God! Where are they to come from?" Cameron exclaimed. Sherman had a ready response, saying that the pool of manpower in the North had barely been tapped, while offers of military assistance from the Northwest had actually been rejected, on the grounds the troops were not needed. Secretary Cameron allowed that this might be, and indicated the policy would be reviewed.

Two weeks later the *New York Tribune,* one of whose men had been in the meeting, published a dispatch highly critical of Sherman, whom

Cameron had carelessly characterized as making an "insane" request. In the manner in which such exaggerations evolve, this offhand remark became a suggestion that Sherman was mentally unstable. Moreover the 200,000 men he had suggested he needed to invade the South and march to the Gulf of Mexico became a demand for 200,000 men just to defend Kentucky. Other Eastern papers took up the dispatch, elaborating further, and then the Western papers joined in.

Now Washington politicians began to question Cump's mental health. "Sherman's gone in the head, he's loony," said one subcabinet officer. His eccentric habits and dress fueled the furor. The continuing press attacks exhausted Sherman. On November 6 he wrote Lorenzo Thomas, saying: "It would be best if some man [of] sanguine mind was here." Within days Don Carlos Buell replaced him, and he was ordered to report to Henry Halleck in Missouri.[31]

Despite his liking and respect for his new subordinate, whom he briefly put in charge of three divisions near Sedalia, Missouri, Halleck was ambivalent about him. True, he downplayed the newspaper charges to Ellen when she journeyed to St. Louis to support her husband, but he saw that Sherman needed rest. "I am satisfied that General Sherman's physical and mental system is so broken down by labor and care," he wrote then general-in-chief McClellan, "as to render him, for the present, unfit for duty; perhaps a few weeks' rest may restore him." Subsequently, when Cump was on leave and back in Lancaster, the *Cincinnati Commercial* on December 11 delivered the harshest attack yet. Topped by the damning headline, "General William T. Sherman Insane," the article rehashed the allegations that had been made about him in Kentucky, and contended that his behavior at Sedalia had been so bizarre that officers would not obey his orders.

Sherman indignantly rebutted the *Commercial*'s assertions. "I write to you," he told Halleck the next day, "because a Cincinnati paper, whose reporter I imprisoned in Louisville for visiting our camps after I had forbidden him leave to go, has announced that I am insane, and alleges as a reason that at Sedalia, my acts were so mad that subordinate officers refused to obey. I know of no order I gave that was not obeyed. . . . These newspapers have us in their power, and can destroy us as they please. . . ." Then he waited. It was not until his return to St. Louis that he learned Halleck, instead of removing him, had restored him to limited command. "He has placed me in charge of Benton Barracks," he wrote his brother, John, on Christmas Eve, "where there are about 12,000 men, mostly awaiting arms. These will be drilled, supplied and sent forward as the service calls for them."

Thus a frustrating, dispiriting 1861 came to a close for Sherman, languishing despite his connections in a training camp backwater, and deemed, for the moment at least, too high-strung for combat. Not until he served under Grant at Shiloh would he prove his mettle. "I am here in a subordinate place whilst others occupy posts that I ought to," he wrote Ellen from Benton Barracks. "I cannot claim [those posts] for having so signally failed in Kentucky, and here I could not demand a higher place. . . . The idea of having brought disgrace on all associated with me is so horrible to contemplate that I really cannot endure it."[32]

Henry Halleck, essential to our story because of the influence he had on the early careers of Grant and Sherman, was born in the Mohawk Valley of Upstate New York on January 16, 1815, the first of thirteen children of Joseph and Catherine Wager Halleck. His father was a struggling farmer, and the teenager so hated the work that, at age sixteen, he fled to the house of Henry Wager, the maternal grandfather for whom he had been named. Wager saw to it his grandson had a proper education, first at Fairfield Academy in Hudson, New York, and then at Union College in Schenectady, where he was elected to Phi Beta Kappa. He also arranged his appointment to West Point.

The cerebral Halleck entered the academy later than most cadets, when he was twenty. There he fell under the influence of Dennis Mahan, the faculty's leading expert in military theory, who besides teaching military and civil engineering expounded on Swiss Baron Henri Jomini's ideas on limited warfare—stressing such principles as short interior lines, concentrated strength, and superior firepower. Both Mahan and Jomini believed that wars could be won by capturing strategic places; toe-to-toe fighting, which involved risk, was to be avoided. "To do the greatest damage to our enemy with the least exposure to ourselves," Mahan told the cadets, "is a military axiom." Halleck became a rigid believer in this truth, not anticipating that the Civil War would unleash, on both sides, all-out passions. He graduated from West Point in 1839, third in a class of thirty-nine, and later was sent to France by Winfield Scott to study military defenses. Out of this grew his aforementioned *Elements of Military Art and Science,* earning him the nickname Old Brains.

Halleck did not see service in the Mexican War but instead served, like Sherman, in California. There from 1846 on he was, sequentially, secretary of state to the military governor, chief of staff, and lieutenant governor of Mazatlan. More importantly, as far as his finances were concerned, his duties gave him free access to land-title records. "In the confused state of transferring sovereignty from Mexico to the United States," said a biographer, "the young officer succeeded in acquiring land and valuable mineral rights." He resigned from the army with rank of captain in 1854 and became a leading California lawyer and businessman, founding perhaps the most respected law firm in the state, turning down a seat in the U.S. Senate, and writing a book on international law that stayed in print for half a century. Meanwhile he married Elizabeth Hamilton, the granddaughter of Alexander Hamilton, served on the boards of a bank and two railroads, and pursued a highly profitable mining venture. In 1860 his worth was estimated at an astounding—for the time—$500,000.[33]

With the outbreak of the Civil War Winfield Scott, sorely in need of senior officers, turned to his long-ago protégé and arranged, in August 1861, for Lincoln to name him a major general. By November Halleck was in St. Louis, replacing the feckless Fremont and bringing order to the Missouri Department. Under his rule, "fraudulent contracts were annulled; useless stipendiaries were dismissed; a colossal staff hierarchy, with more titles than brains was disbanded. . . ." But for all his administrative credentials the flabby-cheeked, bulging-eyed Halleck was not an effective leader. Calculating, brooding, distant—those were the adjectives used to describe him. He eschewed close friendships, and in contacts with others projected a chilly reserve. One officer would remark: "There were two points in his manner which insisted upon notice—a sideways carriage of the head and a habit of looking at people with eyes wide open, staring, dull, fishy even, more than owlish. The effect was of talking to somebody [staring] over my shoulder."

Halleck would not see, as Grant and Sherman already sensed, that the Union could never be restored through Mahan's and Jomini's concept of limited war. At this point he continued to hope that "slavery will still be recognized and protected under the Constitution, and the door kept open for a compromise." But the Confederacy's resolve would not be broken until its singular armies were all but annihilated, and the bloodletting would be terrible to behold.[34]

TWO

* * * *

FORTS HENRY AND DONELSON

In late January of 1862 Grant in Cairo, Illinois, continued to urge Halleck, who knew what had to be done but was reluctant to do it, that the Union forces launch a combined land and water offensive. His plan called for moving up the broad, navigable Tennessee and Cumberland Rivers into west Tennessee and capturing Forts Henry and Donelson, the Rebel outposts on the respective rivers, thereby penetrating into the Confederate heartland and driving the outflanked enemy from Kentucky. He had been rebuffed with icy scorn, as we have seen, at his first meeting with his new chief, but now the timing was mote propitious.

Like George McClellan in the East, Halleck and Don Carlos Buell in the West both were under pressure from Lincoln to strike a blow. Grant, moreover, had a confident supporter. He was Flag Officer Andrew Hull Foote of Connecticut, who was in charge of naval operations on the upper Mississippi. The fifty-five-year-old, grizzled Foote, a God-fearing man given to preaching sermons to his crewmen, was eager to put his spanking-new gunboats to the test. "Fort Henry, on the Tennessee River," he wired Halleck on January 28, "can be carried with four ironclad gunboats and troops, and be permanently occupied." Wired Grant confidently on the same day: "With permission, I will take Fort Henry."[1]

Halleck assented, and the expedition soon got under way. "There were not enough of either boats or [crew] to move at one time the [15,000] men I proposed to take with me up the Tennessee," said Grant. "I loaded the boats with more than half the force, however, and sent General [John] McClernand in command. I followed with one of the latter boats and found that McClernand had stopped, very properly, nine miles below Fort Henry. . . . The transports we had with us had to return to Paducah to bring up a division from there, with General C. F. Smith in command."

Grant's two subordinates could not have been more different. McClernand, a bushy-eyebrowed, black-bearded politician from southern Illinois who had served a number of terms in Congress, had been commissioned by Lincoln—partially at least—to keep his constituents in the Union camp. Though a diligent fighter, he would continually seek to undermine Grant and further his own career. Charles Ferguson Smith had been superintendent at West Point when Grant was a cadet. "Smith was an old-timer," wrote a historian, "a Regular of Regulars, tall and lean and straight, with drooping white mustachios and a parade-ground stiffness to his manner. . . . Grant confessed that he never felt quite right issuing orders to Smith . . . and to the end of his days he seems to have considered Smith the perfect soldier."[2]

Foote's naval flotilla meanwhile proceeded apace up the Tennessee. It consisted of four ironclad—the bows more heavily armored than the sides—and three wooden-hulled gunboats. The ironclads were some 200 feet long, drawing from six to nine feet of water and moving at six to nine miles an hour. Each carried perhaps twelve heavy guns and, to help deflect cannonballs, their sides sloped at a thirty-five-degree angle. The river, swollen by unusually heavy February rains, washed up in the flotilla's path trees and all manner of debris, including several Rebel torpedoes, which today we call mines.

When one of them, laden with seventy pounds of explosives, was brought aboard the *Cincinnati*, Foote's flagship, Grant and others went aboard to see the mechanism taken apart. As the ship's armorer was unscrewing the cap, recounted a seaman, "a quantity of gas inside, probably generated from the wet powder . . . rushed out with a loud sizzling noise. Believing that the hour for evening prayer had arrived, two of the army officers threw themselves face downward on the deck. . . . Foote, with the agility of a cat, sprang up the ship's ladder, followed with commendable enthusiasm by General Grant."

Reaching the top, and realizing that the danger had passed, Foote made light of the incident.

"General, why this haste?"

"That the navy may not get ahead of us," Grant rejoined.[3]

Situated on low ground, haphazardly built and mounting in exposed positions fewer cannon than the oncoming gunboats, Fort Henry was an unexpectedly vulnerable target. The same rainfall that flooded its grounds with river water and impeded its garrison, however, equally slowed the approach of McClernand's and Smith's columns, which were bogged down on the muddy roads. Luckily the troops would not be needed. About noon on February 6, just as Foote was beginning his bombardment, the Rebel commander, fearing he would be overwhelmed, evacuated his 3,000 or so infantrymen to Fort Donelson on the Cumberland and used his cannon to fight a delaying action. "General, I shall have the fort in my possession before you get into your position," Foote told Grant.

The bombardment and return fire from Fort Henry would last some two hours, with the Confederate gunners, initially at least, responding vigorously. Flag Officer Foote during this time was in the pilothouse of the *Cincinnati*, which took thirty-two shells. "Her chimneys, after-cabin, and boats were completely riddled," reported Captain Henry Walke. "Two of her guns were disabled. [But] the only fatal shot she received passed through the larboard front, killing one man and wounding several others. I happened to be looking at the flag-streamer when one of the enemy's heavy shot struck her. It had the effect, apparently, of a thunderbolt, ripping her side timbers, and scattering the splinters over the vessel. She did not slacken her speed, but moved on as if nothing . . . had happened."

The *Essex,* her sister ironclad, sustained the only real Federal damage. "A shot from the enemy pierced the casemate just above the port hole on the port side, then through the middle boiler . . . opening a chasm for the escape of steam and boiling water," said one of her officers. The scene that followed was chaotic. "The steam . . . in the forward gun deck had driven all who were able to get out of the ports overboard, except a few who were fortunate enough to cling to the casemate outside." Within minutes the *Essex* was adrift, her captain badly wounded, and many of her officers and crew dead at their posts. Subsequently, rescuers met horrific sights. The dead helmsman "was found at his post at the wheel, standing erect, his left hand holding the spoke and his right hand grasping the signal-bell rope. A seaman . . . was on his knees, in the act of taking a shell from the box. . . . The escaping steam . . . had struck him square in the face, and he met death in that position."[4] Some forty-eight men were killed or wounded.

Foote and his three remaining ironclads, now firing at close range against Fort Henry's breastworks, soon silenced its guns. True to his word, he accepted its surrender and that of its handful of artillerymen before McClernand's and Smith's infantrymen could arrive on the scene.

Grant took the naval triumph in good part. "Fort Henry is ours," he wired Halleck. "The gunboats silenced the batteries before the investment was complete." Then he added, with studied nonchalance: "I shall take and destroy Fort Donelson on the 8th. . . ." Grant, eager to follow up his success, plainly felt that Halleck, the consummate desk officer, would not openly restrain him. If he took Donelson—eleven miles to the east—it would redound to Halleck's advantage; if he failed, Halleck could say he acted on his own initiative.

One reason for Grant's self-assurance was his knowledge of the two Southerners who would command at Donelson, and the disdain he felt for them. "I had known General [Gideon] Pillow in Mexico," he said, "and judged that with any force, no matter how small, I could march up to within gunshot of any entrenchments he was given to hold. . . . I knew that [John] Floyd was in command, but he was no soldier, and I judged that he would yield to Pillow's pretensions." A third general officer at Donelson would be Simon Buckner of Kentucky, the sole West Pointer of the three and the friend who had loaned Grant money in New York following his resignation from the army. But Buckner, he knew, was only third in command.[5]

Grant did not arrive at Fort Donelson on February 8 after all; the need to wait for supplies and reinforcements held him back, as well as the muddy roads, and he did not get his entire force into position until February 14. Once there he found the Confederate defenses much stronger than those at Fort Henry. On the east Donelson fronted the Cumberland, standing on high ground as much as 150 feet above the river, its twelve guns mounted in two tiers that dominated the water approaches; to the west and south deep lines of rifle-pits and abatis discouraged land assaults; north and south its flanks were protected by streams and ravines. Grant's plan called for Foote, again with four ironclads, to reduce the fort's heavy guns, and his army, which numbered some 27,000, to invest and attack the 21,000 Confederates from the west in a wide semicircle, cutting off any retreat to the south. Brigadiers Charles Smith and McClernand were on the Union left and right; and in the center was the newly arrived brigadier Lewis (Lew) Wallace, an Indiana newspaperman-turned-politician who after the war would write the classic novel *Ben Hur*.

On the late afternoon of the 14th, Foote boldly, perhaps recklessly,

steamed up the Cumberland toward Donelson, seeking a reprise of his triumph at Fort Henry. His flagship now was the *St. Louis,* and the other
ironclads were the *Carondelet, Louisville,* and *Pittsburgh.* Firing broke
out in earnest when the flotilla was a mile or so away from the fort. "We
heard the deafening crack of the bursting shells, the crash of the solid shot,
and the whizzing of fragments of shell and wood," said Captain Walke of
the *Carondelet.* "Soon a 128-pounder struck our anchor, smashed it into
flying bolts, and bounded over the vessel, taking away a part of our
smokestack; then another cut away the iron boat-davits as if they were
pipestems . . . another struck the pilot house, knocked the plating to pieces,
and sent fragments of iron and splinters into the pilots, one of whom fell
mortally wounded." Still the barrage continued. "Our men fought desperately," said Walke, "but under the excitement of the occasion, loaded too
hastily, and the port rifled gun exploded."

A seaman aboard the *Carondelet* recalled the incident. "I was serving
the gun with shell," he said. "When it exploded it knocked us all down,
killing none, but wounding over a dozen men, and spreading dismay and
confusion. . . . For about two minutes I was stunned, and at least five minutes elapsed before I could tell what was the matter. When I found out I
was more scared than hurt . . . I looked forward and found that our gun
had burst, and was lying on the deck split in three places." Soon the cry
rang out that the *Carondelet* was on fire, and he raced to man the pumps.
"While I was there, two shots entered our port bows and killed four men
and wounded others. They were borne past me, three with their heads off.
The sight almost sickened me, and I turned my head away."[6]

Now at point-blank range, no more than four hundred yards from the
fort, Foote and his fellow officers were discovering it was *they* who were
outgunned. "Our pilot house was struck again and another pilot wounded,"
said Walke of the *Carondelet,* "our wheel was broken, and shells from
the rear boats were bursting over us. . . . On looking out to bring our
broadside guns to bear, we saw that the other gunboats were falling back
out of line. The *Pittsburgh* in her haste to turn struck the stern of the
Carondelet and broke our starboard rudder. . . . The pilot of the *St. Louis*
was killed, and the pilot of the *Louisville* wounded. Both vessels had their
wheel-ropes shot away. . . ." The *St. Louis* and *Louisville,* becoming un-
manageable, were compelled to drop out of the fight; the *Pittsburgh* followed. Foote, who was badly wounded in the action, had suffered a major
setback.

Protecting the flotilla's withdrawal as best she could, the *Carondelet*
kept her head to the enemy and continued firing with her two bow guns,

raising a blanket of smoke. By this time all the Rebel shells concentrated on her. "Most of them were fired on the ricochet level," explained Walke, "and could be plainly seen skipping on the water before they struck. The enemy's object was to sink the gunboat by striking us just below the waterline. They soon succeeded in planting two 32-pound shots in the bow . . . which made her leak badly, but her compartments kept her from sinking until we could plug up the holes."

Still the *Carondelet,* even while felling back, kept up a constant barrage. "The warning words, 'Look out!' 'Down!' were often heard, and heeded by nearly all the gun-crews," said Walke. "On one occasion, as the men were at the muzzle of the middle bow-gun, loading it, the [shout] came just in time for them to jump aside as a 32-pounder struck the lower sill, and glancing up struck the upper sill, then . . . bounded on deck and spun like a top, but hurt no one." Some seamen disregarded the shouts, saying they would trust to luck. "The warning words, 'Look out!' 'Down!' were again soon heard," he continued. "Down went the gunner and his men, as the whizzing shot glanced on the gun, taking off . . . the heads of two of the young men who . . . in defiance of the order were standing up." Before the decks were sanded down, "there was so much blood on them that our men could not work . . . without slipping."

One of the Confederate artillery officers at Donelson, H. L. Bedford, could scarcely believe that the Federal flotilla would steam so close to the fort's guns. Only two of the twelve Rebel cannon could be classified as long-range pieces—a 32-pound rifled cannon and his own 10-inch columbiad, each with an effective range of a mile and a half or so. The rest, smoothbore 32-pounders, had a range of some 400 yards. The rifled gun was in the top tier of the river defenses, along with two 32-pounders. The columbiad was mounted some 150 feet below, along with eight 32-pounders.

When the ironclads came within a mile and half, Bedford's columbiad and the rifled gun opened up. "The gunboats returned the fire," he said, "right center boat opening, the others following in quick succession. After the third discharge the rifle remained silent on account of becoming accidentally spiked. This had a bad effect on the men at the columbiad, causing them considerable uneasiness for their comrades at the upper battery." The columbiad continued the action unsupported—one lone gun—"until the boats came with range of the 32-pounders, when the engagement became general. . . . As the [vessels] drew nearer, the firing on both sides grew faster, until it appeared as if the battle [was] a contest of speed in firing. . . . The roar of cannons was continuous and deafening, and commands, if necessary, had to be given by signs."

If Foote had stayed out of range of the smoothbores, Bedford would maintain, he could have concentrated his fire on the columbiad and the rifle, "dismounted those guns, demolished the 32-pounders at his leisure, and shelled the fort to his heart's content. But flushed with his victory at Fort Henry, his success there paved the way for his defeat at Donelson. . . . [Soon] three of the gunboats were seen drifting helplessly down the stream, and a shout of exultation leaped from the lips of every soldier."[7]

Meanwhile the Federals investing Donelson from the landside on the 14th did little but hunker down and wait for orders. "The infantry on both sides are in cover behind the crests of the hills or in thick woods," said Lew Wallace, commanding the Union center, "listening to the ragged fusillade which the sharpshooters and skirmishers maintain against each other almost without intermission. There is little pause in the exchange of shells and round shot. The careful chiefs have instructed their men to lie down. In brief, it looks as if each party [is] inviting the other to begin." Grant, of course, was pondering his next move. "The enemy had evidently been much demoralized by the [naval] assault," he said, "but they were jubilant when they saw the disabled vessels dropping down the river entirely out of the control of the men on board. . . . The sun went down . . . leaving the army . . . anything but comforted over [its] prospects." The weather had turned bitterly cold, and many of his men were without tents, blankets, or even overcoats. "I retired that night not knowing," he admitted, "but that I would have to intrench my position."

In the Confederate camp, however, General Floyd was already planning to evacuate the fort, believing his own situation hopeless. Though an able politician, he was no soldier, and basically had lost his nerve. General Pillow, who was best remembered in the Mexican War for building a parapet with the ditch on the *inside,* concurred with his chief's decision. The Rebel tactics called for Pillow in strength, bolstered by elements of Simon Buckner's command, to assault McClernand's right wing at dawn, roll it back and clear the way for a withdrawal southward to Nashville. "Preparations for the attack occupied the night," said Lew Wallace. "The ground was covered with ice and snow; yet the greatest silence was observed. It seems incomprehensible that columns mixed of all arms, infantry, cavalry and artillery, could . . . not have been heard by some listener. . . . But the character of the night must be remembered. The pickets of the Federals were struggling . . . against the blast, and probably did not keep good watch."

First to feel the enemy onslaught the morning of the 15th was the brigade of Colonel Richard Oglesby on McClernand's extreme right. "Oglesby's Illinoisans . . . held their ground," said Wallace, "returning in full measure the fire that they received. The Confederate [Nathan Bedford] Forrest rode around as if to get in their rear, and it was then give and take, infantry against infantry. The semi-echelon movement of the Confederates enabled them, after an interval, to strike William H. L. Wallace's brigade." Soon this officer, known throughout the army as the "other" Wallace, likewise was hotly engaged. "The first charge against him was repulsed," Lew Wallace continued, "whereupon he advanced to the top of the rising ground behind which he had sheltered his troops during the night." A second assault ensued, and William Wallace again threw the enemy back. "His men were steadfast, and clung to the brow of the hill as if it was theirs by holy right." For the next two hours, while the outcome hung in the balance, "the woods rang with a monstrous clangor of musketry, as if a million men were beating empty barrels with iron hammers."

By 10:00 A.M., however, the whole of John McClernand's right was giving way. "Oglesby was beginning to fare badly," said Lew Wallace. "The 'rebel yell,' afterward a familiar battle-cry on many fields, told of ground being gained against him. . . . Officers were riding to him with a sickening story that their commands were [running] out of ammunition, and asking where they could go for a supply. All he could say was to take what was in the boxes of the dead and wounded." With Oglesby falling back, William Wallace and other units had little choice but to follow. By 11:00 A.M. Pillow not only had opened the escape route to Nashville but was close to collapsing the Federal right.

Responding to McClernand's calls for help, Lew Wallace now dispatched Colonel John Thayer's brigade from the center, then followed up with artillery support. "Hardly had [the battery] unlimbered," he said, "before the enemy appeared, and firing began. For ten minutes or so thereabouts the scenes of the morning were reenacted. The woods [reverberated] with musketry and artillery. The brush on the slope of the hill was mowed away with bullets. A great cloud [of gunsmoke] arose and shut out the woods and the narrow valley below." Given breathing room, William Wallace and Oglesby re-formed their lines behind Thayer and the Rebel assault, which had cost McClernand 1,500 casualties, and came to a sudden halt. "There was a lull in the battle," said Lew Wallace. "Even the cannonading ceased. . . ."

During all the morning Grant had been seven miles away aboard Foote's flagship, conferring with the flag officer, whose wound did not permit him to travel. Alerted by an aide, he rushed back to his command about 1:00 P.M. and surveyed the scene. "I saw no sign of excitement on the portion of the line held by [Charles] Smith," said Grant. "[Lew] Wallace was nearer the conflict and had taken part in it. He had, at an opportune time, sent Thayer's brigade to the support of McClernand. . . . When I came to the right, appearances were different. . . . The enemy had come out in full force to cut his way out and make his escape. . . . It must have been about this time that Thayer pushed his brigade between the [Rebels] and those of our troops that were without ammunition. At all events the enemy fell back within his entrenchments and was there when I got on the field."[8]

Such indeed was the case. With the escape route open, Pillow and Floyd had elected not to withdraw southward immediately, but to return to Fort Donelson. Their reasons are unclear. Perhaps they thought that Grant and his officers, knocked back on their heels, had no fight left in them. Perhaps they felt they could withdraw during the night, almost at leisure. This was not to be.

Coming upon McClernand and Wallace in a clearing during the lull, Grant seemed as imperturbable as ever.

"This army wants a head," muttered McClernand, implying that his commander's absence had been responsible for his problems.

"It seems so," shot back Grant, who then took their reports.

Lew Wallace recalled that Grant was holding a sheaf of papers in his hand when he heard the news that the route southward was open to the enemy. "His face flushed slightly. With a sudden grip he crushed the papers in his hand. But in an instant these signs of disappointment or hesitation . . . cleared away. In his ordinary quiet voice he said: 'Gentlemen, the position on the right must be retaken.' "

For Grant the moment was one not of crisis but of opportunity. If the Confederates had massed their forces on the Union right to effect a breakout, they must have weakened their presence on the left. There is where he would strike with Charles Smith's wing. When Wallace and McClernand heard the sounds of the assault, they were in turn to advance. Meantime he could see that the troops all along the line needed encouragement. Turning to an aide, Colonel Joseph Webster, he said: "Some of our men are pretty badly demoralized, but the enemy must be more so, for he had attempted to force his way out, but has fallen back; the one who attacks first now will be victorious and the enemy will have to be in a hurry if he gets ahead of me."

Grant soon was galloping toward Smith's headquarters, stopping sporadically to make sure that officers were properly distributing ammunition and calling out to the troops, "Fill your cartridge-boxes, quick, and get into line; the enemy is trying to escape, and he must not be permitted to do so." In short order, dazed soldiers began to rally. Remembered Grant: "This acted like a charm. The men only wanted someone to give them a command."[9]

Riding up to Smith, his former commandant at West Point, Grant came to the point: "General Smith, all has failed on our right—you must take Fort Donelson."

"I will do it," the fifty-five-year-old replied, and then proceeded to mass his division, with Colonel Jacob Lauman's brigade at its head and Colonel James Tuttle's 2nd Iowa in the van. "Second Iowa, you must take that fort," he said, pointing toward the high ground and the Rebel entrenchments. "Take the caps off your guns, fix bayonets, and I will support you." Then he trotted to their front, saber held high. During the advance, he turned now and then in his saddle, making sure the men stayed in line. "Damn you, gentlemen, I see skulkers!" he shouted between oaths. "I'll have none here. Come on, you volunteers, come on. . . . You volunteered to be killed for love of your country and now you can be!"

Immediately Smith and his men came under heavy fire. "The defense was greatly favored by the ground," said Lew Wallace, "which subjected the assailants to a double fire from the beginning of the abatis. The men have said that 'it looked too thick for a rabbit to get through.' . . . The air around [Smith] twittered with minie-bullets. Erect as if on review, he rode on, timing the gait of his horse with the movement of his colors. A soldier said: 'I was nearly scared to death, but I saw the old man's white mustache over his shoulder and went on.' "

Smith picked his way through the abatis, "holding his cap all the time in sight; and the effect was magical. The men swarmed in after him, and got through in the best order they could. . . . Up the ascent he rode; up they followed. At the last moment the keepers of the rifle pits clambered out and fled. . . . The four regiments engaged in the feat . . . planted their colors on the breastwork." By 4:00 P.M. the fighting on the left was over. Smith's assault had taken the heights on the left, driving a stake into the fort's defenses; all subsequent attempts to dislodge him would be in vain.[10]

With darkness coming on McClernand now voiced reluctance, despite Grant's clear and stringent orders, to advance on the right and close off the Rebel escape route. "The road ought to be recovered—Grant is right about that," he said to Lew Wallace, indicating he needed additional time to restore his battered division. "But . . . I am not ready to undertake it."

Wallace forthwith took the initiative, sending Morgan L. Smith's minibrigade, comprised of the 11th Indiana and the 8th Missouri, up the sloping ground. "Waiting for a moment for Smith to light a cigar," he said, "I called out, 'Forward it is, then!' " Beginning their climb, the two regiments advanced amid a torrent of lead. "The flank companies cheered while deploying as skirmishers," Wallace continued. ". . . Creeping when the fire was hottest, running when it slackened, they gained ground with astonishing rapidity, and at the same time maintained a fire that was like a sparkling of the earth. For the most part the bullets aimed at them passed over their heads and took effect in the ranks behind them."

Colonel Smith's cigar was shot from his lips. "He took another and called for a match. A soldier ran and gave him one."

"Thank you," Smith said, puffing several times before spurring his horse forward. "Take your place now. We are almost up."

Once the Federals in the van reached the crest, the enemy seemed to melt away. "The whole line then moved forward simultaneously," said Lew Wallace, "and never stopped until the Confederates were within the works. There had been no occasion to call on the reserves. The road [southward] was again effectually shut, and the battle-field of the morning, with the dead and wounded lying where they had fallen, was in [our] possession. . . ." Lieutenant-Colonel Manning Force of the 20th Ohio would write: "The retiring Confederates took with them six captured pieces of artillery, several thousand small arms, and between two and three hundred prisoners; but returned to their trenches weary, disappointed, disheartened."[11]

Inspecting his lines in the gathering gloom Grant came across two of the wounded, a Union officer and a Rebel private, lying side by side. He asked if any of his party had a flask and, when one was produced, dismounted and gave each of the men a sip of brandy.

"Send for stretchers; send for stretchers at once for these men," he told an aide.

Later he noticed that attendants were picking up the Union officer, but seemed disinclined to help the Confederate.

"Take this Confederate, too," he said. "Take them both together; the war is over between them."[12]

Late that night General Floyd called a council of war attended by Gideon Pillow, Simon Buckner, and the Cavalryman Nathan Bedford Forrest. With Union guns and superior numbers dominating Fort Donelson's lines, and supplies fast dwindling, defeat was inevitable. Still the Rebels did not realize that their escape southward again was blocked. "After some recrimination between Pillow and Buckner whether the intention had been to commence the retreat directly from the battlefield," said Manning Force, whose information would come from Southern sources, "or first cut a way out and then retreat to the works, equip for a march and retreat by night, it was agreed to evacuate." Reconnaissance by Forrest soon confirmed, however, that the fort was surrounded.

Here Buckner offered good advice. "It would be wrong to subject the army to a virtual massacre," he counseled, "when no good could result from the sacrifice . . . the general officers owed it to their men . . . to obtain the best terms of capitulation." Floyd and Pillow agreed. But which of them would negotiate the terms of surrender? Both senior generals had their reasons for evading capture. Floyd already was under Federal indictment for malfeasance; he had been Secretary of War in the months before Lincoln took office, and had been instrumental in moving arms from Northern to Southern arsenals. Pillow, a poseur, simply had an exaggerated idea of his importance.

Now occurred a remarkable, even comic, exchange. "General Floyd said he would never surrender—he would die first," reported Force. "Pillow said substantially the same. [But] Buckner said, if he were in command, he would surrender and share the fate of the garrison."

"If the command should devolve on you, would you permit me to take out my brigade?" Floyd asked Buckner.

"Yes, if you leave before the terms of capitulation are agreed upon," Buckner replied.

"Is there anything wrong in my leaving?" Pillow chimed in.

"I turn the command over, sir," Floyd told Pillow.

"And I pass it," said Pillow.

"And I assume it," said the steadfast Buckner.

Floyd subsequently loaded 1,500 of his Virginians aboard two transports and escaped. Pillow left Donelson in a small boat, accompanied by a handful of soldiers. Neither man ever again exercised command. Colonel Forrest, making little effort to conceal his disgust with both senior officers, cut his way out through the flooded terrain with his troopers.[13]

Daybreak found Grant in receipt of a February 16 letter from Buckner asking for terms. "I propose to the Commanding Officer of the Federal forces the appointment of Commissioners to agree upon terms of capitulation of the forces and fort at my command," it read in part, "and in that view suggest an armistice until 12 o'clock today."

"What answer shall I send to this, General?" said Grant, showing the note to Charles Smith.

"No terms to the damn Rebels!" growled Smith.

Grant smiled, and began to write his reply, which eventually would make the name U.S. ("Unconditional Surrender") Grant famous throughout the land. "Yours of this date . . . is just received. No terms except an unconditional and immediate surrender can be accepted. I propose to move immediately upon your works."

"It's the same thing in smoother words," Smith harrumphed.

Buckner must have been taken aback by Grant's no-nonsense communiqué. Theirs was a fast friendship, one that would outlast the war, and the Kentuckian must have felt Grant would show him more courtesy. His reply showed his pique: "The distribution of the forces under my command, incident to an unexpected change of commanders, and the overwhelming force under your command, compel me . . . to accept the ungenerous and unchivalrous terms which you propose."[14]

By early morning white flags were everywhere along the Rebel lines, arms were being stacked, and Grant was sharing a breakfast of cornbread and coffee with Buckner and his officers. "In the course of our conversation, which was very friendly," Grant remarked, "he said to me that if he had been in command I would not have got up to Donelson as easily as I did. I told him that if he had been in command I should not have tried it the way I did. . . . I had relied very much upon [Floyd and Pillow] to allow me to come safely up to the outside of their works."

"Where is he now?" Grant asked Buckner, referring to Pillow.

"Gone," said Buckner. ". . . He thought you'd rather get hold of him than any man in the Confederacy."

"Oh," said Grant, "if I had got him, I'd let him go again. He will do us more good commanding you fellows."[15]

Later he drew Buckner aside, offering him the loan of money to make his imprisonment more bearable. "The episode was characteristic," wrote a Grant biographer. "Up to the moment of surrender, it would not enter Grant's head that his old-time friendship with the opposing commander should in any way affect his attitude; but the once the fighting had stopped . . . the old friendship could be resumed."

To Halleck went the dramatic news from Grant of the capture of an entire army: "We have taken Fort Donelson and from 12,000 to 15,000 prisoners, including Generals Buckner and Bushrod Johnson; also 20,000 stand of arms, 48 pieces of artillery, 17 heavy guns, from 2,000 to 4,000 horses, and large quantities of commissary stores." Later counts would show that the prisoner total was close to 15,000; Grant lost some 3,000 men killed and wounded, the Confederates 2,000. When he received the

dispatch in St. Louis, the normally phlegmatic Halleck permitted himself a
rare show of emotion. "Palmer," he told his clerk, "send up two dozen
baskets of champagne, and open them here for the benefit of the crowd. . . .
And I want you to give public notice that I shall suspect the loyalty of any
male resident . . . who can be found sober enough to walk or speak within
the next half hour."

In the aftermath of the campaign Grant would have nothing but praise
for Sherman, whom Halleck had restored to field command—doubtless
under pressure from Tom Ewing and John Sherman—and sent to Paducah
and thence to the mouth of the Cumberland to support him. "At that time
he was my senior in rank," he said of Sherman's contribution. "But every
boat that came up with supplies or reinforcements brought a note of encouragement from [him] asking me to call upon him for any assistance he
could render and saying that if he could be of service at the front I might
send for him and he would waive rank."[16]

Grant's smashing triumphs at Henry and Donelson, which left all of Tennessee vulnerable to the Union armies, made him an instant hero in the
North. Newspaper accounts were unstinting in their praise, and when
readers learned that he, like Morgan Smith, had lit up a cigar during the
action, box after box of stogies flooded his headquarters as gifts. Previously Grant had used a pipe; now he threw it away and smoked cigars.
Nonetheless his subordinate's sudden fame put Halleck in an embarrassing
position. He and Don Carlos Buell and General-in-Chief McClellan were
bureaucrats and risk avoiders, more comfortable with shuffling papers and
stockpiling men and supplies than going on the attack. During Grant's
march on Fort Henry, Halleck had even been scheming to shunt him aside
and replace him, first with an old comrade-in-arms and then with Sherman. Now he sought simultaneously to diminish Grant's achievement and
aggrandize himself. "Make Buell, Grant and [John] Pope major-generals
of volunteers and give me command in the West," he wired McClellan. "I
ask this for Forts Henry and Donelson." By recommending Grant for promotion along with two officers who had nothing to do with his successes,
Halleck sought to convey the impression *he* was the guiding genius behind
them. Naturally, *his* genius should be rewarded.

For the moment Halleck got nowhere. Lincoln quickly promoted only
one man to major general—U. S. Grant. Though Buell and Pope, and
for that matter Charles Smith, McClernand, and Lew Wallace, soon also
would be named major generals, Grant's commission would predate

theirs, and he would remain the senior commander. Meanwhile Edwin Stanton, the new Secretary of War, bluntly reminded Halleck that Buell would remain his coequal in the West, saying that Lincoln "expects you and General Buell to cooperate fully and zealously with each other, and would be glad to know whether there has been any failure of cooperation in any particular."[17]

Grant's advance along the Cumberland continued apace. "Seccesh is about on its last legs in Tennessee," he told Julia. "I want to push as rapidly as possible to save hard fighting. These terrible battles are very good things to read about . . . but I am decidedly in favor as having as little of [them] as possible." Grant at this juncture informed Halleck "that the way was open now to Clarksville and Nashville; and that unless I received orders to the contrary I should take Clarksville on the 21st and Nashville about the 1st of March."

Moving parallel to Grant was the sluggish Buell, coming down from Bowling Green, Kentucky, toward the same objectives. When William Nelson, one of Buell's division heads, arrived at Donelson after the fighting was over, Grant took it upon himself to send him to Nashville, which the Federals first entered on February 25. This encroachment on his authority did not sit well with Buell, and when Grant encountered him outside the city two days later, the meeting was a strained one. "I said to General Buell my information was the enemy was retreating as fast as possible," Grant recalled. "[He] said there was fighting going on only ten or twelve miles away. I said: 'Quite probably; Nashville contained valuable stores of arms . . . and the enemy is probably trying to carry away all he can. The fighting is doubtless with the rear guard.'" Buell insisted the Rebels might counterattack at any moment. "I said, in the absence of positive information, I believed my information was correct. He responded that he 'knew.'" Grant then let the matter drop.

Soon Halleck muddied the waters in the West still further. Rebuffed in his attempt to bring Buell under his command, he determined to leave the Cumberland to his rival and use the Tennessee to move southward. On March 1, accordingly, he ordered Grant back to Fort Henry. Complicating this strategy was the fact that for weeks communications between Grant and Halleck, unbeknownst to either man, had been partially severed. "From the time of leaving Cairo I had been singularly unfortunate in not receiving dispatches from General Halleck," said Grant. ". . . My dispatches were all sent to Cairo by boat, but many of those addressed to me were sent to the operator at the end of the advancing wire and he failed to forward them. This operator proved to be a Rebel. He deserted his post and went south taking the dispatches with him."[18]

Halleck, a stickler for being kept informed, at this point was working himself into a snit. On March 3 he told McClellan: "I have had no communication with General Grant for more than a week. He left his command without my authority and went to Nashville. . . . It is hard to censure a successful general, but I think he richly deserves it. I can get no returns, no reports, no information of any kind from him." Back came a supporting comment from McClellan: "Generals must observe discipline as well as private soldiers. Do not hesitate to arrest [Grant] at once if the good of the service requires it, and place C. F. Smith in command. You are at liberty to regard this as a positive order. . . ." Thus encouraged, Halleck on March 4 without hard evidence brought up Grant's supposed drinking to McClellan. "A rumor has just reached me that . . . [he] has resumed his former bad habits. If so, it will account for his neglect of my often-repeated orders. I do not deem it advisable to arrest him at present, but have placed General Smith in command of the expedition up the Tennessee."

That same day, out of the blue, Grant got the bad tidings. "You will place . . . C. F. Smith in command of expedition and remain at Fort Henry," Halleck wired him. "Why do you not obey my orders to report strength and positions of your command?"[19]

Grant could not believe what was happening. One friend remembered him as anguished, "with tears in his eyes," saying, "I don't know what they mean to do with me. . . . What command have I now?" In ensuing communications with Halleck, he tried to defend himself, saying, "I am not aware of ever having disobeyed any order from headquarters. . . . I have reported almost daily the condition of my command. . . . You may rely on my carrying out your instructions in every particular. . . ." Halleck nonetheless kept pecking away. "General McClellan directs that you report to me daily. . . . Your neglect of repeated orders . . . has created great dissatisfaction. . . ." Now Grant's dispatches took on an edge. "Every move I made was reported daily to your chief of staff, who must have failed to keep you properly posted. . . . If my course is not satisfactory, remove me at once. . . . Believing sincerely that I must have enemies between you and myself, who are trying to impair my usefulness, I respectfully ask to be relieved." Replied Halleck: "You are mistaken. There is no enemy between you and me. . . ."[20]

The entire contretemps might have ended here, had not Grant received a delayed-in-transit letter from Halleck, which cited an anonymous note alleging the theft of captured Rebel stores at Fort Donelson. "The want of order and discipline and the numerous irregularities in your command since the capture of Fort Donelson are matters of general notoriety," Old Brains sniffed. Grant was outraged. "I refer you to my orders to suppress marauding as the only reply necessary," he said. "There is such a disposition to find fault with me that I again ask to be relieved."

To which Halleck on March 12 replied: "You cannot be relieved from command. There is no good reason for it. I am certain that all the authorities in Washington ask is that you enforce discipline. . . . The power is in your hands; use it. . . ." What accounted for this complete turn-about was startling news from the War Department. Lincoln had just relieved Mc-Clellan as general-in-chief—though keeping him as head of the Army of the Potomac—and had named Halleck commander in the West, in a newly created Department of the Mississippi. The president had made it plain, though, that he was not pleased with the way Halleck was dealing with Grant. Either prefer charges against him, came the stern word from Washington, or restore him to command. Elated over his promotion and his ascendancy over Buell, Halleck chose the latter course. "He forwarded [to me] a copy of a detailed dispatch from himself to Washington entirely exonerating me," Grant would say, "but he did not inform me that it was his own reports that had created all the trouble."

In blissful ignorance of his chief's duplicity, therefore, Grant forthwith proceeded to Savannah on the Tennessee, where Smith and his troops were waiting. "General Smith was delighted to see me and was unhesitating in his denunciation of the treatment I had received," he said. "He was on a sick bed . . . from which he never came away alive." In a bizarre accident, Charles Smith just days before had cut his leg down to the shinbone while moving between boats. Infection would set in, costing him his life. Soon Grant would be without Smith's services while commanding the Army of the Tennessee in its fiercest battle yet. His six division heads would be McClernand, W.H.L. Wallace, Lew Wallace, Stephen Hurlbut, the newly restored Sherman, and Benjamin Prentiss. The political appointees McClernand and Lew Wallace, commanding the 1st and 3rd Divisions, and Sherman, heading the 5th, we have already met. William H. L. Wallace, Stephen Hurlbut, and Benjamin Prentiss, all of Illinois and well connected, would command the 2nd, 4th, and 6th Divisions respectively. Wallace, forty-one, a lawyer and public prosecutor, had ably led a brigade at Donelson and would be replacing Smith. Stephen Hurlbut, forty-seven, bellicose and hard drinking and a friend of Lincoln's, was seeing his first action. Benjamin Prentiss, forty-three, a lawyer whose forebears had come to America on the *Mayflower,* likewise was untested.

Shiloh the two-day battle would be called, after the humble Shiloh Methodist Church around which the Federals were making their camps, at a place called Pittsburg Landing, just below Savannah. The casualties would be horrendous, and cause consternation through the land.[21]

THREE
****

BLOODY SHILOH

Throughout late March and into April, Grant consolidated his forces on the west bank of the Tennessee, using Pittsburg Landing as the staging area for a projected assault on Corinth, a vital rail center some twenty miles to the south just across the Mississippi border. Taking the town not only would isolate Memphis, ninety miles to the west, exposing much of the Mississippi River to the Union incursion, but it would sever the east-west Memphis and Charleston Railroad. Grant's Army of the Tennessee totaled some 42,000 men, and it soon would be reinforced by lead elements of Buell's 37,000-man Army of the Ohio, which was wending its way south from Nashville. Massing at Corinth meanwhile to defend the rail hub was Albert Sidney Johnston's 40,000-strong Army of Mississippi. "When all reinforcements should have arrived I expected to take the initiative," said Grant, ". . . and had no expectation of needing fortifications. . . . The fact is, I regarded the campaign . . . as an offensive one and had no idea that the enemy would leave (his) strong entrenchments."

But Johnston, a strapping Texan who at this point in the war many regarded as the South's finest general, would do just that. Urged on by Pierre Beauregard, the hero of Fort Sumter and his second in command, he resolved to march from Corinth and fall on Grant at Pittsburg Landing before Buell could cross the Tennessee and join him.

Though the Federals were on high ground, with creeks protecting both flanks, their unfortified and widely spaced camps provided tempting targets. Sherman and Prentiss were closest to the enemy—perhaps four miles inland—the former on the right around Shiloh Church, the latter on the left. One of Sherman's brigades, commanded by Chicago lawyer David Stuart, occupied the extreme left, loosely connecting with the river. Backing up Sherman was McClernand. Behind Prentiss and Stuart were William H. L. Wallace, and Hurlbut. Altogether they totaled some 35,000 men. Seven miles north of the staging area, at Crump's Landing and out of the immediate action, was Lew Wallace's 7,000-man division, guarding the army's supply depot.

Grant continued to make his headquarters at Savannah, coming down to Pittsburg Landing by boat each day to supervise operations. Sherman, whom he had placed in overall charge during his absences, received reports on April 4 and 5 of Rebel encroachments, but thought them no more than cavalry raids. "We were conscious that the cavalry in our front was getting bolder and more saucy; and on Friday, the 4th of April, it dashed down and carried off one of our picket-guards . . . but thus far we had not positively detected the presence of infantry."

Sherman, like Grant, believed a full-scale attack most unlikely. Besides, he later acknowledged, he had no wish again to be called crazy for raising a hue and cry. "I have . . . positive orders," he told one uneasy officer, "to do nothing that will have a tendency to bring on a general engagement until Buell arrives." When Colonel Jesse Appler of the 53rd Ohio, a former probate judge, put his unit on alert, Cump summarily dressed him down. "Take your damn regiment back to Ohio," he said. "There is no enemy nearer than Corinth."[1]

In the early hours of Sunday, April 6, the Federals found that this was not the case; Johnston's troops were moving against them in strength, initially falling on Prentiss and Sherman in crushing numbers.

Federal pickets blundered upon the oncoming enemy about 5:00 A.M., one mile south of Shiloh Church, and soon the conflict spread along the lines. On Prentiss's front, Colonel Francis Quinn of the 12th Michigan described the scene: "About daylight the dead and wounded began to be brought in. The firing grew closer and closer till it became manifest a heavy force of the enemy was upon us. The division was ordered into line of battle by General Prentiss and immediately advanced." Now the combatants were at close range. "Volley after volley was given and returned, and many fell on both sides, but their numbers were too heavy for our forces. . . . They were visible in line, and every hill-top in the rear was covered with them. . . . They were advancing in not only one but several lines of battle."

The 6th Division about 9:00 A.M. retreated to its camp and, said Quinn, "although no regular line was formed, yet from behind every tree a deadly fire was poured upon the enemy." Still the Rebels surged forward, forcing another withdrawal north of the Purdy-Hamburg Road. "The division fell back [from the camp] about one-half mile, very much scattered and broken. Here we were posted, being drawn up . . . behind a dense clump of bushes." Behind the bushes was an eroded country lane, later dubbed the Sunken Road. There the Federals dug in.[2]

For Private Leander Stillwell of the 61st Illinois, who had been with Prentiss's division less than a week, the initial assault was an epiphany. "The time we thus stood, waiting the attack, could not have exceeded five minutes," he recounted. "Suddenly . . . there was a long, wavy flash of bright light, then another, and another! It was the sunlight shining on gun barrels and bayonets! . . . We began firing at once. From one end of the regiment to the other leaped a sheet of red flame."

Eventually, Stillwell heard the order to withdraw. "We halted . . . in the edge of the woods, in front of our tents. . . . Here we did our first hard fighting. . . . Our officers said, after the battle was over, that we held this line an hour and ten minutes." Then again came the order to fall back. "We retreated from this position . . . because the troops on our right had given way and we were flanked. Possibly those boys on our right would give the same excuse for their leaving, and probably truly, too." The Rebels were on his heels. "I saw men in gray and brown clothes, with trailed muskets running through the camp. . . . I saw something else, too, that sent a chill all through me. It was a kind of flag I had never seen before. It was a gaudy sort of thing, with red bars. It flashed over me in a second that that thing was a Rebel flag. . . . We observed no kind of order in leaving; the main thing was to get out of there as quick as we could."

Prentiss's riddled units continued to withdraw until, sometime after 10:00 A.M., the last of them came to the clump of bushes behind their camp. Soon they regrouped in the Sunken Road. Here in what would be the Union center, one-half mile north of the Purdy-Hamburg Road and supported on one side by the 2nd Division of William H. L. Wallace and on the other by elements of Hurlbut's 4th Division, the bedraggled remnants of the 6th Division would make their stand.

Leander Stillwell at this point saw his unit's German-American adjutant gesturing toward the oncoming reinforcements, and informing his colonel, in his heavily accented English: *Those are the troops of General Hurlbut.*

"Bully for General Hurlbut," the exhausted Stillwell thought as he settled into the Sunken Road, "Maybe we'll whip 'em yet."[3]

On Prentiss's right, Sherman's 5th Division likewise came under heavy assault. About 7:00 A.M., he reported, "the enemy drove our advance guard back on the main body, when I ordered under arms all my division, and sent word to General McClernand, asking him to support my left; to General Prentiss, giving him notice the enemy was in our front in force; and to General Hurlbut, asking him to support General Prentiss." Minutes later, while Sherman and his staff were riding along the lines, they drew a brisk fire from some skirmishers. His orderly was killed, and a minie ball passed through his palm. He calmly wrapped a handkerchief around the wound and continued his reconnaissance. "About 8:00 A.M.," he said, "I saw the glistening bayonets of heavy masses of infantry to our left front in the woods . . . and became satisfied for the first time that the enemy designed a determined attack."

Sherman next rode to Colonel Appler, who held his left flank, and ordered him to hold at all hazards. "I informed him that he had a good battery on his right and strong supports to his rear. General McClernand had promptly responded to my request, and sent me three regiments, which were posted to protect [Captain Allen] Waterhouse's battery and the left flank."

The clash opened with sporadic cannonading. "I then observed heavy battalions of infantry passing obliquely to the left," said Sherman, "across the open field in Appler's front; also other columns advancing directing upon my division. Our infantry and artillery opened along the whole line and the battle became general. . . . Other heavy masses of the enemy's forces kept passing across the field to our left. . . . I saw at once that the enemy designed to pass my left flank, and fall upon Generals McClernand and Prentiss, whose line of camps were almost parallel with the Tennessee and about two miles back from it."[4]

Soon the sound of battle told Sherman that Prentiss was engaged. At 9:00 A.M., he said, "I judged that [Prentiss] was falling back. About this time Appler's regiment broke in disorder . . . and the enemy pressed forward on Waterhouse's battery thereby exposed." Indeed Jesse Appler, trusted with guarding Sherman's left flank, had been found wanting. Though his own casualties were minor and his regiment's musketry and Waterhouse's cannon had all but decimated the Rebels in his immediate front—the 6th Mississippi would suffer 300 casualties of 425 men engaged—Appler now bolted.

"Retreat, and save yourselves!" he shouted, heading for the rear. Many men in the 53rd Ohio did just that, followed by soldiers in the adjoining 57th Ohio.[5]

Lieutenant Ephraim Dawes, adjutant of the 53rd, eventually found Appler crouching behind a tree.

"Colonel," he urged, "let us go and help the 57th. They are falling back. . . ."

"No, no!" the ashen-faced Appler replied in a trembling voice, pointing over his shoulder to the rear. "Form the men [there]. . . ."

Dawes was incensed. "Our miserable [situation] flashed upon me. We were in the front of a great battle. Our regiment never had a battalion drill. Some men in it had never fired a gun. Our lieutenant colonel had become lost in the confusion of the first retreat, the major was in a hospital, and our colonel was a coward." Dawes cursed Appler and refused to obey his order, whereupon the latter jumped to his feet and "literally ran away," again yelling, "Fall back and save yourselves!"

Largely unsupported, Waterhouse's artillery now came to grief. With its commander wounded and carried from the field, his subordinates waited too long to limber up, allowing the enemy within fifty yards. Musket fire riddled the battery's position, downing cannoneers and horses so fast the guns could not be hitched up. Most were forfeit to the onrushing Confederate tide. From afar one Federal officer noted with considerable chagrin that the Rebels "swarmed around them [guns] like bees. They jumped upon the guns and on the hay bales in the battery camp, and yelled like crazy men."[6]

On Sherman's center and right, Ralph Buckland's Ohioans and John McDowell's mixed brigade of midwesterners nonetheless held firm, keeping the line, temporarily at least, in some semblance of order. "Discovering that [the enemy] was pushing a column up a narrow ravine," said the balding Buckland, a lawyer and politician, ". . . I ordered the 72nd [Ohio] to change front, so as to form a line parallel to the ravine. . . . In this position our line was maintained . . . under a deadly fire from the enemy. . . . He several times recoiled and rallied, but did not advance."

With Prentiss shattered, Sherman refused to budge. "Although our left was thus turned," he said, "and the enemy was pressing our whole line, I deemed Shiloh [Church] so important that I remained by it, and renewed my orders to Colonels [John] McDowell and Buckland to hold their ground." He maneuvered his command coolly during this interval, ignoring the bullets whizzing about him. One ball glanced off his shoulder, wounding him a second time, a third passed through his hat, and three horses were shot from under him. "We did hold these positions until about 10:00 A.M.," Sherman said, "when the enemy got his artillery to the rear of our left flank and some change became absolutely necessary." His resolve nonetheless had forced the Rebels to overcommit troops to the Federal right and disrupted their plan, which called for turning the left and cutting off the retreat to the river.

Covering his withdrawal with his own artillery, Sherman re-formed his depleted division along the Purdy-Hamburg Road, with his right on a deep ravine running to Owl Creek, and his left extending to McClernand. "The scenes on this field would have cured anybody of war," he later wrote Ellen. "Mangled bodies, dead, dying, in every conceivable shape, without heads, legs. . . . The piles of dead gentlemen & wounded & maimed makes me more anxious than ever for some hope of an End, but I know such a thing cannot be for a long, long time."[7]

Sherman's departure from Shiloh Church touched off a fierce Confederate assault against McClernand. Quickly the enemy pushed forward to the Crossroads—the intersection of the Purdy-Hamburg and Pittsburg-Corinth Roads—intent on driving a wedge between the two commands. At 10:30 A.M., said Sherman, "Finding [McClernand] pressed, I moved McDowell's brigade against the left flank of the enemy . . . and then directed the men to avail themselves of every cover—trees, fallen timber, and a wooden valley to our right. We held this position for [about] four long hours, sometimes gaining and at other times losing ground. . . ."

Here at the Crossroads Colonel Julius Raith of McClernand's 3rd Brigade, trying to rally his faltering men, was mortally wounded. Despite the pain he insisted on being left on the field, telling his rescuers they could be of more service in the ranks. "The resistance here . . . was desperate," said Lieutenant Colonel Adolph Engelmann of the 43rd Illinois, reporting that his regiment "maintained its position . . . till the enemy's fire, flanking from the right, compelled it again to fall back." Subsequently, with their ammunition almost exhausted, his men "gathered a scant supply from the killed and wounded of the enemy, who here covered the ground thickly."

McClernand takes up the story: "The situation of the 3rd Brigade at this juncture [about 10:30 A.M.] was most critical. Generals Prentiss's and Sherman's divisions had retired, leaving the brigade exposed to combined attack. . . . In obedience to my order [it] fell back, under command of Lt. Colonel Engelmann, about 300 yards and reformed in front of my headquarters, rejoining the 2nd Brigade, under the command of Colonel [C. Carroll] Marsh and the 1st Brigade, under command of Colonel [Abraham] Hare." To little avail about 11:30 A.M. he launched a counterattack.

"In the course of twenty minutes [our] battery had silenced the enemy's battery in front and to repel the enemy. . . . Major [Adolph] Schwartz, chief of my staff, joined the 34th and 43rd Illinois and boldly charged. . . . Our resistance, however, was overborne by superior numbers, which still continued to flank the right of my line."

To avoid envelopment McClernand like Sherman now began a series of fitful withdrawals from his position behind the Purdy-Hamburg Road, his right under Engelmann bent back on his center and left under Marsh and Hare. "Wholly unsupported on the left, and still outflanked on the right by increasing numbers, to save my command . . . I ordered it to fall back about 200 yards and reform at a right angle with the center of my camp." Rounding up a patchwork force, he nonetheless managed around 1:00 P.M. to launch a second counterattack. "I rode along my line and gave the order, 'Forward!' . . . driving the enemy . . . for half a mile with great slaughter. . . . Within a radius of 200 yards of my headquarters the ground was almost literally covered with dead bodies. . . ."

Once more, however, Confederate pressure drove back McClernand's right flank, leaving him in the same precarious situation. "Here the portion which had first fallen back reformed . . . parallel with the camp and fronting the approach of the enemy from the west, while the other portion formed at right angle with it, still fronting the approach of the enemy from the south," he said. Resigning himself to the inevitable, McClernand now conducted a fighting retreat with Sherman toward Tilgham Branch and the Landing, straightening his refused lines as he went.

By 2:30 P.M. at latest, Johnston's troops had complete control of the Crossroads and the Federal right was humbled. Prentiss's division was in shambles, and Sherman's and McClernand's divisions were perhaps at half strength.

Their stubborn defense, however, had absorbed the enemy's heaviest blows, buying the center and the left much-needed time. Rebel attacks in the morning against the Sunken Road, where William H. L. Wallace's and Prentiss's men were intermingled, were tentative and largely ineffectual, as were those against Stephen Hurlbut. Though David Stuart was pushed back from his camp, he regrouped successfully when the ever-hungry Confederates stopped to feast on his food supplies. In sum, the Union lines were tattered but still extant. From right to left and often widely apart, they stretched for some two miles from Sherman to McClernand, thence to William H. L. Wallace and Prentiss in the Sunken Road and what would be called the Hornet's Nest, thence to Hurlbut, and then to Stuart's 2,000-man brigade near the river.

In the hours to come the Confederate pressure would only increase, the din of battle heighten, and the instances of confusion multiply. Shiloh, in the words of one Union officer, would be a combat of "numberless separate encounters of detached portions of broken lines, continually shifting position and changing direction in the forest and across ravines . . . almost incapable of a connected narrative." The hard-pressed Federal commanders would agree with that assessment.[8]

Grant on the morning of April 6 initially heard the sound of the guns when he was aboard his headquarters boat in Savannah, having his breakfast cup of coffee. Through no fault of his own, just as had happened at Fort Donelson, he was not on the front lines when the battle erupted. He immediately steamed downriver, however, pausing just long enough at Crump's Landing to tell Lew Wallace to ready his division for action. Even though he surmised that he was coming under heavy attack, Grant was not unduly concerned. General William Nelson, commanding the lead division of Buell's army, had arrived the day before and was on the east bank of the Tennessee, just across from Pittsburg Landing. Lew Wallace and Nelson with their additional 15,000 men, he felt, should be enough to deal with any contingency.

The commanding general reached Pittsburg Landing about 9:00 A.M. and with his aides quickly headed toward the front to reconnoiter. A day or two before his horse had lost its footing, pinning Grant's leg underneath and badly twisting his ankle. Because of the injury, he had to be boosted onto his mount, a crutch strapped to the saddle. In short order he saw the situation was much more serious than he had thought. "The Confederate assaults were made with such a disregard of losses on their own side, that our line of tents soon fell into their hands," he said afterward, referring the Union camps, ". . . A number of attempts were made by the enemy to turn our right flank, where Sherman was posted, but every effort was repulsed. . . . But the front attack was kept up so vigorously that . . . the National troops were compelled, several times, to take positions in the rear nearer Pittsburg Landing."

Leander Stillwell, whose unit at this point—perhaps 10:30 A.M.—was supporting an artillery unit, recalled that Grant "went by us in a gallop, riding between us and the [guns] at the head of his staff. The battery was then hotly engaged; shot and shell were whizzing overhead, and cutting off the limbs of trees, but Grant rode through the storm with perfect indifference, seemingly paying no more attention to the missiles than if they had been paper wads."

Not so his aides, who were justifiably worried. One of them tugged at the arm of Captain William S. Hillyer, a senior staff member, saying:

"Go tell the Old Man to leave here, for God's sake!"

"Tell him yourself," replied Hillyer. "He'll think me afraid, and so I am, but he shan't think so."

Finally someone approached Grant, saying: "General, we must leave this place. It isn't necessary to stay here. If we don't we shall all be dead in five minutes."

"I guess that's so," he responded, reluctantly turning from the action.[9]

Grant would range from one part of the battlefield to another during the late morning and afternoon, calmly issuing orders and conferring with his division heads. Though he knew his men were being bloodied, he remained optimistic, perhaps because he momentarily expected Lew Wallace's arrival.

"General, this thing looks pretty squally, doesn't it?" his aide Captain Rowley asked.

"Well, not so very bad," Grant said. "We've got to fight against time now. Wallace must be here very soon."

During these dark hours, the first command Grant visited was the hard-pressed Sherman on the far right, about whom he would say approvingly, "In thus moving along the line . . . I never deemed it important to stay long with Sherman." Going on to the equally beset McClernand, he promised him the last of his reserves, the 15th and 16th Iowa. To Prentiss in the center, who was rallying the remains of his division in the Sunken Road with help from William H. L. Wallace, he gave the order: "Hold at all hazards." To each officer he offered the same encouragement; *Lew Wallace is coming up, William Nelson with Buell's lead division is crossing the river, help is on the way.* "There was no hour during the day," Grant would say of the surrealistic contest, "when there was not heavy firing and generally hard fighting at some point on the line, but seldom at all points at the same time. It was a case of Southern dash against Northern pluck and endurance."

Sergeant Cyrus Boyd of the 15th Iowa, moving up to support McClernand, had come ashore from his transport only that morning. "The enemy lay in ambush at the farther side of the field," he said. "We at first could not see them, only the puffs of white smoke [coming] from the thickets and brush and every log and tree. . . . It was every man for himself." The officers seemed to be the first to fall. "Col. [Hugh] Reid was wounded and fell from his horse with a bullet wound in his neck—Lieut. Col. [William] Dewey I noticed . . . holding the halter to his horse, which seemed to be badly wounded." Without direction, the 15ᵗʰ Iowa soon fell back. "The woods seemed alive with *gray* coats and their victorious cheer and unearthly *yells,* and the concentrated fire . . . caused somebody to give the order for *retreat.* The word was passed along, and we went off that bloody ground in great confusion."

In early afternoon Grant, riding back to Harrison Landing, came upon a dispiriting sight. Thousands of men who had fled the battle were "lying under the cover of the river bluff, panic-stricken, most of whom would have been shot where they lay, without resistance, before they would have taken muskets and marched to the front to protect themselves." Though he dispatched officers to force them back into the lines, Grant understood their fear. "Many of them had arrived but a day or two before," he would write, "and were hardly able to load their muskets. . . . Their officers were equally ignorant of their duties. Under these circumstances it is not astonishing that many of the regiments broke at the first fire. . . . Better troops never went upon a battlefield than many of these, officers and men, afterwards proved themselves to be. . . ."[10]

Grant at this juncture could see that William Nelson's division would need hours to cross the river. Buell had arrived on the west bank ahead of his army but he was unhelpful, just as he had been at Nashville, in expediting their progress.

"What preparations have you made for retreating?" he asked Grant, more than a trifle smugly.

"I have not yet despaired of whipping them, general," was the reply.

But what of Lew Wallace? Earlier Grant had sent word for Wallace through Captain William Rowley to advance up the River Road to Harrison Landing with all haste. His division should have already arrived. Where was it?

Ordered to find Wallace about 2:00 P.M. were James McPherson, Grant's chief engineer, and the aforementioned John Rawlins, his chief of staff. Up they rode the River Road to Crump's Landing, expecting to meet him at any moment. Such was not to be. Wallace had gone off due west, taking a route that would lead him to the Purdy-Hamburg Road and Sherman on the right of Grant's army, or at least where Sherman had been until he had been forced to retreat. That position, unknown to Wallace, was now in the hands of the Confederates.

With the written order lost, it is impossible to determine whether Grant, who gave it verbally, or an intermediary, who scribbled it out, had been imprecise in their instructions, or whether other aides contributed to the confusion, or whether Wallace misunderstood it or even ignored it in the expectation he would gain fame by turning the enemy flank at a critical moment. By the time Rowley, McPherson, and Rawlins all caught up with him it was late afternoon.

Once Wallace heard their protests he ordered his column to countermarch, rather than marching the rear in front, which used up more time. Of course, there were sound reasons for this; marching the rear in front would disrupt the order of battle. All three aides were beside themselves with anger, however, and all too willing to believe that Wallace either was incompetent or disloyal. Rawlins, who throughout the war would be Grant's protector, would insist the order was clear-cut, saying that Wallace was instructed to advance "on the road nearest to and parallel to the river." Later, after they joined him, all three men would complain he did not move with sufficient speed. "Of the character of the march, after I overtook General Wallace, I can only say that to *me* it appeared intolerably slow, resembling more of a reconnaissance . . . than a forced march," said Rowley.

Two decades after the war, Grant and Lew Wallace would still be at loggerheads as to who was responsible for what happened that afternoon. "Wallace did not arrive in time to take part in the first day's fight," Grant would say. "[He] has since claimed that the order . . . was simply to join the right of the army . . . but that is not where I had ordered him nor where I wanted him to go. I never could see and do not now why any order was necessary further than . . . to come down to Pittsburg Landing, without specifying by what route."

In a letter to Grant, Wallace would insist a misunderstanding had kept him from engaging the enemy. Referring to the assertions of Grant's aides, he explained: "They did not understand there was a mistake in your order as it was delivered to me, and while with them I supposed they knew why I was where they found me. Consequently, no explanation took place between us." As to his alleged slowness thereafter: "From 11:30 o'clock until dusk my march was quite fifteen miles. I refer the argument to your calm judgement. I do not wonder my movement seemed slow to your officers. With their anxieties . . . it must have seemed intolerable to them."

Wallace, who all the intervening years had been plagued by the tale of his futile march, concluded: "Finally, general, did you ever ask yourself what motive I could have had to play you falsely that day? It couldn't have been personal malice. Only a few weeks before I had been promoted major general on your recommendation. It couldn't have been cowardice. You had seen me under fire at Donelson. . . . The fact is, I was the victim of a mistake."[11]

The Confederates had been concentrating on the Union right all the morning of April 6, striving for a knockout punch. Now in the afternoon they turned their attention in earnest to the center and left. During these hours, they would hurl perhaps 18,000 men in misguided frontal attacks at Benjamin Prentiss and William H. L. Wallace in the half-mile-long Hornet's Nest, whose numbers would never total many more than 4,000. But the assaults would be piecemeal and at no point would the attackers outnumber the defenders.

Meanwhile the Rebel losses would be horrendous. Yale-educated Colonel Randal Gibson, whose Louisiana and Arkansas brigade would be ordered to assail the Nest "up an elevation covered with an almost impenetrable thicket," outlines the problem: "On the left a battery opened that raked our flank while a steady fire of musketry extended along our entire front. . . . Our line was broken and the troops fell back." Four times his men charged, four times they were repulsed. "The strong and almost inaccessible position of the enemy—his infantry well covered in ambush and his artillery skillfully posted and efficiently served—was found to be impregnable to infantry alone." Gibson's brigade would lose one-third of its men.[12]

While these and other frontal attacks—estimated at anywhere from eight to a dozen—were failing to oust the Federals from the Hornet's Nest, Sidney Johnston about 2:00 P.M. was personally directing a more successful assault against Hurlbut and Stuart on the Union left.

"I will lead you!" he cried to his men, turning in his saddle and beckoning them on, just before the attack on Hurlbut.

Johnston's son, Colonel William Preston Johnston, re-creates the setting: "The line was already thrilling and trembling with that irresistible ardor which in battle decides the day. With a mighty shout [the] brigades moved forward at a charge. A sheet of flame and a roar burst from the Federal stronghold. The Confederate line withered; but there was not an instant's pause. The crest was gained. The enemy were in flight."

Though Johnston's uniform and boots were pierced by bullets in several places, he apparently survived the charge unhurt. Soon thereafter, however, he reeled in his saddle.

"General, are you wounded?" an aide asked.

"Yes, and I fear seriously," was the reply.

Johnston's right leg had been pierced by a minie ball below the knee, severing the main artery. A simple tourniquet might have saved his life, but his boot hid the wound. By the time the injury was found, it was too late. He died within minutes.[13]

Stephen Hurlbut's command was in retreat, but far from routed. About 3:00 P.M., he reported, "Colonel Stuart, on my left, sent me word that he was driven in, and that I would be flanked . . . in a few moments. It was necessary for me to decide at once whether to abandon either the right or left. I considered that Prentiss could, with the help of McClernand's troops, probably hold the right. . . ." He subsequently withdrew along with Stuart. "Perceiving that a heavy force was closing on the left, between my line and the river, while heavy fire continued on the right and front, I ordered the line to fall back. The retreat was made . . . steadily and in good order."

Providing Hurlbut with fortuitous cover during this period was Willard's Battery A, 1st Illinois Light Artillery, commandered by Lieutenant Peter P. Wood. Positioned where it could lay down an enfilading fire on the enemy, it considerably slowed his advance. Sweating gunners sent round after round of canister into the Rebel ranks, loading and discharging with profane gusto. "I had no thought of death or anything else except to hear the old gun talk as fast as possible," said one cannoneer. "We lost about 100 men," stated one Rebel colonel, "and would have been annihilated had not [they] greatly overshot us."

Passing through his camp and approaching the river, Hurlbut re-formed his men behind a protective bulwark of 24-pounder siege guns. "By direction of Major General Grant, I assumed command of all troops that came up. Broken regiments and disordered battalions came into line gradually upon my division. . . . Many officers and men unknown to me, and whom I never desire to know, fled in confusion through the line. Many gallant soldiers and brave officers rallied steadily. . . ."[14]

Late in the afternoon came a lull of about an hour in the Rebel onslaught all along the front, perhaps brought on by the transfer of command from Johnston to Beauregard, perhaps because the enemy was exhausted. Coming upon a "pool of clear blue water," many Confederates threw down their muskets and "rushed to the water with their cups and drank deeply." The body of a dead man on the edge of the pool did nothing to lessen their thirst. "If the water had been mixed with blood," said one soldier of the 15th Mississippi, "it would have been all the same."[15]

Both Federal flanks about 4:30 P.M. had been driven back to the vicinity of Pittsburg Landing. Sherman and McClernand on the right were at Tilghman Branch off Owl Creek; Hurlbut on the left was firming up his new position at Dill Branch off the river. Staying behind, in the increasingly isolated horseshoe that was the Hornet's Nest, were Prentiss and Wallace in the Federal center, surrounded by the enemy on three sides.

"When the gallant Hurlbut was forced to retire," said Prentiss, "Wallace and myself consulted, and agreed to hold our positions at all hazards, believing that we could thus save the army from destruction."

Now the Rebels massed their artillery on the Nest, something they should have done much earlier. Unlimbered and packed wheel to wheel, approximately sixty guns—smoothbores, rifles and howitzers—unleashed a lethal and continuing cannonade that blackened the sky and blasted the entrenchments. Some 180 rounds per minute fell on the Federals for more than an hour, pinning them down and forestalling reinforcements while the encirclement progressed. "The effect of this tremendous concentrated fire was very evident," said a Confederate officer. "The reserves, which could be plainly seen going to Prentiss's relief, fell back in confusion under the shower of shot, shell and cannister that was poured upon them, while our infantry, encouraged by such artillery support, rushed forward with a shout. . . ." Here William Wallace, who just that morning had been expecting a visit from his wife, Ann, incurred a mortal head wound. He would lie that night within the enemy lines, unattended and thought to be dead, while his wife tended the wounded.[16]

With Wallace struck down his officers and men took it upon themselves, with varying degrees of success, to cut themselves out of the trap. Colonel James Tuttle, whose brigade had fought bravely and well in the Sunken Road all day and suffered some 850 casualties, escaped with 2nd and 7th Iowa and marched to the Landing. Colonel William Shaw of the 14th Iowa, knocked from his horse by a tree limb as he made a dash for safety, was not so lucky. Getting groggily to his feet, he found himself face-to-face with Major F. E. Whitfield of the 9th Mississippi.

"Colonel, I think you will have to surrender, as you are entirely surrounded," said Whitfield.

"Well, major, it looks that way," Shaw conceded.

Other Federals behaved less reasonably. "Some of the Union prisoners," wrote one military historian, "refusing to surrender their arms, began smashing their rifled-muskets against the trees. When the Southerners saw what was happening, they opened fire again. . . ."

In the midst of the melee, Prentiss about 5:30 P.M. at last surrendered. ". . . Finding that further resistance must result in the slaughter of every man in the command, I had to yield the fight," he said. "The enemy succeeded in capturing myself and 2,200 rank and file, many of them wounded." Commented Union officer Manning Force: "Prentiss, having never swerved from the position he was ordered to hold, having lost everything but honor, surrendered the little band." In another sense, of course,

Prentiss had gained everything. Just as Sherman's tenacity in the morning at Shiloh Church had forced the Confederates to concentrate on him and abandon their plan of cutting off the Federals from the river, Prentiss and Wallace throughout the day had held the center, permitting the Federal flanks to withdraw in relative order to Pittsburg Landing and re-form their lines.[17]

There on the heights Grant concentrated his own artillery, some fifty guns under Colonel Joseph Webster, intent on protecting his access to the river. "Our men struggled vainly to ascend the hill, which was very steep, making charge after charge without success," said Confederate brigadier general James Chalmers, "but continued to fight until night closed hostilities." For Grant the crisis was over. "There was . . . a deep ravine in front of our left," he said. The Tennessee River was very high and there was water of considerable depth in the ravine. Here the enemy made a last desperate effort to turn our flank, but was repelled. . . . The attack had spent its force."

Preternaturally confident of victory the next day, Grant would direct his division commanders "to throw out heavy lines of skirmishers in the morning as soon as they could see, and push them forward until they found the enemy, following with their entire divisions . . . and to engage the enemy as soon as found." To Sherman he would recount the effectiveness of the counterattack at Fort Donelson, saying, "the same tactics [will] win at Shiloh." His optimism at first seemed unwarranted. His killed and wounded totaled some 7,000, his captured 3,000, and countless others were still huddled along the riverbank, refusing to fight. But Grant knew two things: Confederate casualties likewise had been brutal, totaling thus far more than 8,000, and Lew Wallace, Nelson, and the rest of Buell's command were already filing into his lines, reinforcing him with thousands of fresh troops.

He was sitting in front of a campfire about 10:00 P.M. when Colonel McPherson, his engineering officer, rode up.

"Well, Mac, how is it?" Grant inquired.

McPherson was downcast. He reported that one-third of the army was disabled and much of the remainder disheartened. Grant made no answer.

McPherson pressed the point. "What do you propose to do, sir? Shall I make preparations for retreat?"

"Retreat? No!" was the answer. "I propose to attack at daylight and whip them." Both sides were bloodied, but whoever went on the offensive "was sure to win."

With a heavy rain coming down, Sherman later came upon Grant standing under a large oak tree, his cigar glowing in the darkness. Heeding, he would say, "some wise and sudden instinct not to mention retreat," he made a noncommittal remark.

"Well, Grant, we've had the devil's own day, haven't we?"

"Yes," Grant replied, puffing on his cigar. "Lick 'em tomorrow, though."

Then like his troops he bedded down on the ground, exposed to the elements. "My ankle was so much swollen from the fall of my horse . . . and the bruise was so painful, that I could get no rest." Sometime during the night he rose and wandered toward the field hospital. "Wounded men were being brought in . . . a leg or an arm amputated as the case might require, and everything was being done to save life or alleviate suffering. The sight was more unendurable than encountering the enemy's fire, and I returned to my tree in the rain."[18]

Behind the Confederate lines that same night, the captured Benjamin Prentiss exchanged small talk with his captors.

"Well, sir, we have felt your power today," he told Beauregard, "and have yet to yield."

"You could not expect it otherwise," Beauregard replied. "We are fighting for our homes." The Southern commander was as confident of victory on the morrow as Grant. Erroneous intelligence reports had convinced him Buell's army had been diverted elsewhere. "I thought I had Grant just where I wanted him," he would say.

Bedding down subsequently between two Confederate colonels on a makeshift bed of canvas and blankets, Prentiss remained upbeat about the Union prospects.

"You gentlemen have had your way today," he repeated, "but it will be very different tomorrow. You'll see! Buell will effect a junction with Grant tonight, and we'll turn the tables on you."

Remembered one of the Rebel officers: "This was said evidently with sincerity, and was answered in the same pleasant spirit. . . . Tired as we were with the day's work, sleep soon overtook and held us all until early dawn, when the firing first of musketry and then of field artillery roused us, and General Prentiss exclaimed: 'Ah! Didn't I tell you so! There is Buell!' And so it proved."[19]

On the morning of the 7th then, Buell's Army of the Ohio anchored the Federal left wing, with the division of William Nelson closest to the river and then, from left to right, the divisions of Thomas Crittenden and Alexander McCook. Bull Nelson, a blustery 300-pounder who had once been a naval officer, came from a prominent Kentucky family, as did Crittenden, the son of an U.S. senator and the younger brother of a Confederate general. McCook, one of the fourteen brothers and cousins who during the war comprised the "Fighting McCooks" of Ohio, was a West Pointer and career soldier. Grant's battered Army of the Tennessee—with only four of its original six divisions still operational—comprised the Federal right, with Hurlbut on McCook's right and then, again from left to right, McClernand, Sherman, and Lew Wallace.

The Federals advanced against Beauregard about 7:00 A.M. with some 45,000 men on a broad front, for the most part engaging the enemy head-on. The Confederates, with perhaps half that many to oppose them, initially offered light resistance. Here Wallace's unit took its first casualty. "A round-shot tore past me travelling on a line lower than the horn of my saddle," he said, "and with a sound half swish, half roar, more vicious even than that of a rocket let loose. My horse swerved; yet I heard a sound behind me as if someone were pounding a sand pile with a maul . . . and, turning involuntarily, I was in time to see an arm, torn from the shoulder of a soldier and stiffened like a stick, its fingers all outspread, revolving end over end in the air."

Between 9:00 and 10:00 A.M., however, the Rebel battle lines began to stiffen. On the Union left Nelson found himself bogged down in the vicinity of the Sunken Road, where Prentiss and William Wallace had fought so long and so well, and where the dead and wounded still littered the ground. "Many had died there, and others were in their last agonies as we passed," said one of Nelson's men. "Their groans and cries were heartrending. One poor fellow begged most piteously to be put out of his misery, and another kept repeating, 'O God, have mercy! O God, O God!'"

Chaotic charges and countercharges in Nelson's sector subsequently ensued, as did a deafening artillery duel, before he began to prevail about noon. Crittenden and McCook at this time were similarly successful, driving to the Purdy-Hamburg Road. "The fire of the enemy's infantry was promptly responded to," said Colonel William Gibson of McCook's command. "Our volleys were delivered with rapidity, regularity and effect. The enemy's lines were shaken. . . ." Gibson once more advanced. "Our entire line pushed forward in gallant style, driving the enemy before us a full half mile, and taking possession of the camp from which . . . Sherman's division had been driven the day before."[20]

On the Union right Lew Wallace, Sherman, and McClernand also progressed toward the Purdy-Hamburg Road, though with difficulty. "(The woods) were thick and dark," said Wallace of the terrain. "And darker for the smoke that caught in the foliage and hung there—so dark that neither side could see the other. . . . There was patches of underbrush so thick men had to push themselves through by main strength, making it impossible to preserve their alignment. . . . Men loaded and fired without aim—or rather at the sounds coming from what they thought their front." Wallace, finally seeing action, would observe of the fragmented contest, that "the two armies as a general thing degenerated into mere fighting swarms . . . tactics [were] so limited it may almost be said there (were) no tactics." Whether advancing or retreating "there was but one cohesive principle . . . to watch the flag and stay by it."[21]

It was about noon, too, that the Confederates facing Sherman and McClernand made their strongest counterattack. The place was Water Oaks Pond, about a half mile northeast of Shiloh Church, and near the Crossroads to Corinth. A single Rebel brigade, led by General Sterling Wood of Alabama and numbering no more than 650 men, charged across the water and sent the Federals reeling back. The reversal was only temporary. Reinforcements later flanked Wood and repulsed him with enfilading fire. "Our position . . . was most critical," McClernand acknowledged, "but fortunately the Louisville Legion, forming part of General [Lovell] Rousseau's brigade, came up . . . and supported me. . . . This gallant body poured into the enemy's ranks one of the most terrible fires I ever witnessed."

Just as he had on Sunday under far more perilous circumstances, Grant the second day rode in apparent equanimity all along the lines, seeing for himself how the battle was proceeding. At one point, however, accompanied by Colonel McPherson and Major Hawkins, his commissary officer, he came under sudden attack. "There did not appear to be an enemy to our right," he said, "until suddenly a battery with musketry opened upon us from the edge of the woods. The shells and balls whistled about our ears very fast for about a minute. I do not think it took us longer than that to get out of range and out of sight."

Once Grant and his party reined up, they took stock of the damage. "Major Hawkins [had] lost his hat," said Grant. "He did not stop to pick it up." McPherson's mount, panting and shaking uncontrollably, had taken a ball in the flank that passed straight through him. "In a few minutes the poor beast dropped dead; he had given no sign of injury until we came to a stop." A second ball had hit the metal scabbard of Grant's sword, just below the hilt, breaking it off. "All [of us] were thankful that it was no worse," he remarked.[22]

By 2:00 P.M. the sheer numbers of the Union troops were overwhelming the Southerners who, like Grant's men the day before, were giving ground with the utmost reluctance. "The Rebels fall back slowly, stubbornly," affirmed Colonel Jacob Ammen of Nelson's command. Recognizing the need for a general withdrawal Thomas Jordan, Beauregard's chief of staff, approached him.

"General," he asked, "do you not think our troops are very much in the condition of a lump of sugar, thoroughly soaked with water, but yet preserving its original shape, though ready to dissolve? Would it not be judicious to get away with what we have?"

There was a noticeable pause. "I intend to withdraw in a few moments," the proud Creole eventually replied. Then he gave the formal orders, leaving Jordan with 2,000 infantry and a dozen cannon to cover the retreat back to Corinth. His hopes for a smashing victory had been dashed.

Grant decided his troops were too exhausted to follow on Beauregard's heels. "I wanted to pursue," he said, "but had not the heart to order the men who had fought desperately for two days, lying in the rain and mud whenever not fighting, [to do so]." Though Buell's army was less fatigued, dealing with its laggard commander was a problem. "I did not feel disposed to order Buell, or any part of his command, to pursue. Although the senior in rank at the time [from the date each man had been named a major general], I had been so only a few weeks. Buell was, and had been for some time, a department commander, while I commanded only a district. . . ."[23]

Shiloh, Grant would write, was the most severe battle fought in the West during the Civil War. "I saw an open field in our possession on the second day, over which the Confederates had made repeated charges . . . so covered with dead that it would have been possible to walk across the clearing, in any direction, stepping on dead bodies, without a foot touching the ground." Federal casualties during the bloodletting would total 13,000; Confederates, almost 12,000; altogether, some 25 percent of the men involved in the struggle. William Wallace, found alive on the field that second day, was brought to his wife, Ann, who could do little for his dreadful wound. She held his hand, prayed to God, and consoled herself with the thought that they were together in his final hours. He would die three days later, telling her, "We meet in Heaven."

Sergeant Cyrus Boyd of the 15th Iowa would describe the appearance of the now-deserted battlefield. "We soon came to where the dead lay thick. The first dead Rebel I came upon [was] on his back with his hands raised above his head and had died in great agony. I took a *button* from his coat. . . . Federal and Confederate lay alternately scattered over the ground, some of them wounded and so near dead from exposure that they were mostly insane."

One bizarre scene stuck in his memory. "I saw five *dead* Confederates all killed by one six-pound solid shot. . . . They had been behind a log and all in a row. The ball had raked them as they crouched behind the log. . . . One of them had his *head* taken off. One had been struck at the right shoulder and his chest lay open. One had been cut in two at the bowels and nothing held the carcass together but the spine. One had been hit at the thighs and the legs were torn from his body. The fifth and last was piled up into a mass of skull, arms, some toes and the remains of a butter-nut suit."

Summed up Boyd: "The enemy has retreated and left all his dead and wounded on the field. We have whipped him but at an awful *sacrifice*. The two armies are like two tenacious *bulldogs*. They have grappled and fought until both are exhausted and worn out. One had crawled away to *lie down* and the other one *cannot follow*. This is our condition. We are quite glad to hold the *ground and let him retreat*."

Grant subsequently would defend his decision not to fortify the lines at Pittsburg Landing. "Up to that time," he said, "the pick and spade had been little resorted to in the West. . . . The troops with me, officers and men, needed discipline and drill more than they did experience with the pick, shovel and ax. Reinforcements were arriving almost daily, composed of troops that had hastily been thrown together . . . the men and officers strangers to each other. Under all these circumstances I concluded that drill and discipline were more important to our men than fortifications."[24]

In the weeks to come, this contention and others—and Grant's character as well—would come under harsh criticism.

FOUR
* * * *

CONTROVERSY AND INTRIGUE

That Halleck's military views were in direct opposition to Grant's is nowhere more evident than in the terse instructions Old Brains sent him on April 9 following the Union triumph at Shiloh—for triumph it was, despite the dreadful casualties. "Avoid another battle, if you can," he said, "until reinforcements arrive." For Grant, fighting was what war was all about. For Halleck, who regarded the limited-warfare theories of Baron Jomini as Holy Scripture, slugging it out with the enemy was to be avoided; capturing his strategic strongholds would bring about his downfall. Halleck's judgment, at this point, would prevail. There would be no rushing after Beauregard to destroy him; instead there would be a prudent advance on Corinth. If the Rebels abandoned the rail center and fled, so much the better.

Once he arrived at Pittsburg Landing on the 11th to take personal charge, Halleck, a spit-and-polish garrison commander who could barely sit a horse and had never experienced the detritus of war and the disorder of soldiers in the field, lost no time in finding fault with Grant's leadership. "Immediate and active measures must be taken," he told him, "to put your command in condition to resist another attack." For good measure, he primly advised his subordinate of the proper way to forward official communications: *"Letters should relate to one matter only, and be properly folded."*[1]

Grant took all this in supposed equanimity, though we can conjecture he must have seethed inside. What would affect him with far more immediacy was a devastating 19,000-word article that appeared in the *Cincinnati Gazette* on April 14, written by twenty-four-year-old journalist Whitelaw Reid under the pen name "Agate," that depicted Shiloh not as a Union victory but as a near disaster.

Reid's piece, which may have been fueled by self-aggrandizing slurs from Buell and his men as much as by what he actually saw, maintained in large part that the Federals were still in their beds when the Confederates struck; men had been shot and bayoneted in their tents; Prentiss's division had been captured by 10:00 A.M.; Sherman and McClernand early had been routed and sent packing; soldiers lacking proper direction had little choice but to flee to Pittsburg Landing; Lew Wallace was not ordered up until noon; and Grant had not arrived on the field "after nearly all these disasters had crowded upon us." Implicit in the story was that the Federal commander was a colossal bungler, and that only Buell's arrival had saved the day.

Newspapers East and West picked up the article, reprinting it and adding their own embellishments, some even alleging that Grant had been drinking before the battle, and citing the mishap with his horse as proof. The *New York Herald* flatly stated that "Grant was accountable for the reverse on Sunday. . . . Probably 60 officers, brigade and regimental, have expressed themselves to that effect, while a word in his defense is scarcely to be heard in any quarter." The *Chicago Tribune* added that "the neglect of one man, entrusted with high responsibilities, has left fearful, heartrending testimonials on the savage battlefield of Pittsburg Landing."

Politicians took up the hue and cry. The governor of Ohio, rueful that two Ohio units had broken in the initial stages of the battle, opined that the men's conduct was due to the "criminal negligence" of the commander. Officers who were political appointees—and had fled at the first sound of gunfire—likewise sought to shift the blame. Speaking in defense of such men the lieutenant governor of Ohio declared: "Grant and Prentiss ought to be court-martialed and shot."[2]

Much that Reid wrote in his indignation about the bloodiness of the battle was true, much was not. One historian referred to his dispatch as "a singular blend of great reporting and abysmally bad reporting," and such is undoubtedly the case. That Grant in hindsight erred by not entrenching at Pittsburg Landing—despite his men's need for drill—and that he was surprised by Johnston's and Beauregard's sudden attack is beyond dispute.

But many of Reid's other charges were bunkum. Look at them point by point:

• The Federals were not in their beds. Thanks to the encounters between pickets, Sherman's and Prentiss's divisions—the troops closest to the enemy—had formed battle lines and advanced early Sunday before being thrown back.

• Nor was anyone shot or bayoneted in the tents. It is true that stray bullets passed through some of the shelters, perhaps the most notable of which was occupied by Colonel William Hall of the 11th Iowa, McClernand's command, who was receiving a connubial visit from his wife when the drum roll to arms sounded. Though the balls reputedly pierced several of Mrs. Hall's stays and petticoats as she hastily made her toilette, she was unharmed. Subsequently, she remarked that she and Colonel Hall had not been expecting company.

• Prentiss was not "captured" at 10:00 A.M. This was the approximate time the surviving elements of his command, which admittedly had been overwhelmed, were regrouping in the Sunken Road. Prentiss and William Wallace would hold out in the Hornet's Nest until the late afternoon, and Prentiss would not surrender until 5:30 P.M. Their stout defense in the Union center probably saved the army.

• Sherman and McClernand on the Union right, though continually pushed back toward the Landing, were never routed. By dusk on Sunday they continued to hold along the Savannah-Hamburg Road.

• The soldiers who fled and straggled back to the Landing did not lack direction; they lacked drill and discipline, had been sent to Grant untrained, and were terrified out of their minds. To repeat Grant's assessment: "Under these circumstances, it is not astonishing that many of the regiments broke at the first fire."

• Reid must have been aware that Grant ordered Lew Wallace in early morning to ready his division for combat. He was with Wallace when Grant stopped briefly at Crump's Landing and issued such instructions, and he later stowed away on his transport. When Grant arrived at Pittsburg Landing, of course, he immediately ordered Wallace to the front.

• Grant was not absent during most of Sunday. He arrived at the Landing about 10:00 A.M., and went immediately to the battlefield. Again, Reid must have known this—he debarked with him.

• Grant's decisions at Shiloh, of course, were open to criticism.

But the slow-moving Buell must also be faulted. His march to join Grant should have been far speedier. If his divisions had crossed the river on Saturday night rather than Sunday night the Confederate assault, if it were made at all, would have been stopped in its tracks.[3]

Grant reacted to Reid's charges—for the most part privately—with equally misguided fervor, insisting that there had been no surprise at Shiloh at all and that such assertions were the work of those intent on his ruin. To his father, Jesse, on April 26 he wrote: "There is one thing I feel well assured of; that is, that I have the confidence of every brave man in my command. Those who showed the white feather will do all in their power to attract attention from themselves. I had perhaps a dozen officers arrested for cowardice in the first day's fight. . . . These men necessarily are my enemies. As to the talk of a surprise here, nothing could be more false. . . . Skirmishing had been going on for two days. . . . I did not believe, however, that they intended to make a determined attack, but simply that they were making a reconnaissance in force." To Julia four days later he added: "You need give yourself no trouble about newspaper reports. . . . Most or all that you have seen has been written by persons who were not here and [those] few items collected from persons nominally present, eye witnesses, [were] from those who disgraced themselves and now want to draw off public attention. I am very sorry to say a great [deal] originates in jealousy."

That the assertions wounded Grant was obvious. To his patron Congressman Elihu Washburne he complained: "To say that I have not been distressed by these attacks upon me would be false, for I have a father, mother, wife & children who read them and are distressed by them. . . . Then too all subject to my orders read these charges [which are] calculated to weaken their confidence in me." Here Grant, who because Lew Wallace did not see action on April 6 commanded some 35,000 troops that day against the South's 40,000, permitted himself an exaggeration. "Those people who expect a field of battle to be maintained . . . with about 30,000 troops, most of them entirely raw, against 70,000 . . . whilst waiting for reinforcements to come up, without loss of life, know little of war." His next comment to Washburne, however, revealed the indomitable fighting spirit of the man. "To have left the field of Pittsburg for the enemy to occupy until our force was sufficient to have gained a bloodless victory would have been to [leave] the Tennessee to become a second Potomac— There was nothing left for me but to occupy the west bank . . . and to hold it at all hazards. It would have set the war back six months to have failed. . . ."[4]

Tecumseh Sherman, whose contempt for the press was becoming legendary and whose experiences at Shiloh had forever made him Grant's admirer, lost no time in defending his chief—and himself. "The hue & cry about surprise is wrong," he told Ellen. "I was not surprised and I was in advance . . . and I don't believe [Prentiss] was surprised. . . . In the 302 dead and 1,200 wounded of my division, there was not a bayonet or knife wound. . . . I hope the war won't end until those who caused the war, the politicians and editors, are made to feel it. The scoundrels take good care of their hides. . . ."

To his brother and father-in-law, Sherman was even more caustic. "My hand is still very sore," he wrote Senator Sherman, alluding to his wound, "but I am able to write some. The newspapers came back to us with accounts of our battle . . . as usual made by people who ran away and had to excuse their cowardice by charging bad management on the part of leaders. I see that we were surprised, that our men were bayoneted in their tents, that our officers had not had breakfast &c. This is all simply false." Referring to the two Ohio regiments in his division that had bolted, one led by the hapless Jesse Appler, Sherman said: "The regiments that profess to have been surprised . . . and the two that first broke . . . the 53rd and 57th Ohio—[respectively] lost no officers and only seven men, and two officers and seven men." He stressed that most of his troops had fought well. "Three of my brigades held our original position from . . . when the attack began (10:00 A.M.) till when the enemy had passed my left and . . . I ordered them to fall back. We held our 2nd position until 4 P.M.—and then [withdrew] to the 3rd & last position, more than a mile from the river."

Sherman's letter to Tom Ewing reinforced these points: "Newspapers now rule, and one to prosper must ignore the old government and acknowledge the new power of the press. Their representatives, the reporters, are to me the most contemptible race of men that exist, cowardly, cringing . . . and gathering their material out of the most polluted sources. Thus in our recent operations here, I can hardly realize any description. . . . Even Mr. Lincoln has listened to this tale of surprise and telegraphed to Halleck to know who was to blame for it."[5]

The calumny that Grant had been drinking particularly infuriated his supporters. "As to the story that [Grant] was intoxicated at the battle of Pittsburg," his aide Captain William Rowley wrote a friend, "I have only to say that the man who fabricated that [tale] is an infamous *liar*." To Congressman Washburne, Rowley insisted: "The stories in circulation have their origin in the efforts of cowardly hounds who 'stampeded.'. . . Together with the eagerness of newspaper correspondents to get 'items.' I who was on the field know that had it not been for the almost superhuman efforts of the Gen., added to the assistance he had from his officers, we would have been forced to record a defeat instead of one of the most *brilliant* victories that was ever won. . . ." Colonel J. E. Smith of the 45th Illinois, a Galena resident, in like manner wrote Washburne: "I see also that Grant is severely censured by the public for drunkenness, got up no doubt by those who are jealous of him. There is no foundation for the report."[6]

Congressman Washburne, convinced that Grant was being slandered, soon rose on the floor of the House of Representatives to defend him. He denounced as lies all allegations that Grant had been surprised at Shiloh and had mishandled the struggle, and hailed him as "the general who has recently fought the bloodiest and hardest battle ever fought on this continent . . . evincing, in his dispositions, the genius of the greatest commanders." Debunking the drinking charges, he added, hyperbolically: "There is no more temperate man in the army than General Grant. He never indulges in the use of intoxicating liquors at all. . . . It has well been said, that Falsehood will travel from Maine to Georgia while Truth is putting on its boots.' " Buoyed by Washburne's remarks a grateful Julia Grant wrote: "Permit me to thank you for your bold and gallant effort to right the public mind. . . ."[7]

Though Grant's champions were vociferous, their views at this juncture would not entirely prevail. On April 28 Halleck removed him from the Army of the Tennessee and named him second in command—a meaningless title—of the new combined 120,000-man Federal force at the Landing. Replacing him was George H. Thomas, one of the few Southerners who had renounced his heritage to declare for the Union. Knowing he was not a field commander, Halleck at best may have felt he needed Grant at his elbow for advice; the latter, however, clearly viewed the appointment as a demotion. The tardy Buell continued as head of the Army of the Ohio. Bombastic John Pope, who had just scored successes on the Mississippi at New Madrid, Missouri, and Island Number Ten, capturing 9,000 Rebel prisoners, led the newly arrived Army of the Mississippi. All three army commanders were West Pointers and career soldiers.

Within days Grant, by nature a warrior and entirely unsuited for a staff officer's role, was petitioning Halleck for a transfer. "I deem it due myself to ask either full restoration to duty, according to rank, or to be relieved entirely from further duty with this department. I cannot, do not, believe that there is a disposition on the part of yourself to do me any injustice, but my suspicions have been aroused you may be acting, under instructions, from higher authority, that I know nothing of." Halleck's response was bland. "You have precisely the position to which your rank entitles you," he said. "For the last three months I have done everything in my power to ward off the attacks that were made upon you. If you believe me your friend you will not require explanations; if not, explanations on my part would be of little avail."

Retaining only his staff and a small honor guard, Grant now was an isolated figure within the army life swirling around him. Lew Wallace, passing by his tent one day, noticed him standing by himself. "I recognized General Grant, and rode to him. Bringing a campstool he invited me to sit. The conversation was chiefly remarkable in that he made no allusion to his treatment by General Halleck—neither by voice, look nor manner did he betray any resentment. That very silence on his part touched me the more keenly."[8]

Through the whole of May the Federals, who outnumbered their adversaries two to one, inched their way at a snail-like pace the twenty or so miles southwest to Corinth along a ten-mile front. Pope's men comprised the left wing, Buell's the center, and Thomas's the right. "The movement was a siege from start to close," Grant would say of Halleck's timidity. "The National troops were always behind entrenchments, except of course the small reconnaissance parties sent . . . to clear the way for an advance. Even the commanders of these parties were cautioned, 'not to bring on an engagement.'" The Bluecoats would push forward a short distance, dig in, corduroy and connect the roads behind them, and then repeat the process.

Day after day these spasmodic movements continued. Observed a frustrated Grant: "[We] were thoroughly entrenched all the way from the Tennessee River to Corinth." Snarled Brigadier John "Black Jack" Logan of Illinois, who would become perhaps the toughest fighter of the politically appointed generals from the Midwest: "My men'll never dig another ditch for Halleck except to bury him." Opined a puzzled soldier: "I cannot imagine what our dignitaries are doing that we should lie here so long."

Late in the month, noting that Sherman on the army's right had carried an enemy battery and fortified log-house just two miles from Corinth, Grant took it upon himself to venture some advice to Halleck, proposing that Pope on the left be dispatched to cross over behind Sherman and surprise the Rebels on the right with a flank attack. "The ground, or works, occupied by our left could be held by a thin picket line," he explained, "owing to the stream and swamp in front. To the right the troops would have a dry ridge to march over." Halleck cut him off. "I was silenced so quickly that I felt that possibly I had suggested an unmilitary movement."[9]

Trains had been pulling in and out of Corinth for days, further alarming Halleck, who did not know what they were carrying and thought that Beauregard was being reinforced. The Confederates, to further the ruse, had been instructed to cheer each new arrival. General Logan, whose command had been monitoring the Mobil and Ohio Railroad, insisted that the enemy instead was evacuating the rail center. "Some of the men who had been engaged in various capacities on railroads before the war," said Grant, "claimed that they could tell, by putting their ears to the rail, not only which way the trains were moving, but which trains were loaded and which were empty. They said loaded trains had been going out and empty ones coming in. Subsequent events proved the correctness of their judgment."

Halleck's caution had not only allowed Beauregard and his stricken army to regroup but to get away lock, stock, and barrel. "Corinth was not captured," said Lew Wallace, "it was abandoned to us. At dawn on May 30th we marched into its deserted works, getting nothing—nothing—not a sick prisoner, not a rusty bayonet, not a bite of bacon, nothing but an empty town and some Quaker guns." (This last reference was to blackened logs on wheels meant to be mistaken for cannon.) Halleck was unabashed. In keeping with his views on tactics, he was content that Corinth's fall had cut the Memphis and Charleston Railroad and forced the Confederates to abandon Memphis. Giving no thought to hurling his huge force east against Chattanooga or south against Vicksburg he dug in once more, intent on making the town's fortifications one of the wonders of the world. In the midst of these labors he wired Washington that he had scored a signal victory: "Thousands of the enemy are throwing away their arms," he conjectured. ". . . The result is all I could possibly desire."[10]

This posturing, and his own peculiar status, were more than Grant could bear; he obtained a thirty-day leave, quite likely as a prelude to leaving the service. Hearing this, Sherman visited Grant's campsite. "I found him seated on a cap-stool, with papers on a rude table; he seemed to be employed in assorting letters, and tying them up with red tape into convenient bundles.

"I inquired if it was true that he was going away. He said, 'Yes.'

"I then inquired the reason, and he said, 'Sherman, you know. You know that I am in the way here. I have stood it as long as I can, and can endure it no longer.' I then asked him where he was going to, and he said, 'St. Louis.' I then asked if he had any business there, and he said, 'Not a bit.' "

Sherman here made a fateful decision, urging Grant to reconsider his leave-taking. It was ironic that the one, a brilliant but sometimes manic man, was asking the other, whose steadfast, self-reliant ways he recognized and admired, to stay the course. In so doing, Sherman ensured Grant's place in history.

"I then begged him to stay, illustrating his case by my own. Before the battle of Shiloh, I had been cast down by a mere newspaper assertion of 'crazy,' but that single battle had given me new life, and now I was in high feather; and I argued with him, that if he went away, events would go right along, and he would be left out; whereas, if he remained, some happy accident might restore him to favor and his true place."

Though Grant acknowledges the conversation, his precise response does not survive, but Sherman would write: "He promised not to go without seeing me again, or communicating with me. . . . Very soon after this . . . I received a note from him, saying that he . . . would remain."

To which Sherman on June 6 would reply, doubtless cementing their friendship: "I [rejoice] at your conclusion . . . for you could not be quiet at home for a week when armies were moving, and rest could not relieve your mind of the gnawing sensation that injustice had been done you."[11]

Grant's growing conviction that the war could only be won if the Rebel armies were soundly defeated and hounded into surrender remained anathema to Halleck but, for reasons not spelled out, he was five days later restored to command of the Army of the Tennessee, making his headquarters in Memphis. The "happy accident" mentioned by Sherman had come to pass. Perhaps Washburne had gotten Lincoln's ear; perhaps the Congress and the president, desperate for victories, doubted the wisdom of humiliating the man who—with his victories at Forts Henry and Donelson and at Shiloh—had gained the most significant Union triumphs thus far. "I can't spare this man—he fights!" Lincoln had remarked after the latter battle.

In late June Halleck divided the remainder of his immense army and, in effect, assumed a defensive posture. Buell with the Army of the Ohio, to which George Thomas returned as a division commander, was sent east toward Chattanooga, Tennessee. Pope's Army of the Mississippi, now under William Rosecrans, a West Pointer turned engineer and businessman, was posted south of Corinth; Pope himself had been ordered east, to take command of all troops in Virginia except those under George McClellan.

In July Grant was the beneficiary of a second "happy accident." Lincoln, whose armies in the East had just been defeated in the Shenandoah by Thomas "Stonewall" Jackson and in the Seven Days around Richmond by Robert E. Lee, had for months been in need of a general-in-chief.

McClellan as we have seen had been removed from that role, while remaining in charge of the Army of the Potomac. Lincoln, grasping at straws,
now named Halleck general-in-chief, ordering him to Washington posthaste.
"I am very anxious—almost impatient—to have you here," he told him.
"When can you make it?" Before too long, alas, the president would come
to recognize Old Brain's limitations, characterizing him as "little more than
a first rate clerk."[12]

On the 11th however, a somewhat bewildered Grant received instructions from Halleck to report to Corinth.

"Am I to bring my staff?" he asked.

Halleck was as enigmatic as ever. To be fair, he was also conscious that
the telegraph wires running through hostile country might be monitored.
"This place will be your headquarters," he replied. "You can judge for
yourself."

Within days Grant, so recently in the throes of despair, found himself
by virtue of seniority not only out of Halleck's immediate shadow but
in command of all troops between the Mississippi and the Tennessee
Rivers—principally his own Army of the Tennessee and Rosecrans's Army
of the Mississippi. In the West, only Buell's Army of the Ohio remained
outside his authority.

The promotion nonetheless had been a dicey proposition. Until the last
moment Halleck refused to endorse Grant for the post, asking Washington whether the president wished someone else. He had even sounded out
an aide, Colonel Robert Allen—whose experience was confined to quartermaster duties—as to whether he wanted the job.

"Now, what can I do for you?" Halleck asked his commissary officer,
after informing him that he was being called to Washington.

I'm not sure you can do anything for me, Allen said in so many words.

"Yes, I can give you command of the army," Halleck answered.

When Allen wondered aloud whether he had enough rank, Halleck ignored the objection, saying it could be overcome. Doubtless recognizing
he was not a field commander, Allen begged off, claiming that he was
needed to oversee the army's huge supply operation.

Halleck's high opinion of himself was obvious in such shenanigans.
Writing his wife about this time, he would intone: "It is the strangest thing
in the world to me that this war has developed so little talent in our generals. There is not a single one in the West fit for a great command." This
comment, coming from someone who had seen at first hand the abilities of
such officers as Grant and Sherman, is disturbing. Halleck, despite his administrative talents, was no judge of warriors.[13]

No sooner was Grant established in Corinth that summer than he sent for Julia and the children, a practice he continued throughout the war. They settled into a house owned by a rabid secessionist, a man so vociferous in his support of the Confederacy that he had been arrested and sent north. There Grant set up his headquarters and he and Julia spent several contented weeks, marred only when Buck, then ten, was kicked by a horse. The injury, luckily, was minor. "Men remembered that headquarters was always cheerful when the Grant family was together," wrote a historian. "Grant spent much time with the children, who 'used to play about and over and around the general by the hour,' with neither General nor children saying a word."[14]

It was during this time, too, that the Union authorities began to be more realistic and more adversarial in their policies toward Southern sympathizers in Northern Mississippi and Tennessee. Heretofore the word had been to treat all civilians and their property with respect, even returning runaway slaves to their owners, but this was changing. "If necessary, take up all active sympathizers, and either hold them as prisoners or out them beyond our lines," Halleck at this point wired Grant from Washington. "Handle that class without gloves, and take their property for public use. As soon as the corn gets fit for forage get all the supplies you can from the Rebels. . . . It is time that they should begin to feel the presence of war."

Instrumental in this order was the "taking" of Southern property; Negro slaves were still property, or "contraband," but now they could be removed from their owners. (Lincoln's Emancipation Proclamation, freeing the slaves in the Rebel states, would not take effect until January of 1863; black regiments would not be raised and trained in substantial number until six months after that date.) "The policy is to be terrible on the enemy," said Union general Grenville Dodge, who was already hiring blacks to keep open the Mobile and Ohio Railroad—the main Union supply line. "I am using Negroes all the time . . . as teamsters, and have 1,000 employed. I do it quietly and no fuss is made about it." Enthused Cyrus Boyd of the 15th Iowa: "Contrabands . . . are building forts around here and felling trees across the roads to keep the enemy's cavalry from surprising us. A good many soldiers and people are *bitterly* opposed to having 'Niggers' take any hand in this war. I am not one of those kind of people. If a *colored* man will dig trenches and chop down timber and even fight the enemy he is just the fellow we want, and the sooner we recognize this the quicker the war will *end*." Lieutenant S. D. Thompson of the 3rd Iowa, noting the number of blacks seeking employment, stated: "All that came within our lines were received and put to work and supplied with clothing and subsistence. This policy was viewed . . . with very general approbation."

Many of the Federals, of course, had no love for coloreds, as African-Americans then were called. They came from midwest and border states where abolitionists were unwelcome. But most of them could see that blacks, whether raising crops or repairing infrastructure, were sustaining the Rebel cause. Putting them to work instead for the Union made sense, and Grant concurred. "Every time an expedition goes out many of [the slaves] follow in the wake of the army and come into camp," he wrote. "I am using them as teamsters, hospital attendants, company cooks and so forth, thus saving soldiers to carry the musket."[15]

In the midst of the summer Grant, who normally sought to influence the press rather than suppress it, severely disciplined a reporter for the *Chicago Times,* a Copperhead publication invariably critical of the Union cause. He was W. P. Isham, and there were various explanations of his offense, including a "disrespectful" article he wrote about a Union brigadier who had narrowly eluded capture by the Rebels while patronizing a bordello. The more likely reason for Grant's ire, however, was more military in nature. Isham had concocted a "scoop"—entirely fictional—depicting the arrival in Mobile, Alabama, of a flotilla of English-built Rebel ironclads. The gunboats were ten in number, he claimed, sheathed in all but impregnable armor, mounted thirty guns apiece, and would soon rout the Federal navy on the Mississippi.

Grant, noting that the piece was "both false in fact and mischievous in character," sent a copy to Sherman in Memphis, asking him to take action. This Cump was only too happy to do, and a court-martial sent Isham to jail "until the close of the war, unless sooner discharged by competent authority." Grant subsequently would relent, and Isham, after serving several months of his sentence, would be released.[16]

Perhaps a word is in order here about Civil War reporting. Sylvanus Cadwallader, a *Chicago Times* reporter who soon would earn Grant's trust—and who would be responsible for Isham being freed—would say: "At that time nearly all army correspondents were in bad odor at all army headquarters, and were always secretly held to be a species of nuisance that needed abating. In many cases official hostility was openly expressed, and hindrances put in their way. . . ."

West Pointers, he found, were particularly unfriendly, and often for good reason. "Candor compels the admission that, as a class, the first installment of correspondents deserved no high rank. . . . Some unduly magnified their importance. . . . Some were so lacking in conventional politeness as to make themselves positively disagreeable. . . . Others almost unblushingly took the contract of 'writing up' some colonel to a brigadier, for a specified consideration in dollars . . . [or] were sufficiently ignoble to fasten themselves upon some [officer], and pay their . . . whiskey bills and horse hire by fulsome and undeserved praise."

For Cadwallader the worst of the correspondents were those "who would purloin papers and orders, hang around officers' tents secretly at night hoping to hear conversation that could be used by their papers. . . . A small proportion only of the whole number possessed . . . the ability to discriminate between legitimate and illegitimate news from the seat of war. In the end, the 'survival of the fittest' corrected all this."[17]

By mid-September, however, biased and inaccurate reporting was the least of Grant's concerns. The Confederates again were on the move in the West, courtesy of Halleck's misguided tactics, and Grant had been compelled to weaken himself by sending three divisions to Buell's support in east Tennessee. There Braxton Bragg, a close friend of President Jefferson Davis, had replaced Beauregard as head of the Army of Tennessee and together with General Kirby Smith's command was advancing into Kentucky and even threatening Ohio. (Note that Grant's Federal force was called the Army of *the* Tennessee.) Buell clearly was being outmaneuvered, moving Halleck in Washington to remark that "unless he does something very soon I think he will be relieved. . . . The government seems determined to apply the guillotine to all unsuccessful generals. . . . Perhaps with us now, as in the French revolution, some harsh measures are required."

Grant too was feeling Rebel pressure. On his front in west Tennessee and northern Mississippi his depleted lines extended, left to right, from Rosecrans at Corinth to Major General Edward Otho Ord—a career West Pointer—in the center guarding the north-south Mobile and Ohio Railroad to Sherman at Memphis. Opposing him with increasing boldness were Confederate generals Sterling Price and Earl Van Dorn. Boosting Rebel confidence, of course, were the exploits of Robert E. Lee in the East, who had just humbled John Pope at second Bull Run and was advancing into Maryland, where soon he would face McClellan along Antietam Creek. Grant reacted in character. He resolved to go on the offensive, hoping to catch Price in a pincer movement at Iuka, Mississippi, a village some twenty miles east of Corinth, before he could unite with Van Dorn.[18]

FIVE
* * * *

IUKA, CORINTH, AND ROSECRANS

Grant's battle plan called for William Rosecrans with 10,000 troops to move on Iuka from the south, on a roundabout route, while he and Edward Ord with 8,000 men advanced from the north, catching Sterling Price's 14,000 Rebels between them. To be successful, both Federal columns would have to engage the enemy simultaneously. Ord's column reached Iuka first, on September 18, and was poised to lead off the fight the next morning. Grant at this juncture learned, however, that Rosecrans had been delayed, and would not be ready to close the trap until the next afternoon. Thereupon he instructed Ord to put his assault on hold, and not to advance on the 19th until he heard the sound of Rosecrans's guns. This order was to have unfortunate results, both in the outcome of the battle and in Grant's relationship with Rosecrans.

Descended from Dutch immigrants who had come to America in 1651, William Starke Rosecrans was born in Delaware County, Ohio, in 1819. His father was a storekeeper who had been a militia officer in the War of 1812; his mother was a deeply religious Methodist. When his family could not afford to send him to college, the young man set his sights on West Point. To secure an appointment he walked fifty miles to interview with his congressman, who was so impressed with him that he gave him the place he had been keeping for his son. In 1838 Rosecrans entered the academy, where his classmates included Don Carlos Buell, Earl Van Dorn, and James Longstreet. There he was much admired, with one cadet saying he was "good at everything, his studies, his military duties, his deportment."

There, too, he first met Grant, who was one year behind him. The occasion came one night after taps, when Rosecrans as officer of the day found the newcomer out of his quarters, and asked what he was doing.

"I'm guarding the pump," said Grant, not realizing he was the victim of some hazing. "I've orders to stand here until after the next call."

"You go to bed at tattoo," said Rosecrans, ordering him to his room, "and douse your light at taps."

"But how do I know that you're not playing a trick on me, too?" Grant asked.

"See my chevrons," the upperclassman replied, settling the matter once and for all. "I'm officer of the day."[1]

While still at West Point, Rosecrans converted to Roman Catholicism. For him it was "an intellectual decision," made because he felt the need of "an authorized supernatural teacher." Ever after he was a devoted believer, never tiring of discussing his faith. On his watch chain he carried a small crucifix; in his pocket, a well-worn rosary. Following graduation in 1842 (he was fifth in a class of fifty-six), he taught engineering at the academy, married and began to raise a family, and completed a series of engineering projects for the army. Hoping to increase his income, he applied in 1851 for a professorship at the Virginia Military Institute; ironically, the appointment went to Thomas "Stonewall" Jackson.

In 1853 Rosecrans resigned from the service, later taking a post as chief engineer and superintendent of a coal mining company in western Virginia. Subsequently he established with some partners an oil refinery in Cincinnati. There, trying to develop a more marketable kerosene, he suffered severe burns when a "safety lamp" exploded in his face. The livid scars left him with what contemporaries describe as a permanent smirk. He nonetheless persisted in refinery operations—patenting an odorless oil, an improved kerosene lamp, and an inexpensive chlorine soap.[2]

Following the outbreak of war in 1861, Rosecrans took command of an Ohio brigade, fighting with distinction under George McClellan in the Union victory at Rich Mountain in western Virginia. His fellow general Jacob D. Cox would say of him: "He was tall but not heavy. . . . His aquiline nose and bright eyes gave him an incisive expression, increased by rapid utterance in his speech, which was apt to grow hurried, almost to stammering, when he was excited. His impulsiveness was plain to all who approached him; his irritation quickly flashed out in words when he was crossed, and his social geniality would show itself in smiles . . . when he was pleased." Soon, however, Rosecrans's outspokenness as to how the war should be fought made him enemies. Notable among them was Secretary of War Stanton, no man to take advice from anyone, who was instrumental in transferring him to the West. "To those above him [Rosecrans] was always punctilious, often testy, and at times deplorably indiscreet," Correspondent Whitelaw Reid would write. ". . . This sturdy honesty . . . was at once one of the most striking features of his character, and one of the most potent reasons for his constant embarrassments."[3]

Now on September 19, 1862, with his difficulties with Stanton to some degree behind him, Rosecrans under Grant advanced on Iuka, hoping to trap the Rebels between his own troops and those of Ord's. But this was not to be. Grant and Ord unbeknownst to him would remain in their lines, unable to hear the sound of his guns because of shifting winds and climatic conditions—a relatively common Civil War occurrence. Meanwhile Sterling Price would anticipate the pincer movement, falling back from Ord's front about 4:00 P.M. and hurling himself on Rosecrans, who had only one of his two divisions in place. It was led by Brigadier Charles S. Hamilton, who had graduated with Grant in the West Point class of 1843 but, bitter over his prospects for promotion, soon would revile him. *"Grant is a drunkard,"* he would tell a Wisconsin senator, citing no evidence for the charge. "His wife has been with him for months only to use her influence in keeping him sober. He tries to let liquor alone but he cannot resist."

Hamilton, with Colonel John Sanborn's brigade led by the 5th Iowa in the van, bent but did not break under Price's assault. "Not a moment was lost," Hamilton said. "A second regiment, and a third, with all the rapidity that men could exercise, was added to our little line; and while the Confederates were moving to the front, we managed to get . . . into position. It was then the storm of battle opened." The opposing sides were at close quarters. "[Sanborn's] infantry held their ground against the overwhelming force moving against them. . . . At the first musketry fire of the enemy, most of the horses of our battery [the 11th Ohio] were killed, and the pieces could not be removed from the field." Minute by minute the battle waxed hotter, with Hamilton's troops forced ever backward. "The dead lay in lines along the regiments. . . . The battery under [Lieutenant Cyrus] Sears was doing noble service, but had lost nearly half its men." Not waiting for orders, Sears had unleashed a hail of canister on the foe; his initiative would earn him the Medal of Honor.

By day's end, only six of his fifty-four cannoneers would escape death or wounds.

S. P. Barron of the dismounted 3rd Texas Cavalry depicted the terrible price in turn that the 11th Ohio exacted from the Rebels, with the guns changing hands several times during charges and countercharges. "The entire Federal artillery fire was soon turned on us, using grape and canister shot," he said, "and as their battery was in front of the 3rd Texas, [it] began to play havoc with our people. . . . We charged the battery and with desperate fighting took nine pieces and one caisson." The 3rd Texas, Barron estimated, lost one-quarter of its 388 men.

Here Rosecrans's rearmost division, commanded by Brigadier David Stanley, a West Pointer and former Indian fighter, about 5:00 P.M. came to Hamilton's support "On the crest of the hill stood the 11th Ohio Battery," Lloyd Bryner of the 47th Illinois remembered. "Hamilton [was fighting] three times his own force led by Price in person—the battle became furious. . . . The 'Eagle Brigade' [Bryner's own] came into action on the double quick, the 47th on the left of the 11th Missouri, the 5th Minnesota on the right. . . . Three times the guns on the crest were charged by the Confederates; the cannoneers were bayoneted at the guns. . . . In the last desperate attempt two Mississippi brigades were sent to the work. . . . The smoke of battle hung so heavy that objects could scarcely be seen at five paces."

Though Sears's battery was lost, the Federal infantry held. "On came the brave Mississippians," said Bryner, "but as vainly beat the waves against the rocks as these Confederate[s] . . . against the Illinois boys . . . They were received at the point of the bayonet . . . officers discharged their pistols in the very faces of their foes."[4]

Darkness brought the action at Iuka to a conclusion, with neither side victorious, but with Rosecrans making a mistake of his own. Just as Grant and Ord had not kept in close communication with him, allowing capricious winds to keep them out of the battle, Rosecrans had advanced on just one of the two roads leading south, leaving the other unblocked. During the night Price took advantage of the oversight, escaping with his troops to join Van Dorn down the unguarded route. The Federal occupation of Iuka the next morning was no more than a hollow triumph. Union casualties during the brief engagement totaled some 800, almost all in Hamilton's division; Confederate casualties, some 500.

Grant and Rosecrans, equally disturbed that Price had gotten away, each in varying degree blamed the other. "Word was soon brought to me that our troops were in Iuka," said Grant. "I immediately rode into town and found that the enemy was not being pursued, even by the cavalry. I ordered pursuit by the whole of Rosecrans' command. . . . He followed only a few miles after I left him and then went into camp. . . . I was disappointed . . . but I had so high an opinion of General Rosecrans that I found no fault at the time."

Rosecrans for the nonce held his tongue, but others did his work for him. Recounted the Cincinnati *Commercial,* alleging that Grant did not come to Rosecrans's aid because he was drunk: "How did the enemy get away? . . . You may slightly, but not fully, imagine the bitter curses that went up from our subordinate officers and men when they learned that *Hellish Whiskey* was the whole cause." Writing to Rosecrans's wife, his brother, Sylvester, also a convert to Catholicism and then the auxiliary bishop of Cincinnati, poured fuel on the fire: "The awful charge made against Grant in today's *Commercial* is not so surprising as it is disgusting. I am afraid it is true." These and other fanciful libels about excessive drinking would follow Grant throughout the war; basically he would learn to live with them.

In the days that followed it became obvious that Van Dorn, now united with Price and wrongly thinking he outnumbered the Federals, would be moving to retake Corinth. There Grant, who was making his headquarters in Jackson, Tennessee, continued to entrust Rosecrans with command. The rail center remained the key to the tenuous Federal position in Mississippi; if the enemy retook it Grant would have little choice but to withdraw back into Tennessee. Rosecrans's four division heads were the Iuka veterans Charles Hamilton of Massachusetts and David Stanley of Ohio, together with Brigadier Thomas Jefferson McKean of Pennsylvania, and Brigadier Thomas Davies of New York. Like the first two men, McKean, fifty-two, and Davies, fifty-three, were West Pointers; unlike them, they were relatively old for field command.

On October 3, Van Dorn with 22,000 troops advanced from the northwest on Corinth, where Rosecrans waited with some 23,000 men. The Union line stretched from McKean on the left to Davies in the center to Hamilton on the right, with Stanley on the far left in reserve. Rosecrans's strategy called for meeting the Confederates along an outer line of fortifications several miles from town, damaging them as much as possible, then retreating to a shorter, stronger inner line. The outer fortifications, he explained, "were old Confederate works, which I had no idea of using except as a cover for a heavy skirmish line, to compel the enemy to develop his force." The first major Rebel blows fell about 10:00 A.M. on McKean and Davies. "Finding that the resistance made by [John] Oliver's little command . . . was not stiff enough to determine the enemy's object," Rosecrans continued, "I had ordered [John] McArthur's brigade from McKean's division to go to Oliver's assistance. It was done with a will. McArthur's Scotch blood rose, and the enemy being in fighting force he fought them with the stubborn ferocity of an action on the main line of battle."[5]

Through the morning and afternoon the battle raged, with McKean's and Davies's troops slowly giving ground as they withdrew to the inner line of Corinth's fortifications. One of McKean's men, Cyrus Boyd of the 15th Iowa, describes the fighting: "We could see [the Confederates] advancing toward our position. . . . Our men got upon one knee and had guns all cocked and ready. . . . Then somebody commenced firing and we shot away in the smoke nor knowing exactly where to aim. . . . The Rebs soon closed upon us and came on with countless numbers. They swarmed around on our left and fired from behind trees and logs and kept pressing forward." Boyd's comrades went down all around him. "Middlesworth the 1st corporal in our company stood at my left hand and a ball struck him in the abdomen and he fell with a groan—Corp. Heatley fell shot through the head and Lieut. Cathcart fell dead at almost the first fire. . . . Just as the Regt. began to break Charley Vinton came staggering along. . . . I took Charley by the hand and assisted him for some distance. He was wounded not severely in the head but the blood covered him all over."

In the midst of the conflict, as a bullet struck *splat* on the sapling between them, Lieutenant Colonel William Belknap of the 15th Iowa answered a wistful question from Colonel Marcellus Crocker, the brigade commander.

"Do you know, old fellow, what I am thinking about?" asked Crocker.

"What, colonel?"

"I wish I was back in Des Moines."

"And so did I wish myself back in Keokuk," reflected Belknap.[6]

Davies's division in the center was the hardest hit during the Federal withdrawal; one of its three brigade commanders was killed and the other two wounded, and its casualties that day totaled some 25 percent. So rapid was the fire that rifle barrels grew red hot, in some cases exploding the minie balls during loading. "Let them burst," cried one officer, "there's no time to cool [them] off now." About 3:00 P.M. Stanley's division was ordered to Davies's support. "The cries for help became more and more pressing and frequent," said Lloyd Bryner of the 47th Illinois. "Faster and faster came [mounted] orderlies, excitement grew, aching limbs and blistered feet were forgotten; the boys were now on the run . . . as they swung into line."

"Fix bayonets!" rang out the command from William Thrush, Bryner's regimental colonel. "Charge bayonets, forward, charge!"

Temporarily the Rebel advance was stymied. "God, how the boys fell!" Bryner remembered. "Thrush was killed, shot through the heart. . . . The 47th had lost their leader, and Captain John D. McClure took command. . . . Again the battle took a turn and for a while seemed to hang in even scale. . . . Brave Captain David DeWolf was dead. Captain Harman Andrews and Lieutenant Andrew Tobey wounded—Andrews a prisoner, and McClure alone in command. A portion of the enemy had gained the rear of the line—the 47th was almost without officers, and one-half the men had fallen. . . . The survivors were terribly worn. . . . Slowly [we] retired . . . keeping up a steady fire."[7]

With his left and center falling back to Corinth's inner works, Rosecrans at this point saw an opportunity to fall on the exposed Confederate left with Hamilton's division, which was still in place on the right and had seen little action. "Davies, it appears, has fallen behind the works. . . ." he wrote Hamilton in part. "You will make a flank movement, if your front is not attacked, falling to the left of Davies when the enemy gets sufficiently well in so as to have full sweep. . . ." When Hamilton returned the order, writing on the back, "I cannot understand it," Rosecrans sent his chief of staff, Colonel Arthur Ducat, through a gauntlet of fire to explain it.

Hamilton sent Ducat back to him, requesting a new order in writing. A furious Rosecrans obliged, even though two messengers bearing similar messages had been killed trying to deliver them, saying, "Rest your left on General Davies and swing round your right and attack the enemy on their left flank. . . ." Ducat, ordered by Rosecrans again to run the gauntlet, protested.

"I have four children," he said.

"You knew that when you entered the service," replied his chief.

Ducat, bearing "further explanations of the most explicit kind; and a little sketch to show what ought to be done," quickly galloped off.

So much time was lost in these exchanges, however, that darkness brought the fighting on the 3rd to a halt before Hamilton's division was fully engaged. "Had the movement been executed promptly," Rosecrans lamented, ". . . we should have crushed the enemy's right and rear." Hamilton's excuse that he could not understand the original order, Rosecrans felt, showed the need for "subordinate commanders who instinctively know or are anxious to seek the key of the battle and hasten to its roar."[8]

Though fearsome artillery barrages were exchanged as early as 4:30 A.M. the next morning, the two sides did not immediately reengage. "McKean's division was to hold the left, the chief point being College Hill, keeping his troops well under cover," Rosecrans said. "Stanley was to support the line on either side of Battery Robinett, a little three-gun redan with a ditch five feet deep. Davies was to extend from Stanley's right . . . to Battery Powell, a similar redan . . . Hamilton was to be on Davies' right with a brigade, and the rest in reserve." During the lull he sent forward two regiments to explore the woods where the enemy were concealed. One of them was personally led by Colonel Joseph "Fighting Joe" Mower of the "Eagle Brigade," who was widely known for his pugnacity.

"Feel them, but don't get into their fingers," Rosecrans told him.

I'll feel them! Mower promised, just before galloping off.

Lloyd Bryner of the 47th Illinois takes up the story. "Mower had ridden forward to the skirmish line—no lover more impatient for his mistress than Mower for war's troubles. The 5th Minnesota half-breeds [Colonel Lucius Hubbard's Indians] with the prudence of the white man and the sagacity of the Indian were ideal skirmishers and a portion of them were upon the . . . line with the 47th and here was likely to be trouble to Mower's taste." During the ensuing encounter, Fighting Joe's horse was shot from under him and he was captured. Some thirty minutes later, Bryner recounts, "A rider, bare-headed, spurring his horse at furious pace, burst from the woods through the line of gray straight for the Union lines. From the wood blazed a hundred rifles. The rider reeled for a moment in his saddle, then righted himself and spurred onward." It was Mower, who had seized a Confederate officer's horse, leaped into the saddle and made his escape, suffering only a minor neck wound in the process. "Cheer followed cheer along the whole line. The 'Eagle Brigade' was wild with joy."[9]

Sterling Price launched the main assault on the Federal right about 10:00 A.M., heading straight for Davies's division across open ground with battle flags flying and drums sounding. His closely packed columns, said the correspondent for the Cincinnati *Commercial,* formed a "monstrous wedge" that "drove forward impetuously toward the heart of Corinth." The reporter, noting the casualties the Rebels were taking, wrote that it was "terrible and beautiful to see the [enemy] advance, in spite of a perfect storm of grape and cannister, shell and rifle ball. On they marched and fired, though their ranks were thinned at every step." For a brief time, Price's troops were not to be denied. Crashing through Davies's line, they scattered his men, captured Battery Powell, and entered the north side of the town, where they fought house to house.

Rosecrans reacted with fury. "I had the personal mortification," he said of Davies's collapse, "of witnessing this untoward and untimely stampede." He rode with abandon to the front of the melee, heedless of danger, shouting over and over, "Soldiers! Stand by your country!" One of Davies's men, David Henderson of Iowa, who later would become speaker of the House of Representatives, would say, "[Rosecrans] was the only general I ever knew who was closer to the enemy than we were who fought at the front. . . . By his splendid example . . . he succeeded in restoring the line before it was completely demoralized; and the men, brave when bravely led, fought again." Correspondent Whitelaw Reid was similarly impressed. "It lives in the memory of every soldier who fought that day," he said, "how his general plunged into the thickest of the conflict, fought like a private soldier, dealt sturdy blows with the flat of his sword on runaways, and fairly drove them to stand."[10]

Stand they did, aided by timely reinforcements. Stanley in reserve swiftly sent up troops in support, Hamilton on the right dispatched a brigade, and one of Davies's own brigades rallied and retook Battery Powell. Now Price's men were breaking and running, taking even more punishment in their flight. From his headquarters vantagepoint, Van Dorn uneasily watched the quick reversal of fortune. "That's Rosecrans' trick," he said. "He's got Price where he must suffer."

The attack on the Federal right had been the signal for General Dabney Maury of Virginia to assail the Federal left. Here a series of charges and countercharges were directed against Battery Robinett. "We could see thousands of gray uniforms swarming from the woods and climbing over the fallen timber," said Cyrus Boyd. "Everyone came as best he could toward the works. The cannon at Robinett poured charge after charge into their ranks but they faltered not. . . . The gunners stood to their pieces and many of them *fell there*. A few ran back to the rear where the infantry lay about 200 yards from the fort." The "Stars and Bars" were raised over Robinett, but only for minutes. "The infantry rose from their lair and with fixed and glistening bayonets and one discharge from their muskets rushed on the [enemy] and . . . killed or captured all that were left."

Knowing full well that Corinth was the key to northern Mississippi, a determined Maury regrouped and ordered another charge. "No sooner had the smoke cleared away," said Boyd, "than the second assaulting force . . . bore down on Robinett with the most *terrific yells*. The guns from the fort loaded with grape and cannister mowed them down by the hundreds . . . the gunners this time abandoned their pieces and ran back to the infantry. The Rebs headed by an officer . . . now reached the redoubt and began climbing over its walls." The officer was Colonel William Peleg Rogers of the 2nd Texas, a tall and powerfully built commander. Three of his standard bearers had already been shot in the assault. When the fourth went down he seized the Stars and Bars himself and scaled the works, waving the flag triumphantly. Rogers's elation was short-lived. A Union drummer boy, using a borrowed pistol, killed him with a single shot. Simultaneously the Federal infantry again countercharged. "A long *blue* line of uniforms could be seen rising out of the grass and bushes. . . . Muskets were clubbed and men were killed with the bayonet. The ranks of the Rebels melted like *snow*. . . . How glorious the old flag looked as it again floated over the works."[11]

From his position near Battery Robinett, Oscar Jackson of the 63rd Ohio had helped repulse Rogers's charge. "When I saw the enemy retreating in such confusion, I remarked . . . that we would not have to fight those men any more today, as I thought it would be impossible to rally them again." Jackson was wrong. Just before the Confederates assailed Robinett a third time, he was hurriedly sent to support two guns to the fort's left. "It was like moving into dead men's shoes," he said, "for I had seen one company carried away from there on litters, but without a moment's hesitation we moved up. I had scarce posted my men in rear of the guns when I saw that the enemy was again coming at us. . . . I knew what they wanted and, as the guns were not for close action, I moved my men in front of them."

Facing Jackson was a detachment of some 100 dismounted Texas cavalrymen. "The Rebel officer . . . was marching at the left of his men and when he came nigh he turned and walked backwards and said . . . 'Boys, when you charge, give a good yell.' I heard his command distinctly and it almost made the hair stand up on my head. The next instant the Texans began yelling like savages and rushed at us without firing. . . . I gave them a volley that halted them, cutting down their entire front. . . . The Texan, by a dexterous movement, was putting his bayonets to the front . . . among and literally over his dead and wounded comrades. I saw that he would strike us before we could get another volley at them."

Jackson made a quick decision: "Don't load, boys; they are too close on you; let them have the bayonet."

The young officer remembered his excitement. "The Rebels rushed toward us. . . . I yelled, 'Charge!' in order to give my men momentum to meet the shock. . . . The hostile guns clashed. For an instant we parried like boxers, when the enemy gave back, firing at us now as they retired. . . . Never have I felt so proud of anything as I was of my men. I thought that no such company was in the army." At this point Jackson, who had only eleven men standing, was shot. "One of the Rebels turned towards us and fired. . . . I was struck in the face. I felt as if I had been hit with a piece of timber, so terrible was the concussion, and a stunning pain went through my head. It was my impression that I would never rise . . . but I was not alarmed or depressed by the thought that I was dying. . . ." Subsequently he managed to get to his feet and walk a few dozen yards to the rear, then he collapsed and fell unconscious. Two days later he woke up in a field hospital, only too happy to be alive.[12]

By noon on October 4 the fighting was, for the most part, finished all along the front. The Confederate effort to reclaim Corinth had been bloodily repulsed; soon the Rebels would be in full retreat toward their base at Holly Springs, Mississippi. Van Dorn, with 22,000 men, had lost 4,800. Rosecrans, with 23,000, had suffered 2,350 casualties. Cyrus Boyd, inspecting the ground in front of Battery Robinett that afternoon, counted 126 dead men within forty feet of the fort. "Most of them are in the ditch. . . . One dead man lies just on the slope of the work stiff in death with a hammer in one hand a lot of *rat tail files* in the other. His mission had been to *spike the cannon*. They are so tightly gripped that the fingers can scarcely be opened. Several others I saw with their muskets *gripped* in their dead hands as tight as a vise could hold. Thus they perished with the most unearthly look on their dying faces."[13]

That afternoon, too, Rosecrans publicly castigated the men of Davies's division for earlier giving way. Davies, whose battered unit had lost some 1,000 of its 3,000 men during the two days of fighting, protested the slurs, declaring: "You said upon the battlefield, amid the piles of the dead . . . slain by the Second Division . . . that they were a set of cowards; that they never should have any military standing in your army till they had won it on the field of battle; that they had disgraced themselves, and no wonder the Rebel army had thrown its whole force upon it. . . ." To which Rosecrans grudgingly replied: "They fought nobly the first day, and . . . many of them . . . did the same the second day, and so much so that I shall overlook the cowardly stampede of those under my immediate observation on the second day—which gave rise to the public indignation I expressed in your presence and in theirs." Here Rosecrans again showed the impetuosity and lack of self-control that separated him from Grant. The former, easily riled when he felt himself crossed, could not hold his tongue; the latter invariably kept his own counsel.[14]

Both commanders were eager to pursue Van Dorn and shatter him once and for all, but each approached the task with a different mind-set. Grant wanted to intercept the Confederates before they got to Holly Springs, some sixty-five miles to the northwest. Accordingly he reinforced Rosecrans with five patched-together regiments led by General James McPherson, his engineering officer, and dispatched Stephen Hurlbut's division under Edward Ord to block Van Dorn's path at the Hatchie River crossing. In Grant's mind, Rosecrans and McPherson were nipping at Van Dorn's heels, Ord was in his front, and quick marching would close the trap. "At this distance everything looks favorable," he wired Halleck from his headquarters in Jackson, "and I cannot see how the enemy are to escape without losing everything but their small arms."

Unfortunately, Rosecrans's pursuit ran into obstacles from the start. With McPherson in the van it did not get started until the morning of October 5, Rosecrans's own troops were tired, there was wrangling about the proper route to take and, finally, a massive jam-up ensued at a country crossroads. "Our pursuit of the enemy was immediate and vigorous," Rosecrans maintained, "but . . . the roughness of the country, covered with woods and thickets, made movement impracticable by night and difficult by day." By nightfall he had progressed but ten miles. Meanwhile the outnumbered Ord, thinking that Rosecrans would soon come to his aid, engaged the van of Van Dorn's force at the Hatchie River. In the fighting that followed Ord was severely wounded, the command devolved on Hurlbut, and the Rebels made a successful crossing. Now any hope of immediately catching them was dashed.[15]

Grant was not pleased. "[Rosecrans] traveled with a wagon train to carry his provisions and munitions of war," he said. "His march was therefore slower than that of the enemy, who was moving toward his supplies. Two or three hours of pursuit on the day of the battle, without anything except what the men carried on their persons, would have been worth more than any pursuit . . . the next day could possibly have been. Even when he did start, if Rosecrans had followed the route taken by the enemy, he would have come upon Van Dorn in a swamp with a stream in front and Ord holding the only bridge; but he took the road leading north . . . instead of west, and, having marched as far as the enemy had moved to get to the Hatchie, he was as far from battle as when he started."

Rosecrans now had the bit in his teeth and was intent, however belatedly, on keeping up the chase. "We have defeated, routed and demoralized the army which holds the Lower Mississippi Valley," he wired Grant on the 7th. "We have the two railroads leading down to the Gulf through the most productive parts of the State, into which we can now pursue them with safety. The effect of our return to old position will be . . . to permit them to recruit their forces, advance and occupy their old ground, reducing us to . . . a defensive position, barren and worthless, with a long front. . . ." Rosecrans may well have been right—Holly Springs had been evacuated and even Vicksburg at this juncture was relatively defenseless—but Grant, concerned about a long chase that would unduly extend his lines of supply and communication, decided the risk would be too great. "I regarded the time to accomplish anything by pursuit as past," he said, "and, after Rosecrans reached Jonesboro, I ordered him to return. He kept on to Ripley, however, and was persistent in wanting to go further."[16]

Grant promptly consulted with Halleck. "I . . . submitted the matter to the general-in-chief, who allowed me to exercise my judgment . . . but inquired, 'why not pursue?' Upon this I ordered Rosecrans back." Grant, with the memory of Halleck's own tortuous advance on Corinth five months earlier fresh in his mind, must have winced at his superior's newfound bellicosity. But he had made his decision, and he stood by it.

The friction between Grant and Rosecrans continued to grow. The former, whose official reports on Corinth admittedly slighted Rosecrans, could not have been pleased by a story that appeared on October 9 in the Cincinnati *Commercial,* which read: "And now, to whom is due the honors of the battle of Corinth? The verdict of the whole army is in favor of General Rosecrans. Officers universally assert that it was he who planned the whole series of operations by which the enemy were entrapped. . . . By pretending to be beaten on Friday, he drew them into a place in which he gave them terrible punishment. . . . It would seem from General Grant's dispatches that he claims the honors. . . . There is no doubt that the public will give the credit to General Rosecrans where it belongs."[17]

Over the next few weeks the quibbling between the two men worsened. In one such instance, a contentious Rosecrans insisted that a shipment of new rifles should go to his command, because it had done the fighting at Corinth, rather than where Grant directed. "General," Grant told him,

"I am afraid from many of your dispatches that you regard your command [entitled to] privileges held by others commanding geographical divisions. . . . This is a mistake." Huffed Rosecrans in reply: "You have no truer friend, no more loyal subordinate . . . than myself. Your dispatch does me the grossest injustice."

Officers and staff members fueled the dissension. Colonel Mortimer Leggett of the 78th Ohio, a fervent admirer of Grant, wrote the ever-protective John Rawlins—Grant's chief of staff—of his concerns: "Major General Rosecrans is undoubtedly an excellent officer—and I hope, for his honor . . . that he is not a party in this hellish attempt to ruin General Grant." But, he went on, "I cannot rid my mind of the conviction that he must be at least, privy to the whole devilish scheme." Rawlins, joined by McPherson and Hurlbut, forthwith apprised Julia Grant, who was again visiting her husband, of the situation.

"Mrs. Grant," McPherson said, ". . . We want to reach the General's ear through you. In justice to General Grant—in fact, in justice to ourselves—General Rosecrans ought to be relieved."

When Julia brought up what she had been told, Grant replied that Rosecrans was "a brave and loyal soldier with the best of military training, and of this kind we have none to spare at present. Besides, 'Rosy' is a fine fellow. He is a bit excited now but he will soon come around all right. Do not trouble yourself about me. . . ." Then he added with a smile, "I can take care of myself."[18]

Quite soon the issue of Rosecrans's loyalty vis-à-vis Grant became moot. On October 8 Don Carlos Buell had fought a battle with Braxton Bragg at Perryville, Kentucky, halting the Confederate incursion into that state and forcing Bragg to fall back into east Tennessee. But Buell had largely botched the engagement, getting only nine of his twenty-four brigades into action, and then compounded his mistake by failing to pursue the reeling foe. This was too much for Lincoln and Stanton, and Buell was relieved. Replacing him was William Rosecrans, and Buell's command, formerly known as the Army of the Ohio, was renamed the Army of the Cumberland.

With Rosecrans's promotion, Grant must have felt a burden removed from his shoulders; he was rid of a disputatious subordinate and could concentrate on his next goal—moving deeper into Mississippi and taking Vicksburg, the Rebel stronghold that dominated the Mississippi River at its midpoint. Prospects for the Union at last were getting brighter: Lee in the East had been fought to a draw at Antietam; Bragg had been ousted from Kentucky; Van Dorn in northern Mississippi was on the run.

One more immediate task preoccupied Grant, however—the rehabilitation of Thomas Davies's division—the men whom Rosecrans had so belittled for breaking the second day at Corinth. The heart of this unit were the troops that Charles F. Smith had commanded at Fort Donelson, the men who had given him first major victory. Soon he replaced Davies with the reliable Grenville Dodge, making the telling statement, "I want you to understand that you are not commanding a division of cowards." In truth, Grant never forgot old friends.[19]

SIX
* * * *

CHICKASAW BLUFFS,

MCCLERNAND, AND PORTER

Toward the end of October, three weeks after Corinth, Grant was officially named head of the Department of the Tennessee, which included
western Tennessee and Kentucky and, of course, as much of northern Mississippi as he could seize and occupy. His front stretched along the
Tennessee-Mississippi border, from Memphis in the west to Corinth in the
east, and his headquarters was some forty miles to the rear, in Jackson,
Tennessee. Vicksburg, obviously, would be his next target. Located some
300 winding miles below Memphis and a like distance up from New Orleans, which Union forces had captured months before, the town towered
above the Mississippi on 200-foot bluffs. "Vicksburg was important to
the enemy," Grant said, "because it occupied the first high ground close to
the river below Memphis. From there a railroad runs east, connecting with
other roads leading to points of the Southern States. . . . Vicksburg was
the only channel . . . connecting the parts of the Confederacy divided by the
Mississippi. So long as it was held by the enemy, the free navigation of the
river was prevented."

Grant's original intent was to make his way south solely by land, taking
care to keep his railroad supply lines open. He would be moving parallel
with the Mississippi Central, about sixty miles east of Vicksburg and
the river, heading toward Jackson, the Mississippi state capital. James

McPherson now commanded the left around Corinth, Charles Hamilton the center, and Sherman the right at Memphis. The thirty-four-year-old McPherson's rise in rank had been spectacular; in some eight months he had progressed from lieutenant colonel to major general. Charming and able, he was a particular favorite both of Grant's and his wife's. Julia, in fact, had sewed his brigadiers' stars on his shoulder straps. Hamilton, the officer whose questioning of an order the first day at Corinth had so infuriated Rosecrans, would become one of Grant's severest critics and in a matter of months leave the army. Sherman, of course, remained his chief's staunchest supporter. "We cannot change the hearts of [the] people of the South," he counseled him, "but we can make war so terrible that they will realize that however brave and gallant and devoted to their country [they are], still they are mortal."[1]

In the beginning of November, Grant launched his incursion. "I have commenced a movement on Grand Junction. . . ." he told Halleck. "Will leave here [Jackson, Tennessee] tomorrow, and take command in person. If found practicable, I will go on to Holly Springs, and, maybe, Grenada, completing railroad and telegraph as I go." He would be facing John C. Pemberton of Pennsylvania, who in part because of his wife's and in-laws' Virginia allegiance had elected to fight for the Confederacy, and who had succeeded Earl Van Dorn as head of the Army of Mississippi. (Soon the defensive-minded Joseph Johnston, whom Lee in June had replaced in the East as commander of the Army of Northern Virginia, would be named head of the Department of the West, charged with co-ordinating the activities of Pemberton in Mississippi and Braxton Bragg in east Tennessee.)[2]

Grant's concerns were not limited to the Rebels. The deeper he advanced into Mississippi, the greater became the problem of what to do with the blacks who flocked to the Federal army for protection. "The attempt to fight the war without taking a positive stand on slavery was collapsing," said a historian, "for the peculiar institution was central to the whole military problem. . . . Grant's army was operating in an area where a good many plantations had been hastily abandoned, and the slaves who remained—people who had been left to their own resources, and who had none—were clogging the roads and the lanes, and overflowing into the camps, joined in even greater numbers by slaves who had drifted away from bondage." Here the first idea of a "Freedman's Bureau" got its start. Stated Grant: "The cotton and corn were ripe: men, women and children above ten years of age could be employed in saving these crops. To do this with the contrabands . . . organization under a competent chief was necessary."

Grant found his organizer in the person of Chaplain John Eaton of the 27th Ohio, who at first was reluctant to take on the job. "These were men, women and children in every stage of disease and decrepitude," said Eaton, "often nearly naked, with flesh torn by the terrible experiences of their escapes." He did not believe he could better their lot.

"Oh—you are the man who has all these darkies on his shoulders," Grant said during a meeting. "Sit up and we'll talk." His idiom reflected the prejudices of the time, but it did not negate his goodwill.

Tens of thousands of blacks, he told Eaton, currently were in limbo between slavery and freedom. He wanted them established in clean, regulated camps, put to work on the plantations and in kindred jobs, and paid for their labors. The process would be long and hard, and hampered by setbacks, but it must be initiated. "Never before," said Eaton, "had I heard the problem of the future of the Negro attacked so vigorously and with such humanity combined with practical good sense." He took up his assignment with new enthusiasm. "I gave him all the assistants and guards he called for," said Grant. "We together fixed the prices to be paid for the Negro labor, whether rendered to the government or to individuals. . . . At once the freedmen became self-sustaining. . . . Later [they] were engaged in cutting wood along the Mississippi River to supply the large number of steamers. . . . In this way a fund was created not only sufficient to feed and clothe all, old and young, male and female, but to build them comfortable cabins, hospitals for the sick, and to supply them with many comforts they had never known before."[3]

Concomitant with the contraband problem was that of John McClernand. "At this stage of the campaign against Vicksburg," Grant said, "I was very much disturbed by newspaper rumors that General McClernand was to have a separate and independent command within mine, to operate against Vicksburg by way of the Mississippi River. Two commanders on the same field are always one too many, and in this case I did not think the general selected had either the experience or the qualifications to fit him for so important a position. I feared for the safety of the troops entrusted to him, especially as he was to raise new levies, raw troops. . . ." Grant sought guidance from the general-in-chief. "Am I to understand that I lie still here," he wrote Halleck on November 10 from the vicinity of Holly Springs, "while an expedition is fitted out from Memphis, or do you want me to push as far south as possible? Am I to have Sherman move subject to my order, or are he and his forces reserved for some special service? Will not more forces be sent here?"

To which Halleck replied, encouragingly if enigmatically, "You have command of all troops sent to your department and have permission to fight the enemy where you please."[4]

Grant had reason to be disturbed about McClernand. The Illinois Democrat, a longtime legislator whose political support the Republican Lincoln desperately needed in the southern part of the state, had taken leave at the end of August and returned to Springfield, ostensibly just to raise additional recruits. One month later, however, he was writing the president, submitting a detailed plan for steaming down the Mississippi from Memphis and landing a substantial force a few miles above Vicksburg. Naturally it was understood he would be in command. When Secretary of War Stanton endorsed the proposal at a cabinet meeting, "the President seemed much pleased," according to a participant. Halleck, however, did not think well of McClernand. "He said he is brave . . . but no disciplinarian; that his camp was always full of disorder; that at Corinth he pitched his tents where his men had been buried just below ground. . . . The cause of the evil was that his officers and men were his constituents."

On October 10 and subsequent days McClernand, now in Washington, further refined his plan, calling for an expedition down the Mississippi of some 20,000 infantry and ten batteries of artillery. Lincoln and Stanton were impressed; they considered McClernand that rare political general who was also a skillful commander—he had, after all, been in the thick of the fighting at Fort Donelson and Shiloh. In this their confidence was backed by the wisdom of *The New York Times,* which stated, "Gen. McClernand has inspired the whole West with . . . faith in his courage, untiring energy and military skill."[5]

The son of an immigrant Scottish doctor and a Kentucky woman, McClernand was born in Hardinsburg, Kentucky in 1812, and moved with his family to Illinois when he was four. In his teens he became the protégé of a state senator, began to read law, and in 1832 was admitted to the bar. During the Black Hawk War, he served as a private, and on one risky occasion carried a dispatch across one hundred miles of Indian territory. Turning to politics, he was elected in 1836 for the first of several terms in the Illinois Legislature, where he knew and worked with Lincoln. Seven years later he won a seat in the U.S. Congress and went to Washington, accompanied by his new bride. She was the former Sarah Dunlap, a close friend of Mary Todd Lincoln, and a newspaper described her as "exceedingly fair," asserting that "all that poets fancy . . . is more than realized, in her beautiful countenance."[6]

For the rest of the 1840s and into 1850 McClernand in the House attempted, like Henry Clay in the Senate, to reach a compromise on the debate over the slavery issue. He failed, and left Congress to resume his law practice. In 1858, however, amidst even more acrimonious politicking, he was reelected to the House of Representatives, largely because he condemned John Brown's raid on Harpers Ferry, Virginia, saying it was like "proclaiming war against the people of the South." Once seated, he joined with Stephen Douglas of Illinois in trying to hold the Democratic party together against the gains of Lincoln and the Republicans.

Two years later, while deploring Lincoln's election to the presidency as "a great national calamity," he insisted that Illinois and the other Midwest states remain in the Union, "if not in respect to (Lincoln), in respect for the people and the Constitution itself." With the outbreak of war in 1861, he did not hesitate to write the president, recommending ambitious strategies that the Federal government lacked the means to implement. His biographer would maintain that these schemes revealed the man. He was brash, assertive, energetic, patriotic, confident, visionary—the epitome of the successful politician.[7]

In June of 1861 McClernand and Democratic congressman John "Black Jack" Logan visited the camp of then little-known Colonel Ulysses S. Grant of the 21st Illinois, whose soldiers were at the end of their thirty-day enlistment period. "Both gave rousing patriotic speeches," recounted the biographer, "and the men of the regiment enlisted for three years." Here was the first contact between Grant and McClernand. The latter soon would be named a brigadier, and then a major general, but would always be junior in rank to Grant. During these months the thirty-six-year-old Sarah McClernand, the mother of six, would fall victim to tuberculosis and die. Her husband would soldier on, unable to restrain his ambition.

To John Nicolay, Lincoln's private secretary and biographer, no Democrat in Illinois save perhaps Logan "could bring such a decided and valuable support to the Union cause as McClernand." Lincoln would agree. "There is General McClernand from my state," he would tell a fellow Republican, "whom they say I use better than a radical."[8]

Small wonder then, with this sort of pedigree, that McClernand on October 21 received confidential orders from Secretary Stanton, authorizing him to return to the Midwest, raise and organize troops, and forward them "to Memphis, Cairo, or such other points as may hereafter be designated by the general-in-chief, to the end that, when a sufficient force not required by the operations of General Grant's command shall be raised, an expedition may be organized under General McClernand's command against Vicksburg. . . . The forces so organized will remain subject to the designation of the general-in-chief, and be employed according to such exigencies as the service in his judgment may require." To which Lincoln added, in a handwritten note: "This order, though marked confidential, may be shown by General McClernand, to Governors, and even others, when, in his discretion, he believes so doing to be indispensable to the progress of the expedition. . . . I feel deep interest in [its] success . . . and desire it to be pushed forward with all possible dispatch."

In his elation over receiving these papers, the normally perspicacious McClernand, thinking he was the president's man, did not notice the caveats in their wording: He was to raise troops and have his own command in a Vicksburg assault, if the force was *not required* by Grant; and, regardless, the troops were to *remain subject* to Halleck. In other words Stanton and Lincoln, no political tyros themselves, had left themselves wriggle room. If either—or certainly both—of McClernand's military superiors thought it necessary, his newfound command could be forfeit. Oblivious to these subtleties, he plunged ahead on his assignment. Through November and into December, he continued to work with the Midwest governors in raising an army. Ultimately his efforts in large part resulted in forty-four infantry regiments being created, fourteen of which would participate in the Chickasaw Bluffs, Arkansas Post, and Vicksburg campaigns.[9]

Though Grant received no official copy of McClernand's orders—and apparently neither did Halleck—the record shows both soon became aware of what was going on. In one instance Lieutenant James H. Wilson, who would be Grant's topographical engineer, learned of the Mississippi expedition from McClernand's own lips during a chance October meeting in Washington. Naturally he passed the information on. Meanwhile Lincoln's endorsement of the venture had the curious effect of making Grant and Halleck strong and surprising allies—at least in their opposition to a man operating outside the chain of command, and a non–West Pointer to boot.[10]

One more high-ranking officer privy to these semiclandestine maneuverings, it appears, was the crusty, outspoken Rear Admiral David Dixon Porter, who in April had led the mortar fleet under his foster brother, Rear Admiral David Farragut, during the shelling and capture of New Orleans on the lower Mississippi. In late September Porter was called to Washington, where he was named by Lincoln to head the Mississippi Squadron on the upper Mississippi, the post at one point held by Flag Officer Foote; the latter's wound, suffered at Fort Donelson, had refused to heal and obliged him to give up command.

"I promised that you should see Vicksburg fall," the president reputedly told Porter during a meeting, "and now *you* shall do it. I want to ask you something about your plans. . . ."

"There was a time not long ago," Porter replied, "when Vicksburg could have been easily captured, but it is now a second Gibraltar, and the navy *alone* [can] do nothing."

"Well," said Lincoln, "[who] do you think is the general for such an occasion?"

"General Grant, sir. Vicksburg is within his department; but I presume he will send Sherman there, who is equal to any occasion."

"Well, Admiral," said Lincoln, who had just received McClernand's letter advocating a river assault, "I have in my mind a better general than either of them; that is McClernand, an old and intimate friend of mine."

"I don't know him, Mr. President."

"What! Don't know McClernand? Why, he saved the battle of Shiloh, when the case seemed hopeless!"

"Why, Mr. President," Porter objected, "the impression is that Grant won the battle of Shiloh; as he commanded the army, he would seem entitled to the credit."

"No," said Lincoln, "McClernand did it; he is a natural-born general."

". . . With all due deference," said Porter, ". . . I don't believe in natural-born generals except where they have had proper military training. . . . Besides, if you take troops from Grant and Sherman to give them to McClernand, you will weaken the army."

"Oh, no," said Lincoln, "I don't mean to do that. . . . McClernand is to go to Springfield, Illinois, and raise troops there. . . . In the meantime you can prepare to cooperate with him."[11]

Before leaving Washington, Porter conferred briefly with McClernand, who must have been particularly condescending. The no-nonsense naval officer took an instant dislike to the Illinois politician and his self-important ways, setting up a situation that was to have long-term ramifications. Porter arrived in Cairo, Illinois, to take up his new command in mid-October, shortly before McClernand returned to Springfield to continue his recruiting, and would not get together with Grant until late November. In the interval, even while McClernand's newly formed regiments were arriving in Memphis, he wrote Grant, informing him of the upcoming river operation.

The two men finally met one evening aboard one of Porter's steamers, just as supper was being served. Travel-worn and dressed in civilian clothes, Grant got straight to the point.

"Admiral, what is all this you have been writing me?" he asked. Porter readily spelled out the details of McClernand's expedition.

Grant thought for a moment, then said, "When can you move with your gun-boats, and what force have you?"

"I can move tomorrow with all the old gun-boats and five or six other vessels; also the *Tyler, Conestoga,* and *Lexington.*"

"Well, then," said Grant, "I will leave you now and write at once to Sherman to have 30,000 infantry and artillery embarked in transports ready to start for Vicksburg the moment you get to Memphis. I will return to Holly Springs tonight, and will start a large force for Grenada as soon as I can get it off."

Grant was making decisions, even for him, with unusual dispatch, but he had no intention of being upstaged by a devious subordinate. What he had begun as a land advance on Vicksburg he now would make a two-pronged assault, one that he felt Pemberton and the outnumbered Confederates could scarcely withstand. Sherman would take charge of McClernand's troops, whose commander was still in Springfield, and escorted by Porter steam down the Mississippi. Grant himself would stay with McPherson and Hamilton, driving south down the Mississippi Central Railroad.

"I thought this plan an admirable one," said Porter. "Grant and [I] never indulged in long talks together; it was only necessary for him to tell me what he desired. . . . Here in twenty minutes Grant unfolded his plan of campaign, involving the transportation of over 100,000 men, and, with a good supper staring him in the face, proposed to ride back over a road he had just traveled without tasting a mouthful."[12]

That Porter would take a liking to Grant was not a given. The former came from an elitist family, was garrulous to the point of embellishing on the truth to make a point, and did not suffer fools gladly. Grant's background was humble, he was reserved, and if anything overly tolerant of human weakness. But both men disliked pomp and sham, recognized character, and knew that war was grim business.

David Dixon Porter, the son of Commodore David Porter of War of 1812 fame and the grandson, on his mother's side, of an U.S. congressman, was born in 1813. His father, whose frigate *Essex* had been sunk by two British men-of-war and who had escaped from a prison ship, did not see him until he was fifteen months old. Young Porter grew up in the family mansion, Meridian Hill, located on some 100 acres in Washington, D.C., and through which passed a steady stream of naval heroes. By 1825 the twelve-year-old was at sea with his father in the West Indies, helping rid the Caribbean of pirates. Here Commodore Porter, an exceedingly proud and stubborn man, became involved in a dispute with the Secretary of the Navy, who accused him of exceeding his authority in threatening Spanish citizens.

The resulting court of inquiry resulted in a six-month suspension. Commodore Porter waited out the term, then resigned from the U.S. Navy and stunned his friends by becoming head of the Mexican Navy, taking with him David Dixon as a midshipman. Commodore Porter's decision would be a rash one. He never did succeed in making the Mexican Navy a power, his son during one brush in Cuba in 1828 with the Spanish Navy was captured and thrown into jail, and Meridan Hill had to be sold to pay off his debts.

The next year David Dixon was back in America, where he won appointment as a U.S. midshipman. He served for a time with the Mediterranean Squadron, met his future wife, George Ann Patterson—the daughter of a naval commodore, and endured years of near poverty as a low-ranking officer. Though lack of money meant his marriage had to be indefinitely postponed he never thought of leaving the service. In 1836 he managed to get work with the Coastal Survey, which doubled his pay, and three years later he and George Ann were wed at St. John's Episcopal Church in Washington. Prominent among the guests was his irascible father, now minister to Turkey and back in the government's good graces.

In 1846 Lieutenant Porter fought with distinction in the Mexican War, taking part in the naval assault under Matthew C. Perry on Veracruz and, later, commanding a small gunboat on the Tabasco River. Subsequently, in 1849, he convinced the Navy Department to let him remain in the service while playing a pioneering role in developing U.S. Mail steamships, which then provided the fastest transport between the East and West Coasts. But his father had died, leaving his mother debt ridden, and his own growing family likewise continued to make money a problem. With his naval rank and pay still insufficient, Lieutenant Porter in 1854 took leave from the service and accepted command of the passenger ship *Golden Age,* which he captained on her maiden voyage to set a new record for an Atlantic Crossing.

Further years of humdrum navy life in Washington, D.C., passed by, with Porter in 1860 at last considering resigning from the service and accepting a well-paying position as captain of a Pacific Coast steamer. Then on the night of December 20, he attended a party at the home of Mississippi senator Jefferson Davis, who was celebrating South Carolina's secession.

"You will join us," Davis said facetiously, "and we will make you an admiral."

"Thank you," Porter replied in the same vein, "but I am going to the California gold mines, and when the North and South have done quarreling, and all you seceders have come back and taken your seats in Congress, I will join the navy again."

Soon the war in all its stark reality would intervene, and the Union would badly need Porter's naval expertise—first during the shelling of New Orleans and now the initial assault on Vicksburg. That this contumacious sailor would be lending his support in the latter instance to Grant and Sherman, rather than McClernand, is testimony to his good judgment.[13]

By early December—days after his meeting with Porter—Grant in Oxford, Mississippi, was informing Halleck that, in effect, he intended to commandeer McClernand's troops. "General Sherman will command the expedition down the Mississippi," he said on December 8. "He will have a force of about 40,000 men. Will land above Vicksburg, up the Yazoo [River], if practicable, and cut the Mississippi Central Railroad. . . . I will cooperate from here, my movements depending on those of the enemy. . . ." Halleck, in turn, by not countermanding Grant, was giving his assent. "In regard to the proposed expedition down the Mississippi . . ." he blandly told a curious officer, "I have been informed that the President has selected a special commander and that instructions have been or will be given to him by the War Department. If so they have not been communicated to me, and until I receive them, I shall consider the officer of highest rank as the commander." Left unsaid was what the army pecking order knew full well: Grant was the officer of highest rank.

Sherman, who would be Grant's instrument in this sleight of hand, was equally circumspect. "I repaired at once to Oxford," he would say of his role, "and found General Grant. . . . He explained to me that large reinforcements had been promised, which would reach Memphis very soon, if not already there; that the entire gunboat fleet, then under . . . Admiral D. D. Porter, would cooperate . . . and [that] by a prompt movement I could make a lodgment up the Yazoo and capture Vicksburg from the rear. . . . I also understood, too, that if [General] Pemberton should retreat south, he would follow him up, and would expect to find me at the Yazoo River, if not inside Vicksburg. I confess that . . . I did not dream that General Mc-Clernand . . . was scheming for the mere honor of capturing Vicksburg."[14]

By early December, too, McClernand was beginning to sense that all was not going well for him. Reporting to Stanton that most of his troops were in Memphis, or soon would be, he asked permission to leave Springfield and join them. Stanton replied he would take the matter up with Halleck. More days passed, with McClernand becoming increasingly agitated. On December 16 he wired Halleck directly, asking to be sent downriver to Memphis, "in accordance with the order of the Secretary of War on the 21st of October giving me command of the Mississippi expedition." The next day he wired Lincoln and Stanton: "I believe I am superseded. Please advise me."

Stanton's answer sought to straddle the growing contretemps. While comforting, it could not have been entirely to McClernand's liking. "There has been, as I am informed by General Halleck, no order superceding you. It was designed, as you know, to organize the troops for your expedition after they should reach Memphis. . . . The operations being in General Grant's department, it [was decided] to organize all the troops of that department into three army corps, the first . . . to be commanded by you, and assigned to the operations on the Mississippi under the supervision of the general commanding." Stanton was telling McClernand that, while he was not being removed from the river assault on Vicksburg, he was commanding a corps under Grant, not exercising independent command.[15]

On December 18 Halleck dutifully if not enthusiastically made the reorganization official, ordering Grant to create not three but four corps in the Army of the Tennessee—the 13th under McClernand, the 15th under Sherman, the 16th under Stephen Hurlbut, and the 17th under McPherson. Grant, however reluctantly, promptly wired this information to McClernand in Springfield, confirming that he would be in charge of the river expedition, accompanied by Sherman, who was junior to him in seniority. He wired Sherman in Memphis a similar message. Here fate intervened, in the person of the Confederate cavalryman and raider Nathan Bedford Forrest, who about this time crossed over well behind Grant, wrecking his lines of communication and supply from Jackson, Tennessee, to the Kentucky border. In sum, with the relevant north-south telegraph lines severed for at least ten days, McClernand would receive no orders to report to Memphis; Sherman would receive no directions to wait for him.

McClernand would not wire Stanton again, asking permission to proceed to Memphis, until December 23. This he immediately received. Possibly he was distracted by his marriage earlier that day in Jacksonville, Illinois, to Minerva Dunlap, sister of his late wife and twenty-four years younger than he. His plans called for a shipboard honeymoon on the Mississippi, culminating in the taking of Vicksburg. Long before McClernand and his bride arrived in Memphis, however, Sherman on December 19 had debarked from the city with four divisions on some 100 transports, protected by Porter's Mississippi Squadron. McClernand, it could be said, would be left at the pier. One of his mistakes, of course, was not taking the trouble to establish a rapport with Porter, as Grant earlier had done.

Sherman likewise charmed Porter. Their first meeting, just before the fleet left for Vicksburg, was a memorable one, albeit with comic overtones. "Thinking it probable that Sherman would be dressed in full feather," Porter said, "I put on my uniform coat, the splendor of which rivaled that of a drum major. Sherman, hearing that I was indifferent to appearances and generally dressed in working clothes, thought he would not annoy me in fixing up, and so kept on his blue flannel suit; and so we met, both a little surprised at the appearance of the other." Sherman was his usual energetic self, and Porter recounted his staccato speech with evident gusto.

"Halloo, Porter, I am glad to see you; you got here sooner than I expected; but we'll get off tonight. Devilish cold, isn't it? Sit down and warm up." Stirring up the coal in the grate, Sherman then barked out a rapid-fire series of orders.

"Here, captain,"—to one of his aides—"tell General Blair to get his men on board at once. Tell the quartermaster to report as soon as he has six hundred thousand rations embarked. Here, Dick"—to his servant— "put me up some shirts and underclothes in a bag, and don't bother me with a trunk and traps enough for a regiment. Here, captain,"—another aide—"tell the steamboat captains to have steam up at six o'clock, and to lay in plenty of fuel, for I'm not going to stop every few hours to cut wood. Tell the officer in charge of embarkation to allow no picking and choosing of boats; the generals in command must take what is given them. . . .

"There, that will do," Sherman said, satisfied the coal in the grate was throwing off heat and turning his attention back to the naval officer. ". . . Glad to see you, Porter; how's Grant?"

"My impressions of Sherman were very favorable," Porter would say, delighted by the man's forthright ways. "I thought myself lucky to have two such generals as Grant and Sherman to cooperate with. . . ."[16]

Consider the Federal situation at this juncture. Grant's lines of communication and supply from the North were in the process of being cut by the far-ranging Forrest; McClernand, the Vicksburg expedition's commander, had been left behind—admittedly a not unwelcome development; and Sherman and Porter, lacking all communication with Grant but expecting to rendezvous with him with elements of four divisions, were steaming downriver.

Now on December 20, just a day after Sherman's departure from Memphis, Grant suffered a second blow, one that would bring his land-based advance to a complete halt and put Sherman on the water in an untenable position. Earl Van Dorn, who had been demoted and placed in charge of Pemberton's cavalry, led 3,500 troopers on a raid in Grant's immediate rear at Holly Springs, destroying some $1.5 million in supplies. There some 1,500 defenders of the 8th Wisconsin, badly led, surrendered without a fight; subsequently their commander, Colonel R. C. Murphy, was dismissed from the service. Still not realizing what he would later learn, that an invading army could live off the bountiful Deep South countryside, Grant felt he had no choice but to withdraw and regroup until the railroads were repaired and he could be resupplied. Meanwhile Pemberton, given the respite, fell back from what had been the front lines in northern Mississippi, and hurriedly diverted additional troops and guns to bolster Vicksburg's defenses.

Ignorant of these developments, Sherman and Porter would continue with their river-based assault on the Rebel stronghold. "Sherman's attack was very unfortunate," Grant would say of the action at Chickasaw Bluffs, "but I had no opportunity of communication with him after the destruction of the road and telegraph to my rear. . . . He did not know but what I was in the rear of the enemy and depending on him to open up a new base of supplies for the troops with me."[17]

By December 26 Sherman and his stream of transports were leaving the Mississippi and entering the mouth of the meandering Yazoo River, some half dozen miles north of Vicksburg. Over the next few days he proceeded ten miles up the Yazoo, a waterway crisscrossed by a tortuous maze of bayous, streams, and swamps, landed his men, and felt out the enemy. His division heads were Frederick Steele, George W. Morgan, and two more Smiths—Morgan L. Smith, and Andrew J. Smith. Hitherto Steele, who had been a classmate of Grant's at West Point, had been fighting in Arkansas. George Washington Morgan, a headstrong officer who had served in Texas under Sam Houston and been brevetted a temporary brigadier for gallantry in the Mexican War, soon would have a falling-out with Sherman. Morgan Smith, who entered the war by organizing a regiment of St. Louis longshoremen, had served at Shiloh. Andrew Jackson Smith, a West Pointer and former Indian fighter, had been Halleck's chief of cavalry during the advance on Corinth.

On December 29 Sherman, still not knowing Grant's advance had been stymied, launched the assault on Chickasaw Bluffs, part of the lofty Walnut Hills escarpment north and east of the city. What his maps did not fully prepare him for was the formidable obstacle of Chickasaw Bayou. "As we advanced along the road leading from the Yazoo to the bluffs," said General George Morgan, "the bayou was on our left for some distance; on our right was a forest intersected by sloughs, more or less filled with water. . . . Opposite the point where the bayou turns abruptly to the left, and on the right side of the road, the forest was felled and formed a tangled abatis . . . [there] the bayou divides into two branches, over one of which was a narrow corduroy bridge."

Morgan would claim that Sherman had picked the worst possible point of attack. "The ground on which the battle was fought was a triangle, the apex of which was at the . . . divergence of the two branches of the bayou, the high and rugged bluff in front being the base. . . . Our troops had not only to advance down the narrow apex of a triangle, whose short base of about 400 yards and sharp sides bristled with the enemy's artillery and small arms, but had to wade the bayou and tug through the murky and tangled swamp, under a withering fire of grape, canister, shells, and minie balls, before reaching dry ground. . . ."

Whether Sherman could have selected a more vulnerable target on the Walnut Hills heights, perhaps Snyder's Bluff still further north, is debatable. Certainly Porter did not think so. "No one, at that time, had any idea of the magnitude of the defenses that had been erected. . . . Sherman at every point encountered obstacles of which he had never dreamed. Forests had been cut down, and through the *chevaux-de-frise* the soldiers, standing up to their waists in water, had to cut their way with axes across the dismal swamps. All this, of course, took time; there seemed to be no other way to Vicksburg. . . . To add to [the] difficulties the rain came on—and such a rain! The heavens seemed [to be] trying to drown our army."[18]

Sherman's battle plan called for the two Smiths to keep the Confederate left occupied near Vicksburg, while Porter's gunboats engaged the enemy right farther up the Yazoo. "The first step was to make a lodgment on the foot-hills and bluffs abreast of our position. . . ." he said. "I determined to make a show of attack along the whole front, but to break across the bayou . . . I pointed out to General Morgan the place where he could pass the bayou, and he answered, 'General, in ten minutes after you give the signal I'll be on those hills.' He was to lead his division in person, and was to be supported by Steele's division. The front was very narrow. . . ."

Cannon fire and diversions led off the assault, and by 11:00 A.M. Morgan's men, charging across 300 yards of mudflats, were heavily engaged. "One brigade [Colonel John De Courcey's] of Morgan's troops crossed the bayou safely," Sherman continued, "but took to cover behind the bank, and could not be moved forward. Frank Blair's brigade of Steele's division in support, also crossed the bayou, passed over the space of level ground to the foot of the hills; but, being unsupported by Morgan, and meeting a very severe cross-fire of artillery, was staggered and gradually fell back, leaving about five hundred men behind. . . . Part of [John] Thayer's brigade [under Morgan's command] took the wrong direction, and did not cross the bayou at all; nor did General Morgan cross in person. Had he used with skill and boldness one of his brigades, in addition to that of Blair's, he could have made a lodgment on the bluff, which would have opened the door for our whole force to follow."

Those Federals who did make it across the bayou were trapped beneath the hills. "The men of the 6th Missouri," said Sherman, "actually scooped out with their hands caves in the bank, which sheltered them against the fire of the enemy, who, right over their heads, held their muskets outside the parapet vertically, and fired down. So critical was the position that we could not recall the men till after dark, and then one at a time."[19]

Morgan's account of events at Chickasaw Bluffs differed radically from that of Sherman's—much like the confusion between Lew Wallace and Grant the first day at Shiloh. Even before the attack began, he said, he had led Sherman to the corduroy bridge over the bayou, and "called his attention to our very narrow and difficult front; to the bayou in its course on our left; to the mucky marsh beyond the bayou and bridge, all within easy range of the enemy's guns." For a moment, Morgan would state, Sherman made no reply. "At length, pointing toward the bluffs, he said: 'That is the route to take!' And without another word . . . he rode away to his head-quarters." Moreover, Morgan maintained, he had never boasted he would be on the heights in ten minutes. "A well-mounted horseman," he said, "unobstructed by an enemy, could not have reached the top of those hills in double that length of time."

Not long after their brief reconnaissance, Morgan added, he received a message via one of Sherman's aides: "Tell Morgan to give the signal for the assault; that we will lose 5,000 men before we take Vicksburg, and may as well lose them here as lose them anywhere else." Recounted the reluctant Morgan: "I told [the aide] to say to General Sherman, that I would order the assault; that we might lose 5,000 men, but that his entire army could not carry the enemy's position in my front; that the larger the force sent . . . the greater would be the number slaughtered."

In one respect only, that the attack was a dismal failure, were the two men in complete agreement. "As soon as the corduroy bridge was reached by De Courcey and Thayer, and the bayou to the left by Blair," said Morgan, "the assaulting forces came under a withering and destructive fire. . . . All formations were broken; the [troops] were jammed together, and . . . were mowed down by a storm of [gunfire] that swept our front like a hurricane." However, he added, "all the troops behaved gallantly, and the assault was as valiant as it was hopeless. Each of De Courcey's regiments brought back its colors, or what remained of them. . . . The losses speak for themselves." Indeed, De Courcey suffered 724 casualties; Blair, 603; Thayer, 112. In Morgan's command, of the nine regiments engaged, the casualties totaled 1,439; elsewhere Sherman's losses were only 337—for a total of 1,776. Confederate casualties were just 187.

Morgan subsequently met with Sherman, discussed the repulse, and suggested they send out a flag party asking for an armistice to bring in the wounded and bury the dead. "Sherman said he did not like to ask for a truce, as it would be regarded as an admission of defeat. To this I replied that we had been terribly cut up, but were not dishonored; that the bearing of our troops was superb." Hours later Sherman relented, but, said Morgan, "it had become so dark the flag could not be seen, and the escort was fired upon and driven back. The next morning, December 30th, I sent another flag . . . [and] a truce was promptly granted."[20]

Sherman planned one more improvised attack from his Yazoo River position, this time on Snyder's Bluff, but incessant rain and howling winds brought it to naught. The current was raging, the river was at flood level, and the fog was so bad the gunners could not see the hills above them. He and Porter determined to make the best of a bad situation by withdrawing from the Yazoo, steaming some fifty miles back up the Mississippi, and assailing the 5,000-man Rebel garrison at Arkansas Post, a fort on the Arkansas River. Now the newly wed McClernand belatedly appeared on the scene, in the person of an aide calling on Porter, declaring his chief was taking command of the army.

"I come from General McClernand," the aide said, "who is at the mouth of the Yazoo, and wants you to . . . see him as soon as possible."

"You can tell the general," said Porter, who had not forgotten the politician's overbearing manner, "that my duties at present are so engrossing that I am making no calls, and that it is his place to come and see me."

Soon afterward Porter alerted Sherman to McClernand's arrival.

"Are you going to call on him?" Sherman asked.

"No, I am not making calls just now."

"But I must," said Sherman, "for he outranks me."

When all three men finally got together on Porter's flagship, McClernand lost no time coming to the point. "I find this army in a most demoralized state," he said, "and I must do something to raise their spirits." He then proposed that Porter's gunboats join him in an attack on Arkansas Post.

"Sherman made a remark the purport of which I have forgotten," the admiral said, "but McClernand made a discourteous reply, whereupon Sherman walked off into the after-cabin. I was angry that anyone should dare treat General Sherman with discourtesy in my cabin." Porter informed McClernand that he and Sherman had decided the previous evening to capture Arkansas Post, and insisted that field command of the operation remain with Sherman. "If [he] goes in command of the army, I will go along with my whole force . . . otherwise I will have nothing to do with the affair."

While McClernand was pondering this proposition, Sherman beckoned Porter aside. "My God, Porter!" Cump exclaimed, "you will ruin yourself if you talk that way to McClernand; he is very intimate with the President, and has powerful influence."

"I don't care who or what he is," the admiral replied.[21]

The gist of this story is undoubtedly true, for Porter had inherited his father's disputatious streak, and the navy was independent of the army. In the ensuing engagement on January 11 Sherman and Porter played the major roles, while McClernand remained, according to Cump, "in the woods to our rear, where he had a man up a tree, to observe and report the movements." Porter with three ironclads culminated his three-day-long bombardment of Arkansas Post, also known as Fort Hindman, while the Federal infantry in two columns, one under Sherman and the other under George Morgan, attacked from the rear. Remembering the lesson of Chickasaw Bluffs, Sherman in the early hours of the 11th reconnoitered the terrain himself, noting that the Rebels were constructing a parapet to extend the fort's defenses. "Personally I crept up to a stump so close that I could hear the enemy hard at work, pulling down houses, cutting with axes, and building entrenchments. I could almost hear their words, and I was thus listening when, about 4 A.M., the bugler in the Rebel camp sounded as pretty a reveille as I ever listened to."

The sound of Porter's guns brought the infantry into action. While Morgan's column assailed the fort directly, Sherman on the right moved against the newly built parapet. "The intervening ground between our-selves and the enemy"—some 500 yards—"was dead level, with the ex-ception of one or two small gullies, and our men had no cover but the few standing trees and some logs on the ground. . . . Every tree had its group of men, and behind each log was a crowd of sharpshooters. . . . The fire of the fort proper was kept busy by the gunboats and Morgan's corps, so that all my corps had to encounter was the direct fire from the . . . parapet." This line had three sections of field guns, "that kept things pretty lively, and several round-shot came so near me that I realized they were aimed at my staff."

Overwhelming Union numbers soon brought about a Rebel surrender. Though Sherman had been the first to carry the parapet and the fort, Mc-Clernand now ordered him to stay outside the walls, so Morgan's troops—men he himself had raised—could file into the breastworks and take the credit. "I found General McClernand on the *Tigress,* in high spirits," Sherman wrote. "He spoke [well] of the troops, but was extremely jealous of the navy. He said repeatedly: 'Glorious! Glorious! My star is ever in the ascendant. . . . I'll make a splendid report.' . . . I was very hungry and tired, and fear I did not appreciate the honors in reserve for us. . . . [He] explained to me that by his 'orders' he did not wish to interfere with the actual state of facts; that General A. J. Smith [of Morgan's command] would occupy Fort Hindman . . . and I could hold the lines outside, and go on securing the prisoners and stores."[22]

Arkansas Post made up in part for the debacle at Chickasaw Bluffs. The Federals suffered more than 1,000 dead and wounded, compared to less than 150 Confederates, but they captured 5,000. Grant, who by now had reestablished his communications with Sherman and Porter, was at first critical of the expedition, complaining that it diverted energies from Vicks-burg. But when he learned of the prisoner total, the highest since Fort Donelson, he became far more approving.

Nonetheless McClernand remained a problem. "I received messages from both Sherman and Admiral Porter," Grant said, "urging me to come and take command in person, and expressing their distrust of McClernand's ability and fitness." McClernand meantime was giving as good as he got, saying Grant was "creating confusion," Stanton was guilty of betrayal, and Halleck of "willful contempt." Lincoln replied with his usual patience, announcing he was beset with "too many *family* controversies," and telling the Illinois general, in effect, to mute his grievances. For his part, Grant put the situation in perspective. Though he now had the authority to relieve McClernand, he chose not to do so. "It would not do, with his rank and ambition, to assign a junior over him. Nothing was left, therefore, but to assume the command myself."

In truth, Grant's decision to move his headquarters from west Tennessee and abandon the land assault on Vicksburg was motivated by more than McClernand's petulance. He had come to see he could not control two widely separated armies, particularly in view of the aggressive Rebel cavalry. He resolved to hold the line between Memphis and Corinth with defensive garrisons—leaving Stephen Hurlbut with the 16th Corps in charge—lead the rest of his force 200 miles down the Mississippi himself, and reunite the Army of the Tennessee on the west bank of the river at Young's Point and Milliken's Bend, just above Vicksburg. From now on, his offensive probes would be exclusively from the river.

Out of the hurly-burly then, despite the temporary triumphs of Forrest and Van Dorn, Grant was emerging as the Federal leader in the West. McClernand's star had all but set, Rosecrans in east Tennessee was still unproven. The unassuming Grant had, at the end of 1862 and into January, gained the support of Lincoln, Halleck, and Porter, and, just as importantly, the staunch backing of Sherman. The months ahead would be most difficult, but Vicksburg would be the prize.[23]

1863

ONE

* * * *

WET INTERREGNUM

In the opening months of 1863 Grant was more than cognizant that the Union cause, which so recently had seemed on the upgrade, once again was in peril. The congressional elections in November had gone against the Republican party, Robert E. Lee in the East had routed the Army of the Potomac at Fredericksburg in December, and Chickasaw Bluffs had brought further gloom. "There was nothing left to be done but to *go forward to a decisive victory*," he said. "This was in my mind from the moment I took command at Young's Point."[1] With Grant at this juncture on the west bank of the Mississippi above Vicksburg, or soon to join him, were three of his four corps, some 62,000 men: the 13th under McClernand, the 15th under Sherman, and the 17th under McPherson.

McClernand's division heads were Peter Osterhaus, Andrew Jackson Smith, Alvin Hovey, and Eugene Carr. The conscientious Osterhaus, a German immigrant who had gravitated to St. Louis and would develop into perhaps the best of the foreign-born officers serving the Union, had been fighting in Arkansas. A. J. Smith, of course, had taken part in the Chickasaw Bluffs engagement. Alvin Hovey of Indiana, a jurist and politician and a veteran of Shiloh, had served under Morgan Smith—who had been severely wounded at Chickasaw. Eugene Carr, steady and dependable, was a three-times-wounded West Pointer who had already won the Medal of Honor.

Sherman's commanders would be Frederick Steele, Frank Blair Jr., and James Tuttle. Steele, a graduate of West Point in the same class as Grant, had performed with distinction at Chickasaw, as had Blair, the son of "Old Man Blair," a political power in Washington since Andrew Jackson's day and the man who had offered Lee, at Lincoln's behest, command of the Federal armies in 1861. Tuttle of Iowa had been among the first to occupy Fort Donelson and had exhibited Spartan-like courage at the Hornet's Nest during Shiloh.

James Birdseye McPherson's divisions were led by John Logan, John McArthur, and Isaac Quinby. Black Jack Logan, the Illinois politician who had been fighting since Belmont, was developing into one the army's best field commanders. John McArthur, a brawny Scottish immigrant who had settled in Chicago, had succeeded to command of W.H.L. Wallace's division after the latter's death at Shiloh and had fought under Edward Ord at Iuka and Corinth. Isaac Quinby, who would be plagued by malaria in the months to come, would alternate divisional command with Marcellus Crocker, who had led the 13th Iowa at Shiloh—sustaining 172 casualties, and then a brigade at Corinth, where in the midst of the whistling minie balls, we will remember, he had opined, "I wish I was back in Des Moines."

To understand the complex topography of the Vicksburg area is to understand the challenge Grant faced in capturing the stronghold. The Confederates' right flank—the Walnut Hills escarpment, along which ran Chickasaw Bluffs, Snyder's Bluff, and, finally, Haynes' Bluff—rested on the Yazoo Valley, a vast tract of water-soaked country, 200 miles long and 50 miles wide, crisscrossed by a maze of streams and bayous. "This oval valley," said naval officer James Soley, "was bounded by the Mississippi on the west, and on the north, east and south by what was in reality one long stream, known in its successive parts as the Coldwater, Tallahatchie and Yazoo Rivers. The streams made the valley almost an island, the only break in their continuity being at the northern end of the valley at Yazoo Pass, a bayou which had formerly connected the Coldwater with the Mississippi, but which had been closed by the erection of a levee. . . ."

Most of the Yazoo Valley was impassable for troops, and the streams were most difficult to navigate. "The district was a rich storehouse of Confederate supplies, which were carried in small vessels through obscure passages to Yazoo City, and thence to Vicksburg. At Yazoo City, also, protected from assault . . . by the forts at Haynes' Bluff, was a large navy-yard, where several gunboats were in the course of erection."

If the terrain to the north of Vicksburg made it all but impervious to attack from the water, getting troops in transports past the city's cannon to assail it from the more vulnerable south was equally problematic. Located on a hairpin bend in the Mississippi, Vicksburg's artillery positions, which ran along a three-mile series of bluffs from 150 to 300 feet high, had all the advantage over attackers, in part because gunboats could not elevate their pieces enough to damage the Rebel batteries. That was why Grant originally, before he saw how his supply lines could be cut by enemy cavalry, had intended to advance on the city by land and take it from the rear. Now committed to a water assault, he began looking for ways to turn Vicksburg's right flank, or to slip past its cannon and attack its left flank. "The problem was to secure a footing upon dry ground on the east side of the [Mississippi] from which the troops could operate," Grant said. ". . . On the west side, the highest land, except in a few places, [was] but little above the highest water."[2]

Torrential rains that January and February had raised the Mississippi as much as two feet a week in the environs of Milliken's Bend and Young's Point, flooding the west bank lowlands. The Federal troops, hard pressed to find dry campsites, were strung out for some sixty miles. Rather than wait months for the waters to recede, Grant now began a series of engineering and water-borne probes, hopeful he could use the swollen waters to carry his army around or past Vicksburg. Besides, he said, "it would not do to lie idle all this time. The effect would be demoralizing to the troops. . . . Friends in the North would have grown more and more discouraged, and enemies in the same section more and more insolent."

The first of these initiatives involved the digging of a canal across the De Soto Peninsula, avoiding the river's hairpin bend and transporting the army twenty miles south of the city without coming under its guns. Grant put Sherman's men with shovels and pickaxes to work on the project, eventually bringing in dredges to accelerate its progress. "The distance across was a little over a mile," said Grant of the canal. ". . . I went to Young's Point to push the work of widening and deepening [it]. . . . The work [engaged] about 4,000 men—as many as could be used to advantage—until interrupted by a rise in the river that broke a dam at the upper end, which had been put there to keep the water out until the excavation was completed."

Even if successful, he later admitted, the canal would have been of limited value. "As soon as the enemy discovered what we were doing he established a battery commanding the canal throughout its length. Had [it] been completed it might have been of some use in running transports through, under the cover of night, to use below; they would yet have to run batteries, though for a much shorter distance."

While this effort was going on, Grant set McPherson and his corps to laboring on a second project. This one was 50 miles above Vicksburg at Lake Providence, which ran south through myriad bayous and streams into the Red River, which in turn emptied into the Mississippi some 400 miles below Vicksburg. The idea was to dig a canal from the Mississippi into the lake, clear and deepen the sluggish waterways at the lake's southern end to gain passage into the Red River, and then reenter the Mississippi. "On the 4th of February I visited General McPherson," said Grant. "The work had not progressed so far as to admit the water from the river into the lake, but the troops had succeeded in drawing a small steamer . . . into the lake. With this we were able to explore. . . ."

Grant soon saw, however, that there was little chance of Lake Providence and the Red River being a practical route for getting past Vicksburg. The bayous between the two were choked with underwater stumps, felled trees, and overhanging branches, the distance was too long, and Port Hudson, near where the Red River joined the Mississippi, was in Confederate hands. All along the way, moreover, "the enemy could throw small bodies of men to obstruct our passage and pick off our troops with their sharpshooters. I let the work go on, believing employment was better than idleness. . . ."[3]

Cyrus Boyd of the 15th Iowa, whose diary entries at this point reflect the emergence of the hardened soldier, saw the advantages of keeping busy. "The rain poured down all last night," he wrote of the conditions at Lake Providence. "The hog pens in Iowa do not get in a worse condition than our camp ground. . . . One year ago such times as these would have made us all sick. But we are pretty tough and are not much affected by such small matters. When we landed at Pittsburg we knew nothing about soldiering. We could not cook and we could not eat. Hard bread and *sow-belly* we could not *stomach*. Now we digest all we can get. . . ."

Living in the water-soaked terrain, Boyd explained, required planning. "We can now in two hours after we stack arms have up tents . . . and have up good dry bunks ready to sleep. The soldier can cut four stakes and drive [them] into the ground, take two short pieces—one at the head and one at the foot and lay down small poles wide enough to [sleep]. . . . At his head stands his gun and cartridge box. . . . On a stick having several prongs driven into the ground near his head he can hang his canteen, haversack and the last thing he takes off when he goes to bed—his cap will have the highest prong. In case of a night *alarm* he can put his hand on all his fixtures."

Self-discipline, he stressed—and Grant would have nodded in agreement—was essential. "Whiskey and sexual vices carry off more soldiers than the *bullet*. More men *die* of homesickness than of all other diseases—and when a man gives up and lies down he is a *goner*. Keep the mind occupied with something new and keep *going all the time* except when asleep."[4]

That February, too, Grant and Porter dispatched an expedition of some ten vessels and 5,000 infantry upriver from Vicksburg. Its purpose was to steam 350 miles north on the Mississippi to Helena, Arkansas, blow up the levee at Yazoo Pass and enter the Yazoo Valley, come down the Coldwater, Tallahatchie, and Yazoo Rivers with gunboats and transports, and turn the city's right flank—a circuitous 700-mile-plus incursion. The navy was under the direction of Lieutenant Commander Watson Smith; the army was led by Brigadier Leonard Ross; the destruction of the levee was entrusted to Lieutenant Colonel James H. Wilson of Grant's staff. The latter, an engineering officer who neither drank himself nor approved of others doing so, had forged a close alliance with John Rawlins, the chief of staff and a fellow teetotaler. Both felt it their God-given duty to keep liquor out of Grant's sight.

Opening the levee took Colonel Wilson only two days, but waiting for the waters to flood the lowlands took almost three weeks. Not until February 21 did the flotilla start wending its way through Yazoo Pass, and thence the Coldwater and the Tallahatchie. "Notwithstanding the work which had been done by the army pioneers in removing obstructions," said naval officer Soley, "[progress was] excessively slow—hardly more than three miles a day. The windings of the streams, which imposed the utmost caution on the vessels navigating them in a swift current, and the overhanging branches of the dense growth of trees lining the banks, which damaged the smokestacks and light upper works, made the passage . . . difficult, and caused a number of mishaps." It was not until March 10 that the gunboats, the transports close behind, reached the confluence of the Tallahatchie and the Yazoo.

There the Federals received an unpleasant surprise. General John Pemberton, now personally directing the defense of Vicksburg, had sent 2,000 troops up the Yazoo to block the assault. The Rebel breastworks—called Fort Pemberton—were crisscrossed with fallen trees and bolstered by cotton bales, mounted a dozen guns including a long-range 32-pounder, and were so situated that a land assault was not feasible, or so Brigadier Ross maintained. Nearby, obstructing the waterway, was the sunken hulk of a captured Union gunboat. Lieutenant Commander Smith, with no room to maneuver, found himself forced into ill-advised head-on sorties. "The *Chillicothe* and *De Kalb,*" said Soley, "attacked the fort on three different days, but their guns alone were not enough to reduce it, and the troops . . . could find no firm ground for a landing. The *Chillicothe* was badly wracked by the enemy's fire. . . ."

In the midst of the engagement the frustrated Smith suffered a nervous breakdown. James Wilson, who saw his own chances for glory slipping away, was unsympathetic. Smith's "timid and slow movements," he would complain to Rawlins, had "let one (32-pounder) stop our navy. Bah!" Regardless of who was at fault, the army or the navy, Grant soon called off the impasse, calling the expedition back to the Mississippi. Unlike their subordinates, neither Grant nor Porter indulged in finger pointing. "I told the navy I didn't want to hear anything about it," said the latter. "They did not get through, and didn't get the fort, and the less said about it the better."[5]

Undeterred, Grant and Porter in mid-March launched still a second roundabout river expedition to turn Vicksburg's defenses—this one a mere 200 miles. It involved leaving the Yazoo well below Fort Pemberton at Steele's Bayou, proceeding north through ill-defined waterways with such names as Black Bayou, Deer Creek, and Rolling Fork, and then taking the Sunflower River back south to reenter the Yazoo behind the Rebel right flank on Haynes' Bluff. "Steele's Bayou," said Grant, "empties into the Yazoo River between [Haynes'] Bluff and its mouth. It is very narrow, very tortuous, and fringed with a heavy growth of timber." The connecting streams beyond Steele's Bayou, he continued, "are about of the same nature . . . until the Sunflower is reached; this affords free navigation." Porter's flotilla, which he personally led, consisted of five ironclads—the *Cincinnati, Louisville, Carondelet, Mound City,* and *Pittsburgh,* four tugs and two mortar-boats. Sherman with 5,000 men on transports followed him in support. "It was all very pleasant at first," Porter remembered, "skimming along over summer seas, under the shade of stalwart oaks, but we had no conception of what we had before us."

On March 16, early in the daunting cruise, Porter and Sherman exchanged brief but prophetic greetings.

"Halloo, old fellow," said Sherman, who knew just how hazardous the Yazoo Valley waterways could be, "what do you call this? This must be traverse sailing. You think it's all very fine just now, don't you; but before you fellows get through, you won't have a smokestack or a boat among you."

"So much the better," Porter rejoined. ". . . We will get new ones. All I want is an engine, guns, and a hull to float them."[6]

The admiral soon had cause to regret his bravado. "If the lamented Commander Smith had found the Yazoo Pass route nightmarish," wrote one of Grant's biographers, "he would have been utterly unable to find words to describe this Steele's Bayou business. . . . Porter went ahead, hammering his way through channels where his ironclads had to act like modern-day tanks, [smashing] trees out of the way. . . ." Moving a single mile could take two hours or longer, all manner of snakes, vermin, and wildlife steadily fell from the overhanging tree branches onto the decks and had to be dealt with, and Rebel sharpshooters made sudden death a distinct possibility. "In one intricate little stream, [Porter] found his flagship, which had a 42-foot beam, moving in a channel no more than 46 feet wide. Bridges spanned the watercourse here and there, and had to be butted down . . . now and then a gunboat would get hung up, wedged firmly between two trees, immobilized until the crew could get axes and cut through the thick trunks."[7]

By this time Black Bayou had been passed and the flotilla was entering Deer Creek, with Sherman's troops far behind. Porter's worries thus far had ranged from the enemy cutting down trees in his rear to dumping cotton bales in his front; the latter were intended to act as huge sponges—his vessels barely had two feet of clearance under their keels. Now he had to deal with fire and smoke. Piled up on both sides of the channel were thousands of cotton bales set afire on Confederate orders.

"How long will it take that cotton to burn up?" he asked a black man standing on shore.

Two days, he was told. *Maybe three.*

Porter, on board his flagship the *Cincinnati,* made a quick decision. "Ring the bell to go ahead fast," he told the captain, "and tell those astern to follow after me."

Porter, the ship's captain and the wheelman were the only ones on deck when the *Cincinnati* ran the gamut, "but the heat was so intense that I had to jump inside a small house on deck covered with iron. . . . The boats escaped with some blistering. The smoke was even worse than the heat. . . ."

By the third day, barely a third of a mile from Rolling Fork, the flotilla met a natural obstacle it could not overcome. "I noticed right at the head of the pass a large green patch extending all the way across," said Porter. "It looked like green scum on ponds."

"What is that?" he asked of one of the ubiquitous contrabands.

Nothing but underwater willow switches, he was told. *You can go through like an eel.*

The black man was mistaken, insofar as weighty naval vessels were concerned. Porter sent a tug and a mortar boat on ahead into the underwater willow switches, and then followed. "The tug went into it about thirty yards, began to go slower and slower, and finally stuck so fast that she could move neither ahead nor astern. I hailed her and told them that I would come along and push them through. We started with a full head of steam and did not even reach the tug." The vinelike willows wrapped themselves around the *Cincinnati*'s hull, "and held us as if in a vise. I tried to back out, but t'was no use. We could not move an inch, no matter how much steam we put on. . . . We got saws, knives, cutlasses and chisels over the side, with the men handling them sitting on planks, and cut [the willows] off, steamed ahead, and moved only three feet. Other withes sprang up from under the water."

Compounding Porter's concerns at this juncture was a Rebel artillery bombardment and intensified sniping, as well as news that the enemy had landed 2,000 men at Rolling Fork and was marching to get behind him. He questioned the black man who had brought the report. How did he get his information?

I'm the county telegraph, was the reply.

Could the black find General Sherman somewhere in the flotilla's rear and give him an urgent message?

I can take a note to Kingdom Come if you pay me half a dollar, the man answered.

Porter wasted no time haggling. "Dear Sherman," he quickly scribbled on a piece of paper, "Hurry up, for Heaven's sake. I never knew how helpless an ironclad could be steaming around through the woods without an army to back her."

"Go along the road," he told the black, "and you can't miss him."

I don't go by the road, the man sensibly replied. *I takes the ditches.*[8]

On the night of March 19, even as Porter was striving to free himself from the willows and disengage, Sherman received his message. "The admiral stated," said Cump, "that he had met a force of infantry and artillery. . . . He begged me to come to his rescue as soon as possible. Giles A. Smith had only about 800 men with him, but I ordered him to start up Deer Creek at once. . . . I was almost alone . . . but took a canoe, paddled down Black Bayou . . . and there, luckily, found the (steamer) *Silver Wave* with a load of men just arrived." These troops, preceded by others in a commandeered coal barge pushed by a tug, moved immediately to Porter's aid along the creek, "crashing through the trees, carrying away pilot-house, smoke-stacks, and everything above deck; but the captain . . . was a brave fellow, and realized the necessity. The night was absolutely black. . . ." Sherman and his men disembarked about midnight and marched for several hours through the canebrake, flaming pinecones in the barrels of their rifles lighting the way, until they reached some cotton fields. There they rested. All the next day and through the night, following in Giles Smith's path, they pushed on, often losing their bearings in the unfamiliar terrain.

On March 21, Sherman at last neared the besieged flotilla. "We could hear Porter's guns, and knew that moments were precious," he said. "Being on foot myself, no man could complain, and we generally went on the double-quick." The road along Deer Creek led past several plantations and occasionally ran through swamps, where the water was hip-level. "The smaller drummer-boys had to carry their drums on their heads, and most of the men slung their cartridge-boxes around their necks." In due course Sherman learned that Porter, plagued by obstructions in the water and sharpshooters in the woods, was barely holding his own. Subsequently his men, encountering some Rebels chopping down trees to block Porter's escape, quickly put the enemy to flight. "About that time [an officer] of the 8th Missouri [Smith's brigade] galloped down the road . . . and met me. He explained the situation . . . and offered me his horse. I got on *bareback* and rode up the levee, the sailors coming out of their ironclads, and cheering most vociferously. I soon found Admiral Porter . . . and I doubt if he was ever more glad to meet a friend than he was to see me."[9]

Indeed the days waiting for Sherman had been harrowing ones for Porter. "We kept our mortars hard at work," he said, "but the [enemy] artillery shifted position every three minutes, and were sending among us about twenty shells a minute. The men had to keep between decks. We were in the narrowest part of the pass; it was the same width as the ironclads. . . . The Confederates had completely checkmated us." Making matters worse was the fact that his broadside guns were ineffectual, since his vessels floated below the creek banks. "There was nothing easier than for two thousand men to charge us from the bank and carry us by boarding. Only the enemy didn't know the fix we were in. . . . They didn't know that we had only four smooth-bore howitzers free to work, that our heavy guns were useless."

Eventually the flotilla escaped the clutches of the willows. "I sent a hawser to the tug," said Porter, "and another to the ironclad astern of me, while the latter made fast to another ironclad. Then we all backed together and . . . slipped off the willows into soft water. *Laus Deo!*" Downstream the boats went, stern foremost, "with a four-knot current taking us—bumping badly—down at the rate of two miles an hour—which was twice as fast as we came up." The enemy's cannon fire, while annoying, did little harm. "They . . . failed to understand that we were ironclad and didn't mind *bursting* shell. If they had fired solid shot, they might have hurt us."

Porter during this withdrawal was far more concerned about the Rebel infantry, whom he could clearly see in pursuit. "As our bow guns were bearing astern and *up* the bayou, we could each of us give the enemy now and then, at the turns, a dose of nine-inch shrapnel. . . . They began to find out that our bow guns were . . . doing them some injury." After dark he found a wide spot in the creek that afforded four feet of space on either side of the bank and disembarked 500 men with howitzers, positioning them to repel any attack with enfilading fire.

The next day, toward evening, he interrogated—and entertained—two officers the landing party had captured. Like so many commanders on both sides during the war, Porter prided himself on his mess, and his prisoners found themselves being offered wine and a cold supper.

"You can't escape," one of the officers told him. "How in the devil's name you ever got here is a wonder to me."

"Drink some wine," Porter replied, sliding forward the sherry. "Help yourselves; don't stand on ceremony. . . . How far off are your troops?"

"About four miles. They will bag you at daylight."[10]

Rebel sharpshooters accelerated their fire in earnest the next morning, their minie balls rat-a-tatting off the iron hulls like drops of rain. Porter at this point turned all his guns into mortars by firing them at the greatest elevation. "With short time-fuses and a range of about six hundred yards this had a good effect." Some time later his boats were brought up short, eight large trees blocking their retreat, and the trunks seemed "so interlaced that it was apparently impossible to remove them." The resourceful Porter sent out riflemen along the banks, again driving the enemy away to a safe distance. Still under fire from the sharpshooters, "we removed the eight trees . . . and started to push on, when we found those devils had sunk two large trees . . . under water, and *pinned* them down."

No sooner had his men gotten rid of these further obstructions than the Confederates closed in once more. "We opened mortar fire on them. They didn't mind it. On they came. They were no doubt determined to overwhelm us by numbers, and close us in. Their artillery was coming on with them. Now would come the tug of war. . . . We were jammed up against the bank. . . . Their sharpshooters had taken up positions behind trees about one hundred yards from us. . . . We had picked up a few cotton bales to make defenses . . . and good ones they were."

Suddenly the Rebel forces, taking fire in their rear, fell into confusion. Giles Smith's Federals had arrived, soon to be followed by Sherman's van. "It looked as if [the Confederates] were fighting among themselves," Porter said. "But no! They were retreating before someone. They had run foul of Sherman's army, which was steadily driving them back. The enemy were much surprised at encountering such a force. . . . We would have no more trouble now."

Sherman, when he later rode up to Porter, was as ebullient as ever. "Halloo, Porter, what did you get in such an ugly scrape for? So much for you navy fellows getting out of your element; better send for the soldiers always. My boys will put you through. . . . This is the most infernal expedition I was ever on. . . . But I'm all ready to go on with you again. Your gunboats are enough to scare the crows; they look as if you had got a terrible hammering."

The admiral, however, had swallowed more than his share of the bayou waters. "I have had enough," he said. "The enemy is forewarned . . . they will fill all the rivers with torpedoes, and every hill will be turned into a heavy fort." With that the enterprise came to a close.[11]

Just before conducting the second of these fruitless probes in the Yazoo Valley, Porter had initiated a series of operations on the Mississippi from Vicksburg south to Port Hudson, the 240 miles of waterway and landfall controlled by the enemy. This section included the outlet of the Red River, by which provisions, arms, and detachments of troops were funneled to the Confederate states in the East from Texas, Arkansas, and Louisiana. Up to then Porter had not attempted to get his boats past Vicksburg's guns to challenge this traffic. Now he decided to test the gauntlet. Here a word is in order about Union warships on the rivers. Generally speaking they were paddle wheelers, had relatively flat bottoms and broad beams, and were of three types. Ironclads, as we have seen, were heavily armored throughout, carried perhaps a dozen guns, and drew up to nine feet of water. So-called tinclads, designed to patrol the shallower tributaries, were armored only around their engine rooms and boilers, armed with fewer and lighter cannon, and could be employed, fully loaded, in as little as three feet of water. Rams were just that: fast-moving vessels capable of thirteen or fourteen knots, usually without gunnery but with massive iron prows, braced bow to stern with sturdy bulkheads and designed to smash enemy hulls.

On February 2 the Federal ram *Queen of the West*, commanded by the daredevil nineteen-year-old colonel Charles R. Ellet, steamed into the teeth of the city's batteries. "Her passage . . . alone and by daylight—for her start had been delayed for necessary repairs—was made in the true Ellet fashion," said naval officer James Soley. "She was struck thrice before she got abreast of the town. At this point she turned and delivered a ram-thrust at the enemy's steamer *Vicksburg*, which lay at one of the wharves, and damaged her badly; a second attempt to ram was prevented by a conflagration in the cotton bales which Ellet had placed around his deck. These were pitched overboard, the ram dashed past the lower batteries, and though struck a dozen times by the enemy's shot, in an hour or two was ready for active operations and started down the river."[12]

For once the Confederates were taken by surprise. "Before they knew of his approach, Ellet had run down . . . to the Red River and pounced upon three heavily-laden store-ships. These were burned, and the *Queen*, ascending again until near Vicksburg, coaled from a barge which Porter had set adrift the night before, and which had passed the batteries without mishap. A tender was also found in the *De Soto*, a little ferryboat captured by the army." With her the *Queen* started on a second raid, burning and destroying as she went. Without meeting serious opposition, she roamed at will in the environs of the Red River. The Confederate warship *William H. Webb*, which was thought to be her most dangerous antagonist, was nowhere to be seen.

Then on February 14 Ellet captured the *Era No. 5*, a transport containing 4,500 bushels of corn, a $32,000 payroll, and detachments of troops from Texas and Louisiana. Hearing of a second richly laden transport farther up the Red River he left the *Era* under guard and, with the *De Soto* rashly steamed after another victim. When he turned a bend in the waterway, however, he came to grief under shellfire from a hidden four-gun shore battery. Trying to escape, the *Queen* ran aground.

The ensuing scene was chaotic. "The enemy had our exact range. . . ." wrote a correspondent for the *New York Herald*. "Three huge 32-pounder shells exploded upon the deck and between the smoke stacks. . . . The air was filled with fragments. Soon we heard a crash among the machinery below. . . . Word was passed that the lever which regulates the engines was shot away. . . . Another crash, and we learned the escape pipe was gone. Still another, and the steam chest was fractured. The whole boat shook with the rush of the escaping steam." Men crowded to the stern of the vessel, throwing cotton bales overboard and hanging on to them in an effort to reach the *De Soto,* a mile behind. Many of them, including Ellet, succeeded. Soon Rebel soldiers boarded the *Queen,* commandeering her and taking prisoner those who remained.

With great difficulty the *De Soto* and the survivors made their way back to the Era. Since the ferryboat's size made it unsuitable for a mass withdrawal, they burned it, transferred to the transport, and headed for the Mississippi. Once there, Ellet's bad luck continued. Now the *Era* ran aground. "Here we laid for four mortal hours within ten feet of shore," said the reporter, "liable to capture at any moment from guerillas, until our carpenter could go into the woods, select a tree, and fashion a spar to shove us off." Barely had they again gotten under way when a warship loomed up in the distance. "We at first supposed the *Webb* had passed us in the night and was lying to. . . . I rushed on deck, but as soon as I saw the smokestacks, just visible through the lift of the fog, I knew we had escaped. It was the Union gunboat *Indianola,* sent down to cooperate with the *Queen.*"[13]

With this fortuitous meeting Colonel Ellet and the *Era* on February 16 fade from our story. "Had the commander of the *Queen of the West* waited patiently," wrote Porter bitterly to Navy Secretary Gideon Welles, "he would . . . have been joined by the *Indianola.* . . . This is a serious disappointment to us all here, as we calculated on starving out the garrison at Port Hudson by merely blockading the Red River. . . . I can give orders but cannot give officers good judgment." Sent down the Mississippi by Porter to support Ellet in his isolated position, the *Indianola* had passed Vicksburg without a scratch, but now found herself the only Federal warship downriver, just as isolated in turn. The largest of a new class of ironclads, she was 175 feet long, 52 feet wide, and powered both by paddle wheels and twin screws. Her deck was flat and just above water, her sharply angled casemate three inches thick. Amidships was a towering pilothouse, forward were two 11-inch smoothbores, and aft were two 9-inch guns. Several days of patrol elapsed, and then the *Indianaola*'s captain, Lieutenant Commander George Brown, learned that the Rebels were coming after him. Besides the *Webb,* the flotilla consisted of the *Queen of the West,* which the enemy had repaired and refitted, and two steamers, laden with soldiers and protected by cotton bales.[14]

On the 21st Brown began his run back up the Mississippi, hoping to get by Vicksburg once more and rejoin the rest of the Federal squadron north of the city. A ninety-mile head start soon evaporated, largely because of the coal barges lashed to each side of the *Indianola* and, after nightfall three days later, the Confederates overtook her. "The *Queen of the West* was the first to strike us," said Brown of the ram attack, "which she did after passing through the coal barge lashed to our port side, doing us no serious damage. Next came the *Webb*. I stood for her at full speed; both vessels came together bows on, with a tremendous crash, which knocked nearly everyone down. . . ."

While the steamers filled with soldiers poured heavy fire on the *Indianola,* the two warships circled her flanks and attacked with feral abandon. The *Webb* continued to ram her sides, the *Queen* destroyed her starboard rudder and wheel. During this close-quarter melee the *Indianola*'s powerful guns were relatively ineffective. With each pounding she settled lower in the water, and then the *Webb* "struck us fair in the stern and [crushed] the timbers and starboard rudder-box so that the water [entered] in large volumes. At this time I knew that the *Indianola* would be of no more service to us, and my desire was to render her useless to the enemy."[15]

Soon she would run aground, her crew taken prisoner and the vessel commandeered, the same fate the *Queen* had suffered ten days before. "We heard of the disaster a few hours after," said Porter, "and all my calculations for stopping the enemy's supplies were for the time frustrated." Now he turned his attention to preventing the enemy from salvaging the *Indianola*. "I set the whole squadron at work and made a raft of logs, three hundred feet long, with sides to it, two huge wheel-houses and a formidable log casemate, from the portholes of which appeared wooden guns. Two old boats hung from davits fitted to the 'ironclad,' and two smokestacks made of hogsheads completed the illusion; and on her wheel-house was painted the following: 'Deluded Rebels, Cave In!' An American flag was hoisted aft. . . ."

The mock ram, some 300 feet long and built for under $10, was furnished with big iron pots filled with tar and oakum inside each smokestack to raise black fumes, and at midnight set adrift close to Vicksburg's batteries. "It did not take the sentinels long to discover the formidable monster that was making its way down the river. The batteries opened on her with vigor, and continued to fire until she had passed the range of their guns." The next morning, drifting downstream on the five-knot current, the "ram" encountered the *Queen of the West* who, thinking she was outgunned, turned and fled, the ram in pursuit. Meanwhile the Rebels salvaging the *Indianola,* learning of the oncoming behemoth, mistakenly decided to destroy their prize, rather than see her retaken. "With the exception of the wine and liquor stores," read the enemy report, ". . . nothing was saved."[16]

So ended, with this effective bit of tomfoolery, the futile Federal winter campaign to take control of the Mississippi from Vicksburg to Port Hudson. Grant's detractors—and to a lesser extent Porter's and Sherman's—now were in full cry. Wrote a correspondent for the Cincinnati *Gazette* hyperbolically: "There never was a more thoroughly disgusted, disobedient, demoralized army than this one, and all because it is under such men as Grant and Sherman." For the Louisville *Journal,* the solution was simple: "If Gen. Halleck is unable to find any generals who can take Vicksburg, why doesn't he go and try it himself?" For the persistently insubordinate McClernand, the solution was even simpler: he suggested to Lincoln that the president take direct command. Even General Cadwallader Washburn (for some reason he spelled his name without the final "e"), writing his brother, Congressman Washburne, declaimed: "This campaign is being badly managed. I am sure of it. I fear a calamity. . . . All Grant's schemes have failed. . . ." There is no record, however, that Elihu Washburne ever wavered in Grant's support, which surely earns him more than a footnote in the progress of the war.[17]

The most important figure in this tempest, of course, ruled from Washington with a calm and detachment similar to Grant's. "I think we'll try him a little longer," Lincoln concluded.[18]

Grant meanwhile knew exactly what he was doing, and how he would do it. In early April, with the waters in the Mississippi and the surrounding streams and bayous at last beginning to recede, he set it in motion. "I had in contemplation the whole winter the movement by land to a point below Vicksburg from which to operate," he said, "subject only to the possible but not expected success of some one of the expedients [previously] resorted to. . . . My recollection is that Admiral Porter was the first one to whom I mentioned it." He had no authority to command Porter, but he counted on the latter's proven goodwill. The admiral's flotilla was on the east side of the river above the mouth of the Yazoo, entirely concealed from the enemy by the dense forests that lay between. "It was necessary to have part of his fleet below Vicksburg if the troops were there," Grant said. "Steamers to use as ferries were also essential. The navy was the only escort and protection for those steamers, all of which in getting below had to run . . . miles of batteries."

Porter fell in with the plan at once. "General Grant called a council of war . . . on board my flagship—the *Black Hawk*—and, after informing the generals what he proposed to do, asked their opinions. General McClernand did not attend . . . but wrote . . . approving the [initiative]. I think General Sherman was present, but did not favor the plan, as it would take the army too far from its base of supplies, and for other good reasons which Grant considered it necessary to set aside. . . . All the other generals . . . strongly objected."

Grant was unswayed. The Army of the Tennessee, McClernand's corps in the lead and two divisions of McPherson's following, soon would be on the march down the west, or Louisiana, bank of the Mississippi, from Milliken's Bend to New Carthage and then Hard Times Landing. Sherman for the nonce would be left in front of Vicksburg, pinning down the Confederates in the city. Porter would ready the naval support for the crossing downriver. The crucial battles for Vicksburg were in the offing.[19]

T W O

* * * *

BYPASSING VICKSBURG

That April, too, even while the lead elements of Grant's army were tor-
tuously making their way down the west bank, a so-called special commissioner from the War Department arrived in Milliken's Bend. He was
Charles A. Dana, who for fifteen years had been editor Horace Greeley's
deputy on the *New York Tribune,* and his mission was to keep Lincoln
and Secretary of War Stanton in far-away Washington apprised of Grant's
progress. He was, not to put too fine a point on the matter, a spy. "Grant
was a 'copious' worker and fighter," Lincoln would say in justification of
Dana's assignment, "but he was a very meager writer or telegrapher." The
forty-three-year-old newspaperman would serve as "the eyes of the government at the front." Left unsaid was the stipulation that the president be
kept informed on the extent of Grant's drinking. In this respect Dana,
who came to greatly admire the general and his inner circle, proved a sym-
pathetic observer. "General Grant's seasons of intoxication were not only
infrequent, occuring once in three or four months," he would explain,
"but he always chose a time when his appetite for drink would not interfere with any important movement that had to be directed or attended to
by him." His reports may have contributed to Lincoln's asking, facetiously, what brand of whiskey Grant drank, "for if it made fighting generals . . . I should like to get some of it for distribution."[1]

Dana's mission was an open secret in Grant's camp, and many of his officers at first were for snubbing him. The general would have none of this, however, and through his aide Colonel Rawlins made it clear that the visitor should be shown every courtesy. It was a wise decision, for Dana responded in kind, becoming Grant's booster. "I think Grant was always glad to have me with his army," he said. "He did not like letter writing, and my daily dispatches to Mr. Stanton relieved him from the necessity of describing . . . what was going on. . . . Neither he nor any of his staff or corps commanders evinced any unwillingness to show me the inside of things. . . . The new project, so Grant told me, was to transfer his army to New Carthage, and from there carry it over the Mississippi, landing it at or about Grand Gulf. . . ."

Dana's initial impression of Grant was most favorable, and nothing afterward changed his opinion. "Grant was an uncommon fellow," he would say, "the most modest, the most disinterested, and the most honest man I ever knew, with a temper that nothing could disturb, and a judgement that was judicial in its comprehensiveness and wisdom." Grant was "sincere, thoughtful, deep, and gifted with courage that never faltered; when the time came to risk all, he went in like a simple-hearted, unaffected, unpretending hero, whom no ill omens could deject, and no triumph unduly exalt."

Next to the commanding general, Dana spent most of his time with the assistant adjutant general, Colonel Rawlins, and the topographical engineer, Lieutenant Colonel James H. Wilson, he of the ill-fated Yazoo Pass expedition. "Rawlins was one of the most valuable men in the army. . . . He had but a limited education . . . but he had a very able mind, clear, strong and not given to hysterics. He bosses everything at Grant's headquarters. . . ." Rawlins's suzerainty extended to the commanding general. "He is . . . a townsman of Grant's, and had a great influence over him, especially when he watches him day and night, and whenever he commits the folly of tasting liquor hastens to remind him that at the beginning of the war he gave him [Rawlins] his word not to touch a drop." Wilson, Dana wrote, "was a brilliant man intellectually, highly educated, and thoroughly companionable. We became warm friends at once. Rarely did Wilson go out on a specially interesting tour of inspection that he did not invite me to accompany him."

Grant's staff, Dana observed, ranged from the very good to the very bad. "It is one of his weaknesses," the newspaperman said, "that he is unwilling to hurt the feelings of a friend, and so he keeps him on. . . . Things go much by hazards and by spasms; or, when the pinch comes, Grant forces through, by his own energy and main strength, what proper organization and proper staff officers would have done already."[2]

The man making these judgments had pulled himself up in the world by his own bootstraps. Born in Hinsdale, New Hampshire, and one of several siblings, Dana was the son of an unsuccessful country storekeeper and farmer. His mother died when he was nine, and his father, unable to support the children, parceled them out among relatives. By the time he was twelve he was clerking for an uncle in a general store in Buffalo. Though that business likewise failed, Dana used his years there wisely, reading widely and teaching himself Latin and Greek. In 1839 he entered Harvard, but after two years lack of money forced him to return to Buffalo. Soon thereafter he became a mainstay at Brook Farm, a utopian literary and philosophical community, where he taught and wrote for various publications. There he met his future bride, and first attracted the attention of Horace Greeley, a Brook Farm backer.

By 1847 Dana was working for the *New York Tribune,* where he eventually became Greeley's managing editor. With the onset of the rebellion, tensions began to develop between the two men. Both were against the expansion of slavery to the developing West, but Dana was far more vociferous in his condemnation of secession. "On to Richmond!" became the *Tribune*'s militant cry, one that did not sit well with Greeley, who favored negotiation. The Union defeat at First Manassas in 1861 sealed Dana's fate, and soon afterward he was asked to resign.

Dana was not without friends in high places, however. With Greeley he had helped to establish the New York Republican party, and he knew both Stanton and Lincoln. In 1862 the War Department sent him to Cairo, Illinois, to bring order to a sea of conflicting claims—legitimate and otherwise—against the government for supplies and services. This he did with unusual efficiency. Soon afterward he went into business, intending to purchase much-needed cotton in the Federally occupied area of the Mississippi Valley. Appalled by the corruption these sales were engendering in the army, not to mention the hard currency they were indirectly providing the Rebel cause, he broke off his negotiations and successfully urged Stanton and Lincoln to end the practice. Now he was back in the West, looking over Grant's shoulder.

In his liking for the commanding general, Dana only reflected the opinion of the men. "[Grant's] energy and disposition to do something is what they admire in him," a reporter for the *New York World* snidely conceded, "and he has the remarkable tact of never spoiling any mysterious and vague notions which may be entertained in the minds of the privates as to the qualities of a [commander]." A correspondent for *The New York Times,* writing about the general in the "plain blue suit, without scarf, sword or trappings of any sort, save the double-starred shoulder straps . . . chewing restlessly the end of his unlighted cigar," delivered a fairer appraisal. "The soldiers observe him coming and rising to their feet gather on each side of the way to see him pass—they do not salute him, they only watch him . . . with a certain sort of familiar reverence. His abstract air is not so great while he thus moves along as to prevent his seeing everything without apparently looking at it. . . . However dense the crowd in which you stand, if you are an acquaintance his eye will for an instant rest on yours with a glance of recollection, and with it a grave nod of recognition."[3]

During April, meanwhile, McClernand was moving his 13th Corps down the water-soaked Louisiana side of the Mississippi, heading for New Carthage, some thirty miles below Vicksburg. That he, Grant's most disloyal subordinate, should be in the van of the assault was ironic. Location may have influenced the decision; his troops were better positioned than Sherman's 15th or McPherson's 17th Corps to head south. Then, too, McClernand was the only one of Grant's generals truly enthusiastic about the plan. Knowing the Illinois politician was a close friend of Lincoln's, Grant may even have felt he was placating the powers in Washington. "Sherman, Porter and the other leading officers believed this [decision] a mistake," said Dana, "and talked frankly with me about it. . . . But Grant would not be changed. . . . I believed the assignment of this duty to McClernand to be so dangerous that I added my expostulation . . . and in reporting the case to Mr. Stanton I wrote: 'I remonstrated so far as I could properly do. . . .' "

Back from Stanton came a cautionary message, one that brought Dana's interference to a quick conclusion: "Allow me to suggest that you carefully avoid giving any advice in respect to commands that may be assigned, as it may lead to . . . troublesome complications."[4]

In point of fact, McClernand was doing a commendable job of pushing his column through the stagnant and confusing bayous to New Carthage, improvising a twisting roadbed of pontoons, muddy levees, and bridges. Though opposition from the Rebels was minor, he at one point came under fire from an enemy patrol. When his escort rushed to seek shelter, he spiritedly denounced them. "Damn you, stand fire, don't you run, stand fire, damn you!" He took special care, moreover, in bringing up supply wagons to support the advance. By April 18, ensconced in New Carthage, McClernand was frothing at the bit, petitioning Grant for transports so he could move across the Mississippi to Grand Gulf and "strike the enemy before he could fortify." Later, he was instrumental in the decision to advance his and McPherson's divisions some fifteen miles farther south, to Hard Times, where the debarkation area for the assault would be just across the river from Grand Gulf.[5]

In the interim, Grant and Porter were hatching the naval aspects of the assault. Both men realized that once the vessels bypassed Vicksburg the movement was irrevocable; they no longer could return upriver. Gunboats could make about six knots in still water, and with a four-knot current could achieve a speed of ten knots, meaning that going downriver each would be under the Rebel guns no more than twenty minutes. If the vessels tried to go against the current, however, their speed would be reduced to two knots, exposing them to fire for ninety minutes and making the return trip suicidal. "The great essential," said Grant, "was to protect the boilers from the enemy's shot, and to conceal the fires under the boilers from view. This [Porter] accomplished by loading the steamers, between the guards and boilers . . . up to the deck above, with bales of hay and cotton, and the deck in front of the boilers the same way, adding sacks of grain. The hay and grain would be wanted below. . . ."

By April 16, all was ready. The flagship *Benton,* Porter commanding, led the way, casting off about 10:00 P.M. on a clear night and huddling the east bank, followed at intervals of several hundred yards by the *Lafayette,* with a captured steamer lashed to her side, the *Louisville, Mound City, Pittsburgh,* and *Carondelet*—all these being naval vessels. "Next came the transports," said Grant, "*Forrest Queen, Silver Wave* and *Henry Clay,* each towing barges loaded with coal to be used as fuel by the naval and transport steamers when below the batteries. The gunboat *Tuscumbia* brought up the rear." With the commanding general on his headquarters boat, just beyond the range of Vicksburg's cannon, were Julia and their children. Together with a handful of aides, both seated and standing behind the deck rail, they resembled "an oversized party in the proscenium box of a huge theater. Young Colonel Wilson sat in a chair near Mrs. Grant, with one of the smaller Grant children on his lap." Stretched out for miles behind them on the riverbank were 50,000 Federals troops, watching with silent concern.[6]

Admiral Porter takes up the tale. "I was in the advance, in the *Benton,* and as I looked back at the long line I could compare them only to so many phantom vessels. Not a light was to be seen nor a sound heard throughout the fleet."

He turned to the ship's captain: "We will, no doubt, slip by unnoticed; the Rebels seem to keep a very poor watch."

Just then the whole of Vicksburg seemed to burst into light, as the Confederates on the bluffs torched abandoned buildings, lit bonfires, and ignited barrels of tar. "Every fort and hilltop vomited forth shot and shell," said Porter, "many of the latter bursting in the air and doing no damage, but adding to the grandeur of the scene. As fast as our vessels came within range of the forts they opened their broadsides. . . . The enemy's shells set fire to the transport *Henry Clay,* and she was soon in a blaze, adding her light to the occasion . . . the enemy found her a good target, and showered all their attention on her . . . blazing cotton bales were knocked overboard, and the river was covered with bits of burning cotton, looking like a thousand lamps." The naval vessels, however, ran the gamut with little damage. "The logs on their sides and the bales of hay with which they were packed saved them in many cases. We had few people killed, and the enemy's artillery fire was not much to boast of. . . ."[7]

By midnight the last of Porter's flotilla had cleared the city, and the cannonading was done. Charles Dana, ever the reporter, had counted 525 Rebel artillery blasts. Grant said little, but he must have been elated. The child on Colonel Wilson's lap had fallen asleep, the troops on shore drifted back to their camps.

Porter found that his casualties were few and, oddly enough, most had resulted from musket fire. "The [Confederates] lined the levee and fired into our port holes, wounding our men, for we were not twenty yards from the shore." Just then he was hailed by someone in a small boat: "*Benton,* ahoy!"

"Halloo!" he shouted, soon recognizing the voice of Sherman, his rescuer at Steele's Bayou.

"Are you all right, old fellow?" asked Cump, whose division was still poised opposite Vicksburg, and had commandeered several yawls in the event that it became necessary to pick up survivors.

"Come aboard and see," Porter replied, which Sherman promptly did.

"One man's leg cut off by a round-shot, half a dozen shell and musket ball wounds," the admiral reported.

"You are more at home here than you were in the ditches grounding on willow-trees," said Sherman. "Stick to this, old fellow; it suits Jack better. There are a lot of my boys . . . ready to help you if you want anything. They hauled this boat over for me. Good night! I must go and find out how the other fellows fared." Subsequently one of his yawls rescued a man floating on a piece of timber from the river. It was the *Henry Clay*'s pilot, who had successfully grounded the transport on the Louisiana bank before abandoning ship.[8]

Six days later, on April 22, Grant decided to run Vicksburg's guns again—this time just with supply transports. "It had become evident," he said, "that the army could not be supplied by a wagon train over the single narrow and almost impassable road between Milliken's Bend and Perkins' Plantation." (The latter was halfway between New Carthage and Hard Times Landing.) With civilian crews balking at the risk, he called for volunteers. "Captains, pilots, mates, engineers and deck-hands enough presented themselves to take five times the number of vessels we were moving. . . . Most of them were from [John] Logan's division, composed generally of men from the southern part of Illinois and from Missouri. In this instance, as in all others during the war . . . volunteers could be found . . . to meet every call. . . ." Six more steamers were protected as before, buttressed with bales of hay and cotton, and loaded with supplies. They took twelve barges in tow, loaded similarly. Five of the steamers got through; the one that was lost, unfortunately, carried medical stores.[9]

Grant at this juncture had turned the enemy's left flank on land by sending the bulk of his army through the Louisiana bayous, and had turned the Rebels on the river with the help of Porter's gunboats. Much remained to be done, however. With his supply lines tenuous and his troops dispersed from Milliken's Bend to Hard Times Landing, he must have felt enormous pressure at the prospect of moving across the Mississippi against a resolute foe. Outwardly, he nonetheless remained impassive. One dark night Grant was riding with Charles Dana when his mount took a nasty stumble. "I expected to see the general go over the horse's head. . . ." said Dana. "I had been with Grant daily now for three weeks, and I had never seen him ruffled or heard him swear. . . . When I saw his horse lunge my first thought was, 'Now he will swear.' " But Grant was an expert rider, and instead of going over the animal's head, he kept his seat. "Pulling up his horse," said Dana, "he rode on and, to my utter amazement, without a word or sign of impatience. And it is a fact that though I was with Grant through the most trying campaigns of the war, I never heard him use an oath."[10]

To befuddle Confederate General John Pemberton as to his plans, and dissuade him from sending reinforcements down to Grand Gulf to meet the Federal initiative, Grant earlier had conceived the idea of a cavalry raid in force down the Mississippi heartland, some 100 miles east of the river.

Leading the 1,700-man expedition and leaving La Grange, Tennessee on April 17, one day after Porter's running of the guns, was Colonel Benjamin H. Grierson, a music teacher and storekeeper from Jacksonville, Illinois. The loose-limbed Grierson detested horses—he bore a scar from chin to ear where he had been kicked by an animal as a youngster—but the army in its wisdom had made him a cavalry officer. His command consisted of the 6th and 7th Illinois and the 2nd Iowa, and he would soon be engaged on a daring 600-mile ride to mislead the enemy, destroying railroad track, burning supplies and disrupting telegraph lines as he went. His mission was to make Pemberton think that the Federals were threatening the Mississippi interior, and keep him from concentrating his forces.

For three days Grierson and his column headed south, evading or scattering Rebel patrols and leaving a trail of devastation in their wake. When one enemy detachment finally crossed their path, its officer made the mistake of ordering a charge, urging his men to "make 'em holler." Badly outnumbered, they were put to rout.

"Well, captain, we made one of 'em holler," a Rebel later commented.

"What did he say?" the officer asked.

"He said, 'Forward, skirmishers!' "[11]

On April 20 in Pontotoc, Mississippi, Grierson made the first of several moves to disrupt pursuit. Selecting some 175 of his men, who either were injured or whose mounts were lame, he sent them back north in the column's tracks with the prisoners thus far taken, hoping to give the impression he was ending the raid. The next day he enlarged on the deception, sending an entire regiment—the 2nd Iowa—east with orders to attack the Mobile and Ohio Railroad, and then, if necessary, head back to La Grange. Meanwhile with his remaining 950 men he pushed south through such Mississippi towns as Starkville, Louisville, and Philadelphia. "We moved through a dismal swamp nearly belly-deep in mud," he said of the trek through the soggy bottomlands, ". . . sometimes swimming out horses to cross streams. . . . The inhabitants generally did not know of our coming, and would not believe us to be anything but Confederates."

One reason for the confusion was the so-called Butternut Guerrillas, a small group of scouts who fanned out in advance and on the flanks of Grierson's column and pretended to be Confederates. Wearing captured gray or butternut uniforms, and affecting drawls, they easily gained the Southerners' confidence. Their leader, Sergeant Richard Surby, remembered three pretty sisters—"Secesh Gals"—who with beaming faces told him how their father and brothers were off helping General Pemberton keep that "madman" Grant out of Vicksburg.

Had any other Confederate troops been in the vicinity recently? Surby asked.

"Why, Lawd, it's been two months, hasn't it, sisters?" the oldest replied.

Hearing Surby and his men were hungry, the young women ran into their house "and soon returned, with two black servants following, loaded down with eatables . . . half a ham, biscuits, sweet cakes, fried sausage, and peach pie, all in abundance . . . while one of the young ladies plucked some roses . . . presenting one to each as they bade us adieu, with many blessings and much success in our 'holy cause.' "

The comparatively few Confederates the Butternut Guerrillas met likewise were fooled. "It proved to be the simplest of matters . . . to encounter a Rebel soldier and chat him up about which bridges were burned or the whereabouts of Confederate forces," wrote one historian. "Then came a request to admire the soldier's fine weapon, his willingness to hand it over for inspection, and a pistol point denouement: 'You, sir, are my prisoner.' "[12]

When necessary, however, the scouts offered the opposition a simple choice—give way or die. Reconnoitering the only bridge over the Pearl River, Surby's men reined up before an elderly plantation owner. Courteously, they inquired whether there were any Rebels in the area. Indeed there were, he replied. His own son was one of a handful of militia guarding the bridge, with orders to burn it at the first sight of Federal cavalry. Surby drew his pistol and dropped his drawl. "It lies in your power," he told the Southerner, "to save your buildings from the torch, to save your own life, and probably that of your son, by saving the bridge." With that he sent the man packing, to deliver the message to the guards. Minutes later, he saw the Rebels mounting up, leaving the structure untouched.

Early on April 24, the lead elements of Grierson's cavalry rode into Newton Station on the Vicksburg & Jackson Railroad, some seventy miles east of the fortress, intent on disrupting that vital east-west supply connection. "Lieutenant Colonel [William] Blackburn dashed into the town," Grierson said, "took possession of the railroad and telegraph, and succeeded in capturing two trains in less than half an hour after his arrival. One of these, twenty-five cars, was loaded with ties and machinery, and the other, thirteen cars, [was] loaded with commissary stores and ammunition." The Federals dynamited the locomotives and cars, tore up track and took seventy-five prisoners, all of whom they paroled. Hardly pausing, the column continued on its way. "From information received from my scouts and other sources, I found that Jackson [Mississippi] and the stations east . . . had been reinforced by infantry and artillery; and hearing that a fight was momentarily expected at Grand Gulf, I decided to . . . strike the New Orleans, Jackson, and Great Northern Railroad at Hazlehurst." There on April 27 Grierson came upon rail cars loaded with artillery shells and stores destined for Grand Gulf and Port Gibson. "These were destroyed, and as much of the railroad and telegraph lines as possible. . . . We found the citizens armed to resist us, but they fled precipitately upon our approach."[13]

The remaining six days of the wild ride south through Mississippi were a continuum of raiding and burning, evading the enemy and finding the strength to keep moving. Grierson's smashing of the railroads had infuriated the Confederate high command, but their means of retaliation was limited. Much of Pemberton's cavalry had been transferred to Braxton Bragg in east Tennessee, and his entreaties to Joseph Johnston, the overall Rebel commander in the West, for their return were unavailing. "These raids endanger my vital position," Pemberton at one point desperately wired Johnston. "However necessary cavalry may be for the Army of Tennessee, it is indispensable to keep my communications. The enemy are today at Hazlehurst, on the New Orleans and Jackson Railroad. *I cannot defend every station on the road with infantry. . . .*" The first serious opposition the Federals met during this period occurred on April 28 near Union Church. "While feeding," said Grierson, "our pickets were fired upon by a considerable force. I immediately moved out upon them."

One Union trooper re-created the scene: "The camp was all in confusion, men running as fast as they could in every direction, carrying saddles, leading horses on the gallop, gathering up carbines and sabers and buckling on belts, while the air was filled with cries and oaths and quick impulsive exclamations and sharp stern orders and shouts of 'Fall in here, men, quick!'" Grierson's men drove the attackers, who proved to be the van of the 1st Mississippi Cavalry, through the town, then prudently withdrew toward the New Orleans, Jackson line near Brookhaven. "We moved directly south along the railroad," Grierson said, "destroying all bridges and trestlework. . . . Hearing nothing more of our forces at Grand Gulf, I concluded to make for Baton Rouge [Louisiana]."[14]

With the enemy on its heels, the column raced for the safety of that occupied town, not meeting resistance until it was at the Tickfaw River, within three miles of the Louisiana border. There its lead elements drew the fire of the 9th Louisiana Partisan Rangers; three men were killed and several wounded, Colonel Blackburn and Sergeant Surby among them, when the former ordered the charge, not waiting for support. "The passage of the Tickfaw might have been . . . accomplished without loss," said Grierson, "but for the incident of firing the alarm. . . . Colonel Blackburn, calling on the scouts to follow him, dashed forward to the bridge without waiting. . . ." With the main force's arrival, the Rebels broke and ran. Blackburn's and Surby's injuries were so severe, however, that they had to be left behind. To keep Surby from being shot for being in Confederate gray, his comrades took care to put him in Union blue. He would survive; Blackburn would succumb to his wounds.

Grierson's raiders cantered into Baton Rouge on May 2, their 16-day mission complete. "During the expedition," he reported, "we killed or wounded about 100 of the enemy, captured and paroled about 500 prisoners . . . destroyed between 50 and 60 miles of railroad and telegraph, captured and destroyed over 3,000 stand of arms and other army stores . . . to an immense amount; we also captured 1,000 horses and mules. Our loss during the entire journey was 3 killed, 7 wounded, 5 left on the route sick and 9 men missing, supposed to have straggled." Largely with the help of the Butternut Guerrillas, he explained, "we were always able by rapid marches to evade the enemy when they were too strong and whip them when not too large."

Writing General Halleck subsequently, Grant would say that Grierson's expedition "from La Grange through Mississippi has been the most successful thing of the kind since the breaking out of the rebellion." In the framework of the Mississippi campaign, he was right. Just when a diversion was most needed, Grierson, the former music teacher turned reluctant cavalryman, had kept Pemberton from focusing on the Federal turning movement south of Vicksburg.[15]

Grant, of course, knew nothing of this achievement until later. His own thoughts and energies at the time were directed toward getting his army across the Mississippi with the utmost speed, before Pemberton could anticipate his flanking attack. "On [April] 27th McClernand's corps was all at Hard Times, and McPherson's was following closely," Grant said. "I had determined to effect a landing on the east side of the river as soon as possible. . . . The plan was to have the navy silence the guns at Grand Gulf, and to have as many men as possible ready to debark . . . and carry the works by storm." Here McClernand, attended by his new bride and a retinue of political hangers-on, caused a twenty-four-hour delay by having his men march in review before Illinois governor Richard Yates, who capped the occasion with a speech. Grant was furious, but held off taking disciplinary action. Now was not the time, on the eve of battle, to indulge in a confrontation.

Porter's naval assault on Grand Gulf began at 8:00 A.M. on April 29 and continued for six hours. The result was a standoff. "It was as hard a fight as any that occurred during the war," he said. The Federal gunboats inflicted grave damage on the Rebels atop the bluffs, but suffered greatly themselves. The *Tuscumbia* was hit eighty-one times, the *Benton* and the *Pittsburg* forty-seven and thirty-five times respectively; many sailors were killed and wounded. One shell exploded on the deck of the *Benton,* Porter's flagship, knocking him off his feet; another passed through the wheelhouse, injuring the pilot and temporarily setting the vessel adrift. Retiring to confer with Grant, the admiral reluctantly admitted that Grand Gulf could not be taken by frontal attack.

Sherman meanwhile had been sent to create a diversion of his own. Still in position at Milliken's Bend he made a demonstration in force to the north of Vicksburg, at Haynes' Bluff, to add to Pemberton's confusion. "[Grant] thought I could put in my time usefully," Sherman said, "by making a 'feint' . . . but he did not like to order me to do it, because it might be reported in the North that I had again been 'repulsed, etc.'. . . . Of course I answered him that I would make the 'feint,' regardless of public clamor at a distance." Collecting some barges, he loaded ten regiments of Frank Blair's division aboard them and proceeded up the mouth of the Yazoo. "Sherman spread his command over the decks of the transports, with orders that every man should be in sight and look as numerous as possible," remembered Captain William Jenny, his chief engineer. The accompanying gunboats whistled and puffed, and even brought along a blacksmith shop in tow, to make all the noise and smoke possible. The warships "showed themselves to the garrison at Haynes' Bluff and then drifted back and landed the men, who were marched through the woods . . . until they were seen by the enemy, [then] marched a mile or so down the river, and taken again on board the transports, to go through the same farce again."

The deception worked, and immediately afterward Sherman retraced his route and hastened after McClernand and McPherson. "We later learned," he said, "that General Pemberton . . . had previously dispatched a large force to . . . Grand Gulf and Port Gibson . . . when he discovered our ostentatious movement up the Yazoo, recalled his men, and sent them up to Haynes' Bluff to meet us. This detachment of Rebel troops must have marched nearly sixty miles without rest, for afterward, on reaching Vicksburg, I heard that the men were perfectly exhausted. . . ."[16]

With Porter's failure, Grant now knew he had to put his army across the river somewhere below Grand Gulf. The question was where, for Bayou Pierre formed a watery barrier south of the town. Late that night on the 29th a black man, whose name is lost to history but who knew the countryside well, decided the issue. "Look here," Grant said, pointing to a map in his lamp-lit tent. "Tell me where this road leads to."

That road fetches up at Bayou Pierre, the black man replied, *but you can't go that way, 'cause it's plum full of backwater.*

"Which road would you take if you were to lead me, followed by a great army and trains of loaded wagons and artillery—which road would you take to [cross] Bayou Pierre?"

There is only one way, General, the man answered, *and that is by Bruinsburg, eight miles farther down. There you can leave the boats and the men can walk on high ground all the way. The best plantations in all the country are there, sir, all along that road.*[17]

While Grant was following this advice and issuing orders for his troops to move downriver opposite Bruinsburg, Porter had a curious meeting aboard the *Benton* with Adjutant General Lorenzo Thomas, now serving under Halleck. The fifty-eight-year-old Thomas was one of three dignitaries—the others being Governor Yates and Congressman Washburne—sent by Washington to observe not just the assault on Vicksburg but the conduct of the commanding general. Even at this late date and despite Dana's reports, the powers-that-be—even Lincoln, it seems—were continuing to heed the slanders of Grant's enemies.

Over drinks aboard the *Benton,* Thomas became loquacious. "We stopped first at McClernand's camp. . . ." he told Porter. "He gave us a grand review and a good lunch, but had no ice for his champagne; then we called on Grant, and, Admiral, I'll give you a piece of information."

"Wait a moment," said Porter; "Your throat sounds dry; try this glass of toddy . . . you won't feel the mosquitoes."

Thomas drank the glass down without winking. "I carry in my bag full authority to remove General Grant and place whomsoever I please in command of the army," he confided, waiting to hear if Porter was impressed.

The admiral asked whom he had in mind. "Well, that depends," was the reply, "McClernand is prominent."

"General . . ." said Porter, "let an old salt give you a bit of advice. Don't let your plans get out, for if the army and navy should find out what you three gentlemen came for, they would tar and feather you, and neither General Grant nor myself could prevent it."

". . . I don't intend to do anything," Thomas assured him. "We are delighted with what we have seen. . . . I should have pursued the same course as General Grant had I been in command myself."

"Stick to that, General," said Porter, "and don't forget I am in earnest about the tar and feathers."[18]

The Federal landing at Bruinsburg April 30 was unopposed. "I was now in the enemy's country," said Grant, "with a vast river and the stronghold of Vicksburg between me and my base of supplies. But I was on dry ground on the same side of the river with the enemy. All the campaigns, labors, hardships and exposures from the month of December previous to this time that had been made and endured, were for the accomplishment of this one object." He had with him McClernand's 13th Corps, soon to be reinforced by McPherson's 17th Corps—altogether some 29,000 troops. Besides Vicksburg, Grant continued, "The enemy occupied Grand Gulf, Haynes' Bluff and Jackson, with a force of nearly sixty thousand men. Jackson [the state capital] is fifty miles east of Vicksburg and is connected to it by railroad. My first problem was to capture Grand Gulf to use as a base."

In point of fact Pemberton, whose headquarters was in Jackson, commanded some 54,000 men, but had the disadvantage of having them spread far and wide. Some 5,000 troops were north of Vicksburg on the Yazoo River; 26,000 were in the town; 6,000 were in Grand Gulf; 12,000 were in Port Hudson, the southernmost garrison on the Mississippi; and the rest were here and there. With little cavalry, Pemberton lacked proper reconnaissance, and Grierson's and Sherman's diversions had confused him as to where to meet Grant's threat. Nor were the orders he was getting from his superiors helpful. President Davis was telling him to hold Vicksburg at all costs; General Joseph Johnston, head of the Department of the West, was urging him to leave fixed positions and "unite all your forces." Pemberton's reaction was to temporize. Reluctant to divert troops, he left the Confederates at Grand Gulf, commanded by General John Bowen, with minimal reinforcements.[19]

Early on May 1, the two sides clashed near Port Gibson, several miles southeast of Grand Gulf. "The enemy had taken a strong natural position. . . ." said Grant. "His hope was to hold me in check until reinforcements under [William] Loring could reach him from Vicksburg, but

Loring did not come. . . . The country in this part of Mississippi stands on edge, as it were, the roads running along the ridges except where they occasionally pass from one ridge to another. . . . The sides of the hills are covered with a very heavy growth of timber and with undergrowth, and the ravines are filled with vines and canebrakes. . . . This make it easy for an inferior force to delay, if not defeat, a far superior one." Near the point that Bowen chose to defend, the road to Port Gibson diverged. "This made it necessary for McClernand to divide his force. It was not only divided, but separated by a deep ravine. . . . One flank could not reinforce the other."

McClernand put the divisions of Alvin Hovey, Eugene Carr, and Andrew Jackson Smith on the right-hand road, the division of Peter Joseph Osterhaus on the left. Lawyer-politician Hovey, who had fought gallantly at Shiloh, would be described by Charles Dana as "ambitious, active, nervous, irritable, energetic." Carr, a career West Pointer, was something of an enigma. "He has really been sick throughout the campaign. . . ." said Dana. "This may account for a critical, hang-back disposition." Smith, another West Pointer, was "intrepid to [the point of] recklessness, his head clear though rather thick, his disposition honest and manly." For the German-American Osterhaus, Dana had both praise and criticism. "This general is universally well spoken of. He is a pleasant, genial fellow, brave and quick. . . . [But] on the battlefield he lacks . . . concentrativeness."[20]

On the left-hand road, Osterhaus throughout the morning would accomplish little. The Rebels, though outnumbered three to one, were too well entrenched and too concealed on the high ground crossing his line of march. Hour after hour he and his officers probed the hills and ravines for weaknesses—largely for naught. Colonel Marcus Spiegel of the 120th Ohio made some headway, but then paused. "I advanced as skirmishers some of the best shots from all the companies down into the ravine," he said, ". . . closely supporting them with the remainder of the regiment, and keeping up a constant fire toward the top of the opposite bank. When nearly down, I discovered the exact position of the enemy. . . . I then charged upon them . . . and quickly drove them from the bank to the knoll." Spiegel subsequently drove the Rebels from the knoll, but "did not deem it prudent to pursue them further, being at least 300 yards in advance." By 2:00 P.M. Osterhaus was, in effect, pinned down and asking for reinforcements. Not until late in the afternoon, supported by elements of McPherson's corps, would he turn the enemy's flank and compel a withdrawal.

On the right-hand road the battle likewise proceeded in fits and starts. Carr's men at first enjoyed success, pushing the enemy back from Magnolia Church. "Soon the skirmishers in front come in contact and the roar of musketry is heard," said Sergeant Charles Wilcox of the 33rd Illinois. "We have not *all* got our position yet, but the battle commences in earnest. . . . The enemy has a cross fire upon us and we double quick into line or cover ourselves under the brow of a ridge of land." Now Wilcox saw the rest of the 33rd Illinois, coming up behind him. "I tell the fact to Colonel [Charles] Lippincott. He orders me to bring the Major and his command to join the regiment. I go but dear me! How the shells and shot whiz around me." Soon the order was given to fix bayonets and charge. "The 99th Ill., and the 18th and 24th Ind. make a charge; the order don't reach us so we lie quiet . . . the Rebels break and run."[21]

Bowen at this juncture—about 9:00 A.M.—directed a countercharge on Carr's front, bringing the Federals up short. But McClernand then threw Hovey's and A. J. Smith's divisions into the fight, driving the Confederates back a mile or more. "The second position taken by the enemy on my right front was stronger than the first," he said. "It was in a creek bottom [Centers Creek] covered with trees and underbrush, the approach to which was over open fields. . . ." Here Rebel cannon, hidden in the brush, tore the Federal lines apart.

Later, during the afternoon, McClernand massed his regiments anew, driving toward the enemy center. Seeing this concentration, Bowen promptly sent his reserve, the 3rd and 5th Missouri, commanded by Colonel Francis Cockrell, against the Federal right flank. The two Missouri regiments, said one Union officer, "came down at a charge, with terrific yells, and could not be seen, because of the very thick growth of cane, until they reached a point within 30 yards of my line." Incredibly enough, in the hour-long melee that followed, they succeeded in stymieing ten Federal regiments. Sheer numbers, however, eventually prevailed. By 4:00 P.M. the main fighting ceased, and by dusk the Confederates, on both roads, were stubbornly falling back.

For some twelve hours at Port Gibson, Bowen's men—no more than 7,000 overall, counting meager reinforcements—had held off a vastly superior force. Grant, who had known the Rebel commander in St. Louis during the lean pre-ward years that he and Julia endured there, cited his opponent's gallantry, but added, "My force, however, was too heavy for his, and composed of well-disciplined and hardy men, who know no defeat, and are not willing to learn."[22]

The action at Port Gibson forced the Confederates to evacuate the town and later, on May 2, to withdraw from Grand Gulf and retreat behind the Big Black River. During this period Grant was joined by his twelve-year-old son, Fred, who had been left behind in bed on the headquarters boat at Bruinsburg. (Julia and the rest of the family had by now returned to Illinois.) Waking to the sound of the guns, young Grant determinedly made his way toward the front, at some point making contact with Charles Dana. "We tramped and foraged together until the next morning," said Dana, "when some officers who had captured two old horses gave us each one. We got the best bridles and saddles we could, and thus equipped made our way into Port Gibson." Remembered Grant: "The first time I call to mind seeing either of them, after the battle, they were mounted on two enormous horses, grown white from age"—using rope for bridles. Of Fred he would say: "My son accompanied me throughout the campaign and siege, and caused no anxiety either to me or to his mother. . . . He looked out for himself, and was in every battle. . . ."

If the boy's mood was exuberant, Dana's was reflective. He had just stopped by a makeshift Union field hospital, and the sight of amputated limbs, piled high in the yard outside, had all but sickened him. "I had seen men shot and dead men plenty," he said, "but this pile of arms and legs gave me a vivid sense of war such as I had not before experienced." Later, noting the total absence in the army's path of Southerners capable of bearing arms, he would add: "Only old men and children remained. The young men were all in the army or had perished in it. The South was drained of its youth. An army of half a million, with a white population of only five millions to draw upon, must soon finish the stock of raw material for soldiers."[23]

Grant had little time, or indeed inclination, for this sort of introspection. "When I reached Grand Gulf on May 3rd," he said, "I had not been with my baggage since the 27th of April. . . . The first thing I did was get a bath, borrow some fresh underclothing from one of the naval officers, and get a good meal on the flagship." His orders, now that he had established a beachhead across the Mississippi, called for joining forces with General Nathaniel Banks, who would come north from Baton Rouge. Together the two would reduce the Rebel garrison at Port Hudson. But now, Grant learned, the inept Banks—who had been humbled by Stonewall Jackson in the Shenandoah Valley the year before—could not join him until May 10 earliest, and then with less than 10,000 men. "To wait for his cooperation would have delayed me at least a month," Grant explained. ". . . The enemy would have strengthened his position and been reinforced by more men than Banks could have brought. I therefore determined to move independently . . . cut loose from my base [at Grand Gulf], destroy the Rebel force in rear of Vicksburg and invest or capture the city."

The Federal commander was embarking on a perilous course. It would involve leaving Pemberton's main force in his rear and marching north and east to assail the Confederates at Jackson before the two Rebel forces could unite, all the while moving with utmost speed and largely living off the countryside. Once the state capital was taken, Grant would pivot and fall on Pemberton. "I knew well that Halleck's caution would lead him to disapprove of this course. . . . Even Sherman, who afterwards ignored bases of supplies . . . [advised] me of the impossibility of supplying our army. . . . To this I replied: "I do not calculate upon the possibility of supplying the army with full rations from Grand Gulf. . . . What I do expect is to get what rations of hard bread, coffee and salt as we can, and make the country furnish the balance."[24]

During this first week in May, just as the Confederates were winning their greatest triumph under Robert E. Lee and Stonewall Jackson at Chancellorsville in Virginia, Grant was confidently setting up the destruction of the Rebel army in Mississippi. His would be one of the great strategic decisions of the Civil War.

THREE
* * * *

GRANT GOES ON THE ATTACK

The Federal advance into the Mississippi interior began on May 7. Mc-Clernand's corps along with Sherman's—who by now had rejoined the army—moved northeast along the south bank of the Big Black, using the river as a shield, while McPherson's corps to their right veered off toward Raymond. Grant with some 44,000 men had not yet decided whether he would push toward the Mississippi Southern Railroad, with an eye toward severing the main link between Vicksburg and Jackson, or head directly toward Jackson itself. Pemberton was reduced to wondering where the Union commander was going. He had anticipated that Grant would move north through Warrenton against Vicksburg, and had spread his defensive lines between the Mississippi and the Big Black. Now he worried the Federals were heading toward Edwards Station on the railroad. In sum, the Federals were concentrated and on the march; the Confederates were diffuse and static. "I am obliged to hold back large forces at the ferries on the Big Black," a concerned Pemberton wrote Jefferson Davis from Vicksburg, "lest [Grant] cross and take this place. I am also compelled to keep a considerable force on either flank of Vicksburg, out of supporting distance of Edwards, to prevent his approach in those directions."

Never had the Army of the Tennessee been in higher spirits. Sergeant Osborn Oldroyd of the 20th Ohio, McPherson's command, testified to its morale: "O, what a grand army this is, and what a sight to fire the heart of a spectator with a speck of patriotism in his bosom. I shall never forget the scene of today, while looking back upon a mile of solid columns, marching with their old tattered flags . . . and harkening to the firm tramp of their broad brogans keeping step to the pealing fife and drum, or the regimental bands discoursing 'Yankee Doodle' or 'The Girl I Left Behind Me.'" Oldroyd did not know where he was going but he did not care. "It was all right wherever we went while Grant was leading, for he had never known defeat. Confidence in a good general stiffens a soldier—a rule that ought to work both ways. . . . The enemy are doing all they can to hinder us, but let Grant say *forward,* and we obey."[1]

Living off the countryside was not a problem. Each day on the march wagons were sent out by the hundreds in a ten- to fifteen-mile radius, escorted by infantry for protection. "They returned at nightfall groaning under the weight of impressed supplies," said correspondent Cadwallader, "and increased by the addition of every vehicle . . . that could bear the weight of a sack of grain, pieces of salt meat, or pails full of butter, eggs, honey or vegetables. Fine carriages were often brought in loaded with corn fodder . . . sheaf oats, or anything eatable by man or beast. . . . I frequently saw horses, cattle and mules . . . sheep, goats and lambs; turkeys, geese, ducks and chickens, driven together in one drove. . . . Details of men slaughtered a sufficiency to supply the army each night. . . . If owners could establish their loyalty they were given regular vouchers for everything taken—if not, not."

Black refugees from the plantations seeking freedom and protection continued to swarm into the lines, just as they had during the first Federal incursions into the South. They were of all ages and conditions, on horses and mules, and driving all manner of vehicles, from simple carts to elegant carriages. These last transports were laden with appropriated property—antique furniture, feather beds and tapestries. The army turned a blind eye to these acquisitions, gave the blacks food and shelter and, whenever possible, offered them work.[2]

Thus far Grant had encountered no serious opposition. "My line was now nearly parallel with the Jackson and Vicksburg railroad and about seven miles south of it," he said. "The right was at Raymond, eighteen miles from Jackson, McPherson commanding; Sherman in the center on Fourteen Mile Creek. . . . McClernand to the left . . . his pickets within two miles of Edwards Station, where the enemy had concentrated a considerable force." Indeed, at this juncture, Pemberton with some 22,000 men finally was moving across the Big Black to protect the railroad. The first battle of the advance, however, would not take place at Edwards Station but at Raymond, where on the morning of May 12 McPherson closed in on the enemy. He was met at Fourteen Mile Creek, just outside the town, by John Gregg's Tennessee and Texas Brigade. Both men were spoiling for a fight. Gregg and many of the troops in his three thousand–man unit had surrendered at Fort Donelson; paroled and rearmed, they wanted revenge. McPherson, who had graduated number one in his class at West Point and risen so swiftly to division command, wanted to justify Grant's confidence in him. "He is one of our ablest Engineers," Grant said, "and most skillful Generals." Sherman concurred, adding, "he is as good an officer as I am— is younger, and has a better temper."[3]

Two of McPherson's divisions marched on Raymond, though only one would participate in the engagement, with the Rebels ultimately outnumbered three to one. In the Federal van was the Illinois politician John "Black Jack" Logan, who had become well-known in the army for his courage—and his swearing and drinking. "I saw him on one occasion," Cadwallader would say of Logan's carryings-on, ". . . with nothing on him in the way of clothing but his hat, shirt and boots, sitting at a table on which stood a bottle of whiskey and a tin cup, and playing on the violin for a lot of dusky roustabouts to dance. When the exercise began to flag, which it generally did in the face of such temptations, potations were indulged by player and dancers. Yet he was never accused of drunkenness."

Gregg had concealed his men in a ravine, protected by dense timber and undergrowth, and also along a branch of Fourteen Mile Creek. Suddenly rising and charging forward on the double-quick, they fell heavily on Logan's troops. The 23rd Indiana, taking the full force of the attack, soon broke under the impact. Sergeant Oldroyd of the 20th Ohio, in the midst of the assault, described the scene: "They fought us desperately, and no doubt they expected to whip us early in the fight, before we could get reinforcements." Then, said Oldroyd, "Logan rushed up, and with the shriek of an eagle" restored order.

"For God's sake, men, don't disgrace your country!" he shouted, riding furiously up and down the lines.

The Federals steadied and then rallied. "We dropped on the ground right then and there," said one Union soldier, "and gave those Texans all the bullets we could cram into our Enfields, until our guns were hot enough to sizzle. The gray line paused, staggered back like a ship in collision. . . . Then they too gave us volley after volley, always working up toward us." Oldroyd takes up the story: "For two hours the contest raged furiously, the creek was running red with precious blood spilt for our country. . . . Into another part of the line the enemy charged, fighting hand to hand, being too close to fire and using the butts of their guns." The struggle was vicious everywhere, but in parts of the creekbed it was also bizarre, with Union troops facing and firing in one direction and the Rebels in another, neither knowing the enemy was on his immediate flank because of a bend in the creek.[4]

Once all three of Logan's brigades came into action, however, the outcome was inevitable. Even the aggressive Gregg saw he had no choice but to withdraw toward Jackson. Later in the war he would assume command of the famed Texas Brigade in the East, fighting under Lee with the Army of Northern Virginia. But for now he could only mourn his casualties. In this brief encounter the Confederates had lost some 500 of 3,000 men; the 7th Texas alone had lost half its number. Federal casualties overall were 442, but they were disproportionate. Half of Sergeant Oldroyd's company had been struck down, and Colonel Manning F. Force, his regimental commander, wept openly over his killed and wounded.

Not until sundown did the news of McPherson's victory at Raymond reach Grant, who was making his headquarters with Sherman's corps. Gregg's spirited defense of the town convinced him that the Confederates were buying time to reinforce their troops in Jackson and solidified his plans. He would cut his lines of communications and move on the state capital. "Pemberton was now on my left," Grant said. ". . . A force was also collecting on my right, at Jackson, the point where all the railroads . . . with Vicksburg connect. All the enemy's supplies of men and stores would come by that point. As I hoped in the end to besiege Vicksburg I must destroy all possibility of aid. I therefore determined to move swiftly towards Jackson, destroy or drive any force in that direction. . . ." He would leave Pemberton in his rear, and deal with him another day. Promptly he issued orders. McPherson was to advance on Jackson by way of Clinton; Sherman was to follow. McClernand on the left was to hang back, providing a buffer against the Rebels at Edwards Station.

Late that night Grant entered a tent occupied by Colonel William S. Duff, his chief of artillery, and correspondent Cadwallader. The latter two had become the caretakers of a barrel of whiskey left behind by Illinois Govenor Yates on a recent visit. "General Grant came into the tent . . . and requested a drink of whiskey," said Cadwallader. "Col. Duff drew a canteen from under his pillow and handed it to him. The general poured a generous potation into an army tin cup and swallowed it with great satisfaction. He complained of extraordinary fatigue and exhaustion . . . and took the second, if not the third drink, before retiring." Grant paid no attention to the reporter's presence, and drank the whiskey while making small talk. "His stay in the tent did not exceed twenty or thirty minutes. . . . This was the first time that I ever saw Gen. Grant used any spiritous liquor, and I was a little surprised by his openness in asking for it, and drinking it, before me. My intercourse with him to that time had been casual or accidental . . . yet there was nothing evinced in word or behavior, from which I could infer that he desired the slightest secrecy . . . concerning the object of his midnight call."[5]

If Grant was fatigued, he nonetheless was making decisions—and good ones at that. Pemberton at Edwards Station, on the other hand, was still fence-sitting, reluctant to put further distance between his troops and Vicksburg. Nor was Joseph Johnston, the overall commander in the West, the warrior to stiffen his spine. Summoned by the War Department from Tennessee to take direct charge in the Jackson theater, Johnston did not arrive in the city until May 13. There he found to his dismay that his garrison totaled no more than 6,000 men, including Gregg's battered brigade. The fact that 10,000 additional troops were being rushed to him by rail—including some who would arrive within twenty-four hours—he ignored. No risk taker, he made immediate plans to evacuate the city, putting the reinforcements on hold.

Before doing so, however, he fired off a message to Pemberton that implied he would be making a stand, and that they might catch Grant between them: "I have lately arrived, and learn that Major General Sherman is between us with four divisions at Clinton. It is important to re-establish communication, that you may be reinforced. If practicable, come up on his rear at once. To beat such a detachment would be of immense value. The troops here could cooperate. . . ." To Richmond, however, Johnston wired his true feelings: "I arrived this evening, finding the enemy's force between this place and General Pemberton, cutting off communication. I am too late." Then he prepared to vacate Jackson and retreat to the northeast. What this meant, of course, was that Johnston expected Pemberton to do his fighting for him.[6]

Consider the pressures upon Pemberton at this point. A transplanted Pennsylvanian, and a West Pointer with more talent for administration than field command, he had wrestled with his conscience for weeks before casting his lot with his wife's native Virginia. Moreover he knew there were many Southerners—among them General William Loring, one of his division heads—who questioned both his loyalty and his competence. In this regard the coming of Johnston to the Vicksburg area must have felt like a slap in the face. Initially, however, Pemberton assured his superior that he would advance toward Clinton, albeit with reservations. "I move at once with whole available force . . . from Edwards Depot," he wrote. ". . . [But] I do not think you fully comprehend the position that Vicksburg will be left in." Pemberton had no inkling, of course, that Johnston, instead of advancing from Jackson to support him, actually was withdrawing from the city. He even expected reinforcements.

Only as the morning of May 14 wore on did warning bells sound. Pemberton crafted a compromise, at least in his own mind. He would go on the march, all right, but not on the attack. Instead of moving east, he would march south and cut off Grant's lines of communications—lines he did not know that Grant already had abandoned. "The object is to cut the enemy's communications and force him to attack me," he wrote Johnston in a follow-up dispatch, "as I do not consider my force sufficient to justify an attack on the enemy . . . or to attempt to cut my way to Jackson. . . . Whether it will be most practicable for the reinforcements to come by Raymond . . . or to move them west along the line of the railroad . . . you must determine."[7]

That same day, in a driving rainstorm, McPherson and Sherman closed in on the state capital, the former taking the Clinton Road to the north and the latter the Raymond Road to the south. Opposing them once again was the tenacious John Gregg, whom Johnston had left to fight a delaying action while he retreated with his main force and wagon trains to the northeast. McPherson's corps, with Marcellus Crocker's division in the van, first made contact with the enemy about 9:00 A.M., driving in the Rebel skirmishers. "Crocker . . . was dying of consumption when he volunteered," Grant would say. "[But] his weak condition never put him on the sick report when there was a battle in prospect." At this juncture McPherson, fearful that the heavy rains would make the men's cartridges useless, called a temporary halt. By 11:00 A.M., however, the rain had slackened and both Federal columns moved on the city.

The resulting action, tentative on the part of both McPherson and Sherman, would consume the next two and a half hours, giving Johnston all the time he needed for his retreat. On McPherson's front the well-entrenched enemy contested every bit of ground. The battle there ended when Crocker sent Colonel John Sanborn's brigade forward on the double-quick with fixed bayonets, taking casualties but clearing the road. Sherman on McPherson's right, finding his column blocked by massed cannon, saw he could not advance until he turned them. "Sherman was confronting a Rebel battery which enfiladed the road on which he was marching," said Grant, who was with Cump, ". . . and commanded a bridge spanning a stream over which he had to pass. . . . Appearances did not justify an assault where we were." James Tuttle, whom last we saw in the Hornet's Nest at Shiloh, was ordered to make a flanking movement. "This force, Tuttle's division, not returning," Grant continued, "I rode to the right with my staff, and soon found that the enemy had left that part of the line. . . . Tuttle had seen this and, passing through the lines without resistance, came up in the rear of the artillerists . . . and captured them."[8] By 1:30 P.M. the last of Gregg's troops had fallen back and the roads into Jackson were open. Federal casualties were 290; Confederate, 845.

Shouting and singing, Grant's mud-stained troops marched into the city, their spirits soaring with the knowledge it was the capital of Jefferson Davis's home state. Sergeant Osborn Oldroyd's only complaint was that the honor of being the first to enter went to Sherman's corps, not his own. His chagrin soon turned to compassion, however, when he encountered a dying Confederate on the roadside. Breaking ranks, he took his canteen and gave the soldier a swallow of water. "His piteous glance at me at that time I shall never forget," said Oldroyd. "It is on the battlefield and among the dead and dying we get to know each other—nay, even our own selves." His act was typical of the kindness, even tenderness, each side in the aftermath of battle would show the other's wounded throughout the war.

Fred Grant meanwhile, accompanied by Sylvanus Cadwallader, entered Jackson on a mission of his own. "As soon as the fire of the . . . batteries was silenced," said Cadwallader, ". . . [we] started for the Capitol at full speed to secure the large Confederate flag which waved from a staff on the roof. We supposed ourselves far in advance of anyone connected with the Union army. We dismounted hurriedly in front of the building, ran upstairs till we reached those leading from the garret to the roof, where we met a ragged, muddy, begrimed cavalryman descending with the coveted prize under his arm. To say that our disappointment was extreme but mildly expresses the state of our feelings." Foraging through the building later, the youngster walked into the governor's office and found one of his pipes. "I confiscated it," he would say, "ostensibly for the national service, but actually for my own private use. It had the advantage of being still loaded and lighted."[9]

That the Federal advance was so rapid it forced the Mississippi governor to leave behind a lit pipe is an exaggeration, but there is little doubt that anarchy temporarily reigned in the city. "The streets were filled with people, white and black," said Cadwallader, "who were carrying away all the stolen goods they could stagger under, without the slightest attempt at concealment, and without let or hindrance from citizens or soldiers . . . the era of stealing and plundering lasted through the evening and night of the 14th. . . ." Cadwallader made his way to the Bowman House, Jackson's finest hostelry, where presently he was joined by Grant, McPherson, Sherman, and members of their staffs. There Grant issued orders for Sherman's corps to take up the destruction of the railroads and all military stores. "[Frederick] Steele's division was set to work to destroy the railroad and property to the south and east," said Sherman, ". . . and Tuttle's division that to the north and west. This work . . . was well accomplished, and Jackson as a railroad center or Government depot of stores and military factories, [would] be of little use to the enemy for six months."

Grant himself, on at least one occasion, participated in the razing and burning. "Sherman and I went together into a manufactory which had not ceased work on account of the battle nor the entrance of Yankee troops," he said. "Our presence did not seem to attract the attention of either the manager or the operatives, most of whom were girls. We looked on for a while to see the tent cloth which they were making roll out of the looms, with 'C.S.A.' woven in each bolt. There was an immense amount of cotton, in bales, stacked outside. Finally I told Sherman I thought they had done work enough. The operatives were told they could leave and take with them what cloth they could carry. In a few minutes cotton and factory were in a blaze."

The destruction in Jackson would be widespread—and not entirely confined to military sites. "Foundries, machine-shops, warehouses, factories, arsenals and public stores were fired as fast as flames could be kindled," said Cadwallader. "[But] many citizens fled at our approach, abandoning houses . . . and all their personal property, without so much as locking their doors. The Negroes, poor whites—and it must be admitted— some bummers and stragglers from the ranks of the Union army—carried off thousands of dollars worth of property. . . ." Sherman would admit, reluctantly, to some excesses. "The penitentiary was burned, I think, by some convicts who had been set free by the Confederate authorities. . . . Other buildings were destroyed in Jackson by some mischievous soldiers (who could not be detected) . . . including the Catholic Church and Confederate Hotel—the former resulting from accidental circumstances and the latter from malice. . . . General [Joseph] Mower occupied the town with his brigade . . . and maintained as much order as he could among the mass of soldiers and camp-followers that thronged the place during our short stay there; yet many acts of pillage occurred that I regret. . . ."[10]

Grant spent the night of the 14th in Jackson, occupying the same room that Johnston had just vacated. But he was already making plans to turn on his heels and move west, having learned, through a stolen dispatch, of Johnston's order to Pemberton to take the field and attack his rear. Some months before, it seems, General Stephen Hurlbut, commanding in Memphis, had publicly exiled a man from the city on the grounds that he was a Southern sympathizer. In reality the offender was a Union stalwart, who as a result of the ruse found little difficulty becoming a Rebel courier. He had obtained a copy of Johnston's dispatch and passed it on. Intent on confronting Pemberton, Grant now ordered McPherson to turn about and march the next morning through Clinton to Bolton Station on the railroad—some twenty miles west of Jackson. McClernand was to join him there, and the two commands were then to proceed toward the enemy in the vicinity of Edwards Station. Sherman with two divisions was to stay in the city to finish up his work.

Johnston was not so well informed as Grant. On May 15th, some thirty-six hours after it was sent, he belatedly received Pemberton's message that he was heading south, not east, in a misguided attempt to cut Grant's non-existent lines of communications. Since this further increased the distance between the two Rebel armies, the news sent Johnston into a rage. Ignoring the fact that his withdrawal from Jackson was putting Pemberton in danger, he ordered him to countermarch to Edwards Station and turn east to face Grant in the field. "Our being compelled to leave Jackson makes your plan impracticable," he said. "The only mode by which we can unite is by your moving directly to Clinton, informing me, that we may move to that point with about 6,000 troops." While Pemberton reluctantly was obeying this order, Johnston then continued his retreat to the northeast, actually moving away from Clinton. It is obvious that Pemberton, with all his faults, was getting no support from his superior. With limited troop resources and even less resolve, Johnston would play no battlefield role in the grim days and weeks to come.[11]

Before leaving the Bowman House that morning, Grant and his staff received the bill for their stay. "Sixty dollars was the sum demanded by the proprietor for all their accommodations," said Cadwallader. "Lieut. Colonel Wilson thereupon took out a $100 bill in Confederate paper and handed it to the landlord. The latter seemed thunderstruck, and said that he had expected to be paid in U.S. coin, or greenbacks, or the charges would have been much higher."

"Very well," said Wilson, "charge what you please. We propose to pay you in Confederate money."

The bill was settled, on the latter basis, at ninety dollars.[12]

Daybreak on May 16 found three long Federal columns making their way west toward Edwards Station. The northernmost moved along the Jackson Road, led by Alvin Hovey's division of McClernand's corps, followed by Logan's and Crocker's divisions of McPherson's command. To their immediate left, on the so-called Middle Road, were Peter Osterhaus's and Eugene Carr's divisions, led by McClernand. These two roads would converge near Champion's Hill, where the Confederates were dug in, at a place simply known as the Crossroads. The southernmost column, several miles from the others on the Raymond Road but also under McClernand's command, consisted of Andrew Jackson Smith's and Frank Blair's divisions. All told, the seven divisions comprised sixteen brigades, totaling 32,000 men. Opposing them were Pemberton's three divisions of nine brigades, totaling 22,000. Positioned north to south, they were headed by Carter Stevenson, John Bowen, and William Loring.

The fact that Hovey was in the van of the Jackson Road column was sheer happenstance. "Logan's division had the advance in the morning and moved out of camp early and briskly, expecting to encounter Pemberton in the forenoon and having the honor of opening the battle," said Cadwallader. But such was not to be. "Logan and myself were near the head of his column . . . when we reached a road coming obliquely into ours from the one on which McClernand's advance was to be made, and . . . Hovey's division of the latter's corps was already half past. Logan was compelled to halt . . . then start on squarely in Hovey's rear. I rarely ever witnessed such an exhibition of rage, profanity and disappointment as Logan then gave. The air was just blue with oaths, till speech was exhausted. McPherson's arrival a few minutes after was the signal for another outburst. But there was no apparent remedy. . . ."[13]

Champion's Hill, in actuality a plateau some seventy feet high and midway between Edwards and Bolton Stations, dominated the Jackson Road and the surrounding countryside. Crisscrossed by ravines and gullies, covered by dense woods, it offered the Confederates under Carter Stevenson ideal concealment. If truth be told there might have been no battle there at all—Pemberton already was thinking of retiring to Vicksburg. But so speedily were the Federals coming up that he had little choice but to engage. Under Grant's watchful eye, Hovey's division fanned out across the road, McPherson and Logan moved to his right, and Crocker dispersed his troops in support. These three Federal divisions not only would initiate the fighting but, for reasons we shall see, would do all of it. Sergeant Charles Longley of the 24th Iowa, waiting to go into action, took comfort in Grant's granitelike presence: "The imperturbable face of the great commander appears, and a welcome but brief diversion is afforded as General Grant takes a look, asks a question, and moves on."

For Alvin Hovey the contest would be a defining moment. The Indiana lawyer had fought well at Port Gibson, but it was as a supporting player; now he was on center stage, launching an attack. "He works with all his might and all his mind," Charles Dana said of him, "and, unlike most volunteer officers, makes it his business to learn the military profession just as if he expected to spend his life in it."

The battle began in earnest about 10:30 A.M. "I ordered General [George] McGinnis and Colonel [James] Slack to press their skirmishers forward up the hill," said Hovey, "and follow them firmly with their respective brigades. In a few minutes the fire opened briskly along the whole line, from my extreme left to the right of the forces engaged under General McPherson. . . . For over 600 yards up the hill my division gallantry drove the enemy. The 11th Indiana . . . and 29th Wisconsin . . . captured the four guns on the brow of the hill. . . . The 46th Indiana drove the enemy from two guns on the right of the road . . . [the] 24th Iowa killed gunners and horses as it slashed through a battery of six guns."[14]

General McGinnis of the 1st Brigade gives us his report: "The whole line moved forward, with bayonets fixed, slowly, cautiously and in excellent order when, within about 75 yards of the battery every gun was opened upon us and every man went to the ground. As soon as the volley of grape and canister had passed over us, the order was given to charge . . . and so suddenly and apparently unexpected to the Rebels was the movement that, after a desperate conflict of five minutes . . . the battery of four guns was in our position." Soon, however, the enemy rallied. "The Rebels . . . being strongly reinforced . . . turned upon us and made a most determined stand. At this point occurred one of the most obstinate and murderous conflicts of the war. For half an hour each side took their turn in driving and being driven."

Colonel Slack's 2nd Brigade, caught up in the tangled terrain on McGinnis's left, now moved off the Jackson Road and farther left toward the Crossroads. In the front lines Sergeant Longley re-creates the scene: "We are advancing over rough ground, but steadily touching elbows, while the warming blood begins to be felt bounding through the veins and throbbing at the temples. . . . Onward and upward you go; thicker and faster falls the hissing hail. . . . Suddenly the added elevation brings to view a battery, and at the same instant the horrid howling of grape and cannister is upon us. . . ."

Following a halt to regroup, the assault resumed. "The more accustomed eye now detects here and there a gray-clad enemy marking their line at but a few rods distant. You note one, perhaps, striving to find shelter behind a slender tree—he is reloading, and, hastily withdrawing his rammer, uncovers the upper part of his body—instantly you aim and fire, and when he falls backward, throwing the useless gun over his head, you . . . scream aloud in the very frenzy of self-congratulation."

Initially both McGinnis and Slack were successful, the former taking the crest of the hill, the latter the Crossroads. Stevenson's Rebels on the left were reeling. "Every human instinct is carried away by a torrent of passion," Longley remembered, "while kill, *kill*, KILL seems to fill your heart. . . . Their backs are toward you—they fly—the line becomes a crowd—you pause only to fire—from one end of the regiment to the other the leaden hail converges upon that feted band; you see them plunging down in all directions, and shout with unnatural glee." But Federal charge produced Confederate countercharge, with the enemy throwing in more regiments and the tide of battle waxing and waning. "What next? Alas, there is no leader. . . . Confusion reigns. . . . There comes a new line of gray. Its head of column is already in our rear. . . . See that orderly sergeant in advance . . . Shoot at him? Yes; and all the rest while you may, for now they halt, front, and enfilade the road with a fire that patters in the dust like the big drops of a summer shower. . . ."[15]

For Captain George Wilhelm of the 56th Ohio, who later received the Medal of Honor for his gritty leadership, the battle seemed unending. "Five times a charge was made," he said, "and after each attempt we retreated part of the distance we had advanced. During the fifth charge I received a shot in my left breast, the bullet going through me. I reeled and fell, and was left on the field." Though Wilhelm was captured, he soon turned the tables on his guard. "I sprang forward, seized his musket and fixed it at his breast. . . . Then I led him, by a circuitous route, to the rear of our lines. It wasn't easy, for I could hardly walk myself. My wound pained me considerably. . . . However, I did not betray my own troubles to my prisoner."[16]

It was past noon, and Hovey in the forefront of Champion's Hill needed help if he was to hold his gains. He appealed to Crocker's division, which "was near at hand, and had not yet been under fire. I sent to them for support, but being unknown to the officers of that command, considerable delay (not less than half an hour) ensued." This mix-up had to be settled by Grant, who forthwith ordered a brigade to his support. Meantime Hovey's immediate salvation was the fierce assault that McPherson and Logan were delivering on the right of the Jackson Road lines, forcing Carter Stevenson to turn his attention elsewhere on the hill.

Wearing full-dress uniforms, McPherson and Logan, riding jet black and pure white stallions respectively, were inspirational as they galloped back and forth among their men. How they were not picked off by enemy bullets, God only knows.

"Give them Jesse boys, give them Jesse!" McPherson shouted. "We must whip them here or all go under the sod together!" Logan enjoined. "Give 'em hell!"

The Confederates greeted the Federal advance with a torrent of lead. One staff officer, making a report, "involuntarily and unconsciously screened his eyes with one hand, as one would shield his eyes from a driving rain." Then the cannoneers of the 1st Illinois wheeled four 24-pound howitzers to the front, blasting gaping holes in the enemy lines. Here the Rebels unwisely decided to rush the guns.

General Smith, they are charging with doubled column, said the German-American commanding the cannon with heavily accented English to General John E. Smith, one of Logan's brigadiers. *By damn it,* he added indignantly, *they want my guns.*

"Let 'em come," growled Smith. "We're ready."

The Rebel assault melted under grape and canister. "Forward— double-quick—march!" came Smith's orders, and the blue lines now surged forward in a charge of their own. "[We] plunged into the valley among the brush," said one soldier of the 31st Illinois, "struck and became commingled with the enemy . . . at the base of the hill, and with loud cheers drove them [back] . . . through the double formation that had lost all semblance of order. . . . [We] chased them without stopping to load or fire. . . . Hundreds of prisoners threw down their muskets."[17]

Grant observed the fleeing Rebels on the right with satisfaction. "A direct forward movement carried [Logan] over open fields," he said, "in rear of the enemy and in a line parallel to them. . . . Up to this time I had kept my position with Hovey, where we were the most heavily pressed, but about noon I moved with a part of my staff by our right around, until I came up with Logan himself. . . . He was actually in command of the only road over which the enemy could retreat." Here came Hovey's desperate call for reinforcements. "There were none to spare," said Grant. "I then gave an order to move McPherson's command by the left flank to Hovey.

This uncovered the Rebel line of retreat." It was now about 1:30 P.M., with the battle in the balance.[18]

While this bloodletting and maneuvering was going on, Osterhaus's and Carr's divisions under McClernand on the Middle Road did not enter the fray, though their van since early morning had been five hundred yards south of the Crossroads. There were reasons for this, but none was entirely convincing. Though the terrain was heavily wooded, severely restricting the sight lines, the din of battle had been heard for hours. It is true that Osterhaus was facing an enemy roadblock, but a determined push could have brushed it aside. McClernand's excuse would be, in part, that he was awaiting orders to advance. His 9:30 A.M. dispatch asking permission to do so was not received by Grant until noon; the written reply did not reach McClernand until after 2:00 P.M. Grant had no use for this self-justification, believing that his subordinate should have marched to the sound of the guns. "I sent him repeated orders by staff officers fully competent to explain to him the situation," he said. "These traversed the wood separating us . . . and directed him to push forward; but he did not come."

Whatever McClernand's motives for not advancing, they served Pemberton's purposes. Realizing that the Federal center was immobile, he withdrew John Bowen from his own center—gambling that McClernand would not be a fector—and sent him about 2:30 P.M. to Stevenson's support in a vicious counterattack. In the forefront, falling on Colonel Slack's unit at the Crossroads, was Colonel Francis Cockrell's Missouri brigade. Slack's men, finding themselves under fire from two directions, were forced to fall back. "As I turned to fire, my musket being at prime," said one Ohio soldier, "a bullet from the enemy struck the barrel of my gun, the ball exploding. . . . Four small pieces were buried in the back of my hand. . . . My Enfield was in the right place to save me from the fate of my comrades."

Moving through the Crossroads, with other Confederates on their right, Cockrell's men now headed toward McGinnis on Champion's Hill. "We gave them the Missouri yell," said a sergeant in the 5th Missouri, ". . . We routed them and took after them . . . in about three hundred yards we came to another line . . . they raised on their knees and gave us a fire, we kept crawling on them until we got, in many places, within ten paces of them." Here too the Federals were pushed back. "Having been engaged in a continual conflict for nearly three hours," said McGinnis, "our ammunition being nearly exhausted, many of the men being entirely out . . . and relying upon what they could get from the boxes of the dead and wounded, the 1st Brigade began to fall back. . . ." By 3:00 P.M. the Rebels had retaken the crest of the hill.[19]

To blunt Bowen's thrust, Grant at this juncture found Colonel George Boomer's 1,500-man 3rd Brigade, Crocker's command, and sent it into the maelstrom. "Forward! Forward, double-quick!" came the order as Boomer's men rushed up the hill, passing through McGinnis's riddled brigade. With no time to fix bayonets, said Samuel Byers of the 5th Iowa, "we were charging the enemy's position with bare muskets. . . . A moment more, and we were at the top of the ascent, and among thinner wood. . . . The enemy had fallen back a few rods, forming a solid line. . . . For half an hour, we poured the hot lead into each others' faces. We had forty rounds each in our cartridge boxes and, probably, nine-tenths of them were fired in that half hour. . . . I tried to keep cool, and determined to fire no shot without taking aim; but a slight wound in my hand ended my coolness, and the smoke of the battle soon made aim-taking mere guessing."

In the midst of the fight, Byers encountered a youngster no more than sixteen. "My regiment—my regiment is gone—has run! What shall I do?" the lad asked.

" 'Here's the place,' I said, 'pitch in!' and pitch in he did. He was of metal, that boy, and kept his place with the bravest veteran in the line. Hotter and hotter grew the fight, and soon this same boy cried: 'Look—look behind us,' and, sure enough, the regiment to our left had disappeared and we were flanked." Boomer had fought Cockrell to a draw, losing one-third of his men in the process, but more of Bowen's troops were coming up on his left. " 'Stop! Halt! Surrender!' cried a hundred Rebels," said Byers, "whose voices seem to ring in my ears to this very day. But there was no stopping, and no surrender. We ran, and ran manfully . . . the enemy on flank and rear. . . . We tried to halt, and tried to form. It was no use. Again we ran, and harder. . . ."

Grant already had faced many crises, and this counterattack of Bowen's was just one more to overcome. Calmly, almost analytically, he took stock of his situation. "Hovey's division and Boomer's brigade are good troops," he remarked to an officer, "and if the enemy has driven them, he is not in good plight himself. If we can go in again here and make a little showing, I think he will give way."[20]

Here Grant committed the last of Crocker's units, the brigade of Colonel Samuel Holmes, placing it squarely across the Jackson Road. To the left was Slack's depleted command, which nonetheless had kept good order in its withdrawal from the Crossroads; to the right was another of Crocker's brigades, that of Colonel John Sanborn. Backing them Grant had massed all the cannon he could muster. His position was well chosen. When Bowen's troops emerged from the woods in their headlong charge down the hill, they found themselves funneled into an exposed and narrow front no more than four hundred yards wide. Immediately a hail of grape, canister, and musket balls tore through their ranks. Byers of the 5th Iowa, running for his life, described the 4:00 P.M. turnabout. "Grant had seen it all," he said of the stunning reversal, "and in less time than I can tell a line of cannon had been thrown across our path, which as soon as we had passed, belched [fire] in the faces of our pursuers. They stopped, they turned, and they too ran, and left their dead side by side with our own. Our lines, protected by the batteries, rallied and followed, and Champion's Hill was won."[21]

Losses during the contest were the most severe of the campaign. Federal casualties in Hovey's, Logan's, and Crocker's commands totaled more than 2,400—half of them in Hovey's division; Confederate casualties were even greater—nearly 4,000. "I cannot think of this bloody hill without sadness and pride," Hovey would say in the battle's aftermath. "Sadness for the great loss of my true and gallant men; pride for the heroic bravery they displayed. . . . I never saw fighting like this."

Charles Dana, riding over to John Logan's command along with John Rawlins, would find that Logan could not, or would not, believe the fighting was over. "We found him greatly excited. He declared the day was lost, and that he would soon be swept from his position. I contested the point. 'Why, general,' I said, 'we have gained the day.'

"He could not see it. 'Don't you hear the cannon over there?' he answered. 'They will be down on us right away! In an hour I will have 20,000 men to fight.'

"I found afterward that this was simply a curious idiosyncrasy of Logan's. In the beginning of a fight he was one of the bravest men that could be, saw no danger, went right on fighting till the battle was over. Then, after [it] was won, his mind gained an immovable conviction that it was lost. . . . It did not in the least impair his value as a soldier or commanding officer."

Late that night correspondent Cadwallader, in a letter to his wife back in Milwaukee, summed up the anguish: "We had another terrible battle. . . . The rattle of musketry was incessant for hours. Cannons thundered till the heavens seemed bursting. Dead men, and wounded, lay strewed everywhere. . . . The army is absolutely nomadic. We march and fight alternately. . . . I find it impossible to get a list of the killed. . . . My heart sickens at the suspense many families must suffer."

Samuel Byers, serving in Crocker's division, put the matter in still more personal terms. "It was midnight before we halted for the night," he said, "and then, before lying down, we called the roll, and found how many comrades were left coldly sleeping under the magnolias of [Champion's Hill]. My best friend was killed, and our mess had three that night instead of the six who had shared our rations in the morning at reveille. . . ."[22]

By the next morning, May 17, the two armies again were facing each other, this time at a bridgehead on the east bank of the Big Black River, whence Pemberton had retreated. Grant must have been smarting over McClernand's lack of support the day before, but he still took no disciplinary action against him. "Had McClernand come up with reasonable promptness," he would content himself with saying, ". . . I cannot see how Pemberton could have escaped." The Confederate commander, for his part, had his own disloyal subordinate—the disputatious William Loring, who with his division had been guarding the southernmost Raymond Road, and who throughout the fighting at Champion's Hill had refused to march to the north and engage, leaving the fighting to Stevenson and Bowen. During the night of the 16th, left behind as the rear guard, Loring had simply disappeared. Now Pemberton was holding the east bank behind earthworks, rather than crossing the river with his entire force and burning the Big Black Bridge behind him, in the vain hope Loring would rejoin him.

Meanwhile, the Confederate commander had made a momentous choice. Instead of eventually moving north along the west side of the river with an eye toward joining Johnston, he would defend Vicksburg at all costs. Sensitive to whispers about his Yankee birth, he was taking literally Jefferson Davis's instructions to hold the city, not seeing that circumstances made it impracticable. Perhaps he thought that Johnston, a fine tactician but no hot-blooded fighter, would somehow raise a substantial force and march to his aid. Grant at this point was elated. "We were now assured of our position between Johnston and Pemberton," he said, "without a possibility of a junction of their forces. Pemberton might have made a night march to the Big Black . . . and, by moving north . . . have eluded us and finally returned to Johnston. But this would have given us Vicksburg. It would have been his proper move, however, and the one Johnston would have made had he been in Pemberton's place."[23]

The temporary Confederate position on the Big Black, opposite the

Mississippi Southern Railroad, seemed a strong one. A shallow bayou, felled trees, and earth-covered cotton bales protected the front, while both flanks were anchored on the river. Though Carter Stevenson's division had crossed earlier, rugged John Bowen with five thousand men was holding the bridgehead, fruitlessly waiting for Loring. Facing them were Eugene Carr's division on the Federal right, Peter Osterhaus's in the center, and Andrew Jackson Smith's on the left, all under McClernand; in reserve was McPherson's corps, which had fought so well at Champion's Hill.

Just as the engagement was getting under way, about noontime under a broiling sun, Grant received via courier an order from General-in-Chief Halleck, dated May 11, to return to Grand Gulf and cooperate with Banks to take Port Hudson, and only then to return with a combined force and besiege Vicksburg. He ignored this latest attempt on Old Brains's part to micromanage the war. "I told the officer that the order came too late, and that Halleck would not give it now if he knew our position. The bearer of the dispatch insisted that I ought to obey . . . and was giving me arguments when I heard great cheering to the right of our line and, looking in that direction saw [Michael] Lawler in his shirt sleeves leading a charge upon the enemy. I immediately mounted my horse . . . and saw no more of the officer who had delivered the dispatch."[24]

Michael Kelly Lawler, who came to America from Ireland with his parents when he was two years old, had migrated from the East Coast to Illinois and there married the daughter of a well-to-do landowner. Following service as a company officer in the Mexican War, he began farming on a large scale in Shawneetown, Illinois, where he also opened a general store. Enrolled in the Union army as the colonel of the 18th Illinois, the devoutly Roman Catholic Lawler enforced discipline with an iron hand—knocking down shirkers with his fists, feeding drunks emetics, and threatening violence to naysayers. Irrepressible, flamboyant, hot-tempered; these were the terms used to describe him. Now a 250-pound brigadier who wore his sword belt over his shoulder because he could not get it around his waist, he had both admirers and detractors. "General Lawler was . . . a fine type of the generous, rollicking, fighting Irishman," Cadwallader would say. "His cherished maxim was the Tipperary one: 'If you see a head, hit it.' " Sniffed Charles Dana: "He is as brave as a lion, and has about as much brains." Grant would give him the ultimate accolade: "When it comes to just plain hard fighting, I would rather trust old Mike Lawler than any of them."[25]

Hard fighting it would be indeed when Lawler, serving under Carr, neared the extreme right of the Rebel bridgehead, and—mirabile dictu—found it vulnerable. There heavy rains had washed away felled trees and obstructions from a streambed, providing his troops both passage and concealment. Giving up firepower for speed, he moved his men forward four abreast in column rather than line of battle, using the streambed to narrow the distance to the enemy lines. Then, Lawler said, rang out the command: *Charge!* "Colonel William Kinsman, and at once [the 23rd Iowa] sprang forward to the works. The 21st [Iowa] . . . moved at the same instant, the 11th Wisconsin . . . closely following." A hail of musketry greeted them. "Kinsman fell, dangerously wounded, before half the distance was accomplished. Struggling to his feet, he staggered a few paces to the front, cheered forward his men, and fell again, this time to rise no more, pierced through by a second ball." Colonel Samuel Merrill, the commander of the 21st Iowa, likewise went down, suffering a severe wound.

Despite the loss of these officers the three regiments pressed on, double-quicking 500 yards under unrelenting fire and within minutes coming up to the protective bayou. "Halting here only long enough to pour into the enemy a deadly volley," said Lawler, "they dashed forward through the bayou . . . on to the Rebel works with the shout of victors, driving the enemy in with confusion from their breastworks and rifle-pits. . . ."

These were the cheers that Grant had heard in the midst of reading Halleck's dispatch. Two supporting regiments, the 49th and 69th Indiana, quickly advanced to exploit Lawler's gains. They were followed by other units all along the line, all inspired by his example. One such regiment was the 99th Illinois, which up to this time had been crouching under enemy fire. "Boys, it is getting too damned hot here!" its colonel yelled. "Let's go for the cussed Rebels!" Marveled a soldier in the 33rd Illinois: "Others to the right and left, without a moment's delay or a single command, joined in . . . and thus with wild cheers the entire Union line joined in a charge upon the Rebel works."[26]

If Grant was disturbed that Lawler had initiated the attack without specific orders, he was more than satisfied with the results. "The enemy fled from the west bank of the river," he said, "burning the bridge behind him and leaving the men and guns on the east bank to fall into our hands. Many tried to escape by swimming the river. Some succeeded and some drowned in the attempt. Eighteen guns were captured and 1,751 prisoners. Our loss was 39 killed, 237 wounded and 3 missing. The enemy probably lost but few men except those captured and drowned. But for . . . the destruction of the bridge I have but little doubt that we should have followed the enemy so closely as to prevent his occupying the defenses around Vicksburg."

Even while his troops were hurriedly laying down new spans to take them across the Big Black, Grant sent off a note to Sherman, who by now had rejoined the army, reflecting his belief that the Rebels had lost the will to fight: "The enemy have been so terribly beaten yesterday and today that I cannot believe a stand still will be made [at Vicksburg] unless the troops are relying on Johnston's arrival. . . ." He would be wrong about this, unfortunately, as subsequent events will prove.

Late that night the two men nonetheless watched with pride as the Federal army filed across the river on a pontoon bridge, its march lit by huge fires of pitch pine. "We sat on a log," Sherman said, "looking at the passage of the troops by the light of those fires; the bridge swayed to and fro under the passing feet, and made a fine war picture." They had every reason for their elation. Grant's advance into the Mississippi heartland had been a smashing success. Pemberton would make a stand inside the Vicksburg defenses, but his doom was foreordained.[27]

FOUR
* * * *

SIEGE OF VICKSBURG

By the morning of May 19 the 40,000-man Army of the Tennessee had completely invested the city. Sherman's 15th Corps was on the right, covering the high ground from where it overlooked the Yazoo as far southeast as his troops could extend. McPherson's 17th Corps was on his left, on both sides of the Jackson Road directly east of Vicksburg. McClernand's 13th Corps took up the ground on the far left, extending toward Warrenton in an unbroken line. Now it became evident that Vicksburg's landside defenses were as imposing as its riverside cannon. They stretched for eight miles in the rear of the city, anchored at intervals by small forts. "The main works," said Major Samuel H. Lockett, Pemberton's chief engineer, ". . . had, for the most part, exterior ditches from six to ten feet deep, with rampart, parapet, banquette for infantry, and embrasures and platforms for artillery." Trees had been felled in front—clearing the line of fire—and interlaced with sharpened stakes, creating daunting abatis. While the heavy batteries on the river had been left intact to check Admiral Porter's gunboats, the rest of the artillery had shifted to the landside, which now boasted some 100 guns.

The withdrawal had forced the Confederates to give up Haynes' and Snyder's Bluffs, thereby exposing the Yazoo to the enemy. Pemberton with perhaps 28,000 men at this juncture had just received Johnston's latest discouraging message: "If Haynes' Bluff is untenable, Vicksburg is of no value and cannot be held. . . . Instead of losing both troops and place, we must, if possible, save the troops. If it is not too late, evacuate [the city]." He nonetheless remained resolute, telling Johnston: "I have decided to hold Vicksburg as long as it is possible . . . that the government may yet be able to assist me in keeping this obstruction to the enemy's free navigation of the Mississippi."[1]

Grant meanwhile remained sanguine that Vicksburg would fall without a lengthy siege. Knowing that Johnston was somewhere in his rear, but not knowing his ingrained reluctance to fight, he determined to take the city by storm. At 2:00 P.M. he ordered a general advance. Sherman's troops, who at 500 yards distant were closest to the Rebel lines, promptly pushed forward across open ground on the Graveyard Road, enduring withering cannon and small arms fire as they went. Colonel Thomas Kilby Smith, a former law clerk of Salmon P. Chase, Lincoln's Secretary of the Treasury, was in the van. Now commanding the 2nd brigade in Frank Blair's division, he realized he was in trouble from the outset. "It was almost vain to essay a line," he said, ". . . yet three times, under a most galling and destructive fire, did these regiments halt and dress their colors. . . . Having advanced some four hundred yards, I discovered that the men were thoroughly exhausted, and halted the left wing under the crest of a hill, some sixty-five to seventy-five yards from the ditch and parapet, and where they were comparatively sheltered."

Here Smith chose not to order his troops further, saying, "A few men could have been got over by aid of a ladder of bayonets or digging holes in the embankment, but these would have gone to destruction." Besides, the sharpshooters of the enemy "were picking off our officers with devilish skill."

Captain Charles Ewing of the 13th U.S. Regulars, advancing toward the Stockade Redan, a small fort near the Graveyard Road, met similar resistance. Many of the Rebels had armed themselves with extra muskets, giving them added firepower. "Our brave boys moved over the hill at the double-quick through a most deadly cross-fire," said one of the regulars, ". . . Our comrades were now falling around us at every step, some killed instantly, others having an arm or leg shot off, and wounds of all descriptions." When three of the 13th's color bearers went down within minutes, Ewing seized the flag himself, rushed close to the Stockade Redan and defiantly planted the staff in the dirt—just as a bullet took off one of his fingers. Then he and the survivors huddled in the ditch outside, waiting for nightfall to retreat.

Up and down the lines the Federals likewise were repulsed. "The hard fact was that Confederate morale had not been shattered, as Grant believed," one historian observed. "Days of marching under confused orders, of piecemeal fighting . . . found the back of Johnny Reb stiffening as he fell back into the prepared defenses around Vicksburg. Grant had to come and get him now in a frontal attack, the meanest sort of fight there was. Pemberton's troops . . . still possessed a lot of nastiness." Union casualties this day would total 942—three-quarters of them in Sherman's corps; Confederate losses were some 200.[2]

Still reluctant to launch a siege, Grant over the next two days prepared for a second frontal attack. "The 20th and the 21st were spent strengthening our position and in making roads in rear of the army, from Yazoo River or Chickasaw Bayou," he said. One reason for the roads was to bring up rations; the countryside had provided ample food, but the troops had not enjoyed bread and coffee for some time. "I remember that in passing around to the left of the line on the 21st, a soldier, recognizing me, said in rather a low voice, but yet so I heard him, 'Hard tack.' In a moment the cry was taken up all along the line, 'Hard tack! Hard Tack!' I told the men nearest to me that we had been engaged . . . in building a road over which to supply them. . . . The cry was instantly changed to cheers. By the night all the troops had full rations issued to them."

At 10:00 A.M. on the 22nd, in the midst of a deafening artillery exchange, the Federal assault on the Vicksburg lines resumed. On Sherman's front it was led by 150 volunteers called the "forlorn hope"—essentially a suicide squad carrying logs and planks to span the ditch in front of Stockade Redan and create a pathway for the men behind them. Their ranks leveled by musket balls, no more than a handful reached the ditch, where they crouched impotently at point-blank distance from the enemy, able neither to advance nor fall back. One man, Private Howell Trogden of the 8th Missouri, did manage to climb out of the trench, planting a battle flag beneath the redan's parapet before retiring. "The Confederates tried to capture it by hooking it in with the shanks of their bayonets," said one of his comrades, Corporal Robert Cox of the 55th Illinois, "but failed, owing to the hot fire kept up by the sharpshooters [behind us]. Thereupon Trogden asked me for my gun to give the enemy a thrust. . . . I concluded to try it myself. I raised my head again . . . pushed my gun across the intervening space . . . gave their bayonets a swipe with mine, and dodged down just in time to escape being riddled."

Behind the forlorn hope, Sherman's attacking regiments for two hours could do little but hunker down. One of his officers, Major Gustavus Lightfoot of the 12th Missouri, passed out the last of his cigars. "Take them," he said. "I will have no further use for cigars. This is my last smoke!" Acknowledged Sherman: "The enemy rose behind their parapet and poured a furious fire upon our lines. . . . We had a severe and bloody battle, but at every point we were repulsed."[3]

McPherson's corps on the Jackson Road likewise endured a hail of lead from the Rebel entrenchments. Wilbur Crummer of the 45th Illinois, Logan's division, found himself double-quicking across 200 yards of open ground, his major falling dead by his side at the first volley from the enemy. ". . . There was no one to give the command to halt, or right face and charge; the major was killed and the ranking captain didn't know it. We went as far . . . as we thought sufficient for the regiment to form in line of battle. . . . I kept right on at the head . . . to form in line under the brow of the hill. The ground sloped downhill under the enemy's parapet, and by flattening one's self . . . [I] was comparatively safe from the musketry fire."

Here too the Federals were thwarted. "The order to charge was, after a short time, given by the ranking captain," said Crummer, "and we started up the hill, to be met by a sweeping volley of musketry at short range which mowed the men down in bunches. We could not return the fire, for the enemy was safe behind their breastworks. Some of our men reached the top of the parapet, but fell as fast as they climbed up. No troops could face such a destructive fire. . . ."[4]

Only on McClernand's front, to the far left, did the Union forces achieve modest success. The indomitable General Lawler, attacking the Railroad Redoubt with his Iowa brigade, managed to get a dozen men inside an outlying gun embrasure in hand-to-hand fighting—though at the cost of 368 casualties. The result was a standoff, with the enemy temporarily withdrawing to the main line of defense.

Elsewhere McClernand's advance, said Cadwallader, "had been so mercilessly torn to pieces by Confederate shot and shell that it had lost nearly all resemblance to . . . a storming column. Officers and men were rushing ahead pell-mell without much attention to alignment." The closer his troops got, however, the less the enemy artillery was a factor, since the guns could not be depressed sufficiently. "When they crossed the deep ditch in front of the earthworks . . . they were out of musketry range for the same reason. . . . A straggling line, growing thinner and weaker, finally reached the summit, when all who were not instantly shot down were pulled over the Rebel breastworks as prisoners."

One such fortunate prisoner-to-be was Private Thomas Higgins, the color-bearer of the 99th Illinois. "As fast as practiced hands could gather them up, one after another, muskets were brought to bear," remembered one Texas defender. "The blue lines vanished amid fearful slaughter. There was a cessation in the firing. And behold, through the pall of smoke which enshrouded the field, a Union flag could be seen approaching." It was borne by Private Higgins. "At least a hundred men took deliberate aim at him . . . but he never faltered. Stumbling over the bodies of his fallen comrades, he continued to advance. Suddenly . . . every Confederate soldier seemed to be seized with the idea the man should not be shot down like a dog. . . . Each of them seized his nearest neighbor by the arm and yelled at him, 'Don't shoot at that man again. He is too brave to be killed that way.' "

"Come on, Yank! Come on!" the Texans yelled. Higgins did just that, and once inside the breastworks, completely unscratched, found a hundred elated defenders vying to shake his hand and pat him on the back. Years later, in part because of their recommendations, he was awarded the Medal of Honor.[5]

It was noon, and the fighting should have come to a close everywhere. But McClernand, eager for glory, now exaggerated his minor success at the Railroad Redoubt and sent Grant the following message: "We are hotly engaged with the enemy. We have part possession of two forts, and the Stars and Stripes are floating over them. A vigorous push ought to be made all along the line."

"I don't believe a word of it," said Grant to Sherman, who was with him at the time. Cump, whose mood swings could range from the audacious to the bureaucratic, at this point played the pedant.

"I reasoned with [Grant] that this note was official," he stated, "and must be credited, and I offered to renew the assault at once." Grant hesitated, then gave the go-ahead. Shortly after 2:00 P.M. Sherman and McPherson moved anew toward the Vicksburg defenses. The second assault," said Sherman, "was a repetition of the first, equally unsuccessful and bloody. It also transpired that the same thing had occurred with General McPherson, who lost . . . some most valuable officers and men, without adequate result; and that General McClernand, instead of having taken any single point of the Rebel main parapet, had only taken one or two small outlying lunettes . . . where his men were at the mercy of the Rebels. . . . This affair caused great feeling with us, and severe criticisms on General McClernand."

Just before the second assault Grant had reinforced the Illinois politician with Isaac Quinby's division. Here Cadwallader, an eyewitness to events, takes up the story and censures McClernand all the more: "Instead of using Quinby as a support to his own troops, McClernand ordered them to the front in the . . . hope of retrieving the fortunes of the day, and attempted to make a second assault, with some of his own demoralized troops, on Quinby's flank. One of his colonels flatly refused to obey this order and declared he would take the consequences of his disobedience rather than lead his men to certain death."

Cadwallader, later reporting his observations to Grant and Rawlins, said he would never forget "the grim glowering look of disappointment and disgust [that] settled down on Grant's usually placid countenance, when he was convinced of McClernand's duplicity, and its cost in dead and wounded."[6] Federal casualties would total 3,200—at least half of them coming in the second, needless attack. Confederate casualties were less than 500.

For two days the Federal dead lay on the field, rotting and decomposing, with the wounded suffering unimaginable torment. Grant was unwilling to call a truce to tend to them, lest it be interpreted by the enemy as a sign of weakness. The sight was hideous, the smell was worse. Finally Pemberton on May 25 took the initiative, sending Grant a note: "In the name of humanity, I have the honor to propose a cessation of hostilities for two hours and a half, that you may be enabled to remove your dead and dying men. . . ." His own troops, he added, would help. The offer was accepted, and at the appointed time both sides set about clearing the field, and once it was completed mixed freely in front of the lines. Some Confederates, in fact, even were invited into the Federal camps.

"Here a group of four played cards—two Yanks and two Rebs," noted Osborn Oldroyd of the 20th Ohio. ". . . Everywhere blue and gray mingled in conversation over the scenes which had transpired . . . From the remarks of some of the Rebels, I judged that their supply of provisions was getting low. . . . We gave them from our own rations some fat meat, crackers, coffee and so forth . . . to make them as happy as we could." Officers of both sides, of course, used the truce to record the enemy's positions and possible points of weakness. Sherman, bearing some letters from Northerners to Southern friends, at this juncture approached Confederate Major Lockett. "I thought this would be a good opportunity to deliver this mail before it got too old," he said. Then the two men sat down on a log and made small talk.

"You have an admirable position for defense here, and have taken excellent advantage of the ground," Sherman allowed.

"Yes, General," the chief engineer jibed, "but it is as equally well adapted to offensive operations." To this Sherman cheerfully assented.

"Intentionally or not," admitted Lockett, "his civility certainly prevented me from seeing many other points in our front that I . . . was very anxious to examine."

Elsewhere on the field, with the truce ending, the two sides took their leave. One Union officer, who had been sharing his food and drink with a Confederate captain, extended his hand: "Good day, captain; I trust we shall meet again in the Union of old."

"I cannot return your sentiment," said the Confederate with a smile, taking the proffered hand. "The only union which you and I will enjoy, I hope, will be in kingdom come. Goodbye, sir."[7]

Now the lengthy siege of Vicksburg began in earnest, testing civilians as well as soldiers. "The Federals fought the garrison in part, but the city mainly," said Edward S. Gregory, a resident. "Hardly any [section] . . . was outside the range of the enemy's artillery from any direction except the south. . . . Just across the Mississippi, a few days after the lines were closed, seven 11- and 13-inch mortars were put in position and trained directly on the homes of the people; and if any one of them was silent from that time till the white flag was raised any longer than . . . to cool and load it, I fail to recall the occasion." These mortars were only part of the barrage—which included Admiral Porter's shellfire from the river, but they were particularly demoralizing—"rising steadily and shiningly in great parabolic curves, descending with ever-increasing swiftness, and falling with deafening shriek and explosion; hurling in many a radius their ponderous fragments."

Seeking protection from the cannon blasts, many civilians dug extensive caves in the sloping ground and moved their living and sleeping quarters there. "Imagine to yourself . . . a good-sized parapet, about six feet high, a path cut through, and then the entrance to a cave," said Mrs. W. W. Lord, wife of an Episcopal clergyman, who with her four children was sharing such a refuge with eight or more other families. ". . . Secured strongly with boards, it is dug the height of a man and about forty feet under the hill. It communicates with [a second] cave which is about the same length and opens out on the other side of the hill—this gives us a good circulation of air. . . . I have a little closet for provisions, and niches for flowers, lights and books—inside just by the little walk is our eating table with an arbor over it and back of that our fireplace and kitchen. . . ." Wrote Dora Richards Miller, a Union sympathizer living with her husband for most of the time in her cellar: "The fiery shower of shells goes on day and night. . . . People do nothing but eat what they can get, sleep when they can, and dodge the shells. There are three intervals when the shelling stops . . . for the gunners' meals, I suppose—about eight in the morning, the same in the evening, and at noon. In that time we have both to prepare and eat ours. . . . The cellar is so damp and musty the bedding has to be carried out and laid in the sun every day. . . . The confinement is dreadful."

Mrs. James Loughborough, who had recently arrived in Vicksburg to join her soldier husband, tried to remain in her home, but the shelling finally forced her to flee to a cave. The next morning, returning to her house to inspect it, she found that "the room that I had so lately slept in had been struck and a large hole made in the ceiling." The caves, she said, "were plainly becoming a necessity." Still, they offered no respite from fear. "I endeavored by constant prayer to prepare myself for the sudden death I was almost certain awaited me. My heart stood still as we would hear . . . the rushing and fearful sound of the shell as it came toward us."[8]

Going into the streets on shopping expeditions was a challenge. "You must understand that it was not in the usual way we walked down the street," wrote Emma Balfour in her diary, "but had to take the middle . . . when we heard a shell, and watch for it. You may imagine our progress was not very fast. As soon as a shell gets over your head you are safe for, even if it approaches near, the pieces fall forward . . . but the danger is that sometimes, while watching one, another comes . . . 'ere you are aware."

Food, even in the early days of the siege, was in scarce supply. "I am so tired of corn-bread . . . that I eat it with tears in my eyes," said Mrs. Miller. "We are lucky to get a quart of milk daily from a family who have a cow they hourly expect to be killed. I send five dollars to market each morning, and it buys a small piece of mule-meat. Rice and milk is my main food; I can't eat the mule-meat." Her cellar did have one advantage— a plentiful supply of water. "This place has two large underground cisterns of good cool water, and every night in my subterranean dressing room a tub of cold water is the nerve-calmer that sends me to sleep in spite of the roar. One cistern I had to give up to the soldiers, who swarm about like hungry animals seeking something to devour. Poor fellows! They have nothing but spoiled, greasy bacon, and bread made of musty pea-flour, and but little of that. The sick ones can't bolt it."[9]

By early June the Rebels and their Federal counterparts were settled in their roles—the former stoically enduring the siege, the latter incessantly shelling the city and moving ever closer to the defenses through a network of trenches. They did this in part by the use of "sap-rollers," which essentially were meant to stop enemy bullets while soldiers pushed them forward and dug into the ground behind them. "Suppose we take two empty barrels and lash them together, one on top of the other," said Wilbur Crummer of the 45th Illinois, "then wrap them round and round with willow saplings, fill them with earth, put a cover on, lay them down, and you have a sap-roller." To facilitate the trench construction, Grant directed that all officers who had graduated from West Point, where engineering was a required subject, should besides their other duties supervise the work. He made an exception for the rotund Robert Macfeeley, his chief commissary officer, who claimed there was no kind of engineering he was good for unless it was sap-rolling. "As soldiers require rations . . . and as we would be sure to lose him if he was used as a sap-roller," said Grant, "I let him off. The general is a large man; weighs two hundred and twenty pounds, and is not tall."

The Confederates had their own answer, at least at first, for the sap-rolling devices. "A private soldier suggested a novel expedient by which we succeeded in destroying the rollers," said Major Lockett. "He took a piece of port-fire, stuffed it with cotton saturated with turpentine, and fired it from an old-fashioned large-bore musket into the roller, and set it on fire. Thus the enemy's sappers were exposed and forced to leave their sap and begin a new one some distance back. After this they kept their sap-rollers wet, forcing us to other expedients."[10]

Though Grant did not betray it, he was under increasing strain. The siege work was going slowly, and there was always the nagging worry that Johnston, reinforced, would cross the Big Black and fall on the Union rear. Nonetheless he went about his duties with apparent unconcern. "The common soldiers saw Grant daily," said S.H.M. Byers of the 5th Iowa, "not exhibiting himself for the sake of being cheered and cheaply glorified, but patiently examining the little details necessary to the safety and comfort of the army." Sometimes, making his rounds, he even exposed himself to enemy fire. On at least one occasion a Minnesota private, slow to recognize the rumpled figure, impatiently yelled for him to take cover: "You old _____, you'd better keep down off of there or you'll be shot!"[11]

During this period of relative inactivity we come to the single worst instance by far of Grant's supposed Civil War drinking—one luckily that did no harm to him or to his command. Many have been the reasons advanced for his escapade—his military concerns, his six-week separation from Julia, the temporary absence of the hovering Rawlins. Moreover, convivial off-duty drinking among officers was commonplace—a way of releasing tension. But Grant was not just any officer. He was the commander of the Army of the Tennessee, and the fact was that on June 6 he embarked on a heedless, two-day drinking bout. It all began aboard the steamer *Diligence,* which he was taking on an inspection trip to Satartia, up the Yazoo River. Here Charles Dana, who was with Grant, gives us his discreet—and abbreviated—version of what took place:

"Grant was ill and went to bed soon after he started. We had gone up the river to within two miles of Satartia, when we met two gunboats coming down. Seeing the general's flag, the officers in charge came aboard . . . and asked where the general was going. I told them to Satartia."

"Why," said they, 'It will not be safe. [General Nathan] Kimball has retreated from there, and is sending all his supplies to Haynes' Bluff. The enemy is probably in the town now.'

"I told them Grant was sick and asleep," said Dana, "and that I did not want to waken him. They insisted that it was unsafe to go on, and that I would better call the general. Finally I did so, but he was too sick to decide."

"I will leave it to you," Grant supposedly said. Dana immediately gave the order to head for Haynes' Bluff.

"The next morning," Dana continued, "Grant came out to breakfast fresh as a rose, clean shirt and all, quite himself. 'Well, Mr. Dana,' he said, 'I suppose we are at Satartia now.'

" 'No, general,' I said, 'We are at Haynes' Bluff.' And I told him what had happened. He did not complain, but as he was short of officers at that point he asked me to go with a party of cavalry . . . to find out if it was true, as reported, that Joe Johnston was advancing from Canton to the Big Black." With that, Dana left the *Diligence* and was not privy to subsequent events. "We had a hard ride," he would say of his lengthy scouting expedition, "not getting back to Vicksburg until the morning of the eighth. . . . We found out that Johnston had not moved his main force. . . ."[12]

This was the gist of Dana's account, more interesting for what it left out about Grant's indiscretion than what it contained. Far more lurid was the story related by Sylvanus Cadwallader, who also was aboard the *Diligence*—a tale he did not tell until 1896 when he was in his seventies. On June 6, said Cadwallader, "I was not long in perceiving that Grant had been drinking heavily, and that he was still keeping it up. He made several trips to the bar room of the boat . . . and became stupid in speech and staggering in gait. This was the first time he had shown symptoms of intoxication in my presence, and I was greatly alarmed. . . ."

The reporter first tried to persuade one of Grant's aides to get him into his stateroom on some pretext—"but he was timid, and was afraid the General would resent it"—and then urged the ship's captain to refuse him more whiskey, but was informed "that Gen. Grant was department commander with full power to do what he pleased with the boat, and all it contained." Undeterred, Cadwallader told the captain he would be informing Rawlins of his lack of cooperation. "He knew something of the vindictive feelings Rawlins had for those who supplied Grant with liquor, and finally closed the bar room, and conveniently lost the key in a safe place."

Cadwallader then got Grant into his stateroom himself and locked the door to prevent his leaving. "He became quite angry and ordered me peremptorily to open the door and get out instantly. . . . This order I firmly, but good-naturedly declined to obey. . . . As it was a very hot day, and the stateroom was almost suffocating, I insisted on his taking off his coat, vest and boots, and lying down in one of the berths. After much resistance I succeeded, and soon fanned him to sleep."

Here Cadwallader maintains that the *Diligence,* instead of turning back en route, actually arrived at Satartia. "Before [Grant] had recovered from his stupor we reached Satartia. . . . He was determined to dress and go ashore; and ordered Capt. Osband [who headed his cavalry escort] to debark the men and horses. Poor Osband was now in a dilemma. To . . . land at night in such a miserable little hamlet, filled with . . . Rebel sympathizers, with but a handful of troopers to protect the General, seemed suicidal. . . . I came to his help by promising to take upon myself the responsibility of shooting or hamstringing every horse on the vessel. We soon agreed that under no conditions whatever would we go ashore. . . ." Then the reporter resumed cajoling Grant, in the end persuading him to stay on the boat and go to sleep. During the night the *Diligence* steamed down the Yazoo and by morning was at Haynes' Bluff, where Grant, according to Dana, "came out to breakfast fresh as a rose."

One might think that by now Grant's caper was over. Not so, if we are to believe Cadwallader. "I supposed all necessity for extra vigilance on my part had passed, and was almost 'thunderstruck' at finding an hour afterward that [he] had procured another supply of whiskey from on shore and was quite as much intoxicated as the day before." He used the same tactics with Grant as the previous day, "but I encountered less fierce opposition." Now Grant decided that the boat should go to Chickasaw Bayou. "To be seen in his present condition, would lead to utter disgrace and ruin . . . [the captain] was also alarmed, as to the consequences to himself.

He was now very willing to take orders from me. . . . When Grant's impatience at last threatened to burst all restraints . . . [the captain] was directed to start, but to look for a safe sandbar . . . to stick on for awhile." The beaching was accomplished, and Chickasaw Bayou was not reached until sundown on June 7th—when Grant was in a less boisterous state.

The *Diligence* made a landing near where "Wash" Graham, a sutler, was holding open house on his own vessel for Federal officers, dispensing liquor, cigars, and food. Cadwallader cautioned the sutler against giving Grant drinks, and then went about helping transfer the general's escort and horses to the mainland. Later, however, he could not find him. Going aboard Graham's boat, he started aft in search of Grant, "and soon heard a hum of conversation and laughter. . . . Pushing in among a crowd of officers . . . I found Graham in front of a table covered with bottled whiskey and baskets of champagne and Grant in the act of swallowing a glass of whiskey. I was thoroughly indignant and may have shown scant ceremony in saying to him the escort was waiting. . . . He was not well pleased. . . ."[13]

Grant's displeasure evinced itself, again if we are to believe Cadwallader, in his mounting his horse, spurring the beast into a gallop, and making a wild and dangerous ride toward the lines at Vicksburg. "The horse darted away before anyone was ready to follow. . . . The road was crooked and tortuous . . . but Grant paid no attention to roads or sentries. . . . I took after him as fast as I could go . . . After crossing the last bayou bridge three-fourths of a mile from the landing, he abandoned his reckless gait, and when I caught up with him was riding in walk." With the escort not yet in sight, the two men scuffled over the bridle, Cadwallader claimed, until he gained control. Then, with Grant "unsteady in the saddle," he persuaded him to dismount and lie down on the grass, where he soon fell asleep. When the escort did arrive, the reporter immediately dispatched one of them to Rawlins at headquarters, asking that an ambulance be sent. His intent was to keep the intoxicated Grant from being seen.

For the next few hours, until the ambulance arrived, Cadwallader supposedly kept Grant, now astir, from remounting and riding off. Even then, the general refused to get in the wagon. "We compromised the question by my agreeing to ride in the ambulance also," said the reporter. ". . . On the way he confessed that I had been right, and that he had been wrong throughout, and told me to consider myself a staff officer, and to give any orders that were necessary in his name."

Reaching headquarters about midnight, the two men found a frantic

Rawlins waiting for them. "[Grant] shrugged his shoulders," said Cadwallader, "pulled down his vest, 'shook himself together,' as one rising from a nap, and seeing Rawlins . . . bade [him] goodnight in a neutral tone and manner, and started to his tent as steadily as he ever walked in his life. My surprise nearly amounted to stupefaction. I turned to Rawlins and said I was afraid he would think I was the man who had been drunk."

"No, no. I know, I know him," replied Rawlins fiercely. "I want you to tell me the exact facts. . . . I have a right to know them." Cadwallader repeated all that had transpired, including his usurping of military authority, and voiced the fear that Grant would retaliate by exiling him from the army. With that "Rawlins thanked me warmly for what I had done; told me to dismiss all fear of disagreeable consequences to myself . . . and bidding me 'good night' walked away to his tent."

Cadwallader, of course, never filed a story for his paper on these happenings. In turn, for the rest of his time with the army he was given unsurpassed access to Grant and his aides. "I was always recognized and spoken to," he would say of the general, "as if I had been regularly gazetted. . . . My comfort and convenience was considered; a tent pitched and struck for me whenever and wherever I chose to occupy it; in all provisions for transportation and subsistence I was counted as a member of the staff."[14]

While it is highly unlikely that the correspondent, despite letting some thirty-five years pass before telling this story, made it up out of whole cloth, it is just as likely that he exaggerated the details. Grant doubtless went on a tear; the reporter doubtless helped conceal it—although his "orders" to military personnel ring false, as do his assertions that he was the sole influence on the general. We know Grant was no teetotaler; that he liked a drink or several but in most circumstances controlled his habit. In point of fact, Cadwallader's is the only detailed account of anything involving Grant during the Civil War remotely resembling a spree.

The puritanical Rawlins, moreover, was always more than willing to come down hard on his chief about what he perceived as a grave weakness. In the early hours of the morning on June 6, the same day Grant began his bout, he even wrote him a letter—though it is unclear whether it was ever sent—that read in part: "The great solicitude I feel for the safety of this army leads me to mention, what I had hoped never again to do, the subject of your drinking." Rawlins went on to say he had found wine bottles in the headquarters camp. "I find you where the wine bottle has just been emptied, in company with those who drink and urge you to do likewise. . . ." He reminded Grant of past indiscretions, and then concluded,

"If my suspicions are unfounded, let my friendship for you and my zeal for my country be my excuse for this letter."

That Rawlins was Grant's hair shirt in all matters regarding temperance or lack of it is a matter of record—a fact that reveals as much about the former as the latter. ". . . Whenever he commits the folly of tasting liquor," a seemingly unconcerned Dana would say in a note to Secretary of War Stanton, "Rawlins can be counted on to stop him." The truth seems to be that the aide in this regard was overly zealous, and the general, with the exception of the two-day expedition up the Yazoo, overly maligned. One officer visiting Grant's camp during the siege, yearning for a drink, did not find one until nightfall, being told "Rawlins is death on liquor." Then, sharing a surgeon's tent, he gratefully watched as his host poured out some whiskey for him into a tin cup and placed it on a cracker box. Footsteps suddenly sounded, the tent's flap was disturbed, and the surgeon cried, "It's Rawlins!" Instead the visitor was Grant, who without a word took the cup, swallowed the whiskey, and departed as quickly as he came.

Years afterward, when the officer bumped into Grant on a train trip, the latter asked him if he remembered the episode.

"Perfectly," the officer answered.

"I don't think I ever wanted a drink so much," Grant replied, "before or after."[15]

Early June found the army's so-called Colored troops in their first major engagement. On June 7, while Grant was on his ill-considered jaunt up and down the Yazoo, several thousand Rebels from the Trans-Mississippi attack a joint black and white force at Milliken's Bend. The blacks, officially the 9th and 11th Regiments of Louisiana Volunteers of African Descent, had newly been mustered into the service. Along with the whites they at first gave way but later rallied and routed the Confederates, incensed over reports that those blacks who had surrendered had been executed by the enemy, along with two of their white officers. "It was fought mainly hand to hand," said Dana of the battle. "After it was over many men were found dead with bayonet stabs, and others with their skulls broken open with butts of muskets. . . . The bravery of the blacks in the battle at Milliken's Bend completely revolutionized the sentiment of the army. . . . I heard prominent officers who formerly in private had sneered at the idea of the Negroes fighting, express themselves after that as heartily in favor of it. . . ."

Union General Elias S. Dennis, the commander of the Northwest Louisiana District who witnessed the action, was loud in his praise: "It is impossible for men to show greater gallantry than the Negro troops in this fight." Captain M. M. Miller, a white company commander in the 9th Louisiana, lost sixteen killed and fifteen wounded of his thirty-three men. He described the bloodletting as "a horrible fight, the worst I was ever engaged in, not even excepting Shiloh. The enemy cried 'No quarter,' but some of them were very glad to take it when made prisoners." Grant would say of the engagement: "Most of the troops engaged were Africans, who had little experience in the use of firearms. Their conduct is said, however, to have been most gallant. . . ."

Sergeant Charles Wilcox of the 33rd Illinois was so impressed with the black troops that he resolved to become an officer and command a Colored company, a goal he would achieve in the next few months. Wrote Wilcox: "Talking with an intelligent Negro today about enlisting he said, 'Now, Mr. Wilcox, since this affair [Milliken's Bend] . . . *I feel that I'm as much of a man as anyone.*' The fight had made him our compeer and he felt exceedingly joyful over it. He asked for the privilege of going in my company when I got it up. Of course he shall have the chance. . . ."

The man most responsible for spearheading the enlisting of blacks during the war, which Lincoln considered a top priority, was a most unlikely leader for such an enterprise. He was Lorenzo Thomas, the army's paper-shuffling—and some say bumbling—adjutant general, whom we last saw having a hot toddy with Admiral Porter on the eve of Grant's crossing the Mississippi. Sent to the area with instructions, in effect, to become a recruiting sergeant, he came to relish the role. By the end of 1863 he had organized twenty black regiments, and a year later, thirty more. By the end of the war he had recruited and organized 76,000 blacks, some 40 percent of the 190,000 who served in the Federal armies. Lorenzo Thomas's was a little-appreciated but major contribution to the Union cause.[16]

Grant meanwhile was back in the lines, reconciled to the slow pace of the siege. "We have our trenches pushed up so close to the enemy that we can throw hand grenades over into their forts," he wrote a friend. "The enemy do not dare show their heads above the parapets at any point, so close and watchful are our sharpshooters. The town is completely invested." His only real irritant was McClernand, who continued in ways large and small to challenge his authority. Mindful of his senior corps commander's ties to Lincoln, Grant had decided for the nonce to take no action against him for triggering the second attack of May 22, preferring to avoid his company; the fall of Vicksburg, he felt, would be the proper occasion to settle scores. McClernand, however, was a boiling cauldron of resentments. James Wilson, bearing an innocuous message to him from Grant to shift some troops, at this juncture felt his wrath at first hand.

"I'll be god-damned if I'll do it," McClernand exploded. "I am tired of being dictated to—I won't stand it any longer, and you can go back and tell General Grant!" He then went into a full-blown rage, cursing Grant and all his staff for all his setbacks. Wilson first was taken aback, then enraged himself.

"It seems to me," he interrupted, pulling his horse next to McClernand, "that you are cursing me as much as you are cursing General Grant! If this is so, while you are a major general and I am only a lieutenant colonel, I'll pull you off that horse and beat the boots off you!"

McClernand quickly broke off his tirade. "I was simply expressing my vehemence on the subject matter, sir, and I beg your pardon." The incensed Wilson later recounted the incident to Grant, who found it humorous. No man to use foul language himself, he thought it comical that McClernand had been in a blaspheming rage. For days thereafter, when someone swore in his presence, he would ask facetiously, in so many words, "Are you expressing yourself with vehemence?"[17]

In mid-June, however, McClernand finally made one misstep too many. General Frank Blair Jr. picked up a copy of the *Memphis Evening Bulletin* and read an item titled "Congratulatory Order of General McClernand." In the newspaper account of the proclamation, McClernand praised the bravery of his troops on May 19 and 22, but simultaneously took aim at the supposed deficiencies of Sherman and McPherson for not supporting him on the battlefield, especially on the afternoon of the 22nd. It had always been the role of the stalwart 13th Corps, McClernand implied, to make up for the deficiencies of others and "to redeem previous disappointments." Sherman, sent the paper by Blair, erupted.

"If the order be a genuine production and not a forgery," he wrote Grant, "it is manifestly addressed not to an army, but to a constituency in Illinois, far distant from the scene . . . who might be innocently induced to think General McClernand the sagacious leader and bold hero he so complacently paints himself." Moreover, Sherman went on, the proclamation "pervents the truth to the ends of flattery and self-glorification, and contains many untruths, among which is one monstrous falsehood. It substantially accuses General McPherson and myself with . . . not assaulting on May 19 and 22, and allowing on the latter day the enemy to mass his troops against the 13th Corps alone." McClernand's bogus claim that he had captured two of the enemy's forts on the 22nd, Cump pointed out, was "a mischievous message whereby we lost, needlessly, many of our best officers and men."

McPherson lost no time in expressing his own indignation. "There is a vaingloriousness about this order," he said, "an ingenious attempt to write himself down the hero, the mastermind, giving life and direction to military operations in this quarter inconsistent with the high-toned principles of the solider, *sans peur et sans reproche*. Though born a warrior, <u>as he himself stated</u> [underlining added], he has evidently forgotten one of the most essential qualities [of the soldier], viz., that elevated, refined sense of honor which, while guarding his own rights with zealous care, at all times renders justice to others."

Grant moved with dispatch, obtaining a copy of the proclamation to assure himself that the newspaper account was accurate and then asking McClernand, by letter, why he had published it without his knowledge—a violation of military regulations. The latter's response was that an aide had been neglectful. Grant did not accept the explanation and, at long last, cashiered McClernand for insubordination. Bearing the dismissal order to his tent in the wee hours of June 18 and waking him from sleep was James Wilson, who doubtless performed the task with pleasure.

"Well, sir! I am relieved," McClernand reputedly said. Then, almost to himself, he added, "By God, sir, we are both relieved!"—a double entendre that tacitly acknowledged Grant's state of mind.[18]

Replacing the Illinois politician as 13th Corps commander was the well-regarded West Pointer Edward Otho Ord, now recovered from his wounds at the Hatchie River in the aftermath of the Confederate defeat at Corinth. McClernand, of course, could not believe that the dismissal would stand. From his exile in Springfield he bombarded the president and the War Department with pleas for a hearing. How could a general so well regarded by Lincoln be summarily removed—and on a pretext? "I have been relieved for an omission of my adjutant," he told the president. "Hear me." Lincoln, once and for all coming to the conclusion that he needed Grant's victories in the field more than McClernand's votes in Illinois, responded with forbearance but also with finality. "General Grant and yourself have been conspicuous in our most important successes," he said, "and for me to interfere and thus magnify a breach between you could not but be of evil effect." McClernand would briefly return the following year to command the 13th Corps, when it was widely dispersed in Louisiana and Texas, but his days of influence in Washington were done.[19]

Pemberton's plight during this time, and that of the civilians within Vicksburg, continually worsened. Thousands of his original 28,000 troops were dead, wounded, or incapacitated—although his ranks were, to some degree, strengthened by small units coming into the city from the riverside. It is true that Joseph Johnston, hovering east of the Big Black, now commanded some 30,000 men but, as we will see, he continually deemed this force insufficient to come to the city's aid. The Federal army, also reinforced, at this point totaled perhaps 71,000 effectives.

Roughly speaking, Grant had divided his army, one-half facing west and besieging Vicksburg, the other half under Sherman facing east in case Johnston bestirred himself. In truth the Federal commander need not have worried. While Johnston was a fine tactician, he was exceedingly cautious. One contemporary remembered being with him, before the war, in a hunting party. "He was a capital shot," the man would say of Johnston, ". . . but with Colonel Johnston . . . the bird flew too high or too low, the dogs were too far or too near. Things never did suit exactly. He was too fussy, too hard to please . . . too much afraid to miss and risk his fine reputation as a crack shot." The hunters blasted away, bringing down bird after bird, but Johnston never shot at all. His behavior was much the same during the siege. We do not know if he could have taken Grant in the rear, with Pemberton emerging in support or at least using the diversion to flee the city—because he never made the attempt.[20]

Instead in late May and June there emerged a notable series of communiqués between Pemberton and Johnston—with the former begging for help, and the latter foot-dragging. "My men are in good spirits, awaiting your arrival," Pemberton said on May 29. "I am too weak to save Vicksburg," Johnston replied. "Can do no more than attempt to save you and your garrison. It will be impossible to extricate you unless you cooperate and we make mutually supporting movements." On June 3, Pemberton asked: "In what direction will you move and when? I hope north of the Jackson Road." On June 7, Johnston answered that question with one of his own: "Co-operation is absolutely necessary. Tell us how to effect it, and by what routes." On the 10th, a desperate Pemberton reported: "I shall endeavor to hold out as long as we have anything to eat." On the 15th, still thinking Johnston was coming to his aid, he again urged him to make haste.

That same day Johnston wired Richmond: "I consider saving Vicksburg hopeless." Secretary of War James Seddon's reply was sharp: "Your telegram grieves and alarms us. Vicksburg must not be lost, at least without a struggle. . . . You must hazard an attack. It may be in concert with the garrison, if practicable, but otherwise without." Still Johnston did nothing. By the 19th the Federal sap lines were as close as ten yards to the Rebel defenses. "I hope you will advance with the least possible delay," wrote Pemberton. ". . . We are living on very reduced rations. . . . What aid am I to expect from you?" Replied Johnston on the 23rd: "I will have the means of moving toward the enemy in a day or two, and will try to make a diversion in your favor."[21]

The civilians in the city, knowing little of these exchanges, thought Johnston would be their savior. Meanwhile their days under the cannonading were full of dread. Remembered one resident: "One man had his head shot off while in the act of picking up his child. . . . A little girl, the daughter of a Mrs. Jones, was sitting at the entrance of a cave when a Parrott shell entered the portal and [likewise] took her head off." Wrote Mrs. James Loughborough: "The screams of the women of Vicksburg were the saddest I ever heard." Once death nearly visited her. Huddling in her cave with her baby daughter, she watched as "a Parrott shell came whirling in the entrance and fell in the center of the cave before us all, lying there smoking. . . . We expected every moment the terrific explosion [that] would ensue. I pressed my child closer to my heart. . . ." Then one of the servants rushed forward, picked up the missile and threw it outside. There the fuse sputtered out, making the shell harmless.

The Union sympathizer Dora Miller on one occasion left her cellar to go upstairs and rest on her bed. She was reading the Vicksburg *Daily Citizen,* which having run out of newsprint was being printed on the reverse side of wallpaper, "when a shell burst right outside the window. . . . Pieces flew in, striking all around me, tearing down masses of plaster that came tumbling over me. When H. [her husband] rushed in I was crawling out of the plaster, digging it out of my eyes and hair. When he picked up a piece as large as a saucer beside my pillow, I realized my narrow escape."

Later, on June 25, she lost her composure. "We were all in the cellar when a shell came tearing through the roof, burst upstairs, tore up that room, [with] the pieces coming through both floors down into the cellar. . . . This was tangible proof the cellar was no place of protection." For the first time she quailed. "Every night I had laid down expecting death, and every morning rose to the same prospect, without being unnerved. It was for H. I trembled. But now I first seemed to realize that something worse than death might come; I might be crippled and not killed. Life, without all one's powers and limbs, was a thought that broke down my courage. I said to H., 'You must get me out of this horrible place; I cannot stay;

I know I shall be crippled.' Now the regret comes that I lost control, because H. is worried. . . ."[22]

For the Confederate soldiers in the lines, June 25 was equally trying. That was the day the Federals exploded 2,200 pounds of gunpowder in a tunnel they had dug under the Third Louisiana Redan on the Jackson Road, a Rebel strongpoint. Though the enemy had known about the tunnel for some time, and had sunk countermines to stop it, they had been unsuccessful. "As the hour of 3 (P.M.) approached," said Andrew Hickenlooper, Grant's chief engineer, "the booming of artillery and incessant rattle of musketry . . . suddenly subsided, and a deathlike and oppressive stillness pervaded the whole command. Every eye was riveted upon the huge redoubt standing high above the adjoining lines." The ensuing explosion created a crater some 35 feet in diameter and deep enough to hold perhaps 100 men. "The air was filled with dirt, dust, stockades, gabions, timbers, one or two gun carriages, and an immense surging white cloud of smoke which fairly rose to the heavens," said Cadwallader.

Even before the debris had settled, the Federal assault columns—volunteers from the 23rd Indiana and the 31st and 45th Illinois—were charging into the breach. They descended into the crater, then faced the daunting task of clawing their way up the other side. "There still remained between the new ground which we had gained by the explosion and the main works of the fort an ascent so steep that an assault was practically impossible," said Dana. "The enemy very soon opened a galling fire from within the fort with shells with short fuses, thrown over the ridge by hand. . . . The wounds inflicted by these missiles were frightful."

Though battered by constant shelling and weakened by lack of food, the Rebels still could fight. Down in the crater, Wilbur Crummer found that out firsthand. "They met us with a terrible volley of musketry, but on the boys went, up and over the embankment with a cheer, the enemy falling back a few paces to an inner or second line of breastworks, where are placed cannon loaded with grape and cannister, and these cannon belched forth their death-dealing missiles. . . . The line wavers, staggers, then falls back into the crater. . . . Hand to hand conflict rages for hours. . . . Hand grenades and loaded shells are lighted and thrown over the parapet as you would play ball. . . . Two companies hold the crater for two hours or more, their rapid firing causing the barrels to become hot and foul . . . when another two companies slip in and take their places. . . . What a terrible sacrifice!"

During the night the Federals withdrew, their ill-advised assault emphatically repulsed. Wrote Cadwallader: "Despite the most heroic attempts we were unable to gain any tenable footing with the Rebel works." Black Jack Logan, who had been watching the carnage, was more blunt. "My God!" he exclaimed. "They are killing my bravest men in the hole!"[23]

Nothing disheartened, Grant in the days that followed continued to push his trenches ever closer to the defenses. "By the 1st of July," he said, "our approaches had reached the enemy's ditch at a number of places. At ten points we could move under cover to within from five to one hundred yards of the enemy." What this meant was that most of his troops now were so close to the Rebels that, if they rose up and moved forward, they could overwhelm them; no longer did vast stretches of open ground make frontal attacks suicidal. July 1, in fact, brought the explosion of a second Federal mine. This one, which did less damage than the first, blew a Negro cook in the air and into the Union lines. He landed, unhurt, and found work in Logan's division.

Now events rose to a head. Grant, following a meeting with his generals, set July 6 as the date for an all-out assault on the city—an event that never came to pass. Johnston meanwhile on July 1 finally moved his army in fits and starts toward the Big Black, only to halt and pitch camp after his first encounter with Sherman's pickets. Just as at Jackson, Mississippi, weeks before he had no real intention of engaging the enemy. Pemberton on the same July 1, rightly giving up on Johnston, put the question to his own generals: Should he surrender, or should the army cut its way out? Almost unanimously, they voted for surrender. Carter Stevenson's response was typical. "My men," he said, "are necessarily much enfeebled, and . . . would be unable to make the march and undergo the fatigues . . . [of] a successful evacuation."[24]

"It must have been a bitter moment for the Confederate chieftain," said Dana. "Pemberton was a Northern man, a Pennsylvanian by birth, from which state he was appointed to West Point. . . . In the old army he fell under the spell of Jefferson Davis, whose close friend he was." (Davis, likewise a West Pointer, served as Secretary of War in the 1850s under Franklin Pierce.) The Confederate president appears to have thought Pemberton a military genius; he had jumped him almost at a stroke to the rank of lieutenant general, entrusting him with the defense of Mississippi. Now Pemberton was doubly humiliated, not only that he had failed but, said Dana, "by the knowledge that he would be suspected and accused of treachery by his adopted brethren, and that the result would be used by the enemies of Davis. . . ." [25]

On the morning of July 3, following forty-eight days and nights of siege, white flags appeared on the Vicksburg parapets. Riding toward the Federal lines, bearing a letter from Pemberton proposing an armistice, came the hard-fighting General John Bowen, who within a fortnight would die of illness. "It was a glorious sight to officers and men on the lines where these white flags were visible," said Grant, "and the news soon spread. . . . The troops felt that their long and weary marches, hard fighting, ceaseless watching . . . and, worst of all, the gibes of many Northern papers . . . saying all their suffering was in vain, that Vicksburg never would be taken, were at last at an end." To Pemberton's letter Grant responded much as he had at Fort Donelson: "The useless effusion of blood you propose stopping . . . can be ended at any time you may choose, by the unconditional surrender of the city and garrison."

By 3:00 P.M., the two men and assorted generals and aides were meeting on a hillside within a few hundred feet of the Rebel lines, with Pemberton hoping Grant would soften his stiff terms—essentially the same ones he had offered to Simon Buckner the year before. "Pemberton and I had served in the same division during parts of the Mexican War," Grant said. "I knew him very well, therefore, and greeted him as an old acquaintance. He soon asked what terms I proposed. . . . My answer was the same as . . . in my reply to his letter. . . ."

"The conference might as well end," Pemberton answered snappishly.

"Very well," agreed Grant.

At this juncture General Bowen sought to heal the rift. "His manner and remarks, while Pemberton and I were talking, showed this," said Grant. "He now proposed that he and one of our generals should have a conference." Grant had no objections, and soon Bowen and Andrew Jackson Smith were talking. "After a while Bowen suggested that the Confederate army should be allowed to march out with the honors of war, carrying their small arms and field artillery. This was . . . unceremoniously rejected." The meeting ended with Grant saying he would draft a letter, setting final terms, and send it to Pemberton by 10:00 P.M.[26]

Grant's ultimate offer, after conferring with his officers—and in particular at the urging of James McPherson—was more generous than simple "unconditional surrender," and for this he would be criticized. It called for the Federals to take possession of Vicksburg at 8:00 A.M. the next morning and, he declared, "As soon as rolls can be made out, and paroles be signed by officers and men, you will be allowed to march out of our lines, the officers taking with them their sidearms and clothing, and the field, staff and cavalry officers one horse each. The rank and file will be allowed all their clothing but no other property. . . . Any amount of rations you may deem necessary can be taken from the stores you now have. . . ." In short order, Pemberton accepted these terms.

The criticism would center on Grant's releasing the Rebels on parole—they now totaled some 29,500—instead of shipping them to Union prisons. But there was a rationale to his change of mind. Physically taking them prisoner and sending them hundreds of miles north would tie up his transportation and hinder future operations. But giving them parole—thousands were unfit for service or worried about their loved ones at home—would just as effectively deprive the Confederacy of their services. "To put thirty thousand soldiers on parole was to take a certain chance," wrote one historian. "It was to gamble that no one on the other side would cut any corners." Nonetheless the odds were overwhelming that the parolees, instead of remaining a disciplined force and answering to their officers, would in large number melt away. "Paroled men were very hard to handle, because the soldiers assumed that when they had been captured and paroled they were out of the war." This is precisely what happened to Pemberton's Army of Mississippi. Within weeks after the surrender it no longer existed as a cohesive unit; its officers received quick exchanges, but no more than half of the rank and file returned to service, and then not until the following year.[27]

John Logan's division, given the honor of accepting the surrender marched into Vicksburg the morning of July 4. Wrote a reporter for the *New York Tribune:* "There is no jeering or tormenting from our men. We have even refrained from cheering, and nothing—absolutely nothing—has been done to add humiliation to the cup of sorrows which the Rebels have been compelled to drink." Added Grant: "Our soldiers were no sooner inside the lines than the two armies began to fraternize. . . . I myself saw our men taking bread out of their haversacks and giving it to the enemy they had so recently been engaged in starving out. It was accepted with avidity and thanks."

When Grant met with Pemberton a final time, however, the atmosphere was chilly. The Southern commander and his officers, remembered James Wilson, "were unhandsome and disagreeable in the extreme." Grant was not offered a chair, and when he asked for a glass of water—the day being oppressively hot—was told, in effect, that he could get it for himself. He seemed not to notice the rudeness, well satisfied with the fact that the fall of Vicksburg would be taking some 40,000 Confederate soldiers out of the war. The number included not only those in the city, but the 6,000 or so who had been captured before the siege, and a like number, cut off from support, who would surrender at Port Hudson within a few days.[28]

Soon Grant and his generals rode down to the river, where Admiral Porter—who had been so enthusiastic during the campaign—received them on his flagship. "I opened all my wine lockers—which contained only Catawba—on this occasion," said Porter. "It disappeared down the parched throats which had tasted nothing for some time but bad water. Yet it exhilarated that crowd as weak wine never did before." Grant was a subdued presence in the midst of the gaiety. "There was a quiet satisfaction in his face that could not be concealed, but he behaved . . . as if nothing of importance had occurred. [He] was the only one in that assemblage who did not touch the simple wine offered him; he contented himself with a cigar. . . ."

Sherman now was told by Grant to cross the Big Black and deal with Johnston. This he did forcefully and speedily, driving him back through Jackson in a thirteen-day operation that culminated on July 17, destroying what remained of the railroads, military depots and—alas—private houses in the capital, and forcing him to take refuge in eastern Mississippi. Union soldiers, looking at the city's landscape, dubbed it Chimneyville. Johnston, the consummate military bureaucrat, seemed more disturbed about the presence of Pemberton's parolees in the area than the second sacking of Jackson. "What shall be done with [them]?" he asked Richmond. "They cannot remain in this Department without great injury to us from deficiency of supplying them."

In the period from the battle of Port Gibson on May 1 through the evacuation of Jackson on July 17, the Confederates—besides losing control of the Mississippi—had suffered some 48,000 casualties—killed, wounded, and captured. Grant's losses would be 10,500. Coupled with the stunning defeat of Lee at Gettysburg on July 3, the fall of Vicksburg was the beginning of the end for the Southern cause.

From Lincoln to Grant came the following letter, generous in the extreme: "I do not believe that you and I ever met personally. I write this now as a grateful acknowledgment for the almost inestimable service you have done the country. I wish to say a word further. When you first reached the vicinity of Vicksburg, I thought you should do, which you finally did—march the troops around the neck, run the batteries with the transports, and thus go below; and I never had any faith, except a general hope that you knew better than I, that the Yazoo Pass expedition, and the like, could succeed. When you . . . took Port Gibson, Grand Gulf, and vicinity; I thought you should go down the river and join Gen. Banks; and when you turned northward east of the Big Black, I feared it was a mistake. I now wish to make the personal acknowledgement that you were right, and I was wrong."[29]

Though Grant must have been gratified by the president's words, he kept them in perspective. Many battles would be fought and setbacks endured, he knew, before the Confederacy would be conquered.

REVENGE AT CHATTANOOGA

No sooner was the Union triumph at Vicksburg complete than General-in-Chief Halleck, who still saw himself as a master of grand strategy, begin to break up the army and assume a defensive posture, just as he had after the fall of Corinth the year before. Some 4,000 men and then the entire 13th Corps were sent to Nathaniel Banks in New Orleans, an additional 5,000 went to Arkansas, and two divisions of the 9th Corps—which had reinforced Grant during the siege—were returned to Kentucky. "I felt that the troops that had done so much should be allowed to do more," said a disappointed Grant, "before the enemy could recover from the blow he had received, and while important points might be captured without bloodshed."

What he had in mind was moving against Mobile, Alabama, the last great Confederate seaport on the Gulf Coast. "It would have been an easy thing to capture Mobile. . . . Having that as a base of operations, troops could have been thrown into the interior to operate against [Braxton] Bragg's army." The cautious Halleck demurred. With Johnston pushed out of western Mississippi, the general-in-chief wanted Arkansas and western Louisiana likewise secured before considering additional offensive operations.

In this instance Lincoln sided with Halleck, but for a different reason. Taking advantage of the Civil War, the Emperor Napoleon III had landed a French army in Mexico, preparatory to installing the Austrian Archduke Maximilian as emperor in that country. Facing this kind of European opportunism, Lincoln felt he now had a greater need for Federal forces in Texas and the Trans-Mississippi than in Alabama. "I see by a dispatch of yours," he told Grant on August 9, "that you incline quite strongly toward an expedition against Mobile. That would appear tempting to me also, were it not that, in view of recent events in Mexico, I am greatly impressed with . . . reestablishing national authority in western Texas as soon as possible." Years later, Grant would still insist he was right. "I am well aware that the President was very anxious to have a foothold in Texas, to stop the clamor of some of the foreign governments . . . to recognize belligerent rights to the Confederate States. This, however, could have easily been done without wasting troops in western Louisiana and eastern Texas, by sending a garrison at once to Brownsville on the Rio Grande." The French would stay in Mexico until 1866, when 50,000 U.S. troops massed on the border induced them to leave.[1]

In the first days of September Grant, probably for no other reason than that he was bored by camp life, took a steamer down to New Orleans to confer with General Banks on strategy. Here he suffered a riding accident, which his enemies once more were only too happy to ascribe to excessive drinking. It occurred on the night of September 4, following a colorful and massive troop review and then a relaxing dinner with officers and distinguished guests—admittedly replete with music, wine, and good food. Grant was on his way back to his hotel, riding a powerful, imperfectly broken mount—exactly the kind of challenge he had welcomed since boyhood days. Suddenly a locomotive on nearby railroad tracks sounded a shrill whistle. The horse shied, lost its footing, and fell on Grant's left leg, severely bruising it and knocking him unconscious.

When he came to, with doctors attending him, Grant's leg and side were monstrously swollen, and "the pain was almost beyond endurance. I lay at the hotel something over a week without being able to turn myself in bed. I had a steamer stop at the nearest point possible, and was carried to it on a litter. I was then taken to Vicksburg, where I remained unable to move for some time."

Meanwhile Grant's detractors resumed their whispering. Typical was the artful comment of General William Franklin, who had graduated number one in Grant's West Point class, made a hash of his command at Fredericksburg, and subsequently been transferred from Virginia to the West. The accident was a godsend, Franklin wrote a friend, because "Grant had commenced a frolic which would have ruined his body and his reputation in a week." Commented the sorry Banks, who had failed abysmally against Stonewall Jackson in the Shenandoah and conducted a lackluster campaign against Port Hudson: "I am frightened when I think that he is a drunkard." There seems little rational basis for such charges. Whether Grant abstained altogether, had one glass of wine, or several, before mounting and riding off that night is not the point; the fact is that he had been in the public eye the entire forty-eight hours he was in New Orleans, and no one in his immediate presence, whether officers or thousands of the rank-and-file, saw any signs of drunkenness.

General Lorenzo Thomas would say of the mishap that Grant's horse "threw him over with great violence. The General, who is a splendid rider, maintained his seat in the saddle, and the horse fell upon him." General Cadwallader Washburn, writing his brother, Congressman Elihu Washburne, would strike the same note, saying that "after the review was over and Grant was returning to the city, his horse fell with him and injured him severely." These supporting statements, of course, would not stop the rumors; the malicious and the envious would continue to insist that the rumpled general from Galena, Illinois, was a perennial drunk. Fort Donelson, Shiloh, and Vicksburg had been won not because of his genius but despite his failings.[2]

Following the accident Julia soon joined Grant in Vicksburg with five-year-old Jesse, their youngest child, leaving the three oldest with relatives in St. Louis. Her summer had not been entirely happy. "Our neighbors were all Southern in sentiment," this daughter of a slaveowner would explain, "and could not believe that I was not; no matter how earnestly I denied it, they would exclaim, 'It is right for you to say you are Union, Julia, but we know better, my child; it is not in human nature for you to be anything but Southern.'" Her father, Frederick Dent, only added fuel to the fire, arguing incessantly that the Constitution permitted secession. If Andrew Jackson were still in the White House, he would say, the war "never would have happened. He would have hanged a score or two of them, and the country would [be] at peace. I knew we would have trouble when I voted for a man north of Mason and Dixon's line."

Within a few days of Julia's arrival a relaxed and cheerful Grant was up and about, though forced to use crutches, and resuming his duties. His wife meanwhile was continually being importuned to intercede with him on various civilian matters. One such petition involved an elderly Rebel sympathizer, a Mr. Porterfield, who had been ordered to leave Vicksburg for making seditious remarks. "The daughter of this gentleman came to see me and told me her father had been imprudent enough to say to Surgeon

[John] Moore, who was an inmate of his house, that he was sure that 'yellow jack' [meaning yellow fever] would drive the Yankees out if shot and shell did not. So this with some other little indiscreet speeches was reported to our provost marshall, who at once issued an order that the old gentleman must leave with twenty-four hours or . . . be sent to a Northern prison."

Julia was appalled. She told the petitioner she should see General Grant.

"Oh," replied the weeping woman, "the order is very explicit and says we must not appeal to General Grant."

Julia at once arose, went into her husband's office, and related the story. Then she asked Miss Porterfield to enter.

"Oh, General, this will kill Papa if he must go," the woman begged between sobs.

Grant promptly rescinded the order. "Tell your father to be more careful of his speech in future," he counseled.[3]

The Northern commander's return to relative good health—he still had to be lifted into the saddle—was opportune, for in east Tennessee on September 19 and 20 the Federal Army of the Cumberland under William Rosecrans had suffered a stunning defeat along the banks of Chickamauga Creek in northern Georgia, some miles southeast of Chattanooga, Tennessee. There the normally indecisive Braxton Bragg and his Army of Tennessee had routed Rosecrans, reducing that devout Catholic to crossing himself in the midst of the battle. Only a determined stand by General George H. Thomas, for which he earned the sobriquet "the Rock of Chickamauga," kept the army from complete disaster and permitted its withdrawal into the town, where in subsequent days it came under siege and, eventually, threat of starvation.

Now an Assistant Secretary of War, Charles Dana was with the Army of the Cumberland during this period, instructed by Stanton and Lincoln to evaluate Rosecrans's character and conduct just as he had Grant's. In "Old Rosey's" case, however, Dana's views were negative. "While few persons exhibited more estimable social qualities," he said, "I have never seen a public man . . . with less administrative power, less clearness and steadiness in difficulty, and greater practical incapacity than General Rosecrans. He had inventive fertility and knowledge, but he had no strength of will and no concentration of purpose. . . . He was conscientious and honest, just as he was imperious and disputatious. . . ." The Army of the Cumberland, Dana would report, was both inefficiently run and lacking in discipline. "The former condition proceeded from the fact that General Rosecrans insisted on personally directing each department . . . the latter proceeded from his utter lack of firmness, his passion for universal applause, and his incapacity to hurt any man's feeling by just severity."[4]

With Chattanooga in peril and Rosecrans in bad odor, the War Department by the end of September was assembling some 35,000 troops to reinforce the town. Half would come from the Army of the Tennessee and be led by Sherman; the rest would come from the Army of the Potomac and be headed by Joseph ("Fighting Joe") Hooker, whose sudden loss of nerve when in command at Chancellorsville had permitted Stonewall Jackson to launch the flank attack that decided the battle. Sherman's troops would be much delayed by logistics and terrain, making the 675-mile trip by boat, train, and foot, and not arriving until mid-November. But Hooker's men, helped by an all-out commitment from the Northern railroads, would complete the much longer 1,200-mile trek from Virginia in record time, reaching the town in late October.

Grant meanwhile on October 10 received an enigmatic telegram from Halleck: "It is the wish of the Secretary of War that as soon as General Grant is able to take the field he will come to Cairo [Illinois]. . . ." Escorted by his entire headquarters staff Grant arrived there on the 16th, and the next morning received a second wire, ordering him to proceed to Louisville, Kentucky, to meet with an unnamed War Department official. Before his train reached Louisville, however, it was stopped at Indianapolis, Indiana, where the official, who turned out to be Secretary of War Stanton himself, boarded Grant's car. Presumably all this secrecy and maneuvering were necessary for fear telegrams would be intercepted by the enemy.

Stanton was a man of vast yet calculated contradictions, as both the moderate Democrats and the radical Republicans in Washington could attest, each group considering him to be "one of us." Born dirt poor, the Ohioan was the sole support of his widowed mother and siblings at the age of thirteen, worked his way through Kenyon College, and later became one of the country's foremost lawyers. Moody, asthmatic, opinionated, vehement—he stared at the world through thick spectacles and never settled for less than the answers he demanded. Some thought him too full of himself, but Lincoln urged forbearance. "We may have to treat him as they are sometimes obliged to treat a Methodist minister I know of. . . . He gets wrought up to so high a pitch of excitement in his prayers and exhortations, that they are obliged to put bricks in his pockets to keep him down. We may be obliged to serve Stanton in the same way, but I guess we'll let him jump awhile first."[5]

Through nobody's fault, this first meeting between Grant and Stanton started out awkwardly, with the secretary mistaking Grant's medical director for the general and pumping his hand, telling him he recognized him from photographs. Matters straightened themselves out, however, and Stanton, as the train rolled on to Louisville, came to the point. Lincoln and the War Department were creating a new Military Division of the Mississippi, which would embrace the existing Departments of the Tennessee, the Cumberland, and the Ohio, and Grant would command it. Essentially he now was in charge of all operations from the Alleghenies to the Mississippi, except for Banks in Louisiana. "The Secretary handed me two orders," Grant explained, "saying I might take my choice of them. . . . One order left the department commanders as they were, while the other relieved Rosecrans and assigned [George] Thomas in his place." Remembering his difficulties with the quixotic Rosecrans in the aftermath of Corinth, Grant did not hesitate. "I accepted the latter [order]," he said tersely.

The change in command was immediately telegraphed to Chattanooga. Grant then fired off a second wire to Thomas: "Hold Chattanooga at all hazards. I will be there as soon as possible. Please inform me how long your present supplies will last, and the prospect for keeping them up." Back from Thomas came the answer that he had seven days' rations on hand or nearby, plus some 300 wagonloads of supplies at Bridgeport, Alabama, only some twenty-six miles west of the town but an arduous eight-day trip because of necessary detours around the Rebel lines. While this was not good news, Grant nonetheless must have been cheered by the way Thomas ended his report: "I will hold the town till we starve."[6]

From Louisville Grant took a train south to Stevenson, Alabama, arriving there the night of October 21, preparatory to riding on the next morning to Bridgeport and thence the besieged Chattanooga. While in Stevenson he received a message from Joseph Hooker, who had established his headquarters along the rail lines there, inviting him to dinner, albeit in a pompous manner. The commander lost no time letting his new subordinate know who was in charge. "If General Hooker wishes to see *me* he will find me on this train!" he told the messenger. Recounted Oliver Otis Howard, one of Hooker's division heads, who witnessed the exchange: "The answer and the manner of it surprised me; but it was Grant's way of maintaining his ascendancy where a subordinate was likely to question it. Hooker soon entered the car and paid his respects in person."

Still lame and requiring help to get into the saddle, Grant rode into a shabby and dispirited Chattanooga amid heavy rains on the night of the 23rd and went directly to Thomas's headquarters. Horace Porter, then an aide to Thomas, would say that Grant's face during the brief conference that followed "bore an expression of weariness. He was carelessly dressed, and his uniformed coat was unbuttoned. . . . He held a lighted cigar in his mouth, and sat in a stooping posture. . . . His clothes were wet, and his trousers and top-boots were splattered with mud." Initially he was offered little hospitality, but the slight was not intentional. Thomas, an undemonstrative man, was known as much for his reserve as his rectitude, and he was uneasy in Grant's presence. The latter seemed not to notice. He declined an offer of dry clothes, contenting himself with pulling his chair close to the fire. Then the two men spent the rest of the evening discussing the army's predicament.

The next morning Grant saw for himself the dominant Confederate position around much of the town. Braxton Bragg's troops occupied Missionary Ridge—500 to 800 feet high—to the east, Lookout Mountain—2,200 feet high—to the southwest, and the Tennessee River road as far west as Bridgeport. The Federal troops were entrenched in the Chattanooga Valley, with the Tennessee River at their backs. The enemy, said Grant, occupied "commanding heights to the east and west, with a strong line across the valley from mountain to mountain, and with Chattanooga Creek, for a large part of the way, in front of their line." Union supplies had to be brought in from the north, from the Federal base at Nashville, Tennessee. "The railroad between this base and the army was in possession of the government up to Bridgeport, the point at which the road crosses to the south side of the Tennessee River; but Bragg, holding Lookout and Raccoon Mountains west of Chattanooga, commanded the railroad, the river and the shortest and best wagon roads, both south and north of the Tennessee, between Chattanooga and Bridgeport." What this meant was that all food and ordnance from Bridgeport on had to be hauled, perilously and with considerable delay, over a circuitous and mountainous sixty-mile route north of the river.[7]

Uppermost in Grant's mind was promptly opening up a more direct supply line. Here William F. Smith, the chief engineer of the Army of the Cumberland, proved of inestimable value. The Vermont-born Smith, called Baldy not because of significant loss of hair but to differentiate him from countless other officers of the same name, had been a corps commander in the Army of the Potomac, but a falling out with his superiors after Fredericksburg had resulted in his transfer to the West. Short and rotund, he was described by a contemporary as having "a light-brown imperial and

shaggy mustache, a round, military head, and the look of a German officer, altogether." Now he was urging Grant to send a brigade of Thomas's
troops on flatboats, towing pontoons, nine miles down the Tennessee and
around the hairpin turn called Moccasin Point in a daring nighttime
strike, and there seize a way station called Brown's Ferry. Meanwhile a
second brigade and supporting artillery would move overland from Chattanooga across the base of Moccasin Point in support.

Once crossing Brown's Ferry, the joint force would find itself on a five-
mile-long road cutting through Raccoon Mountain to Kelley's Ferry on
the Tennessee—and a direct connection with Bridgeport. Though both
Brown's Ferry and Raccoon Mountain were thought to be lightly held by
the enemy, the success of the plan was contingent on stealth and timing.
Hooker during this time was to move across the Tennessee at Bridgeport
and advance along the railroad line south of the river toward Wauhatchie
Station and Lookout Valley, catching the enemy in a pincer movement.

"The topographical features [of Brown's Ferry] left nothing to be desired," said Smith. "If Bragg had left it carelessly guarded, as I believed,
we could recover the short line. If I was mistaken, we might be repulsed.
Our desperate situation required us to take any risk on which a hope
might be hung; without action, the end was almost at hand; audacity and
luck might yet bring us through."

Grant quickly approved Smith's plan, which Thomas had previously endorsed, and placed the engineering officer in charge of the 1,600-man advance from Chattanooga. To lead the water-borne troops, Smith selected
Brigadier William Hazen of Ohio, a resourceful fighter who had proved
his worth at Chickamauga. The land-based brigade would be headed by
John Turchin, a former officer in the Czar's Imperial Guard. By 3:00 A.M.
on October 27, the operation was well under way. In the lead boat with
fifty men was Lieutenant Colonel James Foy of the 23rd Kentucky. Some of
the troops covered up their unease with attempts at humor. "No falling
out for water!" cried one. "This reminds me of a picture I saw of George
Washington crossing the Alps," said another, mixing his historical maneuvers.

"Shut up, you damned fools," an officer barked out. "Do you think this
is a regatta?"

Gliding down the river in the darkness, the flotilla suddenly turned a
bend and saw the campfires of the enemy. "The Rebel pickets could be
plainly seen, taking their ease before blazing fires, talking together . . .
with happy unconcern," said an Ohio soldier. By 4:30 A.M., near Brown's
Ferry, Foy's boat came abreast of an immense signal fire on the east bank.

Here he had been instructed to turn, head for the enemy on the west bank, and immediately debark his men. For some reason he did not, revealing the flotilla's presence in the gloom.

"Pull in, Colonel Foy, Pull in! Pull in!" Hazen shouted repeatedly but to no avail.

From the west bank the Rebels fired blindly toward the boats, as did the newly arrived Turchin and his men on the opposite shore, not certain who or what was out there. With lead coming at him from both sides, Foy suddenly remembered his orders. He turned toward the enemy, unloaded his men in record time, and led them up the bank as they scattered the Confederates with surprising ease. Within twenty minutes his troops and those in the boats following were in complete control of Brown's Ferry and the bluffs atop the river. Hours later Hazen and Turchin were reunited—the latter coming across on a pontoon bridge—and it was clear that the Rebels were abandoning Raccoon Mountain; by the afternoon, Federal guns and caissons were rolling across the river. Still, until Hooker came up, the position remained tenuous.[8]

That officer, despite delays on the 27th because of the muddy roads, was making good progress from Bridgeport. With O. O. Howard and his two 11th Corps divisions in the van, Hooker came within ten miles of Brown's Ferry before darkness fell. By 2:00 P.M. the next day he was at Wauhatchie; soon thereafter he was marching through Lookout Valley and by late afternoon was within sight of his objective. General Hazen, seeing Hooker and Howard approach, unfurled his battle flags in welcome. "The thrill of mutual recognition," said Howard, "was a . . . joyous event to us; and not less so to those so lately besieged. As we neared them and could catch their accents, we took in the memorable words: 'Hurrah! Hurrah! You have opened up our bread line.' It was a glad meeting; glad for us, who have accomplished the difficult march; glad for them, who had for some time been growing thin on supplies." Enthused one of Hazen's officers: "The depression which had lasted from the days of Chickamauga was gone. The troops felt as if they had been in prison, and were now free."[9]

The Confederates, however, were not yet done. The tail of Hooker's column, one small division of the 12th Corps under General John Geary accompanied by a large wagon train, was carelessly left exposed the night of the 28th at Wauhatchie, where it was three miles from the main force and vulnerable. Bragg's hope was to smash Geary with one quick assault and then move to regain Brown's Ferry. But his chief lieutenant in making the attack, James Longstreet, who was on detached duty with two divisions from the Army of Northern Virginia, was not up to the task. First he made the attack piecemeal and without overwhelming force—sending John Bratton's 1,500 South Carolinians against a like number of Geary's Federals—and then he allowed rivalries within his command to undermine the operation.

Nonetheless the assault when it came, after midnight, sent Geary's camp into wild confusion. General George Greene, in command on the left, went down early in the battle, a ball breaking his jaw and tearing through his cheek, leaving him gushing blood and gasping for breath. Only a critical decision by Geary's artillery chief—to fire shrapnel with short fuses just in front of the lines—blunted Bratton's charge. Some of the Federals were struck down by the shell bursts, but more were saved. The Confederates, now trying to flank the lines, reacted by delivering a furious hail of lead against the artillerymen and horses, straining to see their shapes amid the cannon fire's glare and the moonlight. Captain Edward Geary, the general's son, swung his gun around to answer the challenge. "Fire!" he bellowed. The order was barely given when young Geary fell dead, a bullet between his eyes.

The struggle went on in the semidarkness for hours, each side slamming the other in punch-drunk fashion. By 3:00 A.M. many of Geary's men had exhausted their sixty rounds of ammunition and were picking up the cartridge boxes of the dead and wounded. At some point the Rebels blundered on the wagon train, partially plundering it before being thrown back. Here the terrified mules reputedly turned the tide, at least on this section of the line. "Fortunately for their reputation and the safety of the command," said Captain Horace Porter, "they started toward the enemy, and with heads down and tails up, with trace-chains rattling . . . they rushed pell-mell upon Longstreet's bewildered men. Believing it to be an impetuous charge of cavalry, his line broke." Subsequently the quartermaster supervising the animals suggested, not entirely facetiously, that the mules for their gallantry be given "the brevet rank of horses."

Even though Bratton believed he was getting the upper hand—"The position of things at this time," he would say, referring to the slackening Federal fire, "was entirely favorable to a grand charge"—he was ordered to withdraw, the result of miscommunication between Longstreet's subordinates. Though not happy to receive these instructions, he complied. The South Carolinians would suffer some 350 casualties; Geary would incur a little more than 200.[10]

Hooker meanwhile assumed personal control of Howard's 11th Corps, moving Carl Schurz's and Adolph von Steinwehr's divisions on the road

to Wauhatchie about 1:30 A.M. Like their commander, his three subordinates had been victimized by Jackson at Chancellorsville, and were more
than eager to strike a decisive blow. This night, however, that would not
be. Part of the problem was Hooker who, in his eagerness to make up for
the gaffe of leaving Geary exposed, was losing control of the tactical situation. Riding with von Steinwehr, he assumed Schurz was in the lead, simply because the latter was closer to Wauhatchie and he had ordered him to
relieve Geary on the double quick. Instead von Steinwehr at this point was
in the van, Schurz having taken a roundabout route to avoid enemy gunfire. "He had hardly set out over the rocks and through the thickets," said
General Howard, ". . . probably not sure in his own mind how to get to
that heavy and continuous firing [at Wauhatchie], when a skirmish fire began, coming upon his advance troops. . . ."

The result would be that von Steinwehr, as he passed what came to be
known as Smith's Hill, marched haplessly into an ambush. "Don't fire on
your own troops!" cried out some Rebel. "What regiment are you?"
yelled another. "The 33rd Massachusetts!" someone unwisely answered.
Out of the gloom came a hailstorm of bullets from a brigade of Alabami-
ans led by Evander McIvor Law. The 33rd Massachusetts and 73rd Ohio
were particularly hard hit, and though Law subsequently fell back and the
Federals regrouped, von Steinwehr did not resume his march for hours.

Schurz in the interim had gotten himself back on the road, and was
again in the army's van, when he came to Tyndale's Hill, a key position he
had been ordered to occupy with a brigade, all the men he had with him.
This he did, overcoming minor opposition. Only then did he discover the
rest of his troops had been held up by Hooker who, overreacting to the
ambush back at Smith's Hill, was rapidly adopting a defensive position.
Puzzled, he rode back for further instructions. When Hooker saw him,
and learned that no help was on the way to Geary, he exploded with rage.
"What were your orders, General Schurz?" he shouted, ignoring the fact
that he was responsible for Schurz's two other brigades being kept from
him. Howard about 3:30 A.M. now decided, either inadvertently or in desperation, to move forward on his own.

"I said to General Hooker: 'With your approval I will take too companies of cavalry and push through to Wauhatchie.'"

"All right, Howard," replied Hooker, oblivious that his troops were in
disarray. "I shall be here to attend to this part of the field."

Reaching Wauhatchie about 4:00 A.M.—hours in advance of the luck-
less relief column—Howard found the fighting all but done. "We broke
through the enemy's cordon and reached [General] Greene, who was

frightfully wounded through the face. I knew him and his excellent work at Gettysburg; his wound now, bad as it looked, did not prove fatal." Howard then went on to see Geary, who at six foot four and some 230 pounds was an imposing-looking officer. "He was a vigorous, strong, hearty and cool-headed man, who was astonished to see me suddenly appear. [But] I was surprised to find that as he grasped my hand he trembled with emotion. Without a word he pointed down and I saw that [his] son lay dead at his feet."[11]

The attack at Wauhatchie would be the enemy's last gasp. Now Lookout Valley was firmly in Union hands and the Tennessee River from Bridgeport to Chattanooga was clear. Wrote Grant to Halleck on October 28: "[The] plan for securing the river and south side road hence to Bridgeport has proven eminently successful. The question of supplies may now be regarded as settled." On October 29 the steamboat *Chattanooga* arrived at Kelley's Ferry, bringing the first load of food, forage, and ammunition, preparatory to its being hauled across by wagon to Brown's Ferry and thence to the town. Later, after some navigational problems were solved, each supply boat came by water directly into Brown's Ferry. Its arrival would be met with wild and raucous cheers, the kind usually reserved for esteemed generals.

"Has Grant come?" asked one Federal soldier, thinking the commander was making an appearance.

"Grant be damned," he was told. "A boatload of rations has come."

The troops called the resumption of supplies the "Cracker Line," so named for the ubiquitous hardtack that was one of the army's basic foodstuffs, and they settled down to serious eating. But the commanding general, now that the army was being fed, was already preparing for another climactic battle. No, he told Julia on November 2, in answer to her plea that she be allowed to move to Nashville, where she would be closer to him: "There is not a respectable hotel and I leave no one of my staff there. You would be entirely among strangers. . . ." Then he went on to muse about his most recent promotion. "I see the papers again teem with all sorts of rumors. . . . This time, however, I do not see myself abused. I do not know whether this is a good omen or not. . . . I feel rather lost when not attacked from some quarter."[12]

Perhaps a word is in order here, at the midpoint of the war, as to how the now-seasoned Grant appeared to an officer new to his command—in this case Captain Horace Porter, who soon would transfer to his staff. "Many of us were not a little surprised," said Porter, referring to Grant's larger-than-life image in the press, "to find in him a man of slim figure, slightly stooped, weighing only a hundred and thirty-five pounds, and of a modesty of mien and gentleness of manner that seemed to fit him more for the court than the camp." Grant spoke little, preferring to listen. "But his face gave little indication of his thoughts, and it was the expression of his eyes which furnished . . . the only response to the speaker who conversed with him." His lips were set in a straight line, and his square-shaped jaw "was highly expressive of his force of character and the strength of his will-power." His hair and beard were chestnut brown, and the beard was worn full, no part being shaven, but both were kept closely trimmed. Though he often appeared careworn, his expression "was in no wise an indication of his nature, which was always buoyant, cheerful and hopeful."

Most importantly, said Porter, "When not pressed by any matter of importance [Grant] was often slow in his movements, but when roused to activity he was quick in every motion, and worked with marvelous rapidity. He was civil to all who came in contact with him, and never attempted to snub anyone, or treat anyone with less consideration on account of his inferiority in rank."[13]

Though he had made all haste, Sherman with four divisions of the Army of the Tennessee did not arrive in Chattanooga until November 14. On the first leg of the journey, while in Memphis, he and Ellen had tragically lost their oldest son, Willie, to the ravages of malaria. Writing to the officer whose battalion had made the boy its honorary sergeant, Sherman revealed the depth of his sorrow: "The child that bore my name, and in whose future I reposed with more confidence than I did in my own plan of life, now floats a mere corpse. But Willie was, or thought he was, a sergeant in the 13th [Regulars]. I have seen his eye brighten, his heart beat, as he beheld the battalion under arms. . . . God only knows why he should die this young. . . . Please convey to the battalion my heart-felt thanks, and assure each and all that if in after-years they call on me or mine . . . they will have a key to the affections of my family . . . that we will share with them our last blanket, our last crust."

Now two weeks later Sherman with his usual energy strode into Grant's headquarters, where the two men bantered with each other like the close friends they were.

"Take the chair of honor, Sherman," said Grant, offering him a cigar and pointing toward a rocking chair.

"Oh, no, that belongs to you, General!"

"I don't forget, Sherman, to give proper respect to age," Grant rejoined, referring to the fact he was two years Cump's junior.

"Well, then, if you put it on that ground," said Sherman, "I must accept."

Oliver Howard, who witnessed the exchange, was impressed with the easy relationship between the two officers, as he was with the way they and George Thomas discussed their future strategy. Matters, he reflected, had not been so relaxed in the spit-and-polish and—despite its recent triumph at Gettysburg—largely unsuccessful Army of the Potomac. Grant's premier military biographer summed up the atmosphere succinctly: "Grant and Thomas and Sherman simply talked things out . . . Sherman bubbling with ideas, as always, Thomas full of solid facts about the roads and mountains and rivers where they would have to fight, Grant listening to both men and now and then putting in an observation of his own. Howard . . . felt it was almost like being in a courtroom: Thomas was the learned judge, Sherman the brilliant advocate, and Grant was the jury whose verdict would always settle everything."[14]

With Sherman in camp at last, Grant had some 70,000 men at Chattanooga. From the Army of the Tennessee, which he now commanded, Cump had brought with him four divisions, three of which were from his old 15th Corps, headed by Frank Blair Jr., son of the Washington insider know as Old Man Blair, and an officer whose military instincts were as sound as his father's political connections.

Blair's division chiefs included some familiar names: the German-born Peter Osterhaus of Missouri; Morgan Smith, also of Missouri, veteran of Shiloh and Chickasaw Bluffs; and Hugh Ewing of Ohio—Sherman's brother-in-law and a son of Tom Ewing. Leading the fourth of Sherman's divisions, from the 17th Corps, was John E. Smith of Illinois, whose father had been an officer under Napoleon, and who had served under Black Jack Logan for much of the war.

Osterhaus's brigades were headed by West Pointer Charles Woods of Ohio and lawyer James Williamson of Iowa. Morgan Smith's units were led by his younger brother, Giles Smith, and Andrew Jackson Lightburn of western Virginia, who had lost out to Stonewall Jackson on a West Point appointment and then joined the Old Army as an enlisted man. Hugh Ewing's commanders were John Loomis, lawyer John Corse of Iowa, and Joseph Cockerill of Ohio.

John E. Smith's brigade heads were Jesse Alexander, lawyer Green B. Raum of Illinois, and Prussian-born Charles L. Matthies of Iowa.

Joseph Hooker had come west, as we have seen, with elements of the 11th and 12th Corps from the Army of the Potomac. Desperate and conniving for command, and warned by Lincoln not to overstep himself—"You are ambitious, which, within reasonable bounds, does good rather than harm"—he had failed at Chancellorsville. Here he was striving to regain his reputation. Oliver Otis Howard of the 11th Corps, a devout Christian and an officer who had lost his right arm at Seven Pines earlier in the war, had with him the divisions of Adolph von Steinwehr and Carl Schurz. The former was a Prussian nobleman and experienced soldier, the latter a brilliant orator without military experience; both possessed the loyalty of large numbers of German-Americans. Leading a single division of the 12th Corps was John Geary, who before the war had been territorial governor of strife-torn Kansas.[15]

Von Steinwehr's brigade heads were Adolph Bushbeck and Ohio railroad executive Orland Smith. Schurz's subordinates were Hector Tyndale, an Irish immigrant and successful businessman; Polish-born engineer Wladimir Krzyzanowski, and Frederic Hecker. Geary's brigades were led by Charles Candy, British-born George Cobham Jr. and David Ireland.

Comprising the Army of the Cumberland under George Thomas were the 4th Corps under the Gordon Granger and the 14th Corps under John Palmer. West Pointer Thomas, born in Southampton County, Virginia, in 1816, was a career soldier who had thrown in his lot with the Union—the reverse decision of the ill-fated Pemberton. In 1852, he had married Frances Kellogg of Troy, New York, a calm, statuesque woman nearly her husband's six feet in height. Following the ceremony he was presented with a sword, "of the truest and prettiest steel," inscribed with the names of the places up to that time he had served his country—Florida, Mexico, and California. His wife and her family, however, unlike Pemberton's, had no influence with his Civil War allegiance. Thomas had made up his mind for himself. So did his two maiden sisters in Virginia, who took his portrait and turned it to the wall, threw away his letters, and suggested he change his name. To them he was dead. His cherished sword was forfeit, he was never forgiven, and never received in their home again.[16]

Gordon Granger, a West Pointer who before the war had been posted on the Indian frontier, had been instrumental in marching to the guns and backing up Thomas in his delaying action at Chickamauga. Leading the 14th Corps, longtime politician John Palmer of Illinois had been a major factor in Lincoln gaining the Republican nomination for the presidency in 1860.

In Granger's 4th Corps his division heads were Charles Cruft of Indiana, a railroad president; Philip H. Sheridan of New York, who had been suspended from West Point for a year after a fight with a fellow cadet, but whose rise in command soon would be second only to Grant and Sherman;

and the diligent Thomas Wood, whose alacrity in obeying a misguided order at Chickamauga had, ironically, led to the rout.

Cruft's brigades were led by Walter Whitaker of Kentucky and politician William Grose of Indiana; Sheridan's by Francis Sherman of Illinois (no relation to William Tecumseh), George Wagner of Illinois and the hard-fighting Charles Harker; and Wood's by August Willich of Cincinatti, Prussian-born and an ardent Marxist; William Hazen, who spearheaded the night attack at Brown's Ferry; and Samuel Beatty, an Ohio farmer with little formal education.

In John Palmer's corps the division chiefs were Richard W. Johnson, who would later become a distinguished academician; the improbably named Jefferson C. Davis of Indiana, who had shot a brother officer to death in a Louisville hotel over a perceived insult; and Absalom Baird of Pennsylvania, another career soldier.

Under Johnson were the brigades of Indian fighter William Carlin, Marshall Moore, and John Starkweather of Wisconsin. Davis's units were headed by James D. Morgan, an Illinois merchant; John Beatty, an Ohio banker; and Daniel McCook, one of the innumerable "Fighting Mc-Cook's" of Illinois. Leading Baird's brigades were John Turchin, whom we met at Brown's Ferry, Ohio lawyer Ferdinand Van Derveer, and Edward Phelps.

Grant's third and by far the smallest command, the Army of the Ohio, at this time was stationed near Knoxville, Tennessee, some 150 miles northeast of Chattanooga. It was led by Ambrose Burnside, another refugee from the Army of the Potomac, who had been relieved from command in the East after the bloody Federal defeat at Fredericksburg the previous December. In one of the more bizarre moves of the war, Longstreet had left Chattanooga on November 4 to lay siege to Knoxville, thus depriving Braxton Bragg and his dissension-wracked Confederate Army of Tennessee of 11,000 crack troops, even while Grant was being heavily reinforced from the Federal Army of the Tennessee. Thus in mid-November an increasingly restive 70,000-strong Federal force found itself facing no more than 50,000 of the enemy.

Grant's plans called for going into action as soon as practicable. "Sherman [on the left] was to disappear on the night of the 18th," said Dana, "and encamp his forces behind the ridge of hills north of the Tennessee, opposite to Chattanooga, and keep them there out of sight of the enemy on the 19th. That same night a bridge was to be thrown over the mouth of Chickamauga Creek, so that on November 20th Sherman's command would be across before daylight. . . . As soon as over he was to push for the head of Missionary Ridge, and there engage the enemy." Simultaneously, Gordon Granger with some 18,000 men in the Federal center was to move forward, and Hooker in Lookout Valley on the right was to ascend Lookout Mountain. From the start, however, hitches developed. Not only were there problems with the bridge, meaning that Cump did not get his command across the creek on the 19th and thereby lost the element of surprise, but then heavy rains began, "which lasted two days and made the roads so bad that Sherman's advance was almost stopped."

Because of these mishaps, and because Rebel deserters had indicated that Bragg was planning to lift the siege and withdraw, Grant adjusted his plans. On November 23, intent on forcing a fight, he assembled some 25,000 troops in front of Chattanooga and ordered Granger in the Union center to send a division forward and make a reconnaissance in force. "Our army lay to the south and east of the town . . . with the river being at our back," said Dana. "Facing us, in a great half circle, and high above us on Lookout Mountain and Missionary Ridge, were the Confederates. . . . The first thing Grant tried to do was to clear out the Confederate lines which were nearest to us on the plain south of Chattanooga, and to get hold of two bald knobs, or low hills, where Bragg's forces had their advance guard."

Colonel Joseph Fullerton, an aide to Granger, found the martial scene inspiring. "Flags were flying; the quick, equal steps of thousands beat equal time. The sharp commands of hundreds of company officers, the sound of drums, the ringing notes of the bugles . . . all looked like preparations for a peaceful pageant, rather than for the bloody work of death." So theatrical were the Federal preparations that Bragg initially thought his foes were staging a review. "General Bragg," said one of his lieutenants in rebuttal, "in about fifteen minutes you are going to see the damnedest review you ever saw," and with that the Confederate officers scattered to their commands.[17]

Leading the attack at Orchard Knob, less than a mile from Missionary Ridge, was Thomas Wood's division, consisting of August Willich's, William Hazen's, and Sam Beatty's brigades. To Wood's right in support was Phil Sheridan's division, to his left, Oliver Howard's.

Shortly before 2:00 P.M. Wood's men moved forward on the double-quick, thousands against hundreds, taking heavy casualties but inexorably rolling on. Within fifteen minutes, with Hazen and Willich in the van, the "reconnaissance" had evolved into a full-scale assault, with the Alabama pickets overwhelmed and the crest of the hill taken. Lieutenant Colonel

Robert Kimberly of the 41st Ohio, which lost one-quarter of its strength in the action, recalled its aftermath: "Most of the enemy were lying flat; a few were standing, some of these having thrown down their guns. . . . One or two who had been lying on their backs and firing over their heads did this after the Union troops were on the breastworks and over it, and a man of the 41st was killed by a wild shot of this kind. The [soldier] who fired that shot was crazed with the fight, not seeing what was going on. . . . It was said that the brother of the man who was thus killed after the surrender [likewise] was maddened . . . and with his bayonet pinned the fear-crazed Southerner to the ground."

Wood forthwith signaled for further instructions: his reconnaissance had, in effect, been too successful. Must he now withdraw? While Grant was debating the issue with Thomas, Rawlins approached his chief and made a passionate plea.

"It will not do for them to come back," he said, insisting the men should not give up ground already won.

Grant for a moment said nothing, then turned to Thomas: "Entrench them and send up support," he ordered.[18]

That night and the morning of the 24th brought new tactical developments. On the Federal left, Sherman during this time had gotten two divisions—those of Morgan Smith and John E. Smith—across the Tennessee at South Chickamauga Creek, but he uncharacteristically paused, waiting for Hugh Ewing to cross before moving toward the upper end of Missionary Ridge. Bragg meanwhile, alarmed by the Union attack at Orchard Knob, had taken one of two divisions from Lookout Mountain and moved it to strengthen his center, thus weakening his left. Now it appeared to Grant that the Confederates would be vulnerable to flank attacks on the 24th by Sherman and Hooker, with Thomas in the center taking a secondary role, and he issued the appropriate orders accordingly.

With the morning wearing on, however, the commander began to wonder why Sherman was not advancing. "Considerable movement has taken place on top of the ridge toward you," Grant wrote him. "Howard has [also] sent a force to try and flank the enemy on our left. . . . Until I do hear from you I am loath to give any orders for a general engagement. . . . Send me word what can be done to aid you." James Wilson, watching Sherman's lack of progress, was less diplomatic. "There was nothing for him to do but move against the enemy," he said. ". . . Nothing could have been more favorable to a direct attack or to a turning movement against the enemy's right flank and rear but . . . Sherman's movements were slow and ineffective."

Not until 1:00 P.M., with Hooker already well engaged at Lookout Mountain, did Cump get under way, and even then—worried that the he might be marching into a hornet's nest—in a halting manner. Two hours later his van was still one-half mile from the upper, or northern, end of Missionary Ridge, which the Confederates, now alerted to their danger, were rushing to reinforce. A word is in order here about the topography of the situation. Upper Missionary Ridge in effect ended at Tunnel Hill, near the Chattanooga and Cleveland Railroad. A cluster of hills apparently extended the ridge farther, up to South Chickamauga Creek, but they were separated from the ridge proper by a steep, half-mile-wide ravine. It was toward this cluster that Sherman about 3:30 P.M. directed his assault, encountering only minor resistance. Only when he was atop it, facing Tunnel Hill, did he realize his error.

With less than an hour of daylight remaining, he decided not to resume the attack. "From studying all the maps," he said of his mistake, "I had inferred that Missionary Ridge was a continuous hill; but we found ourselves on two high points, with a deep depression between us and the one over the tunnel, which was my chief objective point. The ground we had gained, however, was so important that I could leave nothing to chance, and ordered it to be fortified." Scoffed one officer in the Army of the Cumberland, taking a perverse delight in Sherman's and the Army of the Tennessee's discomfort: "It was certainly one of the most remarkable oversights of the war. . . . Every field hand in the vicinity could have given the needed information."[19]

On the Federal right that morning, meantime, an impatient Hooker was chafing at the bit. His orders called for making little more than a demonstration against 2,200-foot Lookout Mountain, but Fighting Joe was intent on routing its defenders—and proving that his defeat at Chancellorsville had been an aberration. Besides John Geary's division of the Army of the Potomac, he commanded Cruft's division of the Army of the Cumberland, together with Osterhaus's division of the Army of the Tennessee. It was a polyglot force, but one that would work well together.

In mist and heavy fog Hooker shortly after dawn began moving Geary's command, together with Whitaker's brigade, Cruft's command, across Lookout Creek and up the western slope of the mountain, hoping to catch the enemy in flank. Once this had been accomplished, his remaining troops were to move up from the base of the mountain, closing the trap. "As soon as [Hooker's] movement was discovered," said Colonel Fullerton, "the enemy withdrew his own troops from the summit of the mountain, changed front, and formed a new line to meet our advance, his left resting at the palisade, and his right at the heavy works in the valley. . . . Whitaker's brigade, being in the advance, drove back the enemy's pickets and quickly ascended the mountain till it reached the foot of the palisade." Here, his right securely anchored, Whitaker reached out on his left to Geary, who in turn had moved up the western side of the mountain, and thus about 11:00 A.M. covered the crossing of Cruft and Osterhaus.

"Hooker's command," Fullerton continued, "now united in the enemy's field, was ready to advance and sweep around the mountain. His line, hanging at the base of the palisades like a great pendulum, reached down the side of the mountain to the valley, where the force that had just crossed the creek was attached to its weight. Now . . . as it swung forward in its upward movement, the artillery of the Army of the Cumberland, on Moccasin Point, opened fire, throwing a stream of shot and shell into the enemy's rifle pits . . . and into the works thickly planted on the 'White House' plateau." This last reference was to the white farmhouse of the Cravens family, located on a plateau halfway up the mountainside.[20]

Though the fog made it impossible to see more than a few yards in his front, Hooker at this juncture pursued the battle in earnest. The "demonstration" had become an all-out assault. "We had to shoot at the flash of the guns, the mist or cloud was so heavy," said Lieutenant Chesley Mosman of the 59th Illinois. "The fog and smoke were so thick we could not see a man two paces from us, but the Rebel bullets flew over us in showers. . . ." When a Union battery mistakenly opened fire on the Federals, Sergeant John Kiggins, color-bearer of the 149th New York, rushed forward between the two lines to wave his flag and avert disaster. Ten bullets riddled his uniform, and one went through his thigh, but he survived.

Outnumbered perhaps four to one but aided by the terrain, the enemy gave ground. "After fighting for nearly two hours, step-by-step up the steep mountain-side, over and through deep gullies and ravines, over great rocks and fallen trees," said Colonel Fullerton, "the earthworks on the plateau were assaulted and carried, and the enemy . . . was forced to fall back." By midafternoon Hooker was more than satisfied with his progress—he was turning and carrying the mountain's eastern face, reopening communications with Chattanooga, and threatening the enemy's left on Missionary Ridge. Nearly out of ammunition, he called a halt.

"In the morning," Fullerton went on, "it had not been known in Chattanooga, in Sherman's army, or in Bragg's camp, that a battle was to be fought. Sherman's men at the other end of the line, intent on the north end of Missionary Ridge, and Thomas' men in the center, fretting to be let loose from their entrenchments, was startled by the sound of artillery and musketry firing in Lookout Valley. Surprise possessed the thousands who turned their anxious eyes toward the mountain. The hours slowly wore away. . . . A battle was being fought just before and above them. They could hear, but could not see how it was going." Then the mist and fog for a few minutes slowly lifted, giving the Federals below a clear view of the action around the White House plateau. "The enemy was seen to be in flight, and Hooker's men were in pursuit! Then went up a mighty cheer . . . that was heard above the battle by their comrades on the mountain."[21]

Hooker did not at this point take the summit of the mountain, but the Confederates there—who had been unable to depress heir cannon barrels enough to be a factor in the fight—had no choice but to vacate the position during the night, lest they be cut off from Missionary Ridge. In truth the battle involved relatively few casualties, with the Federals doing more climbing than fighting, and the enemy's resolve had been less than stalwart. Nonetheless Hooker had every reason to be proud of his triumph, which came to be known as "The Battle Above the Clouds," and he enjoyed it to the fullest, sending a detachment from the 8th Kentucky to the summit the next morning to wave the biggest Stars and Stripes he could find. Then the cheering broke out anew. "Look at old Hooker," said one soldier admiringly. "Don't he fight for keeps?"[22]

Grant's plans for the 25th remained much the same as the previous day. He was confident that Sherman on the left, given a second chance, finally would turn the upper ridge, and he now ordered Hooker on the right to come down from Lookout Mountain, cross Chattanooga Creek, and threaten Bragg's left. George Thomas was told to wait in the works at Orchard Knob, if for no other reason than his Army of the Cumberland was facing three apparently impregnable lines of parallel entrenchments along the 500-foot-plus ridge—one of rifle pits at the base, another halfway up, the third bristling with artillery at the top. But Grant's flanking movements were not to prove successful. It would take Hooker some six hours to repair the bridge the enemy had destroyed behind them, keeping him from being a factor, and Sherman's efforts, in a classic match-up of generals, would be thwarted by a determined foe.

Cump's opponent on the upper ridge was thirty-five-year-old Major General Patrick Cleburne, an Irish immigrant who after serving in the British army had arrived in America some fourteen years before, become a prosperous lawyer, and settled in Helena, Arkansas. At Shiloh his tenacious brigade had fought stubbornly and well, taking casualties of almost 40 percent, the heaviest of any such Southern unit; at Chickamauga his division had likewise distinguished itself. In private Cleburne, who was born on St. Patrick's eve, was mild-mannered and modest; in battle, ferocious and unyielding—so much so that some were calling him the Stonewall Jackson of the West. His 4,000 or so men were considered the shock troops of the army.

But Sherman, though he had the troops to assail the enemy position with four times or more that number, for the second day in a row would be indecisive, instead committing his brigades piecemeal. Ordered first— about 10:00 A.M.—to assault Cleburne at Tunnel Hill was John Corse's brigade, Hugh Ewing's division. "I guess, Ewing, if you're ready, you might as well go ahead," Sherman casually told his brother-in-law. ". . . Don't call for help until you actually need it."

That Corse's men, proud veterans of Vicksburg, would need help as they closed on the enemy would be certain, given that they moved on a narrow front into the teeth of his muskets and cannon. Their ranks steadily evaporated, cut down by minie balls and canister. "To see them blue coats fall is glorious," said Captain Samuel Foster of Texas. "We can see them dropping all along their lines. Sometimes great gaps are made— they can't stand it—and away they go to find shelter from our bullets." Corse went down, wounded in the head, but the Federals regrouped and came on. "They have a flag. . . . Down it came, [yet] another [soldier] picks it up, and down he went. Then another." Foster could only shake his head at the pigheadedness of the frontal attack. "[We] lie here and shoot them down and we don't get hurt—we are behind these logs. We give them fits."[23]

Next to move up an hour and a half later was John Loomis's command, also Ewing's division. The batteries atop Tunnel Hill again were merciless, riddling the brigade as it pushed forward along open ground. Now Loomis sought cover along a railroad embankment, with the men of his Indian and Illinois regiments digging into the dirt with their bare hands. Nearby a ditch began to fill with the wounded. Here two brothers of the 12th Indiana crouched, one dying and the other holding him and listening to his last words. Later the survivor wrote their parents: "I spoke to him about his soul and he did not seem at first to be satisfied to die, but shortly the Lord powerfully blessed him and he was enabled to shout although he suffered intensely. He took from his pocket a Testament and . . . told me to read it and meet him in Glory."

It was 1:00 P.M. Thrown into the melee against Cleburne at this point was the brigade of German-born Charles Matthies—Old Dutchie his troops called him. From a half mile away it came under the enemy's cannon fire.

"We moved now on a charge, running across the open fields," said Lieutenant Samuel Byers of the 5th Iowa, whom we last met at Champion's
Hill. "I had heard the roaring of heavy battle before, but never such a
shrieking of cannonballs and bursting shells. . . . Behind us our own batteries were firing at the enemy over our heads. . . . All the officers were
screaming at the top of their voices; I, too, screamed trying to make the
men hear. 'Steady! Bear to the right! Keep in line! Don't fire! Don't fire!'
was yelled till we all were hoarse. . . ."

Here, as Matthies's bloodied men arrived and hunkered down at the
base of Tunnel Hill, Jenkin Jones of the 6th Wisconsin Battery recalled the
scene: "A terrible struggle followed, wounded men coming back thick and
fast. . . . Our loss is very heavy especially in officers. . . . Our line advanced up the steep side of the bluff time after time; but [was] obliged to
fall back. . . . [My feelings] listening to the noise and rattle of the fight,
mingled with suppressed cheers of charging parties, and the groans of the
wounded as they passed in the long trains of ambulances . . . I cannot describe in words." Matthies himself was hit, and forced to leave the field.[24]

While these Federals crouched under the ridge, enduring not only minie
balls but a fusillade of rocks from the Rebels above them, still a fourth
brigade, that of Green Raum, came up about 2:30 P.M. in support. Together the two units for the next hour and a half inched their way up the
slope, making headway but suffering severe casualties. Now Cleburne decided to roll the dice. Gathering every man he could find—Georgians, Texans, Arkansans, and Tennesseans—he sent his command in a bayonet
charge down the hill, intent on taking the enemy in front and flank and
ending the Union threat once and for all. The effect was magical.
Matthies's and Raum's brigades scattered in wild confusion, some running
for their lives, some falling dead and wounded, others having little choice
but to surrender. Lieutenant Byers found himself in the latter category.

"Come out of that sword!" shouted a big Georgian amid a string of
oaths, taking his blade. "Get up the hill quicker than hell!" yelled another,
grabbing his revolver and shoving him toward the Rebel lines.

For Sherman the engagement had ended in near-total disaster. Raum
had taken a bullet in the thigh—the third of the four brigade commanders
immediately involved to be wounded—and the Federal troops had incurred more than 1,500 casualties. Cleburne's losses were some 220. Observed one Kentuckian of the charge: "They had swept their front clean of
Yankees; indeed, when I went up about sundown, the side of the ridge in
their front was strewn with dead Yankees & looked like a lot of boys had
been sliding down the hill side, for when a line of the enemy would be

repulsed, they would start down hill & soon the whole line would be rolling down like a ball."

Why Sherman did not use all his troops on the 25th, why he did not mass those he did use, and why he attacked Tunnel Hill head-on rather than at least trying to turn the enemy right we do not know. Grant never publicly criticized him for his failure. Perhaps he felt, as the unfortunate George Pickett felt about his repulse at Gettysburg—"I think the Union army had something to do with it"—that in Cump's case Patrick Cleburne and the Rebels had a hand in the outcome.[25]

This is not to say, of course, that Grant was not deeply worried about Sherman's predicament. Sometime about 3:00 P.M. at Orchard Knob he said to General Thomas Wood, "General Sherman seems to be having a hard time. I think we ought to try to do something to help him."

"I think so, too, General," replied Wood, who like all of Thomas's men in the Army of the Cumberland was eager to go on the attack and avenge Chickamauga.

"If you and [Philip] Sheridan were to advance your divisions and carry the rifle pits at the base of the ridge," Grant mused, ignoring that fact that Sherman already had overwhelming superiority in numbers, "it would so threaten Bragg's center that he would [have to] draw enough troops from the right to secure his center, [and] insure the success of General Sherman's attack."

Within minutes, after conferring with George Thomas and with Gordon Granger—the corps commander, Grant ordered Wood and Sheridan forward to take the pits—with Absalom Baird and Richard Johnson in support, some 25,000 men—but to go no further without explicit instructions.

Lieutenant William Morgan of the 23rd Kentucky, an officer in William Hazen's brigade, Wood's division, described the assault: "We see the enemy in the rifle pits . . . prepared to deliver fire. Why so they hesitate? We are in range. They are evidently waiting so that every shot will tell. From the enemy's lower lines now comes a storm of bullets and the air is filled with every sound of battle." Here, with fifty cannon raining shot and shell upon them, a sustained cheer nonetheless rose from the onrushing Federals. "The quick step has been changed to the 'double-quick.' Another cheer, and the enemy's first line of work is ours, together with many of his troops." Grant, however, had made a tactical mistake; once in the pits, the Federals were subject to withering fire from the ridge above. "Shelter is sought on the reverse side of the enemy's works, but the fire from the hilltop makes protection impossible."[26]

For General Hazen, staying at the base was not an option. "The only way to avoid destruction was to go on up . . . the necessity was apparent to every soldier of the command." When Wood rode up to the rifle pits, his men implored him to let them go forward. "General, we can carry the ridge!" someone yelled. "Men, go ahead!" Wood responded. "I frankly confess I was one of the boys on that occasion," he later explained. "I was infected with the contagion of the prevailing enthusiasm."

The flamboyant Phill Sheridan, on Wood's and Hazen's right, likewise sent his men rushing up the slope, stopping only long enough to take a flask filled with whiskey from his pocket, rising in his stirrups and raising it in a toast to the enemy before taking a long swallow.

"Here's to you, General Bragg," he shouted amid the cannonading.

His impudence did not pass unnoticed. The sight of an officer on horseback making such a target redoubled the efforts of the Rebel artillerymen, whose shells missed but showered him with dirt and stones. "That is damned unkind," Sheridan reputedly remarked. "I saw, and heard, the whole performance," groused one nearby noncom, "but instead of thinking it a grand and heroic act, I only wished he would quit his foolishness."[27]

Seeing the troops disregarding his instructions, and fearing that the Army of the Cumberland might be decimated, Grant about 4:15 P.M. reacted angrily. "Thomas," he asked, "who ordered those men up the ridge?"

"I don't know," the stolid Thomas answered, "I did not."

"Did you order them up, Granger?" Grant inquired.

"No, they started up without orders," the hardened Indian fighter replied. Then he added, with pride, "When those fellows get started all hell can't stop them."

Grant turned away, staring stoically at the ridge and muttering that "somebody would suffer" if the sortie failed.

Granger now strode over to an aide, Joseph Fullerton, and dispatched him with a message to Wood and Sheridan. "Ask them if they ordered their men up the ridge, and tell them, if they can take it, to push ahead." Wood and Sheridan both denied initiating the charge, which strictly speaking was true; left unsaid was that they had not restrained it. "They started up on their own account," said Wood of his troops. ". . . Tell Granger, if we are supported, we will take and hold the ridge!" Echoed Sheridan: "I didn't order them up, but we [will] take the ridge!"

Fullerton picks up the story as the Federals moved against the second line of rifle pits and beyond: "The men, fighting and climbing up the steep hill, sought the roads, ravines and less rugged parts. The ground was so broken that it was impossible to keep a regular line of battle. At times their movements were in shape like migratory birds—sometimes in line, sometimes in mass, mostly in V-shaped groups, with the points toward the enemy. At these points [sixty] regimental flags were flying, sometimes dropping as the bearers were shot, but never reaching the ground, for other brave hands were there to seize them."[28]

Helping the advance immeasurably was the fact that the Confederates halfway up the ridge and on the crest at times were constrained to hold their fire, lest they hit their own men fleeing up the slope. The Rebel guns and works atop the crest, moreover, had been erroneously placed against the skyline, instead of just below it. There the men not only were silhouetted, making them vulnerable to musket fire, but the cannon barrels could not be depressed sufficiently to sweep the entire field. Halfway up the hill, blind spots existed where the Federals were safe from artillery fire.

For Major James A. Connolly, an aide to General Baird, the Federal advance through the second line of pits and up the slope was slow but inexorable. "Our flag bearer, on hands and knees, is seen away in advance of the whole line; he crawls and climbs toward a Rebel flag he sees waving above him . . . his regiment follows him as fast as it can; in a few moments another flag bearer gets just as near the summit and his regiment soon gets to him . . . they crouch there and are safe from the Rebels above them, who would have to rise up to fire down at them, and so expose themselves. . . ." The suspense was palpable. "If we can gain that ridge; if we can scale those breastworks, the Rebel army is routed . . . but if we cannot . . . few of us will get down this mountain side and back to the shelter of the woods. . . ."

Bragg at this juncture—about 5:00 P.M.—desperately was hurrying reinforcements from his right, where Sherman had broken off the engagement, to shore up his center. But his efforts were of no avail. "The critical moment arrived when the summit was just within reach," concludes Fullerton. "At six different points, and almost simultaneously, Sheridan's and Wood's divisions broke over the crest. . . . Baird's division took the works on Wood's left almost immediately afterwards, and then Johnson came up on Sheridan's right. The enemy's guns were turned upon those who still remained in the works, and soon [the Rebels] were in flight down the eastern slope." Shouts of "Chickamauga! Chickamauga!" sounded from hundreds of throats. The sun was not yet down, and the Federals had taken Missionary Ridge.

"The storming of the ridge . . . was one of the greatest miracles in military history," Charles Dana enthused. "No man who climbs the ascent by any of the roads that wind along its front can believe that . . . men were moved in tolerably good order up its broken and crumbling face unless it was his fortune to witness the deed. It seemed as awful as a visible interposition of God."

In truth the troops of the Army of the Cumberland, in making the charge, seem to have driven by a messianic fever, a force that transcended physical obstacles. Following the battle a member of the Christian Commission, giving what aid he could to the wounded, stopped some stretcher bearers bringing a sergeant to the rear. "Where are you hurt?" he asked.

"Almost up, sir," answered the man.

"I mean, where are you injured?"

"Almost to the top," the sergeant murmured.

The aid worker pulled open the soldier's coat, and saw for himself the gaping wound.

"Yes," the sergeant said, looking at the wound himself, "yes, that's what did it; but for that I should have reached the top." Then, even as he was borne away, he repeated, "Almost to the top, almost to the top. . . ."[29]

During the three-day campaign, at a cost of some 5,800 casualties (the Confederates lost almost 6,700) Grant had not only lifted the siege of Chattanooga but, just as importantly, deprived the Confederacy of any hope of regaining Tennessee and opened up the route to its vital rail center at Atlanta, Georgia. Two days later, at Ringgold Gap, the Federals strove to follow up on their success by falling on Bragg before he could regroup and destroying his supply wagons. Such was not to be. Joe Hooker, commanding the advance, ran into Patrick Cleburne's nasty delaying action and thought it wise to let the Rebels, without further hindrance, move south into Georgia. Concomitantly, there was the need to relieve Burnside's Army of the Ohio at Nashville, where Bragg had foolishly sent James Longstreet and his superb divisions from the Army of Northern Virginia. This Sherman did in short order, driving Longstreet back into eastern Tennessee.

Grant had been lucky at Chattanooga, and he knew it. Not just because his men at Missionary Ridge had taken it upon themselves to make the final assault but because in Braxton Bragg he had faced an uninspiring commander, one whom his own soldiers had grown to distrust. If Longstreet's divisions had been retained along the ridge, the possibility certainly exists that the Federals, like Pickett's men at Gettysburg, might well have failed. Grant was candid enough to admit this, and he subsequently painted an interesting portrait of Bragg, whose inability to get along with Longstreet or most of his other subordinates had weakened his command.

"Bragg was a remarkably intelligent and well-informed man, professionally and otherwise," he said. "He was also thoroughly upright. But he was possessed of an irascible temper, and was naturally disputatious." Grant went on to tell an anecdote about Bragg from the Old Army, when he held the dual posts of company commander and quartermaster. In the former role he requisitioned some items from the latter—who happened to be himself. Bragg then denied the requisition, giving his reasons for so doing. He then reinstated the requisition, giving his own reasons, and back and forth the requisitions and denials flew. Finally he brought the whole matter to the attention of the camp commander.

"My God, Mr. Bragg," said that worthy, "you have quarreled with every officer in the army, and now you quarreling with yourself!"

Grant nonetheless had won the battle and, as we know, the world loves a winner. "Understanding your lodgment at Chattanooga and Knoxville is now secure, I wish to tender you, and all under your command, my more than thanks, my profoundest gratitude," wired Lincoln. "I congratulate you thus far on the success of your plans," said Halleck. Proclaimed the *New York Herald:* "Gen. Grant is one of the great soldiers of the age. . . ." Not to be outdone, the *New York World* declaimed: "General Grant, out of a maze of tactics more wondrous than ever before . . . had evolved a victory for our arms the importance of which it is yet impossible to estimate." The indefatigable Congressman Washburne, the man who in June of 1861 had started Grant's rise to command in Galena, Illinois, forthwith produced a bill in the House calling for the new rank of lieutenant general—naming no names, but strongly implying who the first beneficiary would be.

The object of this foofaraw found the attention distracting. "I feel under many obligations to you for the interest you have taken in my welfare," Grant wrote Washburne. "But recollect that I have been highly honored already by the government. . . . A success over the enemy is what I crave above everything else. . . ."[30]

1864

ONE
* * * *

LINCOLN MEETS HIS GENERAL

With the coming of 1864 Grant's prospects—personal as well as professional—reached new highs. His salary as a major general was some $6,000 a year, then a handsome sum, and not only was he out of debt but he was amassing savings and making investments, including $5,000 in government bonds and real estate holdings in Missouri. Writing to J. Russell Jones, the United States Marshall in Chicago, a longtime Galena friend who doubled as his financial adviser, he spelled out his monetary ambitions: "I wish to keep what funds I have, collect the interest on the bonds, and retain the gold so collected as a special deposit. I also send herewith $500 more and will continue to send as I can from my pay. At any time you see any little investment for me with the funds on hand, make it without hesitation."

During this period, Grant even was being suggested by anti-Lincoln politicians and journalists in the North as a presidential candidate in the fall elections. ("The next President must be a military man," insisted James Gordon Bennett, publisher of the *New York Herald*.") Replying to Jones's query as to his intentions, Grant was unequivocal: "I am receiving a great deal of that kind of literature, but it soon finds its way into the waste basket. I already have a pretty big job on my hands. . . . Nothing could induce me to think of being a Presidential candidate, particularly as long as there is a possibility of having Mr. Lincoln re-elected."

Lincoln, as it happened, was aware that his general's name was being floated as a rival, and he called in Congressman Washburne to discuss the situation. "About all I know of Grant I have got from you," he complained. "Who else besides you knows anything about [him]?" When Washburne suggested Jones, the president forthwith invited the latter to the White House for a private chat. During their meeting, when he asked about Grant's political ambitions, Jones wordlessly took out his friend's letter and slid it across the presidential desk.

"My son, you will never know how gratifying that is to me," said a relieved Lincoln after reading the note. "No man knows, when that Presidential grub gets to gnawing at him, just how deep it will get until he has tried it; and I didn't know that there was one gnawing at Grant."[1]

By early March Congress passed the bill reviving the rank of lieutenant general—the first such post since George Washington in 1798—Lincoln signed the measure into law, and Grant was called to the capital to accept the promotion. With it came a $2,600 raise and the title general-in-chief, which Halleck relinquished, becoming chief of staff and military adviser to the president—a bureaucratic niche far more suited to his abilities. Halleck's demotion long had been on the horizon. "When [George] McClellan seemed incompetent to the work of handling an army and we sent for Halleck to take command," John Hay, Lincoln's secretary, quoted him as saying, "[Halleck] stipulated that it should be with full power and responsibility as [general-in-chief]. He ran it on that basis until [John] Pope's defeat [at Second Bull Run in 1862]; but ever since that event he has shrunk from responsibility whenever it was possible." In truth, Halleck's fall stemmed directly from the failure of the Army of the Potomac to deal decisively with Robert E. Lee in the East. McClellan, Pope, Ambroise Burnside, Hooker all had been bested, and even George Meade, the victor at Gettysburg, had not destroyed the Army of Northern Virginia's capabilities. Now Grant, ascending to command over his onetime nemesis, would have his chance.[2]

Before leaving for Washington, the new general-in-chief sent off a more than appreciative letter to Sherman: "While I have been eminently successful in this war, in at least gaining the confidence of the public, no one feels more than me how much of this success is due to the energy, skill and harmonious putting forth of that energy and skill, of those who it has been my good fortune to have occupying a subordinate position under me. There are many officers to whom these remarks are applicable . . . but what I want is to express my thanks to you and [James] McPherson as *the men* to whom, above all others, I feel indebted for whatever I have had of success. How far your advice and suggestions have been of assistance, you know. How far your execution of whatever has been given you to do entitles you to the reward I am receiving you cannot know as well as me. . . ."

Back in subsequent days came Sherman's reply, delivered in the near-hyperbolic terms he favored but indicative of their close and mutually respectful relationship: "You do yourself injustice, and us too much honor, in assigning to us too large a share of the merits which have led to your advancement. . . . At Belmont you manifested your traits—neither of us being near. At Donelson, also, you illustrated your whole character. I was not near, and McPherson in too subordinate a capacity to influence you. . . . The chief characteristic of your nature is the simple faith in success you have always manifested, which I can liken to nothing else than the faith a Christian has in his Savior. This faith gave you victory at Shiloh and Vicksburg. When you have completed your preparations, you go into battle without hesitation, as at Chattanooga . . . and I tell you it was this that made us act with confidence. I knew wherever I was that you thought of me, and if I got into a tight place you would help me out, if alive. My only points of doubt [were] in your knowledge of grand strategy . . . but I confess your common-sense seems to have supplied this."[3]

Grant arrived in Washington the evening of March 8 without fanfare—an official welcome had somehow gone awry—accompanied by thirteen-year-old Fred and the ubiquitous John Rawlins, and headed to the Willard Hotel on Pennsylvania Avenue. There a desk clerk, dismissing the rumpled traveler as a nonentity, allowed he might have a small room available on the top floor. When Grant signed the register, however—"U.S. Grant and son, Galena, Ill."—the clerk suddenly remembered the best suite in the hotel happened to be available. Word spread quickly through the Willard. By the time Grant entered the dining room, all eyes were on him. "People scrambled to their feet," said a biographer, "there was a rhythmic shout of "Grant! Grant! Grant!" and someone called for three cheers, which were promptly given. Grant stood up, fumbled with his napkin, bowed impersonally to all points of the compass, and then sat down and tried to go on with his dinner. He did not get much to eat, because too many people were swarming about him, and before long the General and the boy left . . . and went up to their living quarters."

Within minutes a gaggle of politicians arrived at Grant's door, announced that the president was holding a reception for him that very evening, and about 9:00 P.M. hustled him to the White House. Hundreds of curious people were in the East Room when he entered, crowding it to capacity, but initially they hushed and parted before Grant as if for royalty, allowing him to walk its length unimpeded and present himself to a smiling Lincoln.

"Why, here is General Grant!" said the president, taking his hand and shaking it with great vigor. "Well, this is a great pleasure I assure you!"

The meeting was a historical one for the Union, and Captain Horace Porter, who as we know had initially met Grant at Chattanooga, was conscious of its significance. "Standing face to face for the first time were the two illustrious men whose names will always be inseparably associated in connection with the war of the rebellion," he said. "Grant's right hand grasped the lapel of his coat; his head was bent slightly forward, and his eyes upturned toward Lincoln's face. The President, who was eight inches taller, looked down with beaming countenance upon his guest. . . . Each was of humble origin, and had been compelled to learn the first lessons of life in the severe school of adversity. Each had risen from the people, possessed an abiding confidence in them, and always retained a deep hold upon their affections."[4]

Lincoln introduced Grant to Secretary of State Seward, who in turn escorted him to meet Mrs. Lincoln, and various other introductions followed. Meanwhile the crowd was pushing forward, whipping itself into high excitement as it tried to see, and get close to, the visitor from the West. "The vast throng surged and swayed . . . until alarm was felt for the safety of the ladies," Porter said. "Cries now arose of 'Grant! Grant! Grant!' Then came cheer after cheer. Seward, after some persuasion, induced the general to stand upon a sofa, thinking the [people] would be satisfied with a view of him, and retire; but as soon as they caught sight of him their shouts were renewed, and a rush was made to shake his hand." Wrote one Washington correspondent: "It was the only real mob I ever saw in the White House. For once at least the President of the United States was not the chief figure in the picture. The little . . . man who stood on a crimson-covered sofa was the idol of the hour."[5]

The next day Grant, accompanied by his son and aides, returned to the White House to formally accept from Lincoln his commission as lieutenant general. In a ceremony witnessed by cabinet officers and a few others, the president declared in part: "With this high honor devolves upon you, also, a corresponding responsibility. As the country herein trusts you, so, under God, it will sustain you. I scarcely need to add that, with what I here speak for the nation, goes my own hearty personal concurrence."

To which Grant replied, reading from a paper on which he had scribbled his remarks: "With the aid of the noble armies that have fought in so many fields for our common country, it will be my earnest endeavor not to disappoint your expectations. I feel the full weight of the responsibilities now devolving upon me; and I know that if they are met, it will be due to those armies, and above all, to the favor of that Providence that leads both nations and men."

Following these comments, the two men retired for a private chat. He knew full well he was not a military expert, Lincoln told Grant, but the procrastination and bungling of previous commanders in the East had forced him to make military decisions. McClellan, Pope, Burnside, Hooker—all had been found lacking and had been replaced. "He did not know but they were all wrong, and did know that some of them were," Grant would say of the conversation. "All he wanted or had ever wanted was someone who would take the responsibility and act, and call on him for all the assistance needed, pledging himself to use all the power of the government in rendering such [aid]. Assuring him that I would do the best I could . . . and avoid annoying him or the War Department, our first interview ended." Now Grant, victorious in the West, would be directing the war in both theaters.[6]

Lincoln's promise to give his general free rein would be scrupulously observed. On one occasion subsequently, when Secretary of War Stanton tried to dictate how many men should be left in the Washington garrison, Grant demurred.

"I think I rank you in this matter, Mr. Secretary," he told him.

"We shall have to see Mr. Lincoln about that," Stanton answered.

Off the two men went to the White House, where the president heard them out and then rendered his decision: "You and I, Mr. Stanton, have been trying to boss this job, and we have not succeeded very well with it. We have sent across the mountains for Mr. Grant, as Mrs. Grant calls him, to relieve us, and I think we had better leave him alone to do as he pleases."

To be sure, the new general-in-chief was facing an immense challenge. Simultaneously he would be launching an attack into the Southern interior—Georgia and the Carolinas—and moving forward in Virginia against the formidable Lee, who despite the defeat at Gettysburg had retained his near-mythic status in South and North alike.

For Grant the first order of business, following his chat with the president, was traveling to Brandy Station, just north of the Rapidan River, and meeting with George Meade, whom he had known slightly during the Mexican War but had not seen since. The Army of the Potomac had just been reorganized into three corps but, said Grant, "Meade evidently thought that I might want to make still one more change not yet ordered. He said to me I might want an officer who had served with me in the West, mentioning Sherman specially, to take his place. If so, he begged me not to hesitate. . . . He urged that the work before us was of such vast importance . . . that the feeling or wishes of no one person should stand in the way of selecting the right men for all positions." Grant assured Meade he had no intention of supplanting him. "This incident gave me even a more favorable opinion of Meade than did his great victory at Gettysburg the July before. It is men who wait to be selected, and not those who seek, from whom we may always expect the most efficient service."[7]

The future relationship between Grant and Meade, while never close, would be both dutiful and professional. Charles Dana, now attached to the Army of the Potomac, would say of the latter: "He was a tall, thin man, rather dyspeptic, I should suppose from the fits of nervous irritation to which he was subject. He was totally lacking in cordiality toward those with whom he had business, and in consequence was generally disliked by his subordinates." With Grant, however, "Meade got along always perfectly, because he had the first virtue of a soldier—that is, obedience to orders. He was an intellectual man, and agreeable to talk with when his mind was free, but silent and indifferent to everybody when he was occupied. . . ." To Dana, Meade was a perfect number two. "He lacked self-confidence and tenacity of purpose, and he had not the moral authority that Grant had attained. . . . As soon as Meade had a commander over him he was all right, but when he himself was the commander he began to hesitate."

What was called hesitation by some men, however, was considered prudence by others. Criticized both by the government and the press for not pursuing Lee in the aftermath of Gettysburg, Meade had good reasons for his caution. Not only could the Rebels have turned on him at any time, forcing the Federals into the type of bloody frontal attack they had so recently repulsed, but Lee before withdrawing behind the Rappahannock had seen to it that Meade's railroad supply lines were torn up. Months later, when he suspended hostilities for the winter instead of assaulting the entrenched Rebels at Mine Run in Virginia, the criticism intensified. Most of his troops were far more supportive. "Thank heaven that we are back to our old camping ground," said one relieved veteran," and that I still live."

George Gordon Meade was born in Spain in 1815, the son of a wealthy American merchant who subsequently suffered financial ruin during the Napoleonic Wars. Following graduation from West Point, his career was almost exclusively in civil and military engineering. In the initial stages of the war he had commanded a brigade of Pennsylvanians on the Peninsula and at the Seven Days, and had fought in most engagements thereafter. Like McClellan, who would run against Lincoln in his bid for reelection in November, his politics were those of the northern Democrats rather than the radical Republicans—meaning he was adamant about preserving the Union but ambivalent about emancipation and black rights. Brusque, prone to anger, profane, haggard—he did not flourish under the burdens of command. Wrote one correspondent: "His face is almost covered with beard, and . . . is colorless, being of a ghastly pale, with thought, study and anxiety marked upon his every lineament. . . ."[8]

Heading Meade's corps would be Major Generals Winfield Scott Hancock of Pennsylvania, 2nd Corps; Gouverneur K. Warren of New York, 5th Corps; and John Sedgwick of Connecticut, 6th Corps. "Hancock," acknowledged Dana, "was a splendid fellow, a brilliant man, as brave as Julius Caesar. . . . He had more of the aggressive spirit than almost anybody else in that army." Perhaps the most respected of Meade's senior officers, Hancock was, Grant would say, "Tall, well-formed and . . . young and fresh-looking. He presented an appearance that would attract the attention of an army as he passed. His genial disposition made him friends, and his personal courage and his presence with his command in the thickest of the fight won for him the confidence of troops serving under him." In battle, stated one aide, his "dignity gives way to activity; his features become animated, his voice loud, his eyes are on fire, his blood kindles, and his bearing is that of a man carried away by passion."

Warren, an accomplished engineer, possessed a splendid eye for terrain. On the second day at Gettysburg he had instantly noted the significance of Little Round Top and dispatched troops to its defense, arguably averting disaster. He had a prickly nature, however, and "was always willing to set his own judgement against that of his superiors," a defect that ultimately would prove his downfall. He loved limericks, card playing, and drinking in moderation. In appearance he was short and slender, with piercing black eyes, a deeply tanned face and a birdlike manner.

Sedgwick, according to Dana, "was a very solid man, no flummery about him . . . in a battle he was apt to be found where the hardest fighting was. He was not an ardent, impetuous soldier like Hancock, but was steady and sure." One observer found him "quiet, unassuming . . . [with] no pretense, no posing for effect, no stage tricks." Though he was demanding insofar as discipline was concerned, he possessed the affections of his men, who called him Uncle John.

Newly attached to the Army of the Potomac at this time was Ambrose Burnside, he of the muttonchop whiskers, leading the 9th Corps. Burnside was back from Knoxville and the West, relinquishing his role as commander of the Army of the Ohio. Because he was senior in his general's date of commission to Meade he technically did not report to him but, said Dana, "by a sort of fiction . . . [was] acting in concert with Meade." Burnside had first achieved dubious fame at Sharpsburg, where under heavy fire he had failed hour after hour to get his troops across Antietam Creek at the twelve-foot-wide bottleneck later called "Burnside's Bridge." Then he had commanded the Army of the Potomac at the bloodbath that was Fredericksburg, sending wave after wave of Federals against the impregnable Rebel position at Marye's Heights. But he had defended well at Knoxville, and now was being given another chance in the East. "General Burnside," Grant would say, "was an officer who was generally liked and respected. He was not, however, fitted to command an army. No one knew this better than himself. He always admitted his blunders, and extenuated those of officers under him beyond what they were entitled to. . . ."[9]

By March 17, after bowing out of a banquet Lincoln had planned in his honor ("Time is very important now," he told the president, "and I have had enough of this show business"), Grant was back in Nashville, conferring with Sherman, James McPherson, John Logan, Phil Sheridan, and Grenville Dodge—this last general, though an infantryman, being chiefly responsible for rebuilding the railroads and reopening the lines of supply during the fighting in Tennessee and Mississippi. These were men he trusted, and they would figure prominently in his future plans.

During their meetings, Grant spelled out the new table of organization for the Federal armies. His own headquarters would be in the field, with George Meade and the Army of the Potomac in the East. Replacing him in the West, in charge of the three Federal armies there, would be Sherman. Taking over Sherman's old command, the Army of the Tennessee, would be Grant's protégé McPherson; George Thomas would continue to head the Army of the Cumberland; and newcomer John M. Schofield of Illinois, who had been fighting in Arkansas and Missouri, would lead the Army of the Ohio, replacing Burnside.

For McPherson's Army of the Tennessee, the commanders were the indomitable John Logan, 15th Corps; Grenville Dodge, 16th Corps; and the politically connected Frank Blair Jr., 17th Corps. Logan's division chiefs remained Peter Osterhaus and Morgan Smith, and William Harrow replaced Hugh Ewing, the Sherman brother-in-law. Dodge's divisions were led by Thomas Sweeny, a onetime Irish immigrant who had served at Fort Donelson, Shiloh, and Corinth, and James Veatch of Indiana, who had been serving in Memphis; Blair's were newly headed by Mortimer Leggett, an educator and lawyer from Ohio, and Walter Gresham, an Indiana lawyer.

Thomas's Army of the Cumberland included the dutiful but tactically inept Oliver O. Howard, 4th Corps (taking over for Gordon Granger, whose leadership Grant had found unfocused at Chattanooga); John Palmer, 14th Corps; and Joe Hooker, remaining in the West and now commanding the 20th Corps. Howard's divisions were led by David Stanley of Ohio, a career soldier, and John Newton, a hard-fighting Virginian-turned-Unionist, as well as Thomas Wood, one of the heroes of the charge up Missionary Ridge. Palmer's division heads stayed the same: Richard W. Johnson, Jefferson C. Davis, and Absalom Baird. Hooker's top subordinates were Alpheus Williams, a Yale-trained lawyer, John Geary, and Daniel Butterfield, a future Medal of Honor winner, the composer of the bugle call "Taps," and a veteran of Gettysburg.

The small Army of the Ohio, under Schofield, consisted only of the 23rd Corps. Its divisions were led by Alvin Hovey, whom last we saw at Champion's Hill, Henry Moses Judah, the West Pointer son of an Episcopal minister, and Jacob D. Cox of Ohio, a strong abolitionist whose Dutch forebears had been in America since the 1700s.[10]

In a highly dramatic move Grant would be taking Sheridan, with whom he had been most impressed at Chattanooga, with him to the East. Rebel cavalry under Jeb Stuart had long had the advantage there over their opposite numbers, but their superiority at this juncture in the war was vanishing. Not only did Confederate troopers have to pay for their own mounts but they were only reimbursed for them if they were killed; if their horses were sick, half-starving, or broken down—by far the largest number—the problem was theirs. Perhaps half of Stuart's command as a result now was on foot, searching for new mounts or hoping for old ones to regain their health. Sheridan was to take command of all the Army of the Potomac's cavalry, expected to mold its newly confident men and their plentiful and healthy horseflesh into an elite strike force.

The thirty-three-year-old Sheridan, whose unschooled Irish Catholic immigrant parents settled in Somerset, Ohio, when he was an infant, seemed born for warfare. Direct, uncomplicated, brooking no nonsense, he saw the battlefield not as a complicated chessboard but as a game of checkers, whose moves must be simple and fast. Far from being rash, however, he believed in ample intelligence as to the enemy's intent, and he took care that his men arrived on the field well fed. "Put your faith in the common soldier," he would say, "and he will never let you down." He was short, slight, coarse-featured with a predatory look, and he could be as short-tempered and liable to use his fists as any ruffian. Before graduating from West Point, in fact, he served a one-year suspension for assaulting an upper classman, a Virginian he felt was talking to him in a disrespectful manner.

Eight years of service on the frontier followed. With the outbreak of war, he was commissioned a brigadier of volunteers, later fighting at Perryville in Kentucky and at Murfreesboro in east Tennessee. At Chickamauga his command suffered 1,500 casualties out of 4,000 men engaged. Then came Chattanooga and a measure of fame. Whether he could add to his luster in the East, and in the cavalry at that, was still open to question. In subsequent days, after meeting Sheridan, Lincoln was asked his opinion of him. "I will tell you what kind of chap he is," the president replied, obviously withholding judgment. "He is one of those long-armed fellows with short legs that can scratch his shins without having to stoop over."

Grant, however, felt he knew his man. Told by someone in dismissive terms that the diminutive Sheridan seemed "rather a little fellow" to head up the cavalry, the general-in-chief flicked the comment aside like so much cigar ash. "You will find him big enough for the purpose," he promised.[11]

Leaving Sherman with McPherson, Thomas, and Schofield to prepare the Federal armies in the West for the move against Atlanta, Grant returned to Virginia, where for the rest of March and through April he organized a three-pronged attack against Lee. The main thrust, of course, would come from Meade and the 120,000-man Army of the Potomac, which would cross the Rappahannock-Rapidan line and advance on the 62,000-man Army of Northern Virginia, with the intent of crushing it or pushing it back toward Richmond. The second assault would come in Lee's rear from General Benjamin Butler's newly created Army of the James, which would sail up the James River and land at Bermuda Hundred, a peninsula just fifteen miles below the capital. Meanwhile a third action would be launched in the fertile Shenandoah by General Franz Sigel, whose 9,000 troops would be ordered to pillage the valley and deny the enemy much needed produce, livestock, and forage.

This plan would only be as good as the men executing it. Grant had every confidence in George Meade, whom he recognized as a solid if uninspired commander, and besides he would be on the scene if that officer needed prodding. But Butler and Sigel were largely unknown quantities.

The former, who had become known as "Beast" Butler for his harsh treatment of Southerners while military governor of New Orleans, was a political general, gaining his commission through his connections in the Massachusetts legislature. "Even before he reached middle age," said one biographer, "his rotund body, unnaturally short limbs, bloated face, and droopy eyes gave him the look of a dissipated toad." While he had undeniable administrative skills—a keen intellect, a talent for organization, and a persuasive manner—he had so far evinced no tactical abilities. He was further burdened with allegations of corruption, charges that ranged from unseemly purchasing procedures to stealing the silver from the house he had used as his New Orleans headquarters. But his zeal impressed Grant, who may have felt he could count on General William F. "Baldy" Smith, Butler's second-in-command, to provide military expertise.[12]

Franz Sigel, who had been a subaltern in the service of Grand Duke Leopold and later minister of war for the German revolutionary forces, had emigrated to this country in the early 1850s and settled in St. Louis, where he became director of the city's schools and a leader in the German-American community. With the outbreak of war he had enlisted thousands of his countrymen in the Union cause ("I fights mit Sigel" was the rallying cry), and soon became a brigadier. His record thereafter, however, was spotty at best. Now a major general, he seemed more interested in the trappings of military life than in toe-to-toe fighting. Short, ungraceful, speaking with a heavy accent, he did not look the warrior, and his non-German subordinates justifiably resented him for the favoritism he showed his fellow immigrants. Grant recognized Sigel's deficiencies, but hoped on his march up the Shenandoah he could at least tie up some enemy troops. "If Sigel can't skin himself," he said, repeating a favorite aphorism of Lincoln's, "he can at least hold a leg while someone else skins."[13]

By April 27, warm weather had so far advanced as to justify the Federals taking the field. On that day Burnside left Annapolis to occupy Meade's vacated position between Bull Run and the Rappahannock, while Meade himself began pushing further south. On the following day Grant notified Butler that he would cross the Rapidan on May 4, and ordered him to begin his own move up the James. The forty-day Overland Campaign toward Richmond would progress from one bloody battle to another—from the Wilderness to Spotsylvania to the North Anna River to Cold Harbor to Petersburg, with dreadful casualties—and Grant would be sensitive on the subject. "The criticism has been made . . . on the campaign from the Rapidan to the James that all loss of life could have been obviated by moving the army there on transports. [But] Richmond was so fortified and intrenched so perfectly that one man inside to defend was more than equal to five outside besieging."

Here he stated the heart of his approach to warfare, which like Lee's was all about routing the enemy, even at terrible cost, and little about taking and occupying strategic places. "To get possession of Lee's army was the first great object. With the capture of his army Richmond would necessarily follow. It was better to fight him outside his stronghold than in it. If the Army of the Potomac had been moved bodily to the James River by water Lee could have moved a part of his forces back to Richmond, called [Pierre] Beauregard from [Charleston] to reinforce it, and with the balance moved on to Washington. . . ."

To Grant, warfare was going on the attack; staying in defensive positions or in garrison invited disaster. Before moving south, he outlined these thoughts to Lincoln. "I explained to him that it was necessary to have a great number of troops to guard and hold the territory we had captured, and to prevent incursions into the Northern States. These troops could perform this service just as well by advancing as by remaining still; and by advancing they would compel the enemy to keep detachments to hold them back, or else lay his own territory open to invasion."

The president, who had been searching for such a general since First Bull Run, could not have been more pleased. "The particulars of your plans I neither know nor seek to know," Lincoln said. "You are vigilant and self-reliant; and, pleased with this, I wish not to obtrude any constraints or restraints upon you. . . . And now, with a brave army and a just cause, may God sustain you."

To which Grant replied: "I have been astonished at the readiness with which everything asked for has been yielded, without even an explanation being asked. Should my success be less than I desire and expect, the least I can say is, the fault is not with you."[14]

The army that Grant was taking across the Rapidan and into the Wilderness was just getting to know him, and he them. One day just before the campaign started, General Rufus Ingalls, the Army of the Potomac's quartermaster, gained a unique insight into the general-in-chief's working habits. Needing to confer with Grant, he put on his best uniform and boots—everything in that army was spit-and-polish—and rode over to see him in a covered wagon drawn by four well-groomed horses and escorted by resplendent aides. The two men met by accident on the road, and Ingalls explained his mission.

"Very well," said Grant, "We can talk it over here as well as any place," and with that he got down from his horse and Ingalls from his wagon, and

they began to walk together in the rain down the muddy road, Ingalls doing most of the talking and Grant agreeing or disagreeing as the case might
be. They talked for almost an hour, and every time a horse or wagon passed
they were splattered anew with mud.

"That's all," said Grant finally "Goodbye, General." Seemingly oblivious of the circumstances, he remounted and rode off, leaving Ingalls to
shake his head and report the incident straight away to Meade.

"I tell you, Meade, Grant means business," he said, brushing the dirt
from his uniform as best he could.[15]

Meanwhile the men and field grade officers of the Army of the Potomac
were reserving their opinion about the newcomer from the West. "There is
no enthusiasm in the army for Gen. Grant," said one, "and on the other
hand there is no prejudice against him. We are prepared to throw up our
hats . . . when he shows himself the great soldier here in Virginia against
Lee and the best troops of the Rebels."

"Who's this Grant that's made a lieutenant general?" one fellow asked.

"He's the hero of Vicksburg."

"Well, Vicksburg wasn't much of a fight. The Rebels were out of rations and they had to surrender or starve. . . ."

Catching a glimpse of their new commander riding on his rounds, another soldier asked his comrade: "Well, what do you think?"

The second man took in Grant's watchful eyes and hard straight mouth.

"He looks as if he [means] it," he said.

"We'll see for ourselves before long," was the reply.[16]

At this juncture in the war, however, the self-styled intellectual elite—as
usual far removed from the actual fighting—had grave doubts about the
capabilities of both Grant and Lincoln. They seemed so *ordinary!* Could
we not have leaders with *breeding?* Richard Henry Dana Jr., the celebrated author of *Two Years Before the Mast,* now a U.S. attorney in Massachusetts, met Grant in the Willard Hotel during this period and barely
suppressed a well-bred sigh. He "had no gait, no station, no manner,"
Dana sniffed. Besides smoking a large and smelly cigar, he had "rather the
look of a man who did, or once did, take a little too much to drink. . . ."
He was an "ordinary, scrubby looking man with a slightly seedy look, as
if he was out of office or half way." Days later Dana visited Lincoln in the
White House, only to recoil again at what he saw. "Such a shapeless mass
of writhing ugliness as slouched about in the President's chair you never saw
or imagined," he wrote. Lincoln may have some good qualities, such as
they were, but "his weak points may wreck him, or wreck something"—
meaning Dana's convenient, and fastidious, way of living.

No matter. The gangling, gaunt-looking president, who had come up from poverty to the highest office in the land, and the quiet, self-effacing Grant, who had been forced to resign from the prewar army for drinking, now would pursue the war in tandem toward its conclusion. Lincoln had met his general, and in him he was well pleased.[17]

TWO

* * * *

GRANT VERSUS LEE IN VIRGINIA

On May 4 as promised Grant sent the 120,000-man Army of the Potomac across the Rapidan at Germanna and Ely's Fords, some ten to fifteen miles west of Fredericksburg, Virginia, and marched it south into the so-called Wilderness—not so much with the intent of engaging Lee as with turning his right flank and pushing him back toward Richmond. This desolate area, perhaps twelve miles wide and six miles deep, was a densely wooded forest of pitch pine and scrub oak that stretched just west of Chancellorsville, where Stonewall Jackson had scored his greatest triumph the year before, and in so doing been shot by his own men.

The next day, knowing full well the tangled terrain in the Wilderness would impede the Federals and negate their numerical advantage, Lee with the 62,000 men of the Army of Northern Virginia took up Grant's challenge. He advanced two of his three corps—those of Richard Ewell and Ambrose Powell Hill—eastward toward the enemy in head-on thrusts on parallel roads, Ewell on the Orange Turnpike leading to the Wilderness Tavern intersection, Hill on the more southern Orange Plank Road leading to Chancellorsville. Their orders were to avoid a general engagement, if possible, until Longstreet marching from Gordonsville—a good day's march away—could come up in support.

Wheeling to the right to face Lee, the four-mile-long Federal column formed line of battle—Winfield Scott Hancock's 2nd Corps in the lead on the Brock Road comprising the Union left, then Gouverneur Warren's 5th Corps in the center, finally John Sedgwick's 6th Corps on the Germanna Road holding the right. Ambroise Burnside's 9th Corps for the Federals, like Longstreet's for the enemy, was not yet on the field.

Hancock's division heads were Francis Barlow, John Gibbon, David Birney, and Gershom Mott. The Brooklyn-born son of a clergyman, Brigadier Francis Barlow was a Harvard graduate who before the war had been practicing law in New York. Rising from private to brigadier in the Army of the Potomac, he had been severely wounded and left for dead on the battlefield the first day at Gettysburg, only to make a remarkable re-covery. John Gibbon of North Carolina, a West Pointer and the original commander of the Iron Brigade—the only all-Midwestern unit to fight in the East and the near equal of Jackson's Stonewall brigade—had suffered wounds at Fredericksburg and Gettysburg. Though his wife was a Mary-lander and three brothers fought for the Confederacy, he had cast his lot with the Union. Major General David Birney, the son of a prominent abo-litionist, was a Philadelphia businessman and lawyer who had performed ably at Chancellorsville and Gettysburg. Gershom Mott of New Jersey, another businessman, had survived wounds at Second Bull Run and Chancellorsville.

Leading Warren's divisions were Charles Griffin, John Robinson, Samuel Crawford, and James Wadsworth. Griffin, a West Pointer who had been with the army since First Bull Run and was especially well regarded by his troops, was not a man to trifle with. Fearless in combat, he expected no less of others, and could be vitriolic about those he found wanting. Career officer John Robinson, thought by some to be "the hairiest general . . . in a much-bearded army," had fought from the Peninsula Campaign through Gettysburg. On the first day of the last-named battle, even as the Federals were being swept from the field, his division continued to resist, losing some 1,700 of 2,500 men engaged. Samuel Crawford, a graduate of the University of Pennsylvania Medical School, had suffered 50 percent casu-alties while leading a brigade at Cedar Mountain, been severely wounded at Antietam, and fought gallantly at Gettysburg. James Wadsworth of New York, a fifty-seven-year-old landowner and lawyer, was one of the oldest Federal generals. Though without military training, he had fought well at Fredericksburg and Gettysburg.

Horatio Wright, George Getty, and James Ricketts led Sedgwick's divi-sions. Wright, who had graduated second in his class at West Point, was a well-thought-of officer who possessed considerable expertise in military engineering. He had joined the army in time for Gettysburg. George Washington Getty, a West Point classmate of Sherman's who had fought at Antietam and Fredericksburg, was returning to field command after service as the army's inspector general. James Ricketts, another West Pointer, had been shot four times and captured at First Bull Run. A veteran subsequently of Cedar Mountain, Second Bull Run and Antietam—where his wounded horse had reared and pinned him to the ground, badly injuring him—he too had been on detached duty.

Now in midmorning on the 5th, realizing that the concentrated Rebel columns might penetrate his extended line, and perhaps overly confident, Grant reacted characteristically and went on the attack, making Lee's wish to wait for Longstreet moot. The first major clash occurred about 1:00 P.M. near the Orange Turnpike–Wilderness Tavern crossing. Here in the thick underbrush and blinding gunsmoke elements of Warren's 5th Corps, with the divisions of Charles Griffin and James Wadsworth in the van, initially came to grief against Ewell's Confederates. "Officers lost control of their companies and, utterly bewildered, rushed hither and thither, looking for their men," admitted Captain W.H.S. Sweet of the 146th New York. "Troops were passing in our rear from right to left," echoed Private Carrol Waldron of the same regiment. ". . . Suddenly it dawned upon me that they were Rebels and I raised my gun to fire at them." It was too late. Waldron and 130 of his comrades found themselves prisoners.

To Private Theodore Gerrish of the 20th Maine the scene was a deadly game of blind man's bluff. "The Rebels evidently knew but little of our force, position and intention; and it is safe to say we knew less of theirs. And thus the two great masses of men were hurled against each other. The Rebels fought like demons and . . . poured deadly volleys upon us." Minie bullets "went snapping and tearing through the pine limbs; splinters flew in every direction; trees were completely riddled in a moment's time; blood ran in torrents. . . ."

Griffin's men nonetheless persisted, even achieving a breakthrough near a small clearing called Saunder's Field. "The order was given to charge," said Private Gerrish. "The right of our regiment now rested upon the Turnpike. . . . Zip, zip, zip came the bullets on every side. The field was nearly crossed. We dashed up a little swell of land on its farthest side and were under the shadow of the trees. . . . Our lines staggered for a moment but . . . our men threw themselves upon the enemy's guns. . . . Foot after foot the Rebels retreated, their gray forms mantled with fire as they went. Slowly and steadily we advanced. . . . What a medley of sounds—the incessant roar of the rifle, the screaming of bullets . . . men cheering, groaning, yelling, swearing, and praying!"[1]

Ewell and his battle-hardened Confederates, however, soon regrouped. "It so happened that the right of [Griffin] was at this time uncovered," recounted a Federal soldier. "[Horatio] Wright's division of [Sedgwick's] 6th Corps, which should have covered this flank, had not come up, owing to the dense underbrush through which it was compelled to move. On this exposed flank Ewell directed his attack." Meanwhile Wadsworth's division, which should have been advancing due west on Griffin's left, veered off at an angle and came under enfilading fire, forcing it rearward. (Lacking sightlines, Wadsworth had misread his compass and moved not west but southwest.) Unsupported now on both flanks, Griffin's men had no choice but to fall back themselves.

Though elements of Sedgwick's corps late in the afternoon joined the melee on the turnpike, and though the Federals there enjoyed a better than two-to-one advantage, the first day's fighting would ebb and flow and result in stalemate. "I knew the danger of being flanked," said Captain Sweet, "as by charging over the field we broke the continuity of our general line of battle, and the Rebels were adept in finding gaps. Twenty paces to the rear enabled me to look out over the open field we had just crossed. We were not only flanked but doubly flanked. Rebel troops covered the field. . . . Those of our regiment who escaped were principally from the right, where the movement of the Rebels seems to have been discovered in time to make escape possible."

Compounding the confusion were the smoldering fires, brought on by hot lead falling on dry grass and leaves, that now began to race through the woodland. "Swept by the flames," said one soldier, "the trees, bushes and logs which Confederates had thrown up as breastworks [ignited] and dense clouds of smoke rolled across the clearing, choking unfortunates who were exposed to it. . . . The clearing now became a raging inferno in which many of the wounded perished. The bodies of the dead were blackened and burned beyond all possibility of recognition. . . ."[2]

Charles Griffin, whose division had borne the burden of the day's fighting, soon thereafter galloped into Grant's headquarters, rushing into his tent and demanding to know why his troops, after driving Ewell back three-quarters of a mile, had been left unsupported, with both flanks in the air. Where were Sedgwick's men? he raged. Where indeed were Wadsworth's and the rest of Warren's corps?

"Who is this General Gregg?" Grant asked of Meade, misnaming the intruder but little disposed to put up with insubordination. "Why don't you arrest him?" Then he rose to his feet and began to button his uniform blouse, the better to assert his authority. Here Meade interceded on Griffin's behalf.

"It's not Gregg but Griffin," he told the ruffled commander, smoothing his superior's blouse and helping him with his buttons, "—and it's only his way of talking."[3]

Grant sat down, lit a fresh cigar, and lapsed into silence. Presumably Meade lost no time in ushering Griffin from the tent, thereby preserving that valuable officer's services for battles still to come.

Over on the Orange Plank Road, some three miles to the south, the real fighting on May 5 did not begin until 4:00 P.M. There the pugnacious Hancock, nothing deterred by a groin wound incurred at Gettysburg that refused to heal, had been waiting impatiently to advance much of the day, kept from doing so in part because of faulty communications. Now Grant and Meade at last sent George Getty's division of Sedgwick's corps into action against Powell Hill, then moved up Hancock's corps in support.

Once again, despite their numerical superiority, the Federals were stymied. "No one could see the fight fifty feet from him," said one of Hancock's men. "The roll and crackle of the musketry was something terrible, even to the veterans of many battles. The lines were very near each other, and from the underbrush and the tops of trees came puffs of smoke, the 'ping' of the bullets, and the yell of the enemy. It was a blind and bloody hunt to the death, in bewildering thickets, rather than a battle. . . . In advancing it was next to impossible to preserve a distinct line, and we were constantly broken into small groups. The underbrush and briars scratched our faces, tore our clothing, and tripped our feet from under us."

The Rebels were everywhere—and nowhere. "We are playing right into these devils' hands!" cried another Federal. "Bushwhacking is the game! There ain't a tree in our front, twenty feet high, but there is a Reb up that tree!"

Fighting flared up incessantly, and died down just as quickly. "The line pressed steadily forward for about three-quarters of a mile, crossing a swamp under a destructive fire," reported Major Thomas McLaughlin of the 102nd Pennsylvania, Getty's command. "On reaching the crest of a hill, the regiment halted and continued firing, losing very heavily. . . ." Colonel Lewis Grant, leading his all-Vermont brigade, was in the thick of the action: "Our men hugged the ground as close as possible, and kept up a rapid fire; the enemy did the same. The Rebels [were] partially protected by a slight swell of ground. . . . The attempt was made to dislodge them from that position, but the moment our men rose to advance, the rapid and constant fire of musketry cut them down with such slaughter that it was found impracticable."[4]

By now it was past 6:30 P.M. Hill's men, though pummeled and exhausted, were somehow managing to hold their own. "Two, three and four times we rushed upon the enemy," said Union Private Warren Goss, who would attest to the foe's tenacity, "but were met by a murderous fire and with heavy loss. . . . As often as we rushed forward we were compelled to get back. . . ." Lieutenant Colonel Horace Porter, who had been sent by Grant to report on Hancock's progress, would say: "The fighting had become exceedingly severe. . . . General Alexander Hayes, commanding one of Hancock's brigades, finding that his line had broken, rushed forward to encourage his troops, and was instantly killed." Porter bore the news back to Grant, who took it hard.

"Hayes and I were cadets together for three years," the commander finally said. ". . . I am not surprised he met his death at the head of his troops; it was just like him. He was a man who would never follow, but would always lead. . . ."

By 8:30 P.M. darkness brought the battle to an end, buying the Confederates time. On both sides the combatants were scattered and dazed, their lines close and in some cases overlapping. Here on the Plank Road too, just as on the turnpike, cruel fires broke out in the brush and leaves, burning at least 200 of the wounded to death. In front of the 5th Maine, one Union soldier kept screaming for help as the fires neared him. Two of his comrades, rushing to his aid, were brought down by bullets themselves. Finally a sergeant reluctantly took aim and ended the man's suffering.[5]

The next morning at 5:00 A.M. Grant, with Burnside's 9th Corps still in the process of coming up, hurled his army forward once more against Lee's stalwarts. On the turnpike Sedgwick and Warren again encountered stiff resistance from Ewell. For most of the day there the opposing forces would neutralize each other. On the Plank Road, however, Hancock, joined by Wadsworth's division on his right, was more fortunate. There Powell Hill, knowing his men were at their physical breaking point, himself ailing, and expecting to be reinforced by Longstreet's corps during the night, had neglected to put up breastworks. With Longstreet not yet on the field, this would be a near-fatal mistake. "Hancock, Burnside and Longstreet are the principal factors," explained one military analyst. "All three, Union and Confederate, are practically predestined, by their positions . . . to fight on the side of the Plank Road. Hancock, with six

(including Wadsworth) out of the eleven divisions of the Army of the Potomac, was already on the ground, and Longstreet was known . . . to be
aiming in the same direction. Burnside, whose corps was now the only
force in Grant's hand that was free to maneuver, was, as a matter of
course, to be brought into the contest . . . to force the decision."

Hancock at first swept over the bedraggled and near-defenseless Rebels
on the Plank Road with what appeared to be irresistible force. "The roar
of musketry, the hellish yells of the Rebels, and the shouts and cheers of
the Union men mingle together. . . ." said Color Sergeant D. G. Crotty.
"Nothing is thought of but load and fire. The wounded must take care of
themselves. . . . The Rebels now give way, and we chase them through the
dense forest."

"We are driving them, sir," Hancock told Colonel Theodore Lyman of
Meade's staff. "Tell General Meade we are driving them most beautifully.
[David] Birney has gone in and he is just cleaning them out *beautifully*."
But Burnside, who was expected to launch a hammer blow between the
two Confederate commands, was being as much the laggard as Longstreet,
and it was Lyman's unpleasant task to tell Hancock so. "Only one division of Burnside's is up," he said, adding that even that force was not yet
in line.

Hancock's face darkened, and he began to swear. "I knew it!" he cried
out. "Just what I expected! If he could attack *now* we would smash Hill to
pieces!"[6]

The Federal commander's wrath was justified. It was now 6:30 A.M.,
and Burnside's absence had given the lead elements of Longstreet's corps
just enough time to come to Hill's support. Soon Lee, drawing on the
emotional, even mystical, force he had over his army, sent the newly arrived Texas Brigade into the teeth of Hancock's assault. "Lee himself
came in front of us, as if intending to lead us," said John Gregg, the Texans' brigadier. "The men shouted for him to come back, that they would
not budge an inch until he did so. . . ."

"Lee to the rear!" they cried. Reluctantly, and only after Longstreet
added his plea to that of the troops, Lee turned his horse and rode back
through the ranks. In short order the Rebels were forcing Hancock back,
and within three hours they had regained all the ground they had lost.

Now Longstreet, intent on taking the offensive and improving on his
reputation as a purely defensive general, discovered an abandoned railroad
cut on Hancock's left flank. Hastily putting together a patchwork force of
several brigades, he sent it storming through the cut about 11:00 A.M. and
watched as it fell on the Federals. "This movement, concealed from view

by the dense wood, was completely successful," admitted Union General Andrew Humphreys, Meade's chief of staff. Soon the Rebels were rolling up the Federal line, fatally wounding Union general James Wadsworth and sending one brigade after another into a panic. "General Hancock . . . endeavored to restore order and reform his line of battle along the Orange Plank Road . . . but was unable to do so, owing to the great difficulty of adjusting lines under fire in such a dense forest." Hancock did not regroup his command until the afternoon, when he fell back behind his breastworks on the Brock Road.[7]

So devastating was the Confederate turning movement that Grant, who earlier had pulled up most of his pontoon bridges across the Rapidan and thereby impaired his line of retreat, might well have met with disaster but for an accident of war. Longstreet, riding with officers and aides on the Plank Road in the wake of the attack and urging his troops on, fell badly wounded when fired on by his own men, taking a minie ball in the throat that almost choked him in his own blood. The mishap, so similar to Jackson's fatal wounding in the same place the year before, effectively brought the pursuit to a close. Longstreet would not return to duty until October.

Following one more indecisive engagement on the Brock Road about 6:00 P.M. the action in the Wilderness ceased, with both sides tending their wounds. The two days of fighting had cost the Federals 18,000 casualties; estimated Confederate losses ranged from 8,000 to 12,000. "My God! My God!" Lincoln would exclaim when he heard of the numbers, little realizing the worst was yet to come. Early in the Overland Campaign, it was clear, Grant was laying down the gauntlet, unmistakably telling Lee he would give him little room to maneuver, and casualties, though regrettable, be dammed. Heretofore, facing far less gifted generals, Grant had succeeded with minimal losses. Now he was pursuing a strategy calculated to drain the Army of Northern Virginia's lifeblood. The North, with its 22 million population, could replace Grant's losses. The South, with its 5.5 million white population, could not.

During the night of the 6th one exaggerated report after another came into Grant's headquarters of this or that Rebel success along the far-flung lines, this or that Federal failure. "In the darkness of the night, in the gloom of a tangled forest, and after men's nerves had been racked by the strain of a two days' desperate battle, the most immovable commander might have been shaken," said Horace Porter. "But it was in just such sudden emergencies that General Grant was at his best. Without the change of a muscle of his face, or the slightest alteration in the tones of his voice, he quietly interrogated the officers who brought the reports; then, sifting out the truth . . . he gave directions for relieving the situation with the marvelous rapidity which were characteristic of him . . . in the face of the enemy."

Just once did he lose his temper. "General Grant, this is a crisis that cannot be looked upon too seriously," one of his generals would say, insisting that Lee soon would be raining death and destruction upon them. "I know Lee's methods well by past experience; he will throw his whole army between us and the Rapidan, and cut us off completely from our communications."

Grant rose to his feet, took a cigar from his mouth—one of an awesome twenty he had smoked that day—and straight away chastised the worrywart. "Oh, I am heartily tired of hearing what Lee is going to do!" he exploded. "Some of you always seem to think he is going to turn a double somersault, and land in our rear or on both of our flanks at the same time! Go back to your command, and try to think what we are going to do ourselves, instead of what Lee is going to do!"[8]

The offending officer retreated in silence.

The next day was for resting, but in the early hours of May 8 both armies moved a dozen miles south on parallel roads to Spotsylvania Courthouse—and a dozen miles closer to Richmond and the James River. Grant and Meade were continuing what would become a familiar pattern of side-stepping Lee's right, forcing the latter to fall back and block their advance. The Confederates got to Spotsylvania first, fortified and extended their lines from the Po River to the Brock Road, and by the next day both sides were already skirmishing. It was then, while directing the placement of his artillery, that 6th Corps commander John Sedgwick fell victim to a sniper's bullet.

When the first balls whistled by, some of Sedgwick's men ducked their heads. "What! What! Men dodging this way for single bullets!" he chided them with a laugh. "What will you do when they open fire along the whole line. I am ashamed of you. They couldn't hit an elephant at this distance."

Sedgwick was wrong. The snipers undoubtedly were armed with Whitworths, imported English rifles with telescopic sights that were accurate up to 2,000 yards. More balls whistled past, followed by a sickening thud. Sedgwick collapsed in the arms of an aide, blood spurting from a wound under his left eye. He died instantly.

Fighting broke out in earnest late the afternoon of May 10, with Grant launching three separate attacks. First Warren on the right pushed forward, then Hancock on the left; both were repulsed with heavy losses.

(Burnside was on the far left, all but out of the battle, guarding the Fredericksburg Road.) In the center, however, Horatio Wright, who had replaced Sedgwick, enjoyed better luck. There, favored by concealing terrain, he formed an assault force of twelve elite regiments and placed twenty-four-year-old Colonel Emory Upton of New York in command. The redoubtable Upton, who had only graduated from West Point at the onset of the war, at 6:00 P.M. threw his 5,000 men in four waves against the bulging salient—the so-called Mule Shoe—that was the Confederate midpoint, where the enemy were exposed to enfilading fire. Previously he had enjoined his troops not to discharge their pieces until they reached the breastworks. Firing and reloading during the 200-yard charge across open ground would waste precious minutes and lessen the attack's impact. "Many a poor fellow fell pierced with Rebel bullets before we reached the rifle pits," said a soldier in the 96th Pennsylvania. "When those who were left reached the pits we let them have it."[9]

Upton's men surged into and over the works with tidal force, fanning out to right and left and, they thought, carrying the day. But Gershom Mott's 2nd Corps division, the principal unit ordered to exploit the incursion, never came up in support, falling victim to confusing instructions and, later, concentrated Rebel artillery fire during their advance through open fields. Lacking reinforcements and with the enemy rallying, Upton in the growing darkness received orders from Wright to fall back. His troops at first ignored the command, obeying only after several repetitions—and then taking with them more than 1,000 prisoners. "This I assure you was galling to the pride of brave men," said Lieutenant Colonel Samuel Pingree of the 2nd Vermont. "When I got by myself where I would not be ashamed of it I cried like a whipped spaniel—I saw many soldiers cry like girls, and many who took things less to heart, gave vent to their mortification at having lost all they had gained so nobly—by the fault of others, by letting of unnumbered salvos of profanity."

For his leadership Upton, who lost perhaps 1,000 men in the melee, was promoted on the spot to brigadier. "Upton had gained an important advantage, but a lack in others of the spirit and dash possessed by him lost it to us," said Grant, indisposed to accept Mott's excuses.

The next day the commanding general sat down at the mess table for breakfast, which consisted of coffee and a small slice of beef cooked to a crisp, which was the way he liked his meat. There he was joined by Congressman Elihu Washburne, who had accompanied the army across the Rapidan, and was now returning to Washington. What, Washburne wanted to know, should he tell the president? "We are certainly making fair progress," Grant replied, ". . . but the campaign promises to be a long one, and I am particularly anxious not to say anything just now that might hold out false hopes." Then he added: "I will write a letter to Halleck, as I generally communicate through him . . . and you can take it with you." Grant forthwith penned a 200-word communiqué, in the middle of which he revealed his true feelings: *I propose to fight it out on this line if it takes all summer.*[10]

Though repulsed in his first assault on the Mule Shoe, Grant nonetheless was convinced the Confederate position there was a weak one and could be taken. At 5:00 A.M. on May 12, in drenching rain and fog, he sent Hancock's 2nd Corps on the double-quick against the northeast tip of the salient, the Bloody Angle. Though he did not know it, his chances for a breakthrough in the center had been increased immeasurably during the night by a disastrous decision: the pulling back of the Rebel cannon. Thinking the Federals might be turning his left, Lee had ordered most of his guns to be removed from the center and repositioned. Now the cannon were being rushed back, but few would be in place in time to offer resistance. Compounding the enemy's problem was the fact that many of them had allowed their cartridges to grow damp during the rain-soaked night, making their muskets useless.

In sum, Hancock's audacious assault could not have been conducted under more favorable circumstances. Francis Barlow's and David Birney's divisions comprised the van, John Gibbon's and the unfortunate Gershom Mott's commands the second line. Screaming like demons, they rushed with overwhelming force upon the surprised Confederates and quickly scaled the breastworks, striking down and capturing most of the defenders and driving back the survivors. In the mud-filled, narrow trenches, the scene soon became one of total carnage. "A fierce and bloody fight ensued with bayonets and clubbed muskets," said one Federal. "Veteran campaigners had never looked upon such a sight as they beheld when the enemy had been driven out. Dead and dying were heaped in piles."

Stunned by the attack, the Rebels could not believe what was happening to them. Herman Seay of the 23rd Virginia, frustrated beyond care, threw down his weapon and challenged the nearest Yankee to a no-holds-barred wrestling contest. "Damn your soul," he yelled, "and I'll be dammed if I can't throw you down." The two adversaries grappled, and then Seay put his thumbs into his opponent's eyes. "I surrender!" the Yank cried out. Captors and captives alike, doubtless relieved they were still alive, burst into nervous laughter. More sobering, at least to the defenders, was the extent of their losses. Within forty-five minutes the famed Stonewall Division was all but wiped out and some 3,000 men taken prisoner, including two generals.[11]

With his army in danger of being cut in two, Lee shortly after 6:00 A.M. took the field and sought to rally the men, just as he had in the Wilderness. "General Lee knew," said John Brown Gordon, newly named to division command and himself an inspiring officer, "that nothing could rescue [the army] except a counter-movement, quick, impetuous and decisive...." Here Gordon saw to his dismay that Lee, "with uncovered head and mounted on Old Traveler, [looking] a very god of war," intended to lead the charge himself. Gordon instinctively reached out and grabbed his chief's bridle.

"General Lee," he insisted, "You shall not lead my men in a charge.... These men behind you are Georgians, Virginians and Carolinians. They have never failed you on any field. They will not fail you here. Will you, boys?"

"No! No! No!" came the cries from the ranks. "General Lee to the rear! General Lee to the rear!"

Though the entire incident lasted no more than a few minutes, it ignited the men's spirits. Throwing together a line of battle in the pelting rain, Gordon met the Union onslaught head-on, intent on pushing the intruders back and repelling the breakthrough. "Forward! Forward!" he bellowed, and his troops—less than one-third the Federals in number but with the advantage of fighting on a narrow front—fell on Hancock's besieging column with "the fury of a cyclone." Through all the morning the battle raged, with Lee feeding additional brigades piecemeal into the fray, and his men inexorably driving the enemy back toward the Bloody Angle, even while defending their lines elsewhere along the periphery of the Mule Shoe.

Colonel Robert McAllister, leading a brigade in Hancock's assault, remembered the Confederate counterattack: "We soon discovered another line of works, and large reinforcements coming to the aid of the enemy. I ordered 'about face,' and retreated to the first line.... Their massed columns pushed forward to the 'Bloody Angle.' The stars and stripes and the stars and bars nearly touched each other across the works.... The gray and blue coats with rifles in hand would spring on top of the breast-works, take deadly aim and fire, and then fall dead in the trenches below. This I saw again and again. More troops came to our aid...."

Into the afternoon the battle at the Mule Shoe continued unabated, along a front perhaps 1,500 yards, with hand-to-hand fighting the norm. "Here and there the Confederates came all the way up to the line of trenches," one historian would say of the bloodletting, "and there were places where Federals crouched on one side of a log breastwork while Confederates crouched on the other side, not five feet away. Men shot through the chinks between the logs, or jabbed through them with bayonets, or held their muskets overhead at arm's length, muzzles pointed downward, to shoot blindly over the parapet. Now and then soldiers on either side would clamber on top . . . firing at point-blank range until they were killed. There were times when soldiers leaned over the parapet, seized their opponents, and hauled them over bodily, making prisoners of them."[12]

The concentrated mass of Hancock's attacking column, which had enabled him to make the breakthrough in the first place, now rebounded to his disadvantage, and that of Wright's 6th Corps coming up in support. G. Norton Galloway of the 95th Pennsylvania takes up the story: "The great difficulty was in the narrow limits of the Angle, around which we were fighting"—less than two hundred yards—"which precluded the possibility of getting more than a limited number [of men] into action at once. . . . Our ranks were crowded at some points four deep. . . . Our losses were frightful." To keep up the supply of ammunition, dozens of pack mules were used in relays, each of the animals carrying three thousand rounds. "The battle, which during the morning raged . . . on the right and left of this position, gradually slackened, and attention was concentrated on the Angle. So continuous and heavy was our fire that the head logs of the breastworks were cut and torn until they resembled hickory brooms. Several large oak trees . . . were completely gnawed off by our converging fire, and about 3 o'clock . . . fell among the enemy with a loud crash."[13]

Burnside's 9th Corps on the left of the Mule Shoe, meanwhile, and Warren's 5th Corps on the right, accomplished little. In part this may have been because the Rebel firepower on either side of the Angle was too strong, but Grant obviously believed his subordinates were derelict in failing to relieve the pressure on Hancock and Wright. He several times urged Burnside to push forward, and at one point actually considered replacing Warren. But he took no drastic action. Captain Oliver Wendell Holmes Jr., then a young aide to Wright, was less forbearing. "Burnside who attacked on Hancock's left didn't make much [headway]," he said. "He is a damned humbug. Warren, who is a ditto, did about the same." Grant and Meade, he insisted, should have "slapped in all [they] could spare on Hancock's front."

For still more hours and into the night the battle at the Bloody Angle went on—chaotic, feral, unsparing—neither side even considering giving

way. It was a killing ground, a slaughterhouse if you will, in which the
participants suspended belief that their opponents were human. "Toward
dusk," recalled Galloway of the 95th Pennsylvania, who with his comrades
was still nose to nose with the enemy, "preparations were made to relieve
us. By this time we were nearly exhausted, and had fired three to four
hundred rounds of ammunition per man. Our lips were encrusted with
powder from 'biting cartridges.' Our shoulders and hands and hands were
coated with mud that had adhered to the butts of our rifles."

The fighting would not end until 3:00 A.M. on the 13th, some twenty-
two hours after it began. "The moment we would slacken fire" explained
Union Colonel McAllister, "the enemy would close in upon us, so determined were they to carry [the Angle]. Had they succeeded in driving us
from it, all we had gained would have been lost. . . . A dead and dying
mass of humanity was lying in the Confederate trenches, while on our side
the ground [likewise] was covered with the dead."

Lee at this juncture, having constructed new breastworks some three-
quarters of a mile to the rear along the base of the Mule Shoe, ordered the
salient abandoned. Temporarily the battle was over. Inspecting the lines
the next morning, one Union officer was all but dumbstruck by what he
saw. In some parts of the trenches the bodies were piled eight to ten deep.
Riddled with minie balls and coated with mud, they gave mute and ob-
scene testimony to primordial fury. "I never expect to be believed when
I tell . . . of the horrors of Spotsylvania," he said, "because I would be
loath to believe it myself were the cases reversed." Federal losses on May
12 totaled some 9,000; Confederate losses, including the prisoners taken
during the breakthrough, were 8,000.[14]

Major General Phil Sheridan meanwhile was setting off on a boastful
foray, but one in which he would back up his words with deeds. Grant's
new chief of cavalry had not distinguished himself in the Wilderness
against his counterpart, the Rebel Jeb Stuart, and he was eager for vindi-
cation. Part of Sheridan's problem was a fundamental disagreement with
Meade as to how cavalry should be used in the Army of the Potomac. The
former thought he should be given freedom to hit the enemy, whenever and
wherever opportunity presented; the latter, particularly because he was
moving into strange ground, insisted the cavalry be kept closer to home,
guarding the wagon trains and providing intelligence on the enemy's
movements.

On May 8, just before the fighting heated up at Spotsylvania, the two
irascible men got into an expletive-filled argument. "Meade was possessed

of an excitable temper which under irritating circumstances became almost ungovernable," said Horace Porter. "He had worked himself into a towering passion regarding the delays encountered in the forward movement, and when Sheridan appeared went at him hammer and tongs, accusing him of blunders. . . ." Little Phil was equally fiery and, "smarting under the belief that he was being unjustly treated, all the hotspur in his nature was aroused." He insisted that Meade had created the trouble by countermanding his orders, and "declared with great warmth that he would not command the cavalry any longer under such conditions, and said that if he could have matters his own way he would concentrate all the cavalry, move out in force against Stuart's command, and whip it."

Meade shortly thereafter repeated the incident to Grant, including Sheridan's wish to move out and whip Stuart.

"Did Sheridan say that?" said Grant ingenuously, ignoring his protégé's near insubordination. "Well, he generally knows what he is talking about. Let him start right out and do it."

By early the next morning, Little Phil was leaving Spotsylvania and cantering on a single road south toward Richmond, his three divisions of 10,000 troopers stretched out in a thirteen-mile column. Wesley Merritt's unit was in the lead, then James Wilson's, then David McMurtrie Gregg's. The Federal cavalry, so woebegone the first two years of the war, had come of age in June of 1863 at Brandy Station, just before Gettysburg, when it fought Stuart and his men to a draw. Now reorganized under Sheridan, and fitted with superior mounts and arms, it was a potent force. All its commanders were young, most in their early thirties and late twenties.

Brigadier Wesley Merritt, thorough and professional, was leading the First Division in place of the ailing Alfred Torbert; his brigade commanders were twenty-five-year-old George Armstrong Custer of Michigan, who despite graduating last in his class at West Point had jumped from first lieutenant to brigadier; Colonel Thomas Devin, the son of Irish immigrants and a onetime house painter who had risen in the ranks of the New York militia; and Colonel Alfred Gibbs, heading Merritt's old unit. Brigadier David Gregg of Pennsylvania, leading the 2nd Division, had served with the regular cavalry in the old army; his brigade heads were Henry Davies Jr. of New York, and his cousin J. Irvin Gregg, also of Pennsylvania. Commanding the Third Division was General James Wilson, the onetime Grant aide and military engineer who figured in our story at Vicksburg. Before his promotion to the field, he had headed the Cavalry Bureau in Washington, where he lobbied successfully for Union troopers to be issued the seven-shot Spencer repeating carbine, a weapon Stuart's men eyed enviously. Colonels John McIntosh and George Chapman led Wilson's brigades.

Sheridan's lieutenants, despite some complaints that Wilson had little mounted experience, were well regarded. "Torbert had already distinguished himself"—from the Seven Days to Gettysburg—"as an infantry commander," said one cavalry officer. "Gregg . . . possessed the confidence of the whole corps for good judgement and coolness. Wilson . . . was very quick and impetuous; Merritt . . . was with cavalry virtues well proportioned. Custer was the meteoric *sabreur;* McIntosh, the last of a fighting race; Devin, the 'Old War Horse'; Davies, polished, genial, gallant; Chapman, the student-like; Irvin Gregg, the steadfast."[15]

While Sheridan was intent on getting in Lee's rear and raiding the Richmond defenses, as well as doing as much mischief along the way as possible, his chief purpose was to lure Stuart into pursuit. Jeb took the bait, but unaccountably took only half his own force with him, giving the Union commander a two-to-one advantage. Perhaps Lee, remembering how blinded he had been by the absence of the cavalry the first two days at Gettysburg, imposed this decision on him.

By dusk on the 9th Sheridan's van had crossed the North Anna River and fallen on Beaver Dam Station, where it burned two Confederate supply trains and a million and a half rations and irreplaceable medical stores, and freed 400 prisoners. The next day, with one of Stuart's brigades snapping at his rear, Sheridan deliberately covered only eighteen miles, letting two other brigades of the hard-riding enemy circle to his front. "We quietly encamped that night on the south bank of the South Anna, near Ground Squirrel Bridge," said Sheridan. "Here we procured an abundance of forage and . . . men and horses were able to obtain a good rest."

On the morning of May 11, while Sheridan's rear was engaged with elements of the enemy around the South Anna, his van under Wesley Merritt about 11:00 A.M. came upon Stuart at Yellow Tavern, some six miles from Richmond. Here the Union force encountered stiff resistance. Though badly outnumbered, Stuart had placed his dismounted troopers well, concealing them in some woods in front of the Federals and on their left flank, where his cannon could provide enfilading fire. "The enemy," Sheridan acknowledged, "poured in a heavy fire from his line and from a battery which enfiladed the Brook Road, and made Yellow Tavern an uncomfortably hot place." Two of Merritt's brigades—those of Devin and Gibbs—bore the brunt of the battle, slowly pushing back the enemy in their front and straightening the lines. Several hours of fighting, interspersed by lulls, were consumed in this manner, with neither side gaining a clear-cut advantage.[16]

Finally at 4:00 P.M. the third of Merritt's commanders, George Custer, took the initiative. "From a personal examination of the ground," he said, "I discovered that a successful charge might be made upon the battery of the enemy by keeping well to the right."

Galloping over to his superior, he came straight to the point. "Merritt, I am going to charge that battery."

"Go in, general," was the reply. "I will give you all the support in my power."

Sheridan, learning of the imminent charge, was equally enthusiastic. "Bully for Custer!" he cried.

Now all eyes were on the "Boy General." Custer himself continues the story: "The bugle sounded the advance and the three regiments [the 1st Michigan, supported by the 5th and 6th Michigan], moved forward. As soon as the 1st Michigan emerged from the cover of the woods the enemy divined our intention and opened a brisk fire from his artillery. Before the battery could be reached, there were five fences to be opened and a bridge to cross, over which it was impossible to pass more than three at one time. . . . Notwithstanding these obstacles the 1st Michigan advanced boldly to the charge." Recalled one young officer: "My attention was diverted by what appeared to be a tornado. . . . It was the 1st Michigan, in column of squadrons, moving at the trot. . . . In squadron front it covered over two hundred and fifty feet by one hundred and twenty in depth, and it formed a weight of six hundred tons that was about to be hurled across the fields and ravines upon that battery. . . . Away it went toward the guns. It was swallowed up in dust and smoke, a volume of exulting shouts smote the air, the earth shook. . . ."

"Custer's charge," said Sheridan, ". . . was brilliantly executed. . . . Beginning at a walk, he increased his gait to a trot, and then at full speed rushed at the enemy. At the same moment the dismounted troops along my whole front moved forward, and as Custer went through the battery, capturing two of the guns with their cannoneers and breaking up the enemy's left, Gibbs and Devin drove his center and right from the field."[17]

In the aftermath of the breakthrough, while fighting in the midst of the melee with the 1st Virginia and emptying his pistol at the oncoming Yankees, Stuart suffered a mortal wound. "I told him to go away several times," said one officer. "But he would [not] go."

"Give it to them! Give it to them! Stand your ground!" Stuart shouted, waving his saber even as he was struck.

Though the battle continued until dusk, it consisted primarily of delaying actions. Sheridan had won a notable victory, forcing the enemy cavalry to withdraw in disarray to the north, as well depriving the Confederacy of a legendary leader. He would continue on his raid, roaming in the vicinity of Richmond but accomplishing little more, and not returning to the army until May 24. There Grant greeted him with heavy humor. "Now Sheridan evidently thinks he has been clear down to the James River," he told his officers, ". . . and even getting a peep at Richmond; but probably this is all imagination, or else he has been reading something of the kind in the newspapers. I don't suppose he seriously thinks he has made such a march."

Knowing he and his cavalry had proven themselves, the often prickly Sheridan even managed to join in the bantering: "Well, after what General Grant says, I do begin to feel doubtful as to whether I have been absent at all. . . ."[18]

From May 14 to 17, while Lee was solidifying his line at the base of the Mule Shoe, Grant and Meade had been shifting the bulk of their men to the Fredericksburg Road and the right of the Confederate perimeter. Then Grant, thinking that Lee had weakened his center to shadow the move, on May 18 unwisely ordered Hancock's 2nd Corps and Wright's 6th Corps back to the Bloody Angle to duplicate their assault of six days earlier. This time thirty cannon were waiting for them. "All were astonished at this [attack]," said one Rebel artilleryman, "and could not believe a serious attempt would be made to assail such a line. . . . It was welcomed by the Confederates as a chance to pay off old scores." Solid shot greeted the Union infantry at long range, then case shot at 400 to 800 yards, then canister at close range. In less than thirty minutes, some 12,000 infantrymen were driven from the field with heavy losses by artillery alone. "We found the enemy so strongly entrenched," said Meade tellingly, "that even Grant thought it useless to knock our heads [further] against a brick wall. . . ."

The next day brought the last of the clashes at Spotsylvania, with Lee sending out Ewell's corps to reconnoiter. Moving without artillery for speed, the Rebels had no chance when they blundered into Hancock's men, and paid for it heavily. Later that night Grant for the third time sidestepped Lee's right, forcing the Confederates back to the North Anna River. Overall at Spotsylvania the North suffered 18,000 casualties; the South, some 11,000—a number just as staggering considering the relative strength of the armies. "The world has never seen so bloody or so protracted a battle as the one being fought and I hope never will again," Grant wrote Julia. But he would not ease up. "I have reinforcements coming up which will greatly encourage our men," he added, "and discourage the enemy correspondingly."[19] In this latter regard, he would be mistaken; Lee's men were not the sort to lose heart.

What was happening meantime with the second stage of Grant's three-pronged movement into Virginia—the landing of Benjamin Butler's Army of the James in Lee's rear? On May 5 Butler's 40,000-man force—which consisted of the 18th Corps under William Farrar "Baldy" Smith and the 10th Corps under Quincy Adams Gillmore—had steamed up from Fort Monroe and debarked at Bermuda Hundred, the peninsula formed by the convergence of the James and Appomattox Rivers. There Butler was just fifteen miles south of Richmond and seven miles north of Petersburg, and just three miles from the railroad supply line. The area, moreover, was virtually defenseless. Richmond was garrisoned by four infantry brigades, Petersburg by only one, and the Confederate command situation was in flux. "I had given [Butler] to understand," said Grant, "that I should aim to fight Lee between the Rapidan and Richmond if he would stand; but should Lee fall back . . . I would follow up and make a junction of the Armies of the Potomac and the James."

Instead of swiftly advancing against the capital and the breastworks at Drewry's Bluff, however, Butler frittered away his tactical advantage, contenting himself over the next few days with constructing fortifications, reconnoitering and making desultory raids. That the Massachusetts politician was a formidable civilian personality cannot be questioned; Lincoln just weeks before had even offered him the vice-presidential spot on his reelection ticket, an honor he refused. As a military man, however, he was a disaster. Certainly that is what his chief lieutenants, Baldy Smith and Gillmore, believed, and they would give him little respect.

Not until May 9th did Butler move out in any strength, and then it was toward Petersburg. "The enemy was easily driven back to Swift Creek . . . and the railroad and turnpike bridges were reached," Smith said. "The stream was very narrow and with steep banks, and no crossing was possible except by a bridge." Rebel artillery controlled both bridges over the creek, however, leading Smith to suggest to Butler "that if Petersburg was to be taken, the proper way was to throw a bridge across the Appomattox behind our lines and, crossing there, assault the works from the east." Butler rejected the proposal in disparaging terms. "His spoken criticism was of such a character as to check voluntary advice during the remainder of the campaign."

Following more dithering, Butler returned to his lines at Bermuda Hundred on the 11th. Subsequently, when he finally did decide to head toward

Richmond in force, he found that his delays had given Pierre Beauregard, coming up with reinforcements from South Carolina to Drewry's Bluff, the time to give him battle. "On the 16th [Beauregard] attacked Butler with great vigor," Grant would say, "and with such success as to limit very materially the further usefulness of the Army of the James. . . . I afterward ordered a portion of it to join the Army of the Potomac, leaving a sufficient force with Butler to man his works."

The clash on the 16th, daylong and bitter, ended with the Federals suffering 4,000 casualties. Butler was driven back in disorder from Drewry's Bluff and behind his entrenchments at the neck of Bermuda Hundred. Here he was impotent. The Rebels could not get at him, but neither could he subsequently challenge their massed cannon and reemerge from the self-imposed trap. It remained for Grant to sum up the dilemma: "I then asked [General John Barnard, the engineering officer] why Butler could not move out from his lines and push across . . . on the south side of Richmond. He replied that it was impracticable . . . that the position was like a bottle and Butler's line of entrenchments across the neck represented the cork; that the enemy had built an equally strong line immediately in front of him. . . . He was perfectly safe against an attack but . . . the enemy had corked the bottle and with a small force could hold the cork in its place."[20]

For the nonce, Butler had taken himself out of the war.

To General Franz Sigel, another political general, had been entrusted the third of the Federal incursions: defeating the Confederates in the Shenandoah so as to threaten Lee's left through the Blue Ridge Mountains and simultaneously deny him an essential source of produce and livestock. Skirmishing between Sigel's 9,000-man force and some 5,600 Rebels, who were led by John C. Breckinridge of Kentucky, began north of New Market on May 14. Though himself a politician—he had finished second to Lincoln in the 1860 Electoral College voting—Breckinridge nonetheless was a skilled soldier. In the ensuing battle, Sigel would be badly outmatched.

The Federal commander made his first egregious mistake soon after the initial skirmishing, when he divided his force—which was widely spread along the valley pike—and sent nearly one-third of it, under Colonel August Moor, ahead to New Market. There early on the morning of the 15th, after temporarily occupying the town, Moor's troops fell victim to an all-out Rebel assault. Ousted from New Market about noon, the Federals fell back to Manor's Hill on the west of the turnpike. Then, when the enemy pressure continued unabated, they withdrew to Bushong's Hill, where

Sigel, who belatedly had arrived on the scene, was feverishly trying to set up his main defensive line. Though superior in numbers, he had in effect lost that advantage by neglecting to concentrate his command.

It was at Bushong's Hill, bolstered by massed cannon, that Sigel about 2:30 P.M. gave signs of rallying. His gunners sent round after round into the oncoming Rebels, tearing great gaps in their ranks. First the 51st and the 30th Virginia were riddled by Federal canister, later the 62nd Virginia under George H. Smith. Five of the 62nd's color-bearers went down in the space of a few minutes, as did some 100 of his 448 men. Puffing his pipe in the midst of the debacle Smith fell back, telling his men to take cover wherever they could. "The fire," said a survivor, "was the hottest I was ever under."[21]

With the battle in the balance, Breckinridge's aides now urged him to use an untried and unlikely reserve—some 250 teenage cadets from the Virginia Military Institute. "The Federals are right on us," one staff member said. "If the cadets are ordered up, we can close the gap."

Breckinridge hesitated for a long moment. The youngsters were fresh from the parade ground, and new to the horrors of the war. "Put the boys in," he finally said, "and may God forgive me for the order."

Amid thunderclaps and rain, the VMI contingent double-quicked into the breach. Near the Bushong farmhouse the first of many shells fell in their ranks, killing two and leaving a third writhing on the ground, clutching tufts of grass in his agony. Bullets claimed many others. Private Robert Cousins, using the house for cover, remembered that the thud of Federal minie balls made "a sounding board upon its sides." Once past the house and into the fields, their casualties mounted. Private Thomas G. Jefferson took a minie ball in the stomach. When his comrades tried to help him, he waved them away, pointing toward the front. "That is the place for you!" he shouted. "You can do me no good!"[22]

In short order the gap was closed. Now the question was: Which side would give way first?

Here Sigel made his second mistake, again by not concentrating his strength. Instead of hurling Julius Stahel and his 2,000 cavalrymen on the weakened Rebel lines on Bushong Hill, he sent them against a fresh enemy force east of the turnpike. There it was the turn of the Confederate cannon to come into action, shattering the charge of the oncoming horsemen. "Every gun of the enemy was made effective by his use of the smooth ground," said an officer of the 21st New York, "and by rapid maneuvering an enfilading fire was kept up most of the time." Stahel's troopers, caught in front and flank by canister blasts, began milling about in confusion.

Colonel John Wynkoop tried to restore order, bellowing orders and waving his saber, but his men did not respond. Singly and then in groups they began slinking off, making for the rear. "Our cavalry behaved badly," one journalist would admit.

The bewildered Stahel, riding off to make his dismal report to Sigel, could look behind and "see his command utterly routed, so confused that some units would not reform for several hours as they choked the pike in their panic." The sight sickened him. *My God, General Sigel!* he exclaimed in so many words when the two men met. *Where is my cavalry?*[23]

On Bushong Hill the Confederates, given precious minutes to regroup by their comrades to the east, once more gained momentum. Inexorably, with the VMI cadets conspicuous among the grizzled veterans, they gained the crest, turning the high ground to their advantage and pouring down fire on the fleeing enemy. Though the fighting continued the rest of the day, the battle to all intents was over, with Sigel fleeing headlong down the valley. Federal casualties were some 840; Confederate, 530. The cadets suffered 55 casualties, some 20 percent of their number. Thereafter Breckinridge was never able to speak of them without tears coming to his eyes. One of his officers about 5:00 P.M. sought him out. "[Breckinridge] was soon found . . . on foot and muddy to the waist. He had been much of his time off his horse . . . mingling with and cheering his brave, tired, hungry, drenched and muddy infantry and artillery. . . ."

Seldom would such a minor battle have such a major impact. Sigel's failure not only meant that Lee's far left in the Blue Ridge was still secure but it ensured that at least some of the Shenandoah Valley's crops could be harvested over the next few weeks, providing the army with much needed provisions. Combined with Butler's fiasco at Bermuda Hundred, the two defeats would substantially prolong the war.[24]

Back in the vicinity of the North Anna River, meantime, the deadly pas de deux that was Grant's attempt to turn Lee's right would continue. The Federal columns arrived there May 23, only to find their way blocked once more by Rebel breastworks on the south shore. Hancock's 2nd Corps was to the east, marching down Telegraph Road; Warren's 5th Corps and Wright's 6th Corps were five miles to the west, heading for Jericho Ford; Burnside's 9th Corps was between them, moving toward Ox Ford. The sun was shining and the army's spirit, surprisingly enough in view of the heavy losses sustained in the Wilderness and at Spotsylvania, was high. One of Hancock's officers would say: "There was an idea that we were still advancing, that there was a plan that would be carried out. . . . When we reached the North Anna, I think the general feeling was that we should roll on, like a great wave. . . ."

From the commanding officer on down, most men in the Army of the Potomac seemed reconciled to pay the price the Rebel resistance demanded. Grant's troops, in point of fact, seemed more concerned about their inability to rout the enemy than his bulldog tactics. "Now what is the reason that we cannot walk straight through [the Rebels] with our far superior numbers?" one infantryman mused. "We fight as good as they. They must understand the country better, or there is a screw loose somewhere in the machinery of our army. . . ." Grant, of course, found the casualties deeply troubling, revealing his emotions only by his stepped-up cigar smoking. Once, when he did tell Meade of his anxieties, that officer, supposedly the far more sensitive of the two, would hear no more. "Well, General," he relied brusquely, "we can't do these little tricks without losses."[25]

Grant would persist in his master plan, which was to stay in Lee's face, exerting constant pressure and forcing him back toward Richmond. Even the news of Butler's blunder at Bermuda Hundred and Sigel's rout at New Market did not weaken his resolve. By the afternoon of the 23rd the Federal army was successfully crossing the North Anna, where it would eventually constrict the enemy's lines to an inverted V whose apex was at Ox Ford. Here Lee, on the defense, saw a splendid opportunity. "The two wings of Grant's army were safely across the river, but there was no connection between them," said Confederate General Evander McIvor Law. "Lee had only thrown back his flanks and let them in on either side, while he held the river between; and when General Grant attempted to throw his center, under Burnside, across the river, it was very severely handled and failed to gain a foothold on the south side."

Thinking Lee was retreating, the Federals remained oblivious to their danger. "[Grant] had cut his army in two by running it upon the point of a wedge," Law would say. "He could not break the point, which rested upon the river, and the attempt to force it out of place by striking on its sides must of necessity be made without much concert of action between the two wings . . . neither of which could reinforce the other without crossing the river twice; while his opponent could readily transfer his troops as needed . . . across the narrow space between them." That evening Lee made his preparations for a counterattack. "Our holding a half mile of river made the Federal position very bad," said another Rebel officer. ". . . We had the interior lines."[26]

But the counterattack was not to be—still another Civil War what-if.

On May 24, even as Grant's divided army was advancing up the sides of the "V," almost inviting disaster, Lee came down with crippling dysentery. "Lee would gladly have compelled battle," said one of his aides. ". . . He was anxious now to strike a telling blow. . . . But in the midst of his operations on the North Anna, he succumbed to sickness, against which he had struggled for some days. As he lay in his tent he would say, in his impatience, 'We must strike them! We must strike them! We must never let them pass us again!' . . . But Lee in his tent was not Lee at the front." In truth, with Jackson dead and Longstreet severely wounded, the Confederate commander lacked the lieutenants, undirected, who could launch such a telling assault.

Now Grant, belatedly recognizing Lee's threat and the strength of his lines, hurriedly regrouped, throwing up breastworks of his own and halting the Union advance. "Our lines covered his front," he said of his predicament, "with the six miles separating [our] two wings guarded by but a single division. . . . We were, for the time, practically two armies besieging."[27] For several days the impasse went on, with the adversaries perched within pecking distance: Grant frustrated that his drive on Richmond temporarily was stalled; Lee disappointed that his illness had kept him, at a propitious time, from going on the attack.

On May 27 Grant again began moving around Lee's right—his fourth sidestep of the campaign—heading south and the next day crossing the Pamunkey River at Hanovertown. There he found that the Confederates had anticipated him and were dug in along Totopotomoy Creek. Three days of heavy skirmishing followed, until on June 1 Phil Sheridan's cavalry seized the crossroads at nearby Old Cold Harbor, only ten miles from Richmond. Immediately both sides converged on the area, Lee once more falling back to challenge him.

Riding toward the front lines that day, Grant came across a teamster whose wagon was stalled in mud, and who was beating his horses brutally in the face with the butt-end of his whip.

Spurring his mount forward, he angrily galloped toward the man. "Stop beating those horses!" he yelled.

The teamster looked Grant up and down, not knowing his rank, and whacked one of the horses again. "Well, who's drivin' this team anyhow—you or me?" he said.

Grant now completely lost his temper—one of the few occasions he did so during the war. "I'll show you, you infernal villain!" he cried, shaking his fist in the teamster's face and calling for an officer in his escort. "Take this man in charge, and have him tied to a tree for six hours as punishment."

That night, sitting with his staff at their mess table, Grant continued to fulminate about the incident. "If people knew how much more they could get out of a horse by gentleness than by harshness," he said, "they would save a great deal of trouble both to the horse and the man. A horse is a particularly intelligent animal. He can be made to do almost anything if his master has intelligence enough to let him know what is required. . . ."[28]

Though there was hard fighting in the Cold Harbor area in the next thirty-six hours, Grant would not launch his all-out assault against the Confederates, whose breastworks stretched for almost six miles, until June 3. He had some 108,000 troops, Lee some 59,000. Grant's decision to make the frontal attack was not an easy one to make. According to his aide Horace Porter, he could "attempt to crush Lee's army on the north side of the James [River], with the prospect in case of success of driving him into Richmond, capturing the city perhaps without a siege . . . or to move the Union army south of the James without giving battle, and transfer the field of operations to the vicinity of Petersburg." Grant had to consider the question, however, not just militarily but politically. "Many of the people in the North were becoming discouraged at the prolongation of the contest," Porter went on. "If the army were transferred south of the James without fighting a battle . . . people would be impatient at the prospect of an apparently indefinite continuation. . . ."

The soldiers in the Army of the Potomac, by now knowing Grant's ways, on the eve of battle prepared themselves for a bloody contest. Porter, passing among them, saw that many had taken off their coats and blouses and were using needle and thread. "This exhibition of tailoring seemed rather peculiar at such a moment, but upon closer examination it was found that the men were calmly writing their names and home addresses on slips of paper, and pinning them on the backs of their coats, so that their dead bodies might be recognized upon the field, and their fate made known to their families."[29]

Pushing forward at 4:30 A.M., three Federal units would bear the brunt of the attack. Hancock's 2nd Corps was on the left, Wright's 6th Corps in the center, and William Farrar Smith's 18th Corps—newly arrived from Bermuda Hundred—on the right. "Everyone felt that this was to be the final struggle," said Lieutenant Colonel Martin McMahon of Wright's command. "No further flanking marches were possible. Richmond was dead in front." The Federals were advancing into an innocent-looking string of low hills and ridges, behind which the concealed enemy had massed its artillery and muskets to cover every foot of ground. "They are intricate, zig-zagged lines within lines," one newspaperman would write of the Rebel defenses, "lines protecting flanks of lines, lines built to enfilade an opposing line, lines within which lies a battery . . . a maze and labyrinth of works within works . . . each laid out with some definite design. . . ."

Here Horace Porter recounts the futile assault. "Hancock's troops struck a salient of the enemy's works, and after a desperate struggle captured it. . . . The second line, however, did not move up in time to support the first, which was finally driven back. . . . Another division had rushed forward in column . . . but an impassable swamp divided the troops, who were now subjected to a galling fire." Wright's corps managed to capture some rifle pits, but quickly came to grief under an enfilading hail of shot and shell. "Nevertheless, they held a line, and protected it as best they could, at a distance of only thirty or forty yards from the enemy." Smith's troops, advancing through a ravine, initially found themselves some cover. "His men drove the enemy's skirmishers before them . . . but the line had to be readjusted at close quarters, and the same cross-fire from which Wright had suffered made further advances extremely hazardous."[30]

Porter's description of events, while accurate, could not convey the emotions of the troops in the field, who literally were marching to their death. "The men were dropping, wounded, all along the line," said Charles Page of the 14th Connecticut, Hancock's command. "To reach the enemy the men were obliged to pass through a [swamp] very thick and tangled and almost impenetrable." The colonel of the 164th New York, seizing the colors of his regiment, did succeed in reaching the Rebel parapet and planting the flag, then fell mortally wounded. Within minutes the Federal ranks were riddled; those who survived hugged the ground while clawing hollows for their prone bodies.

On Wright's front the situation was much the same. General Emory Upton, one of the heroes of the Wilderness, would condemn the Cold Harbor attack in blunt terms. "We were recklessly ordered to assault the enemy's entrenchments, knowing neither their strength nor position," he wrote his sister. "Our loss was very heavy, and to no purpose. Our men are brave, but cannot accomplish impossibilities."

The 23rd and 25th Massachusetts, Smith's command, got within striking distance of the Confederates, only to be decimated. "The charging column . . . received the most destructive fire I ever saw," said Colonel William Oates of the 15th Alabama, a veteran of the savage fighting for the

Round Tops at Gettysburg. "They were subjected to a front and flank fire from the infantry, at short range, while my piece of artillery poured double charges of cannister into them. . . . I could see the dust fog out of a man's clothing in two or three places at once where as many balls would strike him at the same moment. In two minutes not [one] of them was standing." Recalled Harvey Clark of the 25th Massachusetts: "The first we saw was a line of men shoulder to shoulder waist high above their works, then a . . . shower of shell and bullets. It is hard to describe the sensation I had. It was like being alone in the midst of a whirlwind." Lying among the dead and wounded he managed to crawl backward, inches at a time to avoid notice, until he reached safety.[31]

Lieutenant Colonel McMahon, Wright's adjutant, now realized the Federals were facing disaster. "A strange and terrible feature of this battle was that as the three gallant corps moved on, each was enfiladed while receiving the full force of the enemy's direct fire in front. . . . Each corps commander reported and complained to General Meade that the other corps commanders, right or left, as the case may be, failed to protect him from enfilading fire by silencing batteries in their respective fronts. . . . These dispatches naturally caused mystification at headquarters. . . . The explanation was simple enough, although it was not known until reconnaissance had been made. The three corps had moved upon diverging lines, each directly facing the enemy . . . and the further each had advanced the more its flank had become exposed."

By 7:00 A.M. Meade was asking Grant: "I should be glad to have your views as to the continuance of these attacks, if unsuccessful." Back from Grant came an uncharacteristic reply, in effect clouding the issue and telling Meade *he* should make the call: "The moment it becomes certain that an assault cannot succeed, suspend the offensive. . . ." Perhaps still chafing under the criticism he had received for not pursuing Lee following the victory at Gettysburg, Meade continued the fighting.

Soon Hancock, Wright, and Smith were being told to renew the attack, without respect to coordinating their movements. "Unity of action, so necessary for success," said Lieutenant Colonel McMahon of their understandable foot-dragging, "could certainly not be expected from such an order. The attack was made here and there by the advance of troops that had retired for shelter, and by merely opening fire . . . and the corps commanders duly reported that the attack had been made and had failed." A third time the order was given for a general assault. "It came to the corps headquarters, was transmitted to the division headquarters, and to the brigades and regiments without comment. To move the army further . . .

was a simple and absolute impossibility, known to be such by every officer and man. . . . The order was obeyed by simply renewing the fire from the men as they lay in position."[32]

Mercifully, about 1:00 P.M., the fighting at Cold Harbor came to an end. Grant and Meade would have to share the blame for its failure. Both had rushed into combat without proper reconnaissance; both had given little thought to stabilizing and protecting their line of battle. The bloodletting would mark Grant's nadir as a commander: He lost some 7,000 men; Lee, perhaps 1,500. "I have always regretted that the last assault at Cold Harbor was ever made," he would say—that and little more. Perhaps he subsequently could take comfort in the fact that the battle was Lee's last great triumph.

In this month of continual campaigning, from May 4 to June 3, Grant had lost 50,000 men; Lee, 32,000. The North could supply reinforcements for the Army of the Potomac; the South could do little for the Army of Northern Virginia. "I don't believe the history of the world can afford a parallel to the protracted and severe fighting which this army has sustained for the past thirty days," Meade would write. ". . . I think Grant has had his eyes opened, and is willing to admit now that Virginia and Lee's army is not Tennessee and Bragg's army. Whether the people [of the North] will ever realize this fact remains to be seen."[33]

For the next three days the predominantly Union dead and wounded lay on the ground. "An impression prevails in the popular mind," said McMahon, "and with some reason perhaps, that a commander who sends a flag of truce asking permission to bury his dead and bring in his wounded has lost the field of battle. Hence the reluctance on our part. . . ." The scene was horrendous. "Men lay in places like hogs in a pen—some side by side, across each other, some two deep, others with their legs lying across the head and body of their dead comrades," said one Confederate. ". . . One could not sleep for the sickening sound, 'W-a-t-e-r' ever sounding and echoing in his ears." Not until June 6 did Grant bring himself to ask for a truce, and not until the following day were rescue parties on the field. Concern for the wounded, he belatedly wrote Lee, "compels me to ask a suspension of hostilities for sufficient time to collect them. . . ."

In the midst of these events Grant nonetheless made the time to pen a family note. "We . . . have every prospect of still more fighting to do before we get into Richmond," he told his nine-year-old daughter Nellie. When we do get there I shall go home to see you and Ma, Fred, Buck [Ulysses Jr.] and Jess. I expect Jess rides Little Rebel every day! I think when I go home I will get a little buggy . . . so that you and Jess can ride about the country during vacation. Tell Ma to let Fred learn French as soon as she thinks he is able. . . . It will be a great help to him when he goes to West Point. You must send this letter to Ma to read because I will not write to her today. . . ."[34]

Grant now on June 12 made his fifth and last turn of Lee's right, under cover of night audaciously withdrawing his entire command from the Cold Harbor front and moving it south of the James River. His intent was to seize the rail hub at Petersburg, thereby cutting Richmond's lines of supply. In the first stage of the flanking attack Burnside's 9th Corps, Hancock's 2nd Corps and Wright's 6th Corps pulled back to create breathing room between the armies, even as Warren's 5th Corps swung wide and advanced on the Federal left to Malvern Hill, screening the approaches to the river. Baldy Smith's 18th Corps simultaneously steamed back the way it had come, going down the York River and up the James to rejoin Benjamin Butler at Bermuda Hundred. "The enemy show no sign of having brought troops to the south side of Richmond," Grant informed Lincoln. "I will have Petersburg secured, if possible, before they get here in much force." Replied the president: "I have just received your dispatch. I begin to see it. You will succeed. God bless you all."

For the next few days Lee, in large part because his cavalry's leadership with Stuart's death was impaired, was on the horns of a dilemma. Grant's rapid movements and convincing feints were serving to conceal his aims, so much so that Lee for the nonce felt compelled to stay north of the river. He could not be sure whether Grant was making for Richmond or Petersburg. Meanwhile Baldy Smith was crossing the Appomattox, and the rest of the Federals were completing the fifty-mile trek to Wilcox Landing on the James. There Hancock crossed by boat, while Warren, Wright, and Burnside took advantage of a superbly engineered 2,100-foot pontoon bridge.

Leading the attack from the southeast on Petersburg on June 15 was Smith with 16,000 men. He was advancing on the so-called Dimmock Line, a ten-mile-long, artillery-studded breastwork in the shape of a squat horseshoe whose ends rested on the south bank of the Appomattox River. Opposing him were one brigade of Rebels and some scraped-together militia—some 2,200 men. The fighting began about 7:00 A.M., when James Dearing's cavalry and cannon blocked Smith's advance on the City Point Road. Here the 5th and 22nd U.S. Colored Troops, advancing with speed and daring, flanked the first line of defenses, capturing an artillery piece and sending the foe packing.

Their brigadier, whose wounds had kept him from witnessing the charge, was incredulous. "What has become of the Johnnies?" he asked one black soldier.

Well sir, the man replied, *they just done lit out; didn't care to make our close acquaintance!*

The white troops were impressed. "The problem is solved," one soldier would say about the Union army's controversial decision to mix whites and blacks in combat. "The Negro is a man, a soldier, a hero." Hitherto the blacks had been paid two dollars less a month than the whites; on this day, ironically, Congress rectified the slight. Commented Benjamin Butler approvingly: "The colored man fills an equal space in ranks while he lives, and an equal grave when he falls."[35]

Following this initial contact, however, Smith faltered. Fond of serving champagne at his mess, he could be an unhurried sort. His van did not reach Petersburg's main breastworks until 11:00 A.M., and there it halted. Perhaps remembering the carnage incurred in the frontal attack at Cold Harbor—and not knowing how few were the enemy's numbers—Smith had no stomach for assailing the works without lengthy reconnoitering. He did much of this probing himself—an arduous process—and by the time he finished and informed his three division heads of his findings it was 7:00 P.M., with little light left in the day.

Though his subsequent assault carried a half dozen forts of the extreme left of the enemy's lines, yielding sixteen guns and more than 200 prisoners, Smith broke off the action. It would be more prudent, he decided, to wait until Hancock and the remainder of the army came up in support. "Had he gone ahead . . ." said one Rebel observer, "the chances are that he would have gotten Petersburg. But his chief of artillery had taken all the artillery horses to water, & he lost another hour, during which both night and [reinforcements] were drawing near."

Confederate General Pierre Beauregard, meanwhile, still in command in the Drewry's Bluff–Petersburg area, was frantically rushing fresh troops into the city, at one point even stripping the defenses at Bermuda Hundred. By June 16 his force had grown to 10,000, but he was still facing some 66,000 men.

That day and the next the Federals, even with Grant and Meade now on the scene, made no appreciable progress in breaking through the city's formidable breastworks. The advances were piecemeal, the effort tentative. One reason for the setbacks may have been the physical condition of Hancock, the army's best corps commander. "I can hardly walk or ride," he would admit to Meade, alluding to the groin wound suffered at Gettysburg that had reopened. "[Hancock's] orders to his division commanders . . . threw upon them much responsibility. . . ." reported his aide, Francis Walker. Delays in communications along the far-flung Union lines also played a role. "The enemy have formed in line of battle," Baldy Smith asked at one point. ". . . Shall we attack them in force?" More than two hours passed before he received a response.

How much overall the army's spirit had been dampened by Cold Harbor—despite ringing disclaimers—can be debated, but the casualties incurred there and throughout the Overland Campaign must have given the commanders pause. Grant, under vicious attack for the bloodletting from many of the same newspapers that had previously hailed his genius, would be curiously reticent about the failure to capitalize on his dramatic flanking movement. "During the [16th], Meade assaulted and carried one more redan to his right and two to his left," he would say. "In all this we lost very heavily. The works were not strongly manned, but they all had guns in them which fell into our hands. . . . During the 17th the fighting was very severe and the losses heavy; and at night our forces occupied about the same position they had occupied in the morning. . . ."[36]

Dawn on June 18 found the Rebels gone from their original lines and entrenched closer to Petersburg in shorter and even more imposing works. "By the time new formations could be made," said a disappointed Horace Porter, "Lee's army had arrived [across the James] in large force, great activity had been displayed in strengthening the fortifications, and the difficulties of the attacking party had been greatly increased. . . . Grant realized the nature of the ground and the circumstances that prevented the troops from accomplishing more than had been done. . . ." The four days of fighting cost the Federals an additional 10,000 casualties.

In the months to come both Petersburg and Richmond would fall under a nine-and-a-half-month siege, with both sides shuttling troops back and forth between the two cities for more than a half dozen battles and scores of lesser actions, a story we shall tell presently. Grant accepted the stalemate philosophically: "I will make no more assaults on that portion of the line, but will give the men a rest, and then look to extensions toward our left, with a view to destroying Lee's communications on the south and confining him to a close siege."[37]

THREE
****

THE ATLANTA CAMPAIGN

Back in the West, Sherman during early May was launching his own advance deep into Georgia, intent on seizing the rail and industrial hub at Atlanta. His command, totaling almost 100,000 men and second in size only to Grant's and Meade's in Virginia, consisted, as we know, of three separate armies—those of the Cumberland (50,000 effectives), the Tennessee (35,000), and the Ohio (15,000). They were led, respectively, by George Thomas, James McPherson, and newcomer John Schofield. The Virginia-born Thomas, who had proved his worth at Chickamauga and then, replacing William Rosecrans, again at Chattanooga, was regarded by his family as a traitor for staying with the North. He was big and burly, with a massive presence. On the battlefield he fought with forcefulness and unremitting zeal, but he could not be stampeded into action until his preparations were complete. In the aftermath of the victory at Chattanooga, when asked by a chaplain whether the Union dead should be buried by states, the expatriate [of Virginia] gave a forthright but chilling answer: "No, mix them up. I've had enough of state's rights."

McPherson, the thirty-six-year-old protégé both of Grant's and Sherman's who had led so fiercely on the right at Champion's Hill—and like them an Ohioan—now followed in their footsteps as head of the Army of the Tennessee. Handsome, well liked, number one in his class at West Point, he seemed a man with a limitless future. His deep regret, however, was that the upcoming campaign had forced him to postpone his long-planned wedding to Emily Hoffman, daughter of a prominent Baltimore merchant. "Mac, it wrings my heart, but you can't go now," Sherman told him. "Be patient," Cump wrote Miss Hoffman, "and I know that when the happy day comes for him to stand by your side . . . you will regard him with a high respect & honor. . . ."[1]

John Schofield, three years younger than McPherson, had arrived at West Point from Illinois in 1849, when agitation over slavery already was rising, only to find his Virginia roommates intolerant of "Yankees."

"*You* are not a *Yankee!*" one remarked in mock horror.

"I am from Illinois," Schofield said.

"Oh," replied the roommate, "we don't call Western men Yankees."

"In that remark," Schofield later would write, "I found my mission at West Point . . . to be, as far as possible, a peacemaker between the hostile sections." In his senior year at the academy, because he refused to reveal the names of classmates who had broken some minor rules, he was dismissed. Only the intervention of Illinois Senator Stephen Douglas resulted, the following year, in his reinstatement.

Rotund, bespectacled, highly intelligent, and almost entirely lacking in combat experience, Schofield—whose small command consisted of the 23rd Corps—had Grant's gratitude for the promptness with which he had sent reinforcements to Vicksburg from strife-torn Missouri, where he had been trying to keep the peace.

In the Army of the Cumberland, Thomas's corps were headed by Oliver Otis Howard (the 4th), John Palmer (the 14th), and Joe Hooker (the 20th). Steady, honest, and pious but lacking both dash and tactical skill, Howard—routed at Chancellorsville and a refugee from the Army of the Potomac—had found a home in the West. His divisions were led by David Stanley of Ohio, a perhaps overly confident West Pointer; John Newton, another Virginian fighting for the North; and Thomas Wood, who had been so instrumental in taking Missionary Ridge.

John Palmer, an Illinois Republican party stalwart, was a veteran of New Madrid, Corinth, Murfreesboro, and Chattanooga. His division chiefs included Richard W. Johnson, whose cautionary ways oftimes made him seem more an academic than a soldier; the hair-trigger Jefferson C. Davis, who two years before had shot a brother officer to death but escaped punishment; and able Pennsylvanian Absalom Baird.

Fighting Joe Hooker, like Howard blamed for the loss at Chancellorsville and an outcast from the Army of the Potomac, had to an extent regained his reputation at Lookout Mountain. Hailed by one cabinet officer as "a frank, manly, brave and energetic soldier, of somewhat less breath of intellect than I had expected," he remained inordinately ambitious. Future battles, he felt, would bring him the fame he craved.[2] Hooker's divisions were headed by Alpheus Williams, a Michigan lawyer of uncommon sense and sensibility; six foot four John Geary, a political general who had helped reopen the "Cracker Line" at Chattanooga and who was particularly adept at publicizing his exploits by cultivating, and even bribing, the press; and Daniel Butterfield, who had served as chief of staff both to Hooker and George Meade in the Army of the Potomac, and followed the former to the West.

McPherson's Army of *the* Tennessee (once again, not to be confused with the Confederate Army of Tennessee) had three corps commanders: the hard-hitting, hard-living Illinois politician John Logan, whose exploits we have seen at Champion's Hill and elsewhere (15th Corps); the brilliant railroad-engineer-turned-infantryman Grenville Dodge (16th Corps), whose ability to keep the supply lines open and gather intelligence had contributed so much to Grant's triumph during the Vicksburg Campaign (Dodge was replacing Stephen Hurlbut, who had fought well at Shiloh but whose shady business dealings as an administrator brought about his removal); and Frank Blair Jr. (17th Corps), son of Washington insider "Old Man" Blair, and one of Sherman's close friends. Blair would not join the army until June.

Logan's division commanders remained Peter Osterhaus, the best of the German-American generals and especially prized by the president for his political support; Morgan Smith and John E. Smith, both of whom had been serving as general officers since Fort Donelson; and William Harrow, transferred from the Army of the Potomac. Dodge's divisions were led by crusty Irish-born Thomas Sweeny; who had lost an arm in the Mexican War and later become a career soldier; and James Veatch, a lawyer and legislator. Heading Blair's units were grizzled Ohioan Mortimer Leggett, and Indiana lawyer Walter Gresham.

The Army of the Ohio's twenty-third Corps, under Schofield, consisted of three divisions: those of Alvin Hovey, whom Grant had credited more than any other with the victory at Champion's Hill; Henry Judah, a West Pointer perhaps too ardent for his own good; and Jacob Cox, who by his own account possessed the essential qualities of leadership: "a bold heart, a cool head, and practical common-sense."[3]

This formidable force's weak point was its cavalry, divided into four divisions and nominally headed by Major General George Stoneman. In point of fact, Sherman directed the troopers' operations; Stoneman, a mediocre officer at best, led one of the divisions. The others were headed by Kenner Garrard, who had no cavalry experience in the field; Hugh Judson Kilpatrick, a womanizer so dedicated to his calling that he neither drank nor gambled; and Edward McCook, a Kansas lawyer. Kilpatrick and McCook were aggressive, but often lacking in judgment.

Opposing Sherman with the Army of Tennessee was the defensive-minded Joseph Johnston, whose tepid support of Pemberton at Vicksburg had left so much to be desired. "His military experience and knowledge were large," one Federal officer would say of his opponent, "his mind eminently systematic, his judgment sound, his courage imperturbable. [But] he was not sanguine in temperament, and therefore was liable to lack in audacity." Johnston's force—augmented by the remnants of the Army of Mississippi, headed by Leonidas Polk, a West Pointer turned Episcopal bishop—totaled some 65,000 men. Though badly outnumbered, the Rebel commander possessed several tactical advantages. First and foremost was the fact that he could choose the positions where he wanted to fight, and if forced to give ground would if anything grow stronger, since his lines of supply would shorten and his men would be concentrated. Sherman's numbers on the other hand would lessen as he advanced, since troops would have to be left behind to guard his supply lines—anchored by the Western & Atlantic Railroad—against Confederate cavalry raids.[4]

The Union incursion, moreover, would be made more difficult by the topography of northern Georgia. A series of steep ridges and mountains would have to be turned, and formidable creeks and rivers forded, before Atlanta—no more than 100 miles away as the crow flies, but far more distant in view of the physical obstacles—could be invested. The first such barrier was clifflike twenty-mile-long Rocky Face Ridge, just west of the town of Dalton and its railroad stop. There Johnston's stubborn troops and cannon dominated Buzzard's Roost Gap; clearly, a head-on attack would be suicidal.

Sherman, however, had already determined on another course—flanking the enemy well south of the ridge, at Snake Creek Gap, and marching on Resaca, another stop on the railroad fifteen miles in the Confederate rear. "Before the opening of the campaign," said General Jacob Cox, "Thomas had called Sherman's attention to Snake Creek Gap as a route by which Resaca . . . could be reached, and the position at Dalton be turned. He had offered to lead the Army of the Cumberland by this defile, whilst the Armies of the Tennessee and Ohio occupied Johnston in front."

While he accepted Thomas's suggestion in substance, Sherman decided it would be McPherson who would make the attack on Resaca. Possibly he felt that the stolid Thomas would not move with sufficient speed, possibly he wanted his friend to have what he hoped would be the campaign's initial success. In any event, said Cox, "McPherson . . . [would advance] against Resaca, whilst [Sherman] pressed Johnston in front with his superior force, ready to follow him up the moment he let go of Dalton, and before he could seriously damage McPherson."[5]

Thus it happened that, while Thomas and Schofield were demonstrating in the north against Buzzard's Roost Gap, McPherson on May 9 moved with two corps—thirteen brigades—through Snake Creek Gap with orders to cut the railroad at Resaca. The gap, explained Cox, "is a wild and picturesque defile, five or six miles long. Hardly a cabin was to be seen its entire length. The road was only such a track as country wagons had worn. . . . The forest shut it in, and only for a little while at midday did the sun enter it. . . ." Here McPherson became convinced, understandably in view of the density of the terrain and the difficulty of reconnoitering it, that a superior force blocked his way. Instead only two brigades, many of them raw recruits, confronted him.

Sherman continues the tale: "That night I received . . . notice from McPherson that he had found Resaca too strong for a surprise; that in consequence he had fallen back three miles to the mouth of Snake Creek Gap, and was there fortified." Cump was not pleased. Realizing the Rebels now knew of the turning movement and were evacuating Buzzard's Roost and Dalton, he on the 11th began shifting his entire force to Snake Creek Gap. "McPherson had startled Johnston in his fancied security, but had not done the full measure of his work. He had in hand twenty-three thousand of the best men in the army and could have walked into Resaca . . . and there have easily withstood the attack of all of Johnston's army, with the knowledge that Thomas and Schofield were on his heels. Had he done so I am certain that . . . we should have captured half [Johnston's] army and all his artillery and wagons. . . . Such an opportunity does not occur twice in a single life, but at the critical moment McPherson seems to have been a little cautious. . . ."[6]

When the two men met subsequently, Cump chided his protégé.

"Well, Mac, you have missed the opportunity of a lifetime."

McPherson, knowing he was being rebuked, made no reply, and the two men went into the command tent, presumably to discuss further strategy.

On May 14 with all his force up Sherman closed in on Resaca, located just north of the Oostanaula River, and enveloped it from the north and west along a four-mile front. Schofield with his single 23rd Corps was to the left, Thomas in the center, McPherson on the right opposite the town. Sometime after midday the Federals advanced blindly in heavy underbrush on the left, intent on testing the defenses. The excitable Henry Judah rushed forward his division, Schofield's command, so recklessly that he found himself alone and isolated, pinned down by heavy fire. Trying to lend Judah support Absalom Baird's division, Thomas's command, likewise floundered. Fragmented and sporadic were these and other assaults on the left, and the well-protected enemy easily repulsed them. The experience of the colonel of the 23rd Michigan, in the midst of the shot and shell, was typical. Finding it "impossible to shout orders," he kept his men "on the run," then ordered them to "take refuge."

Within hours the assault on the Rebel right was over, producing nothing but needless casualties. Now the Federal artillery took over, sending barrage after barrage on the enemy works. Meanwhile Johnston, seeing that the extreme left of the Federal line was in the air, in the late afternoon instituted a forceful counterattack. Its target was David Stanley's division, Thomas's command, and it was led by John Bell Hood, perhaps "the best general in the Confederacy for such an enterprise: Hood of Gaines' Mill . . . Second Manassas . . . Antietam . . . Chickamauga."[7]

Hood's resolute charge, accompanied by blood-curdling Rebel yells, in short order threatened to engulf the Federals. Only a bold stand by Stanley's six guns, well positioned in the rear of the lines and directed by Captain Peter Simonson of the 5th Indiana, impeded the onslaught—first with shells and then, at 400 yards, with heavy doses of canister. Six cannon, it seems, were holding off several thousand men, but for how long? That question was answered with the timely arrival of Joe Hooker and the division of Alpheus Williams, whom Sherman had detached from the right of the lines. "I reached the ground just in time to deploy one . . . brigade and to repulse the Rebels handsomely," wrote the Yale-educated Williams, at age fifty-four one of the oldest brigadiers. "They had broken one brigade of Stanley's division and were pressing it with yells and were already near one battery . . . when I astonished the rascals by pushing a brigade from the woods . . . They 'skedaddled' as fast as they had advanced, hardly exchanging a half-dozen volleys."[8]

On Sherman's right, in anticipation of the morrow, McPherson's old 15th Corps under John Logan crossed Camp Creek, closed in on Resaca and established a position near the railroad. Though he had not been told to make the advance, McPherson—eager to atone for his mistake at Snake Creek Gap—took the initiative. His lodgment would be the sole Union success of the day.

May 15 involved rounds of continual skirmishing, which occasionally erupted into costly engagements. Sherman had determined, once again, to advance on his left, and to this end he ordered Hooker's 20th Corps and Oliver Howard's 4th Corps forward. Sergeant Rice C. Bull of the 123rd New York, Hooker's command, had just that morning with some others returned from leave. "We had hardly shaken hands and commenced to answer questions about the homefolks," said Bull, "when General Hooker rode along the rear of our line. . . . Everything was ready and the 'Forward' sounded . . . The timber was heavy so our advance was slow, as we could not lose or sever our contact with the troops on our right and left. After advancing a half mile we came to an open field. . . . At the far end the Rebel breastworks were plainly in view. . . . Our line was in such an exposed position we were ordered to 'Right Oblique' to a knoll just ahead of us where we could lie down out of sight."

Here Bull and his comrades came under an artillery barrage. "They did not do much damage but even for veteran troops it is trying to lie unengaged under artillery fire. . . . [Then] one of our batteries entered the field and silenced the enemy's guns. While this was going on our left . . . was making a right wheel to get on the flank of the Johnnies." By 4:00 P.M. the Federal pressure on the defenders was intense. "They then had their choice: either come out and drive us back or retreat. They . . . jumped over their works and advanced. . . . We surely thought they would be on us and everything was made ready to receive them. All along the line you could hear the click of the hammers on our guns as they were half-cocked to attach the caps. . . ."

The fighting on the left, which again would result in stalement, largely spared Sergeant Bull and his comrades. "When the Johnnies had advanced a third of the way toward our line," he said, "they filed off to the right and entered the woods, where they would not be exposed to the artillery . . . so they made their fight on troops to the left of us. . . . Our position in the open field we thought so unfavorable proved our salvation. . . . After repeated efforts to break or drive our line back, the enemy withdrew into their works that evening. . . . We were fortunate. Our regiment had only ten men killed and wounded."[9]

General Alpheus Williams was in the midst of the main Confederate thrust. "Information was brought to me that the Rebels were moving to our left in force. I changed front and in luck had plenty of time to form my line and place my batteries in position. . . . They came on in masses and evidently without expectation of what was before them. All at once . . . my front line and the batteries (which I had with much work got on the ridge of a high hill) opened upon them with a tremendous volley. The rascals were evidently astounded, and they were tremendously punished. They kept up the attack . . . bringing up fresh troops, but finally gave way. . . ."

His entire division, the widower Williams asserted in a letter to a daughter, behaved gallantly. "Not a man left the ranks unless wounded. In the language of a private of the 27th Indiana (one of my old regiments) we had a 'splendid fight,' and he added, 'Old Pap' (that is I) 'was right amongst us.'"

The fight ended about dusk and, Williams concluded, "In the morning there was no enemy in front. . . . There were scores of dead Rebels lying in the woods . . . and I confess a feeling of pity as I saw them. . . . It is with reluctance that I go over these sad fields. Especially so, when I see a 'blue jacket' lying stretched in the attitude that nobody can mistake. . . . These 'boys' have been so long with me that I feel as if a friend has fallen, though I can recognize no face that I can recollect. . . . But I think of some sorrowful soul at home and oh, Minnie, how sadly my heart sinks with the thought."[10]

Union casualties at Resaca totaled some 3,000; Confederate, 2,800.

That the enemy was nowhere to be seen on the 16th was because the Federals had finally succeeded in throwing pontoon bridges across the Oostanaula River at Lay's Ferry, several miles to the southwest of Resaca. This was due to the efforts of the hot-tempered Irishman Thomas Sweeny, whose division McPherson had assigned to the task. Johnston, seeing that his own rail supply line might be cut behind him, withdrew during the night toward the next natural barrier, the Etowah River some thirty-five miles to the south. "Johnston got his army across the [Oostanaula] bridges, set them on fire, and we entered Resaca at daylight," said Sherman. "Our loss up to that time was about six hundred dead and thirty-three hundred and seventy five wounded."

Moving in several widespread columns on Joe Johnston's heels, the Union armies on May 19 narrowly escaped what could have been a devastating ambush at Cassville, just north of the Etowah. There the Rebel commander, who had decided to go on the attack, massed his forces, intending to fall on the easternmost of Sherman's columns, destroy it, and then take on the others. "In the expectation that a part of the Federal army would follow each road," explained Johnston, "it was arranged that Polk's corps should engage the column on the direct road. . . . Hood's, in position for the purpose, falling upon its left flank during the deployment. . . . [But] after going some three miles, General Hood marched back about two, and formed his corps facing to our right and rear. Being asked for an explanation, he replied that an aide-de-camp had told him that the Federal army was approaching on [the Canton] road."

What had caused the normally bellicose Hood to break off the ambush was a vagary of the battlefield. Elements of Edward McCook's Union cavalry, instructed to tear up the railway line, had wandered onto the scene from the east and come up the Canton Road. Despite their relative innocuousness they caused consternation, even though the Confederate infantry could have blown them away. Instead Hood, and to a lesser degree Johnston, believed it was *they* who were being flanked from the east by the main Federal force. That night, after a contentious council of war, Johnston reverted to type; he continued his pattern of withdrawal, crossing the Etowah and taking up a position at mountainous Allatoona Pass. The graycoats had lost a priceless opportunity.[11]

Sherman at this juncture decided to circumvent Allatoona and swing in an arc farther to the west, leaving the railroad route for the first time. His postings in the South during the 1840s had given him firsthand knowledge of the terrain in the area. "The movement contemplated leaving our railroad, and to depend for twenty days on the contents of our wagons," said Sherman, "and as the country was very obscure, mostly in a state of nature . . . our movements were necessary slow." He was riding with George Thomas, who with the largest command was as usual in the center; John Schofield was on the left, James McPherson on the right.

Once past the Etowah, Sherman's columns crossed Pumpkin Vine Creek, its tributary, and headed for Dallas, "a small town on the other . . . side of this creek and . . . the point of concentration of a great many roads that led in every direction. Its possession would be a threat to Marietta or Atlanta, but I could not then venture to attempt either, till I had regained the use of the railroad, at least as far down as its *debouche* from the Allatoona range of mountains. . . . The movement was chiefly designed to compel Johnston to give up Allatoona."

In this Sherman would be eminently successful. Johnston quickly abandoned Allatoona and headed southwest to intercept him, and the two armies met late on May 25 at New Hope Church, a Methodist meetinghouse at a crossroads four miles from Dallas. Hooker's 20th Corps, Thomas's command, was in the van but, said Sherman, "the woods were so dense, and the resistance so spirited, that Hooker could not carry the position, though the battle was noisy, and prolonged far into the night." Bedding down next to a log in the darkness, without cover under a pelting rain, he got little sleep. "The morning revealed a strong line of entrenchments facing us, with a heavy force of infantry and guns. The battle was renewed, and without success."

During the action on the 25th Sergeant Bull of the 123rd New York saw all the fighting he could wish: "As we moved up to the front, our Colonel McDougall was just behind. . . . On foot as it was impossible to ride through the underbrush. . . . After a discharge from [the enemy's] battery I heard a cry. . . . Turning, I saw the colonel stagger and fall. He was carried to the rear mortally wounded by grapeshot. . . . We took a position a little forward from the line we relieved, and fought [prone] to keep below the grapeshot as far as possible." In an hour darkness came. "Our only light was from the flash of the muskets and the greater light of the artillery in our front. . . . The rain came down in torrents. . . . For a time the thunder drowned out the sound of the artillery. . . ."

Bull's close friend, Sergeant James Cummings, now got to his feet, putting the butt of his musket on the ground and thinking the darkness would protect him.

"Jim, why do you stand there and expose yourself!" Bull yelled.

Back came the ringing answer: "I don't think there is any more danger in standing here than lying in the mud! I have had enough of that!"

Seconds later, Bull heard what he called "a metallic sound, as though one had taken a hammer and hit a tree with it. Cummings's gun dropped from his hands and he and the gun struck the ground at the same time. A bullet had found its mark in his forehead, passing through his brain."[12]

For the next few days the fighting in the confusing terrain would be incessant, with the Confederates entrenched on higher ground and neither side giving an inch. At 5:00 P.M. on the 27th Oliver Howard, Thomas's command, led the 4th Corps forward on the Federal left, several miles northwest of New Hope Church, thus beginning the battle of Pickett's Mill. Opposing them was Patrick Cleburne's tough division, which had so thoroughly roughed up Sherman at Tunnel Hill during the action at Chattanooga. In the van for Howard was Thomas Wood's division, and in Wood's front was the brigade of William Hazen, one of the heroes of the assault on Missionary Ridge.

Wood's troops soon would be taking swift and terrible punishment. "As Hazen pressed on," said Howard, "the left of his brigade still seemed to overlap his enemy's right, and everything appeared to indicate that our tedious march was to conduct us to a great success. But, while Hazen and the remainder of Wood's division were gaining ground, [Richard] Johnson's division, which was at Hazen's left, was going on to Pickett's

Mill. . . . Here the leading brigade received quite a severe fire against its left flank and was compelled to face in the new direction, and so stopped the whole division from moving up abreast of Hazen." This change of direction left Wood uncovered. "Wood was now brought between a front and flank fire. . . . What we had supposed was the end of the Confederate entrenched line was only a sharp angle of it. . . . Wood's men were badly repulsed; he had in a few minutes over 800 killed."

During this assault Howard's other divisions, those of John Newton and David Stanley, made strong demonstrations elsewhere along the line, trying to create a diversion. "But the Confederates there, behind their barricades, did not heed," said Howard ruefully. "The whole engagement, an hour long, was terrible. Our men in this assault showed phenomenal courage. . . ." He himself took a shell fragment in his boot, causing intense pain and badly bruising his foot. "For an instant I believed I had lost my leg," said the general, who had already lost an arm in combat, "and was glad, indeed, to find myself mistaken." The sight of the wounded that night at Pickett's Mill all but sickened him. "That opening in the forest, faint fires here and there revealing men wounded, armless, legless, or eyeless; some with heads bound up with cotton strips, some standing and walking nervously around, some sitting with bended forms, and some prone upon the earth—who can picture it?"[13]

The business of war would go on. Late the next day, in a mirror image of Howard's attack on the Confederate right, the enemy left its breastworks and struck the Federal right just outside of Dallas. There it was the turn of Logan's 15th Corps, McPherson's command, to rain shot and shell on the attackers, inflicting heavy losses. "At about 3:45 P.M.," Captain Charles Wills of the 103rd Illinois wrote, "a heavy column of Rebels rose from a brush with a yell the devil ought to copyright, broke for and took three guns of the 1st Iowa Battery which were in front of the works (they never should have been placed there); the 6th Iowa boys, without orders, charged the Rebels, retook the battery and drove them back. [The enemy] came down on our whole line, both ours and the 16th [Corps], and for two hours attempted to drive us out. We repulsed them at every point without serious loss. . . ."

Wills could not contain his exultation. "It was a grand thing. I did not lose a man and only three companies of our regiment lost any. When the musketry was playing the hottest, Logan came dashing up along our line, waved his hat and told the boys to 'give them hell.' You should have heard them cheer him. It is [William] Hardee's Corps fighting us . . . the same

corps our regiment fought at Missionary Ridge. Our line is very thin . . .
but I guess we can save it now."

The fighting along the six-mile Dallas–New Hope Church–Pickett's
Mill front, in which contests the Federals incurred 4,500 casualties and
the Confederates 3,000, marked a milestone of sorts in the conduct of
the war, at least in the Western theater. Never before had both sides—
attackers and defenders—used entrenchments so extensively and habitually,
or to greater effect. Given a few hours to dig in, an enemy was almost impossible to dislodge. (Grant and Lee in the East, of course, were throwing
up breastworks with equal fervor.) Both combatants, Sherman would say,
were "taking advantage of every species of cover . . . fortifying by night
by rifle-trenches, with head-logs, many of which grew to be as formidable as first-class works of defense. Occasionally one party or the other
would make a sally, but usually it sustained a repulse with great loss of
life. . . ."[14]

By early June, recognizing the impasse and in need of supplies, Sherman
moved back eastward to the rail line; Johnston shifted with him, to the vicinity of Marietta. Soon the enemy was taking up a position along three prominent hills—Pine, Brush, and Lost Mountains. "On each of these hills," said
Sherman, "[he] had signal-stations and fresh lines of parapets. Heavy
masses of infantry distinctly could be seen with the naked eye, and it was
manifest that Johnston had chosen his ground well." On the 14th, while
reconnoitering, he noticed a Rebel battery about eight hundred yards distant atop Pine Mountain. Near it, in plain view, stood a group of the enemy, evidently observing us with glasses." The sight irritated Cump, and
he ordered some nearby artillery—commanded by Captain Peter Simonson,
who had stymied Hood the first day at Resaca—to get off several rounds
and shake up the onlookers.

Only later did he learn that one of the cannon blasts had killed Lieutenant General and Episcopal Bishop Leonidas Polk, a close friend of Jefferson Davis. The solid shell passed straight through Polk's left side,
mangling his arms and ripping open his torso. "The event produced deep
sorrow in the army," said Johnston, "in every battle of which he had been
distinguished." Later, while cataloging Polk's personal effects, his comrades found four copies of a recently published religious tract in his pockets. It was "Balm for the Weary and Wounded," by the Reverend John
Quintard, chaplain of the Army of Tennessee. Polk had written personal
inscriptions in three of the tracts, intending to give them to Johnston,

Hood, and Hardee, his fellow army and corps commanders. Now they received them in the aftermath of his death, soaked with his blood.[15]

For the next two weeks the two armies would jab and counterpunch, endure violent rainstorms, and seek tactical advantages. During this period Sherman summed up his frustrations in a letter to Grant: "My first movement against Johnston was really fine, and now I believe I would have disposed of him at one blow if McPherson had crushed Resaca as he might have done. . . . With that single exception McPherson has done very well. Schofield also does as well as I could ask with his small force. Our cavalry is dwindling away. . . . Garrard is over cautious and I think Stoneman is lazy. . . . Each has had fine chances . . . but was easily checked by the appearance of an enemy." Here Sherman voiced his major grievance: "My chief source of trouble is with the Army of the Cumberland which is dreadfully slow. A fresh furrow in a ploughed field will stop the whole column, and all begin to entrench. I have again and again tried to impress on Thomas that we must assail & not defend. . . . It seems the whole Army of the Cumberland is so habituated to be on the defensive that from its commander down to the lowest private I cannot get it out of their heads. . . ."

On June 22 one of Thomas's corps commanders, Joe Hooker, while helping turn back a sortie at Kolb's Farm, particularly incensed Sherman. "We have repulsed two heavy attacks . . . our only apprehension being our extreme right flank," Hooker wrote him, calling for reinforcements. "Three entire corps are in front of us." Since the Rebel army was composed only of three corps, this last claim was an obvious exaggeration. "I had that very day ridden six miles of their lines," said Sherman, "found them everywhere strongly occupied, and therefore Hooker [and his single corps] could not have encountered 'three entire corps.' " He soon learned that Hooker had used only two of his three divisions in the action, and this increased his anger. "I told him that such a thing must not happen again . . . and from that time he began to sulk. . . . He seemed jealous of all the army commanders, because in years, former rank, and experience, he thought he was our superior."[16]

Still the stalemate with the Confederates continued. Johnston had repositioned his force on an even stronger line two miles back of the Pine Mountain salient, anchoring his left on Kennesaw Mountain and extending it southward along high ground. Opposite him was McPherson on the Union left, Thomas in the center, Schofield on the right. "The whole country is one vast fort," Sherman wired Halleck in Washington, "and Johnston must have at least fifty miles of connected trenches, with abatis and finished batteries. . . . As fast as we gain one position, the enemy has another all ready." Recounted Captain Wills: "This is becoming tedious. Johnston has no regard for one's feelings. We are all anxious to see what is on the other side of these mountains. . . ."

Sherman at this juncture decided, uncharacteristically, on a frontal attack. Perhaps his frustrations were affecting his judgment, perhaps he thought that his flanking probes had forced Johnston to extend and thin his lines, perhaps he thought a head-on thrust would have the advantage of surprise.

"This is too *bad*," Thomas said to his adjutant, William D. Whipple, when he learned of the proposed assault.

"Why don't you send a written protest?" asked Whipple.

"I have protested so often," Thomas said of his differences with Cump, "that if I protest again Sherman will think I don't want to fight."

On June 27 at 8:00 A.M. the battle began on the Federal left, with three brigades of Logan's 15th Corps, assailing Kennesaw Mountain's southern end. They were those of Giles Smith, who had been with the army since Fort Donelson; Joseph Lightburn, once an unsuccessful candidate for the West Point appointment won by Thomas "Stonewall" Jackson; and Charles Walcutt, only twenty-six, who had served under Sherman since Shiloh. The customary artillery barrage preceded their start. "Gun spoke to gun, Kennesaw smoked and blazed with fire, a volcano as grand as Etna," said one staff officer grandly. "It seemed as if the whole earth was upheaving . . ." Another officer was more prosaic. "The day was excessively hot, he said "and the men were [already] exhausted when they reached the enemy's works."[17]

Captain Wills of the 103rd Illinois, Walcutt's brigade, remembered the day well: "The Rebels caught sight of us as we commenced . . . and opened a battery on us. It had the effect to accelerate our movements considerably . . . While forming the line Corporal Myers of my company was killed by a bullet within six feet of me, and one of Company K's men wounded. I don't know how many more. The ground to be gone over was covered with a dense undergrowth of oak and vines of all kinds . . . making an almost impenetrable abatis. To keep a line in such a place was out of the question."

The scene was chaotic. "Not a man in our regiment knew where the Rebel works were when we started. . . . The balls were whistling thick around us, but I could see no enemy ahead. I did not even think of them being on our flank, until one of the boys said, 'Look here, Captain, may I shoot?' I looked to the right, and just across a narrow and deep ravine were the Rebels."

Wills shouted "Charge!" and his men followed him down the ravine and up the hill toward the enemy. Before they were even halfway up, however, a hail of bullets forced them to dive down and take cover. "There was little protection from [the Rebel] fire, though, and if they had done their duty, not a man of us would have gotten out alive. . . . It would have been madness to have attempted carrying the works then, for our regiment . . . were so scattered that we only presented the appearance of a very thin skirmish line."[18]

To Wills's right, Giles Smith's and Joseph Lightburn's brigades fared no better. Some of the attackers overran the enemy's rifle pits, but none could close with the main breastworks. All they could do was hug the ground and take what cover they could. They had gained no more than 100 yards.

Two miles south and an hour behind schedule, the main assault was launched from the Union center. Here the brigades of John Newton's division (4th Corps) and Jefferson C. Davis's division (14th Corps) rushed down the Dalton Road and into a similar reception, one that would result in even greater losses. They were led by George Wagner, whose unit had suffered 700 casualties in the charge up Missionary Ridge; Charles Harker, going into battle conspicuously mounted despite having four horses shot from under him in previous engagements; Dan McCook, one of fifteen brothers and cousins comprising the "Fighting McCooks" of Ohio; and John Mitchell, another twenty-six-year-old, who was a lawyer in civilian life.

Wagner and Harker, making their charge in ranks ten deep, ran into a lethal hail of musketry and canister. "General Harker's brigade," said Oliver Howard, "advanced through the undergrowth . . . in the face of the fire, to the foot of the works but . . . were unable to get in, and fell back a short distance. . . ." Harker made a second advance, then fell mortally wounded from his horse. "Some of his men succeeded in reaching the enemy's works, but failed to secure a lodgment." Wagner's brigade likewise failed to make a breakthrough. His men, reported John Newton, "were compelled to stop their advance a short distance from the enemy's works. . . . Apart from the strength of the lines . . . our want of success is in great degree to be attributed to the thickets and undergrowth . . . which effectually broke up the formation of our columns . . . and deprived [us] of the momentum."[19]

McCook and Mitchell suffered even more grievously. "The air seemed filled with bullets," said one soldier, "giving the sensation of moving swiftly against a heavy wind and sleet storm." McCook was killed, and so were most of his officers. Colonel Mitchell and his brigade, taking fearful losses themselves, now dug in with the survivors. The assault in the center gained no more than 150 yards and, again, left the enemy's main lines intact. "The Yankees seemed," said one Reb, ". . . to walk up and take death as coolly as if they were automatic or wooden men. . . . I was sick as a horse, and as wet with blood and sweat as I could be." Recounts Union general Jeff Davis, conceding that the attack was inadvisable: "Owing to exhaustion produced by too rapid execution of the movement . . . the troops failed to leap over and carry the works. . . ."

During the worst of the fighting, Colonel William Martin of Arkansas, wrapping a white handkerchief around a ramrod, mounted the parapet and called a sudden truce. He had noticed that the underbrush had caught fire, threatening the Union wounded lying on the ground with incineration. "Remove your wounded!" he yelled. "We won't fire a gun till you get them away! Be quick!" Then he leaped down and helped the oncoming rescue party with the task. Once it was finished, a Union major pulled a pair of ornate pistols from his holsters and presented then to Martin, just before the bloodletting resumed, in appreciation of a gallant gesture.[20]

The action at Kennesaw Mountain, which was Sherman's worst mistake of the war, ended in the early afternoon, with the Federals in some places within a dozen yards of Johnston's works but pinned down by unrelenting fire. "The troops are much too exhausted to advance," Thomas reported, "but we hold all we have gained." Could the men attack again, Sherman asked? Thomas answered him bluntly: "One or two more such assaults will use up this army." Though Cump broke off the action, and soon thereafter did what he should have done all along, send a flanking column—in this case Schofield's Army of the Ohio—around the Confederate left, he never admitted his error. "Failure as it was," he said, ". . . I yet claim it produced good fruits as it demonstrated to General Johnston that I would assault, and that boldly."

To Ellen Sherman he was more frank. "Daily for the past two months has the work progressed and I see no signs of a remission till one or both and all the armies are destroyed, when I suppose the balance of the people will tear each other up . . . I begin to regard the death & mangling of a couple thousand men as a small affair . . . and it may be well that we become so hardened. Each day is killed or wounded some valuable officers and men, the bullets coming from a concealed foe."[21]

The battle had cost the Federals 3,000 additional casualties; Confederate losses were less than 1,000.

By July 2 Schofield's turning movement had convinced Johnston to leave Kennesaw Mountain and Marietta and fall back to Smyrna Church.

Three days later Federal pressure caused him to withdraw again, to the north bank of the Chattahoochee River, some seven or eight miles from Atlanta. "[This] proved to be one of the strongest pieces of field-fortification I ever saw," said Sherman, in admiration of Johnston's defensive abilities. "We closed up against it, and were promptly met by a heavy and severe fire. Thomas was in the main road in immediate pursuit; next on his right was Schofield; and McPherson on the extreme right. . . ." Sherman as usual had been prodding Thomas to move more aggressively, but now he saw that the Confederate works were all but impervious to frontal assault. Halting his columns, he began searching for ways to turn the enemy's position.

The first such opportunity presented itself at Isham's Ford, ten miles up-river, which Schofield, shifting from right to left while Thomas held the center, discovered to be lightly guarded. On July 8 he silently brought up guns and troops, concealed them in the underbrush, and prepared to launch his pontoons. "At the appointed time," he said, "the artillery was pushed quickly into position and opened fire, a line of battle advanced, rapidly firing, to the river bank, while the bateaux, loaded with men, were . . . pulled across the river. . . . The astonished Rebels . . . delivered a few random discharges of musketry, and fled, leaving their piece of artillery in our position. The crossing was secured without the loss of a man."

Ten miles farther upriver at Roswell, Kenner Garrard's cavalry division the same day, while effecting a bridgehead, came upon a cotton factory turning out cloth for Confederate uniforms. Garrard had recently been upbraided for Sherman for not getting his men into action fast enough.

"Get out of here quick!" Sherman had yelled at him. Garrard, a transferee from the Army of the Potomac who was accustomed to more formal orders, became flustered. "What shall I do?" he asked. "Don't make a damn bit of difference," he was told, "so [long as] you get out of here and go for the Rebs!"

Up at Roswell, however, Garrard needed no such motivating. He promptly commandeered the factory and tore it down, using the planks to rebuild a bridge across the river. By the time it was completed McPherson, moving from the far right to the far left, had his lead corps up and was marching over the river.[22]

Once more Johnston anticipated the tactic, abandoning the Chatta-hoochee the night of July 9, burning the bridges behind him and falling back behind Peachtree Creek, the last natural obstacle between the Federals and Atlanta. Sherman celebrated by removing his clothes, wading into the river and, like his men, washing away the grime of two months' campaigning. "Great chance for the boys to get cleaned up for Atlanta," he said. He had reason to be pleased. Except for the frontal attack at Kennesaw Mountain, he had handled his army well under trying circumstances, keeping casualties to a minimum—at least in comparison to the slaughter in Virginia—and keeping up the men's morale. "I'd follow Uncle Billy to hell," said one soldier, and most others felt the same way. "Thus far our supplies have been ample," Sherman wrote Ellen, "and the country is high, mountainous, with splendid water & considerable forage in the nature of fields of growing wheat, oats & corn, but we sweep across it leaving it bare as a desert. . . . The task of feeding this vast host is a more difficult one than to fight."[23]

For the next ten days the Federals, hampered by the continuing rains and the muddy roads, accomplished little other than crossing the Chattahoochee and reorganizing. During this period, however, Sherman learned that Andrew Jackson Smith, whom he had sent to Mississippi to deal with the troublesome Nathan Bedford Forrest, had on July 14 and 15 put the Confederate cavalryman to rout. Cump was much relieved, knowing that, temporarily at least, the chances of the enemy cutting his supply lines had been considerably lessened. Then came the equally dramatic news that Johnston had been relieved and replaced by John Bell Hood. Jefferson Davis, fed up with Johnston's series of withdrawals—skilled as they were—wanted a general who would fight. "If the Army of Tennessee," said Davis, "was found to be unable to hold positions of great strength like those at Dalton, Resaca, Etowah, and on the Chattahoochee, I could not reasonably hope that it would be more successful on the plains below Atlanta, where it would find neither natural nor artificial advantages of position."

By promoting Hood, whose offensive inclinations were manifest, Davis hoped to instill new life in the army. The lanky, homespun Texan had received a crippling arm wound at Gettysburg and lost a leg at Chickamauga, but he had lost none of his zeal for combat. Back at Kennesaw Mountain, Hood had firmly resisted retreating. "When we leave our present line," he told Johnston, "we will, in my judgment, cross the Chattahoochee River very rapidly."

"What makes you think that?" asked Johnston, stung by the criticism from a general some twenty years younger.

"Because this line of Kennesaw is the strongest we can get. . . . If we surrender this to Sherman he can reconnoiter from its summit the whole country between here and Atlanta, and there is no such line of defense in the distance. . . ."

Hood, of course, had been proven right. Now Sherman would be facing a different type of opponent. Knowing Schofield had been a classmate's of Hood's at West Point, he asked him what kind of man he was. "[I] learned that he was bold even to rashness, and courageous in the extreme," said Sherman. "I inferred that the change of commanders meant 'fight'. . . . This was just want we wanted, viz., to fight in open ground . . . instead of being forced to run up against prepared entrenchments."[24]

By July 19 the three Union armies were approaching Atlanta in two widely separated columns: Thomas was moving on the city from the north toward Peachtree Creek; McPherson and Schofield from the east toward high ground known as Bald Hill. The first clash took place the next day at Peachtree Creek. There Hood had hoped to fall on Thomas with two of his corps (William Hardee's and Alexander Stewart's, the latter replacing Polk) while he was still crossing the stream, leaving his third corps (temporarily under Benjamin Cheatham) to fight a holding action against McPherson. Positioning and communications woes plagued the Rebels, however, with the result that they did not attack until 4:00 P.M., when Thomas's men were already across, though they were only partially deployed for battle. Newton's division of Howard's 4th Corps was on the extreme left of the front; the divisions of William Ward, Geary, and Williams—all of Hooker's 20th Corps—extended to Newton's right; and finally, on the extreme right, was Richard Johnson's division of Palmer's 14th Corps.

The first wave of Hood's under Hardee men struck Newton's weak left flank, trying to cut him off from Peachtree Creek and, in the process, roll up the entire Federal line. "Yelling like furies . . . like wild beasts let loose," said Oliver Howard—a sea of gray-clad troops raced across open ground and threatened to engulf the defenders. Newton's men, who only moments before had been digging entrenchments, threw down their shovels and grabbed their muskets. Hurriedly moving into some semblance of line of battle, they responded to the attack. "Commence firing!" Newton the Virginian ordered, taking aim at his fellow Southeners. "Fire steady and low! Fire steady and low!"

Here the Federal cannon came into play, buying time for Newton while pouring shells and canister into the oncoming ranks. Thomas had a prominent hand in their placement, urging the horses on with the flat of his sword and directing their fire. Caught in the open, the enemy suffered terribly.

Now the Confederates under Stewart moved on to Ward, Geary, and

Williams. Because Geary's line bulged in a salient, they pushed hard to exploit the gaps between his and the commands on either side. Thomas again rushed up artillery to stymie the assault, putting the guns into play with studious detachment in the midst of the turmoil. Those who knew him nonetheless noted his inner anxiety. Thomas had a habit in times of stress, it seems, of running his fingers through his thick whiskers. "When satisfied he smooths them down," said one officer, "when troubled he works them all out of shape. The Rebels were advancing on us and we on them. . . . The general could see neither party, and . . . at that moment he had his whiskers all [mussed]."[25]

Geary did not admit that his salient invited attack. "With less than 3,000 men I had advanced about 800 yds. in front of the main line of our corps," he would say darkly, "and secured a lodgment upon a fine ridge, easy of defense, if fully occupied. I had the assurance that the 1st Divn would advance that portion of it which extended to my right. *This was not done* . . . [the enemy] soon reached the hill on my right and doubled round in my rear, thus enveloping my command. . . ."

This would be the high-water mark of Hood's assault. Soon Thomas's cannon and the Federal musketry were cutting down the Rebels in brutal fashion. "During the afternoon the enemy made five charges on our line, coming at times within 100 feet; yet I did not see a single Johnnie," said Sergeant Bull of the 123rd New York, Williams's division. "The clouds of smoke from the muskets on both sides and from Winegar's Battery . . . [hid] everything but the flash of the enemy's guns that gave us their position. . . . The gun barrels would get so hot we could scarcely hold them, and I saw many guns discharge as the powder from the cartridge was being placed in the barrel.

"One of the boys near me, after biting off the top of the cartridge, had placed it in the barrel and was ramming it down, when the powder exploded and the bullet and ramrod went together. He looked a good deal surprised, and shaking his fist in the direction of the Johnnies yelled, 'Take that, you _____, and see how you like it!' This expressed the state of men on the firing line, no fear for themselves, just rage."

Though the Confederate onslaught eventually would involve elements of Richard Johnson's division and go on until darkness, its force was spent. "The enemy retreated slowly within his trenches," Sherman would say, "leaving his dead and many wounded on the field. Johnson's and Newton's losses were light, for they had partially covered their fronts with light parapet, but Hooker's whole corps fought in open ground, and lost about 1,500 men. . . . We had, however, met successfully a bold sally, had repelled it handsomely, and were also put on our guard. . . ." Hood in-curred perhaps 2,500 killed and wounded; Thomas, overall, some 1,800.[26]

Two days later on the 22nd, Hood would strike once more, this time east of Atlanta at Bald Hill, sending William Hardee's corps on a fifteen-mile night march around McPherson's left, hoping to take him from the rear. Meanwhile he remained within the Atlanta defenses with the rest of his force, demonstrating and holding off Thomas. Thinking the Confeder-ates were evacuating Atlanta, Sherman would be surprised by Hood's flanking movement. Properly carried out, it could have had a devastating effect, but such was not to be. The night march proved confusing and ex-hausting, and the Rebels did not reach their jumping-off point until dawn. Even then, Hardee needed additional time to feed his troops, distribute ammunition, and reconnoiter, with the result the attack was not made un-til noon.

This delay enabled McPherson to make a fortuitous decision. His lines, from right to left, primarily were composed of Schofield's 23rd Corps, Lo-gan's 15th Corps, and Frank Blair's 17th Corps. Seeing at daylight that the enemy was extending his works beyond Blair's front, he sent Grenville Dodge's 16th Corps—the divisions of Thomas Sweeny and John Fuller—to back him up. This order was countermanded by Sherman, who still had no inkling of Hardee's threat and thought McPherson was being too cau-tious. "Instead of sending Dodge to your left," Cump told him, "I wish you would put his whole corps at work destroying the [Georgia] Railroad back to and including Decatur. . . ." Only his subordinate's personal plea averted possible disaster. Though Frank Blair subsequently would insist that "the Lord placed Dodge in the right place on 22 July," James McPherson was His chosen instrument.[27]

Hardee at noon then, when the so-called Battle of Atlanta began, found his assault blocked not just by Blair but also by the newly arrived 16th Corps. "[General Dodge] saw in an instant that something serious was at hand," said Major W. H. Chamberlin of the 81st Ohio. "He gave General Fuller orders to form his division immediately, facing south-eastwardly, and galloped off toward Sweeny's division. He had hardly reached that command when Hardee's lines came tearing wildly through the woods with yells of demons. As if by magic, Sweeny's division sprang into line. . . . General Dodge's quick eye saw the proper disposition to be made . . . and, cutting red tape, he delivered his orders direct to the colo-nels of the regiments."

The ensuing fight, conducted on open ground with no works to protect either side, was one of the fiercest in the war. Lieutenant Colonel W. E.

Strong, McPherson's chief of staff, takes up the story: "The enemy . . . seemed surprised to find our infantry in line of battle prepared for attack, and after facing for a few minutes the destructive fire . . . fell back in disorder to the cover of the woods. Here, however, their lines were quickly reformed, and they again advanced. . . . The scene at the time was grand and impressive. It seemed to us that every mounted officer of the attacking column was riding at the front . . . of the first line of battle."

Though the Confederates showed great heart, said Strong, "the iron and leaden hail that was poured upon them was too much for flesh and blood to stand, and before reaching the center of the open fields the columns were broken and thrown into great confusion. Taking advantage of this, a portion of Fuller's and Sweeny's divisions, with bayonets fixed, charged the enemy and drove them back to the woods."[28]

Following this repulse a concerned McPherson, fearing that Hardee was trying to exploit the gap between Dodge and Blair's left, rode with two aides to reconnoiter the area. There he encountered enemy skirmishers. Several of them cried "Halt!" and an officer gestured with his sword, signaling him to surrender. McPherson raised his hat as if in agreement, then suddenly wheeled his horse and tried to escape. He was shot low in the back, the bullet ripping open his torso, and died within minutes. "Who is this lying here?" the Confederate officer asked. "Sir, it is General McPherson," replied his orderly. "You have killed the best man in the army." Sherman, when he heard the news, was stunned. "McPherson dead! Can it be?" he cried out.

The battle meanwhile went on. Hardee's men were indeed making another sally, intent on driving a wedge into Blair's left, where the divisions of Mortimer Leggett and Giles Smith were dug in. "On came [Pat Cleburne's] Texans; but they were met by a continuous volley of musketry and shrapnel, shell and cannister," said Richard Tuthill of the 1st Michigan artillery. ". . . It seemed as if no man of all the host that was attacking us could escape alive, and yet they persisted. . . . Many of the enemy reached our line; some got across it; many were bayoneted, many killed with clubbed muskets; hand-to-hand conflicts were frequent. . . . The exact sequence of events that afternoon I cannot give, nor do I believe that any man can. . . ."

Sometime in the melee General Manning Force, worried he might be taking fire from the Federals on his right, called for a flag. One of his aides, thinking he wanted a flag of truce, produced a white shirt. Even the hint of surrender, no matter how mistaken, sent the ordinarily mild-mannered Force into a rage. "*Damn* you, sir!" he screamed. "I don't want

a flag of *truce*; I want the American flag!" One was soon found, and
planted atop the breastworks. Subsequently he was struck by a minie ball,
"which entered just at the lower outer corner of the eye, passed through
his head, and came out near the base of the brain. The blood gushed from
his eyes, nose and mouth. . . ." Force would survive, and later be awarded
the Medal of Honor. Soon a counterattack would throw back this second
enemy initiative.[29]

Thus far all the fighting had been on the left. About 4:00 P.M., however,
the Confederates under Cheatham moved forward from Atlanta and assailed the Federal middle, specifically the divisions of Morgan Smith and
William Harrow, Logan's command. Taking advantage of a railroad cut,
the enemy now penetrated Smith's lines, enveloped him and some cannon,
and forced him rearward. "Sweeping over a small force with two guns,"
said Sherman, "they reached our main line, broke through it, and got possession of De Gress' battery of four twenty-pound Parrots, killing every
horse, and turning the guns against us." The success was only temporary.
Massed Union artillery soon drove back the attackers and closed off this
third incursion.

Though the battle went on until sundown, the Federal lines held firm all
along the front, and the enemy's turning effort, intense as it was, came to
naught. Sherman's grip on Atlanta continued to tighten, despite all the offense that Hood could muster. Both at Peachtree Creek and the environs of
Bald Hill the Confederate commander, with better luck and better timing,
might have routed the divided Union force. But he did not, and his casualties on the 22nd were most worrisome. Estimates put them at some 8,000;
Federal losses were about 3,700. To Ellen, Sherman would write: "Hood
is a new man and a fighter and must be watched. . . . It is wonderful with
what faith [the Rebels] adhere to the belief that they will whip us on all
occasions, though we have them now almost penned up in Atlanta."[30]

Straight away came the problem of who would replace McPherson. "General Logan had taken command of the Army of the Tennessee by virtue of
his seniority, and had done well," said Sherman, "but I did not consider
him equal to the command of three corps. Between him and General Blair
there existed a natural rivalry. Both were men of great courage and talent,
but were politicians by nature and experience, and it may be that for this
reason they were mistrusted by regular officers like Generals Schofield,
Thomas and myself." After discussing the matter with Thomas, Sherman
settled on Oliver Howard, a surprising choice in view of the latter's past
record, as McPherson's replacement. Howard's post as head of the 4th Corps

in the Army of the Cumberland went to David Stanley, one of his division commanders. "I remember well my own thoughts and feelings," Sherman explained, a bit defensively, ". . . and feel sure that I was not intentionally partial to any class. I wanted to succeed in taking Atlanta, and wanted commanders who were purely and technically soldiers, men who would obey orders and execute them promptly."

Once he learned of Howard's promotion, a miffed Joe Hooker asked to be relieved as head of the 20th Corps. "His chances were not even considered," said Sherman. "Indeed I had never been satisfied with him since his affair at [Kolb's Farm], and had been more than once disposed to relieve him . . . because of his repeated attempts to interfere with Generals McPherson and Schofield. . . . He had come to us from the East with a high reputation as a 'fighter,' which he had fully justified at Chattanooga and Peach-Tree Creek, at which latter battle I complimented him on the field for special gallantry. . . . Still, I did feel a sense of relief when he left us." Replacing Hooker in late August would be Henry Slocum of New York, who had fought in the East with Hooker and was one of his most vocal critics. In the interim the able and articulate Alpheus Williams would command.[31]

Sherman continued to mourn McPherson, telling Ellen in one letter "I lost my right bower" and in another that his friend's "death was a great loss to me. I depended much on him." In a note he must have agonized over, he later would tell Emily Hoffman, the young Baltimore woman whose wedding to McPherson he was instrumental in postponing, "I yield to none on earth but yourself the right to excel me in lamentations for our dead hero. Better the bride of McPherson dead than the wife of the richest merchant of Baltimore. . . . Why oh! Why should death's darts reach the young and brilliant instead of older men. . . ."

One more change in the army's command during this period deserves mention. It resulted from a disputatious meeting on July 25 between Grenville Dodge and Thomas Sweeny, one of his division heads. Sweeny, a career soldier, for weeks had resented serving under Dodge, whose own civilian background had largely been confined to railroad building. His ire only increased when Dodge on the 22nd, in the first hectic moments of Hardee's attack, issued orders directly to his regimental commanders, bypassing him and ignoring protocol. Now Sweeny broke out in a tirade against "damned political generals," lacing his remarks with expletives like "son of a bitch." Working himself into a rage the one-armed general then swung at Dodge, who swung back, with the result that the two men had to be pulled apart and restrained by aides. Dodge promptly placed

Sweeny under arrest, though the latter complained that he could not even do this according to regulations, and replaced him with John Corse, who had been Sherman's inspector general.[32]

The last battle in July outside of Atlanta area took place on the 28th, when Sherman ordered Howard to swing the Army of the Tennessee north of the city from east to west, and then move south in an attempt to cut the Macon & Western Railroad. Leaving Hardee's corps in place, Hood dispatched the corps of Stephen D. Lee (newly arrived to replace Cheatham) and the corps of Alexander Stewart to meet them. "The Federal commander continued to move by his right flank to our left, his evident intention being to destroy the only line by which we were still able to receive supplies," Hood would say. "The [Atlanta & West Point] Railroad, because of its proximity to the Chattahoochee River, was within easy reach of the enemy whenever he moved far enough to the right. . . . Therefore the holding of Atlanta . . . depended upon our ability to hold the [Macon & Western]."

That morning Sherman rode to the front, located on a ridge overlooking open fields near a meetinghouse called Ezra Church, where he met with Howard. "As the skirmish line warmed up along the front of Blair's corps, as well as along the 15th Corps [Logan's]," he said, "I became convinced that Hood designed to attack this right flank, to prevent, if possible, the extension of our line in that direction." Howard continues the tale: "I ordered that our front be covered as speedily as possible with logs and rails. . . . Owing to the conformation of the ground Logan's two divisions, Harrow's and Morgan Smith's, which were formed on the right of [Charles] Woods' division [filling in for on-leave Peter Osterhaus], made nearly a right angle with the rest of the line. . . . We had no time to locate our batteries. . . ."

By 11:30 A.M. Howard could see the Confederates approaching. "Next," he said, "without any record of orders given, the fire-at-will began. At first only two or three heavy guns took any part, so that the roar came increasing and diminishing from rapid rifle firing. . . . A few frightened men, as always, sprang away and ran toward the rear, some giving way on our extreme right. Logan became greatly animated, and rushed for all stragglers with drawn saber and, assisted by his officers, drove them back to their commands."

Sherman had been right. With piercing Rebel yells the enemy fell on Howard's right, trying to get in his rear. There the first onrush was met by Major Charles Hipp of the 37th Ohio, who, said Howard, "aided by another regiment, had prepared a log house for defense and thrown out his skirmishers right and left. To the left of him . . . Colonel W. S. Jones had two other regiments, with a section of artillery." Twice wounded before being taken from the field, Hipp conducted a gallant defense, even as Howard reinforced his flank. "As soon as possible my aide, Captain [F.W.] Gilbreth, led up two regiments to prolong the right. Two others, led by [William E.] Strong, followed to the same point. . . . The two regiments led by Colonel Strong were armed with breech-loading rifles, the first used in the war. The Confederates at that point had kept bravely on. Some were tramping the rail piles; a few had passed them when those repeating arms began their [deadly] work. . . ."

Under this firepower the enemy fell in droves, their attack suddenly checked. Leaving nothing to chance, Howard at this point had assembled twenty-six cannons, "arranged so they swept all the ground beyond Logan's right flank," making the assault area a killing ground. "Good! That's fine—just what I wanted, just what I wanted!" an exultant Sherman said to a messenger when he heard of the standoff. "Tell Howard to invite them to attack, it will save us trouble, save us trouble; they'll only beat their brains out, beat their brains out."[33]

This is what Stephen Lee and then Stewart did, continuing to assail the Federal lines piecemeal and to no purpose through the bloody afternoon. Their losses would total some 3,000, compared to some 630 in the Army of the Tennessee, almost all in Logan's corps. Oliver Howard, whose tactical sense had been so lacking at Chancellorsville and to a degree at Gettysburg, had redeemed himself, justifying Sherman's confidence. That Hood would be blamed for the extent of the Rebel casualties was, in view of his aggressive reputation, understandable, but in this case he was not at fault. Stephen Lee (no relation to Robert E.), heading the lead corps toward Ezra Church on the 28th, had plunged into battle without waiting for Stewart to come up, and then had persisted in attacks against an implacable foe.

Despite their dreadful losses, the Confederates not only had succeeded in keeping open the Macon & Western, the last supply line into Atlanta, but in letting their adversaries know they were still dangerous foes.

"Say, Johnnie," one blue jacket called out across the lines after darkness had fallen, "How many of you are there left?"

"Oh, about enough for another killing," some Reb chillingly replied.

During the July 26–31 period, too, Hood's cavalry under the hard-hitting Joseph Wheeler dealt a heavy blow to their Union counterparts, hamstringing two divisions of horsemen. They were the units of Stoneman and McCook, who with 6,700 and 3,000 troopers respectively were sent by Sherman to tear up the Macon railroad south of Jonesboro. Stoneman, who had divided his force and gone off on a fruitless expedition to free the Union prisoners at Andersonville, was brought to bay and surrounded. Wheeler captured him and 700 of his men, and scattered the rest.

McCook's fate was almost as inglorious. Though he did minor damage to the railroad, he likewise was encircled. McCook and his troopers cut their way out and fled north of the Chattahoochee, but lost 500 men, two guns, and their pack train in the process.[34]

Sherman took these setbacks in stride. "Our position before Atlanta was healthy, with ample supply of wood, water and provisions," he would say. "The troops had become habituated to the slow and steady progress of the siege; the skirmish lines were held close up to the enemy, were covered by rifle-trenches or logs, and kept up a continuous clatter of musketry. The main lines were held further back, adapted to the shape of the ground, with muskets loaded and stacked for instant use. The field batteries were in select positions...." But he was far from complacent. Smashing triumphs at Gettysburg and Vicksburg the year before had not sapped the will of the Southern commanders—or their rank and file. In the East at this juncture, as we shall subsequently see, Lee was fighting Grant to a draw outside of Petersburg and Richmond, and Jubal Early was giving the Confederacy new life in the Shenandoah. With Lincoln up for reelection in November, opponents of the war were in full cry. Knowing that the taking of Atlanta would silence them, Sherman redoubled his efforts.

Throughout August the Confederates largely stayed within their lines, enduring heavy bombardment and making it obvious that only a major turning movement aimed at the Macon railroad would bring them out. "Hood has not attempted to meet us outside his parapets," Sherman informed Grant on August 10. "In order to possess and destroy his communications, I may have to leave a corps at the railroad bridge [across the Chattahoochee] . . . and cut loose with the balance to make a circle of desolation around Atlanta. I do not propose to assault the works, which are too strong. . . . I have lost a good many regiments. . . ."

Sherman, in sum, would be risking his own supply line in order to cut Hood's. For the next two weeks, he made his preparations. Then on the 24th he wired Halleck: "Heavy fires in Atlanta all day, caused by our artillery. . . . I will commence the movement around Atlanta by the south, tomorrow night, and for some time you will hear little of us." Stealthily the Federals withdrew from their lines, each unit in an intricate series of maneuvers passing behind the other, the 20ᵗʰ Corps heading toward the Chattahoochee, the others west and south and then east. With daylight the Confederates took no action, not knowing whether Sherman was retreating or flanking. Later, when it became apparent he was moving south and east, Hood faced a new dilemma: Where on the Macon Railroad would he strike? Or was the whole tactic a diversion, to draw the Rebels out of Atlanta and let the 20ᵗʰ Corps take the city?[35]

By August 30 all three commands—from left to right, Schofield, Thomas, and Howard—were approaching the Macon Railroad between Rough and Ready and Jonesboro. Meanwhile Hood, finally discerning their route, was dispatching Hardee with elements of Lee's corps to meet them. "The next morning [August 31] all moved straight for the railroad," Sherman said of his command. "Schofield reached it near Rough and Ready, and Thomas at two points between there and Jonesboro. Howard found an entrenched foe [Hardee's corps] covering Jonesboro, and his men began at once to dig their accustomed rifle pits."

At 2:00 P.M. the Rebels sallied forth from their lines, assailing Howard and the Army of the Tennessee with the same reckless courage they had shown at Ezra Church. "Our veterans understood what was coming," said Howard, "and with confidence awaited the charge. The most determined part . . . was sustained by Logan's front, the enemy approaching to within an average distance of fifty to one hundred paces." Here William Hazen on the Union left, repelling a flanking attempt, took the initial impact. "The first charge was tremendous, some of the enemy getting within Hazen's precincts, and the attack was persistently carried on for three-quarters of an hour. But during this time Hazen's parapet kept up a fire against which no man could stand."

On the Union right meanwhile John Corse withstood another enveloping movement. "Corse restrained [his] command from firing," said Howard, "till the Confederates had cleared the corn field near by, so as to be in plain sight. Then they were met by a terrible sheet of fire. . . ." Here dismounted cavalry and artillery under Hugh Kilpatrick, posted on the extreme right at the Flint River, poured bullet and sheet obliquely on the Rebels, further confusing them. "They enemy was thus decoyed by him and his supports beyond the river, for a Confederate division crossed over and pursued him for a short distance. Nothing, even if I had planned it, could have been better done, to keep an entire . . . division away from the main battlefield."[36]

Taking terrible losses all along the front, Hardee's troops soon fell back to their entrenchments. Some 2,200 of them were killed, wounded, and missing. Federal losses were just 172. "The enemy attacked us in three distinct points," Howard reported to Sherman, "and were each time handsomely repulsed."

With the Macon Railroad irredeemably cut, events now moved swiftly. During the night Stephen Lee's corps was called back toward Atlanta, where it would guard Hood's flank as he evacuated the city on September 1 and fled south. Hardee remained at Jonesboro that day, fighting a holding action from behind his works against Howard and both Jefferson C. Davis (14th Corps, replacing John Palmer, who had quarreled earlier with Sherman) and David Stanley (4th Corps) of Thomas's command, then moved south himself. Sherman was furious. Hardee, he felt, should not have been allowed to escape. "Night was approaching, and the country on the farther side of the railroad was densely wooded," he said. "General Stanley had come up on the left of Davis, and was deploying, though there could not have been on his front more than a skirmish line. Had he moved straight on by the flank . . . he would have enclosed the whole ground occupied by Hardee's corps."

Nonetheless there was every reason for rejoicing. When he heard that Hood had left Atlanta even the normally reserved Thomas snapped his fingers, whistled, and did a little jig. "As the news spread to the army," Sherman said, "the shouts that arose from our men, the wild hallooing and glorious laughter, were to us a full recompense for the labor and toils and hardships through which we had passed in the previous three months." By September 2 Atlanta was firmly in Union hands, Henry Slocum's 20th Corps being the first to enter the city.

"Atlanta is ours, and fairly won," Sherman proudly wired Washington. By his triumph he had all but assured the reelection of Lincoln and the success of the Republican Party in the upcoming campaign. "General [George] McClellan"—who had once headed the Federal armies—"had accepted the nomination of the Democratic Party," he explained, "whose platform was that the war was a failure, and that it was better to allow the South to go free to establish a separate government, whose cornerstone would be slavery. Success to our arms at that instant was therefore a political necessity." Grant concurred. "In honor of your great victory," he wrote his friend on September 4, "I have ordered a salute to be fired with *shotted* guns, from every battery bearing upon the enemy. The salute will be fired within an hour. . . ."[37]

What Sherman would wreak on Atlanta subsequently would be the beginning of what he would unleash on the South. This was a man who appreciated many aspects of the Southern way of life—remember his service and beliefs at the Louisiana Military Seminary—and could tolerate slavery. But he could not abide secession, and he would employ the harshest measures to stamp it out.

Within forty-eight hours of entering the city he requested a ten-day truce, informing Hood, whose army was re-forming some thirty miles away, that he was expelling all civilians. Atlanta henceforth, he declared, would be a "pure military garrison or depot, with no civilian population to influence military measures. I had seen Memphis, Vicksburg . . . and New Orleans, all captured from the enemy, and each at once was garrisoned by a full division of troops, if not more, so that success was actually crippling our armies in the field." To General Halleck he explained: "If the people raise a howl about my barbarity and cruelty, I will answer that war is war, and not popularity-seeking. If they want peace, they and their relatives must stop the war."

Hood accepted the truce—"I do not consider that I have any alternative in the matter"—but bitterly objected to the expulsion of civilians, saying that "the unprecedented measure you propose transcends, in studied and ingenious cruelty, all acts ever before brought to my attention in the dark history of this war. In the name of God and humanity, I protest. . . ." Sherman was unmoved. "I say it is a kindness to these families . . . to remove them now, at once, from scenes that women and children should not be exposed to." Moreover, he added, "In the name of common sense, I ask you not to appeal to a just God in such a sacrilegious manner. You who . . . have plunged a nation into war. . . ." In short order some 700 women, 870 children, and untold loads of household goods were traveling south to Rough and Ready, there to be met by Hood's troops and sent to makeshift camps or the homes of family and friends.[38]

So the Atlanta campaign came to a resounding but curiously inconclusive end. Sherman, rightfully fearing that the army's tenuous railroad supply lines—which now extended more than 300 miles from Nashville—might be cut behind him by Rebel cavalry, detached substantial forces to guard them while he rested and pondered his next move. Simultaneously Hood, hovering nearby and searching for a weak spot in the Federal lines, remained a constant threat.

FOUR
* * * *

PETERSBURG, RICHMOND, AND
THE SHENANDOAH

To the Union lines in the Petersburg-Richmond area on June 21 came a surprise visitor: Abraham Lincoln, who made the journey by boat from Washington. Grant and some officers received him with hearty welcomes, with Grant saying, "I hope you are very well, Mr. President."

"Yes, I am in very good health," Lincoln replied, "but I don't feel very comfortable after my trip on the bay. It was very rough. . . . My stomach has not yet entirely recovered from the effects."

One of the officers in the party offered a suggestion. "Try a glass of champagne, Mr. President. That is always a certain cure for seasickness."

"No, my friend," Lincoln answered, perhaps pointedly in view of all the charges he had heard and ignored about Grant's excessive drinking, "I have seen too many fellows seasick ashore from drinking that very stuff."

All present, including Grant, joined in the laughter that followed, and then the group mounted to visit the troops. "Mr. Lincoln wore a very high black silk hat and black trousers and frock-coat," said Horace Porter in his memoirs. "Like most men who had been brought up in the West, he had good command of a horse. . . . On this occasion, by the time he had reached the troops he was completely covered with dust, and the black color of his clothes had changed to Confederate gray. As he had no straps, his trousers gradually worked up above his ankles, and gave him the appearance of a country farmer. . . . However, the troops were so lost in admiration . . . that the humorous aspect did not seem to strike them. The soldiers rapidly passed the word along the line that 'Uncle Abe' had joined them, and cheers broke forth from all the commands."

Grant soon suggested that they ride on "and see the colored troops, who behaved so handsomely in [Baldy] Smith's attack on the works in front of Petersburg last week."

Lincoln eagerly agreed. "I was opposed on nearly every side when I first favored the raising of colored regiments," he said, "but they have proved their efficiency. . . ." He was not prepared, however, for the wild enthusiasm of the black soldiers. "They beheld for the first time the liberator of their race," said Porter. ". . . They cheered, laughed, cried, sang hymns of praise . . . they crowded around him . . . some of them kissed his hands, while others ran off crying in triumph to their comrades that they had touched his clothes. The President rode with bared head; the tears had started to his eyes, and his voice was so broken by emotion that he could scarcely articulate the words of thanks. . . . The scene was affecting in the extreme."

The next day, traveling with Grant and his party up the James, Lincoln was given a water view of the strong positions the Federals had seized and fortified. The president was impressed. "When Grant once gets possession of a place," he told a nearby officer, "he holds on to it as if he had inherited it." Recounted Porter: "His whole conversation . . . showed the deep anxiety he felt and the weight of responsibility which was resting upon him." Several times, when Lincoln and his general spoke of contemplated battles, the president—again according to Porter—repeated what amounted to a mantra: "I cannot pretend to advise, but I do sincerely hope that all may be accomplished with as little bloodshed as possible."[1]

The two-day visit soon ended, with Lincoln steaming back to Washington. Within days Porter wrote his wife a politically incorrect account of the event, far more irreverent than what he subsequently wrote in his memoirs: ". . . There appeared very suddenly before us a long, lank-looking personage, dressed all in black, and looking very much like a boss undertaker. It was the President. He said, after shaking hands with us all, 'I just thought I would jump aboard a boat and come down and see you. I don't expect I can do any good, and in fact I'm afraid I may do harm, but I'll put myself under your orders and if you find me doing anything wrong just send me right away.' General Grant informed him bluntly that he would certainly do that. The old fellow remained with us till the next day, and told stories all the time. He did not ask and said he did not want to know Grant's plans. On the whole he behaved very well."[2]

Now Grant, unable to take the Petersburg by storm but hoping to avoid a drawn-out siege, began extending the Union lines in a semicircle to the south and west of the city. His intent was to cut the two railroads still bringing Petersburg, and ultimately Richmond, food and supplies. These were the Petersburg & Weldon, which extended to the North Carolina coast, and the Southside, still farther west, which ran inland to Lynchburg.

On June 22 the Federals sent David Birney's 2nd Corps (he was filling in for the ailing Hancock) and Horatio Wright's 6th Corps toward the Jerusalem Plank Road, five miles south of the city. Their orders were to cut the nearby Weldon line and be poised to attack the Southside. Meanwhile General James Wilson, the onetime Grant aide turned cavalryman, rode west in a wide arc with 6,000 troopers to damage the roads as far away as Roanoke. Lee promptly sent his own cavalry under William Henry Fitzhugh "Rooney" Lee, his second-eldest son, to handle Wilson, and dispatched Ambrose Powell Hill, with three divisions, to deal with the infantry incursion.

One of the Rebel divisions was commanded by William Mahone, whose dyspepsia confined him to a diet of milk and eggs, but who was emerging as one of the enemy's best combat officers. Mahone knew the area well from his railroad-building days. Leading his men through a ravine that offered concealment, he about 5:00 P.M. pounced on Birney's left flank and thoroughly routed the Federals, who were halted in a forest waiting further orders. "Suddenly and swiftly, with a wild yell which rang out shrill and fierce in the gloomy pines," said one Confederate gunner, "Mahone's men burst upon the flank—a peaking volley, which roared along the whole flank—a stream of wasting fire, under which the adverse left fell as one man—and the bronzed veterans swept forward, shriveling up [Francis] Barlow's division as lighting shrivels the dead leaves of autumn; then cleaving a fiery path diagonally across the enemy's front, spreading dismay and destruction, rolled up [Gershom] Mott's division in turn, and without check, the woods still reverberating with their clamor, stormed and carried [John] Gibbon's entrenchments and seized his guns."

In what Grant later labeled "a stampede," Mahone inflicted 3,000 casualties, captured four guns and eight regimental flags, and suffered minimal losses. The next day, when the Federals gingerly sought to restore their lines, he struck again, creating similar havoc and taking 600 prisoners in the process.[3]

Wilson at first was more successful, tearing up track many miles to the west. But when he sought to withdraw, he found Rooney Lee nipping at his heels and, on the evening of June 28, Wade Hampton, Stuart's successor as head of cavalry, blocking and harassing him at Sappony Church. Galloping the next day toward Reams Station on the Weldon Railroad, which was ten miles south of Petersburg and which he thought the Federals held, he blundered into two of Mahone's brigades. Wilson at this point was all but surrounded. Said the Rebel gunner: "For a brief space the confused combat, ever receding, went on—shouts of triumph mingling with the dismal cries of stricken men, ringing pistol shots, the chattering fire of cavalry carbines, the dull roar of the guns. . . ." Wrote Union cavalryman George Custer of his colleague; "the upstart and imbecile" Wilson had been defeated through "his total ignorance and inexperience of cavalry." Said Grant ambiguously: "I regret the disaster."

So furious was Mahone's attack that Wilson was overwhelmed. He spiked what guns and burned what wagons he could, and proceeded to cut his way out. When this first action at Reams Station ended the Confederates had killed and wounded hundreds, and taken 1,000 prisoners, thirteen cannon, and many wagonloads of small arms and ordnance. To the Federals Mahone seemed to be everywhere. Complained Meade to Grant about the reports he was receiving: "Mahone's division . . . has now been positively placed on our front, on our left and rear, and on its way to Pennsylvania."[4]

Grant had learned the hard way that Lee and the Army of Northern Virginia might be on the defensive—their thirty-five miles of lines ran from Petersburg north through Bermuda Hundred and Drewry's Heights to Richmond—but they were entirely capable of leaving their works and lashing out with lethal force. Through the summer and into the fall he would have to settle for stretching those lines to the breaking point, making constant probes, and being on the alert for savage counterattacks.

Further bad news came in from the Shenandoah, where Grant had replaced the unfortunate Franz Sigel with David Hunter, instructing him to raze and burn the valley. Hunter with 12,000 men initially had done just that, defeating a small force at Piedmont on June 5, six days later burning down the Virginia Military Institute at Lexington, and then closing in on the supply and rail center at Lynchburg. In reply to John Breckinridge's urgent pleas for help, Lee in the aftermath of Cold Harbor audaciously had sent the entire 2nd Corps under Jubal Early to his aid; counting cavalry, his force totaled 14,000 men. Combined with Breckinridge's command, they considerably outnumbered Hunter, who contented himself with heavy skirmishing at Lynchburg on June 18 before side-stepping west to the Kanawha Valley, clearing the entire Shenandoah for Early's advance.

Lee had given Early the option, after disposing of Hunter, of returning to Richmond or moving down the Shenandoah, crossing the Potomac and threatening Washington. Perhaps this maneuver, he thought, would make Grant send reinforcements to the capital, weakening his operations south of the James. Early chose to push down the valley with great vigor, seeing the destruction that Hunter had caused and cursing the Yankees with every breath. "Houses had been burned, and women and children left without shelter," he said. "The country had been stripped of provisions and many families left without a morsel to eat. Furniture and bedding had been cut to pieces, and old men and women and children robbed of all clothing except what they were wearing."

Like the fast-moving Stonewall of old, Early reached Staunton on June 28, Winchester five days later, and then routed the few ill-prepared Federals at Martinsburg, falling on them so quickly they could not burn or remove their stores. By July 6 he had immobilized the blue coats on the heights above Harpers Ferry, crossed the Potomac at Shepherdstown, and was advancing on Frederick, Maryland, where he eventually bullied the town fathers into paying him $200,000 cash in tribute. "The audacity of Early's enterprise was its safety," said an aide. "No one who might have taken steps to oppose or cut him off would believe his force was so small. . . . The newspapers and scouts represented 'Old Jubal' as moving on Washington with a veteran column of 30,000 to 40,000 troops."[5]

On the morning of July 9, however, on the eastern bank of the Monocacy River just below Frederick, Early found his way blocked by some 6,000 to 7,000 men led by Major General Lew Wallace—the selfsame Wallace who had lost his way at Shiloh two years before and, no favorite of Grant and Halleck, had thereafter been kept from field command. Stationed in Baltimore, he commanded the Middle Department (Maryland, Delaware, and the Eastern Shore of Virginia). Getting word of Early's coming, but fearing his bête noire Halleck would replace him, he had put his troops on alert and advanced without orders to the river. "The truth is I did not care to have my absence [from Baltimore] reported in Washington," he said darkly. "That the junction to which I was going was in my department . . . might not save me. There was no telling how small a thing, under the able management of General Halleck, might be turned to my serious disadvantage."

Digging in with Wallace on the Monocacy was James Ricketts's 6th Corps division, the van of the troops rushed up from Petersburg. Their purpose was to delay the Confederate advance as long as possible, until additional troops could reinforce the Washington garrison. By 10:00 A.M. they were already taking casualties from artillery fire. "While I sat [in the field hospital]," Wallace said, ". . . a man was brought in bloody and screaming. In a moment he lay stripped. A jagged fragment of a shell had torn a furrow across his breast. I could see his lungs clipped and exposed. . . . The chief gave the wound one look, and followed it with a silent wave of the hand; whereupon the under-assistants lifted the doomed subject and took him away to die slowly and in agony."[6]

Early's first assault came shortly thereafter against the Union left, where Ricketts was posted, guarding the Washington Pike. "My eyes dropped involuntarily to the fence—it was of rough rails—toward which the charge was coming," Wallace said. "On the hither side of it . . . I saw indistinctly what looked like daubs of blue pigment. . . . I knew them to be soldiers—our soldiers. They lay ever so still. . . . Behind them other figures in uniform were standing by horses. . . . One man was in his saddle—Ricketts."

Wallace made no secret of his nervousness as he watched the enemy ford the river and advance across open fields; he sucked on a lemon to relieve the dryness in his mouth. "I heard no command given. . . . I saw the gleaming of the burnished gun-barrels as they were laid upon the upper rails. The aim taken was with deadliest intent—never more coolly. . . . Then a ragged eruption of fire, and for an instant smoke interfered with the view. . . . With the return of fair vision we looked for the [Confederate] line. It had disappeared. Not a man of it was to be seen. . . ."

The second charge came about 2:00 P.M., also on James Ricketts, and again the oncoming Rebels were fought to a draw. "Looking from our elevation," Wallace said, "it was to see both the opposing lines engaged. . . . A film of smoke whiter than mist hung over them . . . and through it I could see the combatants, two or three hundred yards apart. . . . I remember the thrill I felt, noticing the enemy brought to a standstill. . . . The firing became an unbroken roll. . . . Both sides were working under a repression too intense for cheering, a repression in which there could only be one intent, load, load and fire, meaning kill, the more the better."

By 4:00 P.M. superior numbers were telling. Soon Early's men were breaking down all resistance, forcing Wallace to retreat toward Baltimore. With the sun coming down the Confederates elected not to pursue but to make camp and reorganize for the drive on Washington. Wallace's staunch stand, which cost him almost 2,000 casualties, had bought the

Federals another twenty-four hours to shift the rest of the 6th Corps, as well as the 19th Corps, to the defense of the capital.[7]

Early arrived outside a panicked Washington on July 11, marching on the Seventh Street Pike through Silver Spring, Maryland, and past a redoubt called Fort Stevens, one of the blockhouses circling the city. Following an inspection of the fortifications, which revealed that the garrison had been much reduced to make up for Grant's losses, he resolved to attack the following morning. Then he and his officers toasted the decision by making inroads into the wine cellar of one of Lincoln's political backers, whose home they had temporarily commandeered.

With the dawn, however, Early's hopes were dashed. Federal reinforcements had arrived during the night and plainly were filing into the Washington lines. Now the outnumbered Rebels were on the defensive, falling back under a determined pursuit in force led by Horatio Wright and the 6th Corps. The Union troops mixed with some of the enemy on July 20, routing them and forcing Early to withdraw farther up the Shenandoah. Wright at this point made a mistake. Thinking the Confederates were rejoining Lee in the Petersburg-Richmond area, he led most of his command back to Washington, preparatory to going to Petersburg himself, leaving behind only George Crook with some 9,500 men.

Early's response was to move down the valley with his 14,000 troops and attack Crook forthwith. The two armies met at Kernstown, just south of Winchester, on July 24—a battle that came to be known as 2nd Kernstown (1st Kernstown had occurred in 1862, when Stonewall Jackson suffered his only defeat). Noon found the opposing forces hotly engaged. Then the Rebels, seeing that the brigade of Colonel (and later President) Rutherford B. Hayes on the Union left was unsupported, struck there with a sudden flanking attack. Hayes had little choice but to fall back, and the entire Federal front began to soften and disintegrate. Crook fled through Winchester to the Potomac in disarray, suffering 1,200 casualties in the process, and again Early was left unchallenged in the Shenandoah.

Old Jube celebrated the victory in a vengeful way, moving north to Martinsburg to tear up track on the Baltimore & Ohio, and subsequently, on July 29 sending two brigades of cavalry to Chambersburg, Pennsylvania. The troopers' orders were to burn down the town unless the citizens paid an indemnity of $100,000 in gold or $500,000 in greenbacks. Still incensed by the destruction Hunter had wreaked in the valley, Early meant to use this money to help the victims rebuild their homes. The indemnity was not forthcoming, and Chambersburg was torched. Early never regretted his conduct, which was still another sign that the conflict was engulfing civilians and evolving into total war. "For this act, I alone am responsible," he would say, "for the officers engaged in it were simply executing my orders."[8]

Back at Petersburg, elements of Ambrose Burnside's 9th Corps for some weeks had been digging a 511-foot tunnel under the enemy works east of the city, eventually packing it with 8,000 pounds of gunpowder. "[Burnside] was induced to do this," said Grant, "by Colonel [Henry] Pleasants of the [48th] Pennsylvania Volunteers, whose regiment was mostly composed of miners, and who was himself a practical miner. . . . His position was very favorable for carrying on this work, but not so favorable for the operations to follow its completion. The position of the two lines at that point were only about a hundred yards apart, with a comparatively deep ravine intervening. . . . [It] was unfavorable in this particular: that the enemy's line . . . was re-entering, so that its front was commanded by their own lines both to the right and the left. Then too, the ground was sloping upward back of the Confederates for a considerable distance, and it was presumable that the enemy had . . . a detached work on this highest point."

Grant and Meade meant to blow a huge gap in the works, which were defended there by only four guns and two regiments, and then hurl Burnside's four divisions—some 15,000 men—one by one into the breach. Earlier they had sent Hancock's 2nd Corps and Sheridan's cavalry north of the James at Deep Bottom to make a demonstration against Richmond and induce Lee to shift the majority of his troops there. In this latter regard they had largely been successful.

Where they would be far less prescient, however, was in drawing up the battle plan for the aftermath of the explosion. Burnside had wanted to lead the charge with Edward Ferrero's division of black troops, the only such division in the Army of the Potomac, because they were fresh and had been trained for the assault. But Meade, fearing there would be criticism that the blacks were being used as cannon fodder, overruled him. Burnside's other division heads then picked straws for the assignment, and the honor went to James H. Ledlie's command. Both Ferrero and Ledlie would turn out to be complete weaklings, the latter being described by one of his officers as "a drunkard and an arrant coward."[9]

On July 30 at 4:30 A.M. the infamous Battle of the Crater began. "It was a magnificent spectacle," Major William H. Powell, an aide to Ledlie, said of the blast, "and as the mass of earth went up in the air, carrying with it men, guns, carriages and timbers, and spread out like an immense cloud as it reached its altitude, so close were the Union lines that the mass appeared as if it would descend immediately upon the troops waiting to make the charge." The first wave of Ledlie's troops—without Ledlie, who was off drinking in a bombproof shelter—could not believe their eyes. The hole in front of them was thirty feet deep, sixty feet wide, and one hundred and seventy feet long, filled with upended guns, broken timbers, and blackened men and limbs.

"Forward!" the men in the lead brigade were told, and forward they went, jumping, sliding, and tumbling into the crater, followed by their comrades in the supporting brigade. Nobody ordered them to skirt the hole so they could breach the works before the enemy could recover, nobody told them much of anything. "When they reached the crater," Horace Porter would say, "they found that its sides were so steep that it was almost impossible to climb out after once getting in. Ledlie remained under cover in the rear; the advance was without superior officers, and the troops became confused. . . . The crater was soon filled with our disorganized men, who were mixed with the dead and dying of the enemy, and tumbling aimlessly about, or attempting to scramble up the other side."[10]

Those blue jackets who did reach the crest found themselves under enfilading fire. "Members of these regiments were killed by musket-shots from the rear," continued Major Powell, "fired by the Confederates still occupying the traverses and entrenchments to the right and left of the crater. . . . A partial formation was made . . . but owing to the precipitous walls the men could find no footing except by facing inward, digging their heels into the earth, and throwing their backs against the side. . . ." The Rebel cannon now started up, adding to the carnage. "It was as heavy a fire of cannister as was ever poured upon a single objective point. It was as utterly impracticable to reform a brigade in that crater as it would be to marshal bees into line after upsetting the hive."

Powell raced back to inform Ledlie of the debacle, but that officer was of no help, boozily insisting his division should "move forward immediately." By 6:00 A.M. Meade was beside himself with frustration, wondering why the advance was stalling. "Our chance is now," he told Burnside. "Push your men forward at all hazards, white and black, and don't lose time in making formations, but make for the crest." Two more of Burnside's divisions, commanded by Generals Robert Potter and Orlando Willcox, then advanced on the crater, some of the columns jumping into the hole, some fanning out to either side and coming under fire from right and left. They too made no headway. When these brave and efficient officers, trying to restore some order, complained to Burnside that he was jamming too many troops into a killing zone, the 9th Corps commander, remembering Meade's instructions, would hear none of it. *Push on! Push on! Push on!* he insisted.

By 7:00 A.M. Edward Ferrero's Colored division likewise was committed—without Ferrero, who had decided to join Ledlie for rum drinks in his bomb shelter. Some of these troops managed to skirt the crater, others did not. "The fire upon them was incessant and severe," said Powell, "and many acts of personal heroism were done here by officers and men. Their drill for this object had been unquestionably of great benefit to them, and had they led the attack, fifteen or twenty minutes from the time . . . the debris of the explosion had settled would have found them [victorious] before the enemy could have brought a gun to bear upon them."[11]

Hours passed. Hopelessly pinned down, the Federals could neither advance nor retreat. What was it like in the crater? A Union lieutenant describes the scene: "[The Confederates] around the crest were loading and firing as fast as they could, and the men were dropping thick and fast, most shot through the head. Every men that was shot rolled down the steep sides to the bottom and in places they were piled four or five deep. . . . The cries of the wounded were piteous in the extreme. An enfilading fire was coming in through the traverse down which we had retreated. General [William] Bartlett ordered the Colored troops to build a breastworks across it. . . . Someone called out, 'Put in the dead men,' and acting on this suggestion a large number of dead, white and black, were piled into the trench. This made a partial shelter."

Bartlett later took a shot, tottered and fell, apparently struck by a minie ball. It was a rare semicomic moment in the center of the chaos. He had lost a leg earlier in the war, and replaced it with a cork peg. "My leg is shattered," he gasped. *Lie down, lie down,* his aides advised. "No, no!" snapped Bartlett. "It's only my cork leg that's shattered!"

About 1:00 P.M. the Confederates delivered the coup de grace, suspending their artillery fire and charging down the sides of the crater. Hand-to-hand fighting was the norm, and what happened next was not the Army of Northern Virginia's finest hour. "It was the first time Lee's army had encountered Negroes," said one officer, "and their presence excited in the troops indignant malice such as had characterized no former conflict. . . . Our men, inflamed to relentless vengeance, disregarded the rules of warfare. . . ." Not all the Rebels forgot their better instincts. One officer of the 8th Alabama, standing in the midst of the clubbing and bayoneting, tried to stop the bloodletting.

"Why in hell don't you fellows surrender?" he shouted to a nearby officer.

"Why in hell don't you let us?" came back the reply.

For the Federals, regardless of race, the white flag soon went up and the carnage ended. "It was the saddest affair I have witnessed in this war," Grant told Halleck. "Such opportunity for carrying fortifications I have never seen and do not expect again to have." The Battle of the Crater had cost 5,000 Union casualties, including 1,500 prisoners. Lee's losses were 1,500.[12]

In the aftermath of this affair Burnside, whose conduct can best be described as ineffectual, would go on leave of absence and no longer serve in the field. "Burnside was usually the personification of amiability," said Horace Porter, "and the scene between [him and Meade] was decidedly peppery, and far into confirming one's belief in the wealth and flexibility of the English language as a medium of personal dispute." Burnside would be replaced as head of the 9th Corps by Major General John Parke of Pennsylvania. Ledlie would be drummed out of the army. Ferrero, amazingly enough, would keep his command and five months later be promoted to major general. Most white officers in charge of colored troops were idealistic and motivated; Ferrero's breach of responsibility was the exception.[13]

In August Grant took strong steps to end the Rebel presence in the Shenandoah once and for all, insisting that Phil Sheridan be sent there and given a unified and semi-independent command. It would consist of Wright's 6th Corps, William Emory's 19th Corps, George Crook's command, and most of the cavalry—some 35,000 men. "[The Shenandoah] was the principal storehouse they now had for feeding their armies around Richmond," Grant would say. ". . . It had been the source of a great deal of trouble to us heretofore to guard that outlet to the North, partly because of the incompetency of some of our commanders, but chiefly because of interference from Washington. . . . General Halleck and Secretary Stanton [kept] any force sent there, in pursuit of the invading army, moving right and left so as to keep between the enemy and the capital; and, generally speaking, they pursued this policy until all knowledge of the whereabouts of the enemy was lost. . . . I determined to put a stop to this."

Neither Halleck nor Stanton much liked the idea, either thinking Sheridan too young for such responsibility or simply being unwilling to cede power, but Grant prevailed. "I want Sheridan put in command," he told Halleck, ". . . with instructions to put himself south of the enemy and follow him to the death. Wherever the enemy goes, let our troops go also."

Sheridan might be only thirty-three, but Grant saw in him the spirited leader who had led the charge at Missionary Ridge and brought down Stuart at Yellow Tavern, and he wanted that kind of initiative in the valley. Lincoln, upon hearing of the general-in-chief's directive, backed him to the hilt. "This, I think," he said, "is exactly right as to how our forces should move."[14]

Sheridan moved to the Shenandoah forthwith, where for the rest of the month and into September he organized his forces and began probing actions in search of Early's movements. Grant meanwhile, partially to keep Lee from reinforcing the Rebels in the valley, continued to engage the enemy in the Richmond-Petersburg area.

On August 13 Hancock with the 2nd Corps and David Birney, now leading the 10th Corps, pushed north of the James in another foray against Lee's far left at Chaffin's Bluff. Though the expedition was a failure, it again had the salutary effect of weakening the Confederate right, and on the 18th Grant and Meade made another attempt to move west and cut the Weldon Railroad, dispatching Gouverneur Warren's 5th Corps to do the job. Warren gained a lodgment near Globe Tavern without difficulty and began tearing up the tracks, but then came under heavy counterattack as both sides rushed up reinforcements. Though the fighting continued for several days, the Federals succeeded in holding their position and severing, for a short distance, the Weldon. This was not the catastrophe for the enemy it seemed at first blush, however, for they quickly set up a wagon line to haul supplies to Petersburg from just south of the incursion. Union casualties were substantial: some 4,450. Confederate losses were 1,600.

Hoping to enlarge the railroad break south of Globe Tavern, Grant now sent Hancock to Reams Station with two divisions, and by August 24 he had destroyed three miles of track. Lee soon responded. "Hancock discovered the enemy massing heavily in his front on the 25th," said Horace Porter, "and concentrated his force at the station, and took possession of some earthworks that had been constructed before . . . but which were badly laid out. That afternoon several formidable assaults were made against [Nelson] Miles, who was in charge of [Francis] Barlow's division, but they were handsomely repulsed. At 5 P.M. [Powell] Hill's Corps made a vigorous attack. Owing to the faulty construction of the earthworks, Hancock was exposed to a reverse fire. . . . A portion of Miles' line finally gave way, and three of our batteries were captured. Our troops were now exposed to attack in flank and reverse, the position of Hancock's command had become exceedingly critical. . . ."

Here John Gibbon's division, decimated by casualties in previous battles and composed of numerous untested men, compounded the problem, turning what could have been an orderly withdrawal into a rout. Soon Reams Station was clear of Federals. "Hancock's want of success was due largely to the condition of his troops," said Porter. ". . . There had been heavy losses during the campaign, particularly in officers, and the command was composed largely of recruits and substitutes." This was true— Hancock's 2nd Corps, once the pride of the army, was a shell of its former self—but it should be pointed out that Lee's men, holding themselves together with grit and guts, were hardly in better shape. Federal casualties were 2,700; Confederate, 720.[15]

By mid-September Grant was chafing at the bit for Sheridan to go on the attack and, if truth be told, paranoid that his orders to Little Phil would be subverted by Halleck and Stanton. Lincoln himself had said of the oncoming action: "I repeat to you it will neither be done nor attempted unless you watch it every day, every hour, and force it." So the 15th of the month found the general-in-chief in the Shenandoah, talking to Sheridan face-to-face and, if necessary, doing a bit of prodding. "I knew it was impossible for me to get orders through Washington to Sheridan to make a move, because they would be stopped there and such orders as Halleck's caution (and that of the Secretary of War) would be given instead. . . ."

Grant speedily found, however, that Little Phil needed no encouragement. Sheridan had learned through a Northern sympathizer in Winchester, a young woman named Rebecca Wright, that Early had been stripped of a crack infantry division and an artillery battalion—troops ordered to the Petersburg-Richmond lines. His reconnaissance also revealed that the overconfident Rebel commander had scattered his forces and left them vulnerable to a concentrated blow. ("The events of the last month had satisfied me," Early would say, "that the commander opposed to me was without enterprise.") Now Sheridan, with a three-to-one advantage, intended to hurl his army on the enemy at Winchester and ensnare them in a trap, turning their right flank and preventing a retreat up the valley.[16]

On September 19 at dawn, in a battle the Confederates would call 3rd Winchester and the Union called Opequon Creek, Wright's 6th Corps and Emory's 19th Corps, with Wright in the van, pushed west toward the town through Berryville Canyon. Crook's 8th Corps was in the rear. Here two impediments substantially slowed their progress. The first was the canyon itself: a narrow, two-mile-long passage that quickly became clogged with thousands of trudging infantrymen. The second was the inexplicable behavior of Wright, who insisted on trailing his wagon trains behind him, further delaying the advance. Emory's repeated pleas that he get them off the road, so his own men could get started, were ignored. Not until Sheridan, in a flaming rage, ordered the wagons dumped into roadside ditches was Emory able to proceed. The upshot was that Early was given time—several hours—to consolidate his forces.

Sheridan's original plan was for James Wilson's cavalry to turn the Confederate right, subsequently followed by Crook, with an eye toward cutting any withdrawal up the Valley Pike. Wright and Emory meanwhile would assail the center along the Berryville Pike, while two cavalry divisions under Alfred Torbert would move north along the Martinsburg Pike and envelop the enemy left.

From the start the assault was troubled. The Confederates under Dotson Ramseur, who absorbed the initial blow, simply refused to budge from dawn to 10:00 A.M., first blunting Wilson's sweeping movement and then bringing the lead elements of Wright's incursion up short. This holding action bought Early more valuable time. "Never," said one of Ramseur's aides, "did that division or any other do better work."

Now all the enemy divisions had arrived on the field and solidified their position; Ramseur was on the Rebel far right, Robert Rodes in the center, John Brown Gordon on the left. By 11:30 A.M. the two sides were fully engaged. "The [Union] advance was pressed in the most resolute manner," said General Wesley Merritt, one of Torbert's division heads, "and the resistance by the enemy being equally determined and both sides fighting without cover, the casualties were very great."

Wright and Emory meanwhile were developing a dangerous gap between their divisions. In part this was because the 19th Corps, delayed by Wright's wagons, was still coming up to the front on the 6th Corps' right. Mostly it was because Wright was guiding himself on the Berryville Pike, which angled south, carrying his troops farther away from the 19th Corps with every step. Into this gap Gordon and Rodes launched a furious counterattack, preceding their assault with double-canister rounds delivered from no more than sixty yards. "We raised our well-known 'Rebel Yell,'" said one Alabamian of the sally, "and continued our onward run. . . . We could see they had a much larger force than ours, but we cared not for numbers." Three Confederate divisions were fighting two Federal corps to a stalemate. "They aimed better than our men," said one Union officer. "They covered themselves more carefully. . . . They could move in a swarm, without much care for alignment and touch of elbows. In short, they fought more like redskins, or like hunters, than we."[17]

From his headquarters, Sheridan sized up the situation. "Gordon and

Rodes struck the weak spot where the right of the 6th Corps and the left of the 19th should have been in conjunction," he admitted, "and succeeded in checking my advance." Here he threw into the melee David Russell's division, spearheaded by twenty-five-year-old Brigadier Emory Upton, who had behaved so gallantly at Spotsylvania. Upton formed his men in some woods at an oblique angle to the oncoming Rebels, waited until they closed on his position, then punished them with volley after volley. In the charge jointly led by Russell and Upton that followed, the Federals threw back the enemy whence they had come. There the Confederates in turn regrouped.

"The charge of Russell was most opportune," Sheridan would say, "but it cost many men in killed and wounded. Among the former was the courageous Russell, killed by a piece of shell that passed through his heart. . . . Russell's death oppressed us all with sadness, and me particularly. In the early days of my army life he was my captain and friend, and I was deeply indebted to him . . . for sound advice and good example. . . ." Just about the same time, while conferring with Gordon, the martial-looking Rodes likewise was killed by a shell fragment. He had served from Seven Pines through Antietam, led Jackson's flank attack at Chancellorsville, and been a bulwark of strength from the Wilderness to Spotsylvania. Now he was no more. "Rodes fell, mortally wounded, near my horse's feet," said his friend Gordon. ". . . To ride away without expressing my deep grief was sorely trying to my feelings, but I had to go. His fall had left both divisions in my immediate control."[18]

By 1:30 P.M. a lull fell on the field and both sides rested. "As my lines were being rearranged," said Sheridan, "it was suggested to me to put Crook into the battle, but so strongly had I set my heart on using him to take possession of the Valley Pike and cut off the enemy that I resisted this advice, hoping that the necessity for putting him in would be obviated by the attack . . . that Torbert's cavalry was to make. . . . No news of Torbert's progress came, however, so yielding at last I directed Crook to take a post on the right of the 19th Corps, and when the action was renewed to push his command forward as a turning column."

Crook with 8,000 fresh troops struck about 4:00 P.M., inexorably driving back Gordon's center and left. Early would commit the last of his reserves at this juncture—the small command of John Breckinridge—but they would be of little help. Sheridan's final crushing blow came when thousands of Torbert's cavalry galloped down the Martinsburg Pike to fall on the enemy left with devastating effect. "The ground which Breckinridge was holding was open," Sheridan said, "and offered an opportunity such as seldom had been presented during the war for a mounted attack, and Torbert was not slow to take advantage of it." Those who saw or made the cavalry charge never forgot it. "Like a thunder-clap out of a clear sky," said a Vermonter, describing the scene. "With a savage yell, we swept down on the trembling wretches like a besom of destruction," added a New York trooper. "The enemy's line broke in a thousand fragments under the shock," summed up General Merritt.

Though Early and his officers made frantic efforts to restore discipline, the fighting was over that day for the Confederates. They streamed through Winchester in broken ranks, even as Gordon's wife, Fanny, shook her fist at them in frustration, calling them cowards and challenging them to make a stand. Gordon barely got her and their six-year-old son into a carriage in time to get them out of harm's way. Then he and some others formed a makeshift line south of the town, intent on slowing down the Union onslaught and protecting their wagons and artillery. But Sheridan and his troops, much fatigued, declined to make a serious pursuit. The Federals suffered some 5,000 casualties during the battle; the Confederates, 4,000.[19]

Early would fall back some fifteen miles during the night to Strasburg and dig in on Fisher's Hill, a high ridge fronted by a fast-running creek. It was an impressive defensive position, no more than three and a half miles long, extending from the Massanutten Mountains on the east to Little North Mountain on the west. When Sheridan subsequently reconnoitered the ridge, he recognized its strength and decided merely to demonstrate in its front, while sending a flanking column around the Confederate left. "The execution of this plan would require perfect secrecy, however, as the enemy from his signal station . . . could plainly see every movement of our troops in daylight," he said. "To escape such observation, I marched Crook during the night of the 20th into some heavy timber . . . where he lay concealed until the 21st."

The next day, while Wright and Emory made sporadic but vigorous feints against Early's center and right, Crook moved unobserved through more dense woods to Little North Mountain. The Rebel commander seemingly gave no thought to Crook's whereabouts, or the possibility that his left might be turned. Indeed, he had posted his weakest troops there, some badly armed dismounted cavalry. "When [James] Ricketts [of Wright's Corps] moved out," said Sheridan, ". . . the enemy, surmising from information secured by his signal-station that my attack was to be made from Ricketts' front, prepared for it there."

Crook's troops surged out of the woods late in the afternoon, the setting sun at their back, astounding the Confederates. "The men rushed on, no line, no order, yelling like madmen," said Colonel Rutherford B. Hayes. "Crook's men quickly crossed the broken stretch in rear of the enemy's left," explained Sheridan, "producing confusion and consternation at every step. . . . About a mile from the mountain's base, Crook . . . was joined by Ricketts, who in proper time had begun to swing his division into the action, and the two commands moved along in rear of the works so rapidly that, with but slight resistance, the Confederates abandoned the guns massed near the center. . . . In a few minutes the enemy was thoroughly routed. . . . The stampede was complete, the enemy leaving the field without semblance of organization."[20]

Early would not rally his army for several days, until its headlong retreat stopped past Staunton. He had lost some 1,200 men, but most of these were missing and would soon return to service. With this second triumph in four days, Sheridan had every reason to think the Rebels would no longer be a factor in the Shenandoah. Through October he applied himself to burning and pillaging the valley, inflicting pain and suffering on a scale deeper and more widespread than ever before. Early, for the most part, could only watch helplessly.

Up and down the Petersburg-Richmond lines, the news of Sheridan's stirring victories provided the Armies of the Potomac and the James with much needed encouragement. The failure to take Petersburg in the early going, and then the Battle of the Crater and the endless skirmishing, had hung like dark clouds over the men's spirits. What was needed at this juncture, Grant decided, was for the newly energized troops along the James to go on the offensive themselves. Besides, the movement might give Lee second thoughts about sending reinforcements to the Shenandoah. "I have never seen the time," said Colonel Charles Wainwright, chief of artillery for Warren's 5th Corps, "when the army thought the war was so near its close. . . . I think they will behave well should anything be attempted."

Grant's primary if unlikely instrument in this regard was the political general Benjamin Butler, whose presidential support had plummeted, just as Lincoln's had soared, following Sherman's capture of Atlanta. Butler had failed miserably, of course, in allowing his Army of the James to become bottled up at Bermuda Hundred. But he had played an important role in sending Baldy Smith south across the Appomattox on pontoon bridges in the first assault on Petersburg, and now he suggested using them again, to push two columns—some 20,000 men—north across the James at Deep Bottom to threaten Richmond. Edward Ord's 18th Corps would comprise one column (Grant had relieved the discontented Smith); David Birney's 10th Corps the other (Quincy Gillmore also had been sent packing).

In truth, Butler's plan was an excellent one—no one doubted his abilities, only his military instincts—and Grant speedily approved it. On the night of September 28, seeking surprise, the Federals crossed the James and early the next morning advanced in a swirling fog. Ord's column, on the left, was to proceed straight toward Forts Harrison and Gilmer, two redoubts in the capital's outer defenses; Birney's initial thrust, two miles to the right, was to be against New Market Heights; then he too was to move against Gilmer. "If they succeeded in breaking through [the enemy's] lines, they were to make a dash for Richmond," said Horace Porter. "While the general did not expect to capture the city by this movement . . . there would be a bare chance, after having once broken through, of creating a panic . . . and getting [to] its inner works."

Birney's corps was led by Brigadier Charles Paine's black division. Opposing them on the heights was John Gregg's much-depleted Texas Brigade, together with some dismounted cavalry. The veteran Texans fired volley after volley at the oncoming blacks, but still they came on, suffering some 850 casualties. "Their charge in the face of the obstacles interposing was one of the grand features of the day's operation," wrote a reporter for the *New York Herald*. "They never halted or faltered, though their ranks were sadly thinned. . . ." By 8:00 A.M., the defenders withdrew to reinforce Fort Gilmer, and the blacks proudly took the summit. Fourteen of them received the Medal of Honor for their heroism. One such man was Corporal James Mills of the 36th U.S. Colored Volunteers. Read the citation: "Having had his arm mutilated, making immediate amputation necessary, he loaded and discharged his piece with one hand and urged his men forward. . . ."

Ord's troops at first did just as well. They drove in the enemy skirmishers, advanced across 1,400 yards of open ground and took Fort Harrison from its outmanned defenders. In this regard, though they did not know it, they were aided immeasurably by the fact that the fort's cannon were few and the gunners ill-trained. While the enemy was falling back, Ord fanned out his men down the captured works. On the left he made some progress, almost reaching Chaffin's Bluff on the river; on the right, moving toward Fort Gilmer, he did not. About 10:00 A.M., after he went down with a bad leg wound, it was apparent his men would advance no farther.

Birney at this point likewise began to have problems. Taking too long to oust small outposts of infantry and artillery, he did not reach Gilmer until noon. There he paused to make a lengthy reconnaissance, permitting Rebel reinforcements to file into the lines. When he did send a division forward, against cannon positioned to sweep the long approach over three ravines, he made the attack even more problematical by stringing out his regiments and surrendering impact. "Death fairly reveled in that third ravine," said a New York sergeant. "Shells hissed and exploded about our ears incessantly, and crushed heads and mangled bodies thickly strewed our pathway."[21]

By now Ord's and Birney's commands had established contact with each other. New attacks against Fort Gilmer, however, continued to be made in piecemeal fashion, resulting in bloody repulses. "The assault was made precisely at 2 P.M.," said the *Herald* of one such sally, "the men giving a cheer and starting forward on the run. They were met with a most murderous fire of grape and cannister, and unceasing volleys of musketry that worked terrible havoc in their ranks." That night the Federals regrouped and concentrated on building up the works at Fort Harrison, content with holding what they had gained in the outer defenses and bracing themselves for Lee's inevitable counterattack.

It came in the early afternoon of the 30th when the Southern commander, taking the field himself, pushed forward eight regiments. Wrote a *New York Times* correspondent: "Formed in three long lines [the Confederates] . . . were met by a fire which sent them staggering back, leaving piles of dead and dying on the field. Rallying again, they renewed the onset, and with such determination that their advance came within two hundred yards of the work. Our men again succeeded in repulsing them, and the slaughter was terrible." Fort Harrison never would be retaken, forcing the enemy to redraw and constrict their lines. Lee had personally urged his troops on, much as he had in the Wilderness and at the Mule Shoe, and he seemed stunned by the battle's outcome, with one of his officers saying that in the aftermath "he had a face on him as long as a gun barrel." Meanwhile the blue jackets celebrated by ascending Harrison's parapets, waving their flags and singing "The Battle Cry of Freedom." Though sporadic fighting would continue north of the James for the next two days, additional Union efforts there would be ineffectual.

South of the Appomattox and of Petersburg during this period, Grant continued to move west against the railroads, using his superior numbers like a boxer's one-two punch. On September 30 Parke and Warren, 9th Corps and 5th Corps respectively, advanced from the Federal position at Globe Tavern toward the Boydton Plank Road, hoping to strike the Southside Railroad. While Ambrose Powell Hill frustrated the assault, it did gain considerable ground, forcing the Confederates to extend their works still farther to Hatcher's Run and necessarily weaken them. The Richmond *Examiner* dismissed Grant's tactics out of hand, as if they were ungentlemanly: "It is, in fact, his single trick—his sole maneuver—a demonstration on the north side to make Lee weaken himself on the Petersburg line, and then a sudden dash to the left flank—always to the left."[22] Union losses on both fronts September 28–October 2 would total some 6,300; Confederate, perhaps 3,000.

Before cold weather brought the fighting on the Petersburg-Richmond front to a close, Grant and Meade initiated one more engagement of note. It took place on October 27, and again it involved attacks both north and south of the James that were designed to take advantage of Lee's widely separated flanks.

North of the river Butler that day set in motion an assault against the Rebels in front of Richmond. Both the 10th and the 18th Corps participated, the former led by Alfred Terry, replacing David Birney, who had died of malaria; the latter by Godfrey Weitzel, filling in for the wounded Ord. But Weitzel, uncertain of the terrain, took too much time to reconnoiter, giving James Longstreet, recovered from the wound he suffered in the Wilderness, ample time to bring up reinforcements.

When Weitzel did engage, about 4:00 P.M., he moved up the Williamsburg Road across open ground and into a blizzard of shot and shell. The Federal force, said Rebel general Charles Field, "got to about 300 yards of my line, when his troops, unable to stand the fire, threw themselves on their faces in a little depression of ground. A portion of [John] Bratton's South Carolina brigade . . . went out in front of my division and captured four hundred or five hundred of them." Soon Weitzel's men were in full retreat. "It was plain enough that we were outnumbered," said a New York soldier, "and finally a confident enemy came out of his works on our flanks and . . . promised our destruction or capture. Word was given for every man to act for himself."

On Weitzel's left Alfred Terry, pushing forward between the Charles City and New Market Roads, fared just as poorly. "It was a terrible place to charge, through thick woods," said Hermon Clark of the 117th New York. "We charged again, but it was useless, and against the judgment of our officers. But old Beast Butler ordered it, and it must be done." Added a soldier in the 203rd Pennsylvania: "The grape and cannister flew over our heads till it made everything rattle. . . . I tell you it took the tree tops off like nothing." Terry too fell back, ending the action north of the James.[23]

On the southside the main Federal thrust, some 43,000 men, moved toward the Boydton Road and Hatcher's Run, where the enemy's works were thought vulnerable to a determined onslaught. John Parke's 9ᵗʰ Corps advanced directly west from the Weldon Railroad; Warren's 5ᵗʰ Corps was on his left; Hancock's 2ⁿᵈ Corps in turn was on Warren's left.

Parke and Warren soon found, however, that the Boydton Road works were far more formidable than they had thought, and about noon were brought up short. "After a conference with Warren," said Horace Porter, "Grant and Meade rode over to Hancock's front, and found that the enemy was there disputing the passage of Hatcher's Run at Burgess' Mill. His troops were strongly posted, with a battery in position in front of the head of Hancock's corps, and another about eight hundred yards to our left." Grant and his retinue soon attracted heavy fire. "As this group of mounted officers formed a conspicuous target," said Porter, "the enemy was not slow to open upon it with his guns. . . . One of our orderlies was killed, and two were wounded."

Grant persisted in his reconnaissance, but what he observed made him call off the attack. "The advance of the troops was impeded by the dense underbrush, the crookedness of the Run, the damming of its waters, the slashed trees, and other obstacles of every conceivable description," summed up Porter. "It was seen by afternoon that an assault under the circumstances would not promise favorable results, and it was abandoned."

The Confederates, however, had other plans. Seeing that Hancock was on the left of the Union lines and dreadfully exposed, they emerged from their works at 4:30 P.M., spearheaded by the ubiquitous Billy Mahone, and fell on his right, trying to cut him off from Warren. Though Hancock's troops at first were thrown into confusion, their superior numbers quickly asserted themselves. "It was like four men getting between four," lamented one Rebel. "After making a brilliant dash . . . General Mahone became surrounded, but cut his way out in a very handsome manner." Nightfall found both sides back in their original lines.²⁴

So the Petersburg-Richmond siege would continue through the winter, with Grant ever tightening the noose, but not getting to the jugular. How long the cities would hold out, or what Lee would do next, no one knew. That his tattered troops were still lethal fighters, with no quit in their bellies, was the only certainty.

In the Shenandoah Valley during October, a rejuvenated Jubal Early was, figuratively speaking, rising from the dead. Not only had his corps regrouped—those tough divisions of Gordon, Ramseur, and the fallen Rodes (now under John Pegram)—but Lee, confident he could handle

Grant's forays against the works north and south of the James, had reinforced Old Jube with Joseph Kershaw's splendid division from Longstreet's corps, plus additional cavalry and artillery. "I have weakened myself very much to strengthen you," Lee had counseled him. "It was done with the expectation of enabling you to gain such success that you could return the troops if not rejoin me yourself. . . . I rely upon your judgment and ability. . . ."

Thus encouraged, Early by October 12—though he was still badly outnumbered—was on Fisher's Hill, observing and fretting as Sheridan moved down the valley, burning and razing as he went. Believing Early to be more an irritant than a threat, the Federal commander in ensuing days, before leaving for consultations in Washington with Stanton and Halleck, took up a position on high ground north of Cedar Creek, just below Middletown. Alfred Torbert's cavalry—three divisions under Wesley Merritt, William Powell, and George Custer—protected the right; Emory's 19th Corps and Crook's 18th Corps were in the center, with the latter extending his lines to the Massanutten Mountains, at whose base ran the North Fork of the Shenandoah; and Wright's 6th Corps was somewhat to the rear.

Climbing to the top of the Massanuttens on October 17, John Brown Gordon inspected the Federal lines through field glasses and found that the enemy left, anchored on the Massanuttens, could be turned. "A dim and narrow pathway was found [along the mountainside]," said Gordon, "along which but one man could pass at a time; but by beginning the movement at nightfall the entire corps could be passed before daylight." Early welcomed the discovery, and quickly drew up a plan of attack. Gordon would take his own division, as well as those of Ramseur and Pegram, along the Massanutten footpath, and be ready to cross the river and fall on the Union left at daybreak on the 19th. Simultaneously Kershaw and other units would attack the center, advancing down the Valley Turnpike, while the bulk of Early's cavalry would demonstrate in force against the right.[25]

The night before the assault, the Federals were unsuspecting. "As evening closed above the valley," recounted A. Bayard Nettleton of the 2nd Ohio Cavalry, one of Custer's troopers, "the soft pleadings of some homesick soldier's flute floated out through the quiet camp, while around a blazing fire an impromptu glee club of Ohio boys lightened the hour and their own hearts by singing the songs of home. An unusually large letter mail arrived that evening and was distributed to the men. . . . The letters were all read and their contents discussed, the flute had ceased its complaining. . . . Taps had sounded, lights were out in the tents, cook-fires flickered low. . . . Midnight came, and with it no sound but the tramp of the relief guard. . . . One o'clock and all was tranquil as a peace convention; two, three o'clock, and yet the soldiers slept. . . ."

Fording the cold waters of the river in dense fog at 5:00 A.M., Gordon's flanking columns fell on Crook's 8th Corps with primeval fury. Simultaneously Joe Kershaw's division, together with Gabriel Wharton's, crossed the high banks of Cedar Creek and assailed Emory's 19th Corps. " 'Boots and saddles!' was blown from division, brigade, and regimental headquarters," said Nettleton of the ensuing confusion. "The darkness rang with the blare of bugles and the shouts of officers hurrying the troopers from their dreams to their dreams. . . . The rattle of musketry in front of the infantry increased to heavy volleys, the volleys thickened into a continuous roar, and now, as day began to dawn, the deep bass of the artillery came in. . . ."

Ordered into the fray, Nettleton and the rest of Custer's men galloped onto a frenetic scene. "The infantry had been surprised in their beds by Early's reinforced army; our best artillery was already in the hands of the Confederates and turned against us; thousands of our men had been killed, wounded or captured. . . ." Gordon's flanking movement had thrown the Federals into panic. "Two entire corps, the 8th and the 19th, broke and fled," the Rebel general enthused, "leaving the ground covered with arms, accoutrements, knapsacks and the dead bodies of their comrades. Across the open fields they swarmed . . . heedless of all things save getting to the rear."[26]

Captain S. E. Howard of the 8th Vermont tells what it was like in the 19th Corps campsite. "I was wakened at the first sounds of day by a terrific clap of thunder," he said, "and sprang into a sitting position and listened. The thunder was the tremendous volley that the enemy was pouring into Crook's camp. . . . I listened for the yell of our men but, alas, it never came; instead the Yi! Yi! Yi! of the Confederates, and—horror of horrors—it seemed to me as if our whole left were enveloped, enfolded by this cry. It was like the howls of the wolves around a wagon train. . . ." Howard's regiment and others were rushed toward the left, with orders to reinforce the 8th Corps. "Here we met the fellows from Crook's camp. . . . Many of them were only partly dressed, some wearing only underclothing, but they generally carried their muskets. . . . They passed around us, through our ranks, and almost over us, insistent, determined. They heeded none of our cries to 'Turn back!' 'Make a stand!' "

Soon Captain Howard, in near-blinding fog and gunsmoke, was in the midst of a fearsome struggle with Gordon's columns. "The regiment flung itself into the boiling cauldron where the fight for the colors was seething," he said. ". . . Again and again the enemy [threw] many times our number against us, only to be forced back. . . . Men fought hand to hand; skulls were crushed with clubbed muskets. Men actually clenched and rolled upon the ground in the desperate frenzy of the contest. . . . Three color bearers were killed." The Rebel onslaught, however, prevailed. "The time came when valor and devotion proved vain. In a moment, without warning and as if by common consent . . . [it was] every man for himself. . . . I had received two severe wounds, and though not wholly disabled, was unable to make anything like good time. . . ."

In the Federal center, meanwhile, Kershaw's troops were demolishing other elements of the 19th Corps, and by 7:30 A.M. both Crook's and Emory's men were in disarray. "Those behind the works would raise their bare heads above the trenches, fire away, regardless of aim or direction, then fall to the bottom to reload," said Captain Augustus Dickert, a South Carolinian of Kershaw's command. "This did not continue long, for all down from our extreme right the line gave way, and was pushed back to the rear and towards our left, our troops mounting their works and following them as they fled in wild disorder. . . . Some of the Confederates were screaming in derision, 'Another Union victory!' "

Once they entered the enemy lines, the Rebels for a time became almost as disorganized as their foes. "The smoking breakfast, just ready for the table, stood temptingly inviting," said Dickert, "while the open tents displayed a scene almost enchanting . . . in the way of costly blankets, overcoats, dress uniforms, hats, caps, boots, and shoes thrown in disorder. . . . All this wealth of provisions and clothing looked to the half-fed, half-clothed Confederates like the wealth of the Indies. . . . But their wants were few . . . at least that of which they could carry." The long-deprived enemy grabbed bacon, an overcoat, a blanket—and then resumed the chase.[27]

Howard of the 8th Vermont at this point despaired. "I had seen the collapse of the 8th Corps. I had seen our whole left swept away . . . our whole army forced out of its works, forced to change its line from front to left, forced far back from its proper position—sullenly on the defensive, dangerous, but clearly out-matched. . . . My heart beat with throbs of grief as I dragged myself painfully to the rear. . . . Unreasonably I attributed the whole disaster to General Sheridan's absence. Had he been there it could never have happened, and thereby I did injustice to the gallant Wright in command. . . ."

Horatio Wright indeed would prove his worth. Positioned to the right and rear of the other commands, the 6th Corps had escaped the initial impact of the Rebel attacks. Wright now ordered these troops into line, taking a determined stand along Meadow Brook, even as the routed 8th and 19th Corps survivors continued to stream to the rear. For the next two hours, they would fight a delaying action. Key to their efforts would be the division of George Getty, on the far left near the Valley Pike. When the other 6th Corps divisions were forced back past Middletown, he hung on tenaciously. "In this emergency—without supports, without orders—in the open indefensible plain where a few moments would bring the Confederates charging upon his defenseless flanks," said Major Hazard Stevens, the 6th Corps assistant adjutant general, ". . . Getty, with prompt and cool decision, moved his troops . . . back across the brook to the foot of the ridge. Then, moving up its slope, he posted them in a single line extending left and right as far as possible."

There Getty's men dug in and fought what arguably was the turning point of the battle. "The gray lines of [John] Pegram's division soon came advancing swiftly up the steep slope," said Major Stevens, "and struck the troops awaiting them on the crest. The heaviest of the attack fell on [James] Warner's brigade. Getty's veterans held their fire until the enemy was close upon them, then delivered it in their very faces, and tumbled the shattered ranks down the hill."

Cannon fire now began to burst upon the ridge, making the Federals scramble for cover. When the Rebels again attacked, said Stevens, "[Getty's] troops sprang to their feet . . . moved forward a few paces to and over the crest, and met the enemy at thirty yards as he struggled, well-winded and tired, up the ascent, with so well-aimed a volley, so thundering a cheer, and so sudden and spontaneous a rush forward that he fell back in great confusion. . . ." Still a third time, following another barrage, the enemy advanced. "Again the troops rose to their feet, dressed their ranks, and gripped their muskets, with bayonets fixed; and again, at the critical moment, just as the charging line, straining up the hill, gained the summit, the steady veterans countered upon it with a terrific threefold blow—a sudden deadly volley, a fierce charge, and a mighty shout—and dashed it to pieces down the slope."[28]

Gordon viewed the resistance of the 6th Corps both with frustration and admiration. "It stood like a granite breakwater, built to beat back the oncoming flood," he said, "but it was also doomed. . . . It was at that hour largely outnumbered, and I had directed every Confederate command . . . to assail it in front and both flanks." Simultaneously he arranged his artillery to unload enfilading fire.

Then, about 10:00 A.M., Jubal Early arrived at the front. "Well, Gordon, this is glory enough for one day," he said. "This is [October] 19th," he added, thinking of the flight from Winchester. "Precisely one month ago we were going in the opposite direction."

"It is very well so far, General, but we have one more blow to strike. . . ." Gordon replied, pointing to the 6th Corps' position.

"No use in that," said Early, indicating he had no wish to assail the Federals further, "they will all go directly."

"That is the 6th Corps, General," Gordon persisted, albeit to no avail. "It will not go unless we drive it from the field."

If this account is to be believed, Early was making a terrible blunder. For the next six hours, thinking the battle had been won, he made no concerted effort to follow up his advantage. He would move forward, a mile or two north of Middletown, but only incrementally. Later, trying to explain his hesitance, he would claim in his report to Lee that his troops had been too disorganized to advance, largely because of looting. "So many of our men had stopped in the camp to plunder," he said, "the country was so open and the enemy's cavalry so strong, that I did not seem it prudent to press further. . . ." That there was looting cannot be denied, but it was not so unchecked as to cause a six-hour delay. In the same report, Early seemed to acknowledge this: "It is mortifying to me," he told Lee, ". . . to make these explanations of my reverses."

Of the decisions that the normally aggressive Early might have made at that juncture—to press forward with abandon, to withdraw to a more defensible position, or to stay in open ground with his flanks unprotected and his back to Cedar Creek—he fatefully chose the third and last.[29]

That morning at 9:00 A.M. Sheridan, unknowing of these events, was just leaving Winchester, where he had spent the night en route from Washington with his escort. "I noticed that there were many women at the windows and doors of the houses," he said, "who kept shaking their skirts at us and who were otherwise insolent in their demeanor. . . . On reaching the edge of town I halted a moment, and there heard quite distinctly the sound of artillery. . . . Concluding from this that a battle was in progress, I now felt confident that the women along the street had received intelligence . . . and were in raptures over some good news. . . ."

One half mile farther on, the Federal commander rode to the crest of a rise and saw the detritus of the 8th and, to a lesser extent, the 19th Corps. "There burst upon our view the appalling spectacle of a panic-stricken army—hundreds of slightly wounded men, throngs of others unhurt but utterly demoralized, and baggage-wagons by the score, all pressing to the rear in hopeless confusion." His first thought was to stop the army on the outskirts of Winchester, form a new line, and fight there. "But as the situation was more maturely considered a better conception prevailed. I was sure the troops had confidence in me, for heretofore we had been successful; and as at other times they had seen me present at the slightest sign of trouble or distress, I felt I ought to try to restore their broken ranks. . . ."

Sheridan's storied ride to rally his army was about to begin. Leaving most of his escort and, later, a cavalry brigade to stem the flow of men down the Valley Pike, he put his black stallion, Rienzi, in a dramatic canter toward Middletown and Cedar Creek. For a while, to make better time, he and some aides took to the fields. "When most of the wagons and wounded were past I returned to the road, which was thickly lined with unhurt men . . . who had halted . . . and begun cooking coffee, but when they saw me they abandoned their coffee . . . shouldered their muskets, and as I passed along turned to with enthusiasm and cheers. To acknowledge this demonstration of affection I took off my hat . . . while every mounted officer who saw me galloped out on either side of the pike to tell the men . . . that I had come back."

Over and over, in response to the cheers, Sheridan shouted the same words of assurance: "If I had been with you . . . this would not have happened! "Face the other way!" "We will go back and recover our camp!"[30]

George "Sandy" Forsyth, one of his aides, knew that he was seeing a great event unfold. "The general would wave his hat to the men and point to the front, never lessening his speed as he pressed forward. It was enough; one glance at the eager face and familiar black horse and they knew him and . . . started after him . . . shouting to their comrades further out in the fields, 'Sheridan! Sheridan!' " Little Phil's swarthy features were determined, his coal black eyes piercing. "We passed through a fringe of woods, up a slight eminence in the road," said Forsyth, "and in a flash we were in full view of the battlefield. In our immediate front the road and adjacent fields were filled with sections of artillery, caissons, ammunitions trains, squads of mounted men . . . all that appertains to . . . the rear of an army in action."

Major Hazard Stevens was standing with George Getty and some troops at a fence-post barricade about 10:30 A.M., wondering why the Confederates were not resuming the assault. Hearing the pounding of horses' hooves, he turned his head and found Sheridan and several aides tearing down upon him at full gallop. "Men, by God, we'll whip them yet!" the newcomer cried out to everyone within earshot. "We'll sleep in our old camps tonight!" The soldiers cheered him lustily. "Hope and confidence returned at a bound," said Stevens. "No longer did we merely hope the worst was over. . . . Now we all burned to attack the enemy."[31]

Sheridan next rode to the northwest, moving behind Getty's line until he came upon Wright and the rest of the 6th Corps, as well as his close friend George Crook, who was trying to re-form the remnants of the 8th Corps, now down to brigade size. "What are you doing way back here?" he inquired of the distraught Crook, throwing his arms around him. "After the embrace of the two men," said an orderly, "I thought I saw moisture in the eyes of both."

Crook's response is unrecorded, but a blood-splattered Wright, as he and Sheridan subsequently clasped hands, volunteered words of apology for the debacle. "Well, we've done the best we could," he said.

"That's all right! That's all right!" Sheridan quickly replied.

William Emory now joined the other commanders, reporting that his 19th Corps, reduced but restored, was ready to cover the retreat. Here the fiery Sheridan reverted to form. "Retreat, hell!" he roared. "We'll be back in our camps tonight!" He galloped back to a hill behind Getty's line, where he established his headquarters and began to draw up his plans. "Go to the right and find the other two divisions of the 6th Corps," he told Major Forsyth, "and also General Emory's command. Bring them up, and order them to take position on the right of Getty."[32]

By this time it was noon, and Sheridan must have been puzzled, like all his officers, that Early was not moving forward in depth. Meanwhile his own line of battle was slowly firming up, from Crook's remnants on the left to Wright in the center to Emory on the right, with Custer's cavalry farther right still. One hour passed without the bugles sounding a counter-attack, however, and an impatient Forsyth, who at this point was with Emory's command, rode to headquarters to find out why not. There he found Sheridan reclining on the ground, taking his ease. His commander looked up, and asked Forsyth what he wanted. "It seems to me, general," the aide blurted out, "that we ought to advance; I have come hoping for orders." Then he stiffened, realizing he was a junior officer giving unwanted advice. Sheridan's eyes flashed with anger, "But gradually an amused look overshadowed the anxious face, and the chief slowly shook his head. 'Not yet, not yet; go back and wait."[33]

Given breathing room by Early's inertia, Sheridan was waiting out the Rebels as long as he dared. "I decided to suspend the fighting," he said, "till my thin ranks were further strengthened by the men who were continually coming up from the rear, and particularly till Crook's troops could be assembled on the extreme left."

Not until 4:00 P.M. did he set the army in motion. Custer and Emory on the right drove toward the Valley Pike south of Middletown in a swinging maneuver, Wright advanced more deliberately in the center, Crook's Corps—still badly mauled—initially was asked only to hold the left and act as the pivot of the assault. Sheridan's purpose was to turn Gordon's strung-out left in the open ground, thereby plunging Kershaw's division and the rest of the Confederate line into confusion, and in this he was soon successful. "Regiment after regiment, brigade after brigade, in rapid succession was crushed," Gordon would say ruefully, "and, like hard clods of clay under a pelting rain, the superb commands crumbled to pieces." Added Captain Augustus Dickert in Kershaw's command: "Seeing no prospects of succor on our right or left, the enemy gradually passing and getting in our rear . . . the men break and fly. . . . The enemy kept close on our heels. . . . There were no thickets, no ravines, no fences to shield or protect us."

Sheridan was elated. "My whole line as far as the eye could see was now driving everything before it, from behind trees, stone walls, and all such sheltering obstacles, so I rode toward the left to see how matters were getting on there." Here he had one more task to perform, restoring the 8th Corps' confidence. "When I reached the Valley Pike Crook had reorganized his men, and as I desired that they should take part in the fight, for they were the very same troops that had turned Early's flank at the Opequon and at Fisher's Hill, I ordered them . . . forward, and the alacrity and celerity with which they moved on Middletown demonstrated that their ill-fortune of the morning had not sprung from lack of valor."[34]

The outnumbered Rebel army, surprised in turn, at this juncture was in complete rout. Harassed by Custer's cavalry it fled south across Cedar Creek, tried unsuccessfully to make a stand at Fisher's Hill and ended up, the next day, at faraway New Market. Though the Federals lost 5,800 men and the Confederates a lesser 3,000, the victors had captured twenty-four guns and hundreds of supply wagons, plus all their own guns and wagons that had been taken in the morning. Moreover, in a matter of hours they had turned defeat into victory. "The Yankees got whipped; we got scared," was the way Early summed up the stunning reversal.

That night Sheridan was in an expansive mood. "You have done it for me this time, Custer!" he shouted, hauling the curly-haired cavalryman with the shoulder-length locks from his horse and pummeling him good-naturedly. Custer returned the roughhousing, seizing Sheridan around the waist, lifting him off the ground and repeatedly whirling him about. "By

God, Phil, we've cleaned them out of their guns—and gotten ours back!" he exulted.[35]

Early had tied down tens of thousands of Union troops for months in the Shenandoah, and inflicted some 14,500 casualties, even when those troops were most needed in the assault on Petersburg, but now his usefulness was at an end. The Confederate presence in the valley, to all intents, had been smashed. Early would remain through the winter with a skeleton force; Gordon, leading the 2nd Corps, together with Kershaw's division, would rejoin Lee in the Petersburg-Richmond area. In the Shenandoah at least, the Federals had eliminated a persistent foe.

FIVE
* * * *

MARCH TO THE SEA

In the West, the war likewise was proceeding at a vigorous pace. On September 20 Horace Porter arrived in Atlanta, sent by Grant from the Petersburg lines to meet with Sherman and exchange information, with an eye toward planning a new campaign. "Colonel Porter will explain to you the exact condition of affairs here better than I can do in the limits of a letter," wrote Grant. ". . . My object now in sending a staff officer is not so much to suggest operations for you as to get your views. . . ." Grant for some time had been pondering a march through Georgia to the sea, which Sherman also advocated, but he realized that such a movement entailed substantial risks. These ranged from how the still dangerous Hood would react—and how he could be neutralized—to what Sherman would do for supplies should he abandon the railroad and plunge more deeply into the Southern heartland.

Porter was meeting Cump for the first time. "His coat was unbuttoned, his black felt hat was slouched over his brow, and on his feet were a pair of slippers very much down at the heels," the aide remembered. ". . . With his large frame, tall, gaunt form, restless hazel eyes, aquiline nose, bronzed face, and crisp beard, he looked the picture of a 'grim-visaged war.'" Following the usual pleasantries, Sherman in his staccato speech made it clear he had lost none of his affection for his chief. "I knew Grant would make the fur fly when he started down through Virginia," he said. "Wherever

he is the enemy will never find any trouble about getting up a fight. . . .
When Grant cried, 'Forward!' after the battle of the Wilderness, I said:
'This is the grandest act of his life; now I feel that the rebellion will be
crushed. . . . ' "

Later Sherman expounded on his proposed March to the Sea—one that
would end in Savannah. "I would feel pretty safe in picking up the bulk of
this army and moving east, subsisting off the country," he told Porter. "I
could move to Milledgeville, and threaten both Macon and Augusta. . . . I
can subsist my army upon the country as long as I keep moving. . . . There
is no telling what Hood will do, whether he will follow me and contest my
march . . . or whether he will start north [to Tennessee] with his whole
army, thinking there will not be any adequate force to oppose him. . . . I
don't care much what he does. I would rather have him start north,
though. . . . I could send enough of this army to delay his progress until
our troops . . . could be concentrated to destroy him. . . . Then with the
bulk of my army I could cut a swath to the sea, divide the Confederacy in
two, and be able to move up in the rear of Lee. . . ."[1]

These recommendations from Sherman went into a lengthy dispatch,
which Porter carried back to Virginia, and which Grant and his aides subsequently discussed. Chief of staff John Rawlins had been ill and on leave
of absence—he was fighting the tuberculosis that in a few years would
take his life—but he returned to duty in early October and weighed in
heavily against Sherman's proposal. "Rawlins always talked with great
force," said Porter. "He had a natural taste for public speaking, and when
he became particularly earnest in the discussion of a question his speech
often took the form of an oration; and as he grew more excited, and his
enthusiasm increased, he would hold forth in stentorian tones."

Porter, who had been much impressed by Sherman, in turn became the
leading supporter of the plan. The debate went on and on, with Rawlins
arguing that the supply lines were so fragile no march should be attempted
until Hood was disposed of, and Porter repeating Sherman's contention
that his army could live off the land and, if Hood chose not to contest the
march and instead moved north into Tennessee, adequate forces could be
detached from the army to defeat him. "The general-in-chief"—not committing himself—"would sit quietly by, listening to the arguments" said
Porter, "and sometimes showed himself greatly amused."

One night someone suggested that Grant, who had kept his own counsel during the arguments, should order Sherman to hold a council of war
with his generals on the subject. "No!" the general-in-chief replied deci-
sively. "I will not direct anyone to do what I would not do myself under

similar circumstances. I never held what might be called formal councils of war and I do not believe in them. They create a divided responsibility. . . . There is too much truth in the old adage, 'Councils of War do not fight!' "[2]

Back in the West, however, the argument in effect would resolve itself. During late September and into October Hood showed that he had no intention of forcing a major battle, instead preferring to move north across the Chattahoochee and harass the Federal supply lines with hit-and-run tactics, tearing up Western & Atlantic track from Marietta to Allatoona to Resaca to Dalton. In effect, he was reversing and retracing the route down which Sherman earlier had advanced with such painstaking effort. Cump chased him, of course, but with conspicuous lack of success. The Federals' sole triumph came on October 5 at Allatoona, where they had a major depot. There the small garrison, hurriedly reinforced by a brigade under General John Corse from John Logan's 15th Corps, held off twice the number of attackers.

"To avoid a needless effusion of blood," the Rebel general besieging had written, "I call on you to surrender your forces at once and unconditionally. Five minutes will allow you to decide." Back came a cool answer from Corse: "I . . . respectfully reply we are prepared for 'the needless effusion of blood' whenever it is agreeable to you." Helped by the fact that many of his men had repeating rifles, Corse roundly repulsed the attack, inflicting some 1,000 casualties on the enemy. Late in the day, he himself suffered a nasty wound in the face. "How is Corse? What news?" semaphored a Sherman aide, desperate to know how the battle was going. "I am short of a cheekbone and one ear," Corse signaled, "but am able to whip all hell yet."[3]

In the midst of his efforts to overtake and corner Hood, and simultaneously thwart the raids of the Confederate cavalry, a frustrated Sherman renewed his case for a March to the Sea. "It will be a physical impossibility to protect the [rail]roads now that Hood, [Nathan] Forrest, [Joseph] Wheeler, and the whole batch of devils are turned loose without home or habilitation," he advised Grant. The proper strategy was not the occupation of Georgia, he stressed, but its destruction. "By attempting to hold the roads, we will lose a thousand men each month, and will gain no result. I can make this march, and make Georgia howl!"

Responded Grant ruminatively on October 11: "If you were to cut loose, I do not believe you would meet Hood's army, but would be bushwhacked by all the old men, little boys, and such railroad guards as are still left at home. Hood would probably strike for Nashville, thinking by going north he could inflict greater damage upon us than we could upon the Rebels by going south. If there is any way of getting at Hood's army, I would prefer that, but I must trust to your own judgment. . . ." Hours later, he endorsed Sherman's proposal more directly. "If you are satisfied the trip to the seacoast can be made, holding the line of the Tennessee [River] firmly, you may make it, destroying all the railroad south of Dalton or Chattanooga, as you think best."[4] Grant was setting two conditions: that adequate troops be left behind to protect Tennessee, and that the railroad be torn up to keep the enemy from using it.

Sherman pursued Hood energetically until October 19, chasing him from north Georgia into Alabama, and then returned to Atlanta, where he immediately began planning his new campaign. Given the task of confronting and defeating Hood, who in weeks to come would surely advance into Tennessee, was the dependable if stolid George Thomas, stationed in Nashville with a token force. In short order, however, he would be reinforced by the 4th Corps of the Army of the Cumberland under David Stanley and the 23rd Corps of the small Army of the Ohio, both under John Schofield's command, and then by Andrew Jackson Smith's detachment of the Army of the Tennessee—in effect the 16th Corps, whose chief, Grenville Dodge, had been wounded outside of Atlanta. Leading the cavalry would be James Wilson. We shall hear more subsequently of the Federal efforts to cope with Hood.

Even with these departures from his immediate command, Sherman during November still led an impressive army of some 60,000 men. Forthwith he organized them into Right and Left Wings. The Right consisted of most of the Army of the Tennessee under Oliver Howard. His 15th Corps, usually commanded by the hard-living John Logan, was led by Peter Osterhaus. Logan, sulking like Joe Hooker over being passed over in favor of Howard, was devoting his time to Lincoln's reelection, and tarrying in Illinois. The 17th Corps was headed by Sherman's trusted friend, Francis Blair.

Osterhaus, who likewise had been unhappy with his rank, was back in the army with a major general's stars. His division chiefs were Charles Woods, William Hazen, John E. Smith, and John M. Corse. Blair's were Joseph Mower, Mortimer Leggett, and Giles Smith. All were tough and experienced officers, and most we have seen before in various engagements.

New Yorker Henry Slocum, replacing Hooker, led the Left Wing. His corps commanders were the hot-tempered Jefferson C. Davis of the 14th and Alpheus Williams of the 20th, both units coming from the Army of the Cumberland. Davis's divisions were led by William Carlin, James Dada

Morgan, and Absalom Baird; Williams's were headed by John White Geary, William T. Ward, and Nathaniel J. Jackson. These officers, too, for the most part had fought long and well.

Chief of Staff Halleck and Secretary of War Stanton, and to a lesser extent Lincoln, during this period voiced grave concerns to Grant about the expedition. Stanton's nervousness was fed at least in part by Rawlins, who stepped out of character in this instance and went behind Grant's back to protest the decision. (Only years later did the general-in-chief learn of this transgression. "My chief of staff . . . finding he could not move me . . . appealed to the authorities in Washington," he icily commented.) Grant nonetheless remained steadfast. "On mature reflection, I believe Sherman's proposition is the best that can be adopted," he told Stanton. To Cump he continued to offer support. "I really do not see that you can withdraw from where you are to follow Hood without giving up all we have gained in territory. I say, then, go as you propose."

Once more it should be noted how well Grant and Sherman—polar opposites in temperament—worked in concert. Each man had near absolute trust in the other's judgment. "Over-zealous partisans of General Grant have claimed that he originated and controlled the entire movement," Horace Porter would say of the March to the Sea, "while enthusiastic admirers of Sherman have insisted that Grant was surprised at the novelty of the suggestion, and was at first opposed. . . . The truth is that the two generals were in perfect accord."[5]

The campaign began on November 15, with the lead elements of the Right and Left Wings streaming out of Atlanta and trudging along the Georgia roads on a front that would extend from forty to sixty miles. Besides the army's tens of thousands of men, its columns consisted of 65 cannons, 2,400 wagons, and 200 rounds of ammunition for each musket and gun. Supplies of food and fodder were kept at a minimum—Sherman, who did not leave the city until the next day, was determined to live off the land. "We rode out of Atlanta by the Decatur Road," he said, "filled by the marching troops and wagons of [Davis's] 14th Corps; and reaching the hill, just outside the old Rebel works, we naturally paused to look back. . . . We stood upon the very ground whereon was fought the bloody battle of July 22, and could see the copse of wood where McPherson fell. Behind us lay Atlanta, smoldering and in ruins, the black smoke rising high in the air, and hanging like a pall over the ruined city. . . ."

Sherman's first major objective would be Milledgeville, then the state capital, more than 100 miles to the southeast. Though his troops were in high spirits, he knew he was striking into the unknown, and he confessed to trepidation. "Some band, by accident, struck up the anthem of 'John Brown's soul goes marching on'," he said, "the men caught up the strain, and never before or since have I heard the chorus of 'Glory, glory, hallelujah!' done with more spirit, or in better harmony of time and place. . . . The day was extremely beautiful, clear sunlight, with bracing air. . . . There was a 'devil-may-care' feeling pervading officers and men, that made me feel the full load of responsibility, for success would be accepted as a matter of course, whereas, should we fail, this 'march' would be adjudged the wild adventure of a crazy fool."[6]

It soon became clear, however, that the army would encounter little in the way of resistance—the Confederates were in the process of scraping together less than 13,000 men, mostly cavalry and ill-trained militia. On November 18, passing through the town of Covington, the troops of the Left Wing closed up their ranks, the color-bearers unfurled their flags, and the bands struck up patriotic airs. "The white people came out of their houses to behold the sight, [in] spite of their deep hatred of the invaders," Sherman said, "and the Negroes were simply frantic with joy. Whenever they heard my name, they clustered about my horse, shouted and prayed in their peculiar style, which had a natural eloquence that would have moved a stone." Here he noticed a soldier carrying a huge ham and a jug of molasses, and munching on a honeycomb.

"Forage liberally on the country," the miscreant intoned, seeing Sherman's eye on him and quoting from the general orders for the army.

"I reproved the man," Cump said, "[and] explained that foraging must be limited to the regular parties properly detailed. . . ."

Sherman was being disingenuous. The Federals cutting their immense swath through Georgia, whether singly or in groups, day after day would terrorize the inhabitants and strip the countryside of food. "It is evident that our soldiers are determined to burn, plunder and destroy everything in their way. . . ." Major James Connolly, an aide to General Absalom Baird, 14th Corps, would say. "Well, that shows that they are not *afraid* of the South at any rate, and that each individual soldier is determined to strike with all his might against the rebellion." Foraging parties were sent out each morning. "They go where they please, seize wagons, mules, horses and harness; make the Negroes of the plantation hitch up, load the wagons with sweet potatoes, flour, meal, hogs, sheep, chickens, turkeys, barrels of molasses, and in fact everything good to eat, and sometimes considerable good to drink."[7]

Dolly Lunt, who before the war had come down from Maine to marry a Covington planter, left us an account of what the residents there and elsewhere would endure. Now a widow, and running the place by herself, she experienced the foraging firsthand. "Slept in my clothes last night," she wrote, "as I heard the Yankees went to neighbor Montgomery's on Thursday night at one o'clock, searched his house, drank his wine, and took his money and valuables.

"As we were not disturbed, I walked after breakfast with Sadai [her daughter], up to Mr. Joe Perry's, my nearest neighbor. . . . Saw Mrs. Laura [Perry] in the road surrounded by her children. . . . She said she was looking for her husband, that old Mrs. Perry [her mother-in-law] had just sent her word that the Yankees went to James Perry's house the night before, plundered his house and drove off all his stock, and that she must [hide] hers in the old fields.

"Before we were done talking, up came Joe and Jim Perry from their hiding-place. Jim was very much excited. . . . As we stood there, I saw some bluecoats coming down the hill. Jim immediately raised his gun, swearing he would kill them.

" 'No, don't!' said I, and ran home as fast as I could with Sadai.

"I could hear [the soldiers] cry, 'Halt! Halt!' and their guns went off in quick succession. Oh God, the time of trial has come!

". . . I hastened back to my frightened servants and told them they had better hide, and then went back to the gate to claim protection and a guard.

"But like demons they rush in. My yards are full. To my smokehouse, my diary, pantry, kitchen and cellar, like famished wolves they come, breaking locks and whatever is in their way. The thousand pounds of meat in my smokehouse is gone in a twinkling, my flour, my meat, my lard, butter, eggs, pickles of various kinds . . . wine, jars and jugs are all gone. My eighteen fat turkeys, my hens, chickens and fowls, my young pigs, are shot down in my yard and hunted as if they were Rebels themselves. Utterly powerless I ran out and appealed to the guard.

" 'I cannot help you, Madam, it is orders.'

". . . A Captain Weber from Illinois came into my house. Of him I claimed protection from the vandals who were forcing themselves into my room. . . . He felt for me, and I gave him and several others the character of gentlemen. . . . I don't believe they would have molested women and children had they had their own way.

". . . Sherman himself and a greater portion of his army passed my house that day. . . . They tore down my garden palings, made a road through my back yard . . . tearing down my fences and desecrating my home—wantonly doing it when there was no necessity for it.

"Such a day, if I live to the age of Methuselah, may God spare me from ever seeing again!"[8]

In the days that followed, while the Federal columns were passing through Georgia, Major Connolly in his own writings made it clear he felt the Rebels were getting what they deserved. "Our stock of Negroes is increasing rapidly," he said of the newly liberated blacks who were flocking to the army. "Many of them travel on horseback now; they furnish their own, i.e., their masters' horses, saddles and bridles, so they are no expense to Uncle Sam; a great many of our privates are getting Negro servants for themselves; the Negro walks along beside the soldier, with knapsack and cooking utensils strapped upon his back, thus relieving the soldier of his load. What soldier *wouldn't* be an abolitionist under such circumstances." The burning and looting, he felt, would shorten the war. "Civilians everywhere look paralyzed and as if stricken dumb as we pass them. Columns of smoke by day, and 'pillars of fire' by night, for miles and miles on our right and left indicate to us . . . the route and location of the other columns. . . . Every 'Gin House' we pass"—referring to cotton gins—"is burned; every stack of fodder we can't carry is burned; every barn filled with grain is destroyed; in fact everything that can be of any use to the Rebels is either carried off by our foragers or set on fire. . . ."[9]

On November 22, even as Sherman's columns were converging on Milledgeville, the Confederates threw themselves on the army's Right Wing at nearby Griswoldsville. There some 600 of 2,000 Rebel assailants, in a series of ill-advised charges, were cut down like wheat before a scythe.

Charles Walcutt's 15th Corps brigade, armed with repeating rifles, did most of the fighting. Captain Charles Wills of the 103rd Illinois describes the action: "We were getting dinner, not dreaming of a fight, when lively musketry opened on the picket line . . . and in a minute more our pickets came in flying. A fine line of Johnnies pushed out of the woods after them. . . . We commenced throwing up logs in our front and did not fire a shot until they were within 250 yards of us. . . . We all felt that we had a sure thing. . . . By the time the first line had got [up] . . . three other lines emerged. . . . We then let loose on them with our muskets. . . . One after another their lines crumbled to pieces, and they took to the run to save themselves. . . ."

Moving onto the battlefield later, Wills was appalled by what he saw. "Old gray-haired and weakly looking men and little boys, not over fifteen years old, lay dead or writhing in pain." What had they hoped to accomplish? "My neighborhood is ruined . . . these people are all my neighbors," a grizzled Confederate in his sixties whispered, gasping his last breaths and gesturing toward the bodies strewn around him. "I hope we never have to shoot at such men again," summed up Wills. "They knew nothing at all about fighting, and I think their officers knew as little. . . ."[10]

In Milledgeville about the same time, the van of the Federal army moved into the capital without firing a shot. "The people of Milledgeville remained at home," said Sherman, "except the Governor [Joseph Brown], the State officers, and Legislature, who had ignominiously fled, in the utmost disorder and confusion. . . . Some of the citizens who remained behind described this flight of the 'brave and patriotic' Governor Brown. He had occupied a public building known as the 'Governor's Mansion,' and had hastily stripped it of carpets, curtains and furniture . . . which were removed to a train of freight-cars . . . leaving behind muskets, ammunition and the public archives."

During his two-day stopover in the town, Sherman found stacks of newspapers from all over the South, and upon reading them "learned the consternation which had filled the Southern mind at our temerity; many charging that we were actually fleeing for our lives and seeking safety at the hands of our fleet on the seacoast. All demanded that we should be attacked 'front, flank, and rear,' that provisions should be destroyed in advance, so that we would starve; that bridges should be burned, roads obstructed, and no mercy shown us. Judging from the tone of the Southern press . . . the outside world must have supposed us ruined and lost."

In short order all warehouses, factories, machine shops, and railroad depots were burned, as well as 2,000 bales of cotton, and the public buildings were plundered, the soldiers helping themselves to Confederate money, valuable law books, and even the inkwell from the Speaker's desk in the state legislature. Sherman did, however, post a guard to protect the Rebel hospitals.

There were some high jinks as well. On one occasion Union officers conducted a sham session of the Georgia legislature, complete with some drinking and much hilarity. "Many of the speakers discoursed in what they thought to be the Southern 'fire-eater' style," wrote one historian. ". . . A number of bills and resolutions were put forward, including one that brought Georgia back into the Union . . . Someone rushed in, shouting, 'The Yankees are coming!' This produced much 'confusion, laughter and mock panic.'" The second bit of fun involved a straight-faced funeral service for the "departed" Governor Brown. "The casket borne by the mourners was an empty crate . . . and the cortege wound through the streets to the accompaniment of drums, finally arriving at the Baptist

Church where Brown worshipped." There an impassioned Union officer delivered the eulogy. "No man . . ." said one attendee, who happened to be a Georgian, "could have done better."[11]

Thursday the 24th had recently been proclaimed by Lincoln as the first national Thanksgiving Day, but officers and men, knowing they were soon moving out, celebrated the event on the 23rd. (The president had much to be grateful for, having been reelected that fall on the Republican ticket with 2.3 million votes; George McClellan, his first general-in-chief, running on the Democratic line and advocating a softer peace policy, amassed 1.8 million.)

Sergeant Rice Bull of the 123rd New York and nine of his comrades bunched their foodstuffs and hired a black woman to cook their feast. "We had several hens, a goose, some fresh pork, a bag of wheat flour and coffee. . . . There was no stove, just a big open fireplace. . . . Nothing could be roasted but she had kettles so our meat was fricasseed and all went into the pot together. . . . We did what we could to help the old [Negro] aunty. . . . With the wheat flour she made biscuits, baked in an iron Dutch oven. All declared they had never eaten anything better than those biscuits. . . . At six in the evening we gathered our things together and after giving a good part of our uneaten food to Aunt Susan, as we called her, bid her goodbye."

Sherman said his farewell to Milledgeville, too, in his own brusque but logical way. He summoned the medical director of one of the hospitals to his headquarters and told him he had a parting gift for him: ten gallons of rye whiskey he had appropriated from the Rebels and now was returning—for medicinal purposes. He also asked a favor. He had twenty-eight men too weak to travel and he wanted the doctor to take care of them.

"If they die, give them a decent burial," Sherman said, "if they live, send them to Andersonville," referring to the prison camp.

The doctor was startled, wondering why a Union officer might condemn his men to Andersonville. "They [would be] prisoners of war," said Sherman, "what else can you do? If I had your men I would send them to prison."

The next day the rested army resumed its march. "About three days' journey from where we were," said Bull, "we would leave the fertile agricultural lands of Georgia and enter the Piney-Savannah region, where there was little farming and no large plantations, the country being largely populated by the 'poor whites.'. . . It had taken eight days to come from Atlanta to Milledgeville, an average of sixteen miles per day. We were now some 175 miles from Savannah. If we continued at the same rate it would take twelve days to reach that city. We could hardly expect to keep up that rate of progress as we were coming into a more difficult country; there were swamps, streams, and large rivers to cross, which would take time. . . ."[12]

Despite the terrain, Sherman kept up the pace. "On the 3rd of December I entered Millen with the Seventeenth Corps [General Frank P. Blair]," he said, "and there paused one day to communicate with all parts of the army. General Howard was south of the Ogeechee River with the Fifteenth Corps, opposite Scarboro'. General Slocum was at Buckhead Church, four miles north of Millen, with the Twentieth Corps. The Fourteenth [General Davis] was at Lumpkin's Station, on the Augusta Road, about ten miles north of Millen, and the cavalry division was within easy support."

Millen was little more than a rail intersection, with a depot, a few houses, and an abandoned hotel, but it was a strategic prize. The Federals promptly set about tearing up track and torching the buildings. "There was a Y or triangle of R.R. tracks at Millen, the roads from Savannah, Augusta and Atlanta [and Macon] all forming junction here," said Major Henry Hitchcock, who had recently become a Sherman aide. "This Georgia Central R.R. was . . . the best managed R.R. in the South, and was the main and vital connection for Richmond with the fertile districts of Georgia and Alabama and Mississippi. Its destruction . . . is a terrible blow to J. D. [Jefferson Davis] & Co. We shall have torn up and destroyed over 100 miles of it, burning long and costly bridges, depot buildings, new ties and material. . . ."

Hitchcock's diary entry for December 3, written in staccato fashion, gives us a sense of the expedition's urgency—and its callousness. "At first camp [Blair's] saw first wounded man—Negro, who went ahead with party of stragglers to show them house to 'forage.' Met fifteen Rebs there, our men skedaddled—Negro was shot in back under right shoulder; our men soon rallied, went back, rescued [him] and drove Rebs off. Poor fellow walked into the camp, doctors examined wound, probably not bad; but that's all I know. . . . On the road today passed a squad digging hole in ground near road. 'Somebody died' was the brief reply to my question. In the army men 'get used to this.' . . . This evening man came to see General [Sherman]—R.R. Supt. of wood and water, native here, plain, frank, sensible man. Same story, house stripped, family left without bread. General invited him to supper. Confirms stories of utter despotism here—says C.S.A. 'gone up,' wants to emigrate, etc."[13]

Sherman would never deny that he was waging all-out war, but insisted it was against property rather than civilians, and in making this distinction he was largely correct. "If the [Confederates] raise a howl against my barbarity & cruelty," he had written General Halleck after his sacking of Atlanta, "I will answer that War is War & not popularity seeking. If they want Peace, they & their relations must stop War." In the North during his march, of course, little was known of Sherman's activities or his progress—telegraphic and railroad communication being impossible. Everyone from Lincoln and Grant on down was relying on Southern newspapers for information, and those accounts were claiming he was on the brink of annihilation. On December 8 a worried Senator John Sherman asked Lincoln for news of his brother. "Oh no, we haven't heard anything from him," the president replied. "We know what hole he went in, but we don't know what hole he will come out of."[14]

John Sherman need not have been concerned. Cump's progress was becoming more and more irresistible—and his confidence all the greater—with every mile he advanced toward Savannah and the sea. "The weather was fine, the roads good, and everything seemed to favor us," he said. "Never do I recall a more agreeable sensation than the sight of our camps at night, lit up by the fires of fragrant pine-knots. . . . No enemy opposed us, and we could only occasionally hear the faint reverberation of a gun to our left rear, where we knew General Kilpatrick [his own cavalry chief] was skirmishing with [Joseph] Wheeler's cavalry, which persistently followed him. But the infantry columns had met with no opposition whatsoever."

Riding along one day, Sherman came upon a young officer whose foot had been splintered and shredded by a torpedo—an early type of land mine—that had been left in the road, and who was waiting for a surgeon to amputate his leg. "There had been no resistance at that point, nothing to give warning of danger, and the Rebels had planted eight-inch shells in the road, with friction-matches to explode them by being trodden on. This was not war, but murder." He reacted with fury, ordering some Rebel prisoners, armed with picks and shovels, to take the lead, and either explode their own torpedoes or dig them up. "They begged hard," he said grimly, "but I reiterated the order . . . and could hardly help from laughing at their stepping so gingerly . . . but [at this point] they found no other torpedoes."[15]

By December 10 the army was in front of the Savannah fortifications, which were commanded by General William Hardee, investing the city on three sides. The 14th Corps was on the left, touching the Savannah River; then the 20th and 17th Corps; then the 15th Corps on the extreme right. Over the last few days, gathering adequate food and fodder had been a problem—testimony to the infertile and largely unproductive land in the area. Sherman now had a hungry army on his hands, one that could have difficulty mounting a lengthy siege without food and fodder from the Yankee fleet, which was lingering somewhere offshore. He straight away resolved to take Fort McAllister, just south of the city on Ossabaw Sound, and thereby bring in supplies from the water.

Given the task of carrying the fort was William Hazen's division of the 15th Corps. "I gave General Hazen, in person, his orders to march rapidly down the right bank of the Ogeechee [River], and without hesitation to assault . . . Fort McAllister by storm," said Sherman. "I knew it to be strong in heavy artillery, as against an approach by the sea, but believed it open and weak to the rear." On the 13th the attack got under way. Hazen reached the vicinity of the fort about 11:00 A.M., but then became bogged down when his troops found torpedoes in their path. "It took some time to dig them out," said Oliver Howard, the Right Wing commander, "for of course the men, after locating them, were obliged to work with extreme caution. Hazen then left eight of his regiments as reserve . . . then slowly worked his way with the remainder to within 600 yards of the work, and there extended his main body into line and pushed out his skirmishers . . . with instructions to creep up . . . under cover till they could approach near enough to watch the gunners through the embrasures. . . ."

The ground in Hazen's front was quite marshy, intersected with streams that connected to the Ogeechee. "His deployment was necessarily . . . difficult," continued Howard, "and . . . it took him till half-past four in the afternoon to get every man in position." At 5:00 P.M. the bugle sounded the assault. "[Hazen] made his line as thin as he could, the result of which was that none of his soldiers were hit by the garrison until they were very near. . . . Not far outside the works other torpedoes were encountered . . . in many instances blowing and scattering the men in fragments."

Hazen sums up the last stages of the attack: "The line moved on without checking, over, under, and through abatis, ditches, palisading, and parapets, fighting the garrison through the fort to their bomb-proofs, from which they still fought, and only succumbed as each man was individually overpowered."[16]

Throughout the afternoon Sherman had been watching Hazen's movements from the roof of a nearby rice mill, where he simultaneously had a clear view of the water. "I received by signal the assurance of General Hazen that . . . he would soon attempt the assault," he said. "The sun was rapidly declining, and I was dreadfully impatient. At that very moment someone discovered a faint cloud of smoke, and an object gliding, as it were . . . along the horizon . . . which little by little grew till it was pronounced to be the smoke-stack of a steamer coming up the river. . . . Soon the flag of the United States was plainly visible, and our attention was divided between this approaching steamer and the expected assault."

"Is Fort McAllister ours?" the vessel signaled.

"Not yet," Sherman replied, "but it will be in a few minutes!"

Just then Hazen's troops came out of the woods, colors flying and pushing forward at a quick, steady pace. Fort McAllister's big guns began to roar, belching clouds of smoke. "On the lines advanced, faintly seen in the white, sulphurous smoke," said Sherman. "There was a pause . . . the smoke cleared away and the parapets were blue with our men, who fired their muskets in the air and shouted so that we actually heard them. . . . Fort McAllister was taken, and the good news was instantly sent to our navy friends."[17]

Sherman celebrated by having dinner with Hazen, who had also invited Major George Anderson, the fort's commander, to sup with him. During the meal Anderson was shocked to see that one of his slaves was waiting table.

Bob, he asked, *have you joined the Yankees?*

I'm working for Mr. Hazen, the man replied.

"General," said Anderson to Cump, "it looks to me as if the game is up."

"Yes," said Sherman, "the game is up. Slavery is gone, and the Southern Confederacy a thing of the past."

One navy steamer soon was followed by others, and by the 16th both supplies and dispatches were being received on shore. Sherman's communications, down since leaving Atlanta, now were fully restored. "Not liking to rejoice before the victory is assured," Grant told him in one letter, "I abstain from congratulating you . . . until bottom has been struck. I have never had a fear, however, for the result."

The general-in-chief subsequently instructed Sherman to rejoin him in Virginia as soon as possible, and there mount an all-out attack on Lee. "My idea now is that you establish a base on the seacoast, fortify and leave in it all your artillery and cavalry, and enough infantry to protect them. . . . With the balance of your command come here by water with all dispatch." Sherman dutifully set about assembling the necessary shipping, which he estimated to be some 100 steamers and sailing vessels, but he did not abandon the idea of taking Savannah. "I have initiated measures looking principally to coming to you with fifty or sixty thousand infantry," he informed Grant, "and incidentally to capture Savannah, if time will allow."[18]

Sherman had good reason to believe General Hardee and his troops were between a rock and a hard place. "I think Hardee, in Savannah," he wrote Grant, "has good artillerists, some five or six thousand good infantry, and, it may be, a mongrel mass of eight to ten thousand militia. In all our marching through Georgia, he had not forced us to use anything but a skirmish-line. . . . In Savannah he has taken refuge . . . behind swamps and overflowed rice-fields. . . . There must be twenty-five thousand citizens . . . that must also be fed, and how he is to feed them . . . I cannot imagine. . . ."

In a note on the 17th Sherman forthrightly asked for Hardee's surrender. "I have already received guns that can cast heavy and destructive shot as far as the heart of your city; also, I have for some days controlled every avenue by which the people and garrison of Savannah can be supplied. . . . Should you entertain the proposition, I am prepared to grant liberal terms . . . but should I be forced to assault, or the slower and surer process of starvation, I shall then feel justified in resorting to the harshest measures, and shall make little effort to restrain my army. . . ."

Sherman did have the heavy guns, which the navy had unloaded and put on shore, but he was exaggerating when he said he had the city surrounded—there was still egress to the east, via a pontoon bridge across the Savannah River into South Carolina. Though Hardee rejected the demand for surrender, his statement was a subterfuge. Even as Cump was making plans to close the exit, the Southern commander evacuated the city the night of the 20th and crossed the river. Sherman marched in the next day and proudly informed Lincoln: "I beg to present to you as a Christmas gift the city of Savannah, with 150 heavy guns and plenty of ammunition; also about 25,000 bales of cotton."[19]

Because Savannah had surrendered, rather than resisted and forced a siege, Sherman would make sure that his army treated the inhabitants with all courtesy. Not only would the soldiers do no looting, but they would keep the city's lawless element in check, pay in cash for their purchases, and even—through the regimental bands—entertain the citizens through the Christmas season. During his occupation of Atlanta and subsequent march Cump had demonstrated he could raze and burn; now he was showing he could be magnanimous. "Savannah was an old place. . . ." he would say. "Its houses were of brick and frame, with large yards, ornamented with shrubbery and flowers; its streets perfectly regular, crossing each other at right angles, and at many of the intersections were small enclosures in the nature of parks. . . ."

Most Southerners realized the war was drawing to a close. "The mayor, Dr. Arnold, was completely 'subjugated,' " said Sherman, "and, after consulting with him, I authorized him . . . to take charge generally of the interests of the people, but warned that all who remained must be strictly subordinate to military law. . . . About 200 persons, mostly the families of men in the Confederate army, prepared to follow the fortunes of their husbands and fathers, and those were sent in a steamboat under a flag of truce . . . to Charleston [S.C.] harbor. . . . But the great bulk of the inhabitants chose to remain . . . and good social relations at once arose between them and the army."[20]

Major Hitchcock, in a letter to his wife, describes the Federal entry into the city and some of the events that followed: "We went first to the 'Pulaski House,' the hotel where *Captain Sherman* used to stay when on duty here many years ago. Very soon a number of the leading citizens called to pay their respects, among them a brother of Gen. Hardee—Dr. Arnold, the mayor—etc., and all were very kindly received. Besides, came Mr. Chas. Green, a wealthy banker . . . who has the finest house in the city, and not only invited but urged the General very earnestly to take up his quarters there—which he finally consented to. . . .

"On Christmas Day the churches—at least five or six principal ones— were open as usual and going with the General to St. John's [Episcopal] . . . I was delighted to see it filled, not only by a large number of our officers and men, but also a considerable number of Savannah people. . . . When the minister came to the prayer for the President of the United States, which I was amused to find in its place in the prayer books in our pew, he simply omitted that prayer altogether. . . . I am glad to say that the . . . conduct of our army here is not only apparent in the streets, but most favorably remarked by the citizens. . . . The General was speaking with great pleasure and feeling of the number of children he met in the Park, playing, etc. . . .

"Christmas evening, Sunday though it was, we had a (military) 'family dinner-party,' Capt. Nichols, our mess caterer, having secured three or four lovely turkeys and sundry other good things—Col. [Henry] Barnum contributing some very good wine presented to him by some winemerchants at whose stores he placed a guard . . . and Mr. Green's handsome china and silver being 'kindly loaned for the occasion.' Including Generals Slocum and Corse, and Mr. Green, we had some twenty at table, Gen. Sherman presiding. . . ."[21]

Hitchcock would marvel at the hundreds of blacks who visited Sherman. "For several days, there was a constant stream of them, old and young, men, women and children, black, yellow and cream-colored, uncouth and well-bred, bashful and talkative—but always respectful and well-behaved—all day long, anxious . . . to pay their respects and see the man they had heard so much of, and whom—as more than one of them told him—God had sent to answer their prayers."

"Well, boys, come to see Mr. Sherman, have you? Well, I'm Mr. Sherman—glad to see you." Cump would say again and again, vigorously shaking each visitor's hand.

Been prayin' for you a long time, prayin' day and night for you, and now, bless God, you are here, more than one caller would respond.

The irony of this situation was that Sherman, and many of his officers, had no especial love of blacks, and certainly did not think the races equal in the sight of God—or man. The slaves were free because their masters had defied the Union and therefore had suffered the consequences, being stripped of their property. He viewed abolitionists with the same contempt he held for reporters. "The Negro should be a free man," he told Secretary of the Treasury Salmon P. Chase about this time, "but not put on any equality with the Whites . . . the effect of equality is illustrated in the character of the mixed race in Mexico and South America. Indeed it appears to me that the right of suffrage in our Country should be rather abridged than enlarged."[22]

Sherman, again it should be admitted, was fighting not for black emancipation—although he accepted President Lincoln's lead in this regard—but to preserve the Union. That he had done with a vengeance on his 300-mile March to the Sea, despite his sparing of Savannah. Traveling in the wake of his expedition just before Christmas, Eliza Frances "Fanny" Andrews, a young Georgia woman, saw mile after mile of wreckage and ruin: "About three miles from Sparta we struck the 'burnt country,' as it is well named by the natives, and then I could understand better the wrath and desperation of these poor people. I almost felt as if I should like to hang a Yankee myself. There was hardly a fence left standing from Sparta to Gordon. The fields were trampled down and the road was lined with the carcasses of horses, hogs and cattle that the invaders . . . had wantonly shot down, to starve out the people and prevent them from making their crops. The stench in some places was unbearable. . . .

"The dwellings that were standing all showed signs of pillage, and on every plantation we saw the charred remains of the gin-house and packing screw, where here and there lone chimney stacks, 'Sherman's sentinels,' told of homes laid in ashes. . . . Hayracks and fodder stacks were demolished, corncribs were empty, and every bale of cotton that could be found was burnt by the savages. I saw no grain of any sort. . . ."

Near Milledgeville Fanny came across a field where 30,000 troops had camped just weeks before. "It was strewn with the debris they had left behind, and the poor people of the neighborhood were wandering over it, seeking for anything they could find to eat, even picking up grains of corn that were scattered around where the Yankees had fed their horses." The sight enraged her. "If all the words of hatred in every language were lumped together into one huge epithet of detestation," she summed up, "they could not tell how I hate the Yankees."

On Christmas Day itself, Sherman conveyed his own strong sentiments on the war to Ellen. "It would amuse you to see the Negroes, they flock to me old & young, they pray & shout—and mix up my name with that of Moses. . . . There are many fine families in the city, but when I ask for old & familiar names, it marks the sad havoc of war. The Goodwins, Teffts, Cuylers, Habershams, Laws, &c. all gone or in poverty, and yet the girls remain, bright and haughty, and proud as ever. There seems no end but utter annihilation that will satisfy their hate. . . . They no longer call my army 'cowardly Yanks' but have tried to arouse the sympathy of the civilized world by stories of cruel barbarities. . . . The next stop in the progress will be 'for God's sake spare us, we must surrender'—When that end is reached we begin to see daylight. . . ."[23]

Grant now would cancel his plan to move Sherman's army to Virginia by boat—assembling such a flotilla, everyone had come to see, would take months—and instead order him to leave a garrison in Savannah and march up through the Carolinas. This movement, which Cump had suggested, would begin February of 1865. "Five thousand men will be plenty and white troops will be best," Sherman told Grant on the 31st, "as the people are dreadfully alarmed lest we garrison the place with Negroes. Now no matter what the Negro soldiers are, you know that people have prejudices which must be regarded. Prejudice like religion cannot be discussed. . . . If you want me to take Charleston I think I can do it for I know the place well. I was stationed there from '42 to '46 and used to hunt a good deal along the Cooper River. . . .

"I am fully aware of your friendly feelings towards me, and you may always depend upon me as your steadfast supporter. Your wish is Law & Gospel to me and such is the feeling that pervades my army. . . ."[24]

SIX

* * * *

LAST HURRAH IN TENNESSEE

While Sherman was pushing through Georgia largely without opposition, George Thomas and his scattered Union command in Tennessee soon would be getting all the fighting they could wish. Hood's reaction in the aftermath of the Federal departure from Atlanta would be to move into middle Tennessee as quickly as possible, cut off and destroy the forward Union forces there under John Schofield, strike north to deal with Thomas in Nashville, and then join Lee in Virginia to turn the tables on Grant. It would be a desperate gamble, but if it succeeded it would more than neutralize Sherman's gains in the South's heartland. "The situation presented an occasion for one of those interesting and beautiful moves upon the chessboard of war," said Hood. ". . . I had beheld with admiration the . . . grand results achieved by . . . [Stonewall] Jackson in similar maneuvers; I had seen his corps made equal to ten times their number by a sudden attack on the enemy's rear. . . ."[1]

On November 21, with Nathan Bedford Forrest's cavalry in the van, Hood sent his three corps—those of Benjamin Cheatham (succeeding William Hardee), Alexander Stewart and Stephen Lee—into Tennessee. Forrest had some 6,000 men; Hood, 33,000. The Confederates forthwith advanced on Lawrenceburg, just west of Pulaski, where Schofield, commanding his own 23rd and David Stanley's 4th Corps, had his headquarters. Schofield, in addition to James Wilson's 5,000 cavalry, had 25,000 infantrymen. (Thomas, defending Nashville some sixty miles to the north with garrison troops, would not be reinforced by Andrew Jackson Smith's 11,000-man corps until month's end, though he did not know this at the time.)

Hood's target in Schofield's rear was Columbia on the Duck River. Divining this tactic, the Federals fell back there themselves on the more direct turnpike, beating the Rebels to the town and arriving on the 24th. "The season of Hood's invasion of Tennessee was extremely unfavorable for offensive operations," Schofield said, "and hence correspondingly favorable for the defense. The ordinary country roads were almost impassable, while the turnpikes were in good condition. . . . Hood was compelled to advance over . . . very bad roads."

Once in Columbia, Schofield threw up entrenchments on the south side of the river, hoping to hold the bridges and go on the offensive, if and when Thomas could come to his aid. The town and its environs were choked with unwilling conscripts, addled residents, and panic-stricken, newly emancipated blacks. The last named, noted one Michigan trooper, were understandably "fleeing from the advancing Rebel army as from a pestilence." Schofield's position was a strong one should Hood attack in his front, but he had the disadvantage of a river at his back. On the other hand, if he did move north of the Duck he would have to destroy the bridges, which would hamper future offensive operations. Moreover, the ground north of the river was low, and dominated by the opposite bank.[2]

For the next few days the situation remained in flux. Grant, of course, during this period and subsequently, was pushing Thomas and Schofield to be more aggressive. "It was still hoped," said Schofield, "that the line of Duck River might be held until reinforcements could arrive. General Thomas was very urgent that this should be done, if possible, as the arrival of General A. J. Smith's corps from Missouri [was] expected daily." Thomas then would "come to the front in person with that corps and all the other troops he could assemble . . . take command, and move against the enemy."

Complicating matters was a breakdown in communications. "The War Department telegraph corps alone was entrusted with the cipher in which General Thomas and I could communicate with each other," said Schofield. "Neither he, nor I . . . were permitted to know the telegraph code. The work was so badly done that from eight to forty-eight hours were occupied in sending and delivering a dispatch. Finally the cipher-operator attached to my headquarters . . . deserted his post. . . . From all this . . . it resulted that my superior at Nashville . . . was able to give me little assistance."[3]

In truth the balding and rotund Schofield, the son and grandson of ordained ministers, welcomed the chance to use his own discretion. A former classmate of Hood's at West Point, he had ranked first in infantry tactics, and thought himself an adept player at "the chessboard of war." Feeling himself vulnerable on the south bank, he crossed over the Duck on the 26th and burnt the bridges behind him, moving to a high ridge a mile and a half behind the shoreline. Even so, the relocation did not resolve his predicament. At 1:00 A.M. on the 29th James Wilson, posted with the cavalry east of Columbia, urgently informed Schofield that the enemy was fording the Duck around his left flank, again trying to cut him off from Nashville. Now Hood's target was the village of Spring Hill, just below Franklin on the Columbia-Franklin Turnpike. "I think it very clear [he] is aiming for Franklin," said Wilson, "and that you ought to get to Spring Hill by 10 A.M . . . Get back . . . without delay."[4]

For one reason or another, Schofield did not receive this dispatch until 7:00 A.M. Nor did he receive a dispatch from Thomas telling him to withdraw, this note being intercepted by Rebel cavalry. Caught between the necessity of blocking Hood's turning movement and following previous instructions from Thomas to hold his ground "if possible," Schofield compromised. He sent Stanley with elements of the 4th Corps—the divisions of Nathan Kimball and George Wagner—north to Spring Hill, but kept the rest of his force in place. Not until dark would he fully realize his danger and withdraw there in haste himself.

Stanley reached Spring Hill about 2:00 P.M. Colonel Henry Stone, an aide to General Thomas, gives us this picture: "On reaching the point where Rutherford Creek crosses the [Columbia-] Franklin Pike, Kimball's division was halted . . . and faced to the east to cover a possible attack from that quarter. . . . Stanley, with [Wagner's] division, pushed on to Spring Hill. . . . As the head of his column was approaching that place, he met [a cavalryman] who reported that . . . Forrest's cavalry was approaching from the east. The troops were at once double-quicked into the town, and the leading brigade, deploying as it advanced, drove off the enemy just as they were expecting, unmolested, to occupy the place. As the other brigades came up, they also were deployed, forming nearly a semicircle—[Emerson] Opdycke's brigade stretching in a thin line from the railroad station north of the village . . . and [John] Lane's from Opdycke's right to the pike below. [Luther] Bradley was sent to the front to occupy a knoll . . . commanding all the approaches from that direction."

Hardly had Wagner's three brigades—numbering no more than 4,000 men—been positioned when Bradley was assailed by the van of Hood's infantry. "At the same time," said Colonel Stone, "an attack was made on a small wagon train heading for Franklin; and a dash was made by a detachment of the Confederate cavalry on the Spring Hill Station. . . . It seemed as if the little band, attacked from all points, was threatened with destruction."

Bradley withstood two charges, but with considerable losses. "The third assault was more successful, and he was driven back to the edge of the village, Bradley himself receiving a disabling wound in rallying his men.

"While attempting to follow up this advantage, the enemy, in crossing a wide corn-field, was opened upon with spherical case-shot from eight guns posted on the knoll, and scattered in considerable confusion. These attacks undoubtedly came from [Pat] Cleburne's division, and were made under the eye of the corps commander, General Cheatham. . . . That they were not successful, particularly as the other divisions of the same corps, [John Calvin] Brown's and [William] Bate's, were close at hand . . . seems unaccountable. . . . Why Cleburne and Brown failed to drive away Stanley's one division before dark; why Bate failed to possess himself of the pike south of the town; why Forrest, with his audacious temper and his enterprising cavalry, did not fully hold Thompson's Station or the crossing of the West Harpeth, half-way to Franklin: these are to this day disputed questions among the Confederate commanders."[5]

The answers to these questions lie in the fact that Hood's communications on the 29th with his officers were as confused and delayed, or perhaps never received, as those of his adversaries. The division of the redoubtable Pat Cleburne did attack, to be sure, but received no help. Cheatham, new to corps command, at this juncture was proving irresolute. Brown and perhaps Bate, his other division heads, gave him reasonable-sounding excuses for *not* pushing forward that he chose not to override. Instead he rode back about 6:00 P.M. to Hood's headquarters, in gathering darkness, to discuss the situation and ask for further orders.

Here he found his superior in a rage. "General, why in the name of God have you not attacked the enemy and taken possession of that pike?" Hood asked. Cheatham reputedly replied that his line was too thin and he was waiting for Alexander Stewart's corps to come up and form on his right. "I could hardly believe it possible," Hood would say, "that this brave . . . soldier, who had given proof of such courage and ability upon so many hard-fought fields, would even make such a report."

Hood would likewise claim that later, about midnight on the 29th, when he learned that Schofield's troops were exiting Spring Hill and moving along the pike to Franklin, Cheatham was equally derelict in not throwing a line of skirmishers along the pike, "in order to throw the Federals into confusion, delay their march, and allow us a chance to attack in the morning. Nothing was done. The Federals, with immense wagon trains, were permitted to march by us the remainder of the night, within gunshot of our lines. I could not succeed in arousing the troops to action."

This curious state of affairs would not play out until days afterward, in early December, when Hood wired the War Department, asking that Cheatham be relieved and another officer assigned to his corps. "Before the receipt of a reply," said Hood, "[Cheatham] called at my headquarters . . . and, standing in my. presence, spoke an earnest avowal of his error, in the acknowledgement that he felt we had lost a brilliant opportunity at Spring Hill to deal the enemy a crushing blow, and that he was greatly to blame." Hood promptly withdrew his application for his wayward officer's removal. Cheatham, however, remembered the meeting differently: "On the morning of the 4th of December . . . I said to him: 'A great opportunity was lost at Spring Hill, but you know that I obeyed your orders there, as everywhere, literally and promptly.' General Hood not only did not dissent from what I said, but exhibited the most cordial manner. . . . The subject was never again alluded to. . . ."

Years later Isham G. Harris, the prewar governor of Tennessee, muddied the waters still further as to who was responsible for letting Schofield escape. "General Hood on the march to Franklin," he asserted, "in the presence of Major [A. P.] Mason"—an aide—". . . censured [Cheatham] in severe terms for his disobedience of orders. Soon after this, being alone with Major Mason, the latter remarked that 'General Cheatham was not to blame. . . . I did not send him the order.' I asked if he had [told this] to General Hood. He answered that he had not. I replied that 'it is due General Cheatham that this explanation be made." Mason thereupon informed his chief of the oversight. "Afterward General Hood said to me that he had done injustice to General Cheatham, and requested me to inform him that he held him blameless. . . ."[6]

Colonel Stone describes the arduous nature of the Union escape: "Just before midnight, Jacob Cox [leading the 3rd Division of the 23rd Corps] started from Spring Hill for Franklin and was ordered to pick up [Thomas Ruger's 2nd Division] at Thompson's Station. At 1 A.M. he was on the road, and the train, over five miles long, was drawn out. At the very outset it had to cross a bridge in single file. So difficult was this whole movement that it was five o'clock in the morning before the wagons were fairly underway. As the head of the train approached Thompson's Station, it was attacked by the Confederate cavalry, and for a while there was consternation."

Thomas Wood's division, 4th Corps, which had followed Cox from Duck River, was marched to the east of the pike to protect the train, and the enemy was driven off. "It was near daybreak when the last wagon left Spring Hill," said Stone. "Kimball's division followed Wood's, and at 4 o'clock Wagner drew in his lines, his skirmishers remaining till it was fairly daylight. The rearguard was commanded by Colonel Emerson Opdycke, who was prepared, if necessary, to sacrifice the last man to secure the safety of the main body. So efficiently did his admirable brigade do its work that, though surrounded by a cloud of the enemy's cavalry, not a straggler or a wagon was left behind."[7]

By noon on the 30th the bulk of the Federal army was entering Franklin, where Schofield decided to make a stand behind breastworks until nightfall, giving his wagons time to cross the Harpeth River on the way to Nashville. Opdycke and his division chief, George Wagner, in truth had done heroic work in bringing up the rear, but they nonetheless were feeling aggrieved. Opdycke was blaming Wagner for making his brigade do most of the division's dirty work during the retreat—not even permitting them breakfast or lunch the next morning—and Wagner was blaming the powers that be for his division bearing the brunt of the withdrawal. Both men had hair-trigger tempers, and when about 2:00 P.M. Opdycke refused Wagner's order to remain in a forward position outside the breastworks, their heated argument stopped just short of violence.

Opdycke marched his men inside the works, however, and a fuming Wagner settled for leaving his two other brigades, those of John Lane and Joseph Conrad (replacing the wounded Bradley), along the pike outside the town. This decision would be foolish in the extreme.

Colonel Stone continues: "As the bright autumn day, hazy with the golden light of an Indian summer wore away, the troops that had worked so hard looked forward to a prospect of ending it in peace and rest, preparatory either to a night march to Nashville, or reinforcement by Smith's corps and General Thomas." Then about 4:00 P.M. the situation became ominous. "In a very short time the whole Confederate line"—some 27,000 men—"could be seen, stretching in battle array, from the dark fringe of chestnuts along the river-bank, far across the Columbia Pike, the colors gaily fluttering, and the muskets gleaming brightly, and advancing steadily, in perfect order, dressed on the center, straight for the works." Hood was rolling the dice, assailing the Federals head-on, hoping to atone for failing to close the trap the night before.

Schofield at this juncture had moved across the Harpeth to supervise the transit operations, taking Stanley with him and leaving Jacob Cox in command at Franklin. "The whole field of operations was plainly visible," said Stone. "Notwithstanding the Rebel demonstrations, the two brigades of Wagner were left on the [forward] knoll where they had been halted, and, with scarcely an apology for works to protect them, had waited until it was too late to retreat."[8]

Such was not precisely true. Lane and Conrad, seeing their peril, had quickly sent a courier into the town, asking Wagner for permission to fall back. Still nettled by his confrontation with Opdycke, and possibly made even more bellicose by several glasses of whiskey, the division head brushed aside their concerns. "Go back," he said to the messenger, "and tell them to fight—and fight like hell!" Even a second messenger, insisting that Hood's whole army was descending on his outlying brigades, failed to sway him. Nor did Cox take positive action.

Within minutes Hood's gray-clad lines, spearheaded by Cleburne's division and by John Brown's unit, were swarming through and over Lane and Conrad's position. Captain John Shellenberger remembered that he and others in the 64th Ohio had time to fire only a few shots. Though his first instinct was "to throw myself flat on the ground and let them charge over us," self-preservation soon took over. "I shouted to my company, 'Fall back! Fall back!' and gave an example of how to do it by turning and running for the breastworks."[9]

Worst of all, the Federals in Franklin could not fire on the oncoming foe lest they shoot down their retreating comrades. "With loud shouts," Colonel Stone writes, ". . . the triumphant Confederates, now more like a wild, howling mob than an organized army, swept on to the very works, with hardly a check from any quarter." Now one of the new, untested regiments, seeing the troops in the forward position streaming to the rear, broke and ran. "The contagion spread . . . the guns, posted on each side of the Columbia Pike, were abandoned, and the works, for the space of a regimental front . . . were deserted. Into the gap thus made . . . swarmed the jubilant Confederates, urged on by Cleburne and Brown."

Here Opdycke's mostly Illinois brigade, refreshed and rested, and aided by the 12th and 16th Kentucky, rushed to the front and succeeded in regaining the works. "Opdycke's horse was shot from under him, and he fought on foot at the head of his brigade. General Cox was everywhere present. . . . General Stanley . . . from the fort where he had gone with

General Schofield . . . galloped to the front . . . and did all that a brave man could until he was painfully wounded. . . ."

Through these efforts the Rebel attack began to stall. "Where there was nothing to hinder the Union fire," said Stone, "the muskets of [Israel] Stiles' and [John] Casement's brigades [23rd Corps] made fearful havoc; while the batteries at the railroad cut plowed furrows through the ranks of the foe. Time after time they came up to the very works, but they never crossed. . . . More than one color-bearer was shot down on the parapet. It is impossible to exaggerate the fierce energy with which the Confederate soldiers . . . threw themselves against the works, fighting with what seemed the madness of despair."[10]

Nathan Bedford Forrest meanwhile sent his cavalry in a sweeping movement across the Harpeth to the north bank, hoping to catch Schofield's wagons unprotected. Met by determined Union troopers, even the storied Forrest was repulsed.

Rebel generals, leading their men, fell with rapidity. In Cheatham's corps and in others, the senior officers, perhaps rankling over Hood's displeasure back at Spring Hill, showed little regard for personal safety. Cleburne—the Stonewall Jackson of the West—died at the head of his division, as did Hiram Granbury, one of his brigadiers. The toll was even worse in John Brown's division: Brown was wounded; three brigadiers— States Rights Gist, John Carter, and Otho Strahl—were killed outright or mortally wounded; and a fourth, George Gordon, was captured. Cheatham's remaining division, that of William Bate, alone emerged with its leadership intact.

Alexander Stewart's corps, which with Cheatham's did most of the fighting, suffered similarly. Brigadier John Adams was killed, his horse astride the works; and Brigadiers Thomas Scott, Francis Cockrell, and William Quarles were severely wounded. In Stephen Lee's corps, Lee was wounded, as were Zachariah Deas and Arthur Manigault.

Hood would continue his unrelenting attacks, to no avail, until 9:00 P.M. Hours later, the Federal army would cross the river and withdraw toward Nashville. Of 27,000 men engaged at Franklin, the Confederates lost over 6,000; of 28,000 men engaged, Schofield suffered 2,300 casualties. Wagner later would be relieved for his obtuseness; Opdycke would be celebrated for his elan.

One historian of the Rebel Army of Tennessee compares Hood's charge at Franklin with that of Pickett's at Gettysburg, and shows that the former's was the bloodier and more difficult by far. Pickett's losses totaled some 1,350, Hood's over 6,000. Pickett's assault was made after a two-hour artillery barrage; the one at Franklin was made without any softening up. Pickett moved forward across a mile of open space; Hood's Army of Tennessee had to cover twice the distance. The Union forces at Gettysburg had only a low-lying stone wall for protection; Schofield's men had breastworks, complete with trenches and parapets. Pickett made his charge but once; Hood kept coming again and again, perhaps as many as thirteen times. "Pickett's charge at Gettysburg has come to be a synonym for unflinching courage in the raw," the historian writes. "The slaughter-pen at Franklin even more deserves the gory honor."[11]

Schofield would disagree that Hood was reckless: "Hood must have been aware of our relative weakness in numbers at Franklin"—actually the count of the men was about the same—"and of the probable, if not certain, concentration of large reinforcements at Nashville. He could not hope to have [in future] anything like so great an advantage in that respect. The army at Franklin and the troops at Nashville were within one night's march of each other. Hood must therefore attack on November 30. . . . It was impossible . . . in a short day to turn our position or make any attack but a direct one in front. Besides, our position, with the river in our rear, gave him the chance of greater result if his assault was successful. . . . The Confederate cause had reached a condition closely verging on desperation. . . ."[12]

During December 1 and the days that followed, Hood and Thomas paused to regroup—the former just south of Nashville and the Cumberland River, the latter within the city's breastworks. "The morning found [Schofield's] entire infantry force safe within the friendly shelter of the works," said Colonel Stone, ". . . where they welcomed the veterans of A. J. Smith, who were just arriving from Missouri. Soon after a body of about five thousand men came in from Chattanooga. . . . They were organized into a provisional division under General J. B. Steedman." Together with Wilson's cavalry, garrison troops and several miscellaneous units, Thomas's army now totaled some 50,000 men, twice the size of the foe.

To say that Hood was regrouping is a misnomer. The truth is he simply did not know what to do other than stand pat and throw up breastworks of his own. He had not the strength to threaten Thomas, or to sidestep him and push into Kentucky, and to withdraw back into Georgia was completely against his nature. He had failed to cut off Schofield while the Federals were dispersed. Now he chose to stand his ground, hoping that raw courage somehow would win out.

Thomas, who did not fully realize his huge numerical advantage, had reasons not to go on the offensive immediately. Perhaps three-quarters of Wilson's cavalry needed mounts or at least replacements; days would be consumed in scouring the countryside. Then, too, there was the need to integrate the various newly arrived commands. Schofield, who during the retreat to Nashville had led both the 23rd and 4th Corps, now reverted to command of the former. "General Stanley, still suffering from his wound, went North," said Stone, "and General [Thomas] Wood, who had been with it from the beginning, succeeded to command of the 4th Corps. General [Thomas] Ruger, who had [led] a division in the 23rd Corps, was also disabled by sickness, and was succeeded by [Darius] Couch . . . who had recently been assigned to duty in the Department of the Cumberland."

The unfortunate General Wagner was relieved, and Washington Elliott given his 4th Corps division. "General Kenner Garrard, who had commanded a cavalry division during the Atlanta Campaign, was assigned an infantry division in [A. J.] Smith's 16th Corps. In all these cases, except in that of General Wood . . . the newly assigned officers were entire strangers to the troops over whom they were placed."[13]

Thomas took care to inform Washington of what he was doing, but his reasoning fell on unsympathetic ears. Late on December 1 he wired Halleck that he would stay within the Nashville fortifications "until General Wilson can get his cavalry equipped. . . . If Hood attacks me here he will be more seriously damaged than he was yesterday." Lincoln and Stanton, reading these words, saw nothing but vacillation in them. Thinking Hood far stronger than he was, and fearing that he—backed up by Forrest— would create havoc in the West and endanger operations in the East, Stanton promptly wired Grant: "This looks like the McClellan and Rosecrans strategy of do nothing and let the Rebels raid the country. The President wishes you to consider the matter."[14]

Grant had high regard for Thomas, but thought him too cautious. To build a fire under him, he began to bombard his subordinate with increasingly impatient instructions. On December 2: "If Hood is permitted to remain quietly about Nashville, you will lose all the [rail]road back to Chattanooga and possibly have to abandon the line of the Tennessee. . . ." Again on December 2: "You will suffer incalculable injury upon your railroads if Hood is not speedily disposed of. Put forth therefore every possible exertion to attain this end." On December 5: "It seems to me whilst you should be getting up your cavalry . . . to look after Forrest, Hood should be attacked where he is. Time strengthens him . . . as much as it does you." On December 6: "Attack Hood at once and wait no longer for a remnant of your cavalry. . . ."

Thomas still delayed. Outfitting the cavalry with new mounts was integral to his plan for cutting off Hood's line of retreat, and he would not be hurried. Finally Grant wired Halleck, saying: "You probably saw my order to Thomas to attack. If he does not do it promptly, I would recommend superceding him by Schofield." To which Halleck replied: "If you wish Thomas relieved . . . give the order. No one here will, I think, interfere." Though the War Department orders were cut, they were never issued, Grant evidently deciding to give Thomas—the famed "Rock of Chickamauga"—one more chance. Influencing the general-in-chief at the juncture, December 9, was that freezing rain was turning the ground around Nashville into a sheet of ice, making maneuvers all but impossible. Instead Halleck sent Schofield this wire: "Lieutenant-General Grant expresses much dissatisfaction at your delay in attacking the enemy. . . ." To which Thomas replied, in a wire directly to Grant: "I have done everything in my power to prepare, and if you should deem it necessary to relieve me I shall submit without a murmur."[15]

With Thomas's future hanging by a thread, Grant over the next few days later sent him words both of encouragement and warning: "I have as much confidence in your conducting a battle rightly as I have in any other officer, but it has seemed to me you have been slow. . . ." He brought up the order that had been cut for Thomas's removal, saying it had been suspended, and "I hope most sincerely that there will be no necessity of repeating [it], and that the facts will show you have been right all the time." Thomas replied, respectfully, that the ice storm precluded attack. Grant's last wire, on December 14, was terse: "Delay no longer for weather or reinforcements."

The general-in-chief, frustrated by what he perceived as Thomas's continuing obstinacy, and possibly by his own failure to take Richmond and Petersburg, now took steps to replace his subordinate. "General [John] Logan, happening to visit City Point [in Virginia] about that time, and knowing him as a prompt, gallant and efficient officer, I gave him an order to proceed to Nashville to relieve Thomas. I directed him, however, not to deliver the order or publish it until he got there, and if Thomas had moved, then not to deliver it at all. . . ."[16]

That same day, December 14, the freezing conditions at Nashville broke. Wired Thomas to Halleck: "The ice having melted away today, the enemy will be attacked tomorrow morning." Key to the Civil War in the West, the two-day assault that followed would be as decisive as Sheridan's in the Shenandoah, wiping out the substantive Rebel presence in Tennessee.

The action on the 15th began with a demonstration by Steedman on

Hood's right, even as Smith's corps attacked the enemy's left, and Wood's corps advanced in the center. "The plan . . . was for General Steedman, on the extreme left, to move out early in the morning, threatening the Rebel right," said Colonel Stone, "while the cavalry, which had been placed on the extreme right, and A. J. Smith's corps were to make a grand left wheel with the entire right wing, assaulting and, if possible, overlapping the left of Hood's position. Wood was to form the pivot for this wheel . . . while General Schofield was to be held in reserve."

Steedman pushed forward in the early morning, under cover of a fog that hid all movements, making his way toward the Murfreesboro Pike. "It was not intended as a real attack, though it had effect," said Stone. "Two of Steedman's brigades, chiefly colored troops, kept two divisions of Cheatham's corps constantly busy, while his third was held in reserve; thus one Confederate corps was disposed of. S. D. Lee's corps, next on Cheatham's left, after sending two brigades to the assistance of A. P. Stewart, on the [far] Confederate left, was held in place by the threatening position of the garrison troops, and did not fire a shot during the day. Indeed, both Cheatham's and Lee's corps were held, as in a vise, between Steedman and Wood."

By 10:00 A.M. the winter sun had burned away the fog, making the salient that was the Rebel left-center on Montgomery Hill, held by Stewart opposite Wood, clearly visible some 600 yards distant. Meanwhile Wilson's cavalry, many of the troopers dismounted, and Smith's corps were enveloping the Rebel left near the Hillsboro Pike, though the wet, swampy ground was substantially delaying their progress. Wilson would have his own way during the battle, Hood having unaccountably sent Forrest and most of his own cavalry off foraging and raiding.

Soon it was 1:00 P.M. "[Sydney] Post's brigade of Wood's old division [now commanded by General Sam Beatty], which lay at the foot of Montgomery Hill . . . had since morning been regarding the works at the summit with covetous eyes," continued Stone. "At Post's suggestion, it was determined to see which party wanted them most. . . . A charge was ordered—and in a moment the brigade was swarming up the hillside, straight for the enemy's advanced works. . . . The color-bearers and those who kept up with them, Post himself at the head, leaped the parapet. As the colors waved from the summit, the whole line swept forward, and was over the works in a twinkling."

Farther to the Confederate left the battle likewise was joined. "[Edward] Hatch's division of Wilson's cavalry . . . was confronted by one of the detached works which Hood had intended to be 'impregnable'; and the right of [John] McArthur's division of A. J. Smith's infantry was also within striking distance of it," said Stone. "[Datus] Coon's cavalry brigade was dismounted and was ordered to assault . . . while [Sylvester] Hill's infantry brigade received similar orders." Though the two commanders took the redoubt, Hill fell dead with a bullet in the forehead. Soon the enemy on that front also was fleeing to the rear. To extend the Union right still more, and give the cavalry even more latitude, Schofield now came up on Smith's right.[17]

It already was 4:00 P.M. The Rebel left was crumbling, but the salient at the center still held. Post's assault had merely driven out or captured the advance line; the main fortifications were intact. Wood at this juncture sent Nathan Kimball's division forward. To make better time across the muddy cornfield that separated them from Stewart's lines, Kimball's men dropped their knapsacks and anything else that might slow them. Shouting like demons, they surged toward the works. Joining in the attack was Washington Elliott's division, led by Opdycke's brigade. Here Lieutenant William Hall of the 36th Illinois, moving with a score of men toward one of the redoubts, noticed that the enemy fire was slackening.

"Now, boys, is the time!" he cried. "I believe we can take that Rebel fort—the Johnnies are more than half whipped! How many of you are ready to go in?"

With screams that chilled the blood Hall's men pushed forward and into the redoubt, killing or capturing the occupants. Everywhere the Federals on the left and in the center similarly were triumphant. "The enemy was driven out with a loss of guns, colors and prisoners," summed up Colonel Stone, "and their whole line was forced to abandon the works along the Hillsboro Pike and fall back to the Granny White Pike. The retreating line was followed by the entire 4th Corps [Wood's], as well as by the cavalry and Smith's troops; but night soon fell, and the whole army went into bivouac in the open fields wherever they chanced to be."[18]

The next day, December 16, found Hood two miles back from his former position, with his lines much shortened. His left was on Shy's Hill and his right on Overton Hill, protecting the Granny White Pike to the west and the Franklin Pike to the east respectively—his principal means of retreat. Why he fought for a second day we will never know, but perhaps it is a measure of the man.

Once again Thomas's plan was to turn the Confederate left, using Schofield and Wilson's cavalry to cut both pikes and catch the enemy in a pincer. The greater part of the day was wasted, however, with Schofield—perhaps haunted by Hood's frantic charge at Franklin—dragging his feet and unreasonably calling for reinforcements, and Wilson accordingly held in place. The delay permitted the impatient Wood, on the Confederate right, to take matters in his own hands at 3:30 P.M. and launch an assault on Overton Hill. His chosen instrument was the aforementioned Colonel Sydney Post, a fierce fighter who this day would win the Medal of Honor. "The brigade was to be supported by fresh troops to be held in readiness to rush the works the moment Post should gain the parapet," said Colonel Stone. ". . . The men dashed on, Post leading, with all speed through a shower of shot and shell. . . . The main line came within twenty steps of the works when, by a concentrated fire of musketry . . . the advance was momentarily checked and, in another instant, Post was brought down by a wound. . . . The leader and animating spirit gone, the line drifted back to its original position, losing in a few minutes nearly 300 men; while the supporting brigade on its left lost 250."

On Post's right the 2nd Colored Brigade of Colonel Charles Thompson, new to combat, suffered even more severely. "As they advanced they became excited," said Stone, "and what was intended as merely a demonstration was converted into an actual assault. . . . But, in their advance across the open field, the continuity of [Thompson's] line was broken by a large fallen tree. As the men separated to pass it, the enemy opened up an enfilading fire on the exposed flanks of the gap thus created, with telling effect. . . . Nothing was left, therefore, but to withdraw as soon as possible to the original position." Thompson's brigade lost 467 men.

Back on the Rebel left at Shy's Hill, Wilson's largely dismounted cavalry now was sweeping in a wide arc and effecting a lodgment on the Granny White Pike, threatening the enemy's rear. "In the midst of the heaviest fighting," Wilson said, "one of our detachments captured a courier from Hood, carrying a dispatch to [James] Chambers"—leading the enemy's sole cavalry division—"directing him 'For God's sake . . . drive the Yankee cavalry from our left and rear or all is lost.'" Wilson sent the note at once to Thomas, then "sent three staff officers, one after the other, urging Schofield to attack the enemy in front and finish up the day's work. . . . But nothing whatever was done as yet . . . to support my movement."[19]

Wilson galloped to Thomas's headquarters, where he found him conferring with Schofield on a knoll, from which both the Rebel defenses and the encircling cavalry to the south could plainly be seen. "I urged Thomas, with ill-concealed impatience," said Wilson, "to order the infantry forward without further delay. Still the stately chieftain was unmoved." Thomas remained hesitant, giving credence to Schofield's contention that a frontal attack against Hood's works would end in disaster. Here John McArthur, commanding one of Smith's divisions on Schofield's left, took the initiative at 4:00 P.M. and sounded the charge, unleashing William McMillan's 1,500-man brigade on Shy Hill's north face. McMillan's success was immediate, as some of Hood's men battled bravely but more fled for their lives—and it revealed how low the morale of the Army of Tennessee had fallen.

Thomas now committed himself, and all the nearby Union forces converged on Shy's Hill and its environs. "Wilson had gone in person to Thomas, to report what his men were doing," said Jacob Cox, one of Schofield's division heads, "and reached him just as McMillan's brigade was seen to rush forward upon the slope of Shy's Hill. At a sign from Schofield, [my] division started also on the run, [Charles] Doolittle's brigade in advance. Wilson turned to gallop back to his command, but before he got halfway there, the whole Confederate left was crushed like an egg-shell. . . . The arch was broken; there were no reserves to restore it, and from right to left the [enemy] peeled away from the works in wild confusion."[20]

Though Thomas sought to pursue his advantage, oncoming darkness brought most of the action to a close. Of 50,000 Federals involved, 3,000 were killed, wounded, and missing. Of 23,000 Confederates, perhaps 1,500 were killed and wounded, and 4,500 captured. By Civil War standards the casualties, for a major battle, were minor. This may have been because so many of Hood's men fled; it may have been because Thomas's men, at this stage of the war, were prudent. That night an exultant Thomas encountered Wilson on one of the roads. "Dang it to hell, Wilson, didn't I tell you we could lick 'em, didn't I tell you we could lick 'em?" he enthused. "This has been a splendid day," was the ambiguous answer. The blow to the Rebels, Wilson obviously thought, should have been delivered earlier and been mortal.

Hood no longer was a presence in the West. Heartsick and weary, he withdrew the remnants of his shattered army across the Tennessee and into northern Alabama. To the tune of "The Yellow Rose of Texas" he endured the withdrawal with his men singing, in part, a double-edged refrain: "But the gallant Hood of Texas played hell in Tennessee." Less than a month later, he resigned. "He might command a brigade, and even a division," one disgruntled officer said of the man who fought so well from Gaines Mill to Gettysburg to Chattanooga, "but to command an army, he is not the man. . . . [To] call him a general is a disgrace . . . to those generals . . . who are worthy to be so called."[21]

Hood, understandably, saw matters differently. "I therefore determined to move upon Nashville, to intrench, to accept the chances of reinforcements from Texas," he would say of his campaign, "and even at the risk of an attack in the meantime by overwhelming numbers, to adopt the only feasible means of defeating the enemy . . . to await his attack and if favored by success, to follow him in his own works." Of the panic on the 16th, he had this to say: "I beheld, for the first and only time a Confederate army abandon the field in confusion. I was seated upon my horse . . . when the breach was effected, and soon discovered that all hope to rally the troops was vain. I did not . . . anticipate a break at that time, as our forces had repulsed the Federals at every point, and were waving their colors in defiance, crying out to the enemy, 'Come on, come on!'"

In the aftermath of Nashville, Hood was both uncomprehending and inconsolable. Earlier in the war he had suffered both a mangled arm and an amputated leg, but now his psychic scars were far deeper. "He was much agitated and affected," remembered one soldier, "pulling his hair with his one [good] hand, and crying like his heart would break." To the end of his life, he never realized he had lost his troops' confidence. His supporters could only mourn.[22]

1865

ONE

* * * *

MOVING UP THE CAROLINAS

In mid-January, just before he would begin his march up the Carolinas, Sherman in Savannah received a visit from Secretary of War Stanton, who had come under political pressure to investigate his treatment of the newly freed blacks. The secretary instructed him to set up a meeting with a score of black leaders, mostly Baptist and Methodist preachers, and then asked a series of probing questions. When the subject came around to Sherman, he asked him to leave the room. "It certainly was a strange fact," Cump would huff, "that the great War Secretary should have catechized Negroes concerning the character of a general who had . . . conducted sixty-five thousand men successfully across four hundred miles of hostile territory, and just brought tens of thousands of freedmen to a place of security; but just because I had not loaded down my army with . . . poor Negroes, I was construed by others as hostile to the black race."

The blacks, however, gave Sherman high marks: "His conduct and deportment toward us characterized him as a friend and gentleman. We have confidence in General Sherman, and think what concerns us could not be in better hands. This is our opinion now, from the short acquaintance . . . we have had." Remarked Sherman: "They understood their own interests far better than did the men in Washington."

Further discussions between Sherman and Stanton followed as to what specifically could be done to ease the plight of blacks in Georgia and South

Carolina, with the result that Cump, with considerable input from the secretary, published Field Order No. 15. Wrote one of Sherman's biographers: "In this statement, Sherman set aside the abandoned lands on the Sea Islands off Georgia and South Carolina for the former slaves, prohibiting any whites, except official personnel, from going there. He encouraged young black males to enlist in the army, promising they would receive their land after the war. It was a revolutionary document, and it is ironic that someone with Sherman's antiblack attitudes should have issued it. But once he promulgated it . . . he did nothing to further its implementation."[1]

More to Sherman's liking was the military and naval support Grant would be providing him. To ease Cump's logistical problems the general-in-chief in January sent the cooperative Admiral Porter, together with 8,000 troops under Alfred Terry of the Army of the James, to capture Fort Fisher in North Carolina. (Political General Benjamin Butler had botched the first attempt to take it, and at long last been relieved of command.) The fort's batteries protected Wilmington, the last important East Coast port still in Confederate hands. Taking it would ensure a forward supply base. "Terry was [told] to communicate freely with Porter and to have entire harmony between army and navy," Grant said, "because the work before them would require the best efforts of both arms of the service."

Fort Fisher, a series of redoubts in the shape of an inverted L, was located on a flat peninsula between the Cape Fear River and the Atlantic. Terry's force landed some five miles to the north on the 13th, then pushed toward the citadel. Admiral Porter's immense fleet, some forty-eight ships in all, meanwhile began a two-day bombardment. By January 15 all was ready for the assault. "The two commanders arranged their signals so they could communicate with each other . . . as they might have occasion," said Grant. "At daylight the fleet [resumed] its firing. The time agreed upon . . . was the middle of the afternoon, and [Adelbert] Ames who commanded the [lead] column moved at 3:30. Porter landed a force of sailors and marines to move against the sea-front in cooperation . . . but [they] were repulsed and very badly handled."

The landside attack proved more fruitful. "[Newton] Curtis' brigade [of Ames's division] charged successfully though met by a heavy fire, some of the men having to wade through the swamp up to their waists. . . . Many were wounded . . . and some killed; but they soon reached the palisades. These they cut way."

More troops came up, taking the parapet. "But the fort was not yet captured," Grant continued. "Traverses . . . had been run until really the work was a succession of small forts enclosed by a large one. The

Rebels . . . had to be driven from these traverses one by one. . . . The fight continued till long after night. . . . The fleet kept up a continuous fire on that part of the fort which was still occupied by the enemy. By means of signals they could be informed where to direct their shots." Fort Fisher surrendered about 10:00 P.M., making the fall of Wilmington only a question of time.[2]

Just as importantly, Grant brought Schofield's 23rd Corps back from Tennessee to pressure the enemy from the North while Sherman was coming up from the South. Bolstered by Terry's men, garrison troops, and conscripts, this force would number some 30,000. In the near future it would occupy Wilmington, then shift its base to New Bern (which had been in Federal hands since 1862), and ultimately join forces with Cump at Goldsboro, North Carolina. "If Wilmington is captured, Schofield will go there," Grant told Sherman on the 21st. "If not, he will be sent to New Bern. In either event, all the surplus forces at the two points will move to the interior toward Goldsboro in cooperation with your movements. . . . All these troops are subject to your orders as you come in communication with them."[3]

Sherman began his march February 1, pushing inland in the direction of Columbia, South Carolina, the state capital, and bypassing Charleston, which the enemy soon would evacuate. His 60,000-man army was organized in much the same way it was when leaving Atlanta. The Left Wing under Henry Slocum was composed of Jefferson C. Davis's 14th Corps and Alpheus Williams's 20th Corps; the Right Wing under Oliver Howard consisted of John Logan's 15th Corps and Frank Blair's 17th Corps. Judson Kilpatrick's cavalry rode on Slocum's left. The division chiefs were seasoned soldiers. Under Davis were William Carlin, James Dada Morgan, and Absalom Baird; under Williams were John Geary, William Ward, and Nathaniel Jackson. Logan's division heads were Charles Woods, William Hazen, John Eugene Smith, and John M. Corse; Blair's subordinates were Joseph Mower, Manning Force, and Giles Smith.

Opposing this confident array would be a ragtag force under General Pierre Beauregard—William Hardee's corps, Joseph Wheeler's horsemen, South Carolina and Georgia militia and cavalry, and elements of the Army of Tennessee, somewhat less than 22,000 men.

Despite the relative lack of resistance—the Rebels usually melting away from various strongpoints as the Federals approached, in many cases burning bridges as they fled—the march from the start was arduous and the landscape bleak. Heavy rains flooded the waterways and collapsed the roads, and Sherman's men pillaged and foraged with even more abandon than they had shown in Georgia. "We seemed to strike rivers, large streams, and great swamps nearly every day, separated by only a few miles," said one New York sergeant. Those plantation houses and dwellings that were not burned to the ground, he added, were gutted and ransacked. "The grudge held against South Carolina and her people by many soldiers was intense, [and] many times they ruthlessly destroyed property when they heard it belonged to an active secessionist. They excused their actions by saying they wished such people to suffer. . . ."

Early on the 7th, in the midst of a rainstorm, the army reached Midway and subsequently severed the Georgia Railroad, which connected Augusta with Charleston. Here General Howard, deploying his leading division in anticipation of a fight, saw a man galloping toward him, riding as hard as he could. Howard recognized him as one of his foragers, mounted on a white horse with a rope for a bridle and laden with food.

"Hurry up, General; we have got the railroad!" the man yelled.

Howard had to laugh, realizing that as he was preparing for battle his foragers, in search of plunder, had gone ahead into the town and found it defenseless.

"We all remained strung along this railroad [for two days]," said Sherman. ". . . Kilpatrick was ordered to demonstrate strongly toward Aiken, to keep up the delusion that we might turn to Augusta; but he was notified that Columbia was the next objective, and that he should cover the left flank against Wheeler, who hung around it. I wanted to reach Columbia before any part of Hood's army could possibly get there."[4]

On the march progressed. The night of February 16 the Right Wing camped on the Congaree River opposite Columbia, near a former prison bivouac called Camp Sorghum, where the mud hovels remained that captured Federals once had used for shelter. Remembered Sherman: "The 15th Corps was then ahead, reaching to Broad River, about four miles above Columbia; the 17th Corps was behind, on the [Congaree]; and the Left Wing and cavalry had turned north toward Alston." The next day, unopposed, he entered the city with elements of the 15th Corps, accompanied by Generals Howard, Logan, Woods, and a retinue of aides. "Near the market-place we found [G. A.] Stone's brigade halted, with arms stacked, and a large detail of his men, along with some citizens, trying to put out the fire in a long line of burning cotton bales, which I was told had been fired by the Rebel cavalry on withdrawing. . . ."

Later he was met by the mayor, who declared Columbia an open city, and begged him not to sack it. Sherman, by his own account, replied that only arsenals and government buildings, the railroad line, and machine shops would be destroyed. "I told him then not to be uneasy, that we did not intend to stay long, and had no purpose to injure the private citizens or private property." The rest of the day and evening was spent on tedious inspections and meetings, and with the coming of darkness an exhausted Sherman returned to his billet and went to bed.

Bright lights flickering on the walls of his room soon awakened him, and he sent an aide for more information. "He reported that the block of buildings directly opposite the burning cotton of that morning was on fire, and that it was spreading. . . . The fire continued to increase, and the whole heavens became lurid. I dispatched messenger after messenger to Generals Howard, Logan and Woods, and received from them repeated assurances that all was being done that could be done, but that high wind was spreading the flames beyond control."

Sherman about 11:00 P.M. went downtown to see the blaze for himself. "The whole air was full of sparks and of flying masses of cotton, shingles, etc. some of which were carried four or five blocks, and started new fires. The men seemed generally under good control, and certainly labored hard to girdle the fire . . . but, so long as the high wind prevailed, it was simply beyond human possibility. . . . Fortunately, about 3 or 4 A.M. the wind moderated, and the fire was got under control; but it had burned out the very heart of the city. . . ."[5] In the aftermath, 30,000 people were homeless.

This account, while accurate, is notable for what it leaves out. That the enemy cavalry originally ignited the cotton is true; that Union discipline subsequently broke down is also true. Major Thomas Osborn, chief artillery officer for the Army of the Tennessee, gives us the full picture of what happened when Charles Woods's division, Logan's 15th Corps, marched into Columbia: "When the [first] brigade occupied the town the citizens and Negroes brought out whiskey in buckets, bottles, and in every conceivable manner treated the men to all they would drink. The men were very much worn and tired and drank freely . . . and the entire brigade became drunk. The enemy had taken the cotton out of the storehouses . . . and set it on fire, which the citizens and soldiers, when we entered, were trying to subdue and had nearly accomplished. But when they became thoroughly intoxicated they began to . . . plunder freely."

Then the wind sprang up, reigniting the flames in the smoldering bales—with help from soldiers holding lighted cigars to the cotton. Forthwith the flames spread to nearby buildings. "By this time all parties were willing to assist [the blaze]. . . . The Negroes piloted the men to the best places for plunder, and both men and Negroes by nightfall were setting fires rapidly. . . . It was well in the evening before the fire gained its greatest height. The first brigade was relieved. . . . The second brigade was also relieved, as they had also become intoxicated. The third brigade was put to work to stop the fire, and consequently were held in better control. They were not allowed to stop long enough to demoralize."

Before the night was over, substantially more Federal soldiers would be required to clear the city of their drunken comrades. "They arrested all the men on the street and frequently had to use force," said Osborn, "and many would not be arrested and were shot. *Forty* of our men were killed in this way, many were wounded, and several . . . drunk men were burned to death."[6]

Major Henry Hitchcock, one of Sherman's aides, likewise cited liquor as the cause of the fire, but blamed Columbia's townspeople for providing it. "[The city] was not burned by orders," he told his wife, "but expressly against orders and in spite of the utmost effort on our part to save it. The streets were full of loose cotton, brought out and set on fire *by the Rebels* before they left. . . . The citizens themselves—like idiots, madmen—brought out large quantities of liquor as soon as our troops entered and distributed it freely among them, even to the guards which Gen. Howard had placed all over the city. . . . Besides there were 200 or 300 of 'our prisoners' who had escaped from Rebel hands before, and when we reached Columbia [they were] burning to revenge themselves for the cruel treatment they had received; and our own men were fully aware of the claims of Columbia to eminence as the 'cradle of secession.'"

Regardless of who or what was responsible for the horrendous conflagration, which shocked the South, there is little question but that Sherman's slash-and-burn tactics, which he had been using since leaving Atlanta, had filtered down into the ranks, hardening his soldiers' hearts against the civilian populace. Captain Charles Wills of the 103rd Illinois, Woods's division, a realistic man we have met before, was far more troubled by the army's boozing than the fact the city was being leveled. "Whiskey and wine flowed like water," he observed, "and the whole division is now drunk. This gobbling of things so, disgusts me much. I think the city should be burned, but would like to see it done decently."[7]

On the army pushed, taking Cheraw, South Carolina, March 5. "The enemy did not attempt to oppose us," said Captain Wills. "The boys say that an intercepted dispatch . . . reads: 'Do not attempt to delay Sherman's march by destroying bridges, or any other means. For God's sake's let him get out of the country as quickly as possible.' Were I one of the S.C. chivalry I'd be in favor of turning out en masse and building up roads for him." Reported Sherman: "Cheraw was found to be full of stores which had been sent up from Charleston prior to its evacuation. . . . Having thus secured the passage of the [Pee Dee River], I felt no uneasiness about the future, because there remained no further great impediment between us and the Cape Fear River, which I felt assured was by that time in the possession of our friends." Before leaving the town he sampled some choice wine at a midday meal.

"Do you like it?" asked General Blair, his host.

"He afterward sent to my bivouac a dozen bottles of the finest Madeira I ever tasted, and I learned that he had captured . . . the wine of some old aristocratic families of Charleston, who has sent it up to Cheraw for safety."[8]

Sherman was correct in thinking that Schofield's supporting force was in control of the Cape Fear and Wilmington. Just about this time, too, there were changes in the Confederate command structure. Beauregard was superceded in the Carolinas by our old friend Joe Johnston, who was highly respected by Lee—newly named as general-in-chief—and restored to duty. The badly outnumbered Johnston would send 8,500 men into a series of delaying actions at Kinston, North Carolina, March 7 to 10, but these would be the last roadblocks in Schofield's path as he and his troops moved inland from Wilmington and New Bern toward the juncture at Goldsboro.

Meanwhile Sherman, prior to making that rendezvous, moved March 11 on Fayetteville, North Carolina. Here some of his foragers, who as one might expect were despised by the enemy, came to grief. "There were about 1,000 Rebel cavalry herein who fell back before our boys skirmishing lively, clear through the town," said Wills, "when they suddenly charged our [foragers] and scooped them [up]. . . . They killed several after they captured them, and one they hung up by the heels and cut his throat. Our boys retreated about a mile from town, and went in again in more solid order. . . . They were successful and routed Johnny, who left six dead in the streets."

The Federals burned the Rebel arsenal and storehouses, together with a score of other buildings, pillaged and confiscated, and then regrouped. "We send from here all the Negroes and white refugees who have been following us, also a large train to Wilmington for supplies," continued

Wills. "The number of Negroes"—whose presence, it must be said, some Union soldiers deeply resented—"is estimated at 15,000. . . . Last night while we were standing around fires by the river, some scoundrel went up to a Negro not 75 yards from us, and with one whack of a bowie knife, cut the contraband's head one-third off, killing him."[9]

From Fayetteville, via steamboat on the Cape Fear River, Sherman reestablished communication with Washington and with Grant. "The army is in splendid health, condition and spirits," he wrote his chief on the 12th, "though we have had foul weather, and roads that would have stopped travel to almost any other body of men I ever heard of. Our march was substantially what I designed. . . . I could leave here tomorrow, but want to clear my columns of the vast number of refugees and Negroes that encumber us. Some I will send down the river in boats, and the rest to Wilmington by land. . . . Jos. Johnston may try to interpose between me here and Schofield [at] New Bern, but I think he will not do that, but concentrate his scattered armies. . . . I expect to make a junction with General Schofield in ten days."

Sherman was mistaken that Johnston would not strike before the two Federal armies converged at Goldsboro. On March 16 his Left Wing under Henry Slocum encountered serious resistance at Averasboro, where Hardee with 11,000 men tried to surprise three times their number. "Our formation had hardly been completed," said Sergeant Bull of the 123rd New York, Williams's 20th Corps, "when from our right and front a body of Kilpatrick's cavalry that had been located on our right flank . . . came down on us in retreat, the yelling Rebels close behind them. We got there just in time to prevent a flanking force getting in the rear of our line. As soon as the cavalry had moved from our front we opened fire and had little trouble stopping [them]." Now Bull and his comrades advanced "and the enemy was driven back into entrenchments. . . . It was nearly dark and our line was halted and we began to build breastworks. . . ." By morning, however, the Confederates had silently stolen away.[10]

More critical was the fight in front of nearby Bentonville, which began on Sunday, March 19. Again Johnston—this time with Hardee, Stewart, and Bragg, perhaps 21,000 men—would assail Slocum's Left Wing, in the desperate hope he could rout it before Howard's force could come to its aid. The Federals were largely unprepared for the attack. Slocum believed there was only cavalry in his front, and so informed Sherman by messenger. Cump for his part did not think that the cautious Johnston, with the Neuse River at his back, would roll the dice.

Slocum learned the truth of the matter about midday, when an emaciated young man dressed in Confederate gray, claiming that Johnston was readying a major assault, was brought before him. "He said he had been in the Union army, had been taken prisoner, and while sick and in prison had been induced to enlist in the Confederate service," recounted Slocum. ". . . While I was talking with him, one of my aides . . . rode up and at once recognized [him] as an old acquaintance . . . I asked [the informer] how he knew Johnston was in command and what he knew as to the strength of his force."

He had seen Johnston riding along the Rebel line that very morning, the man replied, and all the officers were saying that "Old Joe" had caught one of Sherman's wings beyond the reach of support, and that they would smash that wing first and then go for the other one.

Slocum continues: "While [the informer] was making his statement, General [William] Carlin's division with four pieces of artillery became engaged with the enemy. A line for defense was at once selected, and as the troops came up they were placed in position and ordered to collect fence-rails and everything else available for barricades. The men used their tin cups and hands as shovels, and needed no urging to induce them to work. I regretted that I had sent the message to General Sherman assuring him I needed no help, and saw the necessity of giving him the [new] information at once."

While this second messenger was galloping off, Slocum evaluated his situation. "Carlin's division of the 14th Corps had the advance, and as the enemy had exhibited more than usual strength, he had deployed [it]. . . . [James] Morgan's division of the same corps had been deployed on Carlin's right. Colonel H. G. Litchfield, inspector general of the corps, had accompanied these troops. I was consulting with General Jeff. C. Davis, who commanded the 14th Corps, when Colonel Litchfield rode up and, in reply to my inquiry as to what he had found . . . said, 'I have found something more than . . . cavalry—I find infantry intrenched along our whole front, and enough of them to give us all the amusement we shall want for the rest of the day.' "[11]

The most forceful Confederate blow was struck about 3:00 P.M., when Johnston ordered his right under Hardee to move behind concealing woods to turn Carlin's left, throwing some of the Federals into a panic. One New York private confessed his comrades "lost the bonds of discipline and the power to reason." They fell back almost a mile before regaining their composure. There the 14th Corps rallied on the 20th Corps, forming a new line in a thick pine forest, and the Rebels were repulsed in turn. "The enemy fought bravely," Slocum said, "but their line had become somewhat broken in advancing through the woods and, when they came up to [ours], they received a fire which compelled them to fell back. The assaults were repeated over and over again until a late hour, each assault finding us better prepared for resistance."[12]

By the next day, both Union wings were reunited, and Sherman was in perfect position to initiate—and win—a bloody battle. But he did not, perhaps because his scorched-earth tactics had been working so well. Why sacrifice lives in frontal assaults, he may have reasoned, when the enemy can be defeated by burning and razing the countryside. "I would rather avoid a general battle, if possible," he told Slocum. Meanwhile he received messages from Schofield, at Kinston, and Terry, marching up from Wilmington, that both would be in Goldsboro imminently. "During the 20th," he said, "we simply held our ground. . . . The next day (the 21st) it began to rain again, and we remained quiet till about noon, when General [Joe] Mower, forever rash, broke through the Rebel line on his extreme left flank and was pushing straight for Bentonville and the bridge across Mill Creek. I ordered him back. . . . preferred to make junction with Generals Terry and Schofield before engaging Johnston's army. . . . The next day he was gone (moving west into North Carolina) and, the roads being clear, our army moved to Goldsboro."[13]

Bentonville, however, was not fought without the usual casualties. Federal losses were some 1,600; Confederate, 2,600. On the night of the 19th, the Union surgeons did their gory but necessary work at an improvised field hospital. "A dozen surgeons and attendants in their shirt sleeves stood at rude benches cutting off arms and legs and throwing them out of the window where they lay scattered on the grass," said a witness. "The legs of the infantrymen could be distinguished from those of the cavalry by the size of their calves."[14]

Sherman's movement up the Carolinas, covering 425 miles in some fifty days, was an even greater feat than his March to the Sea. "The route traversed embraced five large navigable rivers, viz., the Edisto, Broad, Catawba, Pee Dee, and Cape Fear," he said, "at either of which a comparatively small force, well handled, should have made the passage most difficult. . . . The country generally was in a state of nature, with innumerable swamps, with simple mud roads, nearly every mile of which had to be corduroyed. In our route we had captured Columbia, Cheraw and Fayetteville, important cities and depots of supplies, had compelled the evacuation of Charleston . . . had utterly broken up all the railroads of South Carolina, and had consumed a vast amount of food and forage, essential to the enemy for the support of his own armies."

Though his men were in rags, with their uniforms tattered from the journey, their spirits were high and their bodies sound. As he watched his troops filing into Goldsboro, North Carolina, Sherman could not have been prouder. When an officer expressed concern that their legs could be seen through their torn trousers, he brushed the comment aside. "Splendid legs, splendid legs," he said. "Would give both of mine for any one of them."

To his friend and superior Grant, he would write of Bentonville and his army's condition: "Last night [Johnston] retreated, leaving us in possession of the field, dead, and wounded. We have over 2,000 prisoners from this affair and the one at Averasboro, and I am satisfied that Johnston's army was so roughly handled that we could march right on to Raleigh [the state capital]; but we have now been out six weeks, living precariously upon the collections of our foragers, our men 'dirty, ragged and saucy,' and we must rest and fix up a little. . . .

"Our combinations were such"—Sherman now commanded more than 90,000 men—"that General Schofield entered Goldsboro from New Bern; General Terry got Cox's Bridge, with pontoons laid, and a brigade across the Neuse River entrenched; and we whipped Jos. Johnston—all on the same day. . . .

"We have lost no general officers nor any organization. General Slocum took three guns at Averasboro, and lost three others in the first dash at him at Bentonville. We have all our wagons and trains in good order."[15]

Grant was equally elated, knowing the strategic situation could not be more precarious for the Rebels. "Sherman was no longer in danger," he would write. "He had Johnston confronting him; but with an army much inferior to his own, both in numbers and morale. He had Lee to the north of him with a force largely superior; but I was holding Lee [at Petersburg] with a still greater force, and had he made his escape and gotten down to reinforce Johnston, Sherman . . . would have been able to hold the Confederates at bay for an indefinite period. He was near the seashore with his back to it, and our navy occupied the harbors. He had a railroad to both Wilmington and New Bern, and his flanks were thoroughly protected by streams, which intersect that part of the country and deepen as they approach the sea. Then, too, Sherman knew that if Lee should escape me I would be on his heels. . . .

"The men of both Lee's and Johnston's armies were, like their brethren of the North, as brave as men can be; but no man is so brave that he may not meet such defeats and disasters as to dampen his ardor for any cause, no matter how just he deems it."[16]

On March 27 Sherman steamed up the James to City Point, Grant's headquarters outside Petersburg, for a meeting with his chief. When the ship docked he was the first person off, energetically shaking hands with Grant as they exchanged greetings. Observed Horace Porter: "Their encounter was more like that of two schoolboys coming together after a vacation than the meeting of the principal actors in a great war tragedy." Later Sherman sat down beside a campfire with Grant and his staff and, before a rapt audience, delivered an hour-long, graphic monologue on the march through Georgia and beyond. "The story was the more charming," said Porter, "from the fact that it was related without the manifestation of the slightest egotism. . . . Never were listeners more enthusiastic; never was a speaker more eloquent."

During his discourse Sherman made a point of praising the march's "bummers," explaining they were not just self-appointed foragers but daring volunteers. "They serve as 'feelers' who keep in advance and on the flanks of the main columns, spy out the land, and discover where the best supplies are to be found," he said. "They are indispensable in feeding troops when compelled . . . to live off the country, and in destroying the enemy's communications." To much laughter he told of the bummer who arrived in Goldsboro in advance of Sherman's army, but after Schofield's troops entered the town. The latter force had just set up a telegraph line to the seacoast. The bummer promptly climbed one of the poles and began hacking at the wires.

"What are you doing?" one of Schofield's officers yelled. "You're destroying one of our own telegraph lines."

Nothing nonplussed, the man continued hacking away.

"I'm one o' Billy Sherman's bummers," he yelled back, "and the last thing he said to us when we started out on this hunt was: 'Be sure and cut all the telegraph-wires you come across, and don't go to foolin' away time askin' who they belong to.'"[17]

Grant and Sherman then went off to pay a courtesy call on Lincoln, who was also at City Point, staying aboard the *River Queen*. The meeting was a brief one—their conference would not be until the next day—and they were soon back at headquarters.

Julia Grant was there, and she immediately asked, "Did you see Mrs. Lincoln?"

"We went on a business errand, and I did not ask for Mrs. Lincoln," her husband replied. "And I didn't even know she was aboard," said Sherman.

"Well, you are a pretty pair!" commented Julia.

That evening, before dinner, the two men began discussing future tactics. "Perhaps you don't want me here listening to all your secrets," Julia remarked.

Now began an exchange of repartee, indicative of the friendship of all three. "Do you think we can trust her, Grant?" Sherman asked.

"I'm not sure about that, Sherman. Public documents, in disseminating items of information, are accustomed to say, 'Know all men by these presents.' I think it would be just as effective to say, 'Know one woman,' for then all men would be certain to hear of it."

Sherman now put on a stern face, saying he would find out if Julia knew enough about the war to be of value to the enemy. He began a series of inane questions involving topography and railroads and troop movements, and Mrs. Grant, entering into the spirit of the game, responded in kind.

Eventually the bantering ended. "Well, Grant," Cump said straight-facedly, "I think we can trust her." Turning back to Julia, he remarked, "Never mind, Mrs. Grant, perhaps some day the women will vote and control affairs, and then they will take us men in hand and subject us to worse cross-examinations than that." Julia's reply is not known.[18]

The next day Admiral Porter dropped by, and he and Sherman reminisced about their shared Vicksburg experiences. "When you were in the region of those swamps and overflowed rivers, coming through the Carolinas," Porter finally asked, "didn't you wish you had my gunboats with you?"

"Oh yes," answered Sherman, ". . . those swamps were much like [one] fellow's Fourth of July oration, of which a newspaper said, "It was only knee-deep, but spread out over all creation."

The three men then went to confer with the president, with Porter taking a minor role. There Grant advised Lincoln that the crisis of the war was at hand, and that it was likely that Lee would evacuate Richmond and Petersburg, but if he did he would be in hot pursuit. The president asked if it might be possible to end the conflict without a pitched battle, with attendant loss of life, and was told the enemy must make that decision. Conversation turned to how the Confederates should be treated after the war. The president wanted no reprisals. Horace Porter, to whom Grant related the particulars of the conference, would say: "Lincoln . . . expressed an inclination to lean toward a generous policy. In speaking about the Confederate political leaders, he intimated . . . that it would relieve the situation if they should escape to some foreign country. . . ." On only two points was the president adamant: the South must agree that the Union be preserved, and slavery be abolished.

Sherman returned to his command that afternoon. Grant and some aides subsequently saw Lincoln off, walking him to the train station. "Mr. Lincoln looked more serious than at any time since he had visited headquarters," said Porter. "The lines in his face seemed deeper, and rings under his eyes were of a darker hue. It was plain that the weight of responsibility was oppressing him."

"Goodbye, gentlemen, God bless you all!" the president said in a voice tight with emotion. "Remember, your success is my success!"

"The President is one of the few visitors I have had who have not attempted to extract from me a knowledge of my movements," Grant would say, "although he is the only one who has a right to know them."[19]

TWO

* * * *

GRANT CRUSHES A PROUD FOE

Grant in late March had good reason to think that Lee, despite in-
clement weather and muddy roads, was planning to evacuate Petersburg
and Richmond—where food supplies were low and morale still lower—
and join with Johnston in North Carolina. Up to now President Davis had
stubbornly refused to give the Rebel commander permission to leave the
cities, but every passing day brought the decision closer. Just before Sherman's visit to City Point, Lee had made one last-ditch offensive effort to
break the siege, sending out John Brown Gordon in a March 25 attack on
Fort Stedman, one of the redoubts to the east of the Petersburg lines. Once
the fort was taken, massed infantry were to rush into the adjoining works,
turn captured cannon on the Federals and, hopefully, put them to rout.
But Gordon's assault, though initially successful, failed with dreadful
losses, making evacuation all but inevitable.

"General Grant's chief apprehension," said Horace Porter, "was that
the enemy might suddenly pull out of his entrenchments and fall back into
the interior, where he might unite with General Joe Johnston against Sherman. . . . He did not dare delay his movements against the enemy's right
(at Petersburg) until the roads became dry enough to permit an army to
move comfortably, for fear that Lee himself would take advantage of the
dry roads to start first. Each army, in fact, was making preparations for either a fight or a foot-race—or both."[1]

On March 29 the Federal army was arrayed, from right to left, in a huge semicircle: Godfrey Weitzel, with elements of the Army of the James, was in front of Richmond; John Parke's 9th Corps and Horatio Wright's 6th Corps were holding the works south of Petersburg; Edward Ord's 24th Corps to their left had extended the Petersburg lines to the intersection of Hatcher's Run and the Vaughan Road; Andrew Humphreys (replacing Hancock, whose Gettysburg wound kept reopening) with the 2nd Corps was to Ord's left beyond Dabney's Mill; Gouverneur Warren's 5th Corps was to Humphreys's left at the junction of the Vaughan Road and the Boydton Plank Road; and Phil Sheridan, back from the Shenandoah and again commanding the cavalry, was on the extreme left near Dinwiddie Court House. Though George Meade remained in charge of the Army of the Potomac, Grant continued to make the operational decisions. Altogether the Union forces totaled some 125,000, the Rebels some 57,000.

It would be Sheridan the next day, when he rode up to Grant's headquarters, now located at Dabney's Mill, who would influence him to launch the final thrust against the Petersburg works. "I can drive in the whole cavalry force of the enemy with ease," Sheridan assured the aides who greeted him, "and if an infantry force is added to my command, I can strike out for Lee's right, and either crush it or force him to so weaken his intrenched lines that our troops in front of them can break through and march into Petersburg."

"How do you expect to supply your command with forage if this weather lasts?" asked one officer.

"Forage!" Sheridan cried out. "I'll get all the forage I want. I'll haul it out if I have to set every man . . . to corduroying roads . . . from the [Weldon] Railroad to Dinwiddie. I tell you, I'll ready to strike out tomorrow, and go to smashing things."

Brought into Grant's tent he repeated this claim, full of conviction. "Knowing as I did . . . of what great value that feeling of confidence by a commander was," said Grant, "I determined to make a movement at once . . . for the purpose of extending our lines to the west as far as possible toward the enemy's extreme right." The target would be Five Forks, a vital crossroads near the Southside Railroad. "My hope was that Sheridan would be able to carry Five Forks, get on the enemy's right flank and rear, and force them to weaken their center . . . so that an attack [there] might be successfully made. General Wright's corps had been designated to make this assault"—together with Ord's and Parke's—"which I intended to order as soon as information reached me of Sheridan's success."

Grant did not at this juncture provide his cavalry chief with infantry support, but assured him he would do so the next day, as the turning movement developed. "It is natural to suppose that Lee would understand my design [was] to get to the Southside and ultimately to the Danville Railroad. . . . These roads were so important to his very existence [for supplies] while he remained in Richmond and Petersburg, and of such vital importance to him even in case of retreat, that he would make the most strenuous efforts to defend them. . . ."[2] But Grant would not be content with severing the railroads; he would be aiming to crush Lee's army.

So the stage was set. On March 31 Sheridan departed from Dinwiddie Court House, and with his 13,000 cavalrymen galloped northwest to the neighborhood of Five Forks. His second-in-command was Wesley Merritt, and his division chiefs Thomas Devin, George Custer, and George Crook. At Five Forks he encountered heavy resistance, Lee having divined his purpose and drained his defensive lines to send 19,000 cavalry and infantry— under Fitzhugh Lee [his nephew] and George Pickett respectively—to stop him. This they did, driving Sheridan back to Dinwiddie. Only the timely arrival of George Custer, coming up from guarding the wagon train, kept the retreat from turning into a rout.

"Accompanied by Generals Merritt and Custer and my staff," said Sheridan, "I now rode along the barricades to encourage the men. . . . The cavalcade drew the enemy's fire, which emptied several of the saddles. . . . In reply our horse artillery opened on the advancing Confederates, but the men behind the barricades lay still till Pickett's troops were within short range. Then they opened up, Custer's repeating rifles pouring out such a shower of lead that nothing could stand up against it. The repulse was very quick . . . all danger of their taking Dinwiddie or marching to the left and rear of our infantry line was over, at least for the night. . . ."[3]

To Sheridan's right, meanwhile, Warren and Humphreys were advancing toward White Oak Road and the swamps around Hatcher's Run, where the main Confederate works ended. (To their right Ord, Wright, and Parke—concentrated south of Petersburg—stood poised to assault the city itself.)

Not waiting for the Federals to attack him, Lee now emerged from his lines on White Oak Road and hurled 5,000 troops straight at the capable but methodical Warren. The effect was devastating. Though Warren had 15,000 men, only the first of his three divisions—that of Romeyn Ayres— was anywhere near being in position, the others still being in the rear. To make matters worse, the surprise of the attack prevented Ayres from bunching his brigades. He had little choice but to commit them one by one, and one by one they were sent packing. "Ayres, like a roaring lion, endeavors to check this disorder," said General Joshua Chamberlain, commanding a brigade in the second of Warren's divisions, that of Charles Griffin, "and makes a stand on each favoring crest and wooded ravine. But in vain. His men stream past him. . . . The whole crowd comes back reckless of everything but to get behind the lines on the Boydton Road, plunging through the swampy run. . . . The pursuing enemy swarming down the opposite bank are checked there by the musketry from our line."[4]

Viewing the scene with dismay the tough, volatile Griffin, whom Grant had nearly removed for insubordination at the Wilderness, ordered Chamberlain to launch a counter charge. This he did about 1:45 P.M.

"We sounded bugles 'Forward!' and that way we go; mounted officers leading their commands, pieces at the right shoulder until at close quarters," said Chamberlain, the hero of the second day of Gettysburg at Little Round Top. ". . . What we had to do could not be done by firing. This was foot-and-hand business. We went with a rush, not minding ranks nor alignments, but with open front to lessen loss from the long-range rifles. Within effective range, about three hundred yards, the sharp, cutting fire made us reel and shiver. Now, quick or never! On and over! The impetuous 185th New York rolls over the enemy's right, and seems to swallow it up; the 198th Pennsylvania, with its fourteen companies, half veterans, half soldiers 'born-so,' swing in upon their left . . . and for a few minutes there is a seething wave of countercurrents, then rolling back, leaving a fringe of wrecks—and all is over. We pour over the works . . . and then establish ourselves across the White Oak Road."

One officer of the 198th Pennsylvania gives us a similar picture of the charge: "Only for a moment did the sudden and terrible blast of death cause . . . the line to waver. On they dashed, every color flying, officers leading, right in among the enemy, leaping the breastworks—a confused struggle of firing, cutting, a tremendous surge of force, both moral and physical, on the enemy's breaking lines—and the works were carried. . . . Private Augustus Ziever in mounting one of the parapets captured the flag of the 46th Virginia, and handed it to General Chamberlain . . . who immediately gave it back to him, telling him to keep it and take the credit that belonged to him. . . ." For his daring, Ziever received the Medal of Honor.[5]

Late in the afternoon Horace Porter, dispatched by Grant, rendezvoused with Sheridan just north of Dinwiddie. "He said he had one of the liveliest days in his experience, fighting infantry and cavalry with only cavalry,"

Porter reported, "but that he would hold his position at Dinwiddie at all hazards. He did not stop there, but declared his belief that with the corps of infantry which he expected to be put under his command, he could take the initiative the next morning, and cut off the whole of the force which Lee had detached."

"This [Rebel] force is in more danger than I am," Sheridan insisted, noting that a three-mile gap existed between Pickett and the main Confederate lines. "If I am cut off from the Army of the Potomac, it is cut off from Lee's army, and not a man in it ought to be allowed to get back. We at last have drawn the enemy . . . out of its fortifications, and this is our chance to attack it." Sheridan next told Porter he wanted Wright's corps in support—it had been under his command in the Shenandoah and was familiar with his hard-fighting ways. He was informed this was impossible; Wright was too far to the east. The only corps that could reach him by daylight was Warren's.

Porter rejoined Grant about 7:00 P.M., and subsequently Warren was ordered west from the White Oak Road to join with Sheridan near Five Forks, a distance of perhaps a dozen miles. "It was expected that the infantry would reach its destination in ample time to take the offensive about daybreak," said Porter, "but one delay after another was met with, and Grant, Meade and Sheridan spent a painfully anxious night. . . . Ayres' division of Warren's corps had to rebuild the [Boydton Road] bridge over Gravelly Run, which took till 2 A.M. Warren, with his other two divisions, did not get started from their position on the White Oak till 5 A.M., and the hope of crushing the enemy was hourly growing less. . . . Generals were writing dispatches and telegraphing from dark to daylight. Staff officers were rushing from one headquarters to another . . . making extraordinary efforts to hurry up the movement of the troops."[6]

While it is true that Warren was still another deliberate officer, with a style that could be maddening, it is also true that the confusing and conflicting instructions he received that night made delay inevitable. Recounts Chamberlain: "At 9 o'clock came the order from Grant to Meade: 'Let Warren draw back at once from his position on the [White Oak] Road, and send a division of infantry to Sheridan's relief. The troops to Sheridan should start at once and go down the Boydton Road.' Meade promptly sent orders for the corps to retire and for Griffin to go to Sheridan, and go at once.

"Apparently no one at headquarters seems to have remembered two incidents concerning the selection of Griffin's division . . . first, that [Joseph] Bartlett of this division was already by this time down upon the enemy's rear, by another more direct though more difficult road, and in a far more effective position . . . than could be reached by the Boydton; and secondly, that the two remaining brigades of this division were . . . the farthest off from the Boydton Road, and most impeded by difficult ground. . . . Another circumstance, forgotten or ignored, was that the bridge at the . . . crossing of Gravelly Run was gone, and the stream was not fordable for infantry. Warren, in reporting [he would] comply with the order, reported also the destruction of the bridge and his intention to repair it, but this seems somehow, from first to last, to have added to the impatience felt toward him at those headquarters."

Warren dutifully told Griffin to recall Bartlett and send him down the Boydton Road. Continues Chamberlain: "But as it would take time for Griffin to get his scattered division together and draw back through the mud and darkness to the Boydton Road . . . Warren, anxious to fulfil the spirit and object of the order, sent his nearest division under Ayres . . . to start at once for Sheridan. Meanwhile the divisions of Griffin and [Samuel] Crawford were taking steps to mass on the Boydton Road."

Then at 10:30 P.M. came instructions from Meade that muddled the situation further: "Send Griffin promptly as ordered by the Boydton Road, but move the balance of your command by the road Bartlett is on, and strike the enemy in rear. . . . You must be very prompt." By this last order, Chamberlain says, Warren's corps "was to be turned end for end, and inside out. Poor Warren might be forgiven if at such an order his head swam and his wits collapsed."

"I cannot change my [arrangements] tonight," he wired back, in a message that could not have endeared him to his superiors, "without producing confusion that will render all my operations nugatory."

Finally at 1:00 A.M., came another message from Meade, perhaps the most bizarre of all. "Would not time be gained by sending troops by the Quaker Road? Sheridan cannot maintain himself at Dinwiddie without reinforcements. . . . Use every exertion. . . ." Meade here was suggesting a route that would add another ten miles to the trek, and preclude any possibility of an attack on Pickett's rear.[7]

When dawn broke on April 1, suffice it to say there were hard feelings to spare all around. Sheridan was fuming and wondering aloud when the devil Warren would arrive, the latter was aggrieved, Meade was wringing his hands and, most importantly, Grant rightly or wrongly was in no mood for excuses. "I was so much dissatisfied with Warren's dilatory movements in the battle of White Oak Road and in his failure to reach Sheridan in time," he said, "that I was afraid he would fail Sheridan.

[Warren] was a man of fine intelligence . . . and could make his dispositions as quickly as any officer under difficulties when he was forced to act. But I had before discovered a defect which was beyond his control. . . . He could see every danger at a glance before he encountered it. He would not only make preparations to meet the danger which might occur, but he would inform his commanding officer what others should do. . . ."[8]

Porter at 10:00 A.M. was back with Sheridan north of Dinwiddie, sent by Grant to keep him informed of developments. Ayres and Griffin of Warren's corps were already up, and soon Crawford would join them. Seeing the arrival of Federal infantry, Pickett about noon began to fall back several miles to entrenchments in front of Five Forks. About this time, too, a messenger arrived from Grant and, in Porter's presence, said to Sheridan: "General Grant directs me to say to you that if, in your judgment, the 5th Corps would do better under one of its division commanders, you are authorized to relieve General Warren. . . ." The cavalry chief replied he hoped such a step would not be needed, particularly just before a fight.

Sheridan's plan of battle called for Merritt with the cavalry, mostly dismounted, to make a feint against the enemy's center and right, even as Warren turned his left, cutting off Pickett from communication with Lee's lines at White Oak Road. These orders were given about 1:00 P.M. and Sheridan went over them with Warren in detail, explaining he wanted Ayres and Crawford in the lead, with Griffin in reserve. "General Warren seemed to understand me clearly, and then left to join his command," said Sheridan, "while I turned my attention to the cavalry, instructing Merritt to begin by making demonstrations as though to turn the enemy's right as Warren became engaged. . . . Afterward I rode to Gravelly Run Church and found the head of Warren's column just appearing, while he was sitting under a tree making a rough sketch of the ground."

Furious that the corps commander was not personally hurrying up the infantry, Sheridan resorted to sarcasm. "I expressed to Warren my fears that the cavalry might expend all their ammunition before the attack could be made." He was more concerned, of course, that the daylight hours were being wasted, and that troops from Lee's right, just three miles away, might strike his own rear. "Warren did not seem to me at all solicitous; his manner exhibited decided apathy, and he remarked with indifference that 'Bobby Lee was always getting people into trouble.' With unconcern such as this, it is no wonder that fully three hours' time was consumed in marching his corps . . . to Gravelly Run Church, though the distance was but two miles."[9]

By 4:00 P.M. Warren finally was ready. Porter recounts the assault:

"Ayres threw out a skirmish line and advanced [on the enemy works] across an open field which sloped down gradually toward the dense woods just north of the White Oak Road. He was soon met with a fire from the edge of these woods . . . and the skirmish-line halted and began to waver. Sheridan now began to exhibit those traits which always made him a tower of strength. . . . He put spurs to his horse, and dashed in front of the line of battle from left to right . . . shouting words of encouragement."

"Come on, men!" he cried. "Go at 'em with a will! Move on at a clean jump, or you'll not catch one of 'em. They're all getting ready to run, and if you don't get on to them in five minutes they'll every one get away."

Just then a skirmisher was struck in the neck, his blood spurting from the wound. "I'm killed!" he yelled, dropping to the ground. "You're not hurt!" Sheridan told him. "Pick up your gun, man, and move to the front!"

Porter was amazed. "Such was the effect of his words," the aide said, "that the poor fellow snatched up his musket and rushed forward a dozen paces before he fell, never to rise again."

Now Warren's infantry pushed into the woods, struggling through the swampy ground and dense underbrush. Here they were staggered anew by heavy fire, and Ayres and Crawford began to diverge, leaving a gap in the lines. Sheridan rushed up once more, shouting for his battle flag. "As the sergeant who carried it rode up," said Porter, "Sheridan seized the crimson-and-white standard, waved it above his head . . . and made heroic efforts to close up the ranks. Bullets were now swarming like a swarm of bees above our heads. . . . A musket-ball pierced the battle-flag; another killed the sergeant who had carried it, another wounded an aide. . . . All this time Sheridan was dashing from one part of the line to another, waving his flag, shaking his fist, encouraging, entreating, threatening, praying, swearing. . . ."[10]

Ayres and Crawford soon rallied, helped by Griffin coming up with his division and filling the breech. "Ayres, with drawn saber, rushed forward once more with his veterans, who now behaved as if they had fallen back only to get a 'good ready,'" said Porter, "and with fixed bayonets and a rousing cheer dashed over the earthworks, sweeping everything before them, and killing or capturing every man in their immediate front whose legs had not saved him." Everywhere along the Confederate left the result was the same, the enemy either surrendering or taking to his heels. Federal officers—including Warren, if Chamberlain is to be believed—jumped their mounts over the works, adding to the enemy's panic. Sheridan and his huge black horse landed among a dozen men who had thrown down their weapons.

"Where do you want us all to go to?" one terrified fellow asked, hands in the air. Sheridan's battlefield rage quickly turned to heavy-handed humor. "Go right over there," he said, pointing to the rear. "Get right along. . . . You'll all be safe over there. . . . Are there any more of you? . . . We want every one of you fellows."[11]

On the Confederate left, meanwhile, Devin's cavalry division likewise took the works, driving the enemy before them. "The intermingling infantry and dismounted cavalry swept down inside the entrenchments," said Sheridan, "pushing to and beyond Five Forks, capturing thousands of prisoners. The only stand the enemy tried to make was when he tried to form near the Ford Road. Griffin pressed him so hard there, however, that he had to give way in short order. . . ."

Warren at this juncture sent Sheridan a message that he was at the Ford Road himself, cutting off the enemy's retreat and taking many prisoners. Little Phil, who had not seen the corps commander during his wild dashes along the lines, flew into a rage anew, choosing to believe Warren had avoided danger.

"By God, sir," he thundered at the aide, "tell General Warren he wasn't in the fight!" The messenger was thunderstruck. "Must I tell General Warren that, sir?" he asked. "Tell him that, sir!" was the reply, the words stinging like slaps to the face. "I would not like to take a verbal message like that to General Warren," the aide persisted. "May I take it down in writing?"

"Take it down, sir; tell him, by God, he was not at the front!"

Forthwith Sheridan came across Griffin, and with little or no ceremony told him he was in charge of the 5th Corps. Then he wrote Warren, informing him he was relieved and should report to Grant for further orders.

The Rebel cause, it should be said, was not helped during the Federal assault on April 1 by the fact that Pickett and Fitz Lee were not at their posts. Instead they had ridden two miles to the rear without telling their subordinates where they were going. There they relaxed at an impromptu picnic, feasting on baked shad—the fish had been making their run at a nearby stream—unheeding of Warren's advance. How the two senior Confederate officers on the field could have been so indifferent to their danger, and their duties, remains a puzzlement. Perhaps Grant's relentless pressure had numbed them. Pickett—whose storied charge at Gettysburg had failed so spectacularly—first realized the seriousness of the 4:00 P.M.

attack when some bluecoats materialized seemingly out of nowhere. He leaped on his horse and made it back to the lines, but by then the damage had been done. Fitz Lee never did get through, the Yankees having gotten between him and his command.

Sheridan's triumph was complete; Pickett's expeditionary force, in effect, had become a disorganized mob. Rebel casualties totaled between 4,500 and 5,000, most of them prisoners, and both the Southside and Danville Railroads soon would be severed, threatening Richmond, if it chose to hold out further, with slow starvation. Federal losses were nominal.

Warren now approached in the gathering darkness, the order relieving him clutched in his hand. *Will you not reconsider?* he asked Sheridan.

"Reconsider, hell!" was the reply. "I don't reconsider my decisions. Obey the order!" With that Warren was dismissed. He had been wounded at Gaines' Mill during the Peninsula Campaign, fought at Second Bull Run and Antietam, blocked the Confederate threat to Cemetery Ridge the second day at Gettysburg, fought through the bloody Overland Campaign. But Grant and Sheridan had found him wanting. He would spend the rest of his life trying to clear his name.[12]

Riding back to headquarters at Dabney's Mill about 7:30 P.M., Porter reveled in the victory. "The roads in many places were corduroyed with captured muskets; ammunition-trains and ambulances were still struggling forward; teamsters, prisoners, stragglers and wounded were choking the roadway; the 'coffee-boilers' had kindled their fires in the woods; cheers were resounding on all sides. . . ." He found Grant sitting with his staff before a blazing fire, the ever-present cigar in his mouth. "I began shouting the good news as soon as I got in sight, and in a moment all but the imperturbable general-in-chief were on their feet giving vent to boisterous demonstrations of joy. . . . Officers fell to grasping hands, shouting, and hugging each other like schoolboys." Porter, normally the most proper of officers, found himself whooping and clapping Grant repeatedly on the back. Ironically, several witnesses thought the aide had been drinking.[13]

Following up forthwith on the rout at Five Forks, not waiting the short time it would take for Sherman's formidable force to move up from North Carolina to join him, Grant the next morning about 4:30 A.M. sent the bulk of George Meade's Army of the Potomac forward in an assault on the Petersburg lines. Perhaps he felt that these troops, for so long humbled and then held at bay by Lee's Army of Northern Virginia, deserved to deliver the coup de grace. If so, that is exactly what they would do—the men of Humphreys's 2nd Corps, Wright's 6th Corps and Parke's 9th Corps, with help from elements of the Army of the James under Edward Ord—falling on the stretched-out enemy works with lethal abandon.

Preceding the April 2 attack the Federal cannon, in barrage after barrage, hurled thousand of shells on Lee's still-defiant troops, whose lines ran for a dozen miles south of the Appomattox River, anchored by Petersburg in the east and Hatcher's Run and White Oak Road in the west. Then, as suddenly as it began, the artillery fire ceased. Soon all that could be heard was a distant rustling, described by one Union officer as sounding "like a strong breeze blowing through the swaying boughs and dense foliage of some great forest." This, he finally realized, was the noise made by tens of thousands of advancing men, their footsteps muffled by the soft, moist ground.[14]

The assault on the works, while single-minded, was not as concentrated as folklore would have it. There was thrusting and counterthrusting, sallies and reversals, moves to the front and obliques to the left or right—whatever the circumstances demanded. Meanwhile the musket fire was hot and fierce and men were killed and maimed, and the real question was who would breach the outer line of Confederate entrenchments and how steep would be the price. Storming parties here and there along the works cut their way with axes through the abatis and other entanglements; brigades and regiments followed in their path with various degrees of success. In many places the defenders were few, but invariably they died hard. Hand-to-hand combat was commonplace, lines of battle swiftly dissolved, soldiers blue and gray tested each other's mettle in hundreds of small but murderous firefights.

By most accounts Wright's troops made the initial breakthrough during the melee, smashing the Confederate right at Hatcher's Run and then turning east toward Petersburg. It was during this action that Rebel General Ambrose Powell Hill, making a reconnaissance, was killed. Ord's 24th Corps followed on Wright's heels. To their left Humphreys crossed White Oak Road, then the run, and likewise turned toward the city. Only directly south of Petersburg did the enemy hold, with John Brown Gordon first falling back but then fighting Parke to a standstill. Porter describes the developing action: "At a quarter past five (A.M.) a message came from Wright that he had carried the enemy's line in his front and was pushing in. Next came news from Parke that he had captured the outer works. . . . Soon Ord was heard from as having broken through the entrenchments. Humphreys, too, had been doing gallant work. At half-past seven the line in his front was taken. . . ."

Grant at this juncture rode to the sound of the guns, where he conferred with Meade and, for the next few hours, urged on the attack from a grassy knoll. There he seated himself at the foot of a tree and, surrounded by aides, began writing dispatches. The group soon attracted the attention of the enemy artillery, with shot and shell coming uncomfortably close. "Several of the officers," said Porter, ". . . urged him to move to some less conspicuous position; but he kept on writing and talking . . . apparently not noticing what a target the place was becoming." Not until he finished his writing did Grant pay heed. "Well, they do seem to have the range on us," he conceded, getting on his horse and riding on.[15]

By midmorning Lee was bringing some order out of the chaos, withdrawing to inner lines that could more easily be defended. Noting that Grant had stripped his position at Richmond to bring troops to Petersburg, he quickly summoned Longstreet and his command from north of the James and used them to buttress his hard-pressed right. The redoubtable Gordon continued to hold the left against Parke, withdrawing to the city's inner works and digging in, protecting the key bridge over the Appomattox. By noon, nonetheless, all the outer works except Forts Gregg and Alexander were taken, and these fell in midafternoon. "The result . . . was that the Confederates, having lost their outer system of defenses, were pressed back to a chain of works immediately around Petersburg," wrote one historian. "But as they had here a short and strong line, with their left resting on the Appomattox east of Petersburg and their right on the same river on the west . . . the Union force, weighty as it was, found it impossible to dislodge them."[16]

The harried Lee now had but one thought: to hold his ground until the coming of darkness would enable him to evacuate both Richmond and Petersburg. This he would accomplish. In the works from which the Confederates had been driven, meanwhile, Grant penned a letter to Julia that revealed quiet elation. "I am writing from far inside what was the Rebel fortifications this morning but what are ours now," he said. "They are exceedingly strong and I wonder at the success of our troops carrying them by storm. But they did do it, and without any great loss. We have captured about 12,000 prisoners and 50 pieces of artillery. . . . Altogether this has been one of the greatest victories of the war. Greatest because it is over what the Rebels have always regarded as their most invincible army. . . ."[17]

Lee and his army moved west out of the burning and chaotic cities the night of April 2 to 3 on three separate but converging routes, both north and south of the Appomattox River. Their goal was Amelia Court House, a town south of the river on the Richmond and Danville Railroad some forty miles from the capital and a few miles less from Petersburg. There he expected that rations would await his hungry men. Frail Dick Ewell, who had been in charge of the Richmond garrison, was northernmost, together with elements of the 1st Corps. In the center was Billy Mahone's 3rd Corps division, leaving the works at Bermuda Hundred. Southernmost were Longstreet, Gordon, and Dick Anderson, corps commanders all—at least of what remained of their troops. True believers, amazingly enough, still thought Lee somehow would reverse his fortunes.

"General Lee," one plantation owner's daughter told him, "we shall gain our cause, you will join General Johnston, and together you will be victorious."

"Whatever happens," he answered, "know this, that no men ever fought better than those who stood by me."[18]

For Lee to be resupplied at Amelia, Confederate trains would have to pass through Burkeville Junction and then Jetersville, stops farther west on the Danville Railroad; moreover, if he had any hope of joining Joe Johnston in North Carolina, his most direct route was through these hamlets. But when Lee arrived at Amelia on April 4, he found that his orders had gone awry and the rations were not there. Frantic for food, his reunited army spent the day scouring the picked-over countryside, with little or nothing to show for their efforts. This gave the hard-riding Sheridan the time to throw a cavalry division across the Rebel path at Jetersville and, hours later, for Griffin's infantry corps to reinforce him. The rest of Grant's army was not far behind.

On the afternoon of the 5th, finding his way blocked, Lee decided not to give battle—his all-consuming need at this point was to obtain food and forage—but to make a looping night march around Sheridan's left flank. His intent was to reach Farmville on the Southside Railroad—where rations awaited him—cross to the north of the Appomattox, burn the bridges over the river behind him, then reorganize his army and resume his southward retreat. Lee's column now extended for ten miles. Longstreet with four divisions was in the van; then Anderson and Ewell with the garrison troops and the main wagon train; then Gordon bringing up the rear.

All went well for the Rebels until midmorning on the 6th, when Sheridan's cavalry caught up with them and became a constant irritant. While Longstreet's command forged on ahead, Anderson and Ewell paused to repel the attacks, letting the wagons pass them. Unfortunately this created a gap in the column, which Sheridan took full advantage of, rushing his troopers into the opening at about 2:00 P.M. and creating a roadblock.

Compounding the danger, Ewell had sent the wagons on a northerly route at a fork in the road without informing Gordon, who followed them, leaving Anderson and Ewell without support. Meanwhile Wright's 6th Corps joined the assault.

Desperate and confused fighting began on three fronts about 5:00 P.M. The first engagement was at Little Sayler's Creek, a tributary of the Appomattox, where Ewell's 3,600 men faced Wright's 10,000. Finding the enemy had no cannon, the Federals advanced within 800 yards, opened up a withering fire and charged. "Quicker than I can tell," said one Rebel, "the battle degenerated into a butchery. . . . I saw numbers of men kill each other with bayonets and the butts of muskets. . . ."

Nearby to the southwest, Anderson's 6,300 troops were faring no better against Sheridan's 10,000. Exulted one Yankee cavalryman: "The bugles sounded the advance, and forward up the . . . ridge swept that grand cavalry command with irresistible force . . . the Rebels rose and fired a terrific volley, but . . . before they could reload most of our brigade had leaped the works and were among them." Though Anderson escaped, he lost 2,600 men, most of whom were captured. Realizing that his support had collapsed, Ewell tried to fall back and save his own command. His decision came too late, and his defeat was even worse. Only two hundred of his men escaped, the rest for the most part were taken prisoner, as were Ewell and five other Confederate generals.

The third engagement involved Gordon, who with his 7,000 men had followed Ewell's wagons. Though pushed hard by Humphreys's 16,500-man 2nd Corps, he had largely succeeded in protecting the train, stopping now and then to launch ambushes. When the wagons broke down in the marshland where Little and Big Sayler's Creeks met, however, Gordon came a cropper. He managed to save himself and most of his command, but lost 1,700 men and 200 wagons.[19]

Joseph Kershaw, one of the captured generals, eventually was brought with his fellow officers before George Custer, who greeted them heartily and gave them a good meal. "After supper," Kershaw remembered, "we smoked and talked over many subjects . . . dwelling, however, almost wholly upon the past. The future to us was not inviting, and our host with true delicacy of feeling avoided the subject. We slept beneath the stars, Custer sharing his blankets with me. . . ." The next day he noticed that many of the troopers in the cavalryman's entourage carried Confederate battle flags. "It is my custom after a battle to select for my escort . . . those men of each regiment who most distinguish themselves in action,"

Custer explained, "bearing for the time, the trophies they have taken from the enemy."

"I counted them," said Kershaw, who was one of Lee's most accomplished division chiefs. "There were 31 captured banners representing 31 of our regiments killed, captured or dispersed. . . . It was not comforting to think of. . . ."[20]

Sailor's Creek as the battle came to be known overall cost the Confederates some 7,700 men, and the Federals 1,150. Learning of the debacle Lee rode back from the head of the column and, from a hilltop, surveyed the dismal aftermath of the battle. "My God!" he exclaimed, almost as if talking to himself. "Has the army dissolved?" Late that night and into the morning Lee and his surviving troops—in total numbers now no more than two infantry and one cavalry corps—reached Farmville, withdrawing up both sides of the Appomattox. They failed to burn the Southside Railroad bridges behind them, however, thereby forfeiting the opportunity of keeping the Federals south of the river and, at least to a degree, delaying their relentless pursuit.

Farmville offered the Rebels food, but little chance for rest. With enemy cavalry harassing his flanks and infantry close behind, Lee had no choice but to move his entire force across the Appomattox and head farther west for Appomattox Court House, giving up all hope of moving south. "We reached Farmville on Friday the 7th at 9 A.M.," said one Confederate gunner. "Here we got some bacon and cornmeal, and going on beyond the town toward Cumberland Church I was directed to halt and cook rations. While this was going on an urgent order was received to hurry the battalion forward to Cumberland Church, where the enemy was threatening our trains. Hastily the partly cooked food was seized by all hands, men and officers, and devoured as we marched." Here at the church Lee's still dangerous force won its last battle, with Billy Mahone blunting an attack by elements of Federal cavalry and the 2nd Corps. The latter lost some 600 men, including two generals, one mortally wounded and one captured.[21]

Grant rode into Farmville at midday, even as the contest north of the river was in full sway. "News came in that [George] Crook was fighting large odds with his cavalry . . . and I was directed to go to his front and see what was necessary to be done to assist him," said Horace Porter. "I found that he was being driven back, the enemy . . . having made a bold stand north of the river. Humphreys was also [there], isolated from the rest of our infantry." Because Lee had succeeded in burning the main bridges at Farmville, Grant could not reinforce his men until replacements were built. Toward dusk, however, he sent Wright's 6th Corps across the river in support.

"It was now dark," said Porter, "but [the men] spied the general-in-chief watching them with evident pride from the piazza of the hotel as they marched past. Then was witnessed one of the most inspiring sights of the campaign. Bonfires were lighted on the sides of the streets; the men seized . . . improvised torches; cheers arose from their throats; bands played, banners waved. . . . A regiment now broke forth with the sound of 'John Brown's Body,' and soon a whole division was shouting the swelling chorus. . . . The night march had become a grand review. . . ."22

Earlier Grant had sent Lee a brief but momentous message: "The results of the last week must convince you of the hopelessness of further resistance. . . ." he wrote. "I feel that it is so, and regard it as my duty to shift from myself the responsibility of any further effusion of blood by asking of the surrender of . . . the Army of Northern Virginia." Toward midnight he received Lee's answer: "Though not entertaining the opinion you express of the hopelessness of further resistance . . . I reciprocate your desire to avoid useless effusion of blood, and therefore . . . ask the terms you will offer. . . ."

Before leaving Farmville on April 8 and resuming the chase to Appomattox, Grant sent the Confederate commander a second message: ". . . There is but one condition I would insist upon—namely, that the men and officers surrendered shall be disqualified for taking up arms against the Government of the United States until properly exchanged. I will meet you, or will designate officers to meet any officers you may name . . . at any point agreeable to you, for the purpose of arranging definitely the terms upon which the surrender . . . will be received." For Grant's preeminent biographer, there was a world of difference between this message and the curt demand sent to General Simon Buckner at Fort Donelson three years earlier: "Grant was now offering the easiest terms that could be offered to a beaten army. . . . Far from demanding unconditional surrender, Grant was in effect saying that he would accept almost any conditions. . . ."

Lee responded within hours, but made a semantic distinction. "I did not intend to propose the surrender of the [army]," he wrote, "but to ask the terms of your proposition. . . . As the restoration of peace should be the sole object of all, I desire to know whether your proposals would lead to that end." He suggested a 10:00 A.M. meeting the next morning. Grant did not receive this note until late at night, and when he did he was crestfallen. He had no sanction to negotiate peace terms, only to accept surrender. Lee, he must have felt, was playing games with him. At dawn on the 9th, he replied in his usual straightforward fashion: ". . . I have no authority to treat on the subject of peace; the meeting proposed for 10 A.M. today could lead to no good. . . . The terms upon which peace can be had are well understood. By the South laying down their arms they will hasten that most desirable event, save thousands of human lives, and hundreds of millions of property not yet destroyed. . . ."

Now the Federals were closing on Lee and his exhausted army at Appomattox Court House, and a bloodbath seemed in the offing. Meade was to the north with Humphreys and Wright in the enemy rear, facing Longstreet; Sheridan was to the south with Griffin and Ord, cutting off the head of the Rebel column led by Gordon. Lee at this juncture capitulated, writing a hasty dispatch: "I received your note of this morning on the picket line, whither I had come to meet you. . . . I now ask an interview in accordance with the offer contained in your letter of yesterday." Grant concurred, and the two men would soon thereafter confer. "Damn them, I wish they had held out an hour longer and I would have whipped hell out of them," Sheridan snarled when he heard of the cease-fire. Grant was more perspicacious: "My campaign was not Richmond, nor the defeat of Lee in actual fight," he would say, "but to remove him and his army out of the contest and, if possible, to have him use his influence in inducing the surrender of Johnston. . . ."[23]

Before the generals-in-chief met that Palm Sunday, however, tensions between the armies threatened to explode. One such confrontation involved those bellicose cavalrymen George Custer and Phil Sheridan. Gordon in the van, hearing that Lee was suing for peace, sent an aide forward to inform the enemy. Back with the aide came the twenty-five-year-old Custer, his long blond hair and red scarf making him a conspicuous figure. "I am General Custer," he told Gordon haughtily, "and bear a message to you from General Sheridan. The general desires me . . . to demand the immediate and unconditional surrender of all the troops under your command. . . . He directs me to say to you, general, if there is any hesitation . . . he has you surrounded and can annihilate you. . . ."

Gordon was unfazed, telling Custer that if Sheridan decided to break the cease-fire the responsibility for further bloodshed would be his.

Soon Sheridan himself, an aide bearing a white flag, rode toward the Confederate lines. "Around me at the time were my faithful sharpshooters," said Gordon, "and as General Sheridan and his escort came within easy range of the rifles, a half-witted fellow raised his gun as if to fire. I ordered him to lower his gun. . . . He did not obey my order cheerfully. . . . In fact, he was again in the act of raising his gun to fire at Sheridan when I caught [it] and said, with emphasis, that he must not shoot men under flag of truce."

"Well, general, let him stay on his own side," the man protested.

Sheridan readily enough agreed to honor the cease-fire, but Custer, riding farther into the enemy works, encountered Longstreet and pressed his luck. "I have come to demand your instant surrender!" he called out. "We are in a position to crush you. . . ." Longstreet lost his temper. "By what authority do you come in our lines? General Lee is in communication with General Grant. We will certainly not recognize any subordinate."

"Oh, Sheridan and I are independent of Grant today," Custer persisted, "and we will destroy you if you don't surrender. . . ."

Longstreet grew enraged. "I suppose you . . . have violated the decencies of military procedure because you know no better, but it will not save you if you do so again. Now go and act as you and Sheridan choose and I will teach you a lesson you won't forget! Now go!" Custer said little more, and the fragile truce was preserved.[24]

Grant and Lee, together with various generals and aides, met in the sitting room of a private home belonging to one Wilbur McLean about 1:30 P.M. "When I left camp that morning I had not expected so soon the result that was then taking place," said Grant, "and consequently was in rough garb. I was without a sword, as I usually was when on horseback in the field, and wore a soldier's blouse for a coat, with the shoulder straps of my rank to indicate to the army who I was." Lee, sixteen years his senior, was in full fig, his uniform crisp, his boots and sword of impeccable quality. "I must have contrasted very strangely with a man so handsomely dressed, six feet high and of faultless form," said Grant. "But this was not a matter that I thought of until afterwards."

The Union general-in-chief wondered at the time, instead, what was in his vanquished opponent's mind. "What General Lee's feelings were I do not know. As he was a man of much dignity, with an impassable face, it was impossible to say whether he felt inwardly glad that the end finally had come, or felt sad over the result, and was too manly to show it. . . . My own feelings, which had been quite jubilant . . . were sad and depressed. I felt like anything rather than rejoicing at the downfall of a foe who had fought so long and valiantly, and had suffered so much for a cause, though that cause was . . . one of the worst for which a people ever fought. . . . I do not question, however, the sincerity of the great mass of those who were opposed to us."[25]

Grant seated himself in an armchair in the center of the room, while Lee occupied a cane chair beside a marble-topped table near a window. Their officers walked in softly and ranged themselves along the walls, in the words of one aide, "very much as people enter a sick-chamber when they expect to find the patient dangerously ill." Grant began the conversation. "I met you once before, General Lee, while we were serving in Mexico, when you came over from General [Winfield] Scott's headquarters to visit [Sam] Garland's brigade, to which I then belonged. I have always remembered your appearance, and think I would have recognized you anywhere."

"Yes," Lee replied, "I know I met you on that occasion, and I have often thought of it, and tried to recollect how you looked, but I have never been able to recall a single feature."

Some more small talk ensued, and then Lee suggested that Grant put the terms of the surrender on paper. This he did, saying in part: ". . . I propose to accept the surrender of the Army of Northern Virginia on the following terms, to wit: . . . The officers to give their individual paroles not to take up arms against the Government of the United States until properly exchanged, and each company or regimental commander to sign a like parole for the men of their commands. The arms, artillery and public property to be parked and stacked and turned over to the officers appointed by me to receive them. This will not embrace the sidearms of the officers, nor their private horses or baggage. This done, each officer and man will be allowed to return to his home, not to be disturbed by the United States authorities so long as they observe their paroles. . . ."

Lee then read the document, and when he came to the mention of the officers keeping their sidearms and horses showed he was pleased. "This will have a happy effect upon my army," he said. "There is one thing I would like to mention," he continued after a pause. "The cavalrymen and artillerists own their own horses in our army. . . . I should like to understand whether these men will be permitted to retain their horses. . . ."

"You will find the terms as written do not allow this," Grant replied.

"No, I see the terms do not allow it; that is clear," said Lee, his expression showing how much he hoped for the concession, even though he could not bring himself to ask directly for it.

"Well, the subject is quite new to me," said Grant, picking up on the request. "Of course I did not know that any private soldiers owned their animals . . . [but] I take it that most of the men in the ranks are small

farmers, and the country has been so raided by the two armies, it is doubtful they will be able to put in a crop to carry themselves and their families
through the next winter without the aid of the horses. . . ." He would not
change the terms as written, he went on, but would instruct his officers to
let all men—and there would be many, infantrymen included—"who claim
to own a horse or mule take the animals home with them."

"This will have the best possible effect," said Lee. "It will . . . do much
toward conciliating our people."[26]

Now the talk turned, obliquely, to the immediate issue of providing rations. "I have a thousand or more of your men as prisoners, General
Grant, a number of them officers, whom we have required to march along
with us for several days," said Lee. "I shall be glad to send them into your
lines as soon as possible, for I have no provisions for them. I have, indeed,
nothing for my own men. . . . I telegraphed to Lynchburg, directing several train-loads of rations to be sent by rail from there, and when they arrive I shall be glad to have the wants of my men supplied."

Grant knew full well that Sheridan had captured these trains the night
before. "I will take steps at once to have your army supplied with rations," he said. "Of about how many men does your present force consist?" Lee answered that he did not know, that many of his units were
without officers, and that rosters could not be kept during the forced
march to Appomattox. (Lee's armed and organized troops at this juncture
totaled no more than 7,900; the addition of prisoners, the weaponless,
and the ill would within days swell the number to some 28,000.)

"Sheridan," Grant called out, "how many rations have you?"

"How many do you want?" came the reply.

"How many can you send?" Grant asked.

"Twenty-five thousand."

Would this be enough? Grant wanted to know. "Plenty, plenty, an
abundance," Lee answered.[27]

By 4:00 P.M. the appropriate documents were copied and signed, and
the meeting broke up. Lee rode back to his headquarters in anguished silence, and Grant to his campsite in grateful thanks. "The news of the surrender had reached the Union lines," said Porter, "and the firing of salutes
began at several points, but the general sent an order at once to have them
stopped, using these words: 'The war is over; the Rebels are our countrymen again, and the best sign of rejoicing will be to abstain from all
demonstrations. . . .' This was in keeping with his order issued after the
surrender of Vicksburg. . . ."

Almost immediately the officers present began to purchase souvenirs from the McLean home's owner, who had previously lived where the first and second Battles of Bull Run had been fought and who had, ironically, moved to Appomattox to avoid further warfare. Sheridan paid twenty dollars in gold for the table on which Grant wrote the terms of the surrender and later gave it to Mrs. Custer. Ord paid forty dollars for the table near which Lee sat, and afterward presented it to Mrs. Grant, who declined the gift and insisted it go to Mrs. Ord. Candlesticks, inkstands, even a child's doll were snatched up, the participants jubilantly displaying their prizes.

Grant did not join in the backslapping. Not until after supper did he talk about the surrender at all, and then only to say that he hoped the rest of the Confederate commanders would follow Lee's example, and that the fighting everywhere in the South would end.

The next day he conferred with Lee a second time. "I rode out beyond our lines toward his headquarters, preceded by a bugler and a staff-officer carrying a white flag. Lee soon mounted his horse, seeing who it was, and met me. We had there between the lines, on horseback, a very pleasant conversation of over half an hour, in the course of which Lee said to me that the South was a big country and that we might have to march over it three or four times before the war entirely ended, but that we would now be able to do it as they could no longer resist us. . . . I then suggested to General Lee that there was not a man in the Confederacy whose influence with the soldiery and the whole people was as great as his, and that if he would now advise the surrender of all the armies I had no doubt his advice would be followed with alacrity. But Lee said he could not do that without consulting the President first. I knew there was no use to urge him to do anything against his ideas of what was right."[28]

The formal surrender of the Army of Northern Virginia took place on April 12, four years to the day after the shelling of Fort Sumter off Charleston, South Carolina, touched off the conflict. Brigadier Joshua Chamberlain of the Army of the Potomac, who was given the honor of accepting the stacking of arms, left us a unique and moving account of the event. "The dusky swarms forge forward into gray columns of march," he said. "On they come, with the old swinging route step and swaying battle-flags. In the van, the proud Confederate ensign—the great field of white with canton of star-strewn cross of blue on a field of red, the regimental battle-flags with the same escutcheon following on, crowded so thick, by thinning out of men, that the whole column seemed crowned with red."

The occasion impressed Chamberlain deeply, and he decided to mark it by a salute of arms. "The act could be defended, if needful, by the suggestion that such a salute was not to the cause for which the flag of the Confederacy stood, but to its going down before the flag of the Union. My main reason, however, was one for which I sought no authority nor asked forgiveness. Before us in proud humiliation stood the embodiment of manhood: men whom neither toil and sufferings, nor the fact of death, nor disaster, nor hopelessness could bend from their resolve; standing before us now, thin, worn and famished, but erect, and with eyes looking directly into ours, waking memories that bound us together as no other bond— was not such manhood to be welcomed back into a Union so tested and assured?"

As the head of the Confederate column passed, Chamberlain ordered a bugle call, and the whole Federal line, regiment by regiment, snapped from "order arms" to "carry arms"—the marching salute. John Brown Gordon, leading the procession "with heavy spirit and downcast face, catches the sound of shifting arms, looks up, and taking the meaning, wheels superbly, making with himself and his horse one uplifted figure, with profound salutation as he drops the point of his sword to the boot toe; then facing to his own command, gives the word for his successive brigades to pass us with the same position . . . honor answering honor. On our part not a sound of trumpet more, nor roll of drum; not a cheer, nor word nor whisper of vain-glorying . . . but an awed stillness rather, and breath-holding, as if it were the passing of the dead!"[29]

Each Rebel brigade and regiment—some so painfully depleted as to be unrecognizable—then halted, faced their former foes some twelve feet away across the road and stacked their arms. Concluded Chamberlain: "Lastly—reluctantly, with agony of expression—they tenderly fold their flags, battle-worn and torn, blood-stained, heart-holding colors, and lay them down; some frenziedly rushing from the ranks, kneeling over them, clinging to them, pressing them to their lips with burning tears. And only the flag of the Union greets the sky!"

Grant did not attend this ceremony, but instead was on his way to Washington, where he arrived the morning of the 13th. There he met with Lincoln and the next day, Good Friday, conferred with the president and his cabinet, discussing measures that might be taken to hasten the end of the war. When Grant expressed concern that he had not recently heard from Sherman, Lincoln assured him that good news would soon be forthcoming. He had just had a dream that always preceded glad tidings, he said, in which he was a passenger on a vessel "moving rapidly toward a dark and indefinite shore." This was the same dream the president had experienced before he learned of Antietam, Gettysburg, and Vicksburg.

Then Lincoln invited Grant and Julia to the theater—he and his wife were going that night to see a lighthearted comedy, *Our American Cousin*. Grant begged off, saying that he and his wife were anxious to be off to Burlington, New Jersey, where their children were in school. If he had accepted, and had taken a seat in the president's box, it is likely he, too, would have been John Wilkes Booth's victim. He heard the news of the assassination while passing through Philadelphia. "It would be impossible for me to describe the feeling that overcame me," he said. ". . . I knew [Lincoln's] goodness of heart, his generosity, his yielding disposition . . . and above all his desire to have all the people of the United States enter again upon the full privileges of citizenship with equality among all. I knew also the feeling that [Vice President Andrew] Johnson had expressed in speeches and conversation against the Southern people, and I feared his course toward them would be such as to repel, and make them unwilling citizens. . . . I felt that Reconstruction had been set back, no telling how far."[30]

Grant would be wrong in thinking that Johnson would be a vengeful president, but he would be right in fearing that the radical abolitionists would thwart Lincoln's plans for Reconstruction. On April 19 at the White House, as some 25,000 people paid the slain leader their last respects, he wept unashamedly at his catafalque.

THREE

* * * *

POLITICS AND PLAUDITS

Now all attention turned to Sherman. Following his March 28 meeting with Grant and the president, during which he had been much impressed with Lincoln's wish "to end the war speedily, without more bloodshed or devastation, and to restore all the men of sections to their homes," Sherman had returned to Goldsboro. There he began making preparations for the march north to join with Grant. His organization essentially remained the same: the Right Wing consisting of the Army of the Tennessee under Oliver Howard; the Left Wing, the Army of Georgia under Henry Slocum; the Center, the Army of the Ohio under John Schofield. When he learned of the evacuation of Richmond and Petersburg, and subsequently of Lee's April 9 surrender, these plans necessarily were scrapped.

"Of course, [Lee's surrender] caused a perfect furore of rejoicing," Sherman said, "and we all regarded the war as over, for I knew well that General Johnston had no army with which to oppose mine. So that the only questions which remained were, would he surrender . . . or would he allow his army to disperse into guerilla-bands? . . . On the evening of the 12th I was with the head of Slocum's column . . . and General Kilpatrick's cavalry was still ahead, fighting Wade Hampton's rear guard, with orders to push it through Raleigh."

In the process of occupying the city the next day, Sherman received a delegation of citizens asking for protection. "They had come with a flag of truce, to which they were not entitled; still, in the interest of peace, I respected it . . . and permitted them to assure the Governor and the people that the war was substantially over, and that I wanted the civil authorities to remain in office till the pleasure of the President could be ascertained. . . ." Thus matters stood until from Durham Station, thirty miles west of Raleigh, came a welcome message from Johnston, asking for a truce, "the object being to permit the civil authorities to enter into the needful arrangements to terminate the existing war." To which Sherman replied: "I am fully empowered to arrange with you any terms for the suspension of further hostilities. . . . That a basis of action may he had, I undertake to abide by the same terms and conditions that were made by Generals Grant and Lee at Appomattox Court House. . . ."[1]

He met with Johnston at Durham's on the 17th, just hours after learning of Lincoln's assassination, and before he had the chance to give his own people the news. Once they were alone he showed him the dispatch. "The perspiration came out in large drops on [Johnston's] forehead," Sherman said, "and he did not attempt to conceal his distress. He denounced the act as a disgrace to the age, and hoped I did not charge . . . the Confederate Government." Cump answered that he could not believe that Johnston or Lee, or any other Rebel officers had anything to do with the assassination but that he would not put it past Jefferson Davis. "I explained to him that I . . . dreaded the effect when made known in Raleigh. Mr. Lincoln was particularly endeared to the soldiers, and I feared that some foolish man or woman would say something that would madden our men, and that a fate worse than that of Columbia would befall the place."

Johnston admitted that he could not stand up to the Federals, saying further fighting would be "murder," but suggested surrendering not just his own army but also Confederate units in Louisiana and Texas and guerrilla forces, assuring Sherman he could quickly procure authority from Davis to do so.

That night, after Sherman told his officers and men of the assassination, the torching of Raleigh came close to happening. Several thousand soldiers from John Logan's corps, cursing and swearing and singing "We'll Hang Jeff Davis to a Sour Apple Tree," headed toward the city and had to be blocked by massed artillery. Sherman rode constantly among the various campsites, urging calm. "Had it not been for me Raleigh would have been destroyed," he said.[2]

When Cump and Joe Johnston met the next day, the latter produced proof that he was authorized to surrender all Rebel armies, and the two men discussed the terms. Sherman was a hard man in war, but a soft one at the negotiating table, and the document he drafted went far beyond Grant's concessions to Lee, which covered only the surrender of his army and the parole of his men. Cump in effect drafted peace terms between the Union and Confederate Governments. The agreement, he wrote Grant proudly, "if approved by the President of the United States, will produce peace from the Potomac to the Rio Grande. . . . You will observe it is an absolute submission of the enemy to the lawful authority of the United States. . . ."

Read the terms in part:

- "The Confederate armies now in existence to be disbanded and conducted to their several State capitals, there to deposit their arms and public property in the State Arsenal, and each officer and man to execute and file an agreement to cease from acts of war, and to abide the action of the State and Federal authority."
- "The recognition, by the Executive of the United States, of the several State governments, on their officers and Legislatures taking the oaths prescribed by the Constitution . . . the legitimacy of [which] shall be submitted to the Supreme Court. . . ."
- "The reestablishment of all the Federal Courts in the several States. . . ."
- "The people and inhabitants of all the States to be guaranteed, so far as the Executive can, their political rights and franchises. . . ."
- "The Executive authority of the Government of the United States not to disturb any of the people by reason of the late war, so long as they live in peace and quiet. . . ."
- "In general terms, the war to cease; a general amnesty . . . on condition of the disbandment of the Confederate armies. . . ."

To be fair Sherman headed the document "A Memorandum or Basis of Agreement," but he should have realized not only that he was exceeding his mandate but that his concessions, in the aftermath of the assassination, would make the politicians in Washington, especially the abolitionists, all but froth at the mouth.

Grant read these tidings, which were conveyed by Major Hitchcock, on the afternoon of April 21, and immediately informed Secretary of War Stanton that a meeting of President Johnson and the cabinet should be convened. By 8:00 P.M. this was accomplished, and subsequently all par-

ties concerned were in agreement—some more bombastically than others—
that the memorandum would not do. Grant, anxious to spare Sherman
embarrassment, was soon on his way to Raleigh to explain to his errant
lieutenant how he had gone wrong, and emphatically not, as Stanton
wished, to replace him at the negotiating table. "I find my duties, anxieties
and the necessities of having all my wits about me increasing rather than
diminishing," he wrote Julia before leaving. ". . . What a spectacle it will
be to see a country able to put down a rebellion, able to put half a million
of soldiers in the field, at one time, and maintain them! That will be done
and is almost done already. That nation, united, will have a strength that
will enable it to dictate to all others, *conform to justice and right*. Power I
think can go no further."[3]

Sherman was surprised and welcoming and perhaps a bit relieved when his
friend showed up on his doorstep on April 24. Since drafting the peace
terms he had received a bundle of Northern newspapers, filled with stories
calling for Lincoln's death to be avenged, and become far more aware that
conciliatory gestures would not be tolerated and even be suspect. Indeed,
he had sent a warning to Johnston: "I fear much that the assassination of
the President will give such a bias to the popular mind, which, in connection with the desire of our politicians, may thwart our purpose of recognizing 'the existing local governments'. . . ."

Grant immediately dealt with the matter in hand, explaining to Sherman the bitter feelings in Washington about the South in general and his
memorandum in particular, tactfully omitting the more vituperative
phrases that Stanton and others had used. He suggested that Sherman
meet with Johnston again and draft another agreement, confining himself
to the surrender of the Confederate armies. Cump did so without protest,
Johnston concurred, and on the 26th a new pact was signed. Grant's arrival had been so unobtrusive, his advice so calm and measured, and his
departure so quick, that both he and Sherman must have felt the initial
memo would be forgotten. "I did not wish the knowledge of my presence
to be known to the army generally," Grant said, "so I left it to Sherman to
negotiate the terms of surrender solely by himself, and without the enemy
knowing I was anywhere near the field. As soon as possible I started to get
away, to leave [him] free and untrammeled."[4]

Stanton meanwhile was fulminating against Sherman furiously to the
press, chewing up his original terms to Johnston and spitting them out in
unrecognizable form, all but accusing Cump of treason. Among his
complaints: Sherman was advocating Rebels be seated in the state legisla-

tures, compensating slaveowners for their "property," and forcing the federal government to pay the South's war debts. Newspapers took up his ranting, and spread the allegations far and wide. "It looks very much," said *The New York Times*, "as if this negotiation was a blind to cover the escape of Jeff Davis and a few of his officials"—Davis was still at large and would not be captured until May 10 in Alabama—"with the millions of gold they have stolen from Richmond banks." The *Chicago Tribune* called the memorandum "the hypothesis of stark insanity"; the *Washington Star* said it was "calamitous mischief"; and the *New York Herald* warned that Cump had "fatally blundered."

Henry Halleck, perhaps trying to curry favor with Stanton, likewise roiled the waters. "Generals Meade, Sheridan and Wright are acting under orders to pay no regard to any truce or orders of General Sherman, respecting hostilities," he pompously wired the secretary from Richmond, "on the ground that Sherman's agreement could bind his command only, and no other. They are directed to push forward, regardless of orders from anyone except General Grant. . . ." All this hullabaloo, we must remember, was being raised over a proposal that was in the process, with minimal fuss, of being superceded.[5]

Sherman, as usual, hit back hard. "The tone of all the papers . . . is taken up from the War Department," he wrote John Rawlins, Grant's chief of staff, on the 29th, ". . . which is untrue, unfair, and unkind to me, and I will say undeserved. There has been at no time any trouble about Joe Johnston's army. It fell and became powerless when Lee was defeated; but its dispersion, when the country was already full of Lee's men, would have made North Carolina a pandemonium. I desired to avoid that. . . . The South is broken and ruined, and appeals to our pity. . . . I will fight as long as the enemy shows fight, but when he gives up and asks quarter, I cannot go further."

Cump felt that Stanton was either uninformed or malicious. "If he wants to hunt down Jeff. Davis or the politicians who instigated civil war, let him use sheriffs, bailiffs and catch thieves, and not hint that I should march heavy columns of infantry hundreds of miles on a fool's errand. The idea of Jeff. Davis running about the country with tons of gold is ridiculous. I doubt not he is a beggar, and who will say that if we catch him, he will be punished? The very men who now howl the loudest will be the first to intercede. . . .

"I doubt not efforts will be made to sow dissension between Grant and myself, on a false supposition that we have political aspirations, or, after killing me off by libels, he will next be assailed. I can keep away from

Washington, and I confide in his good sense to save him from the influences that will surround him there. . . ."[6]

Within weeks the charges subsided, but Sherman remained incensed. During May, even as he was leading his army north through Richmond, preparing for the Grand Review of the Armies in Washington, he continued to vent. To Halleck, whom he had long regarded as a supporter, he telegraphed: "After your dispatch to Mr. Stanton . . . I cannot have any friendly intercourse with you." To Ellen he insisted: "I have seen the New York papers of April 24 & 28 but don't mind them much for it is manifest that some deviltry is on foot—the telegraph of Halleck endorsed by Stanton is the worst, but its falsity and baseness puts them at my mercy. . . . I am not dead yet by a long sight and these matters give me new life. . . ." To Grant he confided: "Your private and official wishes when conveyed to me shall be sacred, but there can be no relations between Mr. Stanton & me. . . . You are cool, and have been most skillful in managing such people, and I have faith you will penetrate his designs. . . ."[7]

There is little doubt that Grant stood foursquare behind Sherman in the contretemps with Stanton, but at the time he typically kept his own counsel and made few public statements. Only years later, ruminating on the relationship with Lincoln and the Secretary of War, would he make some telling comments. "They were the very opposite of each other in almost every particular," Grant said, "except that each possessed great ability. Mr. Lincoln gained influence over men by making them feel that it was a pleasure to serve him. He preferred yielding his own wish to gratify others. . . . In matters of public duty, however, he had what he wished, but in the least offensive way." Stanton cared nothing for the feelings of others. "In fact, it seemed to be pleasanter to him to disappoint than to gratify. He felt no hesitation in assuming the functions of the [President], or in acting without advising him."

Most people, Grant went on, supposed the two men complemented each other. "The Secretary was required to keep the President from being imposed upon. The President was required in the more responsible place of seeing that injustice was not done to others." Grant disagreed. "Mr. Lincoln did not require a guardian to aid him in the fulfillment of a public trust." We cannot help but infer from these remarks that the general-in-chief believed that Lincoln, if he had lived, would never have permitted the vilification of Sherman that President Andrew Johnson, albeit briefly, allowed the blustery Stanton to pursue.

"Mr. Lincoln was not timid," Grant summed up, "and he was willing to trust his generals in making and executing their plans. The Secretary was very timid, and it was impossible for him to avoid interfering with the armies. . . . He could see our weakness, but he could not see that the enemy [also] was in danger. The enemy would not have been in danger if Mr. Stanton was in the field."[8]

The Grand Review of the Armies was to take place in Washington May 23 and 24, with Meade's Army of the Potomac marching the first day and Sherman's Army of the West the second. Both commands—some 200,000 troops—pitched their tents in sprawling camps for miles outside the capital well before the event, and found—officers and men alike—that their natural rivalries were still strong. The Easterners, of course, had long chafed at being regarded, however unjustly, as "spit-and-polish" soldiers, good for marching and maneuvering but not so good, under a succession of leaders, at bringing Lee to bay—even after his defeat at Gettysburg. The Westerners, more rustic and rawboned, far less splendidly outfitted, had tasted nothing but victory from Donelson to Shiloh to Vicksburg, and from Chattanooga to Atlanta and the March to the Sea—and to the charge that they had not had to fight Lee, their cocky, confident answer was a whoop and a holler.

Exacerbating these differences was the Sherman affair, which with convoluted reasoning some of the Westerners attributed to a vast East Coast (and Army of the Potomac) conspiracy. Fistfights among the men were common, and at least some of the Western officers in late-night revelry at the Willard Hotel, standing on the bar, demanded that the crowd join them in "Three Groans for Stanton." Grant resolved the situation, in part, by keeping the two armies on opposite sides of the Potomac.[9]

Washington on the 23rd was awash in red-white-and-blue banners and bunting, and the flag of the United States was seemingly everywhere and at full mast for the first time since the assassination. The weather was sunny and clear, spring flowers complemented the picture, and tens of thousands of citizens gathered for the occasion. Grandstands had been erected on Pennsylvania Avenue, in front of the White House, for the president, his cabinet, and distinguished guests. "At nine o'clock the signal gun was fired, and the legions took up their march," said Horace Porter. "They started from the Capitol, and moved along Pennsylvania Avenue toward Georgetown. . . . Martial music from scores of bands filled the air, and when familiar war-songs were played the spectators along the route joined in shouting the chorus. Those oftenest sung and most applauded were,

'When This Cruel War Is Over,' 'When Johnny Comes Marching Home,' and 'Tramp, Tramp, Tramp! The Boys are Marching.'"

Grant did not lead the parade, but sat in the reviewing stand with President Johnson. That honor fell to George Meade, who brought his Army of the Potomac in swinging and awesome cadence, twelve men abreast, down the avenue. "The men preserved their alignment and distances with an ease which showed their years of training in the field," said Porter. "Their movements were unfettered, their step was elastic, and the swaying of their bodies and the swinging of their arms were as measured as the vibrations of a pendulum. Their muskets shone like a wall of steel. The cannon rumbled peacefully along the paved street, banks of flowers almost concealing them." Nothing touched the spectators so deeply as the sight of the old war-flags. "Those precious standards, bullet-riddled, battle-stained, many of them but remnants, often with not enough left of them to show the names of the battles they had seen. . . ."

Meade stopped abreast of the grandstand, temporarily halted his columns, and then joined the dignitaries, as all the senior commanders would do. The victor at Gettysburg, he had offered Grant his resignation when the latter came East, saying he might want his own man in the post. The offer as we know had been refused, and Meade thereafter, in a most difficult chain-of-command position had served his chief well. Now he was enjoying his reward. "I'm afraid my poor tatterdemalion corps will make a poor appearance tomorrow when contrasted with yours," Sherman whispered to him.

Behind Meade came seven miles of cavalry, led by the capable Wesley Merritt. Grant had sent Sheridan down to the Rio Grande, there to lead 50,000 men of the Trans-Mississippi and threaten the French troops keeping Maximilian in power. The gesture would work, and Maximilian's rule soon would collapse, but Sheridan dearly missed his day in the sun. The golden-tressed Custer, his irrepressible protégé, either by accident or design managed to thrill the crown in his stead when "his spirited horse took the bit in his teeth, and made a dash past the troops, rushing by the reviewing officers like a tornado. . . ." When Custer regained control, the crowd screamed with delight.[10]

John Parke's 9th Corps came next. Parke had fought throughout the Overland Campaign and then replaced Ambrose Burnside after the blunders at the Crater during the Petersburg siege. Following Parke was Charles Griffin's 5th Corps, Griffin who had succeeded the unfortunate Gouverneur Warren in the aftermath of Five Forks. Down the avenue

lastly marched Andrew Humphreys's 2nd Corps, Humphreys having replaced Winfield Scott Hancock, the latter forced by his Gettysburg wound
from field service. Horatio Wright and the 6th Corps, who arguably had
saved the day at Cedar Creek, did not parade, remaining on occupation
duty in Virginia. "You think of . . . the scriptural words, 'terrible as an
army with banners,' wrote one reporter. Terrible [this army] is, indeed,
in its strength. One wonders that such a power . . . could have so long
been resisted." Concluded Porter: "For nearly seven hours the pageant was
watched . . . and when it faded from view the spectators were eager for the
night to pass, so that on the morrow the scene might be renewed. . . ."[11]

Sherman, whose appearance was unknown to most people in the East,
led the line of march the next day. But his war-lined face, bristly coppery
hair and tall, spare figure made him all that the spectators had imagined,
and they cheered him with gusto. Accompanying him was Oliver Otis
Howard, who had just been reassigned from command of the Army of the
Tennessee to head of the Freedman's Bureau, and instead of leading his
old troops he rode with Sherman, his armless right sleeve testifying to his
heroism.

With the bands striking up "Marching Through Georgia," Cump dismounted at the grandstand and made his way to the president and the dignitaries, shaking hands and exchanging a few words with each as he
progressed. But it was Edwin Stanton he had on his mind. When the secretary extended his hand, said Porter, "Sherman's whole manner changed
in an instant; a cloud of anger overspread his features, and, smarting under the wrong the Secretary had done him . . . the general turned abruptly
way. This rebuff became the sensation of the day." Reported another observer: "Sherman's face was scarlet and his red hair seemed to stand on
end." Stanton, his face immobile, quickly withdrew his hand. Following
this public display, Cump took his place on Johnson's left, both men content to watch the parade.[12]

Black Jack Logan now came riding down the avenue at the head of the
Army of the Tennessee, that storied force that first Grant and then Sherman once had led. His corps commanders were William Hazen of the 15th,
whom we came to know at Chattanooga, and Frank P. Blair Jr. of the 17th,
who had served with the army since Vicksburg. Hazen's divisions were
headed by Charles Woods, John E. Smith, and John Corse; Blair's were
commanded by Manning Force, Mortimer Leggett, and Giles A. Smith, all
of whom have figured in our story. Next came Henry Slocum, leading the
Army of Georgia. With him were the bold Joe Mower, commanding the
20th Corps, and the bellicose and oddly named Jefferson C. Davis, leading

the 14th. Mower's divisions were led by Alpheus Williams, John Geary, and William Ward; Davis's divisions, by Charles Walcutt, James Dada Morgan, and Absalom Baird, likewise officers we have seen in battles large and small. John Schofield's Army of the Ohio remained on duty in North Carolina.

"It was, in my judgement," said Sherman, "the most magnificent army in existence. . . . Division after division passed. . . . The steadiness and firmness of the tread, the careful dress on the guides, the uniform intervals between the companies . . . all attracted universal notice. Many good people, up to that time, had looked upon our Western army as a sort of mob, but the world then saw . . . that it was an army in the proper sense, well organized, well commanded and disciplined, and it was no wonder that it had swept through the South like a tornado."[13]

The hero of the Grand Review, of course, was Ulysses S. Grant, to whom every eye was turned. Coming out of obscurity at the beginning of the war, he had time and again bent circumstances to his will, and surmounted every problem. "He was possessed of a moral and physical courage which was equal to every emergency in which he was placed," stated Horace Porter. "He was calm amid excitement, patient under trials, clear in foresight, never depressed by reverses or unduly elated by success. He was fruitful in expedients, and had a facility of resource and a faculty of adapting the means at hand to the accomplishment of an end. . . . His singular self-reliance enabled him at critical junctures to decide instantly questions of vital moment. . . ."

Just as important was his innate decency. "His soldiers always knew that he was ready to rough it with them and share their hardships. . . . He wore no better clothes than they, and often ate no better food. There was nothing in his manner to suggest any gulf between him and the men who were winning his victories. He never tired of giving unstinting praise to his subordinates. . . . His fidelity produced a reciprocal effect, and is one of the chief reasons why they became so loyalty attached to him. . . . He never underrated himself in a battle; he never overrated himself in a report."[14]

Ulysses S. Grant, the plainspoken midwesterner once reduced to selling firewood on the streets of St. Louis, had triumphed in his greatest challenge. The United States of America would be forever in his debt.

FOUR
* * * *

THE SURVIVORS

The numbers who perished are awesome. Some 360,000 Federals died in the Civil War defending the Union, and 260,000 Confederates gave their lives to secede from it, and all believed in the righteousness of their cause. We can only marvel at their sacrifice. To make our story complete, let us look now at some Northern survivors, and how they fared in the years thereafter.

Ulysses S. Grant, promoted to full general by President Johnson, had an uneasy working relationship with him from the start. Contrary to the president's wishes, he promptly endorsed Lee's application for amnesty and protested his indictment for treason (the indictment soon was dropped), saying the Confederate leader and his officers otherwise would never have surrendered. When he threatened to resign if the terms agreed upon at Appomattox were not honored, Johnson relented. Later he again bucked the president, a Jacksonian Democrat who was no believer in black suffrage, insisting on keeping Federal troops as occupiers and the Freedmen's Bureau as an administrative authority in the South, noting that these steps were "an absolute necessity until civil law is established."

More and more, despite sharing Johnson's feelings that whites in the South should not be brutalized during Reconstruction, Grant found himself in the camp of Stanton and the radical Republicans, who were determined that white resistance in the former Confederacy should not keep blacks there from gaining equal rights. (In late 1865 the Thirteenth Amendment, following up on Lincoln's Emancipation Proclamation, had abolished slavery; in 1866 the Fourteenth Amendment had given blacks citizenship.) It seemed only natural, then, especially after the House in 1868 impeached Johnson—because of these civil rights' quarrels—that the Republicans should nominate Grant for president. He stood for sound money, government economy, and forceful, but not vengeful, Reconstruction. Campaigning under the slogan "Let us have peace," he was elected with 52.7 percent of the vote.

Once in the presidency, Grant named Sherman general-in-chief, John Rawlins Secretary of War, and Elihu Washburne, his old benefactor, minister to France. But his administration soon drew charges of corruption. Though personally honest, he sometimes appeared to pay little attention to the motives of those around him, and often, his critics contended, ignored their transgressions. One early example of this hands-off attitude occurred in 1869, when the financiers James Fisk and Jay Gould, using their ties to a Grant family member, plotted to corner the gold market. Though he blocked their attempt, he took no other action against them. He nonetheless was handily reelected, with an overwhelming black vote. "We will not find a candidate equal to General Grant," said Frederick Douglass, and his people listened.

Grant's second term likewise was sporadically marked by scandal, including charges of graft taking against William Belknap, Rawlins's successor as Secretary of War, and Orville Babcock, Grant's private secretary. The allegations against Belknap seem to be justified (he resigned), but those against Babcock were overtly circumstantial (he was cleared) and Grant, unruffled as usual, backed him to the hilt, coming forward voluntarily and testifying in his behalf. Hamilton Fish, Grant's well-respected Secretary of State, summed up how most citizens felt about their president. "I do not think it would have been possible for Grant to tell a lie," he insisted, "even if he had composed it and written it down."

Following his presidency, Grant and Julia from 1877 to 1880 traveled widely throughout America, Europe, Africa, the Mideast, and the Far East, meeting dignitaries and being feted everywhere. In 1880, still enormously popular, he came within an eyelash of winning the Republican nomination for a third term, losing on the thirty-sixth ballot to James A. Garfield. The next year he invested all his working capital, perhaps some $100,000, in Grant & Ward, a private brokerage firm founded by Ferdinand Ward and others—including his son Buck, now a grown man and a lawyer—thinking the move would make him financially secure. Initially he prospered, but then in 1884 Ward was revealed as an embezzler and Grant, at age sixty-two, trying to make good the firm's debts, lost everything, including his homes and his Civil War memorabilia. The nation grieved for his losses but Grant, characteristically, simply regrouped.

In 1885, weakened by throat cancer and fortified by frequent injections of cocaine to ease the pain and morphine to let him sleep, he raced against death to write his *Personal Memoirs.* He succumbed within days after completing them. His *Memoirs,* one of the greatest military histories ever written, would earn Julia almost $500,000—then an enormous sum. One last time, Grant had risen to the occasion.[1]

William Tecumseh Sherman, promoted to lieutenant general in 1866 and then to full general and general-in-chief in 1869, did not maintain his close relationship with Grant during the postwar years. Politically, the paths of the two men diverged. Both before and after Grant's election to the presidency, Sherman supported Johnson's policies toward the South, believing that white rule there, so long as it bowed to the supremacy of the Union, was in the natural order of things and that blacks should have little or no voice in government. (The radical Republicans in Congress nonetheless prevailed, carving the South into five military districts in 1867 and imposing martial law; the last Federal troops would not leave until 1871.)

Sherman's tenure as general-in-chief spanned fifteen years, from 1869 to 1884, an amazing statistic when we consider how much he professed to despise politicians. In this capacity he served under Presidents Grant, Rutherford B. Hayes, James Garfield, and Chester Arthur, railed over what he considered lenient treatment of rebellious Indians and harsh reprisals against recalcitrant white Southerners, and fought fruitlessly against drastic reductions in the army's strength. When in Washington he kept gentleman's hours, arriving at the War Office about 10:00 A.M., having a leisurely lunch and departing about four. But he also traveled widely on inspection tours and missions, usually without the home-loving Ellen, who had given him six children, and became involved, for the most part through public flirtations, with a succession of women. "I never saw a man so run after by womankind in my life," a friend remarked. His own *Memoirs,* which like Grant's provide a splendid record of the war, were published in 1875.

Three years later Sherman, who as we know had no use for his wife's Catholicism, learned that his son Thomas had decided to become a Jesuit priest. Devastated by the news, he petitioned John Cardinal McCloskey of New York to intercede. When the cardinal declined to do so, Sherman sank into depression. "Henceforth," he told one of his daughters in his hyperbolic way, "my thoughts will go out more and more to my old army comrades, because they now compose my family. . . ."

Sherman retired from the army in 1884, and many voices urged him to seek the Republican nomination for the presidency. True to his principles, often misguided as they were, he refused, saying, "I will not accept if nominated and will not serve if elected." He settled in New York with Ellen, close to some of his children and grandchildren, joined the Union League Club and helped found the Players', and became a sought-after speaker. His wife's death in 1888 again pushed him into depression. Despite their differences he loved her, and he knew in his heart she was the bedrock in his life. "To her the world was a day—Heaven eternity," he acknowledged. "Could I . . . I would not bring her back. . . ."

Three years later, at age seventy-one, he died of respiratory problems. Thomas subsequently officiated at a private Catholic service, and among Sherman's honorary pallbearers on a bitter February day was Confederate General Joseph Johnston, who doffed his hat and kept his head bared despite the cold and his own shaky health. "If I were in his place and he standing here in mine," the eighty-four-year-old Rebel said, "he would not put on his hat." Johnston was right; Sherman always marched to his own drummer.[2]

The man who exerted so much influence over Grant's and Sherman's early careers, *Henry Halleck,* and whose prewar career, both in the army and in civilian life, had been so brilliant, was all but forgotten in the war's aftermath. Stripped of his chief of staff title by Stanton, he served briefly as commander of occupied Richmond. There his passion for administrative details produced positive results when he personally intervened to save some ten tons of Confederate documents. These later formed the bulk of the Confederate part of the monumental 128-volume *War of the Rebellion, A Compilation of the Official Records of the Union and Confederate Armies,* the all-important bible of the conflict.

Halleck seems to have been universally disliked by the military establishment, in no small measure due to the fact that, first as general-in-chief and then chief of staff, his was the name, notorious for its bureaucratic bent, under which so many confusing and blustering orders were dispatched and officers disciplined. Grant, Sherman, and other high-ranking officers may have had their scapegoats, but they inspired far more loyalty— and, yes, friendship—in their subordinates. Old Brains, a cold fish, never warmed to comradeship. He subsequently was transferred from Richmond to command on the Pacific Coast, with headquarters in San Francisco, where he passed many dreary months dealing with stubborn Indians, dedicating monuments, and presiding over formal dinners.

Transferred to command in the South in 1869, Halleck made his head-quarters in Louisville, Kentucky, where his responsibilities were equally tiresome. Three years later, not yet fifty-seven years old, he suddenly became gravely ill. He embraced Catholicism on his deathbed, and was baptized by his cousin, the bishop of Minneapolis. Neither Grant nor Sherman seems, in any significant degree, to have marked his passing.

Elihu Washburne, the longtime Illinois congressman who was Grant's political mentor, spent a half dozen years after the war as a highly effective minister to France, helped in large measure by his French wife. In 1876 he campaigned for the Republican presidential nomination but lost to Hayes, and four years later tried again (running against Grant, among others), but lost to Garfield. Teetotaler *John Rawlins*, Grant's alter ego, received a brevet major general's commission about the time he learned he had tuberculosis, the disease that had killed his first wife. Travel recommended by his doctors in the High Plains country of the Far West did not improve his health. He died in 1869, five months after he was named Secretary of War.

Morgan Smith, who fought so well at Fort Donelson, Shiloh, and Vicksburg—and is one of many Smiths we have encountered in our story—was appointed consul general to Hawaii by President Johnson. Subsequently he pursued business interests in Washington, where he died in 1874. *Lew Wallace* the man who lost his way at Shiloh but helped block Jubal Early's raid on the capital, was a member of the court-martial trying the conspirators in the Lincoln assassination, and was head of the court-martial that condemned Henry Wirz, commandant of the notorious Confederate prison camp at Andersonville, to death. Later he helped unseat Maximilian in Mexico, was governor of New Mexico, wrote the classic novel *Ben Hur,* and was minister to Turkey. He lived until 1905. *Stephen Hurlbut,* another Shiloh commander, returned to Illinois and became a force in state politics, despite charges of drunkenness and corruption. He was named by Grant minister to Columbia, served in the U.S. Congress, and was appointed by Garfield minister to Peru, where he was again charged with corruption. He died in Lima in 1882.

The journalist who almost wrecked Grant's career in the wake of Shiloh, *Whitelaw Reid,* was hired by Horace Greeley in 1868 as managing editor of the respected *New York Tribune.* Following Greeley's death, Reid gained control of the paper. Subsequently, while continuing to run the *Tribune,* he served as minister to France and ambassador to Great Britain, dying in London in 1912. *Sylvanus Cadwallader,* the Chicago newspaperman who was witness to Grant's supposed 1863 binge on the

Mississippi, became head of the *New York Herald*'s Washington Bureau, moved to Wisconsin and worked in state government, and ended up a sheep farmer in California, where in 1896 he wrote his reminiscences. They were not published, amazingly enough, until 1955.

William Rosecrans, who feuded with Grant at Iuka and Corinth, never did recover, militarily speaking, from his defeat at Chickamauga. He waited out the rest of the war in Missouri and in 1867 resigned his commission. He briefly was minister to Mexico, then took up ranching in California. During the 1880s and early 1890s he served in the U.S. Congress, becoming chairman of the House Military Affairs Committee, and as a Treasury official. He eventually returned to California and devoted himself to his family, in particular his grandchildren. One grandson, who remembered him as "about the most cheerful person imaginable," also said: "He never mentioned Grant." Rosecrans died in 1898, and the Roman Catholic bishop of Los Angeles, officiating at his requiem mass, observed, "He served his country with fidelity, courage and zest."[3]

Black Jack Logan fought his way through the war as a superb field commander. Afterward he served both as congressman and senator from Illinois for many years, was the vice-presidential candidate on the unsuccessful ticket with Grover Cleveland in 1884, and one of the founders of Memorial Day. He died in 1886. *Joe Mower,* who feared nobody and made himself a legend in regimental, brigade, divisional, and ultimately corps command, was assigned in the peacetime army to command of Colored troops—as African-American soldiers then were called. He died of pneumonia, in 1870, on active duty in Louisiana. *Edward Ord,* who was wounded at Corinth and again at the siege of Petersburg, and took charge of the belittled Army of the James from *Benjamin Butler,* stayed in the army until 1881, and died two years later of yellow fever in Havana, Cuba.

The irrepressible Rear Admiral *David Dixon Porter,* to whom Grant and Sherman owed so much in thwarting *John McClernand's* finagling during the Vicksburg Campaign, turned his talents to the rebuilding of the Naval Academy at Annapolis, Maryland, served as its superintendent, and was promoted to vice admiral. In 1870, upon *David Farragut's* death, he was advanced to full admiral. Though his duties thereafter were largely ceremonial, he remained the navy's champion, never ceasing to warn about its downgrading by Congress. (In the aftermath of the rebellion, both the navy and army would be stripped of funds, a decision that ill prepared America for wars of the future.) "It would be much better to have no navy

at all than the one at present," he harrumphed. Porter suffered a heart attack in 1890, and passed away the next year in Washington. Sherman visited his old friend just before his death, but did not see him because he
was sleeping. "I shall be the next one," he told his daughter with a smile,
"and perhaps I may go before Porter." Returning to New York, Sherman
survived his Vicksburg crony by no more than twenty-four hours.[4]

Frederick Steele, George Washington Morgan, Morgan Smith, and *Andrew Jackson Smith* did the fighting at Chickasaw Bluffs, the opening of
the Vicksburg Campaign in December of 1862. *Steele* continued in the
regular army after the war, and by 1869 was in command of the District
of Columbia. He died that year in a fall from his carriage, brought on by
apoplexy. *George Morgan,* no believer in black suffrage, was defeated in
his bid to become governor of Ohio in 1865, but subsequently was elected
three times to Congress on the Democratic ticket and was a determined
Northern opponent of the radical Republicans. He died in 1893. *Morgan
Smith's* end we have already seen. His younger brother, *Giles Smith,* who
likewise served in the Army of the Tennessee, was appointed by Grant to
a Federal post in 1869 but was forced to resign for health reasons; he died
in Illinois in 1876. *Andrew Jackson Smith* at first stayed in the regular
army, but by 1869 was postmaster of St. Louis and, from 1877 to 1889,
city auditor. He passed away in 1897, at age eighty-two.

The dark side of the Vicksburg Campaign, of course, is represented by
the specter of *John McClernand,* whose political ties with Lincoln were so
strong he might have superceded Grant. Banished to the 18th Corps,
which was dispersed in Louisiana and Texas, McClernand resigned from
the army in 1864 and returned to Springfield, Illinois. There he brooded,
practiced law, reentered Democratic politics, was elected a circuit judge,
and, in 1875, brooded anew when the publication of Sherman's *Memoirs*
reinforced his conviction that he had been the victim of a conspiracy. To
George Morgan, his former subordinate, he insisted that Sherman had
"inconsiderately hurried" the troops at Memphis down the Mississippi
"to forestall my arrival to take command"—which, it must be admitted,
was true.

In 1876, McClernand chaired the National Democratic Convention
that nominated Samuel Tilden for the presidency. Tilden won the popular
vote, but lost by one vote to Rutherford Hayes in the Electoral College
when Republicans cut a deal with Southern politicians to remove all
troops from the former Confederacy in return for their support. Outmaneuvered once more, McClernand could only call the election a "crime which
defeated the will of the people." He continued to be a force in Illinois and

national politics, however, and maintained an active life in Springfield with his wife, Minerva and their three children. His last public position was in 1886, when he was named commissioner of the Utah Territory by Democratic President Cleveland. He died four years later, the epitaph on his tombstone reading Lawyer, Legislator, Judge, Soldier, Patriot.[5]

The army's corps at Vicksburg were those of *McClernand, Sherman,* and *James McPherson*—the last named officer, as we know, was killed at Atlanta. *McClernand*'s division heads were *Peter Osterhaus,* the aforementioned *Andrew Jackson Smith, Alvin Hovey,* and *Eugene Carr.* From 1866 to 1877 *Osterhaus* served as consul to France, then returned to America to pursue business interests, and from 1898 to 1900 was vice- and deputy-consul to Germany. He died there in 1917. *Hovey* served with the army through Atlanta but then, disappointed over not being promoted, commanded in Indiana until the end of the war. Thereafter he was appointed minister to Peru, returned to Indiana to practice law, was elected to Congress, and then captured the governorship. He died in office in 1891. *Carr* went on to fight in Arkansas and Mobile, Alabama, then in peacetime served in the West with the 5th and 6th Cavalry. Fighting against the Cheyenne, Sioux, and Apaches he became a storied figure, called War Eagle by his adversaries. He died in 1910, at ninety years of age.

Sherman's divisions during most of the action at Vicksburg were headed by the aforementioned *Frederick Steele,* and by *Frank Blair Jr.,* and *James Madison Tuttle. Blair* resigned his commission in 1865, all but a pauper for having selflessly donated his assets to the Union cause. His opposition to the policies of the radical Republicans, however, led Congress to reject his nominations by Johnson as revenue collector in St. Louis and then as minister to Austria. Blair reacted by reorganizing the Democratic party in Missouri. In 1871 he was elected to the Senate to fill an unexpired term, but two years later failed to win reelection. He died in 1875. *Tuttle* resigned one year before the war ended, engaged in farming and real estate in Iowa, and served several terms in the legislature. In 1877 he branched out into mining in Arizona, where he died in 1892.

The ill-starred *McPherson* had *John Logan, John McArthur,* and *Isaac Quinby* as his division commanders. *Logan*'s postwar career we have seen. *McArthur* returned to Chicago, but failed in reviving his Excelsior Iron Works, which had fallen on hard times in his absence. Later the Great Chicago Fire of 1871 when he was commissioner of public works, and the loss of Federal funds in a bank failure when he was the city's postmaster—for which he was held liable—added to his problems. He nonetheless remained active in veterans' organizations until his death in 1906. Plagued by illness during the Vicksburg Campaign, *Quinby* for two weeks in May, 1863, shared command with *Marcellus Crocker*. He resigned from the army in December 1863 and resumed an academic career, teaching mathematics and science at the University of Rochester (New York) until 1884. Later he was city surveyor of Rochester. He died in 1891. *Crocker,* who himself was ill with tuberculosis, was ordered to New Mexico in 1864 in a vain attempt to restore his health. He died in Washington the next year.

Two more stalwarts, as we know, joined the army in time for Vicksburg: *Charles Dana* and *James H. Wilson.* Lincoln's supposed and sophisticated spy, *Dana* could not have been more supportive for the two years he was with Grant, telling the president the truth: Grant was the man who would win the war. Following Appomattox, he helped found the *Chicago Daily Republican,* then in 1867 arranged to buy the *New York Sun,* which he guided for twenty-nine years and made into the most successful newspaper of the era, establishing its readership in the Democratic working class. His growing wealth enabled him to influence politics, travel abroad, master several languages, and collect both Chinese porcelains and fine wines. He died in 1897.

Wilson, who became Dana's close friend, remained in the army briefly, serving in the Corps of Engineers. He resigned in 1870 to engage in railroad building and management, and thereafter devoted himself to business, public affairs, and writing several books. Both he and Dana during Grant's presidency became increasingly estranged from their friend, whose decisions sometimes blocked their own ambitions. When the Spanish-American War broke out in 1898, Wilson at age sixty-one volunteered and served as a major general. He subsequently helped put down the Boxer Rebellion in China and, in 1902, represented President Theodore Roosevelt at the coronation of Britain's Edward VII. He lived until 1925, the last surviving member of his West Point class of 1860.

Benjamin Grierson, the cavalryman whose raid through the heart of the Confederacy so facilitated Grant's advance into Mississippi, stayed in the regular army postwar and was named head of the 10th Cavalry, fighting Indians in Arizona and New Mexico. He retired in 1890 and died, twenty-one years later, in the Midwest.

George Thomas, the "Rock of Chickamauga" whom Grant later came to believe too slow and plodding, continued to feel the general-in-chief's displeasure in peacetime. Sizable commands during Reconstruction were to go to Sherman and other high-ranking generals, but Thomas was being asked to take a division within Sherman's department. The Virginian, who had sacrificed his family ties in his adherence to the Union, exploded. "I wish you to take the first train to Washington," he instructed an aide, "and tell President Johnson that during the war I permitted the authorities to do what they pleased with me. The life of the nation was then at stake. . . . I [now] demand a command suited to my rank, or I do not want any."

Johnson agreed with Thomas, and eventually gave him the Department of the Cumberland, which included the vital states of Kentucky and Tennessee. Later he served on the Pacific Coast, replacing Halleck. There he died of a stroke in 1870, while penning a response to charges that he had mishandled the Nashville Campaign. He was buried in Troy, New York, his wife's home, with President Grant, Sherman, many high-ranking officers, and representatives of the Army of the Cumberland in attendance. No members of his Virginia family were present.[6]

William Farrar "Baldy" Smith, who was instrumental in opening the "Cracker Line" and then was assigned to the Army of the James, resigned from the army in 1867 and served, successively, as head of a telegraph company, president of the board of police commissioners of New York City, and a civilian engineer on river and harbor projects. He died in 1903. *Ambrose Burnside,* the Army of the Potomac refugee whom we first met at Chattanooga but who soon would transfer back to the East, held many railroad and industrial posts, was three times elected governor of Rhode Island, and served as a senator from that state until his death in 1881.

Two more refugees from the Army of the Potomac were *Joseph Hooker* and *Oliver Otis Howard.* The disgruntled *Hooker* suffered a stroke in 1867 and retired from service the next year, living comfortably on inherited income. He had praise postwar only for Thomas. Sherman was "crazy," Grant had "no more moral sense than a dog," and Howard "would command a prayer meeting with a good deal more authority than he would an army." He died in 1879.[7] The deeply religious *O. O. Howard* made a hash of his appointment to head the Freedman's Bureau, refusing to believe evidence of rampant corruption among his appointees and their associates. A firm supporter of black suffrage, he helped found Howard University, and during the 1870s and 1880s served in Indian country. He retired from the army in 1894, but continued to pursue religious and educational interests. He belatedly received the Medal of Honor for his conduct at Seven Pines—the battle at which he lost his arm—and died in 1909.

John White Geary, who fought so well at Wauhatchie, was elected Republican governor of Pennsylvania for two terms, and suddenly succumbed to illness in 1873.

Various other commanders of the Army of the Cumberland feature in our story. John Palmer, who like Hooker complained about his rank, was elected in 1868 Republican governor of Illinois. A state's rights man at heart, he soon reverted to his Democratic beginnings and in 1888 was a delegate to the convention that nominated Grover Cleveland for the presidency. Later he was elected a Democratic senator from Illinois. In 1896 he and Confederate General Simon Buckner ran unsuccessfully on a minority party ticket for president and vice president. He died in 1900. *Gordon Granger,* whose independence on occasion came close to insubordination, continued in the army, with frequent absences for sick leave, until 1876, the year he died.

Thomas Wood, William Hazen, and *Phil Sheridan* all fought gallantly at Chattanooga and Missionary Ridge, and for that matter throughout the war. *Wood,* largely disabled by his wounds, left the army in 1868 and settled in Dayton, Ohio. Thereafter he was active in veterans' affairs and a member of West Point's Board of Visitors. The first roommate that Grant had at the academy, he was the last survivor of the West Point class of 1845, dying in 1906. Hazen would stay in the army. There for years he coped with Indians and settlers on the frontier, observed the Franco-Prussian War, and testified to the trading-post corruption that brought down Secretary of War William Belknap. In 1880 President Rutherford Hayes named him chief signal officer, a post he held until his death seven years later.

Philip Henry Sheridan, who next to Grant and Sherman won the most acclaim among Northern generals in the conflict, was so rigorous in his occupation policies in Louisiana and Texas after the war that his removal by Johnson and transfer to Missouri caused only slight protest among radical Republicans. "If I am disliked, it is because I cannot and will not cater to Rebel sentiment," said Sheridan. "The more I see of this people the less I see to admire." At the outset of Grant's presidency in 1869 he was named lieutenant general, reporting to Sherman. Thereafter until 1883, with time out to marry a woman exactly half his age, he fought the Indians in the West on a bloody, give-no-quarter basis, becoming something of a pariah in the East in church and humanitarian circles. The next year, upon Sherman's retirement, he nonetheless became general-in-chief and, a few months before his death of heart disease in 1888, was raised to full general. His Catholic funeral mass was held at St. Matthew's Church in Washington, with the battle flag that he had waved to rally the troops at Cedar Creek at the head of his coffin. Military pomp and ceremony, at his wife's request, was kept to a minimum. The cardinal who delivered the eulogy took his text from First Maccabees: "How is the mighty fallen that saved the people of Israel."[8]

Other leaders of the Armies of the Cumberland and the Tennessee were *Richard W. Johnson, Jefferson C. Davis* and *Absalom Baird,* and *John E. Smith* and *Hugh Ewing.* Retiring in 1867 because of wounds, *Johnson* pursued a career as an educator at the Universities of Missouri and Minnesota. He was the unsuccessful Democratic candidate for Minnesota governor in 1881 and died in that state in 1897. *Jefferson Columbus Davis* remained in the army but achieved no further distinction, possibly because of the scandal caused by his slaying of a brother officer early in the war, a killing for which he otherwise was not punished. Described as "brave, quiet and obliging," and "full of ambition, daring, endurance and self-confidence," he died in 1879.[9] *Baird,* who was awarded the Medal of Honor for his actions in the Atlanta Campaign, likewise stayed in service, retiring in 1888 and passing away seven years later.

Still another Smith, *John Eugene Smith,* did not leave the army until 1881, after many years of Indian fighting. He died in 1897. *Hugh Ewing,* one of Sherman's foster brothers, was minister to Holland from 1866 to 1870 and thereafter resumed the practice of law in Washington. His death came in 1905.

Once Grant moved East, the officers of the Army of the Potomac come into our story. *George Meade,* despite his success at Gettysburg, long labored under the accusation: Why did you not finish Lee off? The answer was obvious: Lee and his army were even more deadly in retreat than they were in attack. Their reverses had not lessened their bite. Meade following Appomattox commanded the Atlantic area with headquarters in Philadelphia, and then the South with headquarters in Atlanta. He would be crestfallen when Sherman, not he, was promoted to succeed Grant as general-in-chief in 1869, although the appointment was clearly foreordained. He died three years later of pneumonia.

Winfield Scott Hancock also stayed in the army, commanding in various districts and, in 1877, heading the service in the East, with headquarters in Governor's Island, New York. In 1880 he was the unsuccessful Democratic candidate for the presidency, narrowly losing to Garfield. He died eight years later at Governor's Island. *Horatio Wright* briefly commanded in Texas, then returned to engineering duty. In 1879 he became chief engineer of the army, doing much work in rivers and harbors and completing the Washington Monument. He retired from the army in 1884 and died in 1899. *Gouverneur Warren,* relieved by Sheridan in the aftermath of

Five Forks, continued in the service though he found his advancement blocked, and likewise completed numerous engineering projects. Finally in 1878 a court of inquiry cleared him of all wrongdoing and criticized the way he had been relieved. He died four years later at his home in Newport, Rhode Island. The officer who replaced Warren, *Charles Griffin,* eventually was posted to Texas, where he died, in 1867, in the midst of an epidemic of yellow fever in Galveston.

If Sheridan, who progressed from infantryman to cavalry commander, had a favorite subordinate, it was *George Armstrong Custer,* who mirrored his brash ways. "Curly," Custer was affectionately called by friends because of his shoulder-length locks, but as an Indian fighter with the 7th Cavalry for a decade after the conflict he was as merciless as his adversaries. His last bugle call came in 1876, at Little Big Horn, when the Sioux took their revenge, killing him and his entire 266-man command.

Following the debacle at the Crater, Ambrose Burnside was relieved by *John Parke.* The latter stayed in the army for many years, serving with the engineers, and from 1887 to 1889, when he retired, was superintendent at West Point. He died the next year. *Andrew Humphreys,* who replaced Hancock when he could no longer serve in the field and at age fifty-five was one of the oldest officers when the war ended, was the army's chief engineer from 1866 to 1879, and a member of the American Philosophical Society and the American Academy of Arts and Sciences, and a founder of the National Academy of Sciences. He died in 1883.

Horace Porter, who served on Grant's staff in the East, continued with him in peacetime, and then served as an aide in the White House. He resigned at the end of Grant's first term to become a railroad executive. When several of Grant's friends—especially James H. Wilson—turned against him, Porter found himself testifying in the president's defense in various investigations. In 1880, when Grant took up residence in New York, the two men solidified their friendship, with Porter and his young daughter paying him Sunday visits, and the two families vacationing together. In Grant's last days, he was one of the inner circle who helped him prepare his memoirs. Incensed that Grant's Tomb and Monument on Riverside Drive was still unfinished years after his death, Porter became the driving force in making it a reality, completing the project in 1897. He subsequently was ambassador to France and served as a delegate to the 1907 Hague Peace Conference. He died in 1921.[10]

What of *Benjamin Butler* and *Franz Sigel,* both of whom failed so spectacularly, the one at Bermuda Hundred and the other in the Shenandoah? Butler was sent to Congress by his supporters in Massachusetts in 1866, and kept there by them—except for one term—until 1879, taking a major part in Johnson's impeachment. In 1883 he became governor, and the next year ran unsuccessfully for the presidency. He died in 1893. Sigel settled in New York City, where he pursued publishing and political interests, changed his affiliation from Republican to Democrat, and was named to a Federal pension post by President Cleveland. He died in 1902.

We should not forget *Joshua Chamberlain,* who gave us such a spirited account of the surrender of Lee's army. He was elected governor of Maine in 1866 and served three terms, became president of Bowdoin College in 1871 and stayed on campus until 1885, and thereafter went into railroading.

Sherman's campaigns to Atlanta and beyond brought more officers into the foreground. *John Schofield* ably led his Army of the Ohio (in effect the twenty-third Corps) in these actions, and served briefly as Secretary of War during Johnson's battle with Edwin Stanton over Reconstruction policy. He subsequently commanded in various sectors, recommended that Pearl Harbor be acquired as an army and navy base, served from 1876 to 1881 as superintendent at West Point and, in 1888, succeeded Sheridan as general-in-chief. He died in 1906. *Henry Slocum,* who with Howard led one of Sherman's two wings coming up the Carolinas, left the army and was elected as a Brooklyn, New York, Democrat to three terms in Congress, the last one ending in 1885. He died in 1894. The gifted railroad-engineer-turned-infantryman *Grenville Dodge* in 1866 was named chief engineer of the Union Pacific, which at that time was all but moribund. Three years later he had laid and equipped 1,088 miles of track and made the road a resounding success. In 1873 he joined Jay Gould's company and over the next decade helped lay 9,000 more miles of railroad. He was also a congressman, a railroad surveyor and lobbyist, and a force in Republican politics. He died in 1916.

Thomas Sweeny, the one-armed Irishman who swung on Dodge in a scuffle at Atlanta, got involved after the war in a bizarre plan to invade Canada as a prelude to forcing the British to give Ireland its freedom. Despite these peccadilloes he remained in the army until retirement in 1870. He settled in Astoria, New York, and died in 1902.

John Corse, the hero of Allatoona Pass, was named collector of internal revenue in Chicago. Later he moved to Boston, where he was state Democratic chairman and became postmaster of that city. He died in 1893. *George Wagner,* who had been so gallant at Kennesaw Mountain and so remiss at Spring Hill, began practicing law in Williamsport, Indiana, and resumed his duties as president of the state agricultural society. He died in 1869. *Alpheus Williams* was appointed minister to Salvador, and in 1870 ran unsuccessfully as the Democratic candidate for governor of Michigan. He was elected to Congress in 1874 and reelected two years later. He died in office in 1878. *Manning Force* resumed his law practice in Cincinnati and was elected a judge of the common pleas court. From 1877 to 1887 he served as a judge of the superior court, and then was commandant of the Ohio Soldiers' and Sailors' Home at Sandusky until his death in 1899. He also wrote books on history, archaeology, and legal theory.

Let us end this list with Secretary of War *Edwin Stanton,* the man who came to represent the bitter politics of Reconstruction in the immediate postwar period. In his zeal to give blacks their rights, he may have forestalled them. The unintended consequences of his feud with Johnson, solidifying deep prejudices, resulted in the white South and sympathizers in the North denying blacks their full suffrage rights for the next hundred years. Grant had whipped the rebellion, but he could not whip this mindset. Not that he did not try. Once president, he named Stanton in 1869 to the Supreme Court, where the latter's talents might have reversed the segregationist bias of the other justices. We will never know—Stanton died four days after his nomination.

NOTES

1862

1. GRANT, SHERMAN, AND HALLECK

1. Lincoln, *Speeches and Writings 1859–1865,* Library of America, 1989, p. 295; Sherman, *Memoirs,* Library of America, 1990, p. 279; Stephen E. Ambrose, *Halleck,* Louisiana State University Press, 1962, p. 3; Lloyd Lewis, *Sherman, Fighting Prophet,* Harcourt, Brace, 1932, p. 203.
2. Grant, *Personal Memoirs, Selected Letters 1839–1865,* Library of America, 1990, p. 190; ibid., p. 231; Brooks D. Simpson and Jean V. Berlin, eds., *Sherman's Civil War, Selected Correspondence 1860–1865,* University of North Carolina Press, 1999, p. 236.
3. Grant, *Memoirs,* pp. 21, 22, 27; Hamlin Garland, *Ulysses S. Grant,* Macmillan, 1920, p. 13.
4. Grant, *Memoirs,* pp. 25–26.
5. Grant, *Memoirs,* p. 31; John Y. Simon, ed., *Papers of U. S. Grant,* Southern Illinois University Press, 1967, vol. 1, p. 4; *New York Times,* July 24, 1885; Garland, *Grant,* pp. 43, 51; Jean Edward Smith, *Grant,* Simon and Schuster, 2001, p. 28; Lloyd Lewis, *Captain Sam Grant,* Little, Brown, 1950, p. 94.
6. Grant, *Memoirs,* p. 35.

7. William S. McFeely, *Grant,* Norton, 1982, p. 24; Julia Dent Grant, *Personal Memoirs,* Southern Illinois University Press, 1975, p. 50; Grant, *Memoirs,* pp. 39, 67, 78.

8. Grant, *Memoirs,* pp. 920, 109.

9. Ibid., pp. 85, 94.

10. Ibid., p. 129; Grant, *Memoirs,* p. 71.

11. Grant, *Memoirs,* p. 72; Frank A. Burr, *General U. S. Grant,* G. V. Jones, 1885, as cited in Smith, *Grant,* p. 82.

12. Simon, ed., *Papers of U. S. Grant,* vol. 1, p. 315; Grant, *Memoirs,* pp. 949, 953; Smith, *Grant,* p. 87; Garland, *Grant,* p. 127.

13. McFeely, *Grant,* p. 56; W. C. Church, *Ulysses S. Grant,* Fred Defau, 1897, p. 57, as cited in Smith, *Grant,* p. 92; Grant, *Memoirs,* p. 141; *New York Times,* July 24, 1885.

14. Smith, *Grant,* p. 94; Grant, *Memoirs,* p. 144.

15. George Walsh, *Damage Them All You Can,* Forge, 2002, p. 17; Julia Grant, *Personal Memoirs,* p. 89; Grant, *Memoirs,* p. 160; Garland, *Grant,* p. 175.

16. Grant, *Memoirs,* pp. 165–66; James Crane, "Grant as a Colonel," *McClure's Magazine,* June 1896, p. 43, as cited in Bruce Catton, *Grant Moves South,* Little, Brown, 1960, p. 17.

17. Grant, *Memoirs,* p. 975; Simon, ed., *Papers of U. S. Grant,* vol. 2, p. 96; vol. 3, p. 226.

18. Catton, *Grant Moves South,* p. 69; Simon, ed., *Papers of U. S. Grant,* vol. 2, p. 194; Grant, *Memoirs,* p. 177.

19. Grant, *Memoirs,* pp. 179–80.

20. Grant, *Memoirs,* pp. 180, 183–84; *War of the Rebellion, A Compilation of the Official Records of the Union and Confederate Armies,* 128 vols., Washington, D.C., 1880–1901 (henceforth known as O.R.), vol. 3, p. 289 (all citations are from Series I unless otherwise noted); *Battles and Leaders of the Civil War* (henceforth known as *B&L*), New York, 1887–88, vol. 1, p. 351.

21. Grant, *Memoirs,* pp. 185, 188; Shelby Foote, *The Civil War,* Random House, 1958, vol. 1, p. 152; Smith, *Grant,* p. 131.

22. John F. Marszalek, *Sherman,* Free Press, 1993, pp. 9, 16.

23. Sherman, *Memoirs,* pp. 14, 16; B. H. Liddell Hart, *Sherman—Soldier, Realist, American,* Da Capo, 1993, p. 4; Marszalek, *Sherman,* p. 23.

24. Sherman, *Memoirs,* p. 34; Sherman Family Papers, University of Notre Dame, April 7, 1842, as cited in Marszalek, *Sherman,* p. 41, and Liddell Hart, *Sherman—Soldier, Realist, American,* p. 15.

25. Marszalek, *Sherman,* p. 56; Sherman, *Memoirs,* pp. 70, 95, 133.

26. Sherman, *Memoirs,* p. 138; Marszalek, *Sherman,* p. 119.

27. Liddell Hart, *Sherman—Soldier, Realist, American,* pp. 55, 56; Marszalek, *Sherman,* p. 128; Sherman, *Memoirs,* p. 167; Simpson and Berlin, eds., *Sherman's Civil War,* p. 3.

28. Simpson and Berlin, eds., *Sherman's Civil War,* p. 38; Sherman, *Memoirs,* p. 185.

29. Douglas Southall Freeman, *Lee's Lieutenants,* Scribner's, 1942, vol. 1, p. 82; Sherman, *Memoirs,* p. 204; Liddell Hart, *Sherman—Soldier, Realist, American,* p. 88; Simpson and Berlin, eds., *Sherman's Civil War,* p. 121.

30. Sherman, *Memoirs,* pp. 206–08.

31. Simpson and Berlin, *Sherman's Civil War,* pp. 143, 158; Sherman, *Memoirs,* pp. 219–20; Marszalek, *Sherman,* p. 165.

32. Sherman, *Memoirs,* p. 235; Lewis, *Sherman,* p. 199; Simpson and Berlin, eds., *Sherman's Civil War,* pp. 165, 173.

33. Ambrose, *Halleck,* pp. 5, 8.

34. Herman Hattaway and Archer Jones, *How the North Won,* University of Illinois Press, 1983, p. 55; *Lew Wallace: An Autobiography,* Harper and Brothers, 1906, vol. 2, p. 570; Ambrose, *Halleck,* p. 9.

2. FORTS HENRY AND DONELSON

1. Catton, *Grant Moves South,* p. 130; Jack D. Coombe, *Thunder Along the Mississippi,* Bantam, 1996, pp. 20, 46.

2. Grant, *Memoirs,* p. 190; Catton, *Grant Move South,* p. 50.

3. H. Allan Gosnell, *Guns on the Western Waters,* Louisiana State University Press, 1949, p. 47; Catton, *This Hallowed Ground,* Pocket Books, 1967, p. 114.

4. Catton, *Grant Moves South,* p. 143; *B&L,* vol. 1, pp. 364, 365.

5. *O.R.,* vol. 7, p. 124; Grant, *Memoirs,* p. 196.

6. *B&L,* vol. 1, p. 433.

7. Ibid., pp. 434–35; *Southern Historical Society Papers* (henceforth known as *SHSP*), Richmond, 1876–1959, vol. 13, p. 166.

8. *B&L,* vol. 1, pp. 409, 415, 417, 421; Grant, *Memoirs,* pp. 203–05.

9. *Chicago Tribune,* September 23, 1865, as cited in Catton, *Grant Moves South,* p. 166; *B&L,* vol. 1, p. 422; Grant, *Memoirs,* p. 205.

10. Catton, *Grant Marches South,* p. 169; *B&L,* vol. 1, p. 423.

11. *Lew Wallace: An Autobiography,* vol. 1, p. 412; *B&L,* vol. 1, p. 424; M. F. Force, *From Fort Henry to Corinth,* Broadfoot, 1989, p. 57.

12. John W. Emerson, "Grant's Life in the West," *Midland Monthly,* June 1898, as cited in Catton, *Grant Marches South,* p. 173, and Smith, *Grant,* p. 160.

13. Force, *From Fort Henry to Corinth,* pp. 57–58; *B&L,* vol. 1, p. 425.

14. Grant, *Memoirs,* pp. 207–08; Catton, *Grant Moves South,* p. 175.

15. Grant, *Memoirs,* p. 212; Garland, *Grant,* p. 192.

16. Catton, *Grant Moves South,* p. 177; *O.R.,* vol. 7, p. 625; Ambrose, *Halleck,* p. 33; Grant, *Memoirs,* p. 213.

17. *O.R.,* vol. 7, pp. 627, 652.

18. Grant, *Memoirs,* pp. 215, 217, 219, 985.

19. *O.R.,* vol. 7, pp. 674, 680, 682; vol. 10:2, p. 3.

20. Garland, *Grant,* p. 198; *O.R.,* vol. 10:2, pp. 4, 15, 21.

21. *O.R.,* vol. 10:2, pp. 13, 30, 32; Grant, *Memoirs,* p. 221.

3. BLOODY SHILOH

1. Grant, *Memoirs,* p. 223; Sherman, *Memoirs,* p. 249; Catton, *Grant Moves South,* pp. 218–19.

2. *O.R.,* vol. 10:1, p. 280.

3. John Cannan, ed., *War on Two Fronts,* Combined Books, 1990, p. 81; here and elsewhere I have taken Italian accented speech out of quotes; to leave the accents perpetuates buffoonery.

4. Sherman, *Memoirs,* p. 255.

5. Ibid., p. 257; James Lee McDonough, *Shiloh—In Hell Before Night,* University of Tennessee Press, 1977, p. 109; Larry J. Daniel, *Shiloh,* Touchstone, 1997, p. 159.

6. J. Duke, *History of the 53rd Regiment, Ohio Volunteer Infantry,* Portsmouth, Ohio, 1900, p. 46; Wiley Sword, *Shiloh, Bloody April,* William Morrow, 1974, p. 195; Daniel, *Shiloh,* p. 170.

7. *O.R.,* vol. 10:1, p. 266; Sherman, *Memoirs,* p. 257; Simpson and Berlin, eds., *Sherman's Civil War,* p. 202.

8. *O.R.,* vol. 10:1, pp. 114–17, 143, 250; Force, *From Fort Henry to Corinth,* p. 124.

9. Grant, *Memoirs,* p. 227; Cannan, ed., *War on Two Fronts,* p. 83; Catton, *Grant Moves South,* p. 230.

10. Daniel, *Shiloh,* p. 175; Grant, *Memoirs,* pp. 228–32; *O.R.,* vol. 10:1, p. 279; Mildred Throne, ed., *The Civil War Diary of Cyrus F. Boyd,* Louisiana State University Press, 1953, pp. 30–31.

11. *O.R.,* vol. 10:1, pp. 183–88; *B&L,* vol. 1, pp. 609–10.

12. McDonough, *Shiloh—In Hell Before Night*, p. 143; O.R., vol. 10:1, p. 480.

13. *B&L*, vol. 1, pp. 564–65.

14. O.R., vol. 10:1, pg. 204; Sword, *Shiloh, Bloody April*, p. 280.

15. Sword, *Shiloh, Bloody April*, p. 280.

16. O.R., vol. 10:2, p. 279; vol. 10:1, p. 476.

17. Daniel, *Shiloh*, p. 236; McDonough, *Shiloh—In Hell Before Night*, p. 166; O.R., vol. 10:2, p. 279; Force, *From Fort Henry to Corinth*, p. 146.

18. O.R., vol. 10:1, p. 555; Grant, *Memoirs*, pp. 233–34; Daniel, *Shiloh*, pp. 249–50; Smith, *Grant*, pp. 200–01; Catton, *Grant Moves South*, pp. 237, 241–42.

19. Daniel, *Shiloh*, p. 251; Stacy D. Allen, "Shiloh!" *Blue and Gray*, vol. 14, p. 64, as cited in Smith, *Grant*, p. 201; *B&L*, vol. 1, p. 602.

20. *Lew Wallace: An Autobiography*, vol. 2, p. 550; McDonough, *Shiloh—In Hell Before Night*, p. 204; O.R., vol. 10:1, p. 316.

21. *Lew Wallace: An Autobiography*, vol. 2, pp. 524, 563.

22. O.R., vol. 10:1, p. 120; Grant, *Memoirs*, p. 237.

23. Allen, "Shiloh," p. 17; *B&L*, vol. 1, p. 603; Grant, *Memoirs*, p. 237.

24. Grant, *Memoirs*, pp. 238–39; McDonough, *Shiloh—In Hell Before Night*, p. 300; Throne, ed., *The Civil War Diary of Cyrus F. Boyd*, pp. 37–38.

4. CONTROVERSY AND INTRIGUE

1. O.R., vol. 10:2, pp. 99, 105–06; emphasis added on last citation as in Smith, *Grant*, p. 207.

2. Emmet Crozier, *Yankee Reporters*, Oxford University Press, 1956, pp. 216–18; Catton, *Grant Moves South*, pp. 253–54.

3. Catton, *Grant Moves South*, pp. 255–56; Daniel, *Shiloh*, p. 177.

4. Grant, *Memoirs*, pp. 1005–08.

5. Simpson and Berlin, eds., *Sherman's Civil War*, pp. 206–12.

6. Catton, *Grant Moves South*, p. 259.

7. James Grant Wilson, *The Life and Campaigns of Ulysses Simpson Grant*, R. M. DeWitt, 1897, p. 37; Julia Grant to Washburne, May 16, 1862, Grant Papers, Illinois State, as cited in Catton, *Grant Moves South*, p. 261.

8. Grant to Halleck, May 11, 1862, Missouri Historical Society, as cited

in Catton, *Grant Moves South,* p. 267; *O.R.,* 10:2, p. 182; *Lew Wallace: An Autobiography,* vol. 2, p. 576.

9. Grant, *Memoirs,* pp. 250–52; Allan Nevins, *The War for the Union,* Scribner's, 1960, p. 112; Ambrose, *Halleck,* p. 51.

10. Grant, *Memoirs,* p. 252; *Lew Wallace: An Autobiography,* vol. 2, p. 581; *O.R.,* vol. 10:1, p. 669.

11. Sherman, *Memoirs,* p. 275.

12. Carl Sandburg, *Abraham Lincoln,* Harcourt, 1954, p. 289; *O.R.,* vol. 11:3, p. 311; Ezra J. Warner, *Generals in Blue,* Louisiana State University Press, 1964, p. 196.

13. Grant, *Memoirs,* p. 262; Catton, *Grant Moves South,* p. 287 (some italics added); Halleck to Mrs. Halleck, August 13, 1862, as cited in Catton, *Grant Moves South,* p. 276.

14. Catton, *Grant Moves South,* p. 298.

15. *O.R.,* vol. 17:2, p. 150; Catton, *Grant Moves South,* p. 294; Throne, ed., *The Civil War Diary of Cyrus F. Boyd,* p. 63; S. D. Thompson, *Recollections with the 3rd Iowa,* Cincinnati, 1864, p. 275; Jesse Grant Cramer ed., *Letters of Ulysses S. Grant to His Father and Youngest Sister,* G. P. Putnam's Sons, 1912, p. 88.

16. Crozier, *Yankee Reporters,* p. 319; Catton, *Grant Moves South,* p. 302.

17. Sylvanus Cadwallader, *Three Years with Grant,* University of Nebraska Press, 1996, p. 11.

18. Catton, *Grant Moves South,* p. 308.

5. IUKA, CORINTH, AND ROSECRANS

1. William M. Lamers, *The Edge of Glory,* Louisiana State University Press, 1999, pp. 13, 15.

2. Wiley Sword, *Mountains Touched with Fire,* St. Martin's, 1995, p. 6; Lamers, *The Edge of Glory,* pp. 17–18; Steven E. Woodworth, ed., *Grant's Lieutenants,* University Press of Kansas, 2001, pp. 110–11.

3. Jacob D. Cox, *Military Reminiscences of the Civil War,* Scribner's, 1900, vol. 1, p. 127; Whitelaw Reid, *Ohio in the War,* Moore, Wilstach and Baldwin, 1895, vol. 1, p. 348.

4. Catton, *Grant Moves South,* p. 395; *B&L,* vol. 2, p. 735; Cannan, ed., *War on Two Fronts,* pp. 113, 127.

5. *B&L,* vol. 2, p. 746.

6. Throne, ed., *The Civil War Diary of Cyrus F. Boyd,* p. 72.

7. Lamers, *The Edge of Glory,* p. 140; Cannan, ed., *War on Two Fronts,* pp. 130–31.

8. Lamers, *The Edge of Glory*, pp. 140–41; *B&L*, vol. 2, pp. 746–47, 757.

9. *B&L*, vol. 2, pp. 748, 752; Cannan, ed., *War on Two Fronts*, p. 133.

10. Lamers, *The Edge of Glory*, pp. 148–49.

11. Throne, ed., *The Civil War Diary of Cyrus F. Boyd*, p. 74.

12. Henry Steele Commager, *The Blue and the Gray*, Fairfax Press, 1991, pp. 368–70.

13. Throne, ed., *The Civil War Diary of Cyrus F. Boyd*, pp. 75–76.

14. Lamers, *The Edge of Glory*, p. 154.

15. *O.R.*, vol. 17:1, p. 155; *B&L*, vol. 2, p. 753.

16. Grant, *Memoirs*, pp. 280–81; *B&L*, vol. 2, p. 754.

17. Grant, *Memoirs*, p. 281; Cincinnati *Commercial*, October 9, 1862.

18. Simon, ed., *Papers of U. S. Grant*, vol. 6, pp. 163–67; *O.R.*, vol. 17:2, p. 238; Julia Grant, *Personal Memoirs*, p. 104.

19. Catton, *Grant Moves South*, p. 320.

6. CHICKASAW BLUFFS, MCCLERNAND, AND PORTER

1. Grant, *Memoirs*, p. 283; *O.R.*, vol. 17:2, p. 260.

2. Grant, *Memoirs*, p. 283.

3. Catton, *Grant Moves South*, pp. 356–60; Grant, *Memoirs*, pp. 284–85.

4. Grant, *Memoirs*, p. 285; *O.R.*, vol. 17:1, p. 469.

5. David Donald, *Inside Lincoln's Cabinet: The Civil War Papers of Salmon P. Chase*, Longmans, Green, 1954, pp. 162, 169; *New York Times*, October 30, 1862.

6. *St Clair Banner*, April 23, 1844.

7. Richard L. Kiper, *Major General John Alexander McClernand, Politician in Uniform*, Kent State University Press, 1999, pp. 15, 18, 21.

8. Ibid., pp. 24–25.

9. *O.R.*, vol. 17:2, p. 282; Roy P. Basler, ed., *The Collected Works of Abraham Lincoln*, Rutgers University Press, 1953, vol. 4, p. 468.

10. James H. Wilson, *Under the Old Flag*, D. Appleton, 1912, vol. 1, pp. 120, 144.

11. David Dixon Porter, *Incidents and Anecdotes of the Civil War*, D. Appleton, 1885, p. 122.

12. Ibid., p. 125.

13. Chester G. Hearn, *Admiral David Dixon Porter*, Naval Institute Press, 1996, pp. 1–34; Porter, *Incidents*, p. 10.

14. *O.R.,* vol. 17:1, p. 472; vol. 17:2, p. 404; Sherman, *Memoirs,* p. 303.

15. *O.R.,* vol. 17:2, pp. 415, 420.

16. Porter, *Incidents,* p. 126.

17. Grant, *Memoirs,* p. 292.

18. *B&L,* vol. 3, p. 463; Porter, *Incidents,* p. 128.

19. Sherman, *Memoirs,* pp. 314–15.

20. *B&L,* vol. 3, pp. 466–70.

21. Porter, *Incidents,* pp. 130–31.

22. Sherman, *Memoirs,* pp. 319–25.

23. Grant, *Memoirs,* p. 294; Samuel Carter III, *The Final Fortress,* St. Martin's, 1980, p. 107.

1863

1. WET INTERREGNUM

1. Grant, *Memoirs,* p. 296.

2. *B&L,* vol. 3, p. 561; Grant, *Memoirs,* p. 295.

3. Grant, *Memoirs,* pp. 296–99.

4. Throne, ed., *The Civil War Diary of Cyrus F. Boyd,* pp. 123–25.

5. *B&L,* vol. 3, p. 562; Catton, *Grant Moves South,* p. 384; Porter, *Incidents,* p. 144.

6. Grant, *Memoirs,* p. 301; Porter, *Incidents,* p. 147.

7. Catton, *Grant Moves South,* p. 385.

8. Porter, *Incidents,* pp. 149–50, 159–61; Carter, *The Final Fortress,* pp. 143–47; here and subsequently in this narrative I have taken black speech out of quotes to avoid stereotyping; the quotes were recorded by whites and reflect the prejudices—or at least the tin ears—of the times.

9. Sherman, *Memoirs,* pp. 332–34; Shelby Foote, *The Civil War,* Random House, 1963, vol. 2, p. 210.

10. Porter, *Incidents,* pp. 162–65.

11. Ibid., pp. 166–69.

12. Howard P. Nash Jr., *A Naval History of the Civil War,* A. S. Barnes, 1972, pp. 151–52; *B&L,* vol. 3, p. 564.

13. *B&L,* vol. 3, p. 564; Gosnell, *Guns on the Western Waters,* pp. 186, 189.

14. Hearn, *Admiral David Dixon Porter,* p. 198.

15. Carter, *The Final Fortress,* p. 127.

16. Porter, *Incidents*, pp. 133–35; Carter, *The Final Fortress*, pp. 129–30.

17. Carter, *The Final Fortress*, p. 134; C. Washburn to E. Washburne, April 11, 1863; Gaillard Hunt, *Israel, Elihu and Cadwallader Washburn*, Macmillan, 1925, p. 341.

18. John Fiske, *The Mississippi Valley in the Civil War*, Houghton Mifflin, 1900, p. 225, as cited in Carter, *The Final Fortress*, p. 134.

19. Grant, *Memoirs*, pp. 306–07; Porter, *Incidents*, p. 174; Sherman, in his *Memoirs*, pp. 339–43, insisted that no formal council of war had been held but acknowledged that he had been against Grant's plan; writing Colonel Rawlins, Grant's adjutant, he nonetheless concluded, "Whatever plan of action [Grant] may adopt will receive from me the same zealous cooperation and energetic support as though conceived by myself."

2. BYPASSING VICKSBURG

1. T. Harry Williams, *Lincoln and His Generals*, Knopf, 1952, p. 226; Ida M. Tarbull, "Charles A. Dana in the Civil War," *McClure's Magazine*, October 1887; Smith, *Grant*, p. 231; John Eaton, *Grant, Lincoln and the Freedmen*, Longmans, Green, 1907, p. 64.

2. Charles A. Dana, *Recollections of the Civil War*, University of Nebraska Press, 1996, pp. 30, 61–62, 72–75.

3. *New York World*, February 20, 1863; *New York Times*, June 21, 1863, as cited in Catton, *Grant Moves South*, pp. 390–91.

4. Dana, *Recollections*, pp. 32–33.

5. Kiper, *Major General John Alexander McClernand*, pp. 209–15; *O.R.*, vol. 24:3, pp. 204–07.

6. Grant, *Memoirs*, p. 307; Catton, *Grant Moves South*, p. 414.

7. Porter, *Incidents*, pp. 175–76.

8. Ibid., p. 177.

9. Grant, *Memoirs*, p. 314.

10. Dana, *Recollections*, p. 43.

11. James R. Arnold, *Grant Wins the War*, John Wiley, 1997, p. 84.

12. *O.R.*, vol. 24:1, p. 522ff.; Larry D. Underwood, *The Butternut Guerillas*, Dageforde, 1994, p. 27; Richard W. Surby, *Grierson Raids and Hatch's Sixty-Four Days March*, Rounds and James, 1865, p. 33; Arnold, *Grant Wins the War*, p. 86.

13. Surby, *Grierson Raids*, p. 36; *O.R.*, vol. 24:1, p. 522ff.

14. John C. Pemberton, *Pemberton, Defender of Vicksburg*, University of North Carolina Press, 1942, p. 112; *O.R.*, vol. 24:1, p. 522ff;

D. Alexander Brown, *Grierson's Raid,* University of Illinois Press, 1954, p. 162.

15. Brown, *Grierson's Raid,* p. 191; O.R., vol. 24:1, p. 522ff, p. 33.

16. Grant, *Memoirs,* p. 315; Porter, *Incidents,* p. 180; Sherman, *Memoirs,* p. 345; Cannan, ed., *War on Two Fronts,* p. 172.

17. Catton, *Grant Moves South,* p. 424.

18. Porter, *Incidents,* p. 182.

19. Grant, *Memoirs,* p. 321; Pemberton, *Pemberton: Defender of Vicksburg,* p. 124.

20. Grant, *Memoirs,* pp. 322–23; Dana, *Recollections,* pp. 63–65.

21. O.R., vol. 24:1, pp. 588–89; Edgar L. Erickson, ed., "With Grant at Vicksburg—From the Civil War Diary of Captain Charles Wilcox," *Journal of the Illinois State Historical Society,* January 1938, p. 463ff.

22. O.R., vol. 24:1, pp. 144–46, p. 611; p. 33.

23. Dana, *Recollections,* pp. 45, 51; Grant, *Memoirs,* p. 325.

24. Grant, *Memoirs,* pp. 327–28.

3. GRANT GOES ON THE ATTACK

1. O.R., vol. 24:3, p. 859; Osborn H. Oldroyd, *A Soldier's Story of the Siege of Vicksburg,* privately published, 1885, pp. 9–11, as cited in Carter, *The Final Fortress,* pp. 188–89.

2. Cadwallader, *Three Years with Grant,* p. 72; Dana, *Recollections,* p. 51.

3. Grant, *Memoirs,* p. 330; Woodworth, ed., *Grant's Lieutenants,* p. 159.

4. Cadwallader, *Three Years with Grant,* p. 67; Oldroyd, *A Soldier's Story of the Siege of Vicksburg,* p. 9; Ira Blanchard, *I Marched with Sherman,* San Francisco, 1992, p. 88; Henry O. Dwight, "A Soldier's Story," *New York Tribune,* November 21, 1886, as cited in James R. Arnold, *Grant Wins the War,* p. 133.

5. Grant, *Memoirs,* p. 332; Cadwallader, *Three Years with Grant,* pp. 70–71.

6. O.R., vol. 24:3, p. 870; vol. 24:1, p. 215.

7. O.R., vol. 24:3, p. 877; vol. 24:1, pp. 259–63.

8. Grant, *Memoirs,* pp. 331, 337.

9. Oldroyd, *A Soldier's Story of the Siege of Vicksburg,* p. 21; Cadwallader, *Three Years with Grant,* pp. 73–74; Fred Grant, "Reminiscences," *Vicksburg Evening Post,* July 1, 1963, as cited in Carter, *The Final Fortress,* p. 192.

10. Cadwallader, *Three Years with Grant,* pp., 74–75; O.R., vol. 24:1, pp. 753–54; Grant, *Memoirs,* p. 338.

11. Grant, *Memoirs,* pp. 338–39; Arnold, *Grant Wins the War,* pp. 144–45; Carter, *The Final Fortress,* p. 193; *O.R.,* vol. 24:1, pp. 259–63.

12. Cadwallader, *Three Years with Grant,* p. 75.

13. Ibid., pp. 76–77.

14. Charles Longley, *War Sketches and Incidents,* Des Moines, Iowa, 1893, pp. 208–14, as cited in Earl S. Miers, *The Web of Victory,* Louisiana State University Press, 1984, p. 180ff; Dana, *Recollections,* p. 64; *O.R.,* vol. 24:2, pp. 41–44.

15. *O.R.,* vol. 24:2, pp. 48–50; Longley, *War Sketches,* pp. 208–14.

16. W. F. Beyer and O. F. Keydel, *Deeds of Valor,* Smithmark, 2000, pp. 184–85.

17. *O.R.,* vol. 42:2, pp. 41–44; Arnold, *Grant Wins the War,* p. 164; W. S. Morris, L. D. Hartwell Jr., and J. B. Kuykendall, *History of the 31st Regiment, Illinois Volunteers,* Southern Illinois University Press, 1998, pp. 64–65.

18. Grant, *Memoirs,* p. 345.

19. Ibid., p. 346; T. J. Williams, *The Battle of Champion's Hill,* Broadfoot, 1991–95, vol. 5, pp. 204–12; Arnold, *Grant Wins the War,* pp. 174–75; *O.R.,* vol. 24:2, pp. 48–50.

20. *Annals of the War,* Blue and Grey Press, 1996, pp. 345–46; Arnold, *Grant Wins the War,* p. 180.

21. *Annals of the War,* pp. 345–46.

22. *O.R.,* vol. 24:2, p. 44; Dana, *Recollections,* pp. 53–54; Cadwallader, *Three Years with Grant,* p. 80; *Annals of the War,* p. 346.

23. Grant, *Memoirs,* pp. 347–49.

24. Ibid., p. 350.

25. Cadwallader, *Three Years with Grant,* p. 83; Dana, *Recollections,* p. 65; Catton, *Grant Moves South,* p. 446.

26. *O.R.,* vol. 24:2, pp. 135–39; Cannan, ed., *War on Two Fronts,* p. 188.

27. Grant, *Memoirs,* pp. 352–53; *O.R.,* vol. 24:3, p. 322; Sherman, *Memoirs,* p. 349.

4. SIEGE OF VICKSBURG

1. *B&L,* vol. 3, p. 488; *O.R.,* vol. 24:1, p. 273.

2. Miers, *The Web of Victory,* pp. 203–05; Arnold, *Grant Wins the War,* p. 243; Carter, *The Final Fortress,* p. 213.

3. Grant, *Memoirs,* p. 355; Beyer and Keydel, *Deeds of Valor,* p. 196;

Edwin C. Bearss, *The Campaign for Vicksburg*, Morningside, 1986; vol. 3, p. 843; Sherman, *Memoirs*, p. 352.

4. Wilbur Crummer, *With Grant at Fort Donelson, Shiloh and Vicksburg*, E. C. Crummer, 1915, pp. 110–15.

5. Arnold, *Grant Wins the War*, p. 251; Cadwallader, *Three Years with Grant*, p. 90; Beyer and Keydel, *Deeds of Valor*, pp. 198–99.

6. *O.R.*, vol. 24:1, p. 172; Sherman, *Memoirs*, pp. 352–53; Cadwallader, *Three Years with Grant*, pp. 91–92.

7. John C. Pemberton, *Pemberton: Defender of Vicksburg*, p. 195; Oldroyd, *A Soldier's Story of the Siege of Vicksburg*, pp. 36–37; *B&L*, vol. 3, p. 490; Carter, *The Final Fortress*, p. 255.

8. *Annals of the War*, pp. 116–17; Henry Steele Commager, *The Blue and the Gray*, vol. 2, p. 665; Mary A. Loughborough, *My Cave Life in Vicksburg*, D. Appleton, 1864, pp. 56–58.

9. Carter, *The Final Fortress*, p. 233; Commager, *The Blue and the Gray*, vol. 2, pp. 665–66.

10. Crummer, *With Grant at Fort Donelson*, p. 118; Grant, *Memoirs*, p. 360; *B&L*, vol. 3, p. 491.

11. *Annals of the War*, p. 359; Catton, *Grant Moves South*, p. 459.

12. Dana, *Recollections*, pp. 83–84.

13. Cadwallader, *Three Years with Grant*, pp. 102–07.

14. Ibid., pp. 107–10.

15. Catton, *Grant Moves South*, pp. 463–65; McFeely, *Grant*, p. 135.

16. Dana, *Recollections*, p. 86; Dudley Taylor Cornish, *The Sable Arm*, University Press of Kansas, 1987, pp. 112–14, 144–45; Carter, *The Final Fortress*, p. 250.

17. Carter, *The Final Fortress*, pp. 256–57.

18. *O.R.*, vol. 24:1, pp. 159–64; Miers, *The Web of Victory*, pp. 248–50; Wilson, *Under the Old Flag*, pp. 184–86.

19. *O.R.*, vol. 24:1, p. 158; Wilson, *Under the Old Flag*, pp. 184–86.

20. Walsh, *Damage Them All You Can*, p. 24.

21. Joseph Johnston, *Narrative of Military Operations*, D. Appleton, 1874, pp. 185–204; *O.R.*, vol. 24:1, pp. 249–331; vol. 24:3, p. 971; Miers, *The Web of Victory*, pp. 270–76.

22. Carl Sandburg, *Abraham Lincoln, The War Years*, Harcourt, Brace, 1939, vol. 2, p. 349; Loughborough, *My Cave Life in Vicksburg*, p. 74; Commager, *The Blue and the Gray*, vol. 2, p. 667.

23. *B&L*, vol. 3, p. 542; Cadwallader, *Three Years with Grant*, pp. 121–22; Dana, *Recollections*, p. 92; Crummer, *With Grant at Fort Donelson*, pp. 136–42; Miers, *The Web of Victory*, pp. 281–83.

24. Grant, *Memoirs*, p. 373; Catton, *Grant Moves South*, p. 469; O.R., vol. 24:2, p. 345.

25. Dana, *Recollections*, p. 96.

26. Grant, *Memoirs*, pp. 375–76.

27. Ibid., p. 377; Catton, *Grant Moves South*, p. 473.

28. *New York Tribune*, July 15, 1863; Grant, *Memoirs*, p. 379; Wilson, *Under the Old Flag*, vol. 1, p. 222.

29. Porter, *Incidents*, pp. 200–01; O.R., vol. 24:3, p. 546; Arnold, *Grant Wins the War*, p. 301; Lincoln, *Speeches and Writings*, pp. 477–78.

5. REVENGE AT CHATTANOOGA

1. Grant, *Memoirs*, p. 388; O.R., vol. 24:3, p. 584.

2. Grant, *Memoirs*, p. 390; Bruce Catton, *Grant Takes Command*, Little, Brown, 1968, p. 26; Simon, ed., *Papers of U. S. Grant*, vol. 9, p. 222.

3. Julia Grant, *Personal Memoirs*, pp. 113, 122.

4. Dana, *Recollections*, p. 128.

5. Smith, *Grant*, p. 264; Catton, *Grant Takes Command*, p. 33; Sandburg, *Lincoln*, pp. 281–82.

6. Grant, *Memoirs*, pp. 404–04; O.R., vol. 30:4, pp. 414–15, 455, 479.

7. Oliver Otis Howard, *Autobiography*, Baker and Taylor, 1907, vol. 1, p. 460; Horace Porter, *Campaigning with Grant*, University of Nebraska Press, 2000, pp. 1–2; Grant, *Memoirs*, p. 406.

8. Shelby Foote, *The Civil War*, vol. 2, p. 806; William F. Smith, *Autobiography*, Morningside, 1990, p. 75; Catton, *Grant Takes Command*, pp. 51–52; Peter Cozzens, *The Shipwreck of Their Hopes*, University of Illinois Press, 1996, p. 61.

9. Howard, *Autobiography*, vol. 1, pp. 464–65; Cozzens, *The Shipwreck of Their Hopes*, p. 73.

10. Wiley Sword, *Mountains Touched with Fire*, p. 136; Porter, *Campaigning*, pp. 9–10; Cozzens, *The Shipwreck of Their Hopes*, p. 89.

11. Howard, *Autobiography*, vol. 1, pp. 467–69; Sword, *Mountains Touched with Fire*, pp. 139–41.

12. O.R., vol. 31:1, p. 219; Catton, *Grant Takes Command*, p. 55; Grant, *Memoirs*, p. 1037.

13. Porter, *Campaigning*, pp. 14–16.

14. Sherman, *Memoirs*, pp. 374–75; Marszalek, *Sherman*, p. 238; Howard, *Autobiography*, vol. 1, pp. 473–76; Catton, *Grant Takes Command*, p. 64.

15. Lincoln, *Speeches and Writings,* p. 433.

16. Freeman Cleaves, *Rock of Chickamauga,* University of Oklahoma Press, 1948, p. 50.

17. Dana, *Recollections,* pp. 141–44; *B&L,* vol. 3, p. 721; Cozzens, *The Shipwreck of Their Hopes,* p. 130.

18. *O.R.,* vol. 31:2, p. 717; Howard, *Autobiography,* vol. 1, p. 479.

19. *O.R.,* vol. 31:2, p. 42; Wilson, *Under the Old Flag,* vol. 1, p. 295; Sherman, *Memoirs,* p. 401; Cozzens, *The Shipwreck of Their Hopes,* p. 155.

20. *B&L,* vol. 3, pp. 721–22.

21. Cozzens, *The Shipwreck of Their Hopes,* p. 189; Beyer and Keydel, *Deeds of Valor,* p. 283; *B&L,* vol. 3, pgs. 721–22.

22. Walter H. Hebert, *Fighting Joe Hooker,* University of Nebraska Press, 1999, p. 265.

23. Walter H. Hebert, *Fighting Joe Hooker,* University of Nebraska Press, 1999, p. 265.

24. Shelby Foote, *The Civil War,* vol. 2, pp. 850–51; Sword, *Mountains Touched with Fire,* pp. 243–46.

25. Cozzens, *The Shipwreck of Their Hopes,* p. 220; Samuel Byers, *With Fire and Sword,* Neale Publishing Company, 1911, p. 106; Commager, *The Blue and the Gray,* vol. 2, p. 901.

26. Byers, *With Fire and Sword,* p. 108; Foote, *The Civil War,* vol. 2, p. 851; Gabor S. Boritt, ed., *The Gettysburg Nobody Knows,* Oxford University Press, 1997, p. 122.

27. Thomas Wood, "The Battle of Missionary Ridge," *Sketches of War History,* R. Clark, 1888–1903, vol. 4, pp. 33–35; Commager, *The Blue and the Gray,* vol. 2, pp. 902–03.

28. *O.R.,* vol. 34:4, p. 404; Wood, "The Battle of Missionary Ridge," vol. 4, pp. 36–46; Cozzens, *The Shipwreck of Their Hopes,* p. 277.

29. Commager, *The Blue and the Gray,* vol. 2, pp. 907–08.

30. James A. Connolly, *Three Years in the Army of the Cumberland,* Indiana University Press, 1959, pp. 157–59; Commager, *The Blue and the Gray,* vol. 2, p. 908; Dana, *Recollections,* p. 150; Howard, *Autobiography,* vol. 1, p. 487.

31. Grant, *Memoirs,* pp. 449–50; Lincoln, *Collected Works,* Rutgers University Press, 1954, vol. 7, p. 53; *O.R.,* vol. 31:2, p. 25; *New York Herald,* November 28, 1863; *New York World,* November 26, 1863; Catton, *Grant Takes Command,* p. 103.

1864

1. LINCOLN MEETS HIS GENERAL

1. Ida M. Tarbell, *Life of President Lincoln,* Doubleday and McClure, 1900, vol. 2, pp. 186–88; Catton, *Grant Takes Command,* pp. 110–12; Smith, *Grant,* pp. 285–86.

2. John Hay, *Lincoln and the Civil War in the Diaries and Letters of John Hay,* Dodd, Mead, 1939, p. 164.

3. Grant, *Memoirs,* p. 1046; *O.R.,* vol. 32:3, p. 58.

4. Catton, *Grant Takes Command,* p. 124; Sandburg, *Lincoln,* p. 460–62; Porter, *Campaigning,* pp. 18–20.

5. Porter, *Campaigning,* p. 21; Sandburg, *Lincoln,* p. 463.

6. Grant, *Memoirs,* p. 469; Smith, *Grant,* p. 290.

7. Smith, *Grant,* p. 296; also Sandburg, *Lincoln,* p. 463; Grant, *Memoirs,* p. 470.

8. Dana, *Recollections,* pp. 189–90; Gary W. Gallagher, ed., *The Wilderness Campaign,* University of North Carolina Press, 1997, pp. 68–70.

9. Dana, *Recollections,* pp. 190–91; Grant, *Memoirs,* p. 771; Gallagher, *The Wilderness Campaign,* pp. 83–91; Charles Francis Adams, *An Autobiography,* Houghton, Mifflin, 1916, p. 157.

10. *O.R.,* vol. 32:3, p. 58.

11. Roy Morris Jr., *Sheridan,* Vintage, 1993, pp. 1–3, pp. 21–22; Sandburg, *Lincoln,* p. 464; Porter, *Campaigning,* p. 24.

12. Edward G. Longacre, *Army of Amateurs,* Stackpole, 1997, p. 3.

13. William C. Davis, *The Battle of New Market,* Doubleday, 1975, p. 21; also Catton, *Grant Takes Command,* pp. 142–43.

14. Grant, *Memoirs,* pp. 484–86; *B&L,* vol. 4, p. 112.

15. Catton, *Grant Takes Command,* pp. 162–63; also Smith, *Grant,* pp. 306–07.

16. Catton, *Grant Takes Command,* p. 160; Catton, *A Stillness at Appomattox,* Fairfield Press, 3-volume edition, 1948, pp. 483, 486.

17. R. H. Dana Jr. Papers, April 21 and May 4, 1864, Massachusetts Historical Society.

2. GRANT VERSUS LEE IN VIRGINIA

1. Ezra J. Warner, *Generals in Blue,* Louisiana State University Press, 1964, p. 407; Edward Steere, *The Wilderness Campaign,* Stackpole,

1960, pp. 160–61; Theodore Gerrish, *Army Life: A Private's Reminiscences*, Hoyt, Fogg and Donham, 1882, pp. 93–98.

2. Warren Lee Goss, *Recollections of a Private*, Thomas Y. Crowell, 1890, p. 268; Steere, *The Wilderness Campaign*, pp. 173–74.

3. Steere, *The Wilderness Campaign*, pp. 182–83.

4. Goss, *Recollections of a Private*, p. 270; Steere, *The Wilderness Campaign*, pp. 204–06.

5. Goss, *Recollections of a Private*, p. 271; Porter, *Campaigning*, p. 52; Catton, *Grant Takes Command*, p. 193.

6. C. F. Atkinson, *Grant's Campaigns of 1864 and 1865*, H. Rees, 1908, p. 166; Richard Wheeler, *On Fields of Fury*, HarperCollins, 1991, p. 122; Theodore Lyman, *Meade's Headquarters, 1863–65*, Atlantic Monthly Press, 1922, p. 94.

7. J. B. Polley, *Hood's Texas Brigade*, Neale Publishing Company, 1910, p. 231; Andrew A. Humphreys, *The Virginia Campaign 1864 and 1865*, Da Capo, 1995, pp. 43–44.

8. Sandburg, *Lincoln*, p. 509; Porter, *Campaigning*, pp. 69–70.

9. *B&L*, vol. 4, p. 175; Gordon C. Rhea, *The Battles for Spotsylvania Courthouse*, Louisiana State University Press, 1997, p. 169.

10. Rhea, *The Battles for Spotsylvania Courthouse*, p. 174; Grant, *Memoirs*, p. 550; Porter, *Campaigning*, pp. 97–98.

11. Rhea, *The Battles for Spotsylvania Courthouse*, pp. 235–37.

12. John Brown Gordon, *Reminiscences of the Civil War*, Scribner's, 1903, p. 279; *B&L*, vol. 4, p. 176; Catton, *Grant Takes Command*, p. 227.

13. *B&L*, vol. 4, p. 173.

14. Catton, *Grant Takes Command*, p. 232; *B&L*, vol. 4, pp. 174, 176; Shelby Foote, *The Civil War*, vol. 3, p. 222.

15. Porter, *Campaigning*, pp. 83–84; *B&L*, vol. 4, p. 188.

16. P. H. Sheridan, *Personal Memoirs*, Da Capo, 1992, pp. 205–06.

17. *O.R.*, vol. 36:1, pp. 818–19; Gregory J. W. Urwin, *Custer Victorious*, Blue and Grey Press, 1983, p. 140; William O. Lee, *History of and by Members of the Seventh Regiment Cavalry*, Detroit, 1901, p. 224; Sheridan, *Memoirs*, p. 206.

18. Gary W. Gallagher, ed., *The Spotsylvania Campaign*, University of North Carolina Press, 1998, p. 146; Porter, *Campaigning*, p. 144.

19. *SHSP*, vol. 33, p. 332; George Meade, ed., *Life and Letters of George Gordon Meade*, Scribner's, 1913, vol. 2, p. 197; Grant, *Memoirs*, 1,054.

20. Grant, *Memoirs*, pp. 490–94; *B&L*, vol. 4, p. 208.

21. William C. Davis, *Battle of New Market*, Doubleday, 1975, p. 116.

22. Ibid., pp. 119–20.

23. Ibid., pp. 125–26.

24. *B&L*, vol. 4, p. 485.

25. Catton, *Grant Takes Command*, p. 251; D. G. Crotty, *Four Years Campaigning in the Army of the Potomac*, Dygert Brothers, 1874, p. 132; Dana, *Recollections*, p. 199.

26. *B&L*, vol. 4, p. 135; Edward Porter Alexander, *Fighting for the Confederacy*, University of North Carolina Press, 1989, p. 390.

27. *B&L*, vol. 4, p. 244; Grant, *Memoirs*, p. 567.

28. Porter, *Campaigning*, pp. 165–66.

29. Ibid., pp. 172–74.

30. *B&L*, vol. 4, p. 217; Charles A. Page, *Letters of a War Correspondent*, L. C. Page, 1899, p. 96; Porter, *Campaigning*, pp. 175–76.

31. Charles D. Page, *History of the Fourteenth Regiment, Connecticut Volunteers*, Meriden, Conn., 1906, p. 266; Peter S. Michie, *The Life and Letters of Emory Upton*, D. Appleton, 1885, p. 108; William C. Oates, *The War Between the Union and the Confederacy*, New York, 1905, pp. 366–68; Harvey Clark, *My Experience with Burnside's Expedition and the Eighteenth Army Corps*, Massachusetts, 1914, pp. 66–67.

32. *B&L*, vol. 4, pp. 217–18; O.R., vol. 36:3, pp. 525–26.

33. Grant, *Memoirs*; George G. Meade, *The Life and Letters of George Gordon Meade*, vol. 2, p. 201.

34. D. Augustus Dickert, *History of Kershaw's Brigade*, Broadfoot, 1990, p. 375; O.R., vol. 36:1, p. 638; Grant, *Memoirs*, p. 1,056.

35. Smith, *Grant*, p. 372; Porter, *Campaigning*, p. 199; Longacre, *Army of Amateurs*, p. 147.

36. Alexander, *Fighting for the Confederacy*, p. 426; Noah Andre Trudeau, *The Last Citadel*, Little, Brown, 1991, pp. 49–50; Grant, *Memoirs*, pp. 600–01.

37. Porter, *Campaigning*, pp. 208–10.

3. THE ATLANTA CAMPAIGN

1. Albert Castel, *Decision in the West*, University Press of Kansas, 1992, p. 85; Lewis, *Sherman*, p. 346; Simpson and Berlin, *Sherman's Civil War*, p. 642.

2. John M. Schofield, *Forty-Six Years in the Army*, University of Oklahoma Press, 1897, p. 3; Hebert, *Fighting Joe Hooker*, p. 147.

3. Castel, *Decision in the West*, p. 160.

4. Jacob D. Cox, *Sherman's Battle for Atlanta,* Da Capo, 1994, p. 26.

5. Ibid., p. 31.

6. Ibid., p. 35; Sherman, *Memoirs,* pp. 499–500.

7. Sydney C, Kerksis, ed., *The Atlanta Papers,* Morningside, 1980, p. 341; Castel, *Decision in the West,* pp. 160, 164.

8. Alpheus S. Williams, *From the Cannon's Mouth,* University of Nebraska Press, 1995, p. 308.

9. K. Jack Bauer, ed., *Soldering: The Civil War Diary of Rice C. Bull,* Presidio, 1997, p. 106.

10. Williams, *From the Cannon's Mouth,* pp. 308–09.

11. Sherman, *Memoirs,* p. 503; *B&L,* vol. 4, p. 268.

12. Sherman, *Memoirs,* pp. 512–13; Bauer, ed., *Soldering,* pp. 117–18.

13. Howard, *Autobiography,* vol. 1, pp. 554–56.

14. Charles W. Wills, *Army Life of an Illinois Soldier,* Southern Illinois University Press, 1996, pp. 250–51; Sherman, *Memoirs,* p. 514.

15. Sherman, *Memoirs,* p. 523; *B&L,* vol. 4, p. 270; Castel, *Decision in the West,* p. 276.

16. Simpson and Berlin, *Sherman's Civil War,* pp. 654–55; Sherman, *Memoirs,* pp. 528–30.

17. Sherman, *Memoirs,* p. 530; Wills, *Army Life of an Illinois Soldier,* p. 265; Cleaves, *Rock of Chickamauga,* pp. 221–22; Connolly, *Three Years in the Army,* p. 228.

18. Wills, *Army Life of an Illinois Soldier,* pp. 269–70.

19. Howard, *Autobiography,* vol. 1, p. 583.

20. Francis H. Kennedy, ed., *The Civil War Battlefield Guide,* p. 190; Francis F. McKinney, *Education in Violence,* Americana House, 1991, p. 340; Howard, *Autobiography,* vol. 1, p. 585.

21. Howard, *Autobiography,* vol. 1. pp. 583–84; *O.R.,* vol. 38:4, p. 60; Simpson and Berlin, *Sherman's Civil War,* p. 660.

22. Sherman, *Memoirs,* p. 536; Foote, *The Civil War,* vol. 3, pp. 405–06, 402.

23. Marszalek, *Sherman,* p. 276; Simpson and Berlin, *Sherman's Civil War,* p. 664.

24. Jefferson Davis, *Rise and Fall of the Confederate Government,* D. Appleton, 1881, vol. 2, p. 556; Foote, *The Civil War,* vol. 3, p. 413; Sherman, *Memoirs,* p. 544.

25. Cleaves, *Rock of Chickamauga,* pp. 229, 231; Howard, *Autobiography,* vol. 1, p. 614.

26. William Alan Blair, ed., *A Politician Goes to War,* Pennsylvania

State Press, 1995, p. 188; Bauer, *Soldering*, p. 149; Sherman, *Memoirs*, p. 546.

27. *O.R.*, vol. 38:1, p. 72; Woodworth, *Grant's Lieutenants*, p. 164.

28. *B&L*, vol. 4, pp. 326–27.

29. Castel, *Decision in the West*, p. 400; Foote, *The Civil War*, vol. 3, p. 481; Commager, *The Blue and the Gray*, pp. 945–46.

30. Sherman, *Memoirs*, p. 554; Simpson and Berlin, *Sherman's Civil War*, p. 676.

31. Sherman, *Memoirs*, pp. 558–60.

32. Simpson and Berlin, *Sherman's Civil War*, pp. 672, 676, 682; Castel, *Decision in the West*, p. 418; Sweeny would be acquitted at his court martial but would see no more active service.

33. *B&L*, vol. 4, p. 341; Sherman, *Memoirs*, p. 562; Howard, *Autobiography*, vol. 2, pp. 22–24; Connolly, *Three Years in the Army*, p. 248.

34. Foote, *The Civil War*, vol. 3, p. 490.

35. Sherman, *Memoirs*, pp. 570, 576, 578.

36. Ibid., p. 580; Howard, *Autobiography*, vol. 2, pp. 37–39.

37. *O.R.*, vol. 38:5, p. 727; Sherman, *Memoirs*, pp. 581–83; Grant, *Memoirs*, p. 1,067.

38. Sherman, *Memoirs*, pp. 584–85, 593–94.

4. PETERSBURG, RICHMOND, AND THE SHENANDOAH

1. Porter, *Campaigning*, pp. 217–20, 222–23.

2. June 24, 1864, Horace Porter Papers, Library of Congress.

3. *SHSP*, vol. 2, p. 273; James I. Robertson Jr., *General A. P. Hill*, Random House, 1987, p. 287.

4. *SHSP*, vol. 2, p. 275; Edward G. Longacre, *Grant's Cavalryman*, Stackpole, 1996, p. 144; John S. Wise, *The End of an Era*, Houghton, Mifflin, 1899, p. 319.

5. Jubal A. Early, *Narrative of the War Between the States*, Da Capo, 1989, p. 380; Henry Kyd Douglas, *I Rode with Stonewall*, North Carolina Press, 1940, p. 293.

6. *Lew Wallace: An Autobiography*, vol. 2, pp. 710, 762.

7. Ibid., pp. 768–69, 779–80.

8. Early, *Narrative*, p. 404.

9. Grant, *Memoirs*, p. 607; Catton, *Grant Takes Command*, p. 321.

10. *B&L*, vol. 4, p. 551; Porter, *Campaigning*, p. 264.

11. *B&L*, vol. 4, pp. 552–53, 556; *SHSP*, vol. 2, p. 287.

12. *SHSP*, vol. 18, p. 17; *B&L*, vol. 4., p. 558; Wise, *The End of an Era*, p. 365; *Confederate Veteran*, vol. 15, no. 11, p. 480; Grant, *Memoirs*, p. 1,063.

13. Porter, *Campaigning*, p. 267.

14. Grant, *Memoirs*, pp. 614–15.

15. Porter, *Campaigning*, pp. 281–82.

16. Grant, *Memoirs*, pp. 616, 620; Early, *Narrative*, p. 415.

17. Kyd Douglas, *I Rode with Stonewall*, p. 309; *B&L*, vol. 4, p. 509; *SHSP*, vol. 2, p. 26; Jeffrey D. Wert, *From Winchester to Cedar Creek*, South Mountain Press, 1987, p. 68.

18. Sheridan, *Personal Memoirs*, p. 292; Gordon, *Reminiscences of the Civil War*, p. 321.

19. Sheridan, *Personal Memoirs*, pp. 292–94; Wert, *From Winchester to Cedar Creek*, p. 95.

20. Sheridan, *Personal Memoirs*, pp. 300–01; Wert, *From Winchester to Cedar Creek*, p. 121.

21. Catton, *Grant Takes Command*, p. 365; Porter, *Campaigning*, p. 299; Noah Andre Trudeau, *The Last Citadel*, Little, Brown 1991, p. 209; Kennedy, ed., *The Civil War Battlefield Guide*, p. 267; Wert, *From Winchester to Cedar Creek*, p. 216.

22. Trudeau, *The Last Citadel*, pp. 210, 213, 217; Richard J. Sommers, *Richmond Redeemed*, Doubleday, 1981, p. 148; Catton, *Grant Takes Command*, p. 367.

23. Trudeau, *The Last Citadel*, pp. 239, 241.

24. Porter, *Campaigning*, pp. 309–11; William Pegram to mother, October 28, 1864, Pegram-Johnson-McIntosh Papers, Virginia Historical Society.

25. *O.R.*, vol. 43:2, p. 892; Gordon, *Reminiscences of the Civil War*, p. 335.

26. *Annals of the War, Philadelphia Weekly Times 1877–79*, Blue and Grey Press, 1996, pp. 658–60; Gordon, *Reminiscences of the Civil War*, p. 339.

27. Commager, *The Blue and the Gray*, vol. 2, pp. 1049–51; Dickert, *History of Kershaw's Brigade*, pp. 448–49.

28. Commager, *The Blue and the Gray*, pp. 1052, 1054–55.

29. Gordon, *Reminiscences of the Civil War*, p. 341; *O.R.*, vol. 41:3, pp. 562–63.

30. Sheridan, *Personal Memoirs*, pp. 320–29.

31. George A. Forsyth, *Thrilling Days in Army Life*, Harper and Broth-

ers, 1900, pp. 141–45; Hazard Stevens, *The Battle of Cedar Creek*, Military Historical Society of Massachusetts, 1907, vol. 6, p. 125.

32. Thomas A. Lewis, *The Guns of Cedar Creek*, Harper and Row, 1988, p. 251; Forsyth, *Thrilling Days*, p. 149.

33. Forsyth, *Thrilling Days*, p. 154.

34. Sheridan, *Personal Memoirs*, pp. 332–33; Gordon, *Reminiscences of the Civil War*, p. 348; Dickert, *History of Kershaw's Brigade*, p. 452.

35. Henry Kyd Douglas, *I Rode With Stonewall*, p. 319; Lewis, *The Guns of Cedar Creek*, p. 288.

5. MARCH TO THE SEA

1. Porter, *Campaigning*, pp. 288–93.

2. Ibid., pp. 314–16.

3. Howard, *Autobiography*, vol. 2, pp. 58–62.

4. *O.R.*, vol. 39:2, pp. 113, 152, 412; Porter, *Campaigning*, pp. 317–18.

5. Grant, *Memoirs*, p. 653; Catton, *Grant Takes Command*, p. 390; Porter, *Campaigning*, p. 319.

6. Sherman, *Memoirs*, pp. 654–56.

7. Ibid., pp. 657–58; Connolly, *Three Years in the Army*, pp. 298, 311.

8. Dolly Lunt, *A Woman's Wartime Journal*, Century Company, 1918, p. 20.

9. Connolly, *Three Years in the Army*, pp. 313–14.

10. Wills, *Army Life of an Illinois Soldier*, pp. 323–24; Lee Kennett, *Marching Through Georgia*, Harper Perennial, 1996, p. 255.

11. Sherman, *Memoirs*, pp. 664–65; Kennett, *Marching Through Georgia*, pp. 260–61.

12. Bauer, *Soldering*, pp. 188–89; Kennett, *Marching Through Georgia*, p. 261.

13. Sherman, *Memoirs*, pp. 668–69; Henry Hitchcock, *Marching with Sherman*, University of Nebraska Press, 1995, pp. 135–36.

14. Simpson and Berlin, *Sherman's Civil War*, p. 697; George Templeton Strong, *Diary of the Civil War*, Macmillan, 1962, vol. 3, p. 526.

15. Sherman, *Memoirs*, pp. 669–70.

16. Ibid., p. 672; Howard, *Autobiography*, vol. 2, pp. 88–89.

17. Sherman, *Memoirs*, pp. 673–74; Richard Harwell and Philip N. Racine, eds., *The Fiery Trail*, University of Tennessee Press, 1986, p. 71.

18. Marszalek, *Sherman*, p. 307; Sherman, *Memoirs*, pp. 681–83.

19. Sherman, *Memoirs*, pp. 686–87; Howard, *Autobiography*, vol. 2, p. 94.

20. Sherman, *Memoirs,* pp. 708, 714.
21. Hitchcock, *Marching with Sherman,* pp. 198–201.
22. Ibid., p. 202; Sherman to Chase, January 11, 1865, Chase Papers, Pennsylvania Historical Society.
23. Eliza Andrews, *The War-Time Journal of a Georgia Girl,* D. Appleton, 1908, pp. 32–33, 38, 57; Simpson and Berlin, *Sherman's Civil War,* p. 778.
24. Simpson and Berlin, *Sherman's Civil War,* pp. 783–84.

6. LAST HURRAH IN TENNESSEE

1. Foote, *The Civil War,* vol. 3, p. 656.
2. Schofield, *Forty-Six Years in the Army,* p. 167; Wiley Sword, *Embrace an Angry Wind,* HarperCollins, 1992, p. 101.
3. Schofield, *Forty-Six Years in the Army,* pp. 168–69.
4. *O.R.,* vol. 45: 1, p. 1,143.
5. *B&L,* vol. 4, pp. 444–46.
6. Ibid., pp. 431–32.
7. Ibid., pp. 448–49.
8. Ibid., pp. 450–51.
9. Sword, *Embrace an Angry Wind,* pp. 189–91; John K. Shellenberger, *The Battle of Franklin,* privately published, 1916, pp. 21–22.
10. *B&L,* vol. 4, pp. 452–53.
11. Stanley F. Horn, *The Army of Tennessee,* University of Oklahoma Press, 1941, p. 403.
12. Schofield, *Forty-Six Years in the Army,* p. 184.
13. *B&L,* vol. 4, pp. 454, 456.
14. *O.R.,* vol. 45:2, pp. 2, 15.
15. Sword, *Embrace an Angry Wind,* pp. 290–92; Cleaves, *Rock of Chickamauga,* pp. 297–98; McKinney, *Education in Violence,* p. 400; *B&L,* vol. 4, pp. 454–55; Porter, *Campaigning,* pp. 343–44.
16. Catton, *Grant Takes Command,* pp. 398–99; Grant, *Memoirs,* pp. 659–60.
17. *B&L,* vol. 4, pp. 455–59.
18. Sword, *Embrace an Angry Wind,* p. 341; *B&L,* vol. 4, p. 460.
19. *B&L,* vol. 4, pp. 462–63; James Wilson, *Under the Old Flag,* vol. 2, pp. 99ff.
20. Wilson, *Under the Old Flag;* Jacob Cox, *The March to the Sea— Franklin and Nashville,* New York, 1882, pp. 122–23.

21. Sword, *Embrace an Angry Wind*, pp. 390, 431.
22. *B&L*, vol. 4, pp. 436–37; Sword, *Embrace an Angry Wind*, p. 391.

1865

1. MOVING UP THE CAROLINAS

1. Sherman, *Memoirs*, pp. 725–32; Marszalek, *Sherman*, p. 314.
2. Grant, *Memoirs*, pp. 668–70.
3. Ibid., p. 674.
4. Bauer, *Soldering*, pp. 213, 207; Sherman, *Memoirs*, pp. 754–55.
5. Sherman, *Memoirs*, pp. 759–67.
6. Harwell and Racine, *The Fiery Trail*, pp. 128–29.
7. Hitchcock, *Marching with Sherman*, pp. 268–68; Wills, *Army Life of an Illinois Soldier*, p. 350.
8. Wills, *Army Life of an Illinois Soldier*, p. 357; Sherman, *Memoirs*, p. 773.
9. Wills, *Army Life of an Illinois Soldier*, p. 362.
10. Sherman, *Memoirs*, 779–80; Bauer, *Soldering*, p. 227.
11. *B&L*, vol. 4, pp. 692–95.
12. Ibid., p. 695; Joseph T. Glatthaar, *The March to the Sea and Beyond*, New York University Press, 1986, p. 170.
13. Marszalek, *Sherman*, p. 330; Sherman, *Memoirs*, p. 786.
14. Kennedy, *The Civil War Battlefield Guide*, p. 271.
15. Sherman, *Memoirs*, pp. 788–89, 797–98; Marszalek, *Sherman*, p. 331.
16. Grant, *Memoirs*, pp. 683–84.
17. Porter, *Campaigning*, pp. 417–19.
18. Ibid., pp. 420–21.
19. Ibid., pp. 422–24, 426.

2. GRANT CRUSHES A PROUD FOE

1. *B&L*, vol. 4, p. 708.
2. Porter, *Campaigning*, p. 428; Grant, *Memoirs*, pp. 696–97; Catton, *Grant Takes Command*, p. 441.
3. Sheridan, *Personal Memoirs*, p. 369.

4. Joshua L. Chamberlain, *The Passing of the Armies,* Bantam, 1993, p. 55.

5. Ibid., pp. 59–60.

6. Porter, *Campaigning,* pp. 432–33.

7. Chamberlain, *The Passing of the Armies,* pp. 69–74.

8. Grant, *Memoirs,* pp. 701–02.

9. Porter, *Campaigning,* p. 435; Sheridan, *Personal Memoirs,* pp. 373–74.

10. Porter, *Campaigning,* pp. 437–39.

11. Ibid., pp. 439–40; Chamberlain, *The Passing of the Armies,* p. 113.

12. Sheridan, *Personal Memoirs,* p. 375; Chamberlain, *The Passing of the Armies,* pp. 107, 114; Warren would not get his day in court until 1879, when a military tribunal cleared him of all charges at Five Forks and criticized the manner in which he was relieved.

13. Porter, *Campaigning,* pp. 441–43.

14. Catton, *A Stillness at Appomattox,* p. 670.

15. Porter, *Campaigning,* pp. 445–47.

16. William Swinton, *Army of the Potomac,* Smithmark, 1995, p. 603.

17. Catton, *Grant Takes Command,* p. 447.

18. Douglas Southall Freeman, *Lee's Lieutenants,* Scribner's, 1934–36, vol. 3, p. 687.

19. Robert Stiles, *Four Years Under Marse Robert,* R. Bemis, 1995, p. 333; Noah Andre Trudeau, *Out of the Storm,* Little, Brown, 1994, p. 111; the waterways are spelled Sayler's Creek, the battle and the national park are spelled Sailor's Creek.

20. Urwin, *Custer Victorious,* pp. 248–49.

21. James Longstreet, *From Manassas to Appomattox,* Philadelphia, 1896, p. 615; William Thomas Poague, *Gunner with Stonewall,* Broadfoot, 1987, p. 117.

22. Porter, *Campaigning,* pp. 458–59.

23. Catton, *Grant Takes Command,* pp. 456–63; Grant, *Memoirs,* pp. 727–32.

24. Gordon, *Reminiscences of the Civil War,* pp. 439–42.

25. Grant, *Memoirs,* pp. 735–36.

26. Porter, *Campaigning,* pp. 473–80.

27. Ibid., pp. 482–83; Commager, *The Blue and the Gray,* vol. 2, p. 1,140.

28. Porter, *Campaigning,* p. 486; Grant, *Memoirs,* pp. 743–44.

29. Chamberlain, *The Passing of the Armies,* pp. 195–96.

30. Ibid., p. 196; Porter, *Campaigning,* p. 497; Grant, *Memoirs,* pp. 750–51.

3. POLITICS AND PLAUDITS

1. Sherman, *Memoirs,* pp. 813, 832–33, 835.
2. Ibid., p. 837; Marszalek, *Sherman,* pp. 343–44.
3. Sherman, *Memoirs,* pp. 843–45; Grant, *Memoirs,* p. 1,088.
4. *O.R.,* vol. 47:3, pp. 286–87; Grant, *Memoirs,* p. 756.
5. Marszalek, *Sherman,* pp. 347, 350; Sherman, *Memoirs,* p. 860.
6. Simpson and Berlin, *Sherman's Civil War,* p. 884.
7. Ibid., pp. 892–94.
8. Grant, *Memoirs,* pp. 769–70.
9. Foote, *The Civil War,* vol. 3, p. 1,014.
10. Porter, *Campaigning,* pp. 506–08; Trudeau, *Out of the Storm,* p. 317.
11. Porter, *Campaigning,* p. 509; Trudeau, *Out of the Storm,* p. 319.
12. Porter, *Campaigning,* p. 510; Foote, *The Civil War,* vol. 3, p. 1017.
13. Sherman, *Memoirs,* p. 866.
14. Porter, *Campaigning,* pp. 514–15.

4. THE SURVIVORS

1. Smith, *Grant,* pp. 421, 457, 548, 592.
2. Marszalek, *Sherman,* pp. 412, 417, 489, 496; Sherman, *Memoirs,* p. 1,117.
3. Lamers, *The Edge of Glory,* pp. 448–49.
4. Hearn, *Admiral David Dixon Porter,* pp. 319–21.
5. Kiper, *Major General John Alexander McClernand,* pp. 296, 298, 312.
6. Cleaves, *Rock of Chickamauga,* p. 285.
7. Hebert, *Fighting Joe Hooker,* p. 294.
8. Morris Jr., *Sheridan,* pp. 296, 392.
9. Mark Mayo Boatner III, *The Civil War Dictionary,* David McKay, 1959, p. 226.
10. Porter, *Campaigning,* pp. viii–ix.

INDEX